DECISION 1997

CONSTITUTIONAL CHANGE IN NEW YORK

GERALD BENJAMIN & HENRIK N. DULLEA

EDITORS

D1211807

The Rockefeller Institute Press
Albany, New York

Distributed by The Brookings Institution Press

Rockefeller Institute Press, Albany, New York 12203-1003
© 1997 by the Rockefeller Institute Press
All rights reserved. First edition 1997
Printed in the United States of America

The Rockefeller Institute Press
The Nelson A. Rockefeller Institute of Government
411 State Street
Albany, New York 12203-1003

Library of Congress Cataloguing-in-Publication Data

Decision 1997 / edited by Gerald Benjamin and Henrik N. Dullea.
        p.   cm.
    Includes index.
    ISBN 0-914341-50-2 (paper)
    1. Constitutional law--New York (State) 2. Constitutional
conventions--New York (State)   I. Benjamin, Gerald. II. Dullea,
Henrik N.
KFN5683.D83   1997
342.747 ' 03--dc21   97-5427
                                                          CIP

ISBN: 0-914341-50-2

P4355

Contents

Foreword ix
    Richard P. Nathan

Acknowledgments xi

Introduction xiii
    Peter Goldmark

Decision 1997 xxi
    Gerald Benjamin

Section I   Why State Constitutions Matter **1**

State Constitutions in the Federal System 3
    Richard Briffault

Principal Provisions of State Constitutions:
A Brief Overview 21
    Richard Briffault

New York's State Constitution in
Comparative Context 29
    Robert F. Williams

The Role of the Constitutional Commission
in State Constitutional Change 45
    Robert F. Williams

**Section II   Constitutional Structure and
                    the Process of Government.** **53**

Structures of New York State Government 57
    Gerald Benjamin

State Government Finance 81
    Robert P. Kerker

Legislative Districting and the New York
State Constitution 105
    David I. Wells

New York State's Judicial Article: A Work in Progress 127
    Frederick Miller

The Private Economy 147
    Joseph F. Zimmerman

Intergovernmental Relations 155
    Richard Briffault

Local Government and the State Constitution:
A Framework for Analysis 181
    Richard Briffault

Elections and the Political Process 193
    Jeffrey M. Stonecash

Reforming New York's Constitutional
System of Election Administration 217
    Gerald Benjamin

Section III   Individual Liberties and
                "Positive Rights" **233**

Individual Liberties 235
    Burton C. Agata

Criminal Justice 255
    Burton C. Agata

Education 281
    Robert D. Stone

Social Policy 301
    Gerald Benjamin with Melissa Cusa

The Environment 317
    William R. Ginsberg

Section IV   Amendment and Revision Process:
                Experience and Issues **329**

Amending and Revising the New York State Constitution 331
    Burton C. Agata

A Pandora's Box? Holding a Constitutional
Convention in New York 351
    Peter J. Galie

Constitutional Revision in 1967: Learning the
Right Lessons From the Magnificent Failure 367
    Henrik N. Dullea

The 1967 Constitutional Convention Delegates. 381
    Prepared by Michael Leo Owens

Amending the New York State Constitution
Through the Legislature 385
    Gerald Benjamin and Melissa Cusa

Section V   The Delegate Selection Process **405**

The Delegate Selection Process 407
    *Interim Report of the Temporary State
    Commission on Constitutional Revision*

Delegate Selection and the Problem of Ballot Access........... 435
    Burton C. Agata

The Voting Rights Act and the Election of
Delegates to a Constitutional Convention 445
    Richard Briffault

The Election of Delegates to the Constitutional
Convention: Some Alternatives 473
    Richard Briffault

Public Campaign Financing............................... 491
    Michael J. Malbin

Appendices. **501**

Temporary State Commission on Constitutional Revision

    Commission Members........................... 503

    Commission Biographies......................... 505

    Commission Staff............................... 511

Author Biographies 513

Index 519

Foreword

Democracy is a precious gift that has to be cared for. This large book is a tool for caring for the fundamental political charter of New York State. It is published seven months before citizens of the state will be presented with the ballot question required to be put before them every 20 years as to whether there shall be a convention to revise the state Constitution. This volume, which examines the structure, rights of citizens, and operations of New York State government, was prepared to inform the public discourse preparatory to this 1997 vote. It also serves as a source book on state government. The material presented here grew out of the work of the Temporary State Commission on Constitutional Revision appointed in 1993. The book is being published by the Rockefeller Institute Press along with a companion volume by Henrik N. Dullea, which presents a rich history of the last Constitutional Convention held by New York State, that in 1967.

Richard P. Nathan
Director
The Nelson A. Rockefeller
Institute of Government

March 1, 1997

Acknowledgments

The essays in this volume were written to support the efforts of the New York State Commission on Constitutional Revision. The Commission chair, Peter Goldmark, gave focus and direction to the research agenda reflected in the papers published here. I am grateful to the contributors to this volume, all of whom produced work of high quality under tight deadlines. These essays benefited from the thinking, advice, and comment of the members of the Constitutional Revision Commission and of my staff colleagues at the Commission, Pauline Toole and Eric Lane. Helpful review and advice on specific subjects was provided by Peter Galie, Michael Libonati, Frank Mauro, Kearney Jones, Donald Shaffer, Ted Stein, James W. Lytle, Philip Weinberg, and Gary Weiskopf.

The Rockefeller Institute in Albany, under the direction of Richard Nathan, housed the research effort of the Commission. Administrative support was provided by Liz Praetorius, Director for Finance and Administration of the Institute, and Anne Maloney, Michelle Chabonneau, Michelle Kelafant, Susan Watson, Rich Michaels, and Cathy Halfgood, all working under her direction.

I am particularly appreciative of the research and administrative assistance provided to me by Melissa Cusa, my assistant at the Rockefeller Institute. Irene Pavone's managerial and secretarial skills were essential for the completion of this project. Michael Owens's help was also invaluable. Terri Potente, assistant to Peter Goldmark at the Rockefeller Foundation, was a continuous source of encouragement. Barbara Fanti provided secretarial support at SUNY New Paltz in this project's final stages. Robert Allan Carter, senior librarian at the New York State Library and an expert on the state's constitutional history, was extraordinarily responsive to requests for assistance.

Finally, I am most grateful for the editorial and production work done on this project by Michael Cooper. Michael brought a level of professionalism and dedication to the preparation of this book that significantly enhanced its quality, as have his efforts on all the projects in which I have been involved with him over the years at the Rockefeller Institute.

Gerald Benjamin

Introduction

Peter G. Goldmark, Jr.

Most political analysts would call 1997 in New York an "off year." Of course, there will be local elections across the state, including the election for Mayor of New York City. But in New York State there are no presidential, gubernatorial, congressional, or state legislative races.

The same analysts would say that New York is not a "referendum state." We do not have the initiative. We do not make national headlines with laws enacted directly by popular vote, bypassing the legislature. We are not like California, Colorado, or even Massachusetts.

But in this off year a state constitutional requirement may make a statewide referendum in New York the major political story of the year, and perhaps the decade.

Our state constitution mandates that on this coming Election Day, November 4, 1997, we New Yorkers be asked: *"Shall there be a convention to revise the Constitution and amend the same?"* If we answer "Yes," convention delegates will be elected in 1998 for a state constitutional convention to be held in April 1999. If we say "No," another twenty years will pass before we **must** address this question again (although the Legislature **may** at any time propose a constitutional convention or initiate referenda on constitutional amendments).

The people who added this mandatory convention question to the New York Constitution in 1846 wanted to make sure that there was a way for the state's citizens to review the basics of their governance that was even more direct than by voting for elected officials, and one not dependent on the will of those officials. If the people are truly sovereign, they reasoned, we should consider from time to time whether we want to take a look at the fundamental rules of the game and perhaps change and update them.

This moment of opportunity for a debate on our system of self-governance comes at a time when many New Yorkers, like Americans elsewhere, feel out of touch, disappointed, angry, or impatient with government. Citizens worry about jobs, their children's future and security, conflicts over fundamental values, the absence of opportunity, and the ability of government to address these concerns and to oversee the provision of services.

This volume of essays and the companion history by Henrik N. Dullea of the last Constitutional Convention in New York State in 1967 are being published by the Rockefeller Institute to provide voters and the media with the background information that will help inform this crucial decision in 1997. And surely information is needed. Research has shown that some of those who will vote on the convention question don't even know that there is a state constitution.

Why Should We Care?

From the vantage point of the spring of 1997, a half year before the referendum, those who want a constitutional convention to be called have a job to do. For right now the odds are that the voters will turn down a constitutional convention, but not because they are satisfied with the way things are.

Our state government has done virtually nothing in the last two years to prepare for the possibility of a convention. In fact, it is fair to say that many elected officials are trying to minimize the prospect of a constitutional convention by ignoring it. Having done little or nothing to get ready, some of them will argue with a straight face in the fall that we should avoid a convention because sufficient groundwork for it has not been laid.

Among the organized interests in the state, opponents are organizing and mobilizing; advocates remain scattered and disorganized. In a similar low visibility environment, the last mandatory referendum on whether New York should hold a constitutional convention failed overwhelmingly in 1997. It was 41.3 percent for and 59.7 percent against. But only 62.9 percent of the people who voted in 1977 pulled *either* lever. And those who voted were only 63.3 percent of all eligible voters.

The nature of the opposition and the reasons for it offer insight as to why a convention is needed. No one who opposes a convention says that the quality of New York state government makes it unnecessary. It is not hard to see why. That argument is impossible to make, given our recent experience. For example, divided partisan control has become institutionalized in the state legislature, perpetuated by a self-interested decennial reapportionment process. In the face of enormous, accelerating social and economic change, major issues go unresolved and often unaddressed. The state government's incapacity to do its recurring business in a timely fashion undermines its very legitimacy in the eyes of thoughtful New Yorkers.

But in the face of this general condition those who are beneficiaries of the system as it is now, or who have a stake in a particular provision of the state constitution that they fear may be changed, resist a process that might threaten their interest. The voices speaking for particular interests are numerous; meanwhile few advocate for the common interest in governmental institutions that are truly democratic, effective and accountable. Those who oppose it decry the dangers that they imagine may be associated with a convention, but do not speak of the peril more certainly associated with continued drift down the path of decline, disinvolvement, and deterioration.

There is certain schizophrenia in opposition to a state constitutional convention in New York. Some people say that calling a convention is a waste of time because those already in power will control it, and no real change will occur. Others fear that since you can't predict what people and groups will have power at a convention, it is not smart to open this "Pandora's Box." Both come down to an assessment of risk against benefit. For those of us who do care about improving government in New York, who care about what a convention might accomplish and who do not fear the prospect, the challenge is to forge both a consensus and a coalition on an agenda that makes the potential benefit clear and the assessment of risk realistic.

A vital first step in that direction, and the purpose of this volume, is to shed light on how the process works and help voters understand the areas, issues and opportunities of a constitutional convention. One that is central is fiscal policy and structure. As a former budget director, I cannot help but note that there has been ongoing, deep concern in New York about our budget process and about the borrowing and financing practices of the state. In our state, these are constitutional issues. The full airing of questions of *how* government works, rather than *what* government does, is possible at a constitutional convention; it has proven impossible in regular sessions of the Legislature.

The same point applies to an important related subject. I refer to the structure, workings and fiscal accountability of local governments. Modified incrementally over a century but never thoroughly reformed, the state/local relationship in New York could surely stand the hard scrutiny that a constitutional convention might bring.

State constitutions are long and complex; New York's is one of the longest and most complex of them all. Matters not regarded as constitutional in national government are constitutional at the state level — election reform, equity in education, and redefining the state's approach to criminal justice are three examples. There are other structural, electoral, and substantive issues about which New Yorkers care deeply that a convention might take up, and in doing so convince citizens that government can be structured with greater potential to work legitimately and well for them in the new century.

The Temporary Commission

The Temporary Commission on Constitutional Revision was appointed by Governor Mario M. Cuomo in May 1993 to help voters prepare for the vote they will cast in 1997. It was a strong group — fair, knowledgeable in public affairs but in no way a pawn of the existing political system or the governor who appointed them. They were bipartisan, drawn from many regions and ethnic groups. The Commission included a lawyer, a university professor, a farmer, a labor leader, a newspaper editor, a businesswoman, a city councilman, a former governor, the head of the State League of Women Voters, the head of SUNY's Rockefeller Institute, and the vice chancellor of Cornell University. This was an experienced collection of New Yorkers with no self-interested axes to grind, and with genuine concern for our state and our system of government. The greatest asset we had was time; the scheduled vote was four years off at the time of our appointment. We sought to use that time to engage our fellow New Yorkers in a conversation about what was working and what was not, about what kinds of changes we might like to see in our state government, and about which of these changes might require revising the state Constitution. New York has adopted four Constitutions over its history: in 1777, 1821, 1846 and 1894. Two other conventions have resulted in major constitutional revisions: in 1801 and 1938. Every successful convention has been preceded by a period of intense statewide debate.

A commitment to constitutionalism is at the core of what is historically most distinctive and important about us as Americans and our adventure in self government. American federalism makes our binding institutions our constitutions. We know the fundamental importance of our national Constitution. But we purposely speak here of constitutions, not the Constitution. For there are 51 of them. The 50 state Constitutions affect us where we live every day. They are the basis for our education systems, our provisions for public safety and welfare, the way we govern ourselves in the smallest of rural villages and our greatest cities.

In our state, as nationally, this adventure in self government has three primary ingredients that determine success:

* ❊ The first is the quality of elected leadership we choose. This is not addressed by a constitutional review.

* ❊ The second is the structure of government and the entire public enterprise, and this is directly the concern of constitutional review.

* ❊ The third is the character and extent of citizen attention to and involvement in public affairs. Though perhaps less evident, this too is a concern of constitutional review. For one of the most critical and determinative elements in the process of constitutional revision is the character, intensity, and maturity of the public discussion leading up to it.

As the Temporary Commission on Constitutional Revision proceeded with its work — considering the results of staff research; holding meetings and hearings across the state; debating and deliberating on questions of substance and process — it developed an appreciation of the importance of the state Constitution as New York's social compact. The state's Constitution is the charter that frames the governmental structures of our state and local governments, and which sets forth the duties of state government. It connects with our daily lives in hundreds of ways.

For eighteen months the Temporary Commission examined state government in New York and the state Constitution. We found ambivalence about a constitutional convention among the citizenry of the state. Some strong voices argued for a convention to modernize the Constitution and the state's governmental machinery. Others expressed fears about going through the process. But most clearly and strongly of all we heard about New Yorkers' urgent concerns for rapid, practical action to make government work better in doing its basic jobs: educating children, making neighborhoods safe, keeping taxes fair and reasonable, reaching the state's fiscal decisions in a timely and intelligent way. That concern, which is alive and strong today, could become the animating spirit for a constitutional convention.

Because considerable time might be needed if reform was required, the Commission determined first to focus on the constitutional change process itself. Broad ranging reforms were indeed recommended in an

Interim Report, issued in 1994. The questions addressed included: who might serve as delegates; the compensation of delegates; the financing of delegate campaigns: and the districts and election processes used for delegate selection. Several of the papers in this volume informed commission deliberations on these questions. The Legislature, however, failed to act on commission recommendations.

With the vote now six months off, yea or nay, on a constitutional convention for New York State, this research may appear less useful. But the exploration of the processes the Constitution requires for staffing a possible convention, and their consequences, remains central to a debate over whether a convention should be called. Moreover, some of the commission's reform proposals may still come into play if there is a "yes" vote for a convention at the polls in 1997. They remain pertinent, as well, for thinking concerning future conventions. Remember that a constitutional convention can be called at any time by the Legislature and the Governor, making the research on these questions in this volume as valuable for the future as they are for 1997.

As our commission considered issues raised by voters in hearings around the state, we concluded that the state needed a vehicle that allowed wide public discussion, that could generate broad and coherent proposals for change, and that did not bypass the checks and balances of the deliberative process. The goal was not to replace or short-circuit the existing institutions of state government, but to assist them in shaping and airing approaches to reform in areas where, by common consent, the old ways were no longer serving us well.

Action Panels

We recommended that the Governor and the two houses of the Legislature adopt a new instrument to break logjams in the reform process. Specifically, we proposed the creation of a small number of what we called "Action Panels" charged with developing a coherent reform package in important subject areas. Our list of possible subject areas for such attention contained four topics: fiscal integrity, state/local relations, education, and public safety. There are of course other areas that could be listed, but we chose these as important and illustrative.

Each Action Panel would operate under a rule predetermined by the Governor and the Legislature that would fix a date certain for each panel to report its proposals and fix a following date certain by which the Legislature would have to act on the proposals.

The Action Panels would:

❋ Consist of appointees of the Governor and the Legislature, drawn from the ranks both of public officials and private citizens;

❋ Hold public hearings around the state;

❋ Consult with the Governor and Legislature through the course of their work using defined procedures;

❋ Propose to the Legislature an integrated package of reforms in each area, including constitutional revision, legislation, or regulatory change.

The Commission concluded that if the state could address and solve some of its most protracted problems by use of this special technique, then a constitutional convention would not be needed. But if it could not, then a convention became more attractive. Interested voters are referred to the final report of the Temporary Commission for more information on this approach; the Commission's full report can be obtained from the Rockefeller Institute. I note that in the past year there has been discussion on the use of action panels at both the state and national levels.

New Yorkers have a proud heritage of humane government. New York was for many years recognized as a leader among state governments; reforms and practices pioneered here were emulated around the country and by the federal government. But in the last decades of the twentieth century, new realities and problems have emerged to which present institutions and policies have not responded well. Certainly few students of state government would point to New York today as either a model or a leader. It is not surprising that, like the institutions and practices they themselves once supplanted, our current ones have also, with time, become less effective. In many functional areas of government in New York there has been no serious overhaul or restructuring for upwards of a century. In these circumstances, as one New Yorker who cares about good government and restoring the greatness of our state, I find the case for a constitutional convention increasingly compelling.

*   *   *   *   *

The essays in this book grew out of the work of the Temporary Commission on Constitutional Revision (1993-95), appointed specifically to help prepare New Yorkers for this referendum vote; we are indebted for organizing this material to Gerald Benjamin, who served ably as the Commission's Director of Research. The names and affiliations of members of the Commission on Constitutional Revision, and of Commission staff, are provided in the appendix to this volume. I am pleased on behalf of my Commission colleagues on the Temporary Commission to make the material in this book and the companion volume on the 1967 Convention, written by our fellow Commissioner Henrik Dullea, available as part of the information base for New York's debate this year about assuring quality government for ourselves and those who come after us.

January 1997

Decision 1997

Gerald Benjamin

The materials presented in this volume seek to inform New Yorkers' "Decision 1997." They are organized to focus the reader's attention on the major themes and questions raised when state constitutional change is considered. Organizationally, the book's five sections proceed from the general to the specific, and from questions of substance to questions of process. Each chapter seeks to be comparative in some dimension, placing New York's contemporary constitutional arrangements in the context of the state's constitutional history, and the experience of other states. Each also explores specific constitutional changes that have recently been proposed, or that had come to the attention of New Yorkers because of their consideration or adoption in other states.

Section I of this volume is the most general and broadly comparative. The essays in it discuss what is found in state constitutions and the role and importance of these documents in the American federal system. We examine how commissions have been used as instruments of state constitutional change. Section I also provides a summary comparative overview of those characteristics of the New York Constitution that are unique, and those it shares with the basic documents of other states.

The fundamental structure and processes of New York state and local government are taken up in Section II. The basic design of New York's political and governmental systems is described and analyzed. The essays included give attention to areas that have over the recent history of the state been singled out for reform: budgeting and finance; local government and intergovernmental relations; legislative districting; the organization of the judiciary; the electoral process; and regulation of the private economy.

Section III describes a fundamental difference in the treatment of "rights" under the New York State Constitution and state constitutions generally, and the national document. We include essays on rights as traditionally defined — constitutional protections of the liberties of individuals against governmental intrusion — and also discussions of "positive rights," citizen entitlements from the government in the areas of education, social policy (welfare, housing), and the environment. In modern state government in New York and elsewhere, controversies centering on positive rights under state constitutions are highly charged and have within them enormous consequences for policy and governance.

The constitutional change process is the focus of Section IV. These essays are the most New York-specific in the volume. Several were written to look into questions raised while the Constitutional Revision Commission met about experience with past conventions in the state, especially the most recent convention held in 1967. Chapters in this section detail the methods by which the New York Constitution may be amended or revised, the risks and benefits of the constitutional convention as an amending device, and experience over the state's history with both the convention method and legislatively initiated constitutional amendment.

Section V on the delegates selection process details the steps that would follow if New Yorkers choose to call a constitutional convention. The Commission on Constitutional Revision determined that delegate election procedures required in the state Constitution since 1894 were likely to be in violation of the Federal Voting Rights Act, first passed in 1965 and most recently renewed in 1982. On the basis of this finding, the Commission proposed measures to the New York State Legislature to mitigate this problem and to assure fair, competitive delegate selection elections. This section presents the research on the history and likely operation of the delegate selection process that led to the Commission's conclusions, and the recommendations that it reached.

Appendices to this book contain a brief description of the Constitutional Revision Commission, and background on its members and staff and the authors of the papers presented in this volume. The essays in this book were commissioned and written with the knowledge that Peter Galie had recently published his annotated volume *The New York Constitution: A Reference Guide* (Westport, CT: Greenwood Press, 1991). Because it contains a solid article-by-article description of the development of the modern New York Constitution, there was no need to repeat this in our work. Galie's research, presented in that volume and his more recently published *Ordered Liberty: A Constitutional History of New York* (New York: Fordham University Press, 1995) provide important complements to this volume. Another key source of background for 1997 is Henrik Dullea's *Charter Revision in the Empire State: The Politics of New York's 1967 Constitutional Convention*, published as a companion volume to this collection.

Why State Constitutions Matter

When state constitutions are compared to the national Constitution they rarely come out well. Critics find them to be too long, too prolix, too detailed, too filled with matter that is "not constitutional." But is this comparison appropriate?

Certainly state constitutions lack the symbolic, unifying power within their spheres that the national document has for the nation. In fact, as Richard Briffault points out in his introductory essay to this volume, only a minority of citizens even know of the existence of state constitutions. Moreover, the frequency with which state constitutions are amended suggests that their political and governmental functions are different from those of the national Constitution. Briffault goes on in this essay to look at the role of state constitutions in the American federal system as documents that organize government, protect fundamental rights, and express core political values and goals.

The governmental systems established by the state constitutions are remarkably similar to each other and to the federal model. In his second essay in this section Briffault notes that they all contain a Bill of Rights; all adhere to the separation of powers principle; all but one establish bicameral legislatures; and all create independent judiciaries with the power of judicial review. Briffault also notes, however, that states differ from the national government in their use of the item veto and the constraints they place on their legislatures. And they differ from each other as well in the availability of direct democratic procedures — initiative and referendum.

In his first essay in this section, Robert Williams's close examination of New York constitutional provisions supplements Briffault's overview, showing the specific ways in which this state's approach to governance is unique or unusual. Williams follows with an assessment of how the creation of constitutional commissions has contributed to the state constitutional change process, both in New York and nationally.

State Constitutions in the Federal System

Richard Briffault

Constitutions perform three vital roles in the American political system. They organize the government; they establish fundamental rights that limit the powers of government; and they articulate the basic values and principal concerns of the people with respect to the goals of their government.

Structure: The first role of constitutions is to establish the basic structural framework of the organization being "constituted." They determine the entity's purposes, create its component parts, allocate powers among these components, determine how these parts interact, and provide for participation in the entity's activities and resolution of conflicts within the organization. Constitutions serve this purpose in all sorts of organizations and all sorts of societies, from social clubs to labor unions, political parties to religious denominations. Indeed, any complex collective association can benefit from a fundamental, binding instrument that determines the processes of internal decision making, provides "a set of rules about rulemaking,"[1] and "structure[s] conflict into predictable patterns."[2] Like the "rules of a game," the constitution as framework enables the members of the organization to engage in its ordinary activities free from the burden of having to reinvent, and struggle over, the basic ground rules of the organization each time a conflict within the organization arises.

Although foundational rules and conflict management structures are characteristic of many collective organizations, they are particularly important for governmental bodies, which are responsible for determining public policy and addressing the profound political, economic, and social conflicts within society. "[T]he provision of a publicly known, regularized procedure for decision making takes potential conflict out of the streets

---

1   See Charles R. Adrian, "Trends in State Constitutions," *Harv. J. Legis.* 5 (1968): 311.

2   See Donald Lutz, "The Purposes of American State Constitutions," *Publius* 12 (1982): 27 and 33.

3

and into arenas where calmer reasoning can prevail."[3] As Donald Lutz put it, "a constitution can be viewed as an advanced political technology for managing conflict, regardless of its sources, through well defined processes of legislation, execution, and adjudication."[4]

Fundamental Rights: The second role of constitutions is to establish fundamental rights. The special contribution of the American political tradition to the science of government is the notion that the constitution does not simply organize the polity but that it protects individual freedom and the public's well-being by articulating a set of fundamental rights that place binding restrictions on government. American government is based on popular sovereignty — that the people, not the legislature or the government, are supreme. The constitution vindicates popular sovereignty by providing "a supreme law secure against legislative interference."[5] It cabins the scope of governmental authority, declares and protects fundamental rights, and, ultimately, establishes the principle of limited government. This explains the significance of a written constitution, which seeks to place certain fundamental principles above the ordinary struggles of faction and party in the legislature and thereby secure them from political alteration; and judicial review, which enforces the supremacy of the written constitution against inconsistent legislation or other government action that would overstep the constitution's bounds and abridge or impair the rights and freedoms sought to be secured by the constitution.

Goals: A constitution does not simply establish a government and impose limits on it. It also declares what the government is for, its basic purposes, and the most important policy goals the people wish it to achieve. The third role of constitutions is thus to set forth the principal ends of government.

A constitution is not strictly necessary for this purpose. The important ends of government can be declared and effectuated by statute. Moreover, when it comes to goals "there is no sure standard for distinguishing constitutional from legislative matters."[6]

Indeed, it is often debated whether particular principles and programs ought to be placed in a constitution or left to the regular lawmaking process. Many commentators have criticized the placement of arguably statutory

---

3   *Ibid.*

4   *Ibid.*

5   See Lewis B. Kaden, "The People: 'No!' Some Observations on the 1967 New York Constitutional Convention," *Harv. J. Legis.* 5 (1968): 343 and 345.

6   See John Kincaid, "State Constitutions in the Federal System," *The Annals of the American Academy of Political and Social Science* 496 (March 1988): 19.

material in constitutions, contending that this practice draws the constitution away from "fundamentals," reflects distrust of legislatures, and results in undesirable inflexibility and, ultimately, obsolescence. Much litigation may result over whether goals are mere statements of purpose or are "self executing." Nevertheless, the constitution provides an opportunity for the people to articulate their fundamental principles and policy goals, to give these the greatest legal legitimacy, and to assure that these operate as a mandate on the legislature.

The Role of State Constitutions in American Government

Most discussions of American constitutionalism tend to focus on the federal Constitution. Indeed, one recent survey found that only 44 percent of Americans knew that their state had its own constitution.[7] State constitutions, however, play a crucial role in the American system. The constitutions of the original states predated the federal Constitution and provided examples that the Framers considered during their deliberations. Further, the federal Constitution relies on state governments for the organization of the federal government: The President and members of Congress are elected from the states, and absent federal action state law determines the electorate that can vote for candidates for federal office.[8] The ratification of the federal Constitution, and of subsequent amendments, required the action of the states. One commentator has rightly noted that the importance of the states to the operation of the national government "is apparent from the fact that they are explicitly mentioned in the Constitution at least fifty times in forty-five separate sections."[9]

The federal Constitution presumes the existence of autonomous state governments as part of the ongoing governance of the United States. Moreover, although the federal Constitution requires the states, it does not create them. Federalism is a "central organizing principle" of the federal Constitution.[10] The Framers assumed that most of the work of American government would be done at the state and local level. The enforcement of criminal and civil laws, the regulation of intrastate economic activity, the performance of the police power, and the provision of basic govern-

---

7   See "State Constitutions in the Federal System: Selected Opportunities for State Initiatives," *United States Advisory Commission on Intergovernmental Relations* 17 (July 1989): 2.

8   U.S. Constitution Article I, Section 2, cl. 1; Article II, Section 1, cl. 2; Amendment XVII, cl. 1.

9   See Lutz, "The Purposes of American State Constitutions," *supra*, at p. 40.

10   See Donald S. Lutz, "The United States Constitution as an Incomplete Text," *The Annals of the American Academy of Political and Social Science* 496 (March 1988): 24.

ment services were largely left to subnational governments. The states have residual power over all aspects of government not granted to the federal government. State governments are thus vital to the working of the American political system.

Moreover, apart from the general provision that "the United States shall guarantee to every state in this union a Republican Form of Government,"[11] the federal Constitution says little about the structure, functions, internal procedures, or substantive policy goals of state governments. In contrast, the national government in other federal countries may play a considerable role in organizing the subnational governments. Canada and Australia, for example, do not endow their constituent provinces with locally initiated and enacted constitutions.[12]

Although the federal Constitution imposes limits on the states, state governments are not arms of the national government. They are not like federal administrative agencies or regional offices. The federal government does not appoint or remove state officials, and the federal government cannot give the states direct orders.[13] State governments are limited by the federal Constitution and subordinate to the federal government in most cases of federal-state conflict, but they are in law generally autonomous, free to adopt their own policies and pursue their own goals without being subject to direct federal control. In sum, in the United States, the federal government does not "constitute" the states or direct their activities. That is the function of the state constitutions, or, rather, of the peoples of the states acting through their state constitutions.

Federal Constraints on State Constitutions

Two legal principles govern the relationship between federal law and state constitutions. First is the *supremacy* of federal law within its sphere of authority. Under the supremacy clause of the federal Constitution, the Constitution and federal laws "in pursuance thereof" are the "supreme law of the land," nullifying inconsistent state constitutions or laws. Second is the *autonomy* of the states with respect to matters not in conflict with federal law. Where the federal Constitution and statutes are silent, the states are free to frame their constitutions as they see fit.

---

11 U.S. Constitution Article IV, Section 4.

12 See Ivo Duchacek, "State Constitutional Law in Comparative Perspective," *The Annals of the American Academy of Political and Social Science* 496 (March 1988): 137.

13 See, e.g., *New York* v. *United States*, 112 S.Ct. 2408 (1992).

Supremacy: Although the federal Constitution guarantees to the states a "republican form of government," there has been little constitutional law elaborating the meaning of that guarantee, and a wide variety of state structural innovations that depart considerably from the federal Constitution's organization of the federal government have proven to be consistent with a "republican form of government." Thus, the states enjoy considerable freedom to experiment with new political institutions, different modes of selecting government officers, and drastic alterations of the balance of power among the branches of government. Some examples of state structural innovation that depart from the federal "model" include: voter-initiated legislation and other forms of direct democracy;[14] the unicameral legislature;[15] the item veto,[16] and, by contrast, no provision for a gubernatorial veto of legislation;[17] popular election of judges; state supreme court issuance of advisory opinions on questions of constitutionality; and the plural executive, that is, the independent election of statewide officials to head departments of government rather than their appointment by the governor.

Federal supremacy has had a greater impact in the area of fundamental rights. As a result of the incorporation of most of the protections of the Bill of Rights into the Fourteenth Amendment through expansive interpretations of the Due Process Clause and the Equal Protection Clause, the federal Constitution's fundamental rights now bind the states almost as much as they do the federal government, setting a floor below which the states may not go. Thus, just like the federal government, a state government cannot infringe upon freedom of speech, violate the separation of church and state, take property without providing just compensation, engage in racial discrimination, or deprive criminal defendants of the privilege against self-incrimination.

---

14   Virtually every state provides for some measure of direct citizen involvement in lawmaking. Most state constitutions require voter approval before a state may issue debt. Half the states provide for the suspension of new laws, upon petition, pending their submission to and approval by voters in a referendum. And almost two dozen states authorize citizens to initiate legislation directly, that is, to draft proposals that are then placed on the ballot, and, if approved by the electorate, become law. The Supreme Court has held that such direct democracy is not inconsistent with the guarantee of a republican form of government. *Pacific States Tel. & Tel. Co.* v. *Oregon*, 223 U.S. 118 (1912).

15   Nebraska has a unicameral legislature.

16   Governors in 43 states have the power to veto "items" or "parts" of a bill, while approving the rest of the bill. In most states the item veto is limited to appropriations bills. The particularly expansive item veto in Wisconsin allows the governor to veto individual digits and words. A federal appellate court recently held that the Wisconsin governor's veto power was not inconsistent with a republican form of government. *Risser* v. *Thompson*, 930 F.2d 549 (7th Cir. 1991), cert. denied 112 S.Ct. 180 (1991).

17   North Carolina does not give its governor the power to veto legislation.

Indeed, federal protection of fundamental rights has probably had a greater impact on the structure of state government than any federal provision directly concerned with structure. Under the Fourteenth Amendment's Equal Protection Clause, the Supreme Court has determined that the right to vote is a fundamental right; that this right requires the "one person, one vote" doctrine in legislative representation; and that denials of the franchise and departures from "one person, one vote" are to be subjected to strict scrutiny and invalidated if they are not justified by a compelling state interest. As a result, state constitutional provisions providing for the apportionment of one or more branch of the state legislature on a basis other than population — such as the representation of cities or counties — have been invalidated. This includes provisions still contained in New York's Constitution.[18]

Autonomy: Although the federal Constitution sets the floor for the definition of fundamental rights, and forbids the states from giving less protection, the federal Constitution does not set the ceiling. The states are free to interpret the fundamental rights provisions of their constitutions more expansively than the Supreme Court construes comparable provisions of the federal Constitution. Indeed, the states may add new fundamental rights that have no federal analogue at all. For example many state constitutions explicitly proscribe gender discrimination,[19] provide for a right of privacy,[20] or establish a right to environmental quality.[21] Moreover, many of the provisions of state constitutions declaring the substantive ends of government may also be seen as creating new constitutional rights. Thus, most state constitutions require their legislatures to create free, public schools. In a number of states this has served as the basis of a judicial declaration that there is a fundamental right to equal education or to an adequate education, and the issue continues to be litigated in many other states.[22]

The United States Supreme Court has indicated that as long as the state's new or expanded right does not trench on some other federally protected right the states are free to take a more generous view of

---

18   See the chapter on "Elections and the Political Process" in this book.

19   By one recent count, 17 states have these so-called "little ERAs." See G. Alan Tarr, "Constitutional Theory and State Constitutional Interpretation," *Rutgers L. J.* 22 (1991): 841.

20   See G. Alan Tarr & Mary Cornelia Porter, "Introduction: State Constitutionalism and State Constitutional Law," *Publius* 17 (Winter 1987): 4.

21   See, e.g., *Robins v. Pruneyard Shopping Center*, 447 U.S. 74 (1980) (although the first amendment does not apply to private property, the states may apply their analogous state constitutional protections of free speech to require that a privately owned shopping mall permit individuals on the mall's premises to gather signatures for a political petition).

22   See the chapter on "Education" in this book.

fundamental rights.[23] If a state supreme court interprets a state constitutional right more expansively than its federal constitutional counterpart, the United States Supreme Court will treat the state court's decision as based on an "adequate and independent state ground" and will not review that decision so long as the state court has clearly relied on the state's constitution.[24]

The federal Constitution has relatively little to say about the substantive ends of state government. To be sure, some federal constitutional principles, such as the commitment to national citizenship and a national economic common market, rule out certain potential state ends, such as discrimination against out-of-staters or interference with interstate commerce. Similarly, state constitutional provisions may be preempted by federal statutes. But the Constitution and federal law generally leave state constitutions with enormous discretion concerning the policy and regulatory goals of the states.

Moreover, whereas the federal Constitution is primarily concerned with the procedures for government decision making and the protection of fundamental rights, state constitutions frequently address the substantive ends of state government. As just noted, most state constitutions require their states to provide for free public education. Many others contain substantive provisions dealing with housing and zoning; social welfare and assistance to the poor; unemployment compensation and labor relations; health care; and the conservation of natural resources. Although state courts often interpret these provisions as precatory admonitions rather than enforceable commands, the school finance reform cases indicate that the substantive goal provisions of state constitutions can have a potent impact on state law and policy.[25]

The Federal Constitution and the State Constitutions Compared

Grants v. Limitations

One of the principal points of comparison between the federal Constitution and the state constitutions is theoretical. In principle, the United States government is a government of limited powers. It has only those powers granted to it by the federal Constitution. By contrast, state governments

---

23   *Michigan* v. *Long*, 463 U.S. 1032 (1983).

24   *Ibid.*

25   See Burt Neuborne, "State Constitutions and the Evolution of Positive Rights," *Rutgers L.J.* 20 (1989): 881.

acting through their state legislatures are presumed to have broad, residual, almost plenary governmental power. Thus, state constitutions are seen not as conferring powers on state legislatures but, rather, as limiting those powers the states inherently possess. As the Michigan Supreme Court once put it, "the legislative power of the people through their agent the legislature is limited only by the [state] Constitution, which is not a grant of power but a limitation on the exercise of power."[26] Thus, in theory, the federal government has only those powers that it can trace back to a grant in the federal Constitution, whereas the state legislature can exercise any power unless it is limited by the federal Constitution or by the state constitution.

The "grant/limitation" distinction is less important in practice than in theory. Federal and state judicial interpretations have largely transformed the characters of their respective charters. On the one hand, the federal government has long ceased to be a government of limited powers. The expansive interpretations the Supreme Court has given to the "Necessary and Proper Clause," the "Commerce Clause," the Spending Power, and other provisions of the federal Constitution provide the federal government broad authority to act in areas never contemplated by the Framers. On the other hand, many state courts have interpreted state government powers narrowly. As Robert Williams has observed, "[t]he general characterization of state constitutions as documents of limitation is correct but oversimplified. Many provisions in modern state constitutions were adopted to overcome earlier judicial interpretations of the constitution prohibiting the exercise of the power in question. Such provisions are grants of power, or at least the removal of limitations."[27]

Although the theoretical difference between the federal and state constitutions may be overstated, the notion of state constitutions as documents of limitation rather than grants of power continues to have operative significance when courts interpret them. Within this framework, the provision of a specific power or authorization in a constitution can backfire. Since the state constitution is a document of limitation, constitutional provisions purporting to grant the legislature power to legislate in a particular sphere are unnecessary because the legislature already has the authority. As Frank Grad has noted, "[i]n order to give effect to such special authorizations, however, courts have often given them the full effect of negative implication." That is, courts may hold that authorization

---

26   *Oakland County Taxpayers' League* v. *Board of Supervisors*, 94 N.W.2d 875 (Mich. 1959).

27   See Robert F. Williams, "State Constitutional Law Processes," *Wm. & M. L. Rev.* 24 (1983): 169 and 178-79.

of a particular action precludes other similar actions, so that the explicit power to engage in slum clearance for housing purposes may implicitly preclude clearance for commercial redevelopment, or the express grant of power to levy certain taxes may be interpreted as precluding other taxes.[28] Grad cites a provision in the Oklahoma Constitution that conferred on the state's corporation commissioner power to regulate "all transportation and transmission companies" and then listed railroads, steamboat lines, express companies, and other types of firms engaged in transportation and communications when the provision was adopted. Years later, the Oklahoma Supreme Court held that the commissioner lacked power to regulate airlines since air transportation was not in the list in the constitution.[29]

Length, Frequency of Amendment, and "Statutory" Detail

State constitutions tend to look and feel different from the federal Constitution. They are generally much longer and far more detailed. To the reader accustomed to the broad sweep and majestic general principles of the federal Constitution, state constitutions contain provisions that often seem more "statutory" than "constitutional." The length and detail is, in part, a consequence of the role of state constitutions. Because it does not grant governmental power but structures and limits it, "a state constitution must be explicit about limiting and defining the scope of governmental powers."[30] The greater length may also reflect the nature and scope of state responsibilities. State governments have primary, "frontline" responsibility for protecting life, liberty and property, the provision of education, the administration of justice, the regulation of commercial activity, and a host of "daily services essential to a safe and decent life."[31] The desire to give direction to state governments in these "many and complicated areas" has contributed to the greater length and detail of state constitutions.[32]

The length of state constitutions is also a function of the relative frequency — compared to the federal Constitution — with which state constitutions are amended. These amendments add length and detail. Moreover, as the "document of limitation" doctrine often gives negative implications to amendments, additional amendments may be necessary to

28   See Frank Grad, *The State Constitution: Its Function and Form for Our Time*, New York: National Municipal League, 1969, at pp. 41-42.

29   *Ibid.*, at pp. 42-43.

30   See Daniel J. Elazar, "The Principles and Traditions Underlying State Constitutions," *Publius* 12 (Winter 1982): 11 and 15.

31   See Kincaid, *supra*, at 21.

32   See Tarr & Porter, *supra*, at 2-3.

remove the limitations unintentionally imposed by a prior amendment. Thus, frequency of amendment may give rise to further amendments and an even longer and more detailed document.

1. *Length:* The United States Constitution is approximately 7,300 words long. By contrast, the average length of state constitutions at the end of 1981 was approximately 26,150 words. The only state constitution shorter than the federal Constitution is Vermont's, with an estimated 6,600 words.[33] The longest constitution is Alabama's, with an estimated 174,000 words.[34]

   One 1990 study determined that New York's Constitution is the second longest, at 80,000 words,[35] but this appears to be based on the inclusion of the Statute of Local Governments in the count since a different study in 1981 found the New York Constitution to have 47,000 words[36] — still nearly seven times the length of that of the United States. Among the larger states California's Constitution is approximately 33,000 words; Texas has a 62,000-word constitution; Florida has a 25,000-word constitution; and Pennsylvania's Constitution is 21,675 words.[37]

   After Vermont the shortest constitutions appear to be those of Connecticut, Indiana, Minnesota, and New Hampshire — all of which run between 9,000 and 10,000 words. Large states with relatively short constitutions include Illinois (13,200 words) and New Jersey (17,086 words).[38] The 1967 draft of the New York State Constitution, ultimately rejected at the polls, was about a third shorter than the document in force in the state at the time.

2. *Frequency of State Constitutional Change:* The United States continues to operate under the same Constitution that was adopted in 1787. Since the Constitution's ratification, Congress has submitted 33 amendments to the states for their consideration; the states have ratified 27 of these. The Constitution provides for the

---

33   See Albert L. Sturm, "The Development of American State Constitutions," *Publius* 12 (Winter 1982): 57 and 74.

34   See Janice C. May, "State Constitutions and Constitutional Revision: 1988-89 and the 1980s," *The Book of the States 1990-91,* Lexington, KY: The Council of State Governments, 1991, at p. 40 (Table 1.1).

35   *Ibid.*

36   See Sturm, *supra*, at 76.

37   The 1981 Sturm study and the 1990 May study were in close agreement on each of these counts. In several cases, the 1990 study has a slightly higher word count than the 1981 calculation but that appears to reflect subsequent amendments rather than a difference over what counts as part of the constitution.

38   *Ibid.*

calling of a constitutional convention for proposing amendments on the application of the legislatures of two-thirds of the states, but the state legislatures have never so applied.

By contrast, the 50 states have had 146 constitutions, for an average of nearly three per state. Louisiana has had eleven constitutions, Georgia ten, and South Carolina seven. Three states have had six constitutions; three states five; nine states four; four states three; nine states two; and nineteen states just one. New York's four constitutions were adopted in 1777, 1822, 1846, and 1894.[39]

In 1982, the average age of a state constitution was 82 years. Most constitutions were adopted in the eighteenth and nineteenth centuries, when the colonies declared their independence, territories were admitted as new states, the Civil War and Reconstruction caused the repeated revision of the constitutions of the southern states, and northern states changed their constitutions to adapt to rapid economic, social, and political change. Three New England states[40] continue to use constitutions adopted in the eighteenth century while twenty-nine states are operating under constitutions adopted in the nineteenth century.[41] The remaining eighteen state constitutions were adopted in the twentieth century.

Over the last half century, approximately three new constitutions have been adopted each decade. There were three new state constitutions in the 1940s, two new constitutions in the 1950s, four in the 1960s, and six in the 1970s, and two in the 1980s.[42]

Associated with the large number of state constitutions has been an even larger number of state constitutional conventions. As of January 1, 1992, there have been 233 state constitutional conventions. Again, although much of this activity was in the eighteenth and nineteenth centuries, recent decades witnessed considerable convention activity. There were six conventions in the 1940s, nine in the 1950s, fourteen in the 1960s, twelve in the 1970s, and five in the 1980s.[43] New York has had nine constitu-

---

39 See Janice C. May, "Constitutional Amendment and Revision Revisited," *Publius* 12 (Winter 1987): 153 and 162.

40 Massachusetts, New Hampshire, and Vermont.

41 Sturm, *supra*, at p. 74.

42 See May, *Book of the States 1990-91, supra*, at p. 21.

43 *Ibid.*

tional conventions: 1777, 1801, 1821, 1846, 1867, 1894, 1915, 1938, and 1967.

One reason for the large number of conventions in some states may be that the decision to call a constitutional convention is not entirely up to the legislature. In fourteen states, the state constitution provides that the voters are to be periodically presented with a ballot question asking whether they wish to call a constitutional convention. The period between calls ranges between nine and twenty years, with most states having the periodic call provision utilizing the twenty-year interval. The periodic constitutional call provisions led to the vast majority of conventions over the past half century; five in the 1940s, eight in the 1950s, twelve in the 1960s, ten in the 1970s, and three in the 1980s.[44]

In addition to the large number of new constitutions, the states frequently amend their existing constitutions. The United States Constitution has been amended 27 times; by contrast, one tabulation in 1985 found that the *then-existing* state constitutions (and not the many previous constitutions) had been amended 5,198 times (or approximately 104 amendments per state) even though on average the state constitutions were less than half the age of the United States Constitution.[45] As of 1993, New York's Constitution of 1894 had been amended 213 times.

Whereas most conventions occur without legislative initiative, the vast majority of state constitutional amendments originated as state legislative proposals. According to one study, as of 1985, the legislatures had proposed 90 percent of the total amendments, with the rest resulting from constitutional conventions, standing state constitutional revision commissions that have the power to submit proposals to the voters,[46] and voter-initiated proposals.[47] In recent years, these percentages have remained roughly constant. Currently, seventeen states empower the voters to amend the state constitution through the initiative. From 1984

---

44   *Ibid.*

45   See Janice C. May, "Constitutional Amendment and Revision Revisited," *Publius* 17 (Winter 1987): 153 and 162.

46   Florida has a commission which periodically comes into existence with the power to submit constitutional amendments directly to the voters for their approval. See the chapter on constitutional commissions in this book and May, *Book of the States, 1990-91, supra,* at 23-25.

47   See May, "Constitutional Amendment and Revision Revisited," *supra,* at p. 162.

through 1991, thirty-four state constitutional amendments actually resulted from voter initiatives, out of a total of seventy-five voter-initiated amendment proposals placed on state ballots during this period. During the same time, more than 650 legislative proposals were also adopted as constitutional amendments, as were fourteen proposals from constitutional conventions.[48]

One factor contributing to the frequency of state constitutional change may be the relative ease of amendment, at least when compared to the difficulty of amending the federal Constitution. An amendment to the United States Constitution requires an affirmative vote of two-thirds in each house of Congress, followed by ratification by three fourths of the states. Most state constitutional amendments also emerge out of the legislature, with some requiring super-majorities or other special features, such as New York's requirement that the proposed amendment be passed by two successive legislatures. And in every state except Delaware, constitutional amendments — whether proposed by the legislature, constitutional conventions, constitutional revision commissions, or voter initiatives — must be ratified by the electorate. But except for amendments concerning elective franchise and education matters in New Mexico, which require separate majorities statewide and in two-thirds of the counties to pass, there is no analogue to the "federalist" aspect of federal constitutional revision, that is, there is no requirement of separate approval by a state's component counties or municipalities. This may make the process of ratification less onerous.

Nevertheless, it appears that the principal difference between the federal and state amendment processes is not the rigors of ratification, but the number of proposals that are passed by the legislatures and submitted for ratification. The small number of federal constitutional amendments is primarily attributable to the relatively small number approved by Congress, not the failure of the states to ratify the amendments Congress passed. In the first two hundred years of the federal Constitution, Congress submitted only thirty-three constitutional amendments to the states for ratification.[49] By the same token, although the states have approved an astonishing 5,198 amendments to their existing consti-

---

48   See May, "State Constitutions and Constitutional Revision: 1991-92," *The Book of the States 1992-93*, Lexington, KY: The Council of State Governments, 1993, at p. 2 (Table A).

49   See May, *supra*, at p. 162.

tutions (as of 1985), an even more staggering 8,279 amendments to those constitutions had been submitted to the voters.[50] The ratification rate of proposed federal constitutional amendments is actually somewhat higher than that of their state counterparts (although it could be that the rigors of the federal ratification process discourage Congress from submitting many proposals). What is striking is the enormous number of proposed state constitutional amendments submitted to the voters by state legislatures, constitutional conventions and commissions, and voter initiatives.

3. *"Statutory" Provisions:* State constitutions have long been known, indeed, are notorious, for their detailed, statute-like provisions. Almost a century ago, Lord James Bryce, the famous British commentator on American government, found the state constitutions of that time to include ". . . a great deal of matter which is in no distinctive sense constitutional law but general law, . . . matter therefore which seems out of place in a constitution because it is better fit to be dealt with in ordinary statutes."[51] Reducing the amount of statutory detail in state constitutions has been a major concern of twentieth century constitutional reformers, who have argued that a proper state constitution ought to limit itself to fundamental law, and leave statutory matters to the legislature. Nevertheless, state constitutional amendments continue to address such matters as casino gambling, lotteries, bonds for veterans' housing, liquor by the drink, and the eradication of the boll weevil.[52] And the New York Constitution continues to include language dealing with the tolls on the Erie Canal and the ski trails in the Adirondack park.[53]

The frequency of state constitutional revision and the resulting length of state constitutions are closely intertwined with the detailed quasi-statutory nature of many state constitutional provisions. State constitutions are so long and are so frequently amended because the political majorities of the day may seek to secure their victories from subsequent reverses by enshrining those victories in the state constitution. Detailed, quasi-statutory constitutional amendments transform transient political success

---

50   Ibid.

51   See Lord Bryce, *The American Commonwealth*, I, New York: MacMillan, 1891, at p. 116.

52   May, *supra*, at p. 165.

53   See N.Y. Constitution Article XIV, Article XV. The Adirondack Park provision was most recently amended in 1987; the Erie Canal provision was mostly recently amended in 1991.

into elements of the permanent, constitutional framework of state government. As Janice May has pointed out, "amendment politics is a branch of legislative politics in many states."[54] One result, as one state supreme court justice observed, is that state constitutions are generally perceived as "political documents."[55] They lack the symbolic importance of the national document, a powerful informal barrier to change through amendment. Politics, of course, plays a role in federal constitutional revision as well, but "the politically responsive nature of state constitutions is more directly apparent."[56]

Indeed, state constitutions serve as a sort of Rosetta Stone of state history, displaying the successive political, economic, and social changes in the state as they recorded themselves in the state's fundamental document.

Of course, this very technique of locking legislative victories into the state constitution contains the seeds of its own undoing. As the political wheel turns, and new majorities come to power, they may seek to remove political provisions they oppose or, more commonly, to insert their own statutory provisions to secure the goals they favor. They will, thus, propose additional constitutional amendments. As a result, the constitution becomes longer, more detailed, and more complex. The more detail in the constitution, the more likely constitutional issues will arise in the day-to-day operations of state government. This may lead to more efforts to revise the constitution. As political conflicts get caught up in constitutional questions, the constitution may increasingly be seen as an aspect of the political struggle, and not something outside of or above politics. This makes it still easier to consider constitutional revision as a proper strategy for pursuing political ends. In short, the frequency of amendment and the extensive statutory detail of many state constitutions reflect the extent to which state constitutional change has become part of the ordinary politics of the states.

An alternative, albeit related explanation of the length, detail, and statutory nature of state constitutions centers on the

---

54   May, *supra*, at p. 165.

55   See Justice Robert F. Utter, "Freedom and Diversity in a Federal System: Perspectives on State Constitutions and the Washington Declaration of Rights," *Developments in State Constitutional Law,* Bradley D. McGraw (ed.), St. Paul, MN: West, 1985, at p. 242.

56   See "State Constitutions in the Federal System," *supra*, at p. 1.

role played by voter-initiated amendments and the large number of state constitutional conventions resulting from the voters' power to call them. This view emphasizes the history of popular distrust of state legislatures. Since so much of the "statutory" material in a state constitution is not necessary to empower the government but, instead, operates as a restriction on the legislature — either preventing the legislature from taking some action or compelling the legislature to pursue a particular program — the decision to place such a provision in the constitution is often seen as reflecting the concern that without such a binding constraint the legislature would fail to abide by the people's will on the subject.

As one late nineteenth century commentator observed, writing during a period of extensive state constitutional revision, "one of the most marked features of all recent state constitutions is the distrust shown of the legislature."[57] Indeed, Robert Williams emphasizes that "the transition from early state constitutions granting unfettered legislative power to the more recent constitutions restricting legislative power reflects one of the most important themes in state constitutional law." He sees the theme of distrust of the legislature as manifesting itself in two ways: "the insertion of specific 'constitutional legislation' into state constitutional texts, thereby supplanting legislative prerogatives and sometimes leading to a limitation of legislative alternatives through judicially discovered 'negative implication'" and the adoption of detailed procedural requirements that legislatures must follow when they enact laws.[58]

The Federal "Model" and State Constitutional Reform

Those state constitutional reformers long critical of the length and substantive statutory detail of state constitutions have suggested that the relatively brief and much less detailed federal Constitution ought to be a model for state constitutional reform. As a report issued by the National Municipal League three decades ago put it, "the ideal state constitution expresses *fundamental* law, law which is basic in providing the foundation for a political system and the powers of government. . . . Generally

---

57   See Eaton, "Recent State Constitutions," *Harv. L. Rev.* 6 (1892): 109.

58   See Williams, *supra*, at pp. 201-02.

speaking, fundamental law possesses greater permanence, is less detailed, and requires fewer changes to keep it up-to-date than does statutory law."[59]

In part, this view reflects the concern that a detailed, statutory state constitution embodies distrust of the legislature and the ordinary political process: "The ideal state constitution — short and general — reflects citizen trust of government and citizen assumption of responsibility. Such a constitution vests broad powers in the representatives of the people and holds them responsible through democratic, electoral processes."[60]

But more importantly, the reform position grows out of the concern that excessive statutory detail reduces the elasticity of government, rendering it less capable of adapting to changes and framing new solutions to new challenges. Constitutional restrictions that are desirable in one era might prove too confining to a subsequent generation facing different problems. Constitutional provisions creating a new agency and giving it particular powers or responsibilities might, several decades later, block a desirable governmental reorganization if, as a result of social or technological change, there is less need for the agency, or if government efficiency would be better served by combining several constitutionally created agencies. Even a provision granting the state government a new power might ultimately turn into a restriction rather than an authorization if, due to the negative implications of the "document of limitation" theory, the provisions for the exercise of that new power are too specific, thereby precluding the state's pursuit of alternative avenues to attain the same public goal.

Ultimately, constitutional detail results in inflexibility. Inflexibility may, of course, be the goal — to place the matter included in the constitution beyond change by normal lawmaking processes. The enduring quality of a provision of the state constitution may protect a desirable policy or a fundamental right from capricious legislative action. As the history of fundamental rights indicates, some distrust of the legislature may be necessary for the protection of individual liberty. But when the constitution is too detailed it becomes more difficult for state government to function. In one classic example, the Louisiana Constitution provided in detail for the composition of the New Orleans Civil Service Commission. The members of the Commission were to be appointed from nominees put forward by the presidents of the various colleges in the city. When

59 See John P. Wheeler, Jr., "Introduction," *Salient Issues of Constitutional Revision*, New York: National Municipal League, 1961, at p. xi.

60 *Ibid.*, at p. xii.

one of the named colleges closed, the Commission was unable to obtain a full complement of members.

In short, inflexibility may be desirable with respect to fundamentals, but government's inability to adapt to changing needs is a recipe for obsolescence.

There is no ready metric for distinguishing the "fundamental" from the "statutory," just as there is no ready way of determining what matters ought to be trusted to the legislature and what ought to be protected from legislative change. The definition of "fundamental" is likely to evolve over time and to differ for different groups and interests. What is "fundamental" reflects the needs of government and of the people as conditioned by time and place, the functions of the government, and the history of the community. State constitutions are likely to continue to be longer and more detailed than the federal Constitution because of the greater responsibility of the states for providing government services and regulating aspects of daily life, the long-standing tradition of using state constitutions to limit and guide the substantive actions of state government, and the greater direct role of the people in the processes of constitutional revision. Nevertheless, in setting a "fair balance . . . between the trust implied by a spare constitution and the distrust of legislative action that inspires the 'statutory detail' in a constitution"[61] a central concern must be with both the costs and the benefits of inflexibility that result from the inclusion of detail in the constitution.

---

61   See Kaden, *supra*, at p. 355.

Principal Provisions of State Constitutions: A Brief Overview

Richard Briffault

The Structure of Government

Although the federal Constitution allows the states considerable freedom with regard to the organization of their polities, most states resemble each other and the federal government in basic structure.

All fifty states have adopted the separation of powers, with three separate branches of government. (Indeed, some state constitutions, in addition to providing for three branches of government, also contain a distinct textual provision calling for the separation of powers.) All fifty states have an elected legislature; in forty-nine states it is bicameral. All fifty states have an independently elected governor, although two states provide for legislative selection of the governor from the top two candidates when no candidate has received more than fifty percent of the vote. In all states but Vermont, Rhode Island, and New Hampshire, the governor serves a four-year term. Thirty states limit the number of terms or consecutive terms a governor may serve. The members of the smaller — or upper — house of state legislatures most frequently serve a four-year term, and the members of the larger — or lower — house serve a two-year term. Seventeen states have adopted term limits for their state legislators.

All fifty states have an independent judiciary, although there is considerable variation among the states and departure from the federal "model" in terms of how judges are selected, the length of their terms, and the extent to which the number, size, and jurisdiction of state courts, and the procedures and grounds for taking appeals, are specified in the constitution or left to subsequent legislative enactments. In contrast with the federal judiciary, which is restricted to the adjudication of "cases and controversies," a number of states authorize their state supreme courts to give advisory opinions concerning the constitutionality of proposed legislation.

Three major areas in which most states deviate from the federal "model" are:

1. *Restrictions on Legislative Procedure:* Most modern state constitutions contain detailed provisions regulating the structure and operations of state legislatures. These provisions, which govern the procedures for the enactment of statutes, were not included in the initial state constitutions and reflect a history of distrust of state legislatures. Typical procedural limitations include: requirements that titles of legislative acts provide general notice of their contents; requirements that all bills be referred to committees; requirements that a bill be before the legislature for a certain number of days or read aloud a certain number of times before the legislature may take action; restrictions on alteration of the bill during the process of legislative consideration; prohibitions of acts containing more than one subject; limitations on the method of amending existing statutes; and limitations on the enactment of special laws. These provisions have no parallel in the federal Constitution, which simply designates the presiding officers, defines a quorum, requires that a journal be kept, and provides that "each house may determine the rules of its proceedings."[1] These state constitutional restrictions have also been sharply criticized by reformers, who contend that "legislative procedure should be left for legislative determination."[2]

2. *Item Veto:* A second important distinction between the federal Constitution and most state constitutions is the presence in the latter of the item veto. Forty-three states allow governors to veto "items" or "parts" of bills; in every state but one that provides for this power the item veto is limited to appropriations bills. The most expansive item veto power is enjoyed by the governor of Wisconsin, who may veto individual digits and words. The governor of Washington's partial veto is not limited to appropriations bills. In contrast, the governor of North Carolina has no veto power at all.

3. *The Plural Executive:* The federal Constitution creates only two executive officers — the president and the vice president. The president is the undisputed head of the executive branch, and has

---

1   U.S. Constitution Article I, Section 5.

2   See Patricia Shumate Wirt, "The Legislature." *Salient Issues of Constitutional Revision*, New York: National Municipal League, 1961, at p. 77.

the power to appoint all subordinate executive branch officials, although his appointments for top posts often require Senate confirmation. In contrast, most states provide for numerous independently elected statewide officials, many of whom exercise executive functions independently of the governor. In all but seven states the voters elect the attorney general.[3] Thirty-eight states have an independently elected treasurer or comptroller, while in another four the official with these functions is elected by the legislature.[4] Other state officials that are often independently elected include the secretary of state, the commissioner of education, the commissioner of insurance, and the commissioner of agriculture.

In addition, some state constitutions directly create executive branch offices, agencies, and commissions. Even if these bodies are directed by appointed officials, they may enjoy special constitutional protections from state legislative action.[5]

At the other extreme, eight states dispense with the analogue to the vice president — the office of lieutenant governor. New Jersey, New Hampshire, and Tennessee have just one elected executive branch official, the governor.

Direct Democracy

The federal government is representative in form; the people elect their representatives who then do the governing. Apart from voting for candidates, citizens have no direct role in the ongoing process of government.

Most states, however, provide for some direct role for the people in government. In every state but one, popular approval in a referendum is necessary to ratify changes to the constitution. Two dozen states also permit voter-initiated referenda on new legislation: if a petition initiating a referendum obtains the requisite number of signatures, the effectiveness of the legislation that is the subject of the petition is blocked until the

---

3   See The Council of State Governments, *The Book of the States 1992-93*, Lexington, KY: The Council of State Governments, 1993, at p. 111 (Table 2.17). The attorney general is elected by the state legislature in Maine, and appointed by the judges of the state supreme court in Tennessee. Only five states — Alaska, Hawaii, New Hampshire, New Jersey, and Wyoming — follow the federal model of having the governor appoint the attorney general.

4   *Ibid.*, at p. 120 (Table 2.21). In one state the treasurer/comptroller is appointed by another agency. (Note: The auditing functions of this office are not executive in nature.)

5   See, e.g., *Florida Dep't of Natural Resources* v. *Florida Game & Fresh Water Fish Comm'n*, 342 SO.2d 495 (Fla. 1977).

matter is submitted to the voters for their consideration. In addition, seventeen states provide for voter initiation of amendments to the constitution and twenty-one states permit voter initiation of legislation.[6] In other words, the voters can make law or amend the constitution directly, without any action by the state legislature or the governor.

Fundamental Rights

All state constitutions contain provisions declaring and protecting fundamental rights. Some of these provisions are similar, if not virtually identical, to the Bill of Rights and other fundamental rights provisions of the federal Constitution. Nevertheless, differences in textual detail, state history and tradition, or a state court's constitutional doctrines can result in a state court giving a more expansive interpretation to a state constitutional provision than the federal courts have given to the provision's federal analogue. Moreover, some state fundamental rights provisions have no counterpart in the federal document at all. Some state constitutions ban gender discrimination; apply antidiscrimination principles to private activity; establish a right of privacy; provide for a right to open government; guarantee open access to court; or declare the rights of victims of crime; or the rights of the public to environmental quality.[7]

The Political Process

Traditionally, the states have had the exclusive power to determine who may vote in state elections; most state constitutions still contain articles dealing with the qualifications for the franchise and the procedures for casting a ballot.[8] Over the years, however, voting rights have been substantially federalized. The federal Constitution prohibits race and gender discrimination in voting; prohibits the states from setting a minimum voting age greater than eighteen years; bars discrimination based on wealth, taxpayer status, and durational residency; and generally subjects restrictions on the franchise to strict scrutiny. Federal statutes implement these prohibitions and also address such issues as absentee voting and voter registration in federal elections. The states may continue to regulate those aspects of voting not directly addressed by the federal Constitution and federal statutes, but most of the principal suffrage issues are now

---

6   *Ibid.*, at p. 329 (Table 5.15).

7   Rights under state constitutions are discussed in detail in the chapters "Individual Liberties," "Criminal Justice," and "Social Policy" in this book.

8   In New York, the provision is Article II.

24

controlled by federal law, and federal judicial doctrines will result in strict judicial scrutiny of state rules that restrict the franchise.

Similarly, the apportionment of seats in the state legislature was traditionally a matter for the states, and many state constitutions provide criteria for the districting of state legislatures. As a result of the "one person, one vote" doctrine, the federal Voting Rights Act, and Supreme Court decisions, many of the substantive criteria for legislative apportionment are now determined by federal law. Nevertheless, the states may address other aspects of reapportionment. More than a dozen state constitutions, for example, take the redistricting process out of the legislature and vest it in a constitutionally created districting commission.

Some state constitutions also address other aspects of the state political process, such as campaign finance, lobbying, and ethics in government. Here, too, the range of state constitutional action may be constrained by federal law.

Taxing, Spending, and Borrowing

Most state constitutions give detailed attention to state and local taxation and finance. State constitutions may provide for special procedures or majorities to adopt a tax, restrict the kinds of taxes that may be levied, and limit the rates of taxation that may be imposed. Many constitutions contain a uniformity clause requiring all property to be assessed at the same percentage of value and then taxed at the same rate.[9] Some state constitutions prohibit the use of certain taxes; other states have constitutionalized certain tax exemptions.[10] Some state constitutions may allocate the power to use certain tax sources between state and local government, for example reserving the property tax to local governments. They may also provide for certain taxes and then earmark the proceeds for particular programs, such as the restriction of the revenue generated by the tax on motor fuels to the construction and maintenance of highways.

California's Proposition 13, adopted by initiative and referendum in 1978, provides a dramatic instance of the role of state constitutions in limiting the rate of increase in property assessments; capping the tax rate; and imposing tough procedural requirements on state and local governments that seek either to raise tax rates or impose new types of taxes.

---

9   See Robert Williams, "State Constitutional Law Processes," *W&M Law Rev.* 24, 2 (Winter 1983): 217.

10   *Ibid.*

State constitutions generally address state and local borrowing. Many state constitutions impose debt limits that "severely constrain the ability of state and local governments to borrow money."[11] Some of these set an actual dollar limit on the amount of state debt outstanding. Other constitutional provisions tie local debt to the assessed valuation of local property. Debt above such constitutional limits would require a constitutional amendment. More commonly, debt limits are procedural, providing, for example, that no new debt may be incurred without voter approval.

State constitutional debt restrictions have given rise to a long history of evasion. States have created new entities — public authorities — that are not subject to constitutional restrictions. Similarly, states have created new borrowing instruments, such as revenue bonds, on the theory (accepted by most state courts) that as long as the only claim of bond buyers is to specific pledged revenues, such as those likely to be generated by the project financed by the debt, the general taxing authority of the state is not pledged and therefore the revenue bond does not constitute "debt" within the meaning of the state constitution.

Most state constitutions also contain provisions dealing with some aspects of state spending. Virtually every constitution requires a balanced state budget, and addresses the budget making process. Many constitutions impose restrictions on the subjects of state spending. Typically, spending must be for a "public purpose;" often gifts, loans, or the lending of the state's credit for private purposes has been prohibited. In some states, these provisions have raised constitutional questions concerning state or local economic development initiatives, which involve assistance to private companies, or public-private cooperative ventures.

Local Government

Most state constitutions give considerable attention to local government. Unlike the federal Constitution, which does not create the states or impose extensive restrictions or duties on the day-to-day activities of state government, the states do create their local governments, and determine their form, size, and powers. A state constitution may indicate the types of local governments that can exist within the state; how they are formed; whether, and how, they can expand or contract their borders; how they are to be governed; and the nature of their powers. In addition, many state constitutions try to protect local autonomy by restricting the power of the state

---

11   *Ibid.*, at p. 219.

legislature to act regarding local affairs. Thus, many state constitutions forbid the creation of "special commissions" concerning municipal matters, and bar the enactment of "special laws" that affect specially targeted local governments.

Traditionally, local governments enjoyed only those powers expressly delegated by their state. Many state constitutions, however, now provide for some form of home rule, in which at least some local governments have broad authority over local affairs and do not have to keep returning to the state legislature to obtain specific new powers. The state constitutions, however, display considerable differences concerning which local governments enjoy home rule; the scope of a home rule government's authority to initiate local legislation; and the state's power to displace local action with conflicting state laws.

Substantive Policies

State constitutions provide for an extensive list of substantive programs and policies. These vary considerably from state to state, but provisions in a few policy areas may be found in many, if not most, state constitutions.

Every state constitution contains an education clause that generally requires the state legislature to establish some system of free public schools. Typically, these clauses establish the school system, provide for the management of the schools, and guarantee that the system is nonsectarian. Many also contain language expressing standards for the educational system.[12] These have become the basis for litigation in many states challenging the constitutionality of the state's school financing system.

As another example, many state constitutions contain provisions concerning poverty, shelter, and income assistance for the needy. Section 1 of Article XVII of the New York Constitution provides that "aid, care and support of the needy are public concerns and shall be provided by the state and by such of its subdivisions, and in such manner and by such means, as the legislature may from time to time determine." Although this provision was adopted, in part, to overcome doubts concerning the constitutionality of social welfare programs, and although the provision gives the legislature considerable discretion concerning the amount of aid and the definition of the needy, the Court of Appeals has held that the state constitution "unequivocally prevents the Legislature from simply refusing

---

12 See Molly McUsic, "The Use of Education Clauses in School Finance Reform Litigation," *Harv. J. Legis.* 28 (1991): 307 and 311. See also the chapter "Education" in this book.

to aid those whom it classified as needy."[13] Similarly, the Montana Constitution states that "the legislature shall provide such economic assistance and social and rehabilitative services as may be necessary for those inhabitants who, by reasons of age, infirmities or misfortune may have need for the aid of society." The supreme court in that state relied on this provision to invalidate a state law eliminating general assistance payments to able-bodied childless adults.[14]

Other policy areas addressed in state constitutions include: the regulation of business corporations, public utilities, and intrastate commerce generally; conservation and natural resources, including oil and gas, water, fish, and wildlife within the state and such provisions as New York's requirement that the Adirondack forest preserve be kept "forever wild"; the civil service; the administration of criminal justice; civil litigation and tort reform; and lotteries and casino gambling. As noted, these subjects vary from state to state, according to the history, geography, economy, culture, and traditions of each state.

Constitutional Revision

Finally, most state constitutions contain provisions for their revision. Frequently the legislature, by an extraordinary majority or through action by two successive legislatures, is permitted to propose amendments for ratification by the people. Popular ratification is necessary in every state but Delaware. As previously noted, some states permit initiatives to propose amendments, which become effective if approved by the people. Florida has a standing constitutional revision commission that is periodically convened under a requirement of that state's constitution. It has the power to submit proposed amendments to the people directly. Most state constitutions authorize the calling of new constitutional conventions for the thoroughgoing revision of the constitution. New constitutions generally require the approval of the voters to take effect. In addition, fourteen states periodically present to the voters a ballot question asking the electorate whether they want to call a constitutional convention.

13 *Tucker* v. *Toia,* 43 N.Y.2d 1 (1977).
14 *Butte Community Unions* v. *Lewis,* 712 P.2d 1309 (Mont. 1986).

New York's State Constitution in Comparative Context[1]

Robert F. Williams

The explanation for the comparatively small amount of intensive professional and scholarly interest in at least the basic study of comparative state constitutional provisions lies to a great extent in the nature of the state constitutional documents themselves. This can be proved, for anyone with the necessary time and patience, by reading ...the fifty state constitutions. With some exceptions, the state constitutions are not notable as masterpieces of legal draftsmanship or literary style.[2]

The field of state constitutional research has become in large measure a field of comparative law, and states that propose to amend their constitutions usually look to the constitutional language and experience of other states, either for example or avoidance.[3]

New York State has long and repeated experience with constitution making. Eight of the original thirteen states adopted their first constitutions in 1776. That of New York was effected only one year later, placing it among the states with the longest state constitutional experience. Moreover, New York is about in the middle of the original thirteen in the number of constitutions it has adopted. There have been four to date (that of 1777 and three in the nineteenth century, in 1821, 1846, and 1894).

---

1   The problems of comparative research in state constitutions are very great. Despite the obvious need for such research as background for a state considering amending or revising its state constitution, the indexes and comparative materials are scarce. This paper is thus necessarily only a preliminary, general comparison.

2   See Morris M. Goldings, "Massachusetts Amends: A Decade of State Constitutional Revision," *Harv. J. Legis. 5* (1968): 373. One commentator stated, concerning the New York Constitution, "probably no other large industrial state has such a poorly drafted charter." Robert B. Dishman, *State Constitutions: The Shape of the Document*, New York: National Municipal League, 1968, at p. 69.

3   See Frank P. Grad, "Foreword," in Barbara Faith Sachs, *Fundamental Liberties and Rights: A 50 State Index*, New York: Legislative Drafting Research Fund, Columbia University, Oceana Publications, 1980, at p. v.

Additionally, there was one major revision in the twentieth century, in 1938.

As an original state, New York avoided the exertion of influence over the content of its state Constitution by Congress and the President. (In fact, scholarship has demonstrated that the influence flowed in the opposite direction, with the New York governorship in some measure a model for the design of the presidency.)[4] Therefore, whatever is contained in the New York Constitution is of a New York origin, and not the product of nationally imposed preferences that often were made the price of statehood for the non-original states.[5] As Chief Judge Judith S. Kaye has stated: "The combination of high detail and accessibility to the amendment process gives our Constitution a distinctive New York character. It is a product and expression of this State."[6]

In fact, in addition to influencing the national document, New York's Constitution was a model for other states as they drafted or revised their state constitutions. For example, "the Iowa and New York Constitutions lay behind virtually every section of the Californian's [1849] document."[7]

Each of New York's Constitutions has built on the preceding one, while reflecting the principal political concerns and theories of governance that prevailed at the time of its drafting. Several commentators who studied a number of state constitutional conventions, including New York's 1967 Convention, noted the importance of understanding the political, social, and cultural context of state constitution making and constitutional development:

> . . . [C]onstitutional revision is a political process. As such it does tap the full range of motives and interests called into play by the other political subprocesses at the state level. And like these other forms of state politics, it varies from jurisdiction to jurisdiction in response to local differences in political culture and style.[8]

4　See Charles Thach, Jr., *The Creation of the Presidency, 1775-1789*, Baltimore: Johns Hopkins University Press, 1969.

5　See Peter S. Onuf, *The Origins of the Federal Republic: Jurisdictional Controversies in the United States 1775-1787*, Philadelphia: University of Pennsylvania Press, 1983, at pp. 43-46.

6　See Judith S. Kaye, "Dual Constitutionalism in Practice and Principle," *St. John's L. Rev.* 61 (1987): 399 and 409.

7　See David Alan Johnson, *Founding the Far West: California, Oregon, and Nevada, 1840-1890*, Berkeley: University of California Press, 1992, p. 102.

8　See Elmer E. Cornwell, Jr., Jay S. Goodman & Wayne R. Swanson, *State Constitutional Conventions: The Politics of the Revision Process in Seven States*, New York: Praeger, 1975 at p. 192.

In addition to the successes of the past, the current content of the New York Constitution also displays the influences of ostensibly failed efforts at constitutional revision in the state, for example those of 1867, 1915, and 1967. In fact, these conventions substantially set the constitutional change agenda for New York for decades after their initial proposals were rejected at the polls. Alterations came too in New York as a result of the major waves of state constitutional change that swept the region and nation.

It is therefore evident that New York's Constitution cannot be viewed in a one-dimensional way, as though it were simply drafted at "one sitting." Rather, it must be seen as the culmination of centuries of experience and an enormous array of influences. The result is a layered, or multidimensional, document.[9] As in other states, the state Constitution in New York can be seen as a "mine of instruction for the natural history of democratic communities,"[10] reflecting "the romance, the poetry, and even the drama of American politics"[11] in the unique New York context. Further, it is the very nature of this experience that it is never finished.

One of the leading experts on state constitutions and constitution making in this century, Frank P. Grad of the Columbia Law School, had little patience for the notion that there is an "ideal" state constitution. Rather, Grad wrote:

> ... [W]e must be content with something less that the Platonic ideal; we must aim rather for a constitutional document that is designed to enable the state to carry on its work of government today and in the foreseeable future with efficiency and economy and with minimum interference by unnecessary restrictions. . . .[12]

Because there is no "ideal" state constitution, because political influences are different from state to state, and because the *federal* Constitution performs a different function from state constitutions, com-

---

9   For excellent consideration of each section's origins, see Peter J. Galie, *The New York State Constitution: A Reference Guide*, Westport, CT: Greenwood Press, 1991, and Robert Allan Carter, *New York State Constitution: Sources of Legislative Intent*, Littleton, CO: Fred Rothman Co., 1988.

10 See James Bryce, *The American Commonwealth*, New York: MacMillan, rev. 2d Ed., 1891, at p. 434.

11 See James Q. Dealey, *Growth of American State Constitutions*, New York: DeCapo Press, 1915, at p. 11.

12 See Frank P. Grad, "The State Constitution: Its Function and Form for Our Time," *Va. L. Rev.* 54 (1968): 928-29. See also *Model State Constitution*, New York: National Municipal League, 1963.

parisons should be made with caution. Still, however, there is value to examining New York's current state Constitution in comparative context.

Article I: The Bill of Rights

The New York Bill of Rights did not appear in the original 1777 Constitution. That document, like those of the other original states without separate Bills of Rights, did protect a variety of rights, such as jury trial, freedom of religion, and due process within the body of the Constitution itself.[13] In 1821, however, a separate bill of rights was adopted, forming the basis for the current article which, like in most states now, comes at the *beginning* of the Constitution. New York's Bill of Rights is in many respects similar to those of the other states.[14] The specific provisions reflect amendments adopted over the years to accommodate pragmatic recognition of what are thought to be the necessities of modern state government. For example, Article I, Section 1, concerning disfranchisement was amended in 1959 to permit the legislature to dispense with primary elections under certain circumstances. Article I, Section 2 regarding the right to jury trial has been amended to permit non-unanimous jury verdicts if the legislature so desires. Article I, Section 7, also reflects a similar modern modification in Section (d), a subsection that provides the legislative authority to permit certain private actions to drain agricultural or swamp lands as a public use with just compensation.

The guarantee of freedom of speech contained in Article I, Section 8, is, as in many states, an *affirmative* statement of the right, rather than a negative limitation on government such as is found in Section 9, which prohibits limiting the right to peacefully assemble. This has led some states, with similar provisions, but not New York, to construe them to apply to free speech and assembly activities on certain *private* property such as shopping malls and private universities.

The detailed regulation of gambling in Article I, Section 9, is not unusual for state constitutions, because of its highly political and morally charged content,[15] but it is unusual to find it treated in the Bill of Rights.

---

13 See Peter J. Galie, *supra.*

14 See generally Barbara Faith Sachs, *supra* note 2; Mark L. Glasser and John Kincaid, "Selected Rights Enumerated in State Constitutions," *Intergovernmental Perspective* 17 (Fall 1991): 35; Ronald K. L. Collins, "Bills and Declarations of Rights Digest," *The American Bench* 2483 (1985).

15 See Grad, *supra* note 12, at pp. 950 n. 66; and 955-56.

State constitutional regulation of gambling is more often found in the legislative article.

New York's equal protection provision, Article I, Section 11, is quite unusual because the second sentence, on its face, seems to apply to *private* as well as state action. The courts, however, have not accorded this much recognition.

The search and seizure protection in Article I, Section 12, includes a modern provision extending its protection to "unreasonable interception of telephone and telegraph communications." This provision is found in only a few state constitutions, and is another example of a modern modification of a much older, core constitutional protection.

The Article I, Section 16, prohibition on limiting recoveries for wrongful death is also present in a number of states, reflecting a specific, substantive distrust of the legislature. Under the pressure of powerful railroad employer interests, state legislatures passed statutes limiting recovery for wrongful death at the end of last century, leading to provisions like this. Other examples may be found in the constitutions of Kentucky and Pennsylvania.

The recognition of labor rights in Article I, Section 17, is relatively unusual; it is found in only five other state constitutions.[16] New York led the way in this regard, as it did in constitutionalizing a number of other social policy concerns in 1938. Florida, Missouri, New Jersey, and Hawaii all adopted or modified their constitutions after 1938, perhaps emulating New York's provision in this area.

Finally, the workers' compensation provision, Article I, Section 18, is very common in state constitutions for two reasons. First, like in New York, such a provision was necessary in some states to overcome a decision of the highest state court holding that the legislature was without power to establish a system of workers' compensation. New York's experience in this regard with the famous *Ives* case is among the most well-known examples of a state constitution being amended to "overrule" a state court interpretation of the state Constitution. Other states included similar provisions to eliminate doubt about the constitutionality of statutory workers' compensation schemes.

---

16   See Richard A. Goldberg and Robert F. Williams, "Farmworkers' Organizational and Collective Bargaining Rights in New Jersey: Implementing Self-Executing State Constitutional Rights," *Rutgers L.J. 18* (1987): 729 and 731-32.

Overall, New York's Bill of Rights is comparable to those in most states, subject to the exceptions noted above. However, it does *not* contain a guarantee of equal rights for women (a "state ERA") as is now present in about one-third of the states. The New York Bill of Rights also does not contain constitutional protection for persons with disabilities, which has been adopted in a few states.

Article II: Suffrage

Article II has its origins in the Revolutionary debates over the right to vote, as well as in the 1821 Constitutional Convention, which has been referred to as "one of the great suffrage debates in American history."[17]

The current Article covers much of the same ground as will be found in other constitutions, such as basic qualifications, absentee voting, registration, and disqualification from the right to vote. As noted elsewhere in this volume, many of the New York provisions on suffrage are now invalid because they are in conflict with the U.S. Constitution or federal statutes as interpreted by the U.S. Supreme Court. The special provision contained in Section 9 with respect to presidential elections, quite common in state constitutions, is essentially mandated by federal law. The New York Constitution contains somewhat more detailed provisions regarding voter registration and election administration than generally found in state constitutions.

Article III: Legislature

This Article concerns the basic lawmaking branch of state government, and sets forth its basic structure, the qualifications for service as a legislator, and the method for designing legislative districts. Like in all of the states but one (Nebraska) it establishes a bicameral legislature. In Article III, Section 2, the use of the term "assembly*men*" reflects the absence of gender neutrality, toward which some states have moved in their constitutions.

Part of the responsibility to reapportion the legislature is assigned by Section 4 to the legislature, where it has traditionally resided. Some other states, in recent times, have amended their constitutions to assign the politically difficult task of reapportionment to a commission set up

17   See Peter J. Galie, *The New York State Constitution: A Reference Guide,* (1991), p. 7, quoting Chilton Williamson, *American Suffrage From Property to Democracy, 1760-1860,* Princeton NJ: Princeton University Press, 1960, at p. 195.

specifically for this purpose.[18] These commissions typically develop a reapportionment plan which is then subject to direct review by the state's supreme court, without any involvement by the legislature itself.

The provisions with respect to Senate districts (Section 4) and assembly districts (Section 5) are, as in many states, subject to the overriding mandates of the federal "one person, one vote" decisions and the voting rights act, where it applies. This is confusing. It leaves some but not all aspects of the state constitutional provisions on this subject without force or effect. But it is not an uncommon situation.

The provisions on compensation and expenses (Section 6) and qualifications and the ban on certain civil appointments ("to an office which shall have been created, or the emoluments whereof shall have been increased") are very common among most of the states.

The content of Sections 8-11, concerning the timing of legislative elections, legislative powers and procedures, and the privileges of members, is quite standard in most constitutions, though the provision in Section 12 that "*any* bill may originate in either house" diverges from that of some states which include the more rigid requirement that revenue bills originate in the larger house. The Section 13 requirement that only *bills* are valid to enact law is standard, and reflects the notion that legislative actions short of bills, such as resolutions, are not available to enact a formal law. The limitations on the passage of laws contained in Sections 14-17 are also fairly standard, although states vary on the approach taken to private and local bills (Section 17) and a number of other states expand this prohibition to cover "special" legislation.[19] The special laws provisions in other states are generally aimed at legislative classifications, and in most states are thought to be similar to equal protection guarantees.

The provision in Section 18 permitting the legislature to call itself into session, common in most states, serves as a complement to the governor's power to call special sessions.

The remaining sections of Article III each reflect issues treated in some other state constitutions in comparable ways.[20] Section 24 serves as a substantive limit on the legislature. The provision for emergency gov-

---

18 See Bruce Adams, "A Model State Reapportionment Process: The Continuing Quest for Fair and Effective Representation," *Harv. J. Legis.* 14 (1977): 825.

19 See Robert F. Williams, "Equality Guarantees in State Constitutional Law," *Tex. L. Rev.* 63 (1985): 1195 and 1209-10.

20 See, generally, Barbara Faith Sachs, *Laws, Legislature, Legislative Procedure: A Fifty State Index*, New York: Legislative Drafting Research Fund, Columbia University, Oceana Publications, 1982.

ernment included in Section 25, reflecting the attitudes in 1963, is similar to the relatively untested provisions contained in some other state constitutions.

Legislative term limitation, adopted in almost all states with initiative and referendum, is not present in New York, which does not provide for either technique of direct democracy, or for recall of elected officials, in its Constitution.

Article IV: Executive

The relatively streamlined executive article reflects the standard powers and duties of the governor. Unlike New York, more than half the states limit the number of terms a governor may serve. The policy choice in Section 1, of having the governor and lieutenant governor "chosen jointly," is found in some other states that have lieutenant governors. Other states specify that they run independently. Their joint election notwithstanding, the separate nomination of the governor and lieutenant governor in New York has sometimes led to incompatibility between them.

The mechanisms for succession in office, or the "devolution of the duty of acting as governor," are reflected in fairly standard terms in Section 6.

The executive veto power in Section 7, the original 1777 version of which served as a partial model for the federal Constitution's veto power, now includes a somewhat restricted version of the item veto. The text of the provision seems limited to veto of "items of appropriation of money." Some other states do not so restrict item veto, permitting the governor to veto substantive provisions in appropriation bills, and, under some circumstances, proviso language or "riders" in appropriation bills.[21]

Finally, the limitation on the effectiveness of administrative rules, reflected in Section 8, is found in a number of states, and is a reaction to the importance of lawmaking by agency regulation in the modern administrative state.

Article V: Officers and Civil Departments

This article reflects the reality in many states today — that the governor is not *the* Executive, but is rather a *part* of the Executive. This was one of

---

21   See generally Richard Briffault, "The Item Veto in State Courts," *Temple L. Rev.* 66 (1993): 1171.

Woodrow Wilson's favorite points about executive powers under state constitutions. In fact, however, the executive power is less dispersed among other constitutionally empowered actors in New York than in most other states. Section 1 establishes the comptroller and attorney general as statewide, *elected* officials. In the other sections contained in Article V the constitutional duties of these offices are established. Unlike in some states, California and New Jersey for example, the attorney general in New York has virtually no role in overseeing or coordinating the criminal justice process.

The limitation in Section 2 to "twenty civil departments in the state government" is contained in some other state constitutions, and reflects an attempt to force a reorganization of, and to pinpoint responsibility for, the many administrative agencies in the executive branch.

The appointing and removal powers given the governor in Section 4 are relatively extensive, though this official in New York lacks the constitutional authority to reorganize the executive branch given to the chief executive in a number of other states.

Civil service provisions, such as those contained in Section 6, are fairly common in state constitutions.[22]

Article VI: Judiciary

State constitutional judiciary articles are among the hardest to compare. They often include a high level of detail with respect to the establishment of different courts and their jurisdiction. New York's judiciary article is no exception. It begins to provide for a unified court system (Section 1(a)) — further unification remains a goal — and sets out the basic structure of the state-wide court system. Some detail is required because of special treatment for courts in New York City, making the judicial article another in which the city's presence in the state is manifest constitutionally.

As with other state constitutions, the article deals not only with the establishment of courts and their jurisdiction, but with the selection of judges, their qualifications, their terms, and provisions for their removal. States employ five different systems for the selection of judges: merit selection, appointment by the governor, election by the legislature, nonpartisan election, and partisan election. New York is one of twenty-one states with a variant of merit selection for its high court. The Commission on Judicial Nomination for the Court of Appeals, provided for in Section 2(d), is similar to those in

---

22   See Grad, *supra* note 12, at p. 961.

a few states. Eleven states use partisan election for some level of their judiciary, the system employed in New York for most other judgeships.[23] The Commission on Judicial Conduct in New York, established in Section 22, is less common among the states.

The provisions in Section 24 concerning the impeachment power of the legislature seem oddly placed within the judicial article. Although the content of Section 24 is similar to most states, these provisions are usually contained in the legislative article. The apparent rationale here is the description of the senate trial in an impeachment matter as the "court for trial of impeachments." Technically, though, impeachment is a legislative and not a judicial power.

The provision in Section 30, recognizing the power of the *legislature* over questions of practice and procedure *in the courts*, is somewhat unusual today. Many state constitutions assign this power to the highest court, with only the possibility, in fewer states, of some shared legislative power.

Article VII: State Finances and Article VIII: Local Finances

Sections 1 through 5 of Article VII establish the modern executive budget-making process. There are similar provisions in many other state constitutions, but this is a strong version, and some states (South Carolina, for example) still lack such a process. The second paragraph of Section 1, apparently based on separation of powers concerns, permits the proposed judicial and legislative budgets to be submitted directly to the legislature, subject only to the governor's power to comment thereon. The Section 6 restriction on other appropriations bills being limited to a single object or purpose is contained in a number of other state constitutions, but is often worded differently from this section. The provision in Section 7 that no money should be paid out except pursuant to appropriation by law is very common, as are the limitations on state credit contained in Section 8. The accretion of exceptions reflected in Section 8 is also very common, authorizing the reintroduction of state government financing into a variety of modern activities.

Otherwise, state constitutional provisions on the limitation of borrowing and spending are quite common, but difficult to compare in their detailed provisions. This holds true for the rest of Article VII and the

---

23   See G. Alan Tarr, *Judicial Process and Judicial Policymaking*, St. Paul: West Publishing, 1994, at p. 67.

entirety of Article VIII. Furthermore, Article VIII, Section 7, evidences a recognition of the need to treat a city like New York differently. This reality appears elsewhere in the New York Constitution, and is to a certain extent reflected in other state constitutions where there is the presence of a large, dominant city or a few such cities.

Article IX: Local Governments

Section 1, the "Bill of Rights for Local Governments," is an attempt to set forth a version of constitutional home rule for local government. Importantly, it refers to the "power to adopt *local* laws . . ." (Section 1(a)). These powers seem dependent on legislative implementation (see Section 2), subject to the limitations contained in Section 1. Furthermore, the provision sets up a dichotomy between local matters and statewide matters. This distinction has been abandoned in some state constitutions because of the difficulties in separating state and local matters, leading to the necessity of continuous judicial resolution of disputes.

In other states, the constitutional treatment of local government ranges all the way from self-executing grants of power over any topic that the state legislature could consider (such as Alaska), to essentially no constitutional treatment at all (such as New Jersey).

Article X: Corporations

The state constitutional treatment of corporations is found in a number of constitutions, mostly in states in the West. This article reflects concerns about corporations and banks that date from the Jacksonian era.[24] Like in other states, but in language that is less limiting than that used elsewhere, this article seeks to set forth rules for corporations and banks that are beyond the reach of the legislature, reflecting a lack of trust in the legislature.[25]

Article XI: Education

New York's education article is briefer than those in most states. The Section 1 requirement for "the maintenance and support of a system of

---

24 See David Alan Johnson, *supra* note 6, at p. 102-03; Marvin Myers, *The Jacksonian Persuasion: Politics and Belief,* Stanford, CA: Stanford University Press, 1957, at pp. 199-204.

25 For a strong criticism of the inclusion of even more detailed regulation of corporations in the Oklahoma Constitution, see Robert L. Stone, "Article Nine of the Constitution of the State of Oklahoma of 1907 and Comparative Constitutional Law," *Okla. City U. L. Rev.* 17 (1992): 89.

free common schools" is one of a number of different state constitutional formulations of this legislative mandate.[26] Stronger, more directive language has been critical in decisions of some state high courts to intervene to compel massive restructuring of state educational systems and education financing schemes, but not yet in New York.

The constitutionally based Board of Regents appointed by the legislature, the governance structure for all education set out in Section 2, is one of several models used in the states. Other states employ statewide officials, elected boards, or boards appointed by other means for this function.

Unlike many states, New York lacks a constitutionally prescribed structure for its state university system.[27]

Finally, the Section 3 restriction on public aid to religious schools, with the exception for transportation, can be found in some other state constitutions.

Article XII: Defense

This one-section article, concerning the militia, covers a topic found in many state constitutions. Because of the dominance of federal law in this area, these types of provisions have lost their importance in modern times.[28]

Article XIII: Public Officers

This article contains miscellaneous provisions concerning terms of office, vacancies, oaths of office, removal from office, and compensation for a variety of public officials. These kinds of provisions, in more or less detail, are found in most state constitutions. More recently, modern ethics provisions have begun to appear in state constitutions, though not yet in New York's.

The treatment in Section 13 of sheriffs (as recently amended in 1989 to make counties liable for the acts of their sheriffs), district attorneys, and

---

26 See William E. Thro, "The Third Wave: The Impact of the Montana, Kentucky, and Texas Decisions on Public School Finance Reform Litigation," *J. L. & Educ. 19* (1990): 219.

27 See Joseph Beckham, "Reasonable Independence for Public Higher Education: Legal Implications of Constitutionally Autonomous Status," *J. L. & Educ. 7* (1978): 177.

28 See generally Anthony J. Scaletta, Note: "The Governor's Troops Under the Florida Constitution," *Nova L. Rev.* 18 (1993); and Dishman, *supra* note 1, at pp. 43-47 (these provisions are "obsolete").

other officials is probably a bit more detailed than will be found in most state constitutions.

The provision in Section 14 concerning the power of the legislature to require payment of the "prevailing wage" seems at the very least to be misplaced in this article, being more appropriately contained in the legislative article. Secondly, it is not clear why such a provision is necessary, since presumably the legislature would have the power to provide by law for this matter without specific constitutional authorization. It may be here, of course, to overcome some judicial interpretation or constitutional doubt, or to please groups especially interested in having this subject treated in the constitution.

Article XIV: Conservation
Article XV: Canals

These two articles, dealing with state owned and state controlled lands, and the consequences of the building of state supported canals, are not common in other state constitutions. Provisions aimed at similar problems, however, can be found in some state constitutions.[29]

The Article XIV provisions on conservation reflect an early policy decision to remove certain state lands from legislative control, as well as the later accretions of exceptions, each of which must be voted upon by the people. Few states deal with these matters in as great detail as is found here.

The general policy statements about conservation and natural resources contained in Article XIV, Section 4, are found in a number of state constitutions, utilizing a variety of different language.[30] Some states include these types of provisions in their Bills of Rights.

Article XVI: Taxation

All state constitutions now include detailed provisions on taxation, which serve to limit the range of legislative and local government choice. In fact, perhaps because of the absence of initiative and referendum in New York, the state constitution is less limiting regarding taxation than in many other states.

---

29 In Western states, for example, where water resources are an important issue, the matter of water rights is treated in state constitutions. See Gordon Morris Bakken, *Rocky Mountain Constitution Making: 1850-1912*, Westport, CT: Greenwood Press, 1987, at pp. 65-73.

30 See Jose Fernandez, "State Constitutions, Environmental Rights Provisions, and the Doctrine of Self-Execution: A Political Question?" *Harv. Environmental L. Rev.* 17 (1993): 333 and 361-65.

The exemption provisions in Section 1 are common in most state constitutions. Interestingly, the New York Constitution does not seem to contain an explicit "uniformity" provision for taxation.[31] Section 2 comes the closest to this concept.

Many states have added provisions such as Section 6, that ease the strict limitations on tax exemptions, tax abatements, and debt limitations for the purpose of urban redevelopment projects, which are seen to be included in the role of modern government.

Article XVII: Social Welfare
Article XVIII: Housing

These two articles, recognized around the country as the 1938 Constitutional Convention's contribution to modern social welfare theory, are substantially more detailed than in most state constitutions. Some states have, however, picked up some of the ideas contained in these two articles. They form the basis for what is now seen as the special contribution of state constitutions to "positive rights."[32]

Much of what is contained in Article XVIII with respect to housing consists of exceptions to the rigid limitations on indebtedness, eminent domain, and the general public purpose doctrine.

Section 10 of Article XVIII contains an interesting provision ("shall not be construed as imposing additional limitations") that is aimed at avoiding interpretation by "negative implication."[33]

Article XIX: Amending
the Constitution

Virtually all state constitutions now contain specific provisions concerning the mechanisms for constitutional change. The method used by New York for change through the legislature, passage by two sessions followed by citizen approval at referendum, is one of the two most commonly used. The New York article contains the Jeffersonian idea of an opportunity to revise the state constitution for each generation (Section 2). Not included is a provision for state constitutional change by initiative, which is

---

31 See generally, Wade J. Newhouse, *Constitutional Uniformity and Equality in State Taxation,* 2nd ed., Buffalo, NY: W.S. Hein Co., 1984.

32 See Burt Neuborne, "Foreword: State Constitutions and the Evolution of Positive Rights," *Rutgers L. J. 20* (1989): 881.

33 See Grad, *supra* note 12, at pp. 964-68.

contained in a number of other, mostly western, state constitutions. The detailed New York constitutional provisions for election of delegates to a constitutional convention are paralleled by those in Missouri, but few other states. The constitutions of Ohio and South Dakota provide for nonpartisan election of delegates.

The Role of the Constitutional Commission in State Constitutional Change

Robert F. Williams

Compared to the constitutional convention, that unique, two-hundred-year-old invention of American political practice, the constitutional commission is of recent vintage. It is only about a century old. In fact, in his 1887 Treatise on Constitutional Conventions, Judge John Alexander Jameson described the constitutional commission as "a novel device."[1]

Since Jameson wrote, three distinct permutations of the constitutional commission have evolved, with very different functions. Commissions have been used in conjunction with constitutional conventions, either to help implement their work or lay the groundwork for them; they have been employed as a device for assisting legislatures in avoiding conventions, and thus retain control of constitutional change; and finally they have begun, in Florida, to develop as a method for generating and directly recommending constitutional amendments to the people, bypassing both the legislature and the convention.

Preparing for a Convention or Advising the Legislature

The appointed constitutional commission is not specified in the New York Constitution, nor in any other state constitution except Florida's. (Its unique Constitution Revision Commission can submit proposals directly to the voters and is discussed in detail below.)[2]

Interestingly, the idea to use a constitutional commission seems to have originated in New York, with the 1872 Constitutional Commission,

---

1   See John Alexander Jameson, *A Treatise on Constitutional Conventions: Their History, Powers, and Modes of Proceeding*, New York: Da Capo, 4th Ed. 1887, 1972.

2   See Robert F. Williams, "A Generation of Change in Florida State Constitutional Law," *St. Thomas L. Rev.* 5 (1992): 133 and 137-39.

recommended by the governor and appointed by the legislature.[3] Peter Galie, a leading authority on the history and development of the New York Constitution, describes that Commission as ". . . an innovation in the state's constitutional history, which seemed to fill a gap between a cumbersome convention and the ad hoc legislative amending process. This method allowed distinguished and informed individuals to recommend constitutional change to the legislature and then to the people."[4]

The 1872 Constitutional Commission in New York was able to revive and recommend some of the ideas (such as a longer gubernatorial term and the item veto) from the proposed Constitution that failed at the polls in 1867. After the commission's proposals were approved by the legislature, the people ratified them.[5]

In 1873, New Jersey seemingly emulated the New York commission idea. The legislature there provided for the establishment of a constitutional commission on terms very similar to New York's 1872 statute.[6] This was surely one of the most successful constitutional commissions in history: the New Jersey legislature submitted 28 of the amendments recommended by the commission, all of which were approved by the voters in 1875.[7]

The constitutional commission came into being in New York and New Jersey based on the justifications of efficiency and expertise, neither of which were regarded as attributes of the constitutional convention ("cumbersome") or the legislative amendment process ("ad hoc"). The commission, under these circumstances, served as a research and study group (expertise) and as a technique for agenda-setting in the legislature (efficiency).

But despite these similarities in the New York and New Jersey experience, there seem to have been additional motivations in the use of the commission method in the second case. In New York, the constitutional commission followed a constitutional convention. In New Jersey, in contrast, the commission was a substitute for a convention. This method appears to have been used to diffuse popular pressure on the legislature to

---

3   See Jameson, *supra* note 1, at p. 570.

4   See Peter J. Galie, *The New York State Constitution: A Reference Guide*, Westport, CT: Greenwood Press, 1991, at p. 16.

5   *Ibid.*, at 15. See also Lewis B. Kaden, "The People: No! Some Observation on the 1967 New York Constitutional Convention," *Harv. J. Legis.* 5 (1968): 343 and 364.

6   See Robert F. Williams, *The New Jersey Constitution: A Reference Guide* Westport, CT: Greenwood Press, 1990, at pp. 9-11.

7   *Ibid.*

call a constitutional convention, and therefore to retain control for the legislature over the final recommendations to the voters.[8]

As noted, most commentators on constitutional commissions have emphasized only the efficiency and expertise rationales.[9] But in New Jersey neither was central. Rather the commission was a means for legislative control of the process of state constitutional change. A Utah law adopted in 1969 offers a modified version of this approach. It creates a permanent sixteen-member Constitution Revision Study Commission with heavy representation from the legislature. Commission members serve six-year terms. Three are appointed by the governor and three each by the speaker of the House and the president of the Senate from their respective bodies, with a requirement of bipartisanship. These nine then appoint an additional six. The legislative research director serves ex-officio.[10] The commission selects its own chair.

The Utah commission is authorized in law both to undertake its own initiatives and to consider recommendations from state leaders and "responsible segments of the public." But it may not make proposals directly to the people for constitutional change. Its duties are ". . . to make a comprehensive examination of the Constitution of the State of Utah, and of the amendments thereto, and thereafter to make recommendations to the governor and the legislature as to specific proposed constitutional amendments designed to carry out the commission's recommendations for changes in the constitution." [11]

The technique of retaining legislative control through the use of the commission method for constitutional revision was later noted by such scholars as Albert Sturm and James Henretta.[12] Henretta recently made the following criticisms of commissions that report to and through the legislature and governor:

> In many other states, such as Georgia in the 1940's and Kentucky and California in the 1960's, legislatures dispensed completely with a constitutional convention. To meet the pressing need for the reform of outmoded constitutional structures, the legislatures appointed commissions to consider revisions and to report their

8   *Ibid.*, at p. 9.

9   *See* Jameson, *supra* note 1, at pp. 574-75. But see Bennett M. Rich, W. Brooke Graves, Ed., "Revision By Constitutional Commission," *Major Problems in State Constitutional Revision*, 1960, at p. 86 (criticizing use of constitutional commissions which report to the legislature).

10   Chapter 54, Section 63-1, Laws of Utah.

11   Chapter 54, Section 63-3, Laws of Utah.

12   Albert L. Sturm, "The Development of American State Constitutions," *Publius: The Journal of Federalism* 12 (1982): 57 and 84-85.

recommendations. These commissions were not democratic bodies responsible to the people. Their proposals came before the voters only after being carefully reviewed and revised by legislators, governors, and other state officials.

*   *   *   *

Whatever the gloss . . . the commission revision process . . . represented a diminution of activist popular sovereignty. In a carefully calculated fashion, these maneuvers removed power from the hands of the citizenry. The result was a constitution revised as much through administrative procedures as through constitutional debate and political compromise.[13]

These kinds of criticisms, however, focus on a certain type of constitutional commission — the one created to make recommendations to the legislature. As W. Brooke Graves noted, constitutional commissions have come to be widely "used for a variety of reasons, and in many different ways."[14] New York's experience bears out this observation, as will be discussed presently. Graves went on to describe a different kind of constitutional commission:

Public demand for change is essential before the cumbersome machinery of revision can be put in motion. Such a demand can be developed only by means of a campaign of education, and this in turn, can be effectively conducted only after a great deal of preparatory work has been done.

The usual procedure is to establish a study commission which can serve the two-fold purpose of providing factual information for the campaign information which can be used again later when and if the campaign succeeds in bringing a constitutional convention into existence. Such a commission can be appointed by the governor on his own initiative, or as a result of legislative action, authorizing and directing that such a commission be established. Or it can come about under private initiative, and be privately financed. This procedure is sometimes necessary when the legislature refuses or a least fails to provide the necessary funds.[15]

---

13   See James A. Henretta, "Foreword: Rethinking the State Constitutional Tradition," *Rutgers L. J.* 22 (1991): 819 and 830-31.

14   See W. Brooke Graves, "State Constitutional Law: A Twenty Five Year Summary," *Wm. & Mary L. Rev.* 8 (1966): 1 and 9.

15   *Ibid.*, at pp. 3-4. See also Elmer E. Cornwell, Jr., Jay S. Goodman & Wayne R. Swanson, *State Constitutional Conventions: The Politics of the Revision Process in Seven States*, New York: Praeger, 1975, at p. 190.

This use of the constitutional commission, as an adjunct to the *constitutional convention* rather than to the legislature, seems to answer Dr. Henretta's criticism, and to aid rather than impede the exercise of popular sovereignty.[16]

New York's Experience

In New York, since 1872, constitutional commissions have, as Graves noted in a wider context, been "used for a variety of reasons, and in many different ways."[17] Some were appointed by the governor; others were established by the legislature. Some were created in anticipation of a vote on the mandatory convention question; others resulted from the need to prepare quickly after the question passed. The 1915 and 1938 Conventions — one that produced a Constitution rejected at the polls, the other that resulted in the adoption of major revisions — produced bodies of research that influenced state government's development for decades after.

A second New York commission was established by Governor Samuel J. Tilden in 1875. Only one of its proposals, on debt limits, was recommended by the legislature and approved by the voters. But the work of the 1872 and 1875 constitutional commissions helped lay "the ground work for many of the reforms adopted at the 1894 Convention."[18]

An 1890 commission created by the legislature returned to it with recommendations concerning the judiciary. These were laid aside when the election of a governor and legislature of the same party broke a political deadlock and resulted in the calling of a constitutional convention in 1894 that was authorized at the polls in 1887.[19]

The 1915 Constitutional Convention was authorized by a narrow majority in a very low turnout special election on April 7, 1914, with delegates to be elected at the general election in that same year. Following this vote the legislature created a five-person commission "to collect, compile and print information and data for the Constitutional Convention of 1915."[20] This commission contracted with the Bureau of Municipal

---

16 A constitutional commission was recently used in Oklahoma to develop and recommend initiative petitions seeking state constitutional change. See Robert H. Henry, "The Oklahoma Constitutional Revision Commission: A Call to Arms or the Sounding of Retreat?" *Okla City U. L. Rev.* 17 (1992): 177.

17 *Supra*, note 12.

18 See Galie, *supra* note 4, at p. 16.

19 *Ibid.*, at p. 17.

20 Chapter 261, Laws of 1914.

Research in New York City for what proved to be the most extensive set of studies of state government done to that date.

A commission considered the judiciary again in 1921. A number of its proposals (adapted from the failed 1915 proposals) were recommended by the legislature and approved by the voters.[21]

After the people authorized a constitutional convention when the mandatory question was asked in 1936, Governor Herbert Lehman appointed a committee to prepare background materials for delegates. Chaired by Charles Poletti, who later became lieutenant governor, the New York State Constitutional Convention Committee produced a body of work extraordinary for its depth, breadth, and quality.

In 1956, in preparation for the 1957 vote on whether to hold a constitutional convention, the legislature established a Temporary Commission on the Constitutional Convention. This commission, chaired by Nelson Rockefeller (who later became governor) held public hearings and developed background material. It actually remained in existence after the voters rejected the convention, under the name Special Committee on the Revision and Simplification of the Constitution. It published a number of state constitutional reports before going out of existence in 1961.[22] Some of these provided the basis for amendments later proposed through the legislature and adopted by the people.

After the New York voters approved the call of a constitutional convention in 1965, the legislature created a Temporary Commission on the Constitutional Convention. Galie reports that this commission was "plagued by partisan divisions," and had little impact on the Convention.[23]

No commission was appointed in preparation for the mandatory convention question in 1977, which was defeated at the polls by a substantial margin.

Florida's Constitutionally Based Commission: An Alternative Method for Constitutional Change

In Florida, as earlier noted, the 1968 Constitution provided for an automatic, periodic review of the state Constitution at regular intervals. Article XI, Section 2, provided that ten years after adoption of the Constitution,

21   See Galie, *supra* note 4, at pp. 23-24.

22   *Ibid.*, at pp. 27-28.

23   *Ibid.*, at pp. 28-29.

and every 20 years thereafter, an appointed constitution revision commission would be created. This commission was empowered to submit its recommended revisions *directly to the electorate*, a mechanism of state constitutional revision which was, at the time, unique to American constitutional history.[24]

The Florida Constitution was adopted in 1968. As mandated, the 1977-78 Florida Constitution Revision Commission proceeded to engage in a very open, far-reaching examination of the state Constitution, and proposals for its change. Its proceedings were extraordinarily well documented.[25]

The Commission ultimately made important and well-considered recommendations for change in the state Constitution to Florida's voters.[26] All of the recommendations, however, were rejected.[27] Albert Sturm opined that the defeat resulted from the review coming too soon after the comprehensive 1968 revision, and from the presence on the ballot of another, controversial measure on casino gambling.[28]

On the surface, defeat of the 1978 proposed revisions in Florida seems to be a great state constitutional revision failure. Constitutional Revision Commission Chairman Sandy D'Alemberte, together with others, takes a longer view of the failed 1978 revisions:

The immediate contribution of the commission was less than historic, for its sweeping proposals (including abolition of the cabinet) were lost when presented on a ballot alongside a very unpopular proposal for casino gambling, which was placed there through the initiative process. Although the commission's work was rejected by the voters, a great deal of the agenda for further amendment of the constitution was shaped by the Constitution Revision Commission. As Steve Uhlfelder, executive director of the commission, has observed, in the years following the commission, the legislature proposed and the voters approved proposals in substantially the same format as those developed by the

24 See Talbot D'Alemberte, *The Florida State Constitution: A Reference Guide*, Westport, CT: Greenwood Press, 1991, at pp 15-16.; Steven J. Uhlfelder, "The Machinery of Revision," *Fla. St. U.L. Rev.* 6 (1978): 575.

25 See Harold Levinson, "Interpreting State Constitutions by Resort to the Record," *Fla. St. U. L. Rev.* 6 (1978): 567.

26 See generally "Symposium on the Proposed Revision to the Florida Constitution," *Fla. St. U. L. Rev.* 6 (1968): 565.; Alaine S. Williams, "A Summary and Background Analysis of the Proposed 1978 Constitutional Revisions," *Fla. St. U. L. Rev.* 6 (1978): 1115.

27 See D'Alemberte, *supra* note 22, at p. 15.

28 See Albert L. Sturm, *supra*, note 10, at p. 85.

commission. These included amendments adding a right of privacy to the Declaration of Rights (adopted 1980), extending impeachment to county judges (1988), providing uniform rules for the judicial nominating commissions (1984), extending the widows' exemption to widowers (1988), allowing the legislature to classify inventory for property tax purposes (1980), and providing various changes in the bonding power (1980, 1984).[29]

The commission method of revision has stirred controversy, but Florida voters rejected a legislative proposal in 1980 to abolish the periodic commissions.[30] In fact, in 1988 the voters approved the same mechanism for the Tax and Budget Reform Commission.[31] That commission recently exercised its powers to propose, inter alia, a budget reform amendment that was adopted by the electorate at the November 1992 election, overruling a holding restrictive of the governor's budget powers.[32]

Conclusion

The current Temporary New York State Commission on Constitutional Revision, created by Governor Cuomo, has a long, varied history behind it. Whatever the political context for their creation, the work of many of its predecessor commissions has had considerable impact on government in the state, either immediately or in the decades that followed their deliberations and recommendations.

Constitutional commissions have made substantial contributions in New York and around the country. The recent experience in Florida demonstrates that they may also provide a fourth means to propose constitutional change directly to the people, in addition to the convention, the legislative route, or (where it exists) the initiative process. But even used in this manner, as Bennett M. Rich observed over thirty years ago, "the commission device is no substitute for a convention. No amount of wishing can make it so."[33] Serving as an adjunct to a convention, however, complementing its exercise of popular sovereignty, the commission can be a very important positive component of state constitutional change.

---

29 See D'Alemberte, *supra*, note 22, at p. 15.

30 *Ibid.*, at p. 15.

31 Florida Constitution Article XI, Section 6. *Ibid.* at p. 15, See generally Donna Blanton, The Taxation and Budget Reform Commission, "Florida's Best Hope for the Future." *Fla. St. U. L. Rev.* 18 (1991): 437.

32 See *Chiles v. Children*, A,B,C,D,E & F, 569 Do. 2d 260 (Fla. 1991).

33 See Rich, *supra* note 9, at p. 99.

II

Constitutional Structure and the Process of Government

Defining the structure of and processes for government is the fundamental purpose of any constitution. Even those who argue that state constitutions are too long and detailed do not dispute the need for them to create the state's core governing institutions, distribute powers among them, and regulate their interactions. New York State's institutional arrangements were developed and revised over more than two centuries on the classic American governance model — separate institutions sharing powers. An essay by Gerald Benjamin in this section describes the current constitutional provisions concerning the structure, powers, and relationships among the major governmental institutions of the state, and briefly discusses an array of recent reform proposals.

Three areas of potential change that have been extensively debated in the New York over last quarter century are given detailed treatment in separate essays. Bob Kerker describes the constitutional provisions for budgeting adopted in this century that shifted governmental power substantially from the legislative to the executive branch, and summarizes many of the suggestions for budgetary reform that have arisen out of the failure of New York to adopt timely budgets in recent years. Kerker's essay also looks at constitutional provisions concerning state spending and limitations on borrowing.

New York State's fiscal practices and taxing and spending policies are important in shaping its business climate; political debate in the state for at least a decade has focused on making it more competitive by cutting taxes and reducing the size of government. In a period in which limiting government is regarded as a virtue and skepticism about activist government prevails, it is instructive to remember that, even for conservatives, one generation's prudent constitutional limitation on state government may be the next generation's unnecessary constraint. In his essay on the state Constitution and the private economy, one focus for Joseph Zimmerman is on the way provisions dating to the nineteenth century limiting the use of state and local government credit and resources to benefit private enterprise constrain contemporary economic development efforts.

A key reason that the 1967 Constitutional Convention was called by the state legislature was the political and governmental turmoil produced in New York by U.S. Supreme Court decisions calling for state legislative districting on the basis of "one person, one vote." A new system was adopted by the 1967 Constitutional Convention establishing a Commission to do legislative districting, but was never put into effect as the voters failed to ratify the Constitution offered that year. David Wells reviews this record, explores the issues embedded in how legislative districting is done in New York, and compares current practice in the state to that in other states.

The New York Constitution set out in detail the organization of the state and local court system and methods for selecting judges and holding them accountable. Consequently, most judicial reform may be achieved only through constitutional amendment. This has made unification of the courts and methods for selecting judges a perennial constitutional issue in modern New York government. Fred Miller examines the evolution of constitutional provisions concerning the state court system, and details the successes and failures of the reform efforts of the last quarter century.

Reading these five essays makes it clear that even when it comes to dealing with basic structures and processes, state constitutions are longer and more detailed than the national document. An additional reason is that they deal with matters that the founders purposely avoided; they achieved constitutional brevity in part by leaving some controversial matters for the states to deal with as they chose, through their own constitutions.

Thus, for example, the U.S. Constitution is entirely silent on the subject of local government. In the American federal system the organization of this part of the governmental system, the part with the most immediate impact on citizens' daily lives, is left entirely to the states. The essay by Richard Briffault in this section looks at how local government and the state/local relationship is treated in the New York Constitution. It describes and analyzes the constitutional provisions on the creation of localities, their governance and powers, the consolidation and dissolution of local units, protecting localities against state interference, and their powers to tax, spend, and borrow.

In his essay in this section, Jeffrey Stonecash examines what the state Constitution says about who gets to vote in New York, for whom and on what, and under what conditions. Stonecash also looks at the constitutional dimensions of a number of reform proposals currently under discussion in the state on such subjects as direct democracy (the initiative), term limits, campaign finance and legislative ethics.

The national Constitution is also silent on the question of how "citizenship" is or ought to be defined and elections are to be run. Though power is given to the Congress to act in these areas (and Congress has, over the years, taken many actions to extend and protect the franchise in national elections) decisions about who was to be permitted to vote and under what conditions were initially left to the states. They have important powers not only for state and local elections but also pertaining to national elections. In another essay, Gerald Benjamin looks at the origin of New York's unusually detailed constitutional provisions for bipartisan election administration, and considers possible alternatives.

Structures of New York State Government

Gerald Benjamin

New York State's government, like that of the nation and our sister states, is one of separate institutions sharing governmental powers. Such a system is familiar to most Americans. It provides for executive, legislative, and judicial institutions that are distinct and politically independent of each other, while using each, in some measure, to check the power of the others in their primary spheres of action. Under such an arrangement, arriving at an appropriate balance among these institutions is one of the most significant decisions that faces constitution makers.

This approach contrasts with the distribution of power in parliamentary democracies and most American local governments. There the executive is chosen by and/or from a directly elected legislature, and is responsible to it.

There is no legal or national constitutional barrier to the adoption of parliamentary institutions in an American state. Indeed, the relative merits of the parliamentary and separation of powers systems have been debated at length by scholars and practitioners. But no state has ever adopted a parliamentary system. The persistent adherence of state governments to the separation of powers model over several centuries is a powerful testimonial to the centrality in the American political culture of the idea, expressed by James Madison in *Federalist* #51, that "[T]o control the abuses of government . . . , ambition must be made to counteract ambition. The interest of the man must be connected with the constitutional rights of the place."[1]

Separate Institutions. The "legislative power" in New York is located in the Senate and Assembly (Article III), and the "executive power" in the Governor (Article IV). The state Constitution, though it deals in great detail with the court system, nowhere specifically vests the "judicial power" in it. A change in language accomplishing this was offered in the

---

1   See Roy P. Fairfield, ed., *The Federalist Papers; A Collection of Essays Written in Support of the Constitution of the United States*, 2nd. ed., Baltimore: Johns Hopkins University Press, 1981.

draft Constitution of 1967 (rejected *in toto* at the polls). Separation is further achieved, and the powers of the branches of government defined, by the assignment to each of specific functions.

Separation of the branches is assured by the constitutional prohibition against a serving state legislator accepting a "civil appointment" to a state or city office created during his or her term or for which the "emoluments" were increased as he or she served, and by the requirement, with narrow exceptions, that a legislator resign his or her seat upon acceptance of an elected or appointed post in national, state, or city government (Article III, Section 7). The provision in New York's constitutionally defined budget process that the governor transmit the legislative and judicial budgets along with his executive budget "without revisions" is additional acknowledgment of the separate status of the three major branches of state government (Article VII, Section 1). Judges too are constitutionally barred from other public office, and from political party office, while serving on the bench (Article VI, Section 20. 1(b) and 3).

The constitutional distinctions between the executive and legislative branches are consequential. In 1987, for example, the Court of Appeals found that sweeping state Health Department regulations barring smoking in public places went beyond the powers delegated in law to the department. They were judged unconstitutional as the exercise of legislative power by the executive branch on separation of powers grounds.[2]

Sharing Powers. Separation, however, is not absolute. The clearest example is the power of the executive to veto legislation. The Senate, for its part, must confirm most important gubernatorial appointments. The Assembly has the power of impeachment, with trial before a court that includes members of the Senate. The Court of Appeals is the final arbiter of the constitutionality of state legislation. These are all, of course, purposefully crafted and familiar techniques to limit government that are, as noted, endemic to American systems. (All are discussed in further detail below.)

A number of other New York constitutional provisions do not conform to the separation of powers principle. The gap between the executive and legislative branches is partially bridged by the lieutenant governor, who is elected with the governor but presides over the state Senate and has a casting vote (Article IV, Section 6). The governor submits appropriation bills to the legislature as part of the budget process; on all other matters the submission of legislation is a prerogative of

---

2   *Boreali* v. *Axelrod,* 71 NY 2d 1.

elected members (Article VII, Section 3). As noted below, the legislature appoints the head of the education department, the Board of Regents, though appointing department heads is generally regarded as an executive function (Article V, Section 4). The majority leader of the Senate and the speaker of the Assembly, though legislative branch leaders, are in the line of executive succession, if both the governorship and lieutenant governorship simultaneously become vacant (Article IV, Section 6).

The Electorate: Additional Checks on Government. As a further check on the governor and legislature, the electorate in New York selects the comptroller and attorney general by direct statewide election. This method of filling these offices, instituted in 1846, is designed to assure independence in the execution of their duties. Filling each of these posts by direct election has been the subject of debate on the complex trade-off involved among competing values: efficiency, effectiveness, limited government, and popular control.[3]

Additionally, the electors of the state, voting within cities, towns, counties, and judicial districts, select most judges. This remains a highly debated process, and has been the source of frequent proposals for constitutional change further detailed below. Until 1977 judges on New York's highest court, the Court of Appeals, were also elected. In that year a constitutional amendment was adopted that provided that Court of Appeals judges be appointed by the governor from a group recommended by a panel appointed by him or her, the Chief Judge, and the legislative leaders.

The statewide electorate must be asked once every twenty years if they wish a constitutional convention to be held. Additionally, the electorate must ratify constitutional amendments before they are effected, and approve any pledge of the full faith and credit of the state. Unlike constitutions in 21 other states, however, that of New York does not give citizens the powers of initiative, the right to petition to put policy questions or constitutional amendments on the ballot, or referendum, the right to a popular vote on these questions. A variety of constitutional amendments adding initiative and referendum to the New York Constitution have been proposed in recent years.

Qualifications and Election of State Officers. State legislators, the governor, and lieutenant governor must be American citizens and five-years resident in New York State. Legislators have an additional district

---

3   This debate is detailed in the chapters "Elections and the Political Process" and "Criminal Justice" in this book. The chapter "Elections and the Political Process" details a number of issues mentioned in this section.

residence requirement. All are required to swear or affirm support for the United States Constitution and the New York Constitution. Salaries of offices named in the Constitution may not be increased or reduced during a term of office.

The governor and lieutenant governor must be thirty years old. They are elected in tandem, statewide in even-number nonpresidential years at the general election for a four-year term by a plurality winner system. There is no age requirement for Senate and Assembly members. They are also chosen at the general election, though the date of their election may be altered by legislative action.

The members of both legislative houses are selected within single member districts for two-year terms, also on a plurality winner basis. Legislative districts are reapportioned decennially by the legislature itself in accord with national constitutional and statutory standards and detailed state constitutional provisions. However, many of these state constitutional provisions have been found by federal courts to be in conflict with national standards, and therefore void. The 1967 draft Constitution (not adopted) provided for a legislative districting commission.

There are no term limitations for any state office, though constitutional amendments creating them have recently been proposed.[4]

The Legislature. The New York State legislature is bicameral, as are those of all states except Nebraska. (A constitutional amendment proposing unicameralism in New York is discussed below.) The legislature assembles annually on the first Wednesday after the first Monday in January. The number of Assembly members is fixed at 150 while the number of senators, at least 50 and currently 61, is variable.

The power of the legislature is plenary, except insofar as it is limited in the Constitution. The most important of the legislature's powers is the power of the purse, the authority to both raise and spend funds; it is separately treated in great detail in two articles of the Constitution, and further constrained and defined in the legislative article (Articles VII and XVI and Article III). Additionally, the legislature is explicitly given the power to regulate "practice and procedure" in the courts, and to remove Court of Appeals and Supreme Court judges for cause by concurrent resolution upon two-thirds vote of both houses (Article VI, Sections 23 and 30).

---

4   See the chapter on "Elections and the Political Process" in this book for a further discussion of districting, term limitation, and initiative and referendum.

The legislature is also empowered to provide for filling vacancies in the offices of comptroller and attorney general (Article V, Section 1). The recent use of election by the legislative houses meeting jointly to fill a vacancy in the comptroller's office led to proposals for amendment of the Constitution to alter this procedure, and demonstrated how breaking political events may bring attention to otherwise obscure constitutional provisions.

For bills to become laws they must be passed by a majority of the members elected to each house, following the form of the enacting clause prescribed in the Constitution. In the event of a gubernatorial veto, the legislature may override by a two-thirds vote of those elected to each house (see below for further detail). Proposed constitutional amendments that pass the legislature are not subject to gubernatorial veto, nor are its actions on executive budget bills.

Bills may originate in either house, and be freely amended in either house with a majority required for a quorum to do business, except that many fiscal actions require a quorum of three-fifths. Each house adopts its own rules, is the judge of the qualifications of its own members, and selects its own leaders. By a constitutional change adopted in 1975, two-thirds of the elected members to each house may petition to call the legislature into special session for specified purposes. Neither house may adjourn for more than two days without the consent of the other.

Both the Senate and Assembly must keep and publish a journal and meet in open session, though secrecy is permitted if deemed by the legislature to be in the interests of the "public welfare." To assure free debate on controversial matters, members may not be "questioned in any other place" for remarks made in the legislature.

The Senate must give its advice upon and consent to the appointments by the governor of heads of departments and members of boards and commissions, but has no role in their removal (Article V, Section 5). Upon recommendation of the governor, the Senate can remove judges of the Court of Claims, the county court, the surrogate's court, and the New York City Courts by two-thirds vote (Article VI, Section 23). Additionally, its members sit as a part of the court in trials of impeachment, if charges are brought by a majority of elected Assembly members against the governor, lieutenant governor, or a state judge.

The legislature is restricted in numerous procedural and substantive ways by the state Constitution. Process requirements, often stimulated by past abuses in New York and elsewhere, seek to assure that there is an opportunity for members to familiarize themselves with proposed legislation prior to voting. Thus, bills may not be amended following their final reading nor made applicable by reference. Private bills must be limited to one subject, identified in the title. Similarly, tax laws must clearly identify the nature and object of taxation. Absent a special message of necessity from the governor, bills must be printed and sit on members' desks in final form for three calendar days before passage. Two-thirds of each house must support any appropriation of public money or property for private or local purposes. In budgeting, other appropriations may not be considered until after those offered by the governor are taken up, and then must be made by separate bills, for a single purpose (Article VII, Sections 5 and 6).

Substantively, the legislature is barred from passing private or local bills on fourteen different subjects, for example changing of names of persons, incorporating villages, or granting a person, corporation, or association "any exclusive privilege, immunity or franchise whatever"(Article III, Section 17). The gift or loan of state money or credit for private purposes is prohibited (Article VII, Section 8). A number of key articles or provisions of the Constitution, for example those establishing the "merit and fitness" principle for civil service employment (Article V, Section 6); restricting borrowing authority (Article VII, Section 11); granting powers of home rule to local government (Article IX); establishing a general process of incorporation (Article X); and keeping the forest preserve "forever wild" (Article XIV) are major limits on the legislature's sphere of action.

These substantive limits were adopted for a number of reasons. Constraints on special legislation at once removed opportunities for patronage and corruption and focused the legislature on general matters, making it more efficient. Guarantees of home rule would, it was thought, both advance local democracy and, again, enhance legislative efficiency. (In fact home rule has been greatly weakened by court interpretation.) And the inclusion of broad policy commitments in the Constitution put these beyond the sphere of ordinary politics, making them more enduring.

The Constitution also contains numerous policy directives that the legislature act to give constitutional provisions force and effect, while in other areas it indicates that the legislature may act if it wishes to do so. Thus, for example, the legislature *must* provide for " . . . the maintenance and support of a system of free common schools . . . " (Article XI) but may provide low rent housing and nursing home accommodations (Article XVIII).[5] Requirements that the legislature act in an area are in some

5   See the chapters "Social Policy" and "Education" in this book.

degree limiting on its discretion, though they are not, of course, defining of the action it takes.

The Governor must "take care that the laws be faithfully executed." He or she reports to the legislature annually on the condition of the state, and makes policy recommendations to it that comprise a legislative agenda (Article IV, Section 3). The governor may expedite legislation or allow special legislation applicable to local governments other than New York City, with a message of special necessity (Article II, Section 14; Article IX, Section 2). After the legislature has acted, the governor is presented with legislation for approval or veto. On appropriations bills not originally submitted by him or her, the governor may exercise an item veto, striking one or more "items" without invalidating the entire bill. The definition of an "item" has been the subject of litigation.[6]

If the legislature is in session, a veto must be exercised within ten days of receipt of a measure, and may be overridden by a two-thirds vote of the members elected to each house. During the session there is no pocket veto; if the governor fails to sign a bill within ten days it still becomes law. If the legislature has adjourned, the veto period is thirty days and a bill may not become law without the governor's signature (Article IV, Section 7). One consequence of the legislative practice, since the mid-1970s, of recessing rather than adjourning has been to mitigate the effect of this provision.

The governor's key priorities are often encompassed in the executive budget, produced through a process defined in detail in a separate constitutional provision (Article VII). It requires that annually, by February 1 in gubernatorial election years or by the second Tuesday following the first day of annual meeting of the legislature, the governor submit the executive budget to the legislature, including a "complete plan of expenditures," revenue estimates, the basis of these, and recommendations for additional revenues, if needed. The budget must be accompanied by appropriation bills and proposed implementing legislation. The form of the budget, and the inclusiveness of appropriations bills, have been subjects of dispute between the branches settled in the Court of Appeals.

The governor is the commander in chief of the state's military and naval forces. He or she may call the entire legislature, or the Senate alone, into special session, and set the agenda for that session, though the legislature is not required to act upon the matters brought to it. The

---

6   This and all other gubernatorial and legislative powers concerning state finance are detailed in the chapter "State Government Finance" in this book.

governor may grant reprieves, commutations, or pardons for all offenses except treason and those subject to impeachment, and may suspend execution of a sentence for treason until the legislature has had time to consider and act upon it. With certain exceptions specified in the Constitution and noted below, he or she appoints department heads and, subject to processes prescribed in law, may remove these officials. Following constitutionally prescribed procedures, the governor may also remove elected sheriffs, county clerks or district attorneys for cause (Article XIII, Section 13(a) and (b)).

Regarding the judiciary the governor has considerable appointing authority. He or she appoints judges of the Court of Appeals and the Court of Claims, appoints to fill vacancies in the Supreme Court, appoints four members of the Commission on Judicial Conduct, and designates justices of the Appellate Divisions of the Supreme Court (Article 6, Sections 2(e), 4(c), 9, 21, 22). Additionally, the governor may appoint an extraordinary term of the Supreme Court, designate the presiding justice at such a term, and replace that justice as he or she sees fit (Article VI, Section 27). The governor may recommend to the Senate removal of judges of the Court of Claims, the County Court, the Family Court, the Surrogate's Court, and the New York City Courts (Article VI, Section 23).

The Lieutenant Governor, as noted, presides over the Senate and has a casting vote. He or she *becomes* governor and serves out the term if the governor dies, resigns, or is removed; or *acts* as governor if the governor is impeached, is absent from the state, or is unable to discharge his or her duties, until the temporary condition is meliorated (Article IV, Section 5).

The Comptroller is the head of the Department of Audit and Control. He or she is charged in the Constitution with the pre-audit of all vouchers, the audit of the state's accounts, and the audit of the accrual and collection of revenues. The comptroller also prescribes state accounting methods. Absent an audit by the comptroller, state monies may not be paid out. As provided for by the legislature he or she also supervises the accounts of the state's local governments and oversees some limited aspects of real estate taxation. In aggregate these powers are sources of considerable influence over the management of the governmental system.

The Constitution specifies that the comptroller may not be assigned additional administrative duties by the legislature, presumably to keep the audit function distinct from daily state government operations (Article V, Section 1). The comptroller is also charged with the management of sinking funds for the retirement of certain local debt, and may be required by the legislature to certify local debt that may be incurred outside of ordinary limits (Article 8, Sections 2(a), 4, 5, 7).

Interestingly, the Constitution is silent on the comptroller's very considerable powers in the management of the state retirement system, and his or her role in the incurring of state debt. These are entirely based in statute.

The Attorney General is the head of the Department of Law. The Constitution is almost entirely silent on the powers of this office. When a constitutional amendment is proposed, he or she must within 20 days report to the legislature on its affect on other portions of the Constitution.[7]

The Court System is created in detail in the Constitution, to include at the state level: the Court of Appeals, the Appellate Divisions, the Supreme Court, the Court of Claims, the County Court, the Surrogate's Court, and the Family Court. Court of Appeals and Supreme Court judges serve for fourteen years. Surrogates, County Court judges, and Family Court judges have ten-year terms, and the term of Court of Claims judges is nine years. Whether judges are elected or appointed, long terms are regarded as a necessary condition for judicial independence. All judges on these courts have a mandatory retirement age of 70. Court of Appeals and Supreme Court judges may be certified to continue to perform the duties of a Supreme Court justice for an additional six years, in two-year increments.

The highest court, the Court of Appeals, has a chief judge and six associate judges. Its quorum is five, with four in agreement required for a decision. Upon the Court of Appeals' request, the governor may temporarily appoint up to four Supreme Court judges to serve upon this court and assist with its work, their services to cease upon certification by the court that the need for help has passed. Among the duties of Court of Appeals judges is to sit on courts of impeachment, together with members of the state Senate.

Local courts with constitutional status include a separately defined New York City Court system and district, town, city, and village courts outside New York City. In New York City civil court judges are elected to ten-year terms, while criminal court judges there are appointed by the mayor to terms of the same length. District court judges outside New York City serve six-year terms in districts within counties created by the legislature upon local request and after acceptance at local referendum.

---

7   The chapter "Criminal Justice" in this book discusses alternative models for redefining the attorney general's powers in the state Constitution.

City and village courts may be discontinued by the legislature upon its own decision, but discontinuance of town courts must be approved at referendum in the affected jurisdiction. In towns, justices of the peace are elected for four years.

The four judicial departments, for Appellate Division purposes, and eleven judicial districts, for Supreme Court purposes, are also constitutionally defined.

For all courts, jurisdiction is specified in the Constitution. Processes for appeal, and possible actions on appeal, are also specified.

Administrative supervision of the court system is given to the chief judge of the Court of Appeals who, with the advice and consent of an administrative board of the courts comprised of him- or herself and the presiding judges of the appellate division of each department, appoints a chief administrator of the courts. Judges may be assigned outside of their immediate jurisdiction under the Constitution, and may perform duties of more than one court outside the city of New York if required to do so by the legislature. The Constitution creates an eleven-person Commission on Judicial Conduct, with multiple appointing authorities, to hear complaints concerning judges, initiate investigations, and make independent determinations of their fitness. Upon review of the commission's findings, the Court of Appeals may sanction judges in a range of ways, including removal.

The detailed specification of the state and local court systems in the Constitution contrasts substantially with the broader provisions concerning the judiciary in the national Constitution and that of some other states. There are continuing efforts, described below, to simplify these provisions, further unifying the courts and reorganizing them by constitutional amendment. Another regular object of amendment, also described below, concerns the creation of a fifth judicial department.

Departments and Agencies. The constitution limits departments to twenty in number. (This limitation, designed to constrain the size of government, is in practice overcome by the location of many units, not called "departments," in an omnibus "Executive Department.") Unlike in many other states, the governor is limited in his or her power to reorganize the executive branch. It is the legislature that is constitutionally empowered to reduce the number of departments; create temporary commissions or executive offices of the governor; or enhance, diminish, or alter the powers and functions of departments, officers, boards commissions, or executive offices. Enhanced authority in this area has been sought by the governor through constitutional amendment (Article V, Sections 2 & 3).

As noted above, with the exception of departments headed by elected officials and the department of education, headed by legislatively appointed Regents who in turn select a commissioner to serve as the chief administrative officer, department heads are appointed by the governor with the advice and consent of the Senate. The Senate, however, does not share the removal power (Article V, Section 4). The governor's authority over departments is further solidified by the constitutional requirement that department heads provide him or her with the budgetary information he or she may require, as part of the executive budget process (Article VII, Section 1).

No department rule or regulation, except those entirely for internal management, may be effective until filed with the department of state.

Public Authorities emerged in New York during the Post World War I period, but were first constitutionally regulated by the amendments adopted in 1938. Authorities are autonomous entities delivering service largely outside the departmental structure of state government, and are therefore not subject to many of the rules and regulations that govern the operations of ordinary state departments and agencies. Under the Constitution, authorities must be created by special act of the legislature. They are authorized to contract debt and to collect rentals, charges, rates, or fees to pay for the facilities they build and operate (Article X, Section 5).

The state is not liable for the obligations of public authorities nor can it be made liable for these by legislative act, though the legislature may act to acquire the property of these corporations and assume the indebtedness on this property (Article X, Section 5). The accounts of public authorities are subject to review by the comptroller. Specific exceptions allow state guarantees for authority debt to construct thruways, purchase railroad cars, finance certain economic development activities, and finance housing and nursing home accommodations for low-income persons (Article VII, Section 8.3; Article X, Sections 6-8; Article XVIII, Section 2).

Techniques developed by the state over time to bypass the prohibition of state guarantees of authority debt, including "moral obligation" borrowing and lease purchase arrangements, have made this an area of continuing political and constitutional controversy. State courts have permitted these practices.[8] Numerous constitutional amendments have

---

8   See *Wein v. City of New York*, 36 NY 2d 610 (1975).

been proposed as a result, some to strengthen limits on authority borrowing and the use of *de facto* state guarantees and others to remove existing limits as ineffectual, leaving regulation to the financial markets.[9]

Proposals for Constitutional Change[10]

The Legislature. Most recent constitutional change proposals concerning the state legislature seek to limit that institution. The premises of these efforts are that legislators are self-interested (not public interested); that the legislature's priorities are misplaced; that power within it is too concentrated; and that the institution is not working well to resolve most issues of consequence that face New York. This reform emphasis is abundantly evident from the many widely discussed ideas for change, discussed elsewhere in this volume: initiative and referendum, to bypass the legislature when it cannot or will not act in accord with the majority will; term limitation for legislators, ending or constraining legislative careers; strengthened, constitutionally based ethics requirements for legislators and other elected officials; the creation of a reapportionment commission to decennially redistrict the legislature, taking direct responsibility from the members themselves; the requirement of extraordinary majorities to pass tax increases; and restructuring the budgetary process, to force action in face of repeated fiscal deadlock.[11]

Other suggestions have involved the fundamental restructuring of the legislature, the redistribution of power within it by constitutional prescription, and the creation of alternative decision processes on matters (like reapportionment) where members of the legislature are self-interested.

Unicameralism. A single-house legislature has been regularly proposed in New York in recent years.[12] Advocates argue that the U.S. Supreme Court's "one person, one vote" standard results in the use of the same basis of representation — population — for all state legislative bodies. This, they say, removes the rationale for a bicameral legislature. Such a change, they argue, would ease executive/legislative negotiations by reducing the number of parties involved, thus expediting decision making in the political process. However, sufficient checks would remain

---

9   For a further discussion see the chapter "State Government Finance" in this book.

10   Most issues touched upon in this chapter are detailed in other sections of this book. This summary will confine itself to those not discussed elsewhere in this volume.

11   See primarily the chapters "The Elections and the Political Process" and "State Government Finance" in this book.

12   See A.3690 (1993 introduced by Samuel Colman).

in the internal process of the single remaining house, they think, to prevent excessively hasty decision making. Though present only in Nebraska at the state level, unicameralism is universally employed in American local government without apparent ill effects.

Opponents point out that each legislative house in New York is controlled by a different political party. By deduction, it appears that different district sizes result in different patterns of representation in each house even when population is used to apportion both of them. Bicameralism is the norm for state government, they observe. Its value is in insuring that compromises are forged on policy between the key power centers in the state, and that major actions are not taken until a sufficient consensus has been reached. Such a major institutional reform should not be undertaken, opponents also say, until the nature of the single house to be created is much more clearly defined. Finally, there is a partisan concern. Such a change, Republicans fear, could redound to their disadvantage.

Legislative Openness and Power Sharing. Proposals for constitutional change have augmented numerous ideas for rules changes and statutory initiatives, most often emanating from the minority in each house, to: enhance legislative openness; improve efficiency; and distribute power more widely in the Senate and Assembly. Some examples of constitutional proposals that have been filed include the establishment of a biennial legislative session; the fixing of a definite termination date for each session; and a ban on the passage of bills between midnight and 8 A.M.[13]

The constitutions of other states offer examples of the prescription of legislative procedure in constitutions in ways that may affect the distribution of legislative power. The Hawaii and Michigan Constitutions provide for the discharge of committees, the first by a vote of one-third twenty days or more after referral and the second by a simple majority. Hawaii requires open meetings for committees, as does Montana. The Michigan and Illinois Constitutions require public notice in advance of committee meetings, and in addition in Michigan a record of committee votes must be kept. Finally, in

---

13 13 S.3508 (Hoffmann), S. 1487 (Nolan), A. 4767 (Concurrent) (1993). Rules changes and statutory proposals recently offered, primarily by Assembly Republicans and Senate Democrats, include: itemized legislative budgets; limited bill introduction; full disclosure of legislative mailing costs; limitation on the number of district wide mailings, and restriction on their use close to election; open meetings for political conferences; open meetings of the Assembly Rules Committee, which is the gatekeeper for that body; requirements of timely votes in the second house of matters passed in the first; requirement of conference committees for resolving interhouse differences; increasing public access to legislative records; reduction in the number of committees and subcommittees in each house, with concomitant cost reductions for "leadership" roles; elimination of most special allowances ("lulus") for legislators; and gavel to gavel television of government proceedings on cable television.

Illinois, Pennsylvania, Texas, and Wyoming, all bills must be considered by a committee before they may be passed into law.[14]

Such provisions seek to reduce the control of legislative or committee leadership, and to enhance openness. But leaders are artful about bypassing them. And one expert argues that such constitutional provisions excessively expose substantively controversial legislation to procedural challenge in the courts.[15]

Altering Decision Processes Where Legislators are Self-Interested. Because the legislature is the ultimate repository of all policy making power of the state, except insofar as alternative institutional arrangements or limits are provided in the Constitution, it must necessarily take up matters that touch upon its members' self-interest. In addition to districting, discussed elsewhere and mentioned above, this involves such questions as the compensation of members (pay, benefits, expenses), the staff and resources available to them, and accountability for these. All are matters of enormous political sensitivity in a public already skeptical about the balance incumbent legislators strike between their self-interest and the public interest.

1. *Legislative Compensation.* Six states currently fix legislative compensation in their constitutions.[16] This was the practice in New York until 1947, when a constitutional amendment was passed making the determination of legislative salaries a statutory matter, but prohibiting the alteration of legislative salaries during a term of service.

The $57,500 base salary for New York state legislators, adopted in 1987, is currently the highest in the nation. In downstate areas this level of pay is regarded by many as relatively moderate for professional work. In much of the rest of the state it is seen as relatively generous, especially in the absence of a requirement of full-time legislative service. Additionally, many members receive additional payments for service in leadership

---

14   Hawaii: Article II, Section 12; Illinois: Article IV, Section 7; Michigan: Article IV, Sections 16, 17; Wyoming: Article III, Section 23; Missouri: Article III, Section 22; Montana: Article V, Section 10; Pennsylvania: Article III, Section 2; Texas: Article III, Section 37.

15   See William J. Keefe and Morris Ogul, *The American Legislative Process*, 3rd. ed., Englewood Cliffs: Prentice Hall, 1972, at p. 38.; and Robert F. Williams, "State Constitutional Limits on Legislative Procedure: Legislative Compliance and Judicial Enforcement," *Publius* (Winter, 1967): 92.

16   Alabama, Arkansas, Nebraska, New Hampshire, New Mexico, and Rhode Island. See "Can You Make a Living Making Laws," *Governing* (December 1988): 34-35, cited in Richard D. Bingham and David Hedge, *State and Local Government in A Changing Society*, 2nd. ed., New York: McGraw Hill, 1991 at pp. 107-108.

positions. Proliferation of such positions has been one way of increasing the possibility of higher compensation for members. Fearful of public reaction to salary increases, legislators have taken to voting such increases in lame duck sessions following elections but before the seating of a new legislature. Since incumbent members tend to be reelected in high numbers, they are in effect "giving themselves a raise" by such votes. Very strong public reaction is generated by legislative salary increases, especially by this method, building a reluctance among members to raise salaries for a period of time.[17] This creates the prospect of a higher percentage increase the next time an action is taken, with public reaction focused on this dimension of the matter as well as upon the increase itself.

One answer is to return to specifying legislative salaries in the Constitution. But this makes them far more difficult to change than if they are decided by law. The effect of such provisions is to cause compensation levels to lag even more behind changes in the value of the dollar. One result may be to severely limit the recruitment pool for legislators. Another may be for legislators to seek to compensate themselves in indirect ways, and thus open themselves again to criticism for subterfuge and indirection.

An alternative approach is to establish a constitutionally based legislative compensation commission. In some states this body is empowered to set legislative salaries; in others it makes recommendations for legislative action, with the options left to the legislature constitutionally limited.

The first approach is used in Oklahoma and Idaho. In Oklahoma a commission comprised of five members appointed by the governor (who also designates the chair), two by the president pro tempore of the Senate and two by the speaker of the House, with the chairman of the Tax Commission and the director of State Finance serving ex officio, set legislative salaries every two years. Legislators are specifically barred from service on this group.[18] In Idaho a six-member citizens committee on legislative compensation, three appointed by the governor and three by the

---

17 Constitutional amendments have been introduced to close this lame duck session door to legislative salary increases. See S.1658 (1993), introduced by Senator John Marchi.

18 Article 5, Section 21.

supreme court (but including no office holders) reviews the subject biennially and establishes pay levels.[19]

In Hawaii a legislative veto system is used, which provides the potential of avoiding a vote in the legislature on member salaries, while leaving the legislature a role if it wishes to seize it. There a commission is appointed every eight years by the governor to recommend salary levels, which become effective unless rejected by the legislature by concurrent resolution.[20]

In Utah, Texas, and Maryland the legislature must act on commission recommendations. The Utah and Maryland commissions recommend salary levels, which then provide a ceiling for legislative action. In Utah the governor is the appointing authority of a "citizens'" group; the size of this body and the frequency of its meeting are not constitutionally specified.[21] In Maryland, the commission has nine members who serve for four years. Five are appointed by the governor, two by the president of the Senate and two by the House of Delegates speaker. Again, elected officials cannot serve, but here public employees are also barred.

Finally, in Texas an Ethics Commission made up of eight members serving four-year terms appointed by the governor, from lists supplied by the members and leaders of each of the legislative houses with a requirement of bipartisanship, makes salary and per diem recommendations to the legislature for its members and leaders. These cannot be effected until approved by the people of the state at referendum.[22]

2. *Full-Time Service.* Concerns over levels of legislative compensation have been linked, as noted, to the absence of any requirement, statutory or constitutional, that service in the Assembly or Senate be full time. Additionally, some observers regard the absence of a full-time service requirement as contributory to conflict-of-interest problems that may arise for legislators who retain active roles in law or consulting firms or other private business.[23]

---

19   Article 3, Section 23.

20   Article 3, Section 9.

21   Article 6, Section 9.

22   Article 3, Section 24a.

23   See the discussion of this issue in the chapter "Elections and the Political Process" in this book.

Those who favor a full-time service requirement point to the growing complexity of government in New York, and the need for elected officials to be fully committed to the state's interest to do their job effectively and well. They argue that mechanisms for properly establishing legislative compensation, and justifications for appropriate compensation levels, can only be achieved if there are concomitant requirements of full-time service. They point out, finally, that the state has evolved to a situation in which most legislators have come to identify legislative service as their principal profession, and that therefore a full-time requirement will simply the ratify the status quo.

Opponents suggest, in contrast, that the evolution toward a professional legislature, which has been occurring in New York, is a negative development, not a positive one, and a full-time service requirement would exacerbate this trend. Legislators who are full time and lack ongoing professional experience outside politics, they argue, tend to become too disconnected from everyday experiences of the people they must represent. Moreover, they say, legislators who depend solely on their legislative salaries will be less willing to act independently on difficult matters than those who have other sources of income and independent professional bases.

3. *Term Length.* Though not now much debated, the issue of term length for senators and assembly members offers an interesting example. A four-year term for one house and a two-year term for the other is the modal pattern in the states.[24] A constitutional amendment proposing a four-year Senate term linked to the two-year term for Assembly members (they then had one-year terms) and four-year terms for statewide elected officers was defeated at the polls in New York in 1927. All these proposed changes except the four-year Senate term, which was not offered, were finally accepted by New Yorkers in 1937. The four-year Senate term was rejected again in 1938 and 1941. A proposal for four-year terms for all legislators failed in 1965.

The New York legislature has been criticized in recent years for its inability or unwillingness to make tough decisions on controversial issues. Some would argue that giving members longer terms, though a small sacrifice in democratic accountability, would increase the legislature's institutional capacity to

---

24   See Alan Rosenthal, *Legislative Life*, New York: Harper and Row, 1981 at p. 135.

make such decisions. They argue that such a change would offer members more time to act on controversial matters distant from the next election, and therefore to explain their actions, building support, and softening the negative electoral impact. Moreover, they suggest, if legislators serve the same terms as the governor, and are elected on the same cycle, the entire government could be held accountable for its performance in a more systematic way.

Though its relative merits are by no means self evident, in light of its widespread use elsewhere and the kinds of criticisms of the legislature as an institution currently being made in New York, the four-year legislative term for one or both houses seems a constitutional change worthy of serious consideration. However, legislators already chary of criticism for being self-interested are not likely to bring it forward. (Interestingly, it has appeared in recent years linked to proposals for term limitation.) Such a proposal might be given consideration at a constitutional convention.

The Governor. There are clear consequences for the powers of the New York governorship of reforms discussed elsewhere in this chapter or this volume, for example, a two-term limit for governor, the reallocation of budgetary powers, or altered methods of judicial selection. In general, however, alteration of the powers of the governor has not been the direct focal point of efforts at constitutional change in New York. Perhaps this is because the state is already among those with the strongest gubernatorial powers. Or perhaps there is an underlying consensus among those attentive to politics and government in New York that a strong governor is needed to deal with a socially diverse, economically complex state's broad array of powerful interest groups and institutions.

One exception, however, has been the attempt to give the governor the power to reorganize the state government now specifically left with the legislature. Currently governors in ten states have a constitutionally based power to reorganize their governments by executive order. In eleven others the power is based in statute.[25] Proponents say that this authority properly resides with the chief executive. Opponents fear any further enhancement of gubernatorial power.

A constitutional convention might also be an opportunity for review of the details of the governor's veto power. The reach of the item veto has

---

25   See *Book of the States*, Lexington, KY: Council of State Governments, 1992, Tables 2.4 & 2.5.

been a matter of some contention between the governor and legislature in recent years.[26] One amendment proposed in the legislature, spurred by the annual passage, veto, and override attempts regarding restoring the death penalty, would put to a popular vote any bill passed in the legislature three times and vetoed by the governor three times.[27]

There have been proposals to limit the governor's pardon, reprieve, and commutation powers in cases where the sentence has been life imprisonment without parole.[28] Finally, as noted above, some changes might be offered regarding the governor's power to appoint department heads, both to extend this power and to diminish it. In light of current practice, special constitutional language concerning the appointment of the head of the department of Agriculture and Markets might well be removed from the Constitution.

The Lieutenant Governor. In modern New York history, the effectiveness of this office has been contingent upon the nature of the relationship between the governor and lieutenant governor. Some have therefore suggested that the Constitution be changed to assure that candidates for these offices are nominated as well as elected on the same ticket. Joint election has been the case since an amendment to the Constitution adopted in 1945.

The constitutional provision that the lieutenant governor act as governor when the governor is absent from the state is probably an anachronism in an era of modern communications, and might be considered for removal from the Constitution. Amendments have been proposed in light of national experience to further specify the provisions of the New York Constitution concerning gubernatorial inability to serve. These would affect the lieutenant governorship, as would any effort to formally remove this official from his or her role as Senate presiding officer, making the office purely executive.

Some states, New Jersey for example, do without a lieutenant governor (though there have been recent debates there to restore it). There has been no serious effort in New York in recent years, however, to abolish the office.

The Comptroller. Constitutional changes concerning this office have been proposed to give the comptroller a role in revenue estimating or certification of budget balance, and to provide a constitutional basis for

---

26 For further detail see the chapter "State Government Finance" in the book.
27 A.3938 (1993) offered by Assemblyman Robach and Senator Owen Johnson.
28 S.3556 (1993).

this official's role as sole trustee of state pension funds. The former matter is discussed in detail elsewhere in this volume. Regarding pensions, such a change would be opposed by those who would remove this very great fiscal power from the comptroller, or require it to be shared with others. Toward this end, a constitutional amendment has regularly been introduced in the state Senate that would create in the state Constitution a common retirement fund board of trustees.[29]

The Courts. Recent efforts at court reform have two principal focal points: selection of judges and organization of the court system. Additionally, a number of smaller, more limited proposals concerning civil court jurisdiction and continued service by retired judges have regularly been introduced in the legislature in recent years.[30]

Judicial Selection. Most judges in New York State are elected to long terms in partisan elections at the city, county, or judicial district level. In many jurisdictions dominated by one party, nomination is tantamount to election. Nomination is dominated by party leaders, who therefore control access to the bench, may establish conditions for nomination and renomination, and have claims upon judges after elected. Even where election may be competitive, party leaders frequently enter into cross endorsement agreements under provisions of the state election law to assure that selected candidates of each party are elected unopposed to the offices to which they are nominated.

The realities of the electoral process for judge, reformers therefore argue, belie the premises under which this system was established, for there is no real competition that offers real choice to the voters. But even if the process worked as designed, they argue, it would not be a good one for selecting judges. When it comes to judicial office, voters lack the time and interest to really get to know the alternatives. Moreover, the work of a judge requires special skills and a special temperament. Political campaigns are not a good method for identifying either, and in fact might be compromising insofar as they require candidates to seek favors and raise funds from those most interested in the outcome, lawyers who may appear before them.[31]

---

29 S.4310 (1993, introduced by Senators Farley, Holland, Lack, Larkin, Lavalle, and Volker).

30 A.2080 (1993 Lentol) assigning retired judges as senior judges to courts where they previously served and A.5026 (1993 Weprin) continuing certain judges in service for an additional term. Also S.2175 and S.3769 (1993 Mega) increasing the monetary jurisdiction of the New York City Civil Court and District Courts to $25,000. A number of constitutional issues contained in the judicial article are discussed in the chapter on "Criminal Justice" in this book.

31 See New York State Commission on Government Integrity, *Becoming a Judge: Report on the Failings of Judicial Elections in New York State* (May 1988).

Defenders of the present system argue that it has produced many good judges. It is locally based, and draws on candidates who are deeply rooted in the community, with many years of volunteer service. A change from election to appointment, they say, would not remove politics from the process, but would simply change the locus of politics. The governor would become more powerful. Bar associations would be more powerful.

It is not insignificant, its defenders say, that the current system provides incentives for lawyers to involve themselves in political party activities. Parties need incentives if they are to properly perform their political functions. If parties lose control of these incentives they will ultimately fail, and their effective functioning largely benefits the less advantaged in society.

Those who favor the current system also point to the general research finding that alternative judicial selection methods do not systematically produce judges of background characteristics or abilities different from those for judges selected by the current system.[32] They suggest that different kinds of lawyers, those with more establishment backgrounds, might become judges under alternative methods, but there is no assurance that they would be better judges. The findings of recent research done on New York City trial court judges selected by alternative methods has shown, however, that there " . . . merit selection produces a younger, more representative, better educated, highly qualified and more politically diverse judiciary."[33]

1. *Merit Selection.* One alternative is merit selection. Under such a plan "broad-based, bipartisan nominating commissions — composed of lawyers and laypersons — propose a short list of candidates for appointment to judicial vacancies. In step two, an elected chief executive chooses from the proposed names. Step three is the ratification or disapproval of the appointment by the voters after the judge has been in office long enough to assess actual performance and with all voters having access to an objective evaluation of the judge's record in office."[34]

2. *Partisan Election From Smaller Districts.* The use of judicial districts for judicial selection constitutes at-large election from multimember districts and may therefore deny concentrated minori-

---

32   Research is summarized in M. L. Henry, Jr., *Characteristics of Elected versus Merit-Selected New York City Judges, 1977-92*, New York: Fund for Modern Courts, 1992, at pp. 1-2.

33   *Ibid.*, at p. 16.

34   S.4251 (1993 Goodman). See Fund For Modern Courts.

ties the right to an equal voice in choosing judges, in violation of the federal Voting Rights Act.[35] The Governor's Task Force on Judicial Diversity has suggest that judges be elected from smaller districts, giving minorities a greater say in judicial selection.[36]

3. *Nonpartisan Election of Judges.* A third alternative is nonpartisan election of judges, either from the present districts or smaller districts. Such a method, with nomination by petition, might mitigate the power of party leaders. However, research findings and practical experience in New York State suggest that nonpartisan election in a highly partisan environment often becomes a mask for what is, in fact, a partisan process.

Unified Courts. Reformers argue that though the court system of New York is described as unified in the Constitution, it is in fact highly fragmented. They propose to merge the state's major trial courts.[37] Such a merger, they argue, will " . . . eliminate duplication and jurisdictional disputes, increase efficiency of court administration and raise public understanding of, and respect for, the judicial branch."[38] Opponents stress the value of local administrative autonomy and responsiveness to local values. They say the current system develops specialized judges with special expertise. Proponents suggest in response that most judges are and ought to be generalists seeking to impartially apply the law. Moreover, sufficient specialization can be achieved within a unified system.

Efforts at court merger have a history in New York State reaching back at least forty years. Many distinguished commissions and task forces have made recommendations on the issue.[39] In fact, the effort has been so long and arduous that Arthur Vanderbilt once likened court reform in New York to " . . . jogging down the Ho Chi Minh trail unarmed."[40]

Some consolidation was achieved in 1962. In 1976 Governor Hugh Carey called a special session of the legislature limited to court reform issues, and achieved first passage of three amendments, all later adopted, that: established merit selection for Court of Appeals judges; created the consti-

---

35   This act's requirements are discussed in detail in the interim report of the Temporary State Commission on Constitutional Revision.

36   A.2199 (1993 Friedman).

37   S.4251/A.7145 (1993 Goodman/Koppell).

38   See Committee for Modern Courts, Memorandum in support of A.11 (Weprin) (no date).

39   The Tweed Commission (1953-58); the Dominick Commission (1970-73): The Vance Task Force (1974-75); The Carey proposals (1979); The State Bar Action Unit No. 4 (1979-80); and the Barclay Commission (1983-84).

40   Cited in Frederick Miller, *Court Reform: The New York Experience*, (processed, files of the Temporary Commission, 1979).

tutional office of Chief Administrator of the Courts with the administrative authority until then located in the Appellate Divisions; and set up an eleven-member commission on judicial conduct with authority to discipline judges, subject to review by the Court of Appeals. (A statute establishing Unified Court Budgeting was also passed in that year.) First passage of a constitutional amendment on court merger occurred in 1986, but there was no second passage in 1987. Many now think that further court reform is likely to be achieved only at a constitutional convention.

Creation of a New Fifth Judicial Department. The current Constitution divides the state into four judicial departments, and distributes the judicial districts among them. The 1967 proposed Constitution provided for a minimum of five and a maximum of seven departments, with the legislature empowered to change the number and boundaries of judicial districts within them decennially.[41]

The creation of a fifth department out of portion of the current second Department has long been a goal of leaders of the bar in the tenth judicial district on Long Island and their representatives in Albany, with some support in the Hudson Valley counties of the ninth judicial district. Their claim is that such a change would lead to efficiencies and is justified by the workload of the second department, and distinctions between the nature of cases in the courts outside and within New York City. Opponents suggest that a new department would lead not to greater efficiency but to reduced efficiency in the courts. Other techniques might better be used, they argue, to achieve efficiencies, for example: appointment of additional appellate division judges; transferring appeals among departments to even the workload; and taking steps to reduce the number of appeals. Moreover, they say, the creation of an additional department would increase the number of conflicts in decision, thus driving up the workload of the Court of Appeals.

Attempts to gain constitutional amendments to achieve court merger and merit selection of judges have foundered, in part, over efforts in the Senate to create this fifth department.[42] The creation of a new judicial department comprised of the ninth and tenth judicial districts, with the retention of partisan election for judicial selection, would significantly benefit Republicans in the politics of judicial nomination and election. An alternative proposal under discussion, possibly more politically feasible, would combine Queens with Nassau and Suffolk in the new department.

---

41   Article V, Section 3.

42   S.5841 (1993 Mega).

If left unresolved, the debate over a fifth judicial department would surely continue at a constitutional convention.

Housing Court. A constitutional amendment to create a housing court has regularly been introduced in the legislature in recent years.[43] This creation of a new specialized court to handle housing disputes, of course, is in direct conflict with proposals for unification of the courts.

Justice Courts. From time to time proposals arise to eliminate the justice courts in rural areas. Justices of the peace are elected for four-year terms. They need not be attorneys, but are mandated to take training in the law after elected. These courts are criticized as inefficient and unprofessional, but are deeply rooted and highly valued local institutions in most upstate communities.

State Departments. Proposals might be expected at a constitutional convention that would remove the constitutional restriction on the number of state departments as having little practical effect. Additionally, there have been proposals to give a firm constitutional basis to a process for legislative review of agency rules and regulations for consistency with legislative intent.[44]

43   S.2385 (1993 Hannon).
44   S.3556 (1993 Concurrent).

State Government Finance

Robert P. Kerker

There is no single article or set of related articles on state government finance in the New York State Constitution; provisions bearing directly on this theme appear in 12 of the 20 articles.[1] The 1938 Constitutional Convention did pull together in one article the provisions governing the then-new budgeting system and a variety of sections affecting state borrowing and lending. It also established a new article on taxation. Despite the 1938 Convention's housekeeping (which accompanied some solid substantive changes), many important provisions affecting state finance continued to reside outside the new consolidated articles. The balance of this section discusses all provisions of the Constitution affecting finance in five categories: budgets and appropriations, taxation, debt, public benefit corporations, and gifts and loans.

Budgets and Appropriations

New York adopted an executive budget system in 1927 as a critical component of an extensive reorganization of the executive branch of government. The package of reforms was the product of a decade and a half of work by a bipartisan coalition headed by Governor Alfred E. Smith, former Governor Charles Evans Hughes, Henry L. Stimson, and others. The provisions defining the budget system were initially adopted as Article IV-A and transferred in their entirety to a new comprehensive article on "State Finance," Article VII, in 1938. There were extensive changes in language and some structural revisions in the interest of greater clarity and precision, but fundamentally the system defined by Governor Smith and his allies has remained virtually unchanged since 1927.

Current Provision. The Constitution makes the governor responsible for presenting to the legislature, by a specified date early in the legislative session, a budget containing a complete plan of proposed expenditures and estimated available revenues. Most important, it requires the governor to submit at the same time "a bill or bills containing all the proposed

---

1   Articles I, III, IV, VII, VIII, XIV, XV, XVII, and XVIII.

81

appropriations and reappropriations included in the budget and the proposed legislation, if any, recommended therein." The so-called Article VII budget bills, setting forth revenue proposals, agency reorganizations, and the like, form an integral part of each budget submission.

For Governor Smith, executive responsibility for the appropriation bills was the critical issue, the heart of the executive budget system, and of far greater importance than the presentation of the budget itself. In effect, it makes the governor responsible for determining the format of the appropriations, establishing the level of detail, and defining an "item of appropriation" and the scope of the "single object or purpose" included in an item.

The power to determine the form of an appropriation, and thus the content of items of appropriation, is important because under the Constitution the legislature may not alter an appropriation bill submitted by the governor except to strike out or reduce items therein. It may add items, but must state each of them "separately and distinctly" from the original items of the bill and limit each "to a single object or purpose." Additional items are thus subject to the governor's item veto (Article IV, Section 7), which has been part of the New York Constitution since 1874.

Section 7 of Article VII prohibits the payment of money "out of the State treasury or any of its funds, or any of the funds under its management, except in pursuance of an appropriation by law. . . ." Until 1981, this provision was not considered to require the appropriation of federal funds — other than those state funds included in first-instance appropriation in anticipation of the receipt of federal aid. In that year the Court of Appeals upheld a challenge initiated by the Senate leadership and ruled that Section 7 did indeed apply to federal funds deposited in the state treasury.[2]

Definition of Budgetary Powers Over Time. New York was one of the first states to tackle the issue of budgetary reform seriously, and a strong executive budget system was an integral part of the proposed Constitution submitted to the voters in November 1915. The rejection of the Constitution in its entirety did not diminish interest in budgetary reform, but ten years of experiments with legislative and joint executive-legislative budget systems failed to satisfy the reform coalition. As a result, New York was one of the last of the major states to complete a comprehensive overhaul of its budgetary processes. The system that eventually did emerge was anchored in the Constitution (Governor Smith rejected all suggestions to settle for statutory authorization alone), comprehensive in its scope, and strong in its commitment to executive initiative and control.

---

2   *Anderson v. Regan,* 442 NYS 2d 404 (1981).

Format of Appropriation Bills. The governor's power to determine the format of appropriation bills seems to have been upheld in 1939, although the decision was not as explicit as advocates of the executive's prerogatives would have liked.[3] Implicit or explicit challenges to the governor's right to determine the form and content of appropriations, beginning in the late 1960s, failed because the plaintiffs lacked standing to sue or because of a judicial reluctance to involve the courts in the budget process short of a finding that the legislature had been in some way prevented from performing its role. But at the same time the Court noted that "we do not suggest by our decision . . . that the budget process is per se always beyond the realm of judicial consideration."[4]

Too Much Detail in the Constitution? Questions have been raised from time to time by reformers about the need for the detail in Sections 1-4 of Article VII. In the fiscal crisis of the 1970s the "detail" served the state well. Writing for the Court of Appeals in *Wein* v. *Carey*, Chief Judge Charles Breitel argued that "it would be ludicrous to deny prima facie validity to this constitutionally mandated and meticulously directed process."[5]

Item Veto. Governors have varied in their reliance on the item veto since the establishment of the executive budget system. For example, Governors Franklin D. Roosevelt and Herbert H. Lehman, facing hostile legislatures, used it extensively. Governor Thomas E. Dewey, benefiting from his party's firm control over both houses during his 12 years, rarely if ever used it. Governors have extended the power inherent in the item veto to include striking out language that seeks to limit their use of appropriations. Although no cases have dealt head-on with this issue, Governor Roosevelt's use of the item veto in this way was implicitly endorsed in the first *Tremaine* case.[6] Governor Hugh L. Carey's right to do so was supported by opinions of the attorney general in 1978 and 1982. In the latter opinion, Attorney General Robert Abrams concluded that in adding restrictive language to items of appropriation in the governor's budget, the legislature "did not follow the procedures for action on appropriation bills required by the Constitution." He noted, however, that "no New York cases dealing with the distribution of power between the Legislature and the Governor over the budgeting process are squarely on point, and the issue

---

3   *People* v. *Tremaine*, 281 NY 1 (1939).
4   See, for example, *Saxton* v. *Carey*, 406 NYS 2d 732 (1978), which focused on the level of itemization. The passage quoted is at p. 735.
5   393 NYS 2d 955 (1977), at p. 960.
6   *People* v. *Tremaine*, 252 NY 27 (1929).

is not entirely free from doubt." Although he found Attorney General Louis Lefkowitz's argument in 1978 persuasive, Abrams noted that court decisions elsewhere (in Maryland, for example) had supported a legislature's right to place conditions on the use of appropriations.[7]

Impoundment. The importance of the item veto has been enhanced, however, by the so-called "impoundment case," *Oneida* v. *Berle*.[8] In it the Court of Appeals ruled that "under the State Constitution, the executive possesses no express or inherent power . . . to impound funds which have been appropriated by the Legislature." The Court acknowledged that the state had faced a financial crisis and thus had an interest in restraining expenditures. It noted, however, that the Governor had the power to use his item veto to strike the legislative addition to his appropriation bill. He had chosen not to use it, and had approved the bill presented to him. "Once the appropriation was approved, . . . the Governor and his subordinates were duty bound [to] take care that [it was] faithfully executed."[9]

Appropriating Federal Aid. Despite the explosive growth of federal aid, which began in the 1960s, a trend among state governments everywhere to appropriate federal funds, and occasional irritation over the alleged executive abuse of its administrative control over federal funds to thwart legislative intent, no attempt was made to change this situation until 1981. In its decision in *Anderson* v. *Regan*, the Court acknowledged that legislative behavior had not always been consistent with its stance in the suit, and that "the clear and unambiguous working of a statute or constitutional provision may be overlooked entirely when it is seemingly inconsistent with the practice and usage of those charged with implementing the laws." Nevertheless, it ruled, once money was in the treasury there was only one way to get it out, and there was "no logical justification" for excluding federal funds from the "ambit" of Section 7. It agreed that there were funds that were withheld from the treasury, but types of such funds were listed in Section 121 of the State Finance Law and did not include federal funds.[10]

Balanced Budget. Although there is a consensus that the governor must submit a balanced budget, there is less agreement on the equally important questions of whether or not the legislature must enact a balanced budget

---

7   1978 Op. Att'y Gen., (f. 78-76) and 1982 Op. Att'y Gen., (f. 82-F5).

8   427 NYS 2d 407 (1980).

9   *Ibid.*, at page 412.

10   442 NYS 2d 404 (1981).

and avoid taking subsequent steps that would disturb that balance, and whether or not the governor, with or without legislative concurrence, is required to maintain budget balance throughout the fiscal year. These issues were canvassed during the fiscal crisis of the 1970s when the state's shortfalls, the specter of default, and the state's relationships with the financial community and the purchasers of state debt kept the state's books under day-to-day scrutiny.

Several court cases focused on this issue, of which the most important was *Wein* v. *State*.[11] Chief Judge Breitel, writing for the Court, observed that "Critical to understanding State finances is that the Constitution mandates a balanced budget. . . . There is no express treatment in the Constitution governing appropriations made after the regular session and during the fiscal year at extraordinary sessions, but the implication is, and an essential one, that additional appropriations must be covered by matching revenues, or else the balanced budget of the regular session would be a device easily evaded. . . ." By implication, one might at the least conclude from this that the legislature must enact a balanced budget.

Four years later, in *Oneida* v. *Berle*, the Court noted that it had previously recognized the governor's constitutional obligation "to *propose* a balanced budget. . . . But at no time has the Court suggested that, once a budget plan is enacted, revenues and expenditures must match throughout the fiscal year." There must, practically, "be some gap between the two. Recognizing this reality, the Court has but recently disclaimed any obligation on the part of the State to *maintain* a balanced budget. . . . There must in every year be either a deficit or surplus" (emphasis in original; the Court was quoting from the decision in *Wein* v. *Carey*). As there was no obligation to maintain a balanced budget, there can be — *Oneida* v. *Berle* contended — no justification for unlawful actions to that end.

Taxation

For so highly charged an issue, the constitutional provisions governing state taxation are relatively sparse. Article XVI, "Taxation," was developed as a new article by the Convention of 1938. It makes clear that the state cannot surrender its power to tax, or give it away through some subterfuge, and that tax policies are not "contracts" that would restrict subsequent legislatures. Other provisions affecting the state protect the right of nonresident individuals and out-of-state corporations to keep

---

11   383 NYS 2d 225 (1976), at p. 227.

money, securities, and "other intangible property" in the state without fear that New York will tax such property, and prohibit the levy of *ad valorem* or excise taxes on intangible personal property, taxes on undistributed profits, discrimination against enterprises incorporated under federal law, and the taxation of pensions of employees of the state, its subdivisions, and "agencies" (i.e., public authorities).[12]

In addition to the provisions of Article XVI, the most important section of the Constitution bearing explicitly on state taxation is Section 22 of Article III, the article defining the powers and responsibilities of the legislature. Dating from 1846, Section 22, requires every tax law to be clear and distinct as to its nature and the object to which it applies. It prohibits satisfying these requirements by simply referring to another law. The section was amended in 1959 to authorize the legislature to adopt federal definitions for income tax purposes. This addition was consistent with a national trend toward conformity at the time. Its selling point was that it would simplify individual income tax preparation: the Department of Taxation and Finance termed it the "five-minute form." Although the amendment did not affect tax rates, it did simplify the exchange of data among revenue agencies. For example, because the definitions of income, allowable deductions, and other items were more or less consistent, conformity has facilitated the exchange of audit findings and tax rulings between the Tax Department and its federal counterpart.

Unlike the constitutions of many states, New York's Constitution affords the state "great freedom in selecting subjects of taxation and in granting exemptions" and in devising "reasonable tax policies."[13] The result has been a flexible revenue system, with few constitutional obstacles to the introduction of new taxes, the establishment of rates, or the use of the revenue collected. Section 23 of Article III now requires both a roll call vote and a quorum consisting of at least three-fifths of the elected members of each house in the case of acts that — among other things — impose, continue, or revive taxes, create debt, or appropriate money.

Debt

Restrictions on the state's ability to incur debt, exceptions to the restrictions, authorization to incur debt for particular purposes, and procedural requirements are scattered through the Constitution in Articles III, VII, X,

---

12   The U.S. Supreme Court has ruled in a Michigan case that states must extend the same exemption to the pensions of federal employees (*Davis* v. *Michigan Department of Treasury*, 109 US 1500 1989). New York State has enacted legislation that does so (Chapter 664, Laws of 1989).

13   *American Bible Society* v. *Lewisohn* 386 NYS 2d 49 (1975).

XVII, and XVIII. The core of the provisions governing state debt, and the center of the current controversy over debt policy and procedure, lies in Article VII, especially Sections 9 and 11.

Short-Term Debt. Section 9 of Article VII authorizes the legislature to incur short-term debt, to be repaid within one year, in anticipation of tax receipts or other revenues. It also authorizes the state to issue bond anticipation notes (BANs) to be repaid from the proceeds of the sale of bonds within two years of the date of issue. The Constitution has had a provision authorizing the state to borrow funds "to meet casual deficits or failures in revenues, or for expenses not provided for" since 1846. In pre-budget days, however, the size of such borrowing was controlled by establishing a cap on the aggregate amount ($1 million in the 1894 Constitution) rather than by requiring repayment within a specified period. An amendment in 1920 established the time requirement.

Long-Term Debt: Single Work or Purpose and Popular Referendum. Perhaps the most controversial issue with respect to debt emerges from Section 11 of Article VII, which provides that

> no debt shall be . . . contracted by or in behalf of the State, unless such debt shall be authorized by law, for some single work or purpose, to be distinctly specified therein.

It further provides that the law shall not take effect until it has been approved by the voters at a general election. This is an ancient section, dating from the Constitution of 1846 and reflecting the alarming growth in the period of state debt for canal construction and other internal improvements.

In requiring voter approval of long-term debt, New York's Constitution is not unique. In his recent study of public authorities, Donald Axelrod notes that 40 of the 50 states "are in constitutional debt shackles."[14] Only ten rely solely on legislative authorization — as New York did prior to 1846.

Over the years several amendments to Section 11 have tried to increase its flexibility. In 1905, for example, the time limit on state debts was successfully extended from 18 to 50 years, and it was made possible to place a law authorizing debt and a constitutional amendment also authorizing debt on the ballot at the same time (the time limit on repayment

---

14   See Donald Axelrod, *Shadow Government: The Hidden World of Public Authorities — and How They Control Over $1 Trillion of Your Money*, New York: John Wiley and Sons, 1992, at pp. 36-37.

was subsequently reduced from 50 to 40 years and transferred to Section 12 of the Constitution in force today). Also removed from the section over the years was a requirement that a law authorizing debt must impose a tax sufficient to pay the interest and discharge the principal of the debt.

In 1938 an amendment substituted the broader term "single work or purpose" for the original "single work or object." Peter Galie notes that this phrase, designed to prevent multipurpose debt, "has been anything but clear," and has been the subject of much litigation.[15] On occasion, supporters of contracting debt for broader purposes (e.g., for the construction of public buildings in 1925) submitted a constitutional amendment rather than a simple debt law to reach their goal because of this provision.

Of the remaining sections of Article VII affecting state borrowing practices, Section 16 is the most important; it requires annual appropriations to cover interest and installments of principal on all long-term debt. If the legislature fails to make such an appropriation, the comptroller is required to set aside revenues in amounts sufficient to meet the state's obligations. It is this provision, coupled with the procedural requirements of Section 11, that defines the meaning of "full faith and credit."[16]

Other Provisions Concerning Debt. The relevant provisions of the other articles have proven less controversial. Article III, Section 23, requires a roll call vote, with a quorum of three-fifths of the elected members in each chamber, to authorize debt — the same test that must be passed for taxes or appropriations. Article X includes specific provisions (Sections 6-8) authorizing and setting dollar limits for debt for particular purposes: the Thruway Authority, the purchase of railroad cars by the Port Authority of New York and New Jersey, and — by inference — the Job Development Authority. Section 7 of Article XVII, the "Social Welfare" article, author-

---

15   See Peter J. Galie, *The New York State Constitution: A Reference Guide*, New York, Westport, CT: Greenwood Press, 1991, at p. 176.

16   See also sections 8, 10, 12, 13, 14, 15, 16, 18, and 19. Section 8, which prohibits the gift or loan of state credit or money except for specified purposes, is discussed in the final section of this chapter. Section 10 authorizes the state to contract debt to meet certain emergencies (e.g., insurrection). Section 12 requires the state to repay debt in equal annual installments over a period of not more than 40 years (consistent, it was assumed, with the expected life of the generation authorizing the debt). Section 13 authorizes the legislature to include a call provision in any state debt at the time it is contracted. Section 14 authorizes the state to create debt up to $300 million for the elimination of railroad grade crossings. Section 15 sets forth procedures for establishing and managing sinking funds for debt retirement; no sinking fund debt has been issued since 1920 and the section is essentially obsolete.

    Two other sections authorize the state to create up to $400 million in debt to pay cash bonuses to veterans of World War II (Section 18) and up to $250 million in debt to expand the State University (Section 19). This last provision was approved by the electorate in 1957, and was more or less made redundant by the establishment of the State University Construction Fund, which permitted the enormous expansion of the SUNY system in the 1960s.

izes loans for hospital construction. It was adopted in 1969 in response to a perceived shortage of hospitals and other health care facilities.

Section 2 of Article XVIII, the "Housing" article, authorizes the state to incur debt for low-income housing, slum clearance, and nursing home accommodations. The state's low-income housing program was initiated in 1934; the 1938 Convention gave it a constitutional basis to forestall potential conflicts with the restrictions on incurring debt set forth in the State Finance article. An amendment in 1965 extended the powers granted to the state by this article to nursing home accommodations. Other parts of Article XVIII affecting the state directly include Section 3, which authorizes the state to contract debt up to a sum of $300 million without approval of the electorate for housing, slum clearance, or nursing homes, and Section 5, which makes municipalities liable for repayment of any state loan to a housing authority or urban renewal agency that had acted as the municipality's agent.

Issues Concerning Short-Term Borrowing and Response. The use of tax-and-revenue anticipation notes (TRANs) to fund school aid and some other forms of local assistance beginning in the late 1960s, and their use in successive years to cope with revenue shortfalls during the fiscal crisis of the 1970s, brought the state's short-term borrowing practices under increasing scrutiny and criticism. Although the Court of Appeals was generally understanding of the state's plight and supportive of its efforts to patch together the fragile plans to aid New York City and troubled state authorities, it appeared to do so with misgivings. "If properly observed," wrote Chief Judge Breitel in Wein v. State, "temporary obligations may not become long-term and a burden on future taxpayers who undoubtedly will have their own fiscal problems to solve." The Court did note, however, that in avoiding constitutional violations "the State . . . has been driven to the brink of valid practice."[17]

It has been argued that the state's ability to authorize and pay school aid in one state fiscal year without paying for it until the next (taking advantage of the "magic window" afforded by differences in the state and school district fiscal years) enables the state to roll over its debt each spring, contravening the spirit, if not the letter, of Section 9. The state has essentially acknowledged this problem, and has initiated a program through a new agency, the Local Government Assistance Corporation (LGAC), to convert some $4.7 billion in short-term debt to long-term debt. A challenge to this program in the courts failed on technical grounds (lack

---

17   383 NYS 2d 225 (1976), at p. 227.

of standing to sue), but the setback probably did not forestall additional suits.[18]

Bypassing Long-Term Borrowing Limits. Active governors with ambitious building programs, such as Alfred E. Smith and Nelson A. Rockefeller, found the "shackles" of state long-term full-faith-and-credit borrowing limits particularly irksome; Governor Rockefeller actively sought and found ways to shake them off.

The Rockefeller administration, which took office in 1959, launched a vast, capital-intensive effort to acquire park land; build middle-income housing; create an extensive public university system (which dwarfed that envisioned in the program authorized by the voters in 1957); reconstruct and modernize the state's old and much-criticized network of mental hygiene facilities; expand mass transit; initiate a pure waters program of breath-taking scope; develop residential treatment centers for narcotic addicts; and literally rebuild downtown Albany with an enormous office-building complex.

It was apparent from the start that the administration's targets would not be reachable under the prevailing pay-as-you-go financing of capital construction. In 1961, when this multipronged attack was still in its formative stages, 98.4 percent of the state's capital program was being funded from current revenues. Comptroller Arthur Levitt remarked critically in his annual report that it would be unfair "to resort to a system of excessive taxation in order to free the next generation from the burden to pay for buildings" that would last for 50 to 100 years, implicitly endorsing more borrowing.

Although the electorate approved a $75 million bond issue for park land acquisition in 1960, it rejected two new bond proposals in 1961. The defeat of these propositions led the administration to pursue a wide array of other options. Debt was incurred by public authorities and supported by earmarking of charges, lease-purchase agreements (often with the state itself), and rentals (with the state often the tenant). Because it did not directly obligate the state, this borrowing was not backed by its "full faith and credit," as it would have been if created under Article VII. Rather it was backed by so-called "moral obligation" arrangements first proposed in 1959 to finance the construction of middle-income housing. The debt of the Housing Finance Agency (HFA), which had been created to facilitate the financing of the construction of such housing, was not "a

---

18   State of New York, Court of Appeals, unpublished opinion of Judge Bellacosa *In Matter Of Schulz* v. *State*: see *infra*, fn 21.

legally enforceable obligation on part of the State of New York." However, if revenues proved insufficient to meet debt service, HFA would bring the matter to the attention of the legislature for such action as it deemed appropriate.

By 1967 the Temporary State Commission on the Constitutional Convention pointed out in a staff report that any review of state debt policies would have to take into account the debt created by public authorities. "Much of the major capital construction in recent years," it noted, "has been financed outside the constitutional debt system."[19] It is estimated that by 1992 almost half the states had followed New York's lead and used some form of moral obligation debt as an alternative to the quantitative, qualitative, or procedural restrictions in their constitutions.

In 1975, the default of one of the state's authorities — the Urban Development Corporation (UDC) — brought moral obligation financing and, indeed, the entire network of authorities under scrutiny by scholars, financial analysts, and the public. This has continued in the 1980s and 1990s as the state has sought ways to satisfy perceived public needs, such as the demand for more prison space, in the face of voter resistance to new debt or higher taxes.

Constitutional Challenges to Borrowing Practices. What originally appeared to be a quixotic assault on state financial practices may bring some of these issues to a head, long before a constitutional convention. Beginning in the 1980s, a Washington County resident, Robert Schulz, initiated suit after suit challenging the state's borrowing practices as a violation of the constitutional provision requiring voter approval of proposed long-term debt. He also challenged the state's right to promote an environmental bond issue and an economic development issue; to issue bonds to phase out the annual spring borrowing; to issue TRANs to cover end-of-the-year deficits (contending — as had Leon Wein in the 1970s — that the state was simply rolling over its debt); and to present a bond act to the voters for economic development on the ground that this violated the restriction in Section 11 to a "single work or purpose." Schulz also litigated against the state's plan to sell an interstate highway to the Thruway Authority and the Attica Prison to the UDC (in the latter case, UDC bought the prison for $200 million, issuing bonds to pay for it, and leasing it to the state) and a plan to sell $6 billion in bonds through the

---

19 See State of New York, "Report on State Finance," *Temporary State Commission on the Constitutional Convention*, 8, (March 1967): 71 (herein after cited as "Report on State Finance," *TSC* March, 1967).

Thruway and Metropolitan Transportation authorities to finance the state's comprehensive highway and transit programs.

Schulz lost the early cases — in part because of a 1975 law enacted to fend off the challenges of Leon Wein to the state's New York City and public authority rescue program. The 1975 law, which prohibited "citizen taxpayer" challenges to state bond issues and bond anticipation notes, was upheld by the courts in 1978 and 1979, and on this basis it was ruled that Schulz lacked the standing to sue.[20]

On May 11, 1993, however, the Court of Appeals handed down what may live up to its billing as a "landmark ruling." In the particular case — *In the Matter of Robert L. Schulz et al.* v. *The State of New York* — the Court, in an opinion written by Judge Joseph Bellacosa, dismissed Schulz's challenge to the sale and leaseback of Attica Prison and Interstate Highway 287 on the technical ground ("laches") that the suit had been brought too late. But more importantly, the Court overturned its 1979 ruling and upheld the right of citizens to challenge the state's borrowing practices — including the network of financial devices that have been used as alternatives to voter-approved full-faith-and-credit debt:

> Serious concerns accompany a complete cloak of immunity that would preclude access to judicial review of challenged public financing schemes. Extension of the "taxpayer" standing limita-tions, to the extent urged by the State here . . . logically and practically confers on the Legislature and Executive the power never again to submit their long-term financing schemes to the voters. The core provision of Article VII, section 11, directing a voters' constitutional referendum as protection against imprudent public financing, would be rendered not just moribund but dead. Since that protection emanates from the People and reserves that ultimate check to themselves, we cannot allow that right to become a dead letter, a mere set of hollow words.[21]

In the eyes of some observers, *The New York Times* reported on May 12, "the judge almost seemed to be inviting new lawsuits." A repre-sentative of Moody's Investors Service added that the procedural hurdles that had been imposed in the past are now down.

20 Chapter 827, Laws of 1975, which created a new Article 7-A of the State Finance Law. The enactment of Article 7-A triggered a significant body of litigation on the issue of "citizen taxpayer" suits. See *Wein* v. *Levitt,* 405 NYS 2d 915 (1978) and *Wein* v. *Comptroller,* 413 NYS 2d 633 (1979).

21 State of New York, Court of Appeals, *In The Matter of Robert A. Schulz, et al.* v. *The State of New York, et al.,* prepublication opinion of Judge Bellacosa, May 11, 1993, at p. 7. As published, the case will appear in 81 NY 2d 336 (1993).

Public Authorities

Closely related to the issue of debt is the question of public authorities. The importance of this issue was recognized as early as 1938 when the Constitutional Convention Committee perceptively observed in its "Report on State and Local Government" that:

> Some time or other the courts might possibly decide that the public may be held responsible for the obligations of all those relatively uncontrolled authorities which have been set up, regardless of the magnitude of those obligations.[22]

In light of this concern, the Constitution was amended to provide that general governments shall not lend their credit to public authorities (Article X, Section 5).

The events of the mid-1970s probably demonstrate the futility of trying at this point to isolate one part of the public fiscal structure from the rest, but it was important that the dangers inherent in relatively uncontrolled debt-incurring agencies were recognized. Article X, Peter Galie notes, represents the first attempt to regulate authorities constitutionally, and the reaction of former Governor Smith to the effort is instructive and might be echoed by other activist governors. The article, Smith said, would "paralyze the one method we have discovered of getting work done expeditiously without taxing our people."[23]

The situation had grown much more complex by the time of the 1967 Constitutional Convention. The increase in the number and importance of authorities, the introduction of moral obligation debt in 1960, which in essence enabled the state to bypass both the normal budgetary process and constitutional restrictions on the creation of debt, and the apparent lack of accountability in the case of many authorities were all disturbing. In summing up the arguments for taking some form of corrective action (it also listed the arguments against taking action), the 1967 Commission's staff report observed that existing provisions had "permitted massive circumvention of necessary limits on State debt . . . [and] that the present constitutional prohibition [had] been inadequate to prevent the State from engaging in 'backdoor' financing without approval at referendum."[24]

It may be argued that the concerns expressed in 1938 and 1967 were more than justified in light of the events of the 1970s. The "independence"

---

22 See "Report on State Finance," *TSC* (March 1967): 171.

23 See Galie, *op. cit.*, at p. 227.

24 See "Report on State Finance," *TSC* (March 1967): 181.

of authorities was in many ways a fiction. The reality was "interdependence." Peter Goldmark, then budget director, noted in October 1976 that "the whole fiscal crisis of the past 18 months . . . has really ripped off the covering that lay over the skeleton of fiscal interrelationships in this State."[25] The financial markets were clearly aware of the linkage. The inability of an authority, the Urban Development Corporation, to meet payments on bond anticipation notes drove all other authorities from the municipal bond market and undermined the credit of the state's own securities.

Gifts and Loans

Article VII, Section 8, prohibits the state from giving or loaning money or property to private corporations or associations and from giving or loaning its credit to any individual, public or private corporation or association, or private undertaking. The provisions date from the 1846 Constitution, reflecting contemporary concern about abuses in loans or grants of the state's credit to railroads and other enterprises. Particularly galling were instances in which companies failed and the state had to make good on its contingent liability. Its original formulation was stark and to the point: "The credit of the State shall not, in any manner, be given or loaned to or in aid of any individual association or corporation."

The Constitutional Convention of 1867, whose work was rejected by the voters in 1869, and the Constitutional Commission of 1872 (created to address issues left unresolved by the defeat of the Constitution) went further. If the Constitution prohibited the loan of credit, it did nothing to prevent loans of money or property. Grants to sectarian institutions, including many engaged in eleemosynary work, and the depredations of the Tweed Ring were at center stage in the early 1870s and the commission added prohibitions against gifts and loans of money and property to the fundamental law. At the same time, it took steps consistent with the broader view of state responsibilities that was emerging in the last third of the nineteenth century, the Constitution was amended to authorize the legislature to extend aid for the education and support of the blind, deaf, and dumb, and juvenile delinquents, and to add certain educational purposes to the list of exemptions from the general prohibition.

As it stands now, Section 8 has three subdivisions that:

---

25 See Proceedings, *Board of Education, Levittown Union Free District, Nassau County, et al.,* Plaintiffs, v. *Ewald B. Nyquist, Commissioner of Education, et al.,* Defendants, Supreme Court, Nassau County, Trial Term, Part IV, Mineola, NY, October 21, 1976, at p. 17167.

1. Prohibit gifts or loans of state money to or in aid of any private corporation or association, or private undertaking; or gifts or loans of the credit of the state to or in aid of any individual, or public or private corporation or association, or private undertaking. Excepted from these bans are funds or property held by the state for education, mental health, or mental retardation purposes.

2. Enumerate specific exemptions from the prohibition that, with additional classes covered in Articles XVII (Social Welfare) and XVIII (Housing), reflect the breadth of the state's present-day educational, health, and social welfare activity.

3. Authorize loans to a public corporation (i.e., the Job Development Authority) that may make loans to nonprofit corporations or guarantee loans by banks to finance the construction of buildings for a wide variety of economic purposes. Article X, Section 8 authorizes the legislature to make the state liable for the principal and interest on JDA obligations up to an aggregate specified in the section. It was last raised in 1985 and now stands at $600 million.

In 1975, at the height of the fiscal crisis, Leon Wein sued the state alleging that appropriations by the 1975 legislature of $250 million to New York City and $500 million to the Municipal Assistance Corporation to be funded (although the Court noted that this had not been specified in the statute) by short-term state borrowing (TRANs) constituted a gift or loan of the credit of the state to a public corporation in violation of Section 8 of Article VII.[26] In the course of his opinion, Chief Judge Charles Breitel included an extensive historical and philosophical as well as legal analysis of the gifts and loans provision (pp. 227-230). The history of this prohibition, Judge Breitel wrote, indicates that it

> was intended to protect the State from the uncertain and possibly disastrous consequences of incurring future contingent liabilities, liabilities easy for a current generation to project but a burden on future generations.[27]

In the instant case he found no violation, provided that any monetary assistance is given pursuant to an appropriation. "It is undisputed that the

---

26 *Wein v. State,* 383 NYS 2d 225 (1975).

27 *Ibid.,* at p. 229.

State may give or lend money, as distinguished from its credit, to assist a municipal or other public corporation in a public purpose."[28]

Proposals for Constitutional Change

Considerable attention has been given in recent years to changing the state constitutional provisions concerning budgeting and finance summarized above. The causes for this are numerous: the legacy of the mid-1970s fiscal crises; the difficulties recently encountered by the legislature and governor in producing a timely budget; the emphasis on economic development that has arisen as a consequence of New York State's economic difficulties; the rapid growth of the public benefit corporation as an agent of state policy; the increasing complexity of federalism, and concomitant importance of intergovernmental funding streams; professional trends in internal financial management; greater private market sophistication about state finance and debt practices; and a growing body of litigation generated by challenges to the processes as well as the purposes of state financial activity.

Budget Process Changes

The recurrent stalemates in the state's budget approval process since the mid-1970s have generated a variety of suggestions for constitutional revision.[29]

1. *Open the Process Further.* In 1991, the state Senate's leadership recommended a constitutional amendment that would make agency budget requests public and would open up the executive's constitutionally required budget hearings.[30] Proponents argued the value of open government. Opponents suggested that the result would be a more difficult process and more political posturing, and that access to the process by the legislature under present constitutional provisions is sufficient. Most important, opponents see this as impairing the executive's ability to balance

---

28 *Ibid.*, at p. 230; for additional information on the gifts and loans provisions, see the chapters "The Private Economy" and "Social Policy" in this book.

29 This summary relies heavily on the "Preliminary Draft Report of the Constitutional Revision Committee, Capital Area Chapter, American Society for Public Administration" (ASPA), Subcommittee on State and Local Finance, August 21, 1991; and Frank Mauro, "Finance and Budget Issues (Both Good and Bad Depending on Your Perspective) that might be Considered by a Constitutional Convention," November 1993 (Fiscal Policy Institute, copy in files of the Commission).

30 S.5725-A (1991)

ends against means and present a coherent as well as complete financial plan.

2. *Alter the Budget Timetable.* This change may be accomplished by statute. A *later beginning of the state fiscal year* has been advocated at various times by the governor, the Assembly, and the Senate; July 1 is the date most often mentioned. Such a change, it is argued, would give the legislature more time to consider the executive budget; help correct certain cash flow imbalances; enhance accuracy in revenue forecasting; and reduce the need for short-term borrowing. Opponents note that the legislature receives copies of agency budget submissions at the same time that the Division of the Budget receives them, in reality enters the process much earlier than the date the budget is submitted, and that it therefore has sufficient time under existing law; that a shift would negatively affect local government budgeting; that cash flow needs could be dealt with in other ways; and that this change would simply shift the chronic budget crisis from the spring to the summer.

A second approach would be to *adopt biannual budgeting,* which is the practice in 18 states. This would require a constitutional amendment. It might produce greater efficiency (some budgeting tasks need be performed only once in two years) and improve planning. Longer-term budgeting would bring less accuracy into fiscal projections, however, and would require regular updates to be viable.

One idea is to adopt both an earlier start to the fiscal year — beginning, say, in October — and do biannual budgeting in a cycle that overlapped the electoral cycle. This would allow mid-budget cycle adjustments by a newly elected governor, and would allow the chief executive ample time to develop his or her budget for the next biennium.

3. *Require the Governor to Submit a Balanced Budget.* It has been commonly understood that the "complete plan" of proposed expenditures and required revenues (Section 2, Article VII) means that the governor must submit a balanced budget. Just as important, in his first budget message in 1943, Governor Dewey observed that "The Constitution of the State requires a balanced budget. This requirement is not specifically stated," he noted, "but it is implied in the provision permitting temporary borrowing only for a maximum period of a year." Each budget must therefore

provide for the liquidation of any outstanding short-term debts, producing balance, though it is not precisely constitutionally required that the governor submit a balanced budget.

There have been proposals to make the "balanced budget" requirement in the Constitution more explicit. If this is done, conditions for determining if "balance" has been achieved must be set out, including presentation of sufficient detail within the state financial plan and in the budget. Information should include past actual, current expected, and projected revenues and expenditures in usable categories so that an independent judgment may be made. Some have suggested that balance according to "generally accepted accounting principles" (GAAP) should be specified. Others regard this as too constraining and too detailed for a constitutional provision. Skeptics also note that the rules laid down in GAAP are subject to frequent revision.

4. *Disincentives to Lateness in Completing the Budget.* Fines, salary forfeiture, or prohibition against running for reelection for a period of time have all been proposed as penalties for the governor, lieutenant governor, comptroller, and the leaders or members of the legislature for failure to pass a budget by the start of the fiscal year. Critics have noted that this idea fails to address the causes of budget deadlocks, may punish those with no real control over budget timing, and offers incentives for ill-considered action.

Other proposals designed to produce more timely budget action include *automatic adoption of some version of the budget,* and necessary revenue and appropriation measures — last year's, the governor's proposal, a baseline budget prepared by the governor or a "current services" budget— or an *immediate special session* governed by special constitutionally prescribed procedures to resolve budget differences. A third idea is to *require the legislature to meet in continuous session* until a budget is passed.

5. *Alternative Methods for Estimating Revenue.* A number of proposals have sought to reduce the level of controversy over revenue estimating in New York by specifying in the Constitution that a binding estimate be made by an institution or person other than the governor and the legislative houses. A 1985 study of the Public Policy Institute proposed a consensus approach to revenue estimating that "involves both houses of the legislature, the comptroller, the executive branch, the business community, and

economists from outside of government."[31] Others have suggested that this power be given to the state comptroller, as it is in Texas.

Proponents of a consensus model regard this task as technical, not political, and say such a change would build public confidence and refocus budgetary debate where it belongs, on the expenditure side of the budget. Those who would give this responsibility to the comptroller suggest that it would help this statewide fiscal officer function as a constraining force on spending. Opponents argue that revenue estimating is integral to budgeting, and should be left to those who have been elected specifically so that they can exercise political judgment. As it happens, the comptroller's revenue estimates might themselves reflect a political as well as an economic perspective, and might compromise other, less politically charged, responsibilities of the office such as auditing, accounting, and debt management.

6. *Balanced Budget Certification by the Comptroller.* A constitutional requirement of certification of the budget by the comptroller is another way that this statewide elective official could be given power to assure fiscal accountability in the state government. Proponents suggest that this highly visible role for an elective official, with an actual capacity to block budget adoption if he or she is not satisfied, would be an effective check on excesses in budgeting. Opponents resist giving a budgetary role to an official responsible for auditing, and question the basis on which the comptroller could certify balance unless much more information on the state's actual budgetary and financial situation was available to and required of the executive branch.

7. *Global Budgeting for State Government.* This idea conceives of all New York State and local governmental budgets as interactive and mutually dependent, and therefore suggests that their consideration should be integrated into the state budget process. If it were adopted, the Constitution would require preparation and presentation of the state budget with full consideration of its linkage with and impact on all local governments and other governmental entities in the state. Implementation of this proposal might require bringing state and local fiscal years into

---

31 See "An Analysis of State Revenue Forecasting Systems," Albany, New York: Nelson A. Rockefeller Institute of Government (1985).

conformance, which in turn might make local budgeting more difficult.

8. *Require the Legislature to Adopt a Balanced Budget.* There is no such provision currently in the Constitution. As discussed above, it would be necessary to define the term "balanced budget" in detail.

9. *Specify Executive and Legislative Roles.* Constitutional changes may be adopted to clarify ambiguities that heretofore have been the subject of litigation, or may provoke litigation in the future. These include specifically requiring the appropriation of all funds; defining the extent and limits of legislative power to specify terms and conditions of spending in appropriations; define the item veto power; and specify the governor's impoundment power. Opponents to action in these areas would argue that many of these matters are settled, and that excessive specificity in the Constitution would weaken the capacity of the political system to respond to new problems and needs.

10. *Cap Spending.* Such a proposal would link the growth of total state spending to growth in personal income, the cost of living, or another measure of the growth of the state economy. The detail of any proposal, of course, would determine its impact. Excess revenues in any year would be placed in a reserve fund. Proponents argue that this is the only effective way to curb the propensity of governments to increase spending. Opponents argue that such a measure would further increase the level of conflict in state government, making it even more difficult to reach decisions. Ultimately, they add, it would simply transfer costs to localities, a pattern already evident in New York and other states, and — the states collectively might contend — within the federal system itself.

Taxation Changes

Suggested changes have focused on proposals to limit the tax base or define the permissible subjects of taxation; earmark certain revenue sources (such as the gas tax) and restrict their use to certain programs; cap tax rates; adopt a clause requiring "equality and uniformity" in taxation (some states have adopted such a clause as a barrier to discriminatory taxation); or require extraordinary legislative majorities to increase taxes.

1. *Constitutional Tax Limitations.* These have been adopted in a number of states that have initiative and referendum procedures. As with a spending limit, such a cap would be linked to some measure of the state's economy. The effectiveness of a cap is conditional on its actual design. The issues of displacement of tax pressure onto local government and other revenue sources and the impact on state government capacity, politics, and priorities are similar to those for a spending cap.

2. *Extraordinary Majorities or a Referendum Requirement or Both for Tax Increases.* Super-majorities for tax increases are in place in seven states (Arkansas, California, Connecticut, Louisiana, Minnesota, South Dakota, and Washington). These two barriers to tax increases are favored by those who seek smaller state government. The arguments concerning them are substantially similar to those concerning tax and spending limits. Requiring a two-thirds majority, for example, would give an extraordinary power to block any change to one-third plus one of the voting members of either house of the legislature.

3. *Constitutional Earmarking.* Recent experience with state transportation "locked box" funds has led some to propose the earmarking of revenues from certain sources in the Constitution to ensure they are spent for the purposes they are raised. Earmarking is generally opposed by those who regard it as the role of government to weigh alternative priorities and allocate resources to meet the most pressing needs in the context of a given set of circumstances. Additionally, they perceive it as potentially wasteful, requiring spending in specified areas "because the money is there." Earmarking is favored by those who wish to assure a certain or predictable level of funding for desired programs, those who are hostile to or suspicious of decision making in the political branches, and those who favor certain programs — such as highway construction and maintenance — over other claims on public resources.

Debt Proposals

No aspect of state finance is likely to prove more controversial at a constitutional convention than the debt of the state and its public authorities. State debt policies are at the center of an increasingly acerbic debate, which, on the surface at least, focuses less on the objects of government action (e.g., incarceration, public transportation, economic development) than on the means chosen to achieve them. The debate is taking place against a backdrop of slow economic growth, tighter federal budgets, accelerating demand for services, and taxpayer resistance.

1. *Debt Reform Constitutional Amendment.* Governor Cuomo and other officials have been widely quoted as agreeing with at least some of Robert Schulz's argument that the state should limit — if not end — so-called "backdoor financing" under which the state sells properties to an authority, which issues bonds to finance the purchase, and leases the property to the state. The suits, the governor reportedly acknowledged, raised valid points that ought to be taken up by a constitutional convention. A constitutional amendment, which would revise Section 11 extensively, has gained first passage in the legislature (it must also pass the next elected legislature before being placed on the ballot at a general election). Aimed not only at meeting the current wave of criticism but at providing a more sound foundation for the debt policy of a modern industrial state, the amendment includes features that would:

    ❋ require the governor to submit a detailed multiyear capital program and financing plan to the legislature within 30 days following the submission of the executive budget;

    ❋ authorize submitting more than one debt proposition at a single election;

    ❋ authorize the state to issue special revenue bonds with dedicated revenue sources;

    ❋ place a cap on the amount of such bonds outstanding equal to 5 percent of the state's personal income;

    ❋ exempt from the cap general obligation debt or the existing debt of authorities;

    ❋ ban the use of "backdoor" debt with a handful of listed exceptions, mostly involving debt undertaken in support of local government (e.g., bonds of the Municipal Assistance Corporation);

    ❋ restrict the use of general obligation or revenue bonds to capital construction; and

✳ authorize the state to borrow without voter approval to meet economic emergencies, court judgments above a specified floor, or natural disasters.

Essentially the amendment would cover all borrowing, by the state or its authorities, with relatively few exceptions: these include the Municipal Assistance Corporation, HFA's Distressed Hospital Program, and local court facility debt.

Schulz has voiced his opposition. He argues that no reform is necessary; simple adherence to current constitutional requirements is what is needed. Others see too many loopholes in the proposal, including a cap on borrowing so high that it effectively bypasses the referendum requirement and excessive exceptions to the bar to "backdoor" borrowing.

2. *Limit Amount of Debt or Debt Service.* One approach would limit the amount of debt that might be outstanding at one time. Another would limit the amount that the state might spend annually on debt service. Constitutional debt limits linked to the property tax base exist for most local governments in New York. Adoption of such a provision would cap debt in a manner similar to that used in the state Constitution before "process limitations" were put in place, and might help gain public acceptance for easing such limitations. However, caps might be a barrier to needed long-term investments or action in emergencies. To work as intended, they would have to be crafted to avoid borrowing by the state outside the cap, in the manner detailed above, or in a similar manner.

3. *Remove the Referendum Requirement for Borrowing.* This would leave the regulation of borrowing to the marketplace. Advocates argue that it would be a more straightforward approach than that recommended by the governor, and would give state government the power it says it needs to meet the demands upon it. Such a step might be linked to *super-majorities in the legislature to authorize debt.* Opponents would argue that governors and legislatures ought not to be granted this level of discretion (reopening, in effect, issues that faced the 1846 Convention). Moreover, it might be argued, the financial markets could not be relied on to discipline borrowing until it was too late, and a crisis had occurred.

Public Authorities

Constitutional changes offered in this area are designed to integrate public authority and state government activity more effectively. As noted, *limi-*

tations on "backdoor" borrowing in the Constitution would directly affect authorities, as would *comprehensive capital planning.* The constitutionalization of current legislative *limits on authority borrowing,* or requirements to *coordinate authority borrowing* may also be considered at a constitutional convention.

Legislative Districting and the New York State Constitution

David I.Wells

New York State has failed to bring its century-old state constitutional provisions for legislative districting and apportionment into accord with United States constitutional requirements in the three decades since "one person, one vote" became the law of the land. The state constitutional questions left in the wake of *WMCA* v. *Lomenzo* and the follow-up ruling by the State Court of Appeals were the chief reasons that the New York Legislature, in 1965, initiated action leading to a constitutional convention.[1] When the Convention met in 1967, the Constitution's districting provisions were changed substantially. However, the subsequent rejection by the voters of the entire proposed Constitution left the State with a truncated, patchwork process.

Parts of the constitutionally prescribed procedures were no longer operative. Others were still in effect. Still others were in effect "conditionally" — provided that their implementation did not necessitate population inequalities. For example, prior to the 1960s decisions, determination of the size of the Senate was one function of a complex formula that had the overall effect of limiting the representation of the most heavily populated counties. While seats may no longer be distributed among the counties on the basis of that formula today, *the total number of seats* must still be calculated by adding up the numbers that *would have been* allocated to each county or group of counties had the formula still been in effect. Thus, an unconstitutional formula has for three decades continued to be an operative part of the Constitution.

The failure to adopt the 1967 proposal, and the absence of any action since to revise or amend the state's constitutional provisions for apportionment and districting, means that the problem which faced that year's convention — the need to reconcile the constitutional provisions with the 1960s rulings and to integrate and rationalize the districting procedures

---

1   377 U.S. 633 (1964). *Matter of Orans*, 15 N.Y. 2d 339 (1965).

as a whole — remains essentially unresolved. Meanwhile, each passing decade produces new districting, and new layers of litigation, further complicating the legal environment and obscuring the meaning of state constitutional provisions in this area.

The Pre-1964 Districting Process

The formulae for allocating Senate and Assembly seats among the counties and the rules for drawing district lines were set forth in Article III of the Constitution in 1894, and remain largely unchanged since that time.

The Senate formula established a two-tier system — one for the populous counties, another for the more rural ones — that made severe urban underrepresentation inevitable. At the Assembly level, rural over-representation was assured by the fact that regardless of population, every county but Hamilton was guaranteed at least one seat out of a fixed total of 150.[2]

The formulae for *apportioning* seats among the counties were self-executing. The Constitution gave the Legislature itself the power to delineate Senate *district boundaries*. In counties entitled to more than one Assembly seat, the job of drawing the Assembly district lines was given to the local governing body (the City Council within the five boroughs and county boards of supervisors elsewhere).

The Constitution also provided "ground rules" for the placement of district lines.

In the Senate, each district had to have approximately equal population[3]; districts had to consist of contiguous territory in as compact form as practicable; no county could be divided in the process except to create districts wholly within the same county (that is, no district could contain *parts* of more than one county); no town[4] or city block could be divided in drawing district lines; and adjacent districts within the same county could not differ in population by more than the population of a town or block along their common border (that is, towns and blocks along a boundary had to be placed in one district or the other in a way which minimized the population difference between the two).

---

2   For purposes of Assembly representation, it was combined with adjacent Fulton County.

3   Because this requirement was modified by the apportionment formula, it meant in effect only that there had to be approximate equality of district populations *within counties.*

4   With minor exceptions.

Rules for the Assembly required that districts be composed of "convenient" and contiguous territory "in as compact form as practicable," and again that no town or block could be divided and no adjacent districts within a county could vary in population by more than the population of a town or block along their border.

The W.M.C.A. and Orans Rulings

On June 15, 1964, the U.S. Supreme Court ruled that the equal protection clause of the fourteenth amendment required that state legislatures be apportioned substantially on an equal population basis, and that, because it made wide population disparities unavoidable, New York's districting machinery was constitutionally invalid.[5]

Ten months later, the State Court of Appeals, in *In re Orans*[6], sought to clarify which parts of the state Constitution's districting rules survived and which did not. The actual language of the state Constitution could not, of course, be changed by the *Orans* ruling. Rather the court indicated that certain state provisions, because they conflicted with the federal Constitution, were "dead letters" and could no longer be implemented. Nevertheless the invalidated parts as well as the still-operative ones remain part of the document. In summary, the Court of Appeals said:

1. The violations of the federal Constitution found by the Supreme Court related almost entirely to the formulae for *apportioning seats among the counties.*

2. The formula for determining the total number of Senators remained in effect, but *for that purpose only — not for apportioning seats.*

3. The provision requiring Assembly districts to be "compact...convenient and contiguous" remained in effect.[7]

4. The "town and block rules" (prohibiting the division of towns and blocks and limiting the population differences between adjacent districts in a county to the population of a town or block along their border), also survived.

---

5   *WMCA* v. *Lomenzo,* 377 U.S. 633 (1964).

6   *Matter of Orans,* 15 N.Y. 2d 339 (1965).

7   The decision made no explicit mention of the rule that Senate districts too had to consist of "contiguous territory" in "as compact form as practicable," but the reasoning underlying retention of the Assembly wording made the continued validity of the Senate requirement clear as well.

5. A full Assembly seat could no longer be guaranteed to each county.

6. It would no longer be possible to construct all districts wholly within county boundaries.

7. Because some districts would now overlap county lines, it would no longer be possible to give local legislatures the power to delineate Assembly districts.

8. Nevertheless, "the historic and traditional significance of counties in the districting process should be continued where and as far as possible."

The 1967 Constitutional Convention

When the Constitutional Convention met in 1967, questions relating to the districting process fell within the jurisdiction of the Committee on the Legislature. The single most controversial issue was, "Who would have the authority to draw district lines?"

After much deliberation, the Committee majority voted to send to the convention floor a provision that:

❋ kept power over redistricting in the hands of the Legislature, but provided that if the Legislature failed to redistrict by a specified date, authority was to pass to a bipartisan commission;

❋ eliminated gubernatorial veto power over districting statutes (both legislative *and Congressional*);

❋ provided that the rules regarding state legislative districting were to be applicable to Congressional districting as well; and

❋ explicitly "prohibited gerrymandering . . . for any purpose."[8]

Six of the Committee's 27 members, however, signed a draft minority report vigorously opposing retention of the Legislature's power to

---

8   This unique provision "goes to the heart of the redistricting problem," stated the official accompanying explanatory analysis. "Except for the principle of equality of population," it continued, "all formulations of standards for districting are in essence efforts to prevent what we call 'gerrymandering.' It seemed appropriate to cut through to the heart of the problem by explicitly prohibiting gerrymandering. Dictionaries and scholarly writings accept 'gerrymandering' as a word with a definite meaning. A sampling of judicial opinions demonstrated that the courts use the word without quotation marks, indicating judicial acceptance of the word as expressing a generally understood process. . . . The words 'for any purpose' are included to make it crystal clear that the word is to be read not in its original 19th Century sense of 'partisan political' gerrymandering, but in its 20th Century sense of any unfair districting aimed at a particular group — political, racial, religious, economic, or any other." *State of New York, Constitutional Convention 1967, Document No. 51*, New York State Library, Albany.

redistrict and elimination of gubernatorial veto power. "Just as a judge will disqualify himself in a case in which he has a personal stake," said the report, "so legislators should be disqualified from being involved in a process in which they have such an obvious, direct — and understandable — political and personal interest."[9]

Neither the minority report nor a majority report was ever sent to the convention floor. In a move reportedly designed to block introduction of the former, the Committee on the Legislature filed *no* report, and the districting proposal was instead introduced by the Rules Committee.

Initially, the convention leadership of both parties had favored retention of the districting power by the Legislature, but then, in a reversal, which *The New York Times* editorially labeled a "near miracle at Albany,"[10] the substance of the *minority* report, transferring the districting power to a bipartisan commission, was introduced by the Convention's powerful Democratic Majority Leader. That proposal was immediately and vigorously denounced by the Republican Minority Leader. Within a day, however, the GOP leadership too appeared to have had a change of heart and the proposition was passed unanimously.[11] Strong press support around the state favorable to the idea of removing the Legislature from participation in the process of redrawing its own district lines had reportedly motivated the shift of position by the Democratic leadership. The Republican minority then apparently became reluctant to be perceived as opposing what was widely acclaimed as a desirable reform.[12] Thus there was incorporated into the proposed Constitution a provision that:

1. fixed the Senate's membership at 60 while retaining a 150-member Assembly;

2. removed the Legislature's authority to redistrict itself and placed the line-drawing power instead in the hands of a five-member Redistricting Commission, four members of which would be appointed by the Democratic and Republican leaders of each house with the fifth, the chairperson, to be designated by the Court of Appeals;

---

9   Because it was never formally issued, the draft minority report is not part of the official convention record or archives. A copy is in the possession of the author. Among the delegates who signed it were Leonard Sand, the attorney who had successfully argued the *WMCA* case before the Supreme Court, and David Dinkins, the future New York City Mayor.

10   *New York Times,* Aug. 9, 1967, p.38.

11   *New York Times,* Aug. 8, 1967, p.1, and Aug. 9, 1967, p.1.

12   See League of Women Voters of New York State, *Seeds of Failure — A Political Review of New York State's 1967 Constitutional Convention,* 34-37.

3. included *Congressional* districting among the Commission's responsibilities, thus giving that function constitutional status for the first time;

4. required that districts be "as nearly equal as practicable in total population," "contiguous and compact," and that "wherever practicable, boundaries of pre-existing political subdivisions and natural geographic boundaries" be used as district lines;

5. "prohibited gerrymandering" by explicit reference;[13]

6. provided that the Commission's plan was to have the immediate force of law, with no need for gubernatorial or legislative approval.[14]

All came to naught, however, when the electorate turned down the entire proposed new Constitution in November (a decision having been made to submit it for voter-approval as a single ballot item rather than in the form of separate proposals grouped by subject-categories). Although the rejection was clearly based on controversial issues unrelated to districting, it left the existing provisions as modified by the *Orans* ruling as the only constitutional guidelines.

Redistricting In New York Since Orans

Since the *Orans* ruling, the Legislature has been completely redistricted four times: in 1966, 1972, 1982, and 1992. (In addition, Congressional districts were also redrawn in 1968, 1970, 1972, 1982, and 1992.) Each of these actions has been subjected to legal challenge in either the federal or state courts, or both.

While the state court litigation has been based primarily on alleged violations of the constitutional rules dealing with contiguity, compactness, and the integrity of counties, the underlying controversies have stemmed largely from three sources: 1) charges of partisan gerrymandering (drawing district lines to provide one party with an advantage); 2) charges of "incumbent" or "bipartisan gerrymandering" (drawing lines to provide special advantages to particular individuals

---

13   *State of New York, Constitutional Convention 1967, Document No. 51*, New York State Library, Albany.

14   Subject only to the original and exclusive jurisdiction of the Court of Appeals at the suit of any citizen.

— usually incumbent legislators regardless of party); and 3) charges of "racial injustice" by some and "racial gerrymandering" by others.

The Senate and Assembly, under divided political control in 1966, were unable to agree on a districting plan. Instead, a specially appointed Judicial Commission drew new district lines for the elections of 1966, 1968, and 1970. In 1971[15] the Legislature, then under complete Republican control, enacted a plan for the elections of 1972 through 1980. (That plan, along with the 1972 Congressional redistricting, was partially revised in 1974 in the wake of federal court action relating to the racial aspects of districting.) In 1982, following an extended partisan deadlock, multi-faceted litigation and intervention by the U.S. Department of Justice, a politically divided Legislature adopted a plan establishing districts for elections from 1982 through 1990. And again in 1992, after lengthy disputes involving both political and racial factors and after intervention by both federal and state courts as well as the Justice Department, the Legislature, still politically divided, adopted a plan for the Senate essentially drawn by that house's Republican leadership and one for the Assembly drafted by its Democratic leadership. A congressional districting arrangement initially devised by a commission appointed by a state court was adopted after much political haggling. (In both 1982 and 1992, federal courts also appointed "special masters" to draw lines in light of the continuing inability of the Senate and Assembly to come to agreement, but the masters' plans did not go into effect because in both instances the Legislature took last-minute action to avert their imposition).[16]

The fact that the Legislature has been under politically divided control during the past two redistricting periods[17] points up a noteworthy aspect of districting in New York. In many states, when a politically split legislature is faced with the need to redistrict, the usual result is the kind of bipartisan gerrymandering in which incumbents of both parties in both houses are "accommodated." In New York, however, that circumstance has led instead to a rather unique hybrid of partisan and bipartisan gerrymandering at the state legislative level. With neither party willing to jeopardize its majority in the house it already controlled, the impasses have been resolved by each party unilaterally taking charge of drawing the lines for that house. This has resulted, according

---

15   The redistricting bill was actually passed by the Legislature in December 1971 but not signed until January 1972.

16   The appointment of a special master in 1992 involved Congressional districting only.

17   The Legislature has actually been politically divided, with Republicans controlling the Senate and Democrats the Assembly, since January 1975.

to critics, in a kind of "double partisan gerrymander": Senate district lines drawn to maintain a Republican advantage and Assembly lines carved to keep Democratic control. The advantages secured for the dominant party in each house in 1982 were arguably the chief reason each party was able to retain control of that house straight through to the next redistricting a decade later, when the process was repeated. The redistricting pattern of the 1980s and 1990s is thus in good measure (though not solely) responsible for the development of what appears to be a *permanently divided legislature*.[18] Some view this as an impediment to effective government; others see it as a way to guard against the exercise of unlimited power by either party.

Potential Constitutional Districting Issues

The following are among the aspects of the districting process that may warrant consideration by a constitutional convention:

Population Equality

Approximate equality among district-populations is already guaranteed by the federal Constitution as interpreted by the Supreme Court. The one person-one vote rulings of the 1960s laid down the basic rule that all districts in a legislative chamber had to have approximately equal populations. In one sense, therefore, state action in this sphere is merely minor "tinkering." Nevertheless, much subsequent litigation centered around the question of precisely what *degree* of equality was required: Did all districts have to have *exactly* the same populations or was *some* leeway permissible?

At the Congressional level, the present status of the matter is that districts must be exactly equal *except* that there may be very minor departures from precise equality provided that *each* such departure is *explicitly justified*.[19]

The standard regarding state legislative districts is looser. "Application of the 'absolute equality' test...to state legislative redistricting may impair the normal functioning of state government,"[20] the Supreme Court

---

18 Gerrymandering cannot, however, permanently guarantee control of a legislative chamber. Unforeseeable events can intervene and upset all expectations. In the election of 1974, for example, the Assembly, whose lines had been drawn by a Republican majority less than three years earlier, fell to the Democrats — the apparent result of an unusually strong Democratic tide running all across the country the year in the wake of the "Watergate scandal."

19 See *Karcher* v. *Daggett,* 462 U.S. 275 (1983).

20 *Mahan* v. *Howell,* 410 U.S. 315 (1973).

ruled in 1973. It expressly reaffirmed an earlier holding that at the state level, "deviations from the equal population principle are constitutionally permissible . . . so long as the divergences . . . are based on legitimate considerations incident to the effectuation of a rational state policy."[21] Subsequent rulings have interpreted this to mean that a state may have a small range of allowable departure from precise equality — up to about 10 percent from the least- to the most-populous district.[22] Within these rough parameters, variations have been permitted provided that they are rationally based, nondiscriminatory, and uniformly applied.

> QUESTIONS: *Should the State Constitution supplement or interpret the "one person, one vote" principle? If so, should it specify a population-deviation range? On what factor(s) ought such a range be based?*[23]

Contiguity

The concept of geographic contiguity — of a legislative district being composed of a single piece of territory — would seem to be inherent in the word "district" itself. Yet over the years the requirement that districts be contiguous has given rise to much controversy.[24] The standard of "contiguity" (like compactness, discussed below) has merely been stated. It is a required but undefined goal. This has made consistent implementation by the Legislature and meaningful interpretation by the courts difficult.

> QUESTIONS: *Is district contiguity always necessary or desirable? If so, should it be guaranteed absolutely or modified under certain circumstances — for example, to take account of racial factors? Should it be defined more precisely? Should the contiguity of over-water districts be dealt with explicitly, and if so, how? Should there be a requirement, such as that in the New York City*

---

21 *Reynolds* v. *Sims,* 377 U.S. 533 (1964).

22 See NCSL Reapportionment Task Force, *Reapportionment Law: The 1990s,* Denver: National Conference of State Legislatures, 1989: 25-40.

23 Among the factors that the Supreme Court has indicated would be acceptable to justify population deviations of reasonable dimensions are affording representation to political subdivisions, making districts compact, respecting municipal boundaries, preserving the cores of prior districts, and avoiding contests between incumbent legislators. (Only the first three of these would appear to be conducive to constitutional recognition.)

24 There have been continuing disputes regarding the contiguity (or lack thereof) of districts that took in territory whose parts were separated by bodies of water. At different times in the past, for instance, insular Richmond County has been included in Senate districts with distant Rockland and Suffolk Counties. Currently as well, there are districts whose component areas lack a direct connection.

Charter, that when the equal-population rules necessitate joining territory separated by water, only areas connected by bridges, tunnels, or regular ferry service may be combined in a district?

Compactness

The requirement that Senate and Assembly districts be "in as compact form as practicable" was first inserted into the Constitution by the Convention of 1894. Although many districts established by redistricting statutes enacted since then have been attacked as lacking in compactness and a number have been challenged in court on those grounds, there has been only one instance of a *successful* challenge based on this standard.[25] This is in part due to the fact that, like "contiguous," the term "compact" is nowhere given constitutional definition.[26] In addition, inclusion of the modifying word "practicable" in the constitutional language has rendered interpretation of the provision even more subjective.

Moreover, as issues of race and ethnicity have become increasingly central in districting in recent years, some have come to believe that the compactness requirement operates to inhibit establishment of districts in which ethnic minorities can compose a majority or plurality. Those with this view think the requirement should either be eliminated or made clearly subordinate to one taking account of districts' racial characteristics. Others, however, believe that downgrading the compactness standard (thus weakening a rule which limits the Legislature's discretion) might well permit more gerrymandering.

QUESTIONS: *Should the constitutional provisions dealing with compactness be strengthened, kept as is, weakened, or deleted altogether? If they are to be strengthened, should the word "practicable" be eliminated from the constitutional language? Should the term "compact" be defined? Should the Constitution prescribe some type of compactness rule or method by which the degree of compactness in competing plans may be gauged and compared?[27] Or, in the alternative, should all reference to compactness be eliminated or made explicitly subordinate to other considerations?*

---

25 *Matter of Sherrill v. O'Brien*, 188 N.Y. 185 (1907).

26 Indeed, the Court of Appeals has taken explicit judicial notice of the fact that the term is constitutionally undefined. See *Schneider* v. *Rockefeller*, 31 N.Y. 2d 420 at 429 (1972).

27 Colorado, for example, requires that the statewide aggregate linear distance of all district boundaries be as short as possible (Colo. Const., Art. V, Sec.47, part 1). The New York City Charter imposes the same rule with regard to Council districts.

Integrity of Counties and Towns

Prior to the 1960s decisions, constitutional rules effectively guaranteed the integrity of all counties and almost all towns in the districting process by precluding the division of those units except under very limited circumstances. The *Orans* ruling modified those guarantees to conform with the equal population principle. Over the intervening years, despite the admonition in *Orans* that attention should still be paid to county lines in the placement of districts, the anti-division rules have been disregarded with increasing frequency.[28] Some contend that dividing a county or town among districts does no harm and that indeed such division can actually multiply a county or town's influence by having parts of it represented by additional spokespersons. Others believe *any* division dilutes an area's political "clout." They also argue that complex and overlapping jurisdictional boundaries are confusing to citizens and make it harder for them to understand the political process and hold elected officials accountable.

> QUESTIONS: *Is county and town integrity desirable in districting? Are such units really weakened if portions of their territory are separated among legislative districts? Is the need to equalize district populations in any way impeded by a requirement that attention be paid to county and town lines when possible? If not, should the Constitution reassert and strengthen the rules designed to safeguard those governmental units from division unless there is an unavoidable conflict with federally guaranteed rights? How could such rules be worded? And if there is such protection, which other guarantees should it supersede? To which should it be subordinate?*

Integrity of Cities and Villages

The protection against being "carved up" in the districting process that the State Constitution provides to counties and towns was never extended to cities — which are therefore vulnerable to being subdivided. (Because it is composed of whole counties, this absence of protection has no effect

---

28 In its most recent decision on the subject, the Court of Appeals rejected a challenge to the 1992 legislative redistricting brought primarily on the grounds that the statute needlessly contravened the surviving state constitutional provisions regarding county integrity. *Matter of Wolpoff* v. *Cuomo, 80 N.Y. 2d, 70 (1992)*.
In a dissenting opinion, however, one judge wrote that "the tolerance the majority has today expressed for a plan that all but disregards the integrity of county borders will be read by many as a signal that our State Constitutional provisions no longer represent serious constraints on the critically important redistricting process." *Matter of Wolpoff* v. *Cuomo, 80 N.Y. 2d, 70 at 85*.

on New York City, but it does affect cities elsewhere in the state.) Villages too have no constitutional protection against subdivision in the districting process. Their situation, however, is different from that of cities. Under the State's system of government, cities and towns cannot occupy the same territory. Even though cities are often geographically *surrounded* by towns, their jurisdictions do not overlap. But *villages* and towns can and do overlap. Some villages are themselves divided, being partially in one town and partially in another. Indeed, the territory of some villages is even divided between *counties*. A prohibition against dividing villages would therefore have the potential to vastly complicate application of the existing provisions on county and town integrity.

> QUESTIONS: *Should whatever constitutional protection is provided for counties and towns be accorded to cities as well? Are there any disadvantages in doing so? And if such protection is extended, should cities and towns have equal status? (That is, should cities be subdivided in preference to towns or vice versa — or should such determination depend only on population level and/or geographic location?)*[29]

Special Criteria

A number of states, either in their constitutions or by statute, have adopted special requirements for determining which areas may be joined to form districts. (The New York City Charter also includes such guidelines, calling, for example, for keeping intact "neighborhoods and communities with established ties of common interest and association, whether historical, racial, economic, ethnic, religious or other.") However, such overlapping, subjective criteria are very difficult to give force and effect to, and therefore generally have little significance in practice.

> QUESTION: *Should the Constitution specify any factors to be considered in selecting areas to be joined into districts?*

Race and Ethnicity

In recent decades, the racial component of the districting process has been its most controversial, volatile aspect. As with the question of disparities

---

29 The proposal submitted by the 1967 Constitutional Convention spoke merely of adherence to the boundaries of "political subdivisions," with no specific reference to counties, towns, cities, or villages *per se*.

in district populations, the subject is in the first instance a matter of federal law and constitutional protections, but states may codify or expand those protections.

Applicable federal law in this area consists of two parts of the Voting Rights Act of 1965. Section 5 of the Act includes a formula based on 1968 voter turnout and the existence at that time of barriers to voter participation (including literacy tests in English). Its purpose was to determine which states and localities would be required to submit redistricting laws (and other enactments affecting voting) to the Justice Department for "pre-clearance." Although the formula was aimed primarily at the South, several non-Southern jurisdictions, including three New York counties — Bronx, New York, and Kings — are affected by it. Thus, since the 1970s, portions of New York legislative and Congressional districting laws have required federal approval — and several have been initially rejected.

In 1982, Section 2 of the Act, which affects not just selected areas but the entire country, was amended to give the Justice Department the power to overturn enactments that in its judgment effectively failed to provide minorities with equal voting *opportunities* — whether such laws were *intended to discriminate or not.* All state enactments on districting are therefore now subject to challenge by federal authorities. (At the same time, however, language was added stating that it was not Congress' purpose to require that a racial group's percentage of officeholders elected reflect its proportion of the population.)

New York's 1992 redistricting was the first enacted since the 1982 amendments. The extent to which the new lines were required to — or should — be based on considerations of race, engendered much controversy. Some read the law as mandating creation of the maximum possible number of districts in which ethnic minorities protected under the Voting Rights Act[30] constituted the majority or plurality of the population — even if carving out such districts necessitated disregarding other state constitutional provisions. Others believed, however, that such an interpretation was more than the Act called for: that it did not require a "maximization" of predominantly minority districts but merely that minority rights not be jeopardized. In addition, many assert that to require that districts be drawn on a racial basis contravenes the drive for deseg-

---

30 In New York, three groups — African-Americans, those of Spanish-speaking origin, and Asian-Americans — are numerous enough and sufficiently concentrated geographically to qualify for protected status in the districting process under the Act.

regation that has characterized much of the Civil Rights movement of the past half century.[31,32]

> QUESTIONS: *Should the Constitution expand on the language of the Voting Rights Act by explicitly requiring establishment of numbers of minority-majority or minority-plurality districts in exact or rough proportion to the minorities' statewide or county-wide percentage of the population? If so, how could such rules be framed? Or should matters of race in districting be left to federal law and judicial interpretation?*

Explicit Reference to Gerrymandering

The failure of the present Constitution to provide definitions of contiguity and compactness has made interpretation, implementation, and enforcement of those standards difficult. As indicated above, the districting proposal adopted by the 1967 Convention included a provision that explicitly "prohibited gerrymandering" — by name. Such reference could provide a court with a way of striking down districting arrangements perceived to be discriminatory in ways not clearly covered by other federal or state constitutional provisions.[33] On the other hand, giving the courts such wide latitude could give rise to endless litigation and enmesh the court system in what Justice Felix Frankfurter referred to as a "political thicket."[34]

> QUESTION: *Should the Constitution strengthen the safeguards against gerrymandering by making explicit reference to the practice?*

Order of Priority Among Criteria

Whatever districting criteria are included in the Constitution, it is virtually inevitable that in applying them, some will conflict with others, and

---

31   See Jim Sleeper, "In Defense of Civic Culture," The Progressive Foundation, Washington, 1993, 7-10; *The Wall Street Journal,* Aug. 31, 1994, A12; *The New York Times,* Sept. 19, 1994, B8; and Abigail Thernstrom, "Redistricting in Black and White," *The New York Times,* Dec. 7, 1994, A23.

32   The question of whether or not districts may — or must — be deliberately drawn to create majorities for specific racial groups has not yet been definitively decided by the Supreme Court. Its most recent pronouncement on the subject came in *Shaw* v. *Reno,* 61 L.W. 4818 (1993), but further clarification is expected when the Court rules on several cases currently scheduled for argument in early 1995.

33   The U.S. Supreme Court has ruled political gerrymandering to be a justiciable issue (*Davis* v. *Bandemer,* 478 U.S. 109 [1986]), but as of this writing the ways in which unconstitutional gerrymandering may be proven to the satisfaction of a court remain unclear.

34   See *Baker* v. *Carr,* 369 U.S. 186 at 266 (1962).

that it will therefore not be possible to apply them all to the same extent. In addition, merely setting forth a list of rules without specifying an order of priority in their application would not effectively serve the purpose of inhibiting gerrymandering, for it would enable those who draw the lines to choose from among the various rules those which are most politically advantageous to whatever group may be in control of the process, and to pay little or no heed to those that are perceived as disadvantageous. To address this concern, the New York City Charter, for example, explicitly states that the districting rules it includes are to be applied *in the order listed.*[35]

QUESTION: *Should there be a specified priority-order among whatever districting rules are included in the Constitution? If so, what should that order be?*

Size of the Houses of the Legislature

As previously noted, the Constitution specifies the size of the Assembly (150) but leaves determination of the number of Senators to a now-archaic formula. There is therefore a clear need at least to write a new provision establishing the number of upper house members. In addition, there may be reason to consider whether a change in the number of Assembly members is warranted as well.

It has long been recognized that there are no objective standards upon which to base decisions about the size of a legislative house, or the relative size of houses in a bicameral system. These decisions have profound consequences for the nature of representation in a polity, and the internal dynamics of a legislature.[36] Regarding districting, two factors — racial and ethnic considerations and "coterminality" — arise out of the question of size. The latter is discussed separately below.

When there are a greater number of districts, each one is smaller in population, making it more likely that some can be drawn in which specific racial or ethnic groups, if they are sufficiently concentrated geographically, can predominate. This was the primary motivation in expanding the

---

35   Charter of The City of New York (1989), Chapter 2A, Section 52.

36   For one summary see Douglas Muzzio and Tim Tompkins. " On the Size of the City Council: Finding the Mean," in Frank J. Mauro and Gerald Benjamin. *Restructuring the New York City Government: The Reemergence of Municipal Reform,* New York: Academy of Political Science, 1989, pp. 83-96.

membership of the New York City Council in that city's 1989 Charter revision.[37]

Some regard smaller, more homogeneous districts as a positive prospect. Others fear that the greater the number of ethnically homogeneous districts, the fewer the incentives of representatives to cooperate across racial lines to deal with common problems. They also suggest that a public hostile to politics and politicians would not receive well a proposal to create additional legislative seats.

For those who favor smaller, more homogeneous districts, this final point leads to consideration of the possibility of the creation of a single-house legislature, with a number of members larger than the current Assembly but fewer than the Assembly and Senate combined. Such a change would achieve smaller districts, and also a smaller net number of state legislative posts.

QUESTIONS: *Should the membership of either or both houses be expanded to make more likely the creation of a greater number of districts in which racial or ethnic minorities can make up the majority or plurality? If so, how much larger should the houses be? And in any event, at what level should the Senate membership be set? Should a unicameral legislature be considered along with consideration of appropriate district size?*

Coterminality

Prior to the *WMCA* and *Orans* rulings, the New York Constitution required that Assembly districts be placed wholly within Senate districts — that is, that Senate and Assembly districts be "coterminous." But the equal-population requirement, coupled with the fact that the number of Assembly seats (150) cannot be evenly divided by the number of Senate seats (which has at various times within the past several decades stood at 57, 58, 60, and 61), has made adherence to that provision impossible. If it were decided that bicameralism be retained; that coterminality[38] is desirable; that there be three Assembly districts per Senate district; and that the number of members should remain roughly in the present range; the following would be among the possible dimensions:

---

37   New York City Charter Revision Commission, *Final Report of the New York City Charter Revision Commission, January 1989-November 1989*; New York, 1990: 11-13.

38   Sometimes referred to as "nesting."

Senate Seats	Assembly Seats	Total Legislators
50	150 (present size)	200
53	159	212 (closest to present total)
61 (present size)	183	244

The most often-heard arguments in favor of coterminality are that it would make it easier for voters to identify their representatives and would facilitate cooperation between Senate and Assembly members in working on matters of common local interest. Additionally, there is some evidence that coterminality may be a serious constraint upon gerrymandering in the larger house. On the other hand, coterminality might also mean that any advantages or disadvantages for particular groups in the districting arrangements for the larger house would automatically be transmitted to the smaller. In addition, as the above figures demonstrate, coterminality at a 3:1 ratio would require either a sizeable reduction in the number of Senators or a substantial increase in the size of the Assembly. Any altered ratio would raise similar issues of negatively impacting incumbents and reducing political opportunity, or, alternatively, increasing the number of political jobs and the cost of the legislature. Such matters are always controversial.

> QUESTION: *Should the coterminality of Senate and Assembly districts be restored by changing the membership of one or both houses? If so, how?*

The Districting Agency

As noted above, the question of whether the Legislature should continue to exercise the power to delineate districts was the single most controversial districting issue at the 1967 Constitutional Convention. Many continue to advocate the position which carried the day then: that only by removing the Legislature from participation in the process by which its own districts are shaped can gerrymandering — partisan or bipartisan — be effectively inhibited.[39] Others believe that redistricting has traditionally and properly been and should remain a legislative function. Still others contend that simply transferring the districting power to a bipartisan commission would have only a limited deterrent effect

---

39　Detail on constitutionally based commissions provided for in other states may be found in *The New York State Constitution: A Briefing Book,* Albany: The Commission on Constitutional Revision, 1994, pp.151-152.

on gerrymandering.[40] Because gerrymandering is facilitated by discretionary powers in the hands of *whoever* draws the lines, they suggest, the really effective way to deter the practice would be to *limit* discretion by making the districting rules more explicit and easier to enforce.

> QUESTIONS: *Should the power to draw districts stay with the Legislature or be transferred elsewhere? If the latter, should the authority be vested in a bipartisan commission jointly appointed by the parties or legislative leaders, or composed in some other way; or, alternatively, in some type of nonpartisan body?*

The Role of the Governor

The procedures by which statutes establishing legislative (and Congressional) districts in New York are enacted are the same as those for all other legislation: passage by simple majorities in each house and signature by the governor (or overriding of a veto). The role played by governors has been significant in past years and has related primarily (though not exclusively) to the issue of partisan gerrymandering. Although there has been only one time since the 1960s decisions when redistricting was undertaken by a Legislature in which one party held majorities in both houses, that situation was quite common in prior decades.[41] Under such circumstances, the veto power, if held by a governor of the opposite party from the one which controls the Legislature, can be the only bulwark against one-party gerrymandering.[42] Even without its actually being employed, the mere existence of gubernatorial veto power can inhibit the actions of a legislative majority of the opposite party — and can provide a governor with influence over the actions of his own party in the districting process as well. Nevertheless, some believe the governor ought not be a participant in the process at all — that in line with the "separation of powers" concept, districting should be a purely legislative function. As indicated, this was the initial position of the leadership of the 1967 Convention, and indeed there are fully ten states in which the governor plays no role in

---

40 This view is premised on two factors: that the positions of commission members would be likely merely to reflect the preferences of those who appointed them; and that even if districting by a bipartisan commission diminished the threat of *partisan* gerrymandering, there is little reason to believe it would have any effect on *incumbent* gerrymandering.

41 One party has made up the majority in both houses during 70 of the hundred years that the Constitution of 1894 has been in effect. The opposite party has held the governorship for 23 of those years.

42 Indeed, there was *no* legislative redistricting from 1917 until 1943 primarily because for almost that entire period one party controlled the Legislature while the other held the governorship.

the process, having neither veto power nor *any* say in the promulgation of a plan (see footnotes 50 and 51, below).

> QUESTIONS: *Should the governor's power to veto districting legislation be maintained or eliminated? Or, as an intermediate position, might the strength of the veto power be modified — perhaps by permitting the Legislature to override gubernatorial vetoes by margins of less than the two-thirds now required?*

Extraordinary Majority Requirement

There is yet another way to build a potential procedural brake on partisan gerrymandering into the districting machinery: a requirement that districting legislation be passed by *extraordinary* rather than simple legislative majorities. In Connecticut, for example, unless a two-thirds majority can be attained, the districting responsibility passes to a commission.[43]

> QUESTIONS: *Should the legislative majorities required to pass districting legislation be changed? If so, how large a majority should be required?*

Districting Provisions In Other States

In considering possible changes in the State's districting machinery, the following brief summary of ways in which other states, either constitutionally or by statute, handle some aspects of the subject, may be useful.[44]

1. *The Districting Agency.* In 37 states, as in New York, districting is primarily a legislative function, but the number of states that have given authority over the process to non-legislative agencies has increased markedly since the court rulings of the 1960s.

Commissions, the make-up of which varies from state to state, hold initial power to draw legislative district lines in eight states.[45] In most, the legislative leaders of the major parties play a leading role in the appointment of commission members. In five other states[46] the governor, in some cases together with other

---

43   Conn. Const., Amendment XVI, Sec. 2a.

44   See NCSL Reapportionment Task Force, *Redistricting Provisions: 50 State Profiles,* Denver: National Conference of State Legislatures, 1989; and Legislative Drafting Fund of Columbia University, *Constitutions of the United States — National and State,* Dobbs Ferry, N.Y., 1989.

45   Colorado, Hawaii, Maine, Missouri, Montana, New Jersey, Pennsylvania, and Washington.

46   Alaska, Arkansas, Maryland, Ohio, and Vermont.

statewide officials, either has initial responsibility for delineating districts or plays the major role in determining the composition of the body that does so.

2. *Congressional Districting.* Whereas New York's Constitution makes no mention of Congressional districting, leaving that task to be dealt with statutorily, the constitutions of 17 states[47] do deal with the subject — generally by applying the same type of guidelines to the process of delineating Congressional districts as are applicable to the legislative districting process. Five state constitutions[48] place the responsibility for drawing Congressional lines in the hands of the same commission charged with legislative districting responsibility.

3. *Gubernatorial Veto.* Whereas New York's governor has the power to veto districting statutes passed by the Legislature, as do the governors of 35 other states, the constitutions of 14 states[49] do not provide their governors with such power. In five of these, however,[50] the Governor plays a major or exclusive role in the initial districting process itself. In five,[51] the absence of veto power extends to Congressional districting as well.

4. *Coterminality.* As indicated, coterminality requires that the number of lower house members be evenly divisible by the number of Senators. Coterminality is constitutionally required in 20 states.[52]

5. *Compactness and Contiguity.* The constitutions of all but 13 states[53] contain some reference to geographic compactness and/or contiguity in the construction of legislative districts (and in some cases Congressional districts as well). The requirements vary considerably in the degree of specificity with which they are

---

47   California, Colorado, Connecticut, Hawaii, Kentucky, Maine, Minnesota, Missouri, Montana, Rhode Island, South Carolina, South Dakota, Utah, Virginia, Washington, West Virginia, and Wyoming.

48   Hawaii, Maine, Montana, Ohio, and Washington.

49   Alaska, Arkansas, Colorado, Connecticut, Florida, Hawaii, Maryland, Missouri, Montana, New Jersey, North Carolina, Ohio, Pennsylvania, and Washington.

50   Alaska, Arkansas, Maryland, Missouri, and Ohio

51   Connecticut, Hawaii, Montana, North Carolina, and Washington

52   Alabama, Arkansas, Arizona, Hawaii, Idaho, Illinois, Iowa, Maryland, Minnesota, Montana, New Hampshire, New Jersey, North Dakota, Ohio, Oregon, Rhode Island, South Dakota, Washington, Wisconsin, and Wyoming.

53   Arizona, Delaware, Florida, Kansas, Louisiana, Maine, Nevada, New Hampshire, New Mexico, Oklahoma, Oregon, South Carolina, and Utah

phrased. Some, like New York's, merely state the concepts as undefined goals; others are considerably more precise.

* * * * * * * * * * *

Though there are a host of questions concerning legislative districting, and a great variety of possible answers, the most compelling in recent years have related to just a few particularly controversial aspects of the process — population inequality, partisan and bipartisan gerrymandering (and New York's unusual amalgam of the two), and the role of racial factors in the process.

To all intents and purposes, the population-inequality issue has been solved by federal action. Partisan gerrymandering is harder to address. Changing the districting agency offers one possible approach, but experiences in other states indicate that such a change by itself may be of limited effectiveness. The remaining problems — bipartisan gerrymandering and the role of race and ethnicity in districting — are far less tractable and likely to require innovative, imaginative approaches.

It may be helpful for those dealing with constitutional proposals in these areas to pose to themselves the most basic kinds of questions and to examine each suggestion in light of the answers: Does the proposal speak to the problem of partisan gerrymandering more effectively than the system now in place?; Can it deal more effectively with "bipartisan gerrymandering"?; Would it protect against discrimination and promote the search for racial justice more fairly and effectively? Proposals that can elicit affirmative answers to these questions can render the Constitution better able to serve the people of the state by bringing greater fairness, logic, and common sense to a process that lies at the very core of our system of representative democracy.

New York State's Judicial Article: A Work in Progress

Frederick Miller

Introduction

The Empire State has a large and complex court system, the busiest in the nation and perhaps the western world. The trial courts accept more than four million new cases each year, and render a like number of determinations in pending actions. Issues brought to the system for resolution range from minor infractions of municipal ordinances to multi-billion dollar commercial disputes and constitutional cases of landmark dimension.

More than a quarter of the state Constitution is given up to a detailed blueprint in Article VI for the structure of the judicial branch, and the distribution of powers and responsibilities within it. The ostensible purpose for this level of detail is to protect the judiciary from encroachments by the political branches of government. But the detail of Article VI also serves the pragmatic function of protecting some judges and courts from encroachments by other judges and courts, and keeping them in their places.

It is therefore no accident that Article VI permits judges to be partisan candidates for election as delegates to a constitutional convention, notwithstanding the fact that there is nothing judicial in the work of drafting a constitution. This provision, like numerous others in Article VI, is the handiwork of the many judges who have served as delegates, or on government committees and commissions that have proposed amendments to the Constitution.

The present judiciary article, adopted in 1962, declared the court system to be a "unified court system." It then proceeded to establish, or continue, a broad array of discrete trial and appellate courts, an administrative authority that was shared by four regional and independent appellate courts, a mixed and complicated system of state and local government funding, no central rule-making authority for court procedures, and about 120 separate personnel and budget systems.

These are not the usual characteristics of a "unified court system." In the parlance of court administrators, a "unified" system is supervised by a central management and rule-making authority and has a bare minimum of trial courts with specialized jurisdiction. Moreover, it is funded with a single judicial budget with effective controls. Other features that often complement a unified system include so-called "merit systems" rather than partisan election for the selection of judges, and efficient procedures, not legislative impeachment, for dealing with judicial misconduct and disability.

The history of court reform in New York since 1962 can be viewed as an effort to correct the constitutional fiction that the state has a unified court system. That effort has been waged on at least three fronts: by amendments to Article VI through legislative initiative, by statutes to complement Article VI structures and procedures, and with rules of court that attempt to force unity into the administration and processes of the system.

This essay focuses upon the more memorable efforts to achieve structural reform through constitutional changes since World War II. These are, of course, important in their own right. But more generally, because these efforts have been a persistent theme in state government over the last half century, they also provide insights into the promise of, and limits to, government restructuring through constitutional amendment.

The Existing Court System

The seven member Court of Appeals is at the apex of New York's court system. Below it, four Appellate Divisions of the Supreme Court serve as intermediate appellate tribunals for the trial courts within multicounty regions, which are called judicial departments. Judicial departments, in turn, are divided into 12 judicial districts consisting of one or more of the state's 62 counties. The bulk of all appellate review is provided by the Appellate Divisions.

In the trial court structure, there are 11 distinct courts, each with its jurisdiction and procedure. The Supreme Court, analogous to the superior court in most states, is the principal trial court. Its 330-plus justices are elected by the voters in the judicial districts where they serve. While the Supreme Court possesses unlimited, original, and statewide jurisdiction, the court generally deals with cases that do not fall within the jurisdiction of other courts. Examples of Supreme Court cases include contract and tort actions; divorce, separation and annulment proceedings; and equity disputes involving mortgage foreclosures and injunctions.

Within New York City, the Supreme Court hears both civil and serious criminal cases. Elsewhere in the state, it usually exercises only civil jurisdiction. Upstate — that is, outside New York City — felonies are generally tried in the County Courts. Family law matters including child support, neglect and juvenile delinquency proceedings, and foster-care placements are heard by the county-level Family Courts. Proceedings involving the estates and affairs of dead persons are heard by the Surrogate's Court in each county. In many upstate counties, the County Court has been consolidated with the Family and Surrogate's Court, or both. Tort and eminent domain suits against the state (but not other government units) must be tried in the Court of Claims.

New York City has two other citywide courts with limited civil and criminal jurisdiction. The Civil Court tries cases involving disputes up to $25,000, and has special parts for small claims, landlord-tenant disputes, and housing-code violations. The Criminal Court has jurisdiction over misdemeanors and violations.

Upstate there are city, town, and village courts that exercise limited civil and criminal jurisdiction and, in Nassau and Suffolk County, a District Court system that supplants many city and town courts.

The Unified Court System has 3,410 judges. Of these, about two-thirds are town and village justices, formerly called justices of the peace. They are elected locally and need not be lawyers. Most serve part time. Their salaries and the operating costs of their courts are paid by their local units of government.

All judges above the town and village court level are required to be lawyers. Most are elected by partisan ballot, although some are appointed by the governor and some by the mayors of cities, including the 47 judges of the Family Court and 107 judges of the Criminal Court in New York City.

Judges serve for terms of varying length, as prescribed by the Constitution or by statute. Terms are substantial, 10 to 14 years, or until age 70 when mandatory retirement expires a term. Judges may be disciplined by the legislature in impeachment cases, but the usual method is through a prosecution by the State Commission on Judicial Conduct, which is also an Article VI instrumentality.

Since 1978, section 28 of Article VI has provided that the chief judge of the Court of Appeals is the chief judge of the state and its chief judicial officer. Section 28 also provides for the chief judge to appoint a chief administrator of the courts, who may be a sitting judge. The chief administrator's appointment requires the advice and consent of the Administrative Board of the Courts, a consultative body consisting of the chief judge and the presiding justices of the four Appellate Divisions.

The chief administrator, on behalf of the chief judge, is responsible for supervising the administration and operation of the trial courts. Statewide administrative policy is approved by the Court of Appeals in consultation with the Administrative Board of the Courts.

If a judge, the chief administrator is called the chief administrative judge. The principal responsibilities of the office include the preparation of the system's annual budget, establishment of court terms, assignment of judges, promulgation of rules of judicial conduct, regulation of court practice, hiring and supervision of nonjudicial personnel, labor relations and collective bargaining, the collection of statistics, intergovernmental relations, continuing education programs for judges and court staffs, and the development of court improvement projects and facilities.

The chief administrative judge heads a management office called the Office of Court Administration (OCA), and currently has four principal deputies: two judges who supervise the trial courts in New York City and upstate; a deputy who supervises the management units within OCA; and a counsel who directs OCA's legal and legislative efforts.

In 1976, the legislature unified the judiciary's operating budget and personnel systems with the enactment of the Unified Court Budget Act. All courts were included except town and village courts. The act merged 120 separate municipal court budgets into a single statewide budget funded by the state. It also transferred 9,500 local court employees to the state's payroll, and obligated the court system to establish a statewide personnel and salary structure for them. The Act relieved county and city governments of the personnel and operating costs they had previously borne, but it left them responsible for providing courthouses and other physical facilities.

The chief administrative judge supervises the preparation of the judicial budget, which, in turn, requires the approval of the Court of Appeals before its transmittal to the governor and legislature on December 1 of each year. The governor is constitutionally obligated to present the budget to the legislature without revision, but with whatever recommendations he or she deems proper. The legislature determines the final appropriations, subject to the governor's constitutional veto powers. The judiciary's budget in 1979 approached $325 million. By Fiscal Year 1994-95, it had grown to $908 million.

Historical Development

Origins in the 1846 Constitutional Convention. The 1846 Convention adopted many reforms that were considered modern at the time, laying the basis of New York State's current court system. These included the popular election of judges, the transfer of procedural rule-making authority from the courts to the legislature, and legislative removal of judges for cause.

The 1846 convention also established the Court of Appeals as the state's high court of appellate jurisdiction, and abolished independent chancery and circuit courts, merging their jurisdiction into the Supreme Court, the then-new statewide court of complete and original jurisdiction.

Additionally in 1846 "General Terms" of the Supreme Court were established to serve as intermediate appellate courts. These ultimately evolved into the present Appellate Divisions of the Supreme Court. County Courts, then courts of common pleas, narrowly escaped abolition through merger, but their jurisdiction was substantially curtailed. And for the first time, the state's probate courts, also of colonial origin, were incorporated into Article VI as Surrogate's Courts. The convention also continued local city, town, and village courts.

The 1846 convention produced a judicial system of remarkable durability. Its organizational structure paralleled the political boundaries of local government (towns, villages, cities, and counties). In both administration and jurisdiction, trial courts were largely independent. The state's financial obligation to the system was minimal. By and large, each local court looked to its local unit of government for its financial needs and facilities.

Consistent with this attitude of local responsibility, the legislature imposed few standards or administrative controls over the judiciary. Over time, one consequence of this passivity was the proliferation of specialized courts. In New York City, for example, there were 19 separate trial courts by the 1950s, each with its own jurisdiction, administration, budget, and personnel.

The Post-World War II Crisis. The trial court system that evolved in the century following the 1846 convention ultimately proved too rigid and specialized to adapt to the flood of litigation that poured into the courts after World War II. Great shifts in population, the disintegration of families, increased poverty, and rising crime rates soon translated into persistent congestion and delay in the criminal and family law courts.

To cite an example from just one area of law, postwar vehicular traffic nearly doubled the number of traffic injuries between 1944 and 1948, causing a corresponding increase in negligence litigation. Economic inflation added substantially to the costs of litigation, and jury awards increased dramatically. Litigants avoided the lower trial courts, with their limited monetary jurisdiction, in hope of greater financial success in the Supreme Court, which has no fixed limits on the amount of its judgments.

Beginning in the late 1940s, judicial and legislative leaders responded by fashioning an array of procedural devices to speed the flow of cases: pretrial conferences, preferences for cases considered more deserving of Supreme Court processing, pretrial discovery, and the use of special referees as substitute judges. These patches proved inadequate. Four-year delays in civil case processing were commonplace. Basic reforms were clearly necessary.

The Tweed Commission. In his 1953 State of the State message, Governor Thomas E. Dewey remarked "...that we have arrived at a time that cries out for improvement in the administration, procedure, and structure of our courts." Dewey called upon the legislature to create a temporary commission to evaluate the state's court system on a scale comparable to the 1846 revisions, and consider a range of reforms including merit selection of judges.

The legislature responded by creating the Tweed Commission, named for its chairman, Harrison Tweed, a prominent member of the New York City bar. Over a five-year period, that commission conducted the most thorough court reform project in the state's history. Highlights of the commission's final plan included the continuation of the Court of Appeals and the Appellate Divisions; merger of the Surrogate's Court and the Court of Claims into the Supreme Court; consolidation of all New York City courts into a single court; an upstate system of county courts with civil, criminal, family, and probate jurisdiction; a system of magistrates' courts in upstate towns and cities for traffic and minor criminal proceedings; a system of central court administration; and a central court budget financed with state appropriations.

Forty years later, this is hardly radical stuff. Nonetheless, the Commission's plan quickly slipped into a political morass. Predictably, political leaders were fearful of a loss of their traditional influence in the courts, particularly in the selection of judges, the appointment of court staff and the patronage dispensed by Surrogate's Courts. A look at the 1952 payroll of the New York City courts suggests the extent of that influence. Of 199 leaders of both parties, 57 held court jobs. More than 70 percent of the legal positions were held by non-lawyer politicians. And according to the State Crime Commission, political leaders routinely selected both judges and their staffs.

Fearing outright rejection of its plan, the Commission sought to accommodate special interests with revisions on revisions. To many observers, its final proposal was but a shadow of the original. Near the end of the 1958 legislative session, the plan passed the Senate overwhelmingly. But four days later it was defeated by a one-vote margin in the Assembly.

At a post-session press conference, Commission chairman Tweed blamed judges and politicians for killing the plan. Another analysis suggests that the Commission's willingness to compromise, coupled with a lack of public and political support from the Harriman Administration, were equally responsible. It was also important that public support for the Commission's work seemed to erode with each announcement of another compromise. Even the League of Women Voters jumped ship. It withdrew its support and denounced the final plan as "wholly unacceptable."

All was not lost however. A storm of protest arose from the editorial pages and good government groups. An embarrassed Governor Harriman reacted by requesting the Judicial Conference, itself the product of a Tweed Commission recommendation, to draft a comprehensive court reorganization plan. The League of Women Voters and the Citizens' Union commissioned experts to devise their own plan of reorganization. Later both the Democrat and Republican legislative leaders added to this mix proposals of their own.

The Judicial Conference, then a nine-judge agency chaired by the Chief Judge, unveiled its proposals for reorganization in November 1958. The plan borrowed heavily from the Tweed Commission's work. It called for continuing the existing appellate court structure, abolishing the Court of Claims, continuing the Supreme and Surrogate's Courts, establishing a statewide Family Court and consolidating the trial courts in New York City. Upstate, the local court structure would consist of County Courts and, on the municipal level, City Courts in large cities and a District Court system to replace town and village courts.

With respect to administration, the Judicial Conference proposed that statewide policy be formulated by the Conference and be executed in the management of trial courts by the Appellate Divisions in their respective judicial departments. Despite obvious compromises, these proposals received wide support from influential citizen groups, prominent members of the judiciary and the legal community. But once again, the politicians went to work to gut the plan.

The Rockefeller Reforms. The election of Governor Nelson A. Rockefeller in November 1958 proved to be a boon to the state's long-suffering court reformers. Rockefeller promptly overhauled the Judicial Conference's proposals and sent his program to the legislature for first passage. It included many of the Conference's recommendations and, not surprisingly, left intact the largely Republican upstate court system. The program passed the Republican-controlled legislature over the near-solid opposition of the Democrats. But in the public arena and the press, Rockefeller scored a notable political victory in his first year in office: engineering the first reorganization of the state's judicial system in 113 years.

Two years later, when the package required second passage by the legislature, fewer than 10 votes were cast against it. With the aggressive public support of Rockefeller, the chief judge, good government groups, and the press, the voters approved the submission by a plurality of 1.8 million votes, the largest in the history of the state for a constitutional amendment.

The 1967 Constitutional Convention. The ill-fated Constitutional Convention of 1967 produced an unremarkable proposal for reforming the courts. Judicial reform issues were debated on the floor until the last minutes of the convention. The Democrats were deeply divided on the issues, and the President of the convention, Anthony J. Travia, the Democrat speaker of the Assembly, gave no clear direction to his party members.

When the convention was organized, Travia appointed his close friend Appellate Division Justice Henry L. Ughetta to chair the Judiciary Committee. Ughetta fell seriously ill during the convention and much of the work of his committee fell to a subcommittee of the Rules Committee. Moreover, two-thirds of the delegates were either judges or lawyers. They shared keen but disparate interests in the organization and operation of the court system.

Notwithstanding the articulate advocacy of retired Chief Judge Charles Desmond and Bernard Botein, the respected presiding justice of the Appellate Division in Manhattan, most sitting judges and state legislators who served as delegates opposed court merger and the merit selection of judges, and succeeded in blocking both reforms.[1] Although shorter in length, the convention's judicial article was highly detailed. Administrative authority was centralized in the Court of Appeals. The legislature could create up to seven judicial departments. State financing of the major trial courts was to be phased in over ten years. A district court system outside New York City was authorized (instead of city and justice courts), but only at local option and with protections for incumbent judges. But when presented to the voters, the convention's entire handiwork was rejected, including the judiciary article.

The Dominick Commission. Responding to a proposal of the League of Women Voters for a fresh look at the court system, Governor Rockefeller in 1970 submitted legislation to establish a temporary study commission. The result was an 11-member body chaired by Republican Senator D. Clinton Dominick, with a reporting deadline of February 1, 1971.

Nearly two years past that deadline the Commission released a three-volume report containing 180 reform recommendations. They included central court administration by a chief administrative judge appointed by the chief judge; state financing of all but town and city courts; discipline of judges by a state commission on judicial conduct and a permanent Court on the Judiciary; merger of the Supreme Court, the Court of Claims, the County Court, the Family Court, and the Surrogate's Court; and the establishment of a district court system in larger counties to replace town, village, and city courts.

With respect to judicial selection, the Commission proposed only modest changes. Judicial nominating conventions for the Supreme Court would be eliminated but otherwise judges would run in partisan elections. Appointed judges would continue to be appointed, but from lists proposed by nominating commissions.

Governor Rockefeller endorsed the proposals for improved judicial discipline procedures, but went much further with respect to the selection of judges and the administration and financing of the court system. His reforms included gubernatorial selection of judges of the Court of Appeals and the Supreme Court, but with screening panels and Senate confirmation; central court management by a court administrator appointed by the

1   Henrik Dullea, *Charter Revision in the Empire State: The Politics of New York's Constitutional Convention*, Maxwell School, Syracuse University, PhD. Dissertation, 1982, pp. 279-288, 453-481. A revised version of this dissertation is being publish as *Charter Revision in the Empire State: The Politics of New York's 1967 Constitutional Convention*, Albany, NY: Rockefeller Institute Press, 1997.

chief judge with approval of the Senate and the governor; and court funding by the state to be financed by a reduction in state aid to local governments.

The Dominick Commission and Rockefeller proposals were apparently too much for the legislature to digest in a single year, particularly when the 1973 agenda included a massive overhaul of the state's laws on drug abuse. Another complicating factor was Rockefeller's resignation. Court reform was shelved at the end of the session with the legislature creating yet another joint legislative committee to study the issues.

The Last Election of a Chief Judge. Outside the legislative arena, a political event occurred in 1973 that greatly influenced the New York history in court reform: the election of Charles D. Breitel as chief judge.[2]

Since 1870, judges of the Court of Appeals had been selected by statewide election. But there also developed a political tradition whereby Democrat and Republican leaders filled vacancies on the high court by agreement. This was possible because election laws permitted the cross endorsement of candidates, and because statewide party nominations were made at political conventions with political leaders in command. The tradition was particularly strong with the office of chief judge: title passed to the senior associate judge on the court, regardless of political enrollment. One reason that tradition persisted was that it produced great judges.

In 1972, however, New York changed its laws to allow primary election challenges. This permitted an aspirant to the high court to outflank a judicial convention and secure a major party nomination by winning a statewide primary. To the dismay of the legal community, good government groups, and editorial page writers, the result was a series of election spectaculars for seats on the Court of Appeals.

In 1973, Chief Judge Stanley H. Fuld retired. The senior associate judge, also near mandatory retirement age, announced that he would not be a candidate for the top job. Next in seniority was Charles D. Breitel, a renowned legal scholar, a former prosecutor, a former counsel to Governor Dewey, and a Republican. Breitel had served 12 years on the Court of Appeals, and earlier on the trial and appellate benches in Manhattan.

In accord with longstanding practice, Breitel might have expected to be the nominee of both major parties. But he got only the Republican

---

2   See Frederick Miller, "Court Reform: The New York Experience" in *Court Reform in Seven States,* Lee Powell, ed. National Center for State Courts, 1980.

nomination. A Democrat primary, with six candidates, was won by Jacob D. Fuchsberg, a successful trial lawyer from Manhattan. In the hotly contested general election that followed, Breitel defeated Fuchsberg (and a Conservative Party candidate) and became chief judge on January 1, 1974.

That same year Fuchsberg waged a second primary race and won a seat on the high court as an associate judge. A notable loser in the 1974 election was the court's only black judge, Harold A. Stevens. A Democrat and former presiding justice of the Appellate Division in Manhattan, Stevens had been appointed to the Court, on an interim basis, by Republican Governor Malcolm Wilson. Outspent in the Democratic primary, Stevens lost his party's nomination and ran, unsuccessfully, on the Republican, Liberal, and Conservative lines.

The Breitel-Fuchsberg race was bitter, and it strained relationships within the high court when Fuchsberg won his seat as associate judge. Moreover, Steven's loss had nothing to do with his credentials as a judge but rather the influence of money and partisan politics. These events stiffened Breitel's resolve to use the clout of his office to shape public policy against the partisan ballot for selecting judges of the Court of Appeals.

The Carey-Breitel-Gordon Reforms

Meanwhile in the legislature, the talk of court reform continued. The successor to the Dominick Commission was a Joint Legislative Committee on Court Reorganization, chaired by Republican State Senator Bernard G. Gordon. Drawing upon earlier studies, the Gordon Committee promptly produced four major proposals: appointment of judges of the Court of Appeals by the governor, subject to Senate confirmation; an overhaul of judicial discipline machinery; central court management by a chief administrator of the courts appointed by the chief judge, subject to Senate confirmation; and state financing of the courts with partial reimbursement from local governments.

While these developments were unfolding in the legislative arena, Breitel was serving his first weeks as Chief Judge. From the beginning, it was clear that he had an agenda, and that he was not a bashful advocate. One of his first moves was to appoint Richard J. Bartlett as his state court administrator. Bartlett was a respected former Republican Assemblyman from the North Country who had recently been elected to the Supreme Court.

Breitel then arranged for the four Appellate Divisions to delegate to Bartlett their substantial management authority over the trial courts. With this move — not unlike a treaty — Breitel administratively centralized the management of New York's massive court system. In a related act, a single administrative judge was appointed to supervise all the trial courts within New York City, notwithstanding judicial department boundaries. The practical effect of this appointment was an administrative merger of the New York City trial courts.

In yet another bold stroke, Breitel arranged for an invitation to address the legislature, the first (and only) event of its kind for a chief judge. Breitel used the occasion to advance five fundamental court reforms: unified administration, consolidated trial courts, state funding, merit selection of judges, and the administrative handling of judicial discipline cases subject to judicial review.

The chief judge's campaign for court reform was well timed. The 1962 reorganization had not produced the anticipated efficiency, and by 1974 the need for major repairs was obvious. Indeed, Governor Hugh L. Carey, elected in 1975, campaigned vigorously on a plank of court reform. And it proved to be a campaign promise that the governor did not neglect once he was elected. He assigned court reform a high priority in his administration and appointed the future United States Secretary of State, Cyrus Vance, then president of the Association of the Bar of the City of New York, to chair a gubernatorial task force on court reform and to work with the counsel to the governor, Judah Gribetz, on the effort.

Amendments One, Two, and Three. The legislature in 1974 gave first approval to constitutional amendments encompassing three of the Gordon Committee's proposals: the overhaul of judicial discipline machinery, central court administration, and first-instance financing of the courts by the state. Second passage came in 1975, with presentation to the voters in the November general election. Only the judicial discipline proposal was approved by the voters. They narrowly rejected a bundled proposal for central court management and first-instance financing by the state, probably because of fiscal concerns in that crisis year.

When negotiators returned to the drawing board at the 1976 legislative session, the issues were narrowed to eliminating the partisan ballot for the Court of Appeals, central court administration, and further improvements in judicial discipline procedures. The struggle to reach agreement was intense and continued literally into the final hours of the session, when negotiations collapsed. To most observers familiar with New York's complex amendment process, it appeared that constitutional reform had again been stalled for several years.

They were wrong, doubtless underestimating Carey's resolve and commitment to court reform. In midsummer, the governor called the legislature into Extraordinary Session with an agenda that he limited to Article VI proposals: adoption of a merit selection system for the Court of Appeals, creation of the constitutional office of chief administrator of the courts, and establishment of a Commission on Judicial Conduct with authority to discipline judges, subject to final review by the Court of Appeals.

There was one other important product of the midsummer session: a proposal from Bartlett to unify the court system's budget by statute, avoiding the need for amendments to Article VI. The proposal was well-received as the shift of local court costs to the state helped financially strapped local governments, particularly in New York City where fiscal problems were at a crisis level.

Notwithstanding that Governor Carey called the session without a prior commitment by the legislative leaders to deal with his proposals, the two-day special session produced extraordinary results. The legislature approved all three constitutional proposals, and a version of Bartlett's Unified Court Budget Act. Second passage of the constitutional reforms by a separately elected legislature occurred in 1977.

The next challenge was selling the amendments — numbered One, Two, and Three on the ballot — to the voters at the November 1977 referendum. Good government groups, led by the League of Women Voters and the Committee for Modern Courts, responded with statewide public information campaigns. Also, a number of prominent New York City law firms, at Breitel's urging, organized a committee called Court Reform Now, and raised money to support voter approval of the amendments. One theme of the reformers was: "Take the clubhouses out of the courthouses." But the campaign was not all one-sided. An Ad Hoc Committee for Preservation of an Elected Judiciary spent $17,000 for its media campaign to reject the amendments.

The reform efforts succeeded. All three amendments were handily approved by the voters. They also survived a vigorous court challenge (by supporters of an elected judiciary) concerning the method by which the amendments were submitted to the voters.[3]

---

3   *Frank* v. *New York*, 44 NY 2d 687, 405 NYS 2d 454 (1978).

There followed a brief administration under the new structures as Chief Judge Breitel was obliged to retire on December 31, 1978, upon reaching mandatory retirement age. On December 15, 1978, the new State Commission on Judicial Nomination provided Governor Carey with the names of seven nominees to replace Breitel. On January 1, 1979, the governor announced his selection: Lawrence H. Cooke, an associate judge of the high court and a Democrat.

The Cooke and Wachtler Years. Neither Cooke, who served through 1984, nor his Republican successor Sol Wachtler (1985-1992) aggressively pushed the legislature to achieve the remainder of the reform agenda: trial court merger and abolishing the partisan ballot for selecting judges. Both leaders had more pressing management challenges.

For Cooke and his administrative judges, a massive effort was required to implement the fiscal, personnel, and collective bargaining provisions of the Unified Court Budget Act. In addition, they undertook a logistically difficult and unpopular program to assign upstate judges to busier courts downstate.

Chief Judge Wachtler served in economic hard times for the state. Indeed, times were so hard on the court system that he engaged in bitter litigation with the governor and legislature for additional funding. These fiscal problems were compounded by soaring increases in new filings in the criminal courts. Given that cost estimates for court merger alone ranged between $30 and $90 million, it is understandable that the judicial branch followed the lead of the other branches in searching for other fields to plow.

One of those fields was the problem of aging and inadequate court facilities. The problem was first attacked by a task force appointed by Cooke to inventory existing facilities and develop space and maintenance standards. In 1987, Wachtler and Administrative Judge Joseph W. Bellacosa succeeding in persuading the legislature to enact the Court Facilities Act, which provides state fiscal incentives to local governments to maintain, improve and construct capital facilities for the courts. It will be a multi-billion dollar effort well into the twenty-first century.

There were amendments to Article VI following the 1978 reforms. They are reflective of the kind of lesser concerns that must be addressed through the amendment process when a constitution is highly detailed. One proposal approved by the voters in 1983 increased the monetary jurisdiction of the County Court and the New York City Civil Court (from $10,000 to $25,000); and of the District Court (from $6,000 to $15,000).

Another authorized the temporary assignment of Family Court judges to the Supreme Court. In 1985, the voters approved an amendment to permit the Court of Appeals to provide other state and federal high courts with interpretations of New York law. This is not the stuff that one usually considers to be fundamental law requiring statewide voter referendums.

The Cuomo Years

Since his election in 1982, Governor Mario M. Cuomo crafted a consistent public record of support for the two unfinished pieces of court reform: court merger and the merit selection of judges. However, that support was not expressed in actual constitutional change. Chief Judge Judith S. Kaye, who succeeded Chief Judge Wachtler in 1993, endorsed the governor's merger and merit selection proposals, which were introduced by them jointly as part of their 1994 legislative programs.[4]

Additionally, Governor Cuomo supported the creation of one or two new Appellate Divisions to relieve serious caseload congestion in the Second Judicial Department. He proposed that Article VI be amended to provide the legislature with a two-year period in which to create one or more additional judicial departments, beyond the existing four.

Cuomo's reform package would have achieved merit selection and court merger immediately, while leaving the business of restructuring the appellate court structure to the legislative process, but with a deadline that appeared to assure action. Because partisan control of the legislature was (and is likely to remain) divided, a bipartisan compromise was needed. Additionally, the Cuomo proposal created a role in appellate court restructuring for the chief executive, through the veto power. (A governor has no formal role in amending the Constitution by legislative initiative.)

A Near Miss?: 1986-87. During the last year of Governor Cuomo's first term, many observers believed that the legislature had finally come to grips with the unfinished pieces of court reform. On the last day of the 1986 session, a concurrent resolution containing the governor's Article VI proposals received first passage. But second passage following election of a new legislature in 1986, a requisite for amending the Constitution, never happened.[5]

These events provide a classic example of legislative maneuvering. Near the close of the 1986 session, the legislative leaders failed to reach

---

4   Senate 7028 (1994 Goodman); Assembly 10867 (1994 Weinstein).
5   Senate 9618 (1986 Dunne), Assembly 11733 (1986 Weprin).

agreement on a new program to help local governments finance capital projects for court facilities. At the eleventh hour, almost literally, the governor's court reform package was dusted off, passed, and hailed as a major legislative achievement. Unannounced was the apparent understanding that the resolution would not be resuscitated at the 1987 session.

The 1994 Proposals

The governor, chief judge, Assembly, and Senate all had court reform proposals on the table during the 1994 legislative session.

Merger. In its current formulation, the Cuomo-Kaye package provides for a staged unification process. First the County, Family, and Surrogate's Court would be merged into the Supreme Court. Merger of the Court of Claims would occur nine months later; and one year thereafter, the New York City Civil and Criminal Courts, all City Courts having full-time judges, and the District Courts in Nassau and Suffolk Counties. Upon merger, the incumbent judges would become Supreme Court justices for the balance of their terms.

James J. Lack, Republican chairman of the Senate Judiciary Committee, offered an alternative plan in 1994 that was far different from the Cuomo-Kaye and Assembly majority packages.[6] Lack proposed to merge the Supreme Court, County Court, Surrogate's Court, and Court of Claims into a new Superior Court, preserving a second tier of lower courts consisting of the Family Court, New York City Civil and Criminal Courts, and upstate City and District Courts.

Judicial Selection. The governor's proposed merit selection system would apply to all vacancies occurring after the lower courts are merged into the Supreme Court. The Cuomo system would complement the statewide process that generates nominees for the Court of Appeals with important adaptations to accommodate participation in the nomination process by mayors and county executives.

For example, the governor would appoint Supreme Court justices within New York City upon nomination by the mayor from a list of candidates found to be well-qualified by a citywide judicial nominating commission. Similar procedures would apply upstate: gubernatorial appointments would be made upon the nomination of county chief elected officers from lists of well-qualified candidates screened by judicial district nominating commissions.

---

6   Senate 8185 (1994 Lack).

All judicial appointments would be subject to Senate confirmation. Moreover, the members of the various nominating commissions would be structured to include persons selected by the governor, the chief judge, legislative leaders, ranking regional judges, and local government and bar leaders. The overall composition of each commission is intended to be bipartisan and include both lawyers and non-lawyers in the membership of the panels.

The Cuomo-Kaye package includes an unusual twist for New York: nonpartisan retention elections. These are a feature of the so-called "Missouri Plan" of judicial selection. After a judge has served two years on the Supreme Court, local voters would be asked at the general election, "Shall..., a Justice of the Supreme Court, be retained in office?" Only if a majority voted "yes" would the incumbent continue in office for the balance of the term (the earlier of 14 years or until age 70 is reached). Reappointment to successive terms would be automatic, provided the incumbent wins a well-qualified rating from the appropriate judicial nominating commission.

At the 1994 session, the Democratic Assembly leadership endorsed most, but not all, of the reforms advanced by the governor and chief judge. Helene E. Weinstein, chairwoman of the Judiciary Committee, introduced the Cuomo-Kaye concurrent resolution, but with an important revision that would alter the selection system for the 50-odd justices of the Appellate Divisions.[7] Article VI currently gives the governor the authority to select these justices from the corps of elected Supreme Court justices. There is no constitutional screening or nominating process, or Senate confirmation.

The Assembly alternative would continue gubernatorial appointment of these judges, but would require screening by nominating commissions that could recommend the appointment of any judge or lawyer with ten years experience at the bar. According to Weinstein, this change is intended to increase the number of women and minorities on these appellate courts. Senator Lack's concurrent resolution, on the other hand, would retain all existing judicial selection systems, whether appointive or elective.[8]

One other significant proposed amendment to Article VI dealing with judicial selection was introduced at the 1994 session. It would empower the legislature to divide any or all of New York City's four

---

7   Assembly 10867 (1994 Weinstein).
8   Senate 8185 (1994 Lack).

judicial districts into political subdivisions for the purpose of electing Supreme Court justices.[9] The sponsors' memorandums in support of this amendment say that its purpose is to "assure minority representation on the bench." Many civil rights experts believe that the current system of electing Supreme Court justices at-large from multicounty districts may violate the federal Voting Rights Act. Should the existing electoral system be declared illegal in litigation, this proposed amendment to Article VI might provide the state with a procedural remedy to cure the illegality.

Appellate Organization. The Second Department's caseload is generated by the civil and criminal courts in Kings, Queens, and Richmond counties in New York City, Nassau and Suffolk counties on Long Island, and the suburban counties of the lower Hudson Valley. As a result, the Second Department handles about 40 percent of the state's entire intermediate appellate intake, with a persistent backlog of more than 40,000 undecided appeals. In fact, it is the busiest appellate court in the United States, with delays for litigants in civil appeals fast approaching two years. In New York's other three judicial departments, the wait for litigants is measured in months.

No one disputes that the court's caseload is excessive. The principal problem is how to recast the overall appellate structure without tipping the balance of political elective power. Supreme Court justices (including all Appellate Division justices) are elected from judicial districts, which consist of one or more counties. The five counties of the lower Hudson Valley comprise the Second Department's Ninth Judicial District, which is reliably Republican. The same is true in the Second Department's Tenth Judicial District, which consists of the counties of Nassau and Suffolk. In contrast, the New York City portion of the Second Department is largely Democrat.

While public discourse on the subject of appellate delay seldom includes the nitty gritty of politics, the solution of creating a Fifth Judicial Department involves major political risks: a miscalculation in redrawing these geographical appellate boundaries could have a terminal effect on the careers of countless judges and other court personnel and affect the patronage opportunities that abound in the trial and appellate courts. It is a risk that most politicians would prefer to avoid altogether.

Assemblywoman Weinstein's concurrent resolution[10] includes the governor's proposal to give the legislature a two-year period in which to

---

9   Senate 6528 (1993 Connor); Assembly 9166 (1994 Friedman).

10   Assembly 10867 (1994 Weinstein).

create one or two additional judicial departments. In contrast, Senator Lack's resolution would expressly provide for five judicial departments, with the fifth department to consist of the counties of Queens, Nassau, and Suffolk.[11] This embraces a recommendation advanced by the presiding justice of the Second Department, Guy J. Mangano. The population of these three contiguous boroughs is roughly half of the Department's existing population, and perhaps of more importance, the voting population in these three is roughly balanced between the Democrats and Republicans.

Conclusion

As close observers expected, none of the Amendments to Article VI offered in 1994 were approved before the legislature recessed in early July. Partisan deadlock remains on key components of the major issues, and the energy and enthusiasm that was so evident during the mid-1970s is more a memory than an exigent political force.

But there are reasons beyond partisan deadlock for the waning appetite for additional court reform. One is that the 1978 reforms have worked so well. The court system's aggressive use of its post-1978 administrative powers, for example, has undoubtedly mitigated the pressure to tackle structural court merger within Article VI. At the same time, contemporary political and demographic forces make new groups skeptical about the promises of merit selection. As minorities have become more successful in electoral politics, their leaders find less reason to abandon that system for another untested method that may, in fact, serve them less well, except at the atypical level of the Court of Appeals.

It is also worth observing that the variety of specialized courts and elected benches, in itself, does not now prevent court administrators from managing these institutions effectively. The court system's ability to transfer cases and trial judges among the various courts of the system, and to pay them salary differentials, are powerful tools that produce many of the practical traits that are typical of a consolidated system.

A related and somewhat unexpected reality is that changes wrought by statute have proven as powerful and important for court reform in New York as long sought constitutional amendments. The 1978 Unified Court Budget Act and the 1987 Court Facilities Act are examples of key structural reforms that have been achieved by ordinary legislation.

---

11   Senate 8185 (1994 Lack).

Despite changes in the political leadership and dynamics of New York following the 1994 general election, some things are certain. One of them is the inevitability that pending court reform proposals will resurface in some incarnation or another during the 1995 legislative session. But the earliest that any constitutional change by way of legislative initiative can become part of Article VI is a far distant January 1, 1998. That assumes first passage in 1995 or 1996, second passage in 1997, and voter approval at the general election in November 1998. And one must add to the 1998 effective date the years it will actually take to implement the text of any constitutional amendments.

Alternatively, the judicial branch would certainly be a major concern in a new constitutional convention. If a convention is called by the voters in response to the mandatory referendum on this question in 1997, delegates will be elected in 1998. The convention will meet and proffer the voters a new judiciary article in 1999. If approved by the voters, the state's new charter will likely take effect in the year 2000, again with additional time that would be needed for practical implementation.

But the experience of the 1967 convention serves as evidence that achieving judicial reform by the convention process will be highly dependent upon the delegates, and their agendas. Sitting judges, of course, are still constitutionally eligible to run and to serve, and there is every reason to believe that many will be candidates for this extra-judicial part-time public office, and the additional salary, pension, and other benefits that go with it.

One final thing that should be clear from this survey of court reform is that the movement in the Empire State needs its Lochinvars. Whatever progress that has been achieved since World War II is a tribute to the leadership and tenacity of a handful of uncommon public citizens — lawyers, legislators, judges, and chief executives.

For all of its history, Article VI has been a work in evolving progress. While substantial structural work remains undone, and the pace remains frustratingly slow to many, there should be comfort in the words of Arthur Vanderbilt who, as chief justice of New Jersey, encouraged the modernization of state courts there and nationwide. Court reform, Vanderbilt judiciously observed, is not a sport for the short-winded.

The Private Economy

Joseph F. Zimmerman

State constitutional arrangements concerning taxing, spending, borrowing, and social policy all fundamentally affect the business climate in New York. This chapter will confine itself, however, to the five articles of the New York Constitution that relate directly and purposefully to private business activities. They are Articles III (Legislature), VII (State Finance), VIII (Local Finance), X (Corporations), and XVI (Taxation). The first four restrict the state's capacity to aid private business with public resources. They are a legacy of excesses of the nineteenth century. The fifth specifically limits the state's taxing power as it applies to certain corporations.

New York State is currently seeking to retain and expand its economic base in competition with other states. As a consequence, the contemporary political environment is once again supportive of the use of state incentives to attract business firms to New York and keep existing firms here. One result has been repeated attempts, several successful, to amend the Constitution to provide state government greater leeway in the use of public funds and public credit for promoting economic development. There has, however, been no direct frontal attack on constitutional constraints in this area.

Current Provisions

Restrictions on the Legislature. Article III, Section 17, contains a number of restrictions on the legislature's power to enact a special or local law granting special privileges to specific firms or individuals. These were adapted in 1874, in the midst of the Industrial Revolution, to fight corruption and enhance governmental efficiency. Under these provisions the legislature is barred from enacting a special or local bill to: regulate the rate of interest on money; grant any corporation, association, or individual the right to lay down railroad tracks; grant any private corporation, association, or individual any exclusive privilege, immunity, or franchise whatever; grant to any person, association, firm, or corporation an exemption from taxation on real or personal property; or provide for the building of bridges, except over the waters forming a part of the boundaries of the state, by other than a municipal or other public corporation or a public agency of the state.

Gifts and Loans by the State. Article VII, Section 8, added in 1846 and amended in 1894 and 1938, forbids the gift or loan of state funds or the credit of the state in aid of any private corporation, association, or undertaking, with the exception of funds or properties held by the state for educational, mental health, or mental retardation purposes.

In 1961, Subsection 3 of this section was added by amendment, simultaneous with the addition of Article X, Section 8, to overcome this restriction for job creation purposes. It permits state loans or loan guarantees to not-for-profit entities of up to a total of $50 million for the construction or rehabilitation of manufacturing facilities (but not retail space or hotel accommodations) to create employment in depressed areas. This subsection was the constitutional basis for the state Job Development Authority (JDA).

Further amendments to Articles VII and X in 1969, 1973, 1977, 1981, 1985, and 1991 increased the scope of the agency and its borrowing authority. (Other proposed amendments to increase the JDA's borrowing authority passed the legislature but failed at the polls in 1967, 1977, and 1979.) The total limit of potential loans grew by increments, reaching the current $900 million level in 1991 (see Article X, Section 8). Currently, the Authority may loan up to 60 percent of the costs of qualifying acquisition, rehabilitation, or improvement projects (secured as specified in the Constitution), and guarantee bank loans for realty or machinery and equipment for up to 80 percent of their cost.

Gifts and Loans by Localities. Article VIII, Section 1, in a manner similar to the restriction on the state, bars localities from giving or loaning money, property, or credit to a private person, corporation, association, or undertaking. It has been a widespread local government practice to find ways around this restriction (for example, by receiving some consideration to avoid a governmental contribution as a "gift"). Localities also may not take ownership in the stocks or bonds of a private corporation or association.

Formation of Corporations. Article X, Section 1, added in 1846, allows the formation of corporations by general law and not by special act except where, "in the judgment of the legislature, the objects of the corporation cannot be attained under general laws." An earlier provision required an extraordinary majority of two-thirds of the members of each house to create a corporation by special act. The legislature retains regulatory power over corporations by the provision that "All general laws and special acts passed pursuant to this section may be altered from time to time, or repealed."

Chartering of Banks. Article X, Section 3, dating to 1846 and amended in 1874 and 1983, reflects a special fear of abuse in that era in the chartering of banks. It prohibits the legislature from chartering banks by special act, its power to charter other corporations in this manner notwithstanding. Additionally, the article requires the legislature to "conform all charters of savings banks, savings and loan associations, or institutions for saving, to a uniformity of powers, rights and liabilities." The 1983 change placed savings and loan associations within the scope of this article, and removed restrictions on the issuance of capital stock by savings banks and institutions and restrictions on trustees from sharing in bank profits.

Corporations' Powers and Liability. Article X, Sections 2 and 4, deal with corporate liability, the definition of corporations, and their right to sue and be sued. They are currently regarded as of little practical import because of the development of state law and the adoption, after these provisions were added to the New York Constitution, of the equal protection clause of the Fourteenth Amendment of the United States Constitution.

Taxation of Certain Corporations. Article XVI, Sections 3 and 4, prohibit the taxation of undistributed corporate profit and bar discrimination by the state between U.S. chartered corporations and other corporations doing "substantially similar" business in New York. Section 4 was added in 1938 specifically to ensure that proposed bank taxes that might discourage out-of-state deposits could not be imposed on New York chartered banks.

Historical Origin of the Provisions

With the exception of the Bill of Rights, few restrictions were placed on the statute-making powers of the state legislature until 1846 when voters adopted a new Constitution containing provisions relative to state finance and corporations.

Commencing in 1790, the state legislature provided financial assistance to private corporations undertaking public works that were unable to secure adequate private financing. State grants and loans of credit enabled private firms to construct canals, railroads, and highways, and state grants were used to help finance banks. The state's credit, for example, was pledged as support for bonds issued by railroad companies in exchange for mortgages on railroad properties. Lacking a reserve fund to pay interest or bond principal, railroad companies defaulted on most of their state-supported bonds during the financial panic of 1836-1837, and the state legislature was forced to levy a special tax to obtain funds to meet the state's obligation to bondholders.

This period was the era of Jacksonian Democracy. The state's fiscal problems, public disapproval of grants and pledges of state credit to benefit private firms or entrepreneurs, and demands for democratization of state government combined to produce public pressure on the state legislature to call a constitutional convention. It drafted the new Constitution that was ratified by the voters in 1846. Included in that Constitution was a section (Article VIII, Section 1) relating to the chartering of private corporations.

Although Section 9 of Article VII of the new Constitution stipulated "the credit of the State shall not, in any manner, be given or loaned to, or in aid of, any individual, association, or corporation," the state legislature was able to evade the prohibition and gave or loaned money to private corporations, particularly sectarian charities and railroads.

Continuing citizen unhappiness with the state legislature resulted in the convening in 1867-68 of the first constitutional convention called by the voters. The Convention drafted a new document and submitted it in two parts to the voters who in 1869 ratified only the judicial article. The rejected part included a section requiring a two-thirds vote in each house to appropriate money for other than "purposes of government."

In 1872, Governor John T. Hoffman, with Senate approval, appointed a constitutional commission, which recommended that many of the provisions of the rejected part of the proposed Constitution be placed on the referendum ballot by the state legislature. Six proposed amendments were ratified by the voters in 1874, including one prohibiting the giving or loaning of its money or credit by the state legislature or a local governing body to aid any private organization or individual with stated exceptions. The state legislature could make grants or loan its credit ". . . for the education and support of the blind, the deaf and dumb, and juvenile delinquents. . . ." Similarly, local governments were granted an exception relative to aiding the poor if authorized by the state legislature.

The present Constitution, adopted in 1894, continued the restriction on the giving or loaning of money or credit, but added an exception for the issuance of local government bonds for the purpose of water supply. Amendments ratified in 1938, 1964, and 1965 authorize additional exemptions from the constitutional prohibitions, but these amendments directly affect only certain classes of individuals and nonprivate business activities.

Impact Upon Private Business Activities

The restrictions contained in Section 17 of Article III have no major impact upon private business activities with the possible exception of the provisions preventing private firms from building and operating toll bridges.

The prohibition of the loan of the state's money or credit may have hindered the ability of the state to promote industrial development prior to 1961 when a constitutional amendment authorized a limited loan of such money or credit to a nonprofit corporation formed for the purpose of financing new manufacturing plants.

Until these restrictions were added to the new Constitution in 1846, the "public purpose" doctrine was the only constitutional limitation on the appropriation of funds of the state and local governments to private parties or entities. In 1855, the Court of Appeals opined that the state legislature has broad but not limitless authority to determine what are public purposes.[1]

The Association of the Bar of the City of New York in 1967 recommended that "except for a public purpose" be added to the current provisions concerning the gift or loan prohibition. The committee argued that ". . . an ever-expanding concept of governmental function and technique has required and will continue to require the kind of constant reevaluation of the doctrine which only a broad constitutional phrase, like 'public purpose,' can authorize without the constant recourse to constitutional amendment which has so long plagued the present Section 1 of Article VIII and Section 8 of Article VII."[2]

The current provision relative to the formation of corporations in effect allows the state legislature to determine when a private corporation should be formed by a special act instead of a general act as the provision only expresses a preference for incorporation by general law.

---

1 *Town of Guilford v. Supervisors of Chenango County*, 13 NY 143 (1855).

2 See Special Committee on the Constitutional Convention, *Local Government and Finance*, New York: The Association of the Bar of the City of New York, 1967, at p. 22.

The sentence authorizing the state legislature to amend or repeal a general or special law forming a corporation is attributable in origin to the Dartmouth College case in which the United States Supreme Court opined that the New Hampshire state legislature could not modify the royal charter establishing Dartmouth College because the charter was a contract protected by Section 10 of Article I of the United States Constitution.[3] The 1958 Inter-Law School report on the Constitution concluded that the dictum expressed in the Dartmouth College case had been superseded by the due process and equal protection clauses of the Fourteenth Amendment to the United States Constitution, and observed that federal and state courts in recent decades had allowed the state legislature to use the police power to promote the public interest in ways affecting contracts.[4]

Section 3 of Article X, dating to the Constitution of 1846, forbids the state legislature to charter a corporation for "banking purposes" by special law whereas the legislature in its wisdom can charter any other type of corporation by special law. This provision simply gave constitutional status to a law enacted in 1838 establishing a general method for incorporating banks.[5]

The part of the section dealing with savings banks was inserted in the Constitution by an 1874 amendment and was the product of concern that abuses were associated with the chartering of savings institutions and granting them different privileges. The state legislature had established uniform standards for chartering such institutions in 1869 and the amendment simply elevated the legislative policy to constitutional status.[6] The Inter-Law School Committee concluded in 1959 that there was "no need for preserving now the admonition that was already tardy when first given in 1874."[7]

Until 1983, Section 3 also forbade a savings bank from having capital stock and its trustees from sharing in the bank's profits or from having any interest "in any loan or use of any money or property" of the bank. The Inter-Law School Committee pointed out that these institutions were designed to be public service institutions serving the thrifty poor, but

---

3   *Trustees of Dartmouth College* v. *Woodward*, 4 Wheaton 518 (1819).

4   See Inter-Law School Committee, *Report on the Problem of Simplification of the Constitution*, Albany: Special Legislative Committee on the Revision and Simplification of the Constitution, 1958.

5   Chapter 260, Laws of 1838.

6   Chapter 213, Laws of 1869.

7   See Inter-Law School Committee, *Report on the Problem of Simplification*, Albany: Special Legislative Committee on the Revision and Simplification of the Constitution, 1958, at p. 113.

questioned whether "these matters of legislative detail, no matter how wisely conceived, should be embodied in the constitution."[8]

Proposals for Constitutional Change

Though efforts to ease the constitutional limits upon the state's capacity to aid private business have been relatively frequent in recent years, there is no active movement to amend or repeal the above provisions of the state Constitution relating to private business activities. The Business Council of the State of New York is unaware of any interest in the above constitutional provisions among its members.

1. *Delete Outmoded Provisions.* Observers have pointed out that a number of provisions are dead letters, including the prohibition of granting to a private individual or corporation the right to lay down railroad tracks. Similarly, as noted, the provision relative to the chartering of corporation by general law does not restrict the state legislature in using its judgment to charter a corporation by a special law. It is most unusual to have such provisions in a modern state constitution.

2. *Delete Unneeded Restrictions on the Legislature.* The Constitution proposed by the 1967 Constitutional Convention did not include the restrictions on the legislature's use of special acts contained in the current Section 17 of Article III, described above. Except for banking associations and corporations, general provisions relative to corporations were also removed.

The Constitution proposed in 1967 retained limits on the grant or loan of state resources to private persons, associations, or corporations, but following the recommendations contained in earlier studies an exception was made for "public purposes" (Article II, Section 18(a)). More generally, the draft Constitution gave authority to state government, local government, or public corporations to ". . . grant to any person, association or private corporation in any year or periodically by contract, or loan its money for economic and community development purposes . . ." (Article X, Section 12(a)) thus enhancing their discretion to act in the area of economic development.

The Model State Constitution, drafted by the National Municipal League (now National Civic League), reflects the best judgments of

---

8   *Ibid.,* pp. 113-14.

leading state constitutional experts and contains none of the restrictions on state and local government referred to above.[9]

---

9   See *Model State Constitution*, New York: National Municipal League, 1968. The League has moved its headquarters to Denver, CO.

Intergovernmental Relations

Richard Briffault

Principal Themes and Provisions

There are four principal themes concerning local government in the New York State Constitution: (a) local popular control of local governments; (b) the authority of local governments to adopt laws concerning local matters, and the authority of the state legislature to adopt laws concerning local governments; (c) the formation and restructuring of local governments and intergovernmental cooperation; and (d) local finances. These themes are addressed primarily in Article IX, the so-called "home rule" article, and Article VIII, which regulates local finances.

Article IX defines "local government" to consist of counties, cities, towns, and villages. It does not include school districts, special districts, or public authorities (Article IX, Section 3(d)(2)). It declares "effective local self-government and intergovernmental cooperation are purposes of the people of the state"; creates a "Bill of Rights" for local governments; provides local governments with local lawmaking authority; sets forth the legislature's power to create and organize local governments; and addresses the power of the legislature to act with respect to local matters.

In contrast, most of the provisions of Article VIII apply to school districts as well as to counties, cities, towns, and villages. It restricts the purposes of local spending, lending, and lending of credit; determines how local governments may incur debt; and sets limits on the amount of local debt and on the amount of revenue local governments may raise from the tax on real estate.

Other provisions affecting local governments are scattered throughout the Constitution, including Article III, Section 17 (restrictions on legislature's power to pass private or local bills); Article X (Corporations); Article XIII (Public Officers); Article XVI (Taxation); and Article XVIII (Housing).

Local Control of Local Government

The first two provisions of the first section of Article IX establish the principle of local popular control of local government. Section 1(a) provides that every local government "shall have a legislative body elective by the people thereof" and "shall have the power to adopt local laws as provided by this article." In Section 1(b), Article IX provides that all officers of every local government, the selection of whom is not otherwise provided for in the Constitution, shall be elected by the people or appointed by the officers of the local government "as may be provided by law."

Local control over local officers is, however, somewhat limited by Article XIII. Section 3 authorizes the legislature to provide for filling vacancies; Section 5 authorizes the legislature to provide for removal from office for misconduct; and Section 8 provides that city officers are to be elected in odd-numbered years. Section 13 addresses the terms, powers and duties, and removal of certain county officers, including the sheriff, the county clerk, the register, and district attorney. Section 14 authorizes the legislature to regulate and fix the wages, hours, and health and safety conditions of local public employees and contractors or subcontractors performing work for local governments.

Home Rule: Local Legislative Powers and State Legislation With Respect to Local Governments

Home rule consists of both the grant of power to local governments and the restriction of the state legislature's power to act concerning local matters. The Constitution expressly grants local governments certain powers; it authorizes the legislature to grant local governments additional powers; and it limits the ways in which the legislature may act in relation to local matters.

1. *Direct Constitutional Grant of Authority to Local Governments:* Article IX, Section 1 — the "bill of rights for local governments" — gives localities the power to take private property by eminent domain within their boundaries (Article IX, Section 1(e)). Section 2 provides local governments with the "power to adopt and amend local laws not inconsistent with the provisions of this constitution or any general law relating to its property affairs, or government" (Article IX, Section 2(c)(i)). In addition, local governments can adopt and amend local laws "not inconsistent with the provisions of the constitution or any general law" with respect to ten enumer-

ated subjects whether or not they relate to local property affairs or government except that the legislature may restrict the adoption of local laws with respect to matters other than the property, affairs or government of a local government. The ten enumerated areas of local lawmaking, whether or not they relate to local property, affairs or government, are:

a. The powers, duties, qualifications, number, mode of selection and removal, terms of office, compensation, hours of work, protection, welfare, and safety of its officers and employees.

b. In the case of a city, town, or village, the membership and composition of its legislative body.

c. The transaction of its business.

d. The incurring of its obligations.

e. The presentation, ascertainment, and discharge of claims against it.

f. The acquisition, care, management, and use of its highways, roads, streets, avenues, and property.

g. The acquisition of its transit facilities and the ownership and operation thereof.

h. The levy, collection, and administration of local taxes authorized by the legislature and of assessments for local improvements, consistent with laws enacted by the legislature.

i. The wages or salaries, the hours of work or labor, and the protection, welfare, and safety of persons employed by any contractor or subcontractor performing work, labor or services for it.

j. The government, protection, order, conduct, safety, health, and well-being of persons or property therein. (Article IX, Section 2(c)(ii)).

Article IX, Section 3 provides that the "rights, powers, privileges and immunities granted to local governments" by Article IX "shall be liberally construed."

2. *Authorization to Grant Additional Powers*: Article IX, Section 2, also provides that the legislature "shall enact" a "statute of local governments" granting local governments additional powers "including but not limited to" matters of local legislation and administration. A power granted in the statute of local governments can be repealed or reduced only by a law passed and approved by the governor in each of two successive calendar years (Article IX, Section 2(b)(1)). The legislature may also confer on local governments powers not relating to their property, affairs, or government and not limited to local legislation and administration "in addition to those otherwise granted by or pursuant to this article" and it may withdraw or restrict such additional powers (Article IX, Section 2(b)(3)).

    Other constitutional provisions authorize the legislature to grant additional powers to local governments, including the power to apportion the cost of a government service or function upon any portion of the area within the local government's jurisdiction and exercise of eminent domain outside local boundaries (Article IX, Section 1(e)(g)). Article XVIII authorizes the legislature to grant various powers to cities, towns, and villages for the financing of low-rent housing and nursing home accommodations for persons of low income.

3. *Restriction on Legislative Power to Act With Respect to Local Matters*: Article IX also limits the power of the legislature to act in relation to the "property, affairs, or government" of local governments in Section 2. It can pass general laws relating to local property, affairs, or government. A law is "general" if "in terms and in effect" it applies alike to all counties, all cities, all towns, or all villages. The legislature may act in relation to the property, affairs, or government of a local government by special law — that is, by a law "which in terms and in effect applies to one or more, but not all" counties, cities, towns, or villages — *only* (a) on request of two-thirds of the membership of the local legislative body or of the local chief executive officer concurred in by a majority of the membership of the local legislature — a so-called "home rule request"; or (b) on certificate of necessity from the governor "reciting facts which in his judgment constitute an emergency requiring enactment of such law" and with the concurrence of two-thirds of each house of the legislature. The second option — the governor's message and legislative super-majority

— is unavailable for special laws concerning New York City (Article IX, Section 2(b)(2)).

In addition, the "bill of rights" bars the legislature from prohibiting any local government from making a fair return on the value of property used in a public utility service or from using utility profits to pay refunds to consumers or "any other lawful purpose" (Article IX, Section 1(f)).

More generally, Section 3 provides that nothing in Article IX shall restrict or impair the power of the legislature to act in relation to "the maintenance, support or administration of the public school system" (including any retirement system relating to a public school system); the courts; or matters other than the property, affairs, or government of a local government.

Local Government Formation, Restructuring, and Cooperation

1. *Formation of Local Governments:* Article IX, Section 2(a), provides that the "legislature shall provide for the creation and organization of local governments in such manner as shall secure to them the rights, powers, privileges, and immunities granted to them by this constitution." The Constitution contains no other general standards or procedures for the formation of local governments, but it does provide some restrictions.

Article III, Section 5, prohibits the formation of a new county unless it has a sufficient population to entitle it to an Assembly seat.[1] Article III, Section 17 bars the incorporation of villages by "private or local bill."[2] There is no similar ban on the formation of other local governments, and Article X, Section 1 exempts "corporations . . . for municipal purposes" from the general ban on the creation of corporations by special act.[3] Article X, Section 5, provides that no public corporation (other than a county, city, town, village, school district, fire district, or improvement district) possessing both the power to contract indebtedness and the power to collect rentals, charges, rates, or fees for services

---

1   The same provision explicitly exempts Hamilton County from the requirement that every county be large enough to have one seat in the Assembly.

2   Twelve villages are currently incorporated under special charters. These apparently predate the adoption of the constitutional ban on such special charters. In addition, six other villages were first incorporated by special charters and then reincorporated under general law.

3   All the cities in New York have been incorporated by special laws.

furnished by it shall be created except by a special act of the legislature.

2. *Restructuring Local Government:* (a) *Boundary Change.* The local government "bill of rights" provides that no territory of any local government shall be annexed without (i) the consent of the people, in a referendum, of the area proposed for annexation, and (ii) the approval of the governing board of each local government whose area is affected by the annexation.[4] The legislature must provide for judicial review, applying an "over-all public interest" standard, of the refusal of a local governing board to consent to an annexation (Article IX, Section 1(d)).

(b) *Change in Form of County Government and Transfer of Function.* The "bill of rights" also directs that counties shall be empowered by general law, or special law enacted upon county request, to adopt, amend, or repeal alternative forms of county government provided by the legislature or to prepare, adopt, or repeal alternative forms of their own. Any such change of form of government may entail the transfer of functions or duties of the county or of any local government unit within the county and the abolition of local offices, departments, agencies, or units of government. However, no change in the form of county government can become effective unless approved in a referendum by both (i) a majority of the votes in the county cast outside of cities and (ii) a majority of the votes cast in the cities of the county considered as a unit. Moreover, if an alternative form of government involves the transfer of a function from a village, or the abolition of a village office, the double referendum becomes a triple referendum. Changes affecting villages must be approved in a referendum of a majority of the votes cast in all the villages so affected, considered as one unit (Article IX, Section 1(h)(1)).[5]

3. *Intergovernmental Cooperation:* Article IX provides that local governments shall have the power to agree, "as authorized by act of the legislature," with the federal, state, or one or more local governments within the state "to provide cooperatively, jointly

---

4 The consent of the governing board of a county is required only where a boundary of the county is affected.

5 After the adoption of an alternative form of county government, any subsequent amendment, by either state or local law, which abolishes or creates an elective county office, changes the voting or veto power or the method of removal of a county officer during his term, transfers his function to another county officer or agency, or changes the form or composition of the county legislature shall be subject to a permissive referendum, as provided by state law. (Article IX, Section (1)(h)(2)).

or by contract any facility, service, activity or undertaking which each participating local government has the power to provide separately." In so doing, each participating local government "shall have power to apportion its share of the cost thereof upon such portion of its area as may be authorized by act of the legislature." (Article IX, Section 1(c)).

Two sections of Article VIII address the financing of inter-local cooperative and contractual projects. Section 1 provides an exemption from the general constitutional ban on a local government's giving or lending its credit by allowing two or more local governments[6] to "join together pursuant to law in providing any municipal facility, service, activity or undertaking which each of such units has the power to provide separately." In financing such joint projects each involved local government may contract joint or several indebtedness, pledge its faith and credit for the payment of the indebtedness of the joint undertaking, and levy real estate or other taxes or charges.[7] In addition, Article VIII, Section 2(a), enables the legislature to authorize any county, city, town, or village to incur indebtedness to provide water supply or sewage treatment, and disposal in amounts greater than the local government's own needs so that the locality may sell the excess capacity to any other public corporation or improvement district. Further, the legislature may authorize any two or more public corporations and improvement districts to provide for such facilities in common and to contract joint indebtedness for such purposes (or to contract indebtedness for specific proportions of the cost).

Local Finances

Home rule concepts do not apply to local finances. Local governments are dependent upon the legislature for the power to tax. Local spending, borrowing, and taxing are tightly regulated by the Constitution and subject to the plenary power of the legislature to impose further restrictions.

1. *Restrictions on Local Spending and Lending:* Article VIII, Section 1, contains two important prohibitions. First, no local government may give or loan any money or property to or in aid of

---

6   Article VIII, Section 1 includes school districts in the category of local governments that can incur indebtedness to finance joint undertakings.

7   The legislature is empowered to regulate the amount of such indebtedness and the manner in which it is incurred, and to provide a method for allocating and apportioning such debts among the local governments participating in a joint project.

any individual, private corporation or association, or private undertaking, or become the owner of the stock or bonds of any private corporation or association. Second, no local government may give or loan its credit in aid of any individual, public or private corporation or association, or private undertaking.

There are numerous exceptions to these prohibitions. As noted in the discussion of interlocal cooperation, two or more localities may join together pursuant to law in providing any municipal facility, service, activity, or undertaking that each has the power to provide separately. In addition, Article VIII, Section 1, makes numerous exemptions for health and welfare programs and for the payment of pensions and benefits to certain public employees and their survivors. Further, Article XVIII allows the legislature to authorize cities, towns, and villages to make payments to, and guarantee the debts of, public corporations that provide housing facilities or nursing home accommodations, and to make loans to the owners of existing multiple dwellings for their rehabilitation and improvement.[8]

2. *Restrictions on Local Borrowing:* Article VIII also restricts how local governments contract debt, and imposes limitations on the amount of local debt.

(a) *Restrictions on Contracting Local Indebtedness.* Local governments may contract debt only for local public purposes (or as part of cooperative projects with other local governments). No debt shall be contracted for longer than the period of probable usefulness of the object or purpose for which the debt is incurred, to be determined by state law, but in no event greater than forty years. No debt may be contracted unless the local contract "shall have pledged its faith and credit for the principal thereof and the interest thereon." Local debts are to be repaid in annual installments starting no more than two years after the debt was contracted (Article VIII, Section 2).

Article VIII also regulates the time and method of repayment of debts. It provides for local sinking funds, subject to such requirements as the legislature shall impose by general or special law, and for annual local appropriations into the sinking funds to cover the cost of servicing the debt. Debt service is made the first claim on local revenues (Article VIII, Section 2).

---

8   For further detail see the chapter "Social Policy" in this book.

(b) *Limitations on the Amount of Local Indebtedness.* Article VIII, Section 4, provides that no county, city, town, village, or school district shall contract debt for any purpose if such debt, taken together with existing debt, shall exceed an amount equal to the following percentages of the full valuation of taxable real estate in such locality:

- ❋ New York City — 10 percent.
- ❋ Nassau County — 9 percent.
- ❋ Cities with population greater than 125,000, other than New York City — 9 percent.
- ❋ Counties other than Nassau — 7 percent.
- ❋ Cities with population under 125,000 — 7 percent.
- ❋ Towns — 7 percent.
- ❋ Villages — 7 percent.
- ❋ School districts wholly or partly within cities with populations under 125,000 — 5 percent, but this limit can be increased with the approval of (i) 60 percent of local voters in a referendum; (ii) the Regents; and (iii) the Comptroller.[9]
- ❋ There is no constitutional debt limit for school districts wholly outside cities.[10]

The full valuation tax base that is used to calculate the debt limit is the average of the local valuation for the five preceding years. Indebtedness contracted by smaller cities for education purposes is excluded from those cities' limits and assigned to the appropriate school districts.

Generally exempt from the debt limitations are: short-term debt (to be repaid within two years); debt contracted for the supply of water or for sewage treatment and disposal projects; debt contracted for a self-supporting local public improvement or service district; and debts related to certain local pension or retirement systems (Article VIII, Section 5). There are also certain specific historic exemptions from the limits for particular debts of Buffalo, Rochester, Syracuse, and New York City (Article VIII, Sections 6, 7, 7(a)).

In addition, Article XVIII empowers the legislature to authorize any city, town, or village (but not counties) to contract

---

9 For further detail see the chapter on "Education" in this book.

10 There are no independent school districts operating in cities with populations greater than 125,000.

indebtedness in an amount up to 2 percent of the local assessed valuation for low-income housing and slum clearance projects. For cities and villages, this 2 percent debt may be in addition to the debt limit imposed by Article VIII, provided that these municipalities levy a tax, other than an *ad valorem* tax on real estate, sufficient to provide for the payment of the principal and interest of the debt. Note that in Article XVIII the debt limit is calculated based on a five-year average of *assessed* valuation, whereas the Article VIII debt limit is based on the five-year average of full valuation.

Further, Article XVI, Section 6, provides that the legislature may authorize local governments to incur debt to redevelop "economically unproductive, blighted or deteriorated areas" through tax increment financing. A locality may pledge for the payment of a redevelopment project's debt "that portion of the taxes raised by it on real estate in such area which, in any year, is attributed to the increase in value of taxable real estate resulting from such redevelopment." Such redevelopment debt may be excluded from the debt limitations of Article VIII.

3. *Restrictions on Local Taxation:* (a) *The Power to Tax.* As noted, the power to tax is not one of the home rule powers of local government. Indeed, Article XVI expressly provides that the "power of taxation shall never be surrendered, suspended or contracted away" and any state laws that delegate the taxing power "shall specify the types of taxes which may be imposed thereunder and provide for their review." This prohibits blanket enabling acts empowering localities to impose taxes at their own discretion. In addition, exemptions from taxation may only be granted by general laws (Article XVI, Section 1).

(b) *The Property Tax.* The principal tax delegated to local governments is the *ad valorem* tax on property. The legislature must provide for the supervision, review, and equalization of assessments for purposes of taxation; assessment "shall in no case exceed full value." (Article XVI, Section 2). *Ad valorem* taxation of intangible personal property is forbidden (Article XVI, Section 3), as is any alteration or repeal of the exemptions from taxation of real or personal property used exclusively for religious, educational, or charitable purposes and owned by a corporation or association organized for one of those purposes and not operating for profit (Article XVI, Section 1).

(c) *Limitations on the Amount of Real Property Tax Levies.*
Article VIII, Section 10, imposes limits on the amount of real
property taxation by most local governments. Like the debt limits,
the property tax limits are calculated based on a rolling five-year
average of full valuation of taxable real estate within the jurisdiction. The limits are:

* ❋ New York City: 2.5 percent
* ❋ Other cities with population greater than 125,000: 2.0
  percent
* ❋ All other cities: 2.0 percent.
* ❋ Counties: 1.5 percent (which the legislature may raise
  to 2 percent).
* ❋ Villages: 2.0 percent.
* ❋ There are no limits on town taxation.

Local governments subject to tax limits may make appropriations for capital expenditures or improvements for which they
might otherwise borrow and exclude the taxes raised for such
appropriations from the tax limits. In effect, property taxes for
capital expenditures are not under the constitutional limit. For
New York City, however, such appropriations for capital purposes
are counted against the debt limit.

To protect the tax and debt limitations, Article VIII, Section
3, provides that "no municipal or other corporation (other than a
county, city, town, village, school district or fire district, or a river
improvement, river regulating, or drainage district established by
or under the supervision of the department of conservation)
possessing the power (a) to contract indebtedness and (b) to levy
taxes or benefit assessments upon real estate or to require the levy
of such taxes or assessments shall be created." Counties and
towns, however, may create improvement districts provided that
the county or town pledges its faith and credit for the improvement
district's debts, and the debts are counted against the county's or
town's debt limit.

Moreover, nothing in Article VIII shall be construed to
prevent the legislature "from further restricting" local powers
with respect to contracting indebtedness or levying taxes on real
estate (Article VIII, Section 12).

History

Home Rule

Article IX, though adopted in its present form in 1963, has antecedents in New York's constitutional history.

1. *Local Control of Local Officers.* The concern for local control of local officers may be seen in the Constitution of 1777, which, although it did not grant local elections, confirmed that town officers should continue to be elected by the people (Section 20). The Constitution of 1821 (Article IV, Section 15) extended the practice of filling local offices by election to counties, cities, and villages. The Constitution of 1846 provided for the local election or appointment of local officers whose selection was not provided for in the Constitution — the forerunner of the current provision. The 1894 Constitution prohibited the legislature from transferring the local functions performed by locally elected officials at that time from those officials.

2. *Home Rule.* Home rule was a major issue in New York State for much of the nineteenth century. Constitutional provisions adopted in 1874 foreclosed local bills and required general laws in some areas of concern to cities. The first more general constitutional provision for a measure of home rule, adopted in 1894, resulted from reactions, especially in New York City, to legislative interference with city governance.[11] The 1894 Constitution's home rule provision, applicable to cities only, embraced two concepts that shaped all subsequent constitutional restrictions on legislative power to act concerning local matters. First, it sought to protect cities' "property, affairs, and government" from legislative meddling. Second, it focused on the legislature's ability to act by special laws, e.g., those targeted on some subset of local governments. (Note that the Constitution has never restricted the legislature's power to use general laws to affect local property, affairs or government.)

    The 1894 Constitution divided cities into three classes based on population; a special law was one that related to less than all cities in a class. A special law relating to the property, affairs, and government of a city had to be submitted to the city's

---

11   For historical background see Gerald Benjamin and Charles Brecher (eds.), *The Two New Yorks*, New York: Russell Sage, 1988, at pp. 114-123.

mayor, who had 15 days to determine whether or not the city accepted it. If the city accepted the bill, it would be submitted to the governor; if not, the legislature would have to re-pass the bill before it could be submitted to the governor. The mayor, thus, had a "suspensory veto." The charter of the greater City of New York was passed over such a suspensory veto in 1897.

The 1923 Home Rule Amendment revised the limitation on the legislature's authority to pass special laws relating to cities, and provided the first constitutional grant of local lawmaking authority. It provided that the legislature could pass a special law relating to a city's property, affairs, or government only on a message from the governor declaring that an emergency existed, and then only with a two-thirds vote in each house of the legislature. Moreover, the 1923 amendment gave cities power to adopt local laws relating to a number of distinctly local matters; the legislature was authorized to confer upon cities by general laws such further power of local legislation and administration as it deemed expedient.

Amendments adopted in 1938 extended home rule to counties, and the legislature was directed to extend it to villages of more than 5,000 people by 1940. Local legislative power was widened to include the entire area of local "property, affairs or government." This made home-rule-as-local-legislative-power coextensive with home-rule-as-protection-from-special-laws. The provision for protection from legislative interference was revised. All special laws relating to local property, affairs, or government would require the approval of two-thirds of each house of the legislature. Moreover, no special law concerning a city could be adopted without a local request; no special law concerning a county could be adopted without both a local request and a gubernatorial message of necessity; and no special law concerning a home rule village could be adopted without either a local request or a gubernatorial message.

Article IX in its current form, adopted as noted in 1963, extended home rule to towns and to all villages. It added the express declaration that "effective local self-government and intergovernmental cooperation are purposes of the people of this state," and most of the provisions in the Bill of Rights for local governments described above. Article IX expanded local legislative powers to include the ten enumerated subjects whether or not they were the property, affairs or government of local governments, and it authorized the Statute of Local Governments.

Article IX also revised the procedure for the adoption of special laws concerning local property, affairs or government to permit legislative action by a simple majority on a home rule request. The legislature may still act without a home rule request, but that requires a message of necessity from the governor and a two-thirds vote in each house. There is no procedure for legislative adoption of a special law concerning the property, affairs, or government of New York City without a home rule request.

Finally, Article IX adopts a rule of liberal construction of local rights, powers, privileges, and immunities — thereby repudiating Dillon's Rule, or the traditional judicial rule of interpretation that local powers are to be narrowly construed.

Local Finances

The first constitutional provision concerning local finances was adopted in 1846, when the legislature was given the mandate to restrict localities in "taxation, assessment, borrowing money, contracting debts, and loaning their credit, so as to prevent abuses in assessments, and in contracting debts." Much of this language has been carried forward into current Article VIII, Section 12. The provision was a response to the borrowing excesses of the 1820s and 1830s, especially for the financing of railroads and canals, which created a financial crisis for the state in the aftermath of the Panic of 1837. The 1846 measure prohibited the gift and loan of *state* funds, and the lending of *state* credit, to private activities, and restricted the *state's* power to incur indebtedness. It did not, however, impose restrictions on local governments. Thus, private enterprises, especially railroads, seeking public support turned to local governments.

In the aftermath of the Tweed Ring scandal, abuses in the local financing of railroads, and the Panic of 1873, the Constitution was amended in 1874 to prohibit municipalities from giving any money or property or lending their money or credit to private undertakings, except in aid of the poor. Reflecting concerns about the growth in the use of public benefit corporations, the 1938 amendments prohibited local governments from giving or lending their credit to public corporations.

In 1884, continued concern over the graft and corruption of the Tweed era, the overextension of local credit during periods of boom leading to subsequent defaults, and the increase in taxes caused by debt service obligations led to the adoption of the first debt and tax limitations. Debt was limited to 10 percent of local assessed valuation for cities with populations over 100,000 and for the counties in which they were located; real estate taxes were limited to 2 percent of local valuation. The 10 percent debt limit was extended to all cities and counties in 1894.

The local finance article was comprehensively revised in 1938 in response to the fiscal difficulties occasioned by the Depression. With respect to debt, the 1938 amendments required that local governments pledge their full faith and credit for the payment of the principal and interest on local indebtedness; assured bondholders of the first claim on all available local revenues; required that original or refunded debt be retired within the period of probable usefulness of the object or purpose for which it was contracted; imposed the restriction on the creation of new jurisdictions with powers to tax and incur debt; extended the debt limits to towns and villages; generally lowered the permissible debt percentage; and changed the base for the calculation of the debt limit from current assessed valuation to the five-year moving average. (The 1938 amendments also added Article XVIII and its special provisions for the financing of low-income housing and slum clearance projects.) In 1951, the base was changed from assessed valuation to full valuation, thereby substantially raising the debt limit; at the same time, the percentage limit was lowered for all the covered units except Nassau County and the big cities. Article VIII has been amended several times since 1938 — e.g., to permit borrowing by localities for common or cooperative purposes with other localities, and to exempt water supply and sewage projects from the debt limits — but the basic policies and structure of the debt limitations have not changed over the past 55 years.

The history of the limits on real property taxes parallels the evolution of the debt limits. As noted, the first tax limits were adopted in 1884, and applied just to large urban counties. In 1938, the limits were made applicable to all cities and to villages; and the base was changed from annual assessed value to a five-year average. This was designed to prevent rapid fluctuations in taxing power during times of recession. In order to provide relative equality of treatment with areas served by independent school districts, the legislature was empowered to exclude amounts raised for educational purposes from the limitations applying to cities with fewer than 100,000 people and to villages. Where a school district was wholly or partly within a city, the property tax levy raised within the city for educational purposes was excluded from the city's limit. By this time, personal property had been removed from the property tax base by statute, and another 1938 amendment prohibited the *ad valorem* taxation of intangible personal property and the alteration of charitable exemptions.

In 1949, the base for the tax limit was changed from assessed valuation to full valuation, effectively increasing the limit, and a 1½ percent limit was imposed on counties, with the proviso that the legislature could raise it to 2 percent. In 1953, the limit for New York City and its component counties was set at 2½ percent. With other slight modifications, the 1938 amendments continue to set the basic structure of local property tax limits.

Contemporary Meaning and Policy Consequences

Court of Appeals decisions in three critical areas — home rule, local government restructuring, and local finance — are critical in defining the meaning of the New York State Constitution's provisions concerning the state/local relationship.

Home Rule

1. *The Doctrine of State Concern:* Though it does not appear in the Constitution, the legal doctrine of "state concern" strongly affects the scope of local home rule. As noted, the Constitution appears to give local governments autonomy with respect to matters of local "property, affairs, or government" and to limit the power of the legislature to act with respect to such local matters by special law. The Court of Appeals, however, has long held that matters of state concern and questions of local property, affairs, or government are not mutually exclusive. That is, a matter may be of state concern even if it also affects local property, affairs, or government. As then-Chief Judge Benjamin Cardozo put it in the leading case of *Adler* v. *Deegan*, the state may legislate by special law — and without a home rule request, gubernatorial message, or legislative supermajority — "if the subject be in a substantial degree a matter of State concern . . . though intermingled with it are concerns of the locality."[12] The court has found that housing, local taxation, municipal sewers, planning and zoning, cultural institutions, and the residential mobility of municipal civil servants are all matters of state con-

---

12   *Adler* v. *Deegan*, 251 NY 467 (1929).

cern sufficient to sustain the state's power to legislate concerning these matters by special law without either a home rule request or a legislative supermajority.[13]

Although the state concern doctrine long predates the adoption of Article IX, the scope of the doctrine has been largely unaffected by the new home rule provision. Indeed, the Court of Appeals has continued to apply the state concern doctrine vigorously over the last three decades, notwithstanding the apparent intent of Article IX to expand local autonomy. Thus, as long as the state is able to make a colorable case that it is acting with respect to a matter of state concern, the constitutional home rule provision provides little restriction on the legislature's ability to act by special law.

2. *Conflict and Preemption:* The sources of home rule authority generally provide that local enactments must not be inconsistent with the Constitution or general laws. In other words, although a subject may fall within the grant of home rule authority, local action may be preempted by state law. It will often be difficult to tell, however, whether state and local laws are inconsistent.

There are two strands to contemporary preemption doctrine: outright conflict and occupation of the field.

(a) *Outright conflict* focuses on whether the state and local governments have issued conflicting commands. A clear case of conflict would be a statute requiring a motorist to drive on the right side of the road and a local ordinance requiring that she drive on the left. The motorist cannot comply with both laws at the same time. Most state-local conflicts, however, are more subtle than this. The most difficult issue is whether a limited state prohibition conflicts with a local measure extending that prohibition to conduct the state left alone.

Thus, in the 1962 case *Wholesale Laundry Board of Trade, Inc. v. City of New York,* the court held that New York City's local law setting a minimum wage in the city of $1.25 an hour was in conflict with the state's $1.00 minimum wage. As the Appellate

---

13 See, e.g., *Adler v. Deegan, supra* (multiple dwelling law for New York City); *New York Steam Corp.* v. *City of New York,* 268 NY 137 (1935) (local taxation); *Robertson* v. *Zimmerman,* 268 NY 52 (1938) (Buffalo Sewer Authority); *Floyd v. Urban Development Corporation* 33 NY 2d 1 (1973) (housing, planning, and zoning); *Wambat Realty Corp.* v. *State,* 41 NY 2d 490 (Adirondack Park and local zoning); *Hotel Dorset Co.* v. *Trust for Cultural Resources,* 46 NY 2d 358 (1978) (special legislation to aid the Museum of Modern Art); *Uniformed Firefighters Ass'n* v. *City of New York,* 50 NY 2d 85 (1980) (legislature's restrictions on City's power to require local residency for certain public employees).

Division, in an opinion subsequently adopted by the Court of Appeals, put it, "[g]enerally speaking, local laws which do not prohibit what the State law permits nor allow what the State law forbids are not inconsistent. . . . However, where the extension of the principle of the State law by means of the local law results in a situation where what would be permissible under State law becomes a violation of the local law, the latter law is unauthorized."[14] The effect of a *Wholesale Laundry* approach is to narrow local lawmaking autonomy significantly. If any limited state prohibition is held to constitute an affirmative authorization of all conduct not prohibited, then, once the state has passed a law on a subject all local action that goes beyond mere duplication of the state would be preempted.

In recent years, the courts appear to have recognized the narrowing effect of such an approach and have tended to reject a finding of outright conflict when the locality adopted a more extensive regulation than the state. Thus, in 1987, in *New York State Clubs Association* v. *City of New York*, the Court of Appeals upheld New York City's ban on discrimination in certain private clubs even though such discrimination had been exempted from the antidiscrimination requirements of the state's human rights law.[15] Similarly, in *Council for Owner Occupied Housing, Inc* v. *Koch*, New York City's requirements that the sponsor of a cooperative conversion establish a reserve fund for capital repairs and post notice of the building's housing code violations were sustained notwithstanding the argument that the state's law governing cooperative conversion did not include these rules, and that since the city law would prohibit conversions the state law would allow the city's law was "inconsistent" with the state's. The court found that "silence on this issue should not be interpreted as an expression of intent by the legislature. To interpret a statute in that manner would vitiate the concept of home rule."[16]

Although a concern for home rule appears to be leading the courts to avoid finding that more extensive local laws automatically conflict with state regulation, the doctrine in this area is far

---

14   17 A.D. 2d. 327, 234 NYS 862, 864-65 (1st Department 1960), *aff'd*, 12 NY 2d 998, 239 NYS 2d 128 (1963).

15   69 NY 2d 211 (1987).

16   61 NY 2d 942 (1983).

from clearly settled. The concern that local ordinances may be inconsistent with state law may chill local initiatives.

(b) *"Occupation of the field"* is the second strand in pre-emption. Although the courts may be less inclined to find that a state law constitutes affirmative permission of all conduct not proscribed — so that additional local law would be in conflict — they have also refused to endorse the logical converse; that is, that local legislation will be held "inconsistent" with state law only when the state has explicitly banned local lawmaking. Preemption, the Court of Appeals said in *Consolidated Edison v. Town of Red Hook*, "need not be expressed. It is enough that the Legislature has impliedly evinced its desire to do so."[17] It is through the tension between the principles that state law is not automatically preemptive of local initiative, but that state law may be preemptive even when preemption is not officially declared in the statute, that the doctrine of preemption by implication, or occupation of the field, has developed.

The courts have treated the question of whether the state has occupied the field, thereby precluding local lawmaking, as a question of interpreting the intent of the state legislature. They have relied on two indicators to divine the legislature's intent: statements of legislative policy and the scope of the state's regulatory scheme. These criteria, however, have often proven to be uncertain guides. The legislature rarely makes a clear declaration of policy. The courts therefore have no clear standard for determining whether the extent and nature of state regulation of an area is "comprehensive," and therefore preemptive, or "piecemeal," and therefore not preemptive. The result is ad hoc judicial decision making and considerable uncertainty as to when state legislation will be considered preemptive of local action.

The combination of the state concern and preemption doctrines may narrow local home rule considerably. In theory, the Constitution gives local governments broad powers to act and limits the state's power to act on local matters to general laws. But under the doctrine of state concern, the legislature can adopt special laws with respect to most matters, including local property, affairs, or government. Such laws can preempt inconsistent local laws either through a finding of outright conflict or a

---

17   60 NY 2d 99 (1983).

determination that the state has occupied the field. This possibility of preemption casts a shadow over local autonomy, often leading local governments to question whether they have the authority to act. As a result, local governments may fail to exercise fully their constitutional home rule powers.

On the other hand, the state can provide for a form of "reverse preemption" — that is, state laws, that provide general rules for local governments but which provide that localities can adopt alternative rules in lieu of the state's. Thus, a number of provisions of the Municipal Home Rule Law allow towns and villages to supersede various general provisions of the Town Law and Village Law. These supersession statutes do grant real home rule powers to towns and villages but they can be repealed by ordinary legislation.[18]

3. *County Charters and Local Officers:* One area in which the adoption of Article IX appears to have led to a modest expansion in local autonomy has been the power of counties with respect to county officers. Relying on the provisions of Article IX, Section 1(h), concerning county power to adopt alternative forms of county government, the courts upheld the power of a county to authorize the setting of real property tax equalization rates by the county executive rather than by the board of assessors, as provided by the state's Real Property Law;[19] to shorten the term of the sheriff by merging that office with another office;[20] and to provide for the filling of vacancies in the office of county legislator in a manner inconsistent with the state's County Law.[21] More importantly, in *Resnick v. County of Ulster*, the Court of Appeals extended to noncharter counties the power to provide for the filling of vacancies in county office, despite an inconsistent provision of state law. The court relied on the general "bill of rights" principle of local power to select local officers, rather than on the specific provision dealing with alternative county charters.[22]

On the other hand, in *Matter of Kelly v. McGee*,[23] the Court of Appeals sustained state legislation concerning the salaries of

---

18   See Peter J. Galie, *The New York State Constitution: A Reference Guide*, Westport, CT: Greenwood Press, 1991, at p. 219.

19   *Matter of Heimbach v. Mills*, 67 A.D.2d 731 (1979).

20   *Westchester County Civil Service Employees Ass'n v. Del Bello*, 47 NY 2d 886 (1979).

21   *Nydick v. Suffolk County Legislature*, 36 NY 2d 951 (1975).

22   44 NY 2d 279 (1978).

23   57 NY 2d 279 (1978).

district attorneys. The court determined that although district attorneys are local officers, the adequacy of the salary for that office implicates the state's concern for the enforcement of the state's laws. Similarly, in *Carey v. Oswego County Legislature*, the court upheld the governor's exclusive right under state law to appoint an interim district attorney.[24] Arguably, these cases suggest a judicial inclination to treat local law enforcement as a matter of state concern, while granting counties greater autonomy with respect to the structure of county government. One commentator, however, has suggested that the district attorney cases "severely limited" the significance of the earlier county officer decisions.[25] In any event, the relationship between local power to determine terms and duties of local officers and state power over the same subject is not clearly resolved.

Local Restructuring

The provisions of Article IX make certain forms of local restructuring difficult. The annexation provision requires the consent of both the people of the area proposed for annexation and of the governing boards of affected local governments. Although the refusal to consent of affected local governments can be overcome by judicial review, the need for an affirmative vote in referendum of the people in the area proposed for referendum is an absolute requirement. Similarly, the double referendum requirement for the adoption of an alternative county charter, and the triple referendum requirement for the transfer of functions from villages to the county or other local governments is also a barrier to local government restructuring.

Local Finance

1. *Lack of Local Autonomy:* Among the striking features of New York's intergovernmental relations is the relative lack of local autonomy with respect to fiscal matters. Local governments have no constitutionally based power to levy taxes other than the tax on real property. If a local government seeks an additional source of revenue, or to raise the rate of any nonproperty tax the legislature previously authorized it to levy, it must go to Albany for the necessary authority. At the same time, local governments have no power to resist the state's imposition of new functions or service

---

24   59 NY 2d 847 (1983).

25   See Galie, *supra*, at pp. 220-21.

delivery requirements on them or to require that the state supply the funds necessary to meet the costs of such new mandates.

2. *Tax Limits:* The constitutional limits on the levels of taxation have two features: they are *not* cumulative, and they only apply to real property taxation. As a result, their effectiveness in limiting the amount of local taxation is uncertain.

As to the first point, the limits are imposed with respect to categories of local government and not with respect to the rate or amount of tax an individual taxpayer can be required to pay. Many areas of the state fall within the jurisdiction of two or three general purpose local governments simultaneously. An area may be within a county and a city; or within a county, a town, and a village. Additionally, most school districts and fire districts have independent authority to levy property taxes, the former subject to popular referendum, the latter to statutory spending limits. Thus, these taxes can be far greater than the 2 percent of full value city or village limit. (Recall, there are no limits on town property taxes.)

As to the second, there are no constitutional limits on the aggregate amount of local taxation from all sources. Thus, localities near their property tax cap may, with state approval, impose other kinds of taxes. The combination of tax limitations that apply solely to the property tax and the complete local dependence on the state legislature for authorization to impose nonproperty taxes — county and city sales taxes, for example — can give the state enormous power with respect to local finances.[26]

3. *Debt Limits:* Some of the points made with respect to the tax limits are equally applicable to the debt limits: they are not cumulative, and they are based entirely on the locality's property wealth. For example, although the debt limit for most general purpose local governments is 7 percent, the effective limit for an area that is in both a city and a county is 14 percent. Again, some significant borrowers — school districts, for example — face no constitutional limit, though they do have a referendum requirement for the approval of new debt. The theory of the debt limits is to limit

---

26 On the other hand, the Court of Appeals has limited one avenue of evasion of the tax limits by twice invalidating legislative efforts to assign a period of probable usefulness of three years to amounts paid by the City of Buffalo for pensions and social security benefits so that these expenditures would be characterized as capital expenditures and thus exempted from the property tax limit. *Hurd* v. *City of Buffalo,* 34 NY 2d 628 (1974); *Bethlehem Steel Corp.* v. *Board of Education,* 44 NY 2d 831 (1978).

local debt to the local government's "carrying capacity." On the assumption that local revenues are based on local real estate, the constitutional debt limits are calculated in terms of local taxable real estate. But many local governments derive substantial revenues from nonproperty taxes, such as the sales tax or the personal income tax. For these localities, the base for the debt limit may understate the ability of the locality to carry the debt. The range of criteria used by rating agencies to evaluate municipal credit worthiness is illustrative of the limitations of the surrogate standard employed in the state Constitution.[27]

More than the tax limits, it appears that the debt limitations have been evaded, primarily through the public authority device. Public authorities not subject to the debt limitations may be created to issue bonds to finance new facilities, with the debt payable from revenues generated by the projects financed by the authorities. Not debt of the local governments themselves, this borrowing is not subject to the constitutional debt limits. Thus, the local government debt limits may have contributed to the proliferation of such public authorities, and to public authority control of revenue-generating infrastructure projects and facilities.

4. *Restrictions to Local Public Purposes:* A central theme in the local finance article is to restrict local spending, local borrowing, and local debt guarantees to local public purposes. The courts, however, have liberalized these restrictions by frequently upholding state laws that enable or require one local government to contribute to the support of another, such as public authorities or nonself-sustaining public corporations created to get around restrictions or limitations on local spending or local debt. Thus, in *Comereski* v. *City of Elmira*,[28] a public parking authority was authorized to sell bonds and construct and operate parking lots in the city; the City of Elmira, in turn, was authorized to contract with the authority to pay any yearly deficits incurred by the authority up to a limit. The Court of Appeals sustained this arrangement against the challenge that it fell afoul of the prohibition of the lending of credit to another public entity. *Comereski* was subsequently extended in *Wein* v. *City of New York*,[29] which

---

27   See Moody's Investors Service, *Issuer's Guide to the Rating Process* (March 1993).
28   308 NY 248 (1955).
29   36 NY 2d 610 (1975).

sustained a state law requiring New York City to commit its funds to maintain the debt service reserve fund of the Stabilization Reserve Corporation even though the bonds and other obligations of the SRC were, by law, not the debt of the city. Although it can be argued that in such cases the local government expenditure does benefit the people of the local government, the assisted entity is not subject to the direct control of the popularly elected local government, and the local government's new financial obligation does not count against its debt limit.

Proposals for Constitutional Change

Though many of these proposals were not adopted, the record of the 1967 Constitutional Convention, augmented by constitutional amendments offered or discussed since that time, provides a good outline of constitutional issues still pending in intergovernmental relations in New York State.[30]

1. *Home Rule:* The Convention considered a proposal to shift the constitutional basis for local power to legislate from the traditional focus on local "property affairs or government" and specific areas designated as local to a broad delegation of all legislative power (except taxation) to local governments, subject to the legislature's power to limit local legislative authority by general law. The theory behind this so-called "legislative home rule" approach was that it would provide more power to local government, and eliminate the danger of narrow judicial construction of local powers, while still preserving to the state power to act on matters of state concern.

2. *Local Restructuring:* To facilitate the restructuring of local government, the Convention considered a proposal to authorize every county outside New York City to transfer any function possessed by any city, town or village therein to the county government, subject to a single countywide referendum — thereby eliminating the double and triple referendum procedures of Article IX.

3. *Local Finances:* The convention considered proposals to grant local governments power to levy nonproperty taxes; to liberalize the tax and debt limits; and to provide for single, consolidated areawide tax and debt limits rather than different overlapping

---

30   See generally Donna Shalala, *The City and the Constitution: the 1967 New York Convention's Response to the Urban Crisis*, New York: National Municipal League, 1972.

limits for each type of local government. (A narrower proposal — to remove the 5 percent debt limit on school districts outside the largest cities — also failed at the Convention, although a similar amendment was adopted by the voters in 1985.) More recent efforts at amendment have focused on allowing the use of contemporary techniques for contracting, paying, and refunding local debt.[31] Other proposed amendments, generated by controversial issues in particular budget years, have sought to limit the state's capacity to cut local aid after school budgets are adopted, or to reallocate earmarked highway trust funds by legislation.[32]

The 1967 Convention actually did vote to amend the restrictions in Article VIII, Section 1, to permit local gifts and loans "for public benefit purpose in aid of programs and facilities relating to economic and community development," but the defeat of the entire Constitution at the polls blocked this change.

4. *Transfer of Functions to the State:* In contrast with the situation in most other jurisdictions, in New York State, the City of New York, and counties outside the city pay up to half the state share of public assistance and medicaid costs. The local jurisdictions involved favor full state assumption of these costs. The 1967 Convention adopted a proposal directing a phased-in state takeover of local government's share of welfare costs. An amendment to Article VII offered in 1993 would make the state responsible for all costs associated with medical assistance to needy persons currently paid by counties and the City of New York.[33]

5. *Constitutional Prohibition of Unfunded Mandates:* Litigation by Monroe, Nassau, and Ulster counties is now pending that challenges unfunded state mandates as violative of both the home rule and taxation articles of the state Constitution. The 1967 Convention considered and rejected a proposal to limit the ability of the state to mandate new local expenditures. Prior to and since that time fourteen states have adopted constitutional provisions limiting or barring some or all unfunded mandates. Some of these require local action, by affected governments or popular referendum, before mandates can be effected. This is the case in Alabama for state law increasing city or county spending or decreasing revenues in the current year, and in Alaska for special acts

---

31   A.3524 (1993).

32   S.1430 (1993); A.3456 (1993); S.4214 (1991-92).

33   A.6776 (1993).

necessitating local appropriations.[34] Others require partial or full state funding, or the provision by the state of local authority to access a new source of funding, to meet newly mandated costs.[35]

In California, a provision adopted as a result of a 1979 initiative requires the legislature or any state agency that ". . . mandates a new program or higher level of service on any local government . . ." to provide ". . . a subvention of funds to reimburse such local government . . .," except if the mandate was requested by the local agency or the result of defining a new crime or redefining a crime.[36] The Florida provision, adopted in 1990, requires a two-thirds vote in the legislature mandating expenses on counties or municipalities and prohibits such action unless there is an important state interest and state funding or a new local revenue source is provided. Additionally, the mandate must either be specifically responsive to a federal requirement of localities or applicable equally to all persons similarly situated, "including the state and local governments."[37]

In New York, an amendment to Article IX has been offered annually since 1989 in the Senate and Assembly that would prohibit the legislature from ". . . enacting any general law which would impose a direct or indirect fiscal burden on local governments unless an estimate of such fiscal burden is computed. The extent of the fiscal burden shall appear on the face of the bill and an appropriation shall be made to each local government sufficient to hold it harmless from any part of such fiscal burden."[38]

---

34 Alabama: Amendments numbers 474 and 491. Alaska: Article 2, Section 19.

35 Examples are Hawaii: Article 8, Section 5; Louisiana: Article 6, Section 14. See generally, Joseph F. Zimmerman, "State Mandated Expenditures Distortions: Is There a Remedy?" (Presented at the Annual Legislative Conference of the Association of County Commissioners of Georgia, January 13, 1994, files of the Commission).

36 Article XIII, Section 6.

37 Article VII, Section 18.

38 A.4575 (1993); S.7139 (1992).

Local Government and the State Constitution: A Framework for Analysis

Richard Briffault

The operation of general purpose local government in modern New York reflects an underlying duality that has never been reconciled. On the one hand, New York's local governments are autonomous entities, headed by officials elected by and responsive to the sovereign people within each locality. On the other, these local governments are "branch offices" created by the "central office," the sovereign state government, to serve the state's purposes in accord with the authority it has from the people.

The "Bottom Up" Perspective

Whether acting autonomously or as agents of the state, local governments typically provide many of the public goods and services that most affect people in their families, homes, and neighborhoods. Many citizens are therefore particularly concerned that they be able to have a voice in shaping public policy with respect to these matters, though few understand the dual role of local governments. (Indeed, this dual role is often not well understood by local officials.) The "localness" of local governments, their closeness to the grass-roots, increases the possibilities for popular oversight of government and popular involvement in the decision-making process. Moreover, the relatively small size of most local governments — compared to the state and the federal government — enhances the potential ability of individuals to have impact on their actions. In a democracy, such popular participation is valuable in itself; it also may increase the responsiveness and accountability of government to the people.

In addition to being relatively small and relatively close to the people, local governments in New York State are numerous. The multiplicity of local governments permits a variety of different local rules, or different mixes of taxes, services, and regulation, tailored to the preferences of the people of different localities. Given the variations in local needs, circumstances, and desires, a large number of localities with independent decision-making power may result in greater overall satisfaction with government actions than would be the case if one rule were applied uniformly throughout the state.

In short, this "bottom up" tradition in thinking about local governments emphasizes local decision-making autonomy, local variation, local government accountability to a local electorate, and local immunity from state interference.

The "Top Down" Perspective

The state role in establishing local governments is fundamental. From this "top down" perspective, local governments are established by special state action or in accord with general law, and derive their legal authority, their regulatory powers and their public service responsibilities from the state Constitution, state statutes, and state-granted charters.

Local governments are territorially based communities, but there is no generally accepted principle for determining what the territorial dimensions of a community are, or whether a particular piece of territory ought to be in one local government or another. Put another way, the concept of local self-government does not automatically suggest who is the "self" that does the governing. A higher level government — the state — must determine which local government, and how many local governments, will have jurisdiction over what territory.

There are 62 counties (57 outside New York City) in New York State, and 62 cities. The number and the borders of the counties have not changed in eighty years (or more than a century, if changes related to the creation of Greater New York City are excluded), and the number and borders of the cities have not changed in fifty years. There have been slightly greater fluctuations in the number and borders of towns and villages — there are now about 930 of the former and 550 of the latter — but overall the pattern has been one of great stability for most of this century. This is because there is little capacity in state government in New York to reorder local boundaries in light of changing patterns of settlement, new technologies of transportation, communication, and production, new economic relationships, and other developments that affect the geographical dimensions of the efficient performance of local government functions essential to the effective operation of the local government system.

For much of the last century three categories of developments have been at the forefront in local government in New York: a convergence of the powers of different classes of governments; an increased freedom of these governments to reorganize themselves internally; and an increase in the use of specially created entities (public authorities, special districts) to provide services or meet needs that could not or would not be met within the existing general purpose governmental structure. All these may be seen as means of incrementally adapting an entrenched system to changing circumstances.

Although it is possible that the matrix of general purpose local governments established well before the Second World War remains suitable for addressing most contemporary needs and concerns, it seems likely, in light of the vast changes in social, economic, and political life in New York over this period, that some other arrangement might be better.

With the population highly mobile, and with so many local governments overlapping and adjacent to each other, local government actions inevitably have effects on people, jurisdictions and interests beyond their borders, imposing costs and providing benefits. Yet inherent in the "bottom up" concept of democratic local self-government is the assumption that all the people significantly affected by a local governmental action have the right to participate in its decision making. To be subject to the jurisdiction of a local government when one is excluded from the electorate that selects that government is not self-government but colonialism.

The state government — legally superior to local governments and electorally accountable to **all** the people in the state — must deal with concerns that, to local governments, are "externalities." State limits on the ability of local governments to impose costs on outsiders; state requirements that localities be compensated for benefits they provide for other jurisdictions, or those living beyond their borders; or state judgments about whether the aggregate benefits of local responsibility for a certain government function are greater than the aggregate costs of externalities of local action all are necessary to assure that local governments live up to the very accountability and responsiveness values that underlie the "bottom up" vision of local autonomy.

The Task for a State Constitution

Taking the "top down" and "bottom up" models together — and recognizing that a state Constitution ought to set up a general framework but not a detailed blueprint for governance — the Constitution ought to provide local governments autonomy in the exercise of the powers delegated to them, but also ought to provide for the capacity to revise local borders and shift powers from one local government to another in light of changing political, economic, social, demographic, and technological circumstances. The state would set up local governments, give them their powers and responsibilities, provide them with legal authority and fiscal resources adequate to their governmental role, and then step aside. Local governments would be protected from state interference in their exercise of their powers and from state impositions that would impinge on local government accountability to local residents. The state, however, would be empowered to monitor the system and to step back in to alter local borders and redistribute powers among different levels of government in light of new settlement patterns, changes in the ability of particular areas (or local governments generally) to efficiently and effectively perform the functions entrusted to them, or increases in the scope and significance of local spillovers.

To a considerable degree, the New York State Constitution gets these basic principles backwards. Local governments have relatively limited autonomy, limited fiscal resources, and precious little protection from state interference or state impositions. On the other hand, the Constitution places constraints on the realignment of local borders and the transfer of functions among different local governments. Moreover, even where system reorganization is not constitutionally restricted and the legislature is free to alter local boundaries and responsibilities, political inertia may inhibit the possibilities for change. The two goals of local government constitutional reform in New York, then, should be to: (1) enhance local autonomy in the performance of the powers vested in local governments; and (2) facilitate the restructuring of local borders and local powers in light of changes in those circumstances that affect the ability of local governments to carry out their powers in an effective, efficient, and accountable manner.

Local Autonomy

Local autonomy has three components. First, local governments must have broad power to initiate action in the areas entrusted to them. They must have no doubt about their powers to act, and ought to be able to take action without having to get specific permission from the state. This is the gist of "home rule." Second, local governments must have some immunity from state interference. They must be protected from state actions that would impair the structural integrity of local governments, local performance of local functions, or local government accountability to the local electorate. Third, local governments must have the fiscal resources sufficient to carry out the functions and to provide the services for which the state has made them responsible.

The state Constitution fails to provide any of these elements of local autonomy. With respect to the first — local initiative — Article IX does contain a number of general and specific grants of power to local governments. But Article IX is an extremely complex provision, reflecting layer upon layer of drafting, revision, and amendment over the period of a century, and incorporating several different, and conflicting, theories of home rule. By raising questions concerning the extent of local autonomy, Article IX gives the courts a considerable role in determining the scope of home rule. In the past, the courts have tended to construe home rule narrowly. As a result, many local governments doubt whether they have sufficient authority to initiate new programs without first obtaining the approval of the state.

Presumption in Favor of Local Authority to Act: One way to assure local power to initiate measures, without need for state approval, would be to simplify constitutional home rule by replacing the complex structure of Article IX with a provision — similar to that in several other states — that simply grants to local governments all legislative powers not specifically denied to local governments by the legislature. This would greatly reduce the role of the courts in determining whether local governments have power to act. It could also embolden local decision making by clarifying that local governments presumptively have the power to act, with the burden of persuasion on those opposed to a particular action to demonstrate that the state has specifically denied to the local government the power to take the action in question.

Immunity Against State Interference — No Ready Solution: The second component of local autonomy — local immunity from state interference — is more problematic. Article IX provides that the state can act with respect to local "property, affairs or government" by general laws only, and not by special laws, e.g., laws that apply to one or more, but not all, counties or cities or towns or villages. This gives local governments next to no protection. There is no limit on general laws, and, as a result of judicial interpretation, the restriction on special laws does not apply if the special law — aimed, for example, at just one city — addresses a matter of "state concern." The courts have given a very broad interpretation to the notion of state concern: A matter can be of state concern even if it also affects local "property, affairs or government," and the fact of a state concern will nearly always outweigh the local interest.

There is no ready solution to the problem of state interference in local government actions. Strong local immunity from state action would require a sharp demarcation between local matters and state matters, but that line is inherently difficult to draw, will certainly change over time, and should not be frozen into the Constitution. Local spillovers are endemic in a state containing thousands of local governments. The resulting interlocal conflicts will often require state action, including state limitation on local powers, or state requirements that local powers be exercised according to state specifications that would require local governments to take extra-local interests into account. Moreover, many problems can arise in many localities simultaneously. Even if these do not have cross-border effects, statewide treatment of a problem that exists statewide may permit a more economical or more effective response.

At the heart of the immunity problem is the conundrum of a multitier government system in which a higher level government includes the lower ones. The state includes all the local governments, all local residents are also state residents and New York is among those states with the greatest amount of layering of general purpose local governments. It is appropriate for the state to be accountable to its citizens, including those who reside within local units. Often, the most interfering state legislation is a response to interests within a particular locality that failed to achieve political success at the local level. But the ability of losers in local politics to refight their battles by taking an appeal to the state legislature, or even to Congress, may be endemic to our multilevel system. It thus is extremely difficult to write a constitutional provision that would secure local immunity from state interference without limiting the state's ability to address statewide problems or mediate interlocal conflicts, and without locking in a state/local distinction that would almost certainly become out of date with the passage of time.

Constitutional Ban on Special Acts: One response to the inability to craft a general shield for localities against state action would be to focus on specific problem areas. One problem is the ability of the state to interfere with particular local governments. General legislation interfering with all local governments may be resisted politically since it may prompt all local governments to unite in opposition. By contrast, a special law focused on one or a few localities may be easier to pass since a target that is alone and without allies may be particularly vulnerable. Article IX attempts to condition some special laws on the approval of the target locality, but this provision has been eroded by judicial interpretation. One solution might be to revitalize the constitutional ban on special acts by making it clear that it applies to all special acts, regardless of whether there is a "state concern." This would not interfere with the state's ability to adopt general laws.

True Local Control of Local Government: A second focus could be on state actions that interfere with the ability of local people to control their own local government. As already indicated, the Constitution should not determine what is "state" and what is "local," or guarantee local governments particular powers. The state should be able to shift responsibility for different functions among the different levels of government in light of changing circumstances. Thus, any local immunity from state action ought to be limited. But the Constitution should guarantee that local governments are controlled by and accountable to local people. The Constitution should, thus, protect the power of local people to decide on the basic institutions and procedures of their governments, and, for those functions entrusted to local governments, to formulate and carry out local decisions.

A frequent impediment to local control of local government is state regulation of local government contracting practices and the local public employment relationship, particularly the state imposition of obligations on local governments that have no analogue to the obligations the state imposes on private firms. To perform their public service functions local governments typically must hire workers and contract with vendors and other private providers. State regulations that drive up local public employment and contracting costs drain local revenues and interfere with the ability of local governments to perform their functions. These regulations divert local funds to programs chosen by the state rather than by local constituencies, thus interfering with local accountability. The Constitution ought to protect the structural integrity of local governments, broadly defined to include employment, contracting, and other "housekeeping" aspects of local performance of local government functions. State cost-imposing regulation of local public employment and contracting is also one piece of the unfunded mandates problem, which is addressed more fully below.

Fiscal Autonomy for Localities: The third piece of local autonomy is fiscal. Local governments must have the resources necessary to carry out their functions. To give a local government the legal authority to undertake various activities without also assuring that it has the funds necessary to pay for those activities is a cruel trick.

The question of local fiscal resources is also an issue of interlocal inequality. Due to enormous interlocal differences in tax base, some localities have far greater resources than others. Local government is far more able to advance the programs of local residents and provide high quality public goods and services where there are substantial local fiscal resources than where local resources are lacking. At least partly as a result of differences in local resources, there are enormous differences in local government effectiveness and in the quality of local services. The sufficiency of local fiscal resources, then, is essential both for local autonomy and as a matter of fairness to the residents of different localities.

The state Constitution, however, utterly fails to provide local governments with fiscal autonomy, with regard to both local resources and grants from the state. Local governments have very limited power to raise their own funds. Currently, home rule concepts do not apply to local taxation and borrowing. Although the state has delegated to local governments the *ad valorem* tax on property, local property taxation is subject to constitutional levy limits (much as local borrowing is also subject to constitutional caps), to state regulation of the collection and assessment processes, and to the legislature's power to create exemptions from taxation (without providing localities an offsetting payment for revenues lost).

Additionally, local governments have no constitutional authority to levy taxes other than the tax on real property. If a local government seeks an additional source of revenue, or to raise the rate of any nonproperty tax previously authorized by the legislature, it must go to Albany for the necessary authority. Nor is the state under any obligation to assure that local governments have tax bases adequate to their needs or to furnish localities with funds if the local governments are unable to raise sufficient revenues locally. Indeed, the state has unlimited authority to impose new functions, new service delivery requirements, or other expenses on local governments without having to supply the localities with the funds necessary to meet the costs of such mandates.

Home Rule for Taxation: There are several ways to increase local fiscal autonomy. One would be to increase local power to tax, either by placing authority to levy specific taxes in the Constitution, or by providing that home rule includes the power to tax. The prime constraint on local taxation would then be local politics and interlocal competition rather than the Constitution or state law. This would increase autonomy for most local governments, although it would be less valuable for poor areas with fewer taxable resources.

State Aid for Basic Local Service Levels: Second, and more dramatic, the Constitution could require that the state assure that all local governments have the resources to perform their functions. The state would be obligated to provide the funds where local resources were inadequate. The state could be required to determine a basic level of local public services for all communities; to determine the cost of that basic level; and to determine whether each locality has the resources, including both the taxing power and the tax base, to provide the basic level of services. If a given locality lacked sufficient revenue-raising power, the state would be required to provide additional taxing authority. Further, to address the interlocal inequality problem, the Constitution might provide that no locality collect in local revenues more than a certain percentage of the local tax base in order to meet the state-set service minimum. A locality that taxes at this levy limit but is unable to pay for the service minimum would be entitled to state funds to make up the difference. Localities would, however, be free to tax and spend above the service minimum if they so choose.

Such a constitutional provision would guarantee all localities the fiscal resources — in terms of taxing power and mandatory state assistance — necessary to carry out their state-delegated responsibilities, but would not interfere with the ability of localities to provide additional services if they were willing to pay for it. This proposal is based on some initiatives in the school finance reform area that would require the state to guarantee every school district the resources necessary to meet a state-set standard of basic education, but it would not be limited to education.

Prohibit Unfunded Mandates: Third, the Constitution could prohibit unfunded mandates. Unfunded mandates can be a major infringement on local fiscal autonomy, as they commandeer local governments to state ends and divert local resources from local control to state-determined programs. Unfunded mandates impair government accountability in general, since the state legislature is free to impose costs on local taxpayers without paying any political penalty while local officials are held accountable for costs over which they have no control. To protect local governments, the Constitution could authorize localities to ignore mandates unaccompanied by the funds necessary to carry them out.

Local Restructuring

The provisions of Article IX make certain forms of local restructuring difficult. The annexation provision requires the consent of both the people of the area proposed for annexation and of the governing boards of the affected local governments. Although the refusal of the affected local governments to consent can be overcome by judicial review, the requirement of an affirmative vote of the people in the area proposed for annexation is absolute. Similarly, the double referendum requirement for the adoption of an alternative county charter, and the triple referendum requirement for the transfer of functions from villages to the county or other local governments is also a barrier to local government restructuring.

Easing Impediments to Boundary Changes: One first step to greater flexibility in reordering local governments would be to reduce or eliminate many of the existing impediments to boundary change and the transfer of powers. Functions could be transferred from local units to a county government subject only to a single countywide referendum, thereby eliminating the double and triple referendum procedures of Article IX. Indeed, the referendum requirement for the transfer of functions, as well as the referendum requirement for annexations, could be eliminated.

Boundary and Powers Commission: More dramatically, the state could take a more active role in reviewing, and ultimately, reordering the configuration of local governments.

The Constitution ought to provide for some state-level institution responsible for actively examining the boundaries of particular local governments and the powers delegated to categories of government, proposing changes to the current structure, and, perhaps, implementing those changes. Most important is that such an entity — a boundary and powers review commission — have the power to initiate changes, such as the merger of existing local units, the shifting of territory from one locality to another, or the transfer of functions.

Although about a dozen states have boundary review commissions, they are primarily reactive. They pass judgment on locally initiated proposals for boundary change. These commissions can block changes — such as the incorporation of new communities on the metropolitan fringe — that may be undesirable from the perspective of the region or the state as a whole, but they cannot initiate changes that might reduce the large number of adjacent or overlapping governments in a region. To be most useful in assuring that local boundaries and powers are appropriate to meeting local service and regulatory responsibilities, a boundaries and powers commission needs the authority to launch a process of restructuring, even over the opposition of current local officials.

To be sure, it is unlikely that such a commission would be (or ought to be) able to force changes unilaterally. The Constitution ought to provide standards that would govern a commission's proposals for local restructuring; affected local governments ought to have procedural rights to participate in the commission's deliberations and to challenge the commission's proposals; and there ought to be some review — either judicial or legislative — of the commission's recommendations before they could take effect. But the central idea would be to have the structure of the local government system, and its relationship to the underlying values of effective and accountable government, subject to comprehensive examination from a regional or state perspective in a setting that emphasizes the possibilities for adapting the local government system to economic, demographic, and technological change. New York may thereby enhance the ability of local governments to meet local needs and perform their functions in an efficient and responsive manner, rather than continuing the current combination of constitutional impediments and political resistance to reorganization that threatens to extend into the next century a structure adopted many decades ago.

Elections and the Political Process

Jeffrey M. Stonecash

New York's Constitution plays a major role in defining the fundamental parameters of the state's political process. First, it specifies what substantive matters the public votes upon (the state's limited arena for direct democracy), and what areas of action are left to the governor and the legislature. Second, it defines who may vote and how such voters are to qualify. Third, it indicates which offices are elective and when elections are to be held to fill those offices. Finally, it delegates to the legislature the authority to enact additional legislation regulating the political process.

While the New York Constitution establishes this framework, it is not, in fact, the direct basis for a number of current political practices and procedures.[1] First, many of its provisions have been preempted or overridden by federal statutes, court rulings, or constitutional amendments, rendering certain language in it obsolete. (For example, the 26th Amendment to the federal Constitution, establishing 18 as the voting age, nullifies the state's constitutional requirement that voters be at least 21.) Second, many aspects of the political process that are the object of considerable public attention and criticism are not prescribed in the state's Constitution. Three examples are campaign finance practices, conflicts of interest, and barriers to ballot access that arise from detailed election law provisions and judicial construction of them. Absent new constitutional provisions, any attempts to address alleged defects in the political process based in

---

I appreciate the research assistance of Michael L. Owens of the Commission staff in the preparation of this essay.

[1] The New York Constitution has gone through many changes. The history of constitutional changes is covered in other documents. The concern here is the current Constitution. For those interested in the history of provisions relating to elections and the political process, see New York State Constitutional Convention Committee, "Problems Relating to Home Rule and Local Government," *Revised Record* XI (August 1938); State of New York Temporary Commission on the Revision and Simplification of the Constitution, Staff Report on Suffrage and Elections, Report No. 30 (New York, August 1959); and Peter J. Galie, *The New York State Constitution: A Reference Guide*, Westport, CT: Greenwood Press, 1991.

such provisions or practices must be made either in the legislature or the courts.

There is considerable dispute about the condition of the political process in the Empire State. Its adherents argue that it works reasonably well. Elections are held. Leaders are chosen. The government functions. The process is far from perfect, these defenders would agree. But much of the criticism of it arises out of ignorance, or hostility towards the kinds of compromises that representative democracy demands. Most of the larger difficulties in the working of state government that trouble the political process's critics, its defenders argue, do not stem from the nature of the process itself, but are outgrowths of serious divisions in the society at large.

In contrast, critics say that New York's political process is fundamentally flawed, and indeed at times works in ways that are antithetical to democratic values. Election law, campaign finance regulation, redistricting methods, statutory ethics codes, and election administration, they say, all tend to perpetuate the powerful in power and reward those specially skilled at manipulating the system. Strict and arcane rules of ballot access, for example, produce political exclusion and citizen disengagement rather than individual involvement in politics and government. While they understand that the progress made in a democracy is normally achieved incrementally, critics strongly argue that experience demonstrates how difficult it is to induce those in control of the political process to enact constraints upon themselves that are more than symbolic.

With an understanding that there is no consensus on the basic issue of how well New York's democracy works, this paper is designed to: 1) review what the New York Constitution specifies regarding the electoral process; 2) discuss current issues concerning the election system; and 3) examine potential constitutional changes in this area.

The Current System

What Does the Public Vote On?

New York's Constitution specifies limited areas in which the public must directly vote to decide policy. The Constitution provides for two separate categories of voting — statewide referendums and local referendums. All matters not designated in the Constitution as requiring a public referendum are left to the legislature and the governor for decision.

1. *Statewide Voting on Substantive Issues.* The Constitution mandates that the following issues must be placed on the ballot and voted upon directly by the electorate of the state:

   a. *Any debt contracted by or on behalf of the state* (Article VII, Section 11). Debt must be for a specific purpose. The Constitution also contains a number of exceptions to this requirement. [2]

   b. *Final approval of amendments to the Constitution* (Article IX, Section 1). Amendments must be presented to the public for a vote after their passage by two consecutive legislative sessions, separated by an intervening election.[3]

   c. *Calls for a constitutional convention and approval of any proposed Constitution or revisions* (Article IX, Section 2).

The courts have ruled that the use of referenda on statewide issues in New York is limited to those areas mandated in the Constitution. The permissive referendum is not available to the legislature for statewide matters.[4]

2. The Constitution requires a referendum of local voters in affected localities to:

   a. *Approve local games of chance, or gambling, for religious, charitable, or nonprofit purposes* (Article I, Section 9 [2]);

   b. *Annex one area to another.* If an area is to be annexed, the change must be approved by a majority of the electorate within the area considered for annexation, and the governing boards of the affected areas (Article IX, Section 1(d));

---

2   The public does not have to vote on debt that is: short term and issued in anticipation of revenue or proceeds from sale of bonds; on account of invasion, insurrection, war, or forest fires (Article VII, Sections 9 and 10); a maximum of $250 million for the expansion of the state university (Article VII, Section 19); issued by a corporation created as an instrument of the state, or assumed by the state on behalf of a corporation (Article X, Section 58). For further detail see the chapter on "State Government Finance" in this book. For those interested in public corporations, or public authorities, see Keith M. Henderson, "Other Governments: The Public Authorities," in Jeffrey M. Stonecash, John K. White, and Peter W. Colby, *Governing New York State*, Third Edition, Albany: SUNY Press, 1993.

3   See the chapter on "Amending and Revising the New York State Constitution" in this book.

4   *Barto* v. *Nimrod and Lovett* 8 NY Reports 483 (1853).

c. *Adopt alternative forms of county government, or the transfer of functions within a county, or the abolition of any local agency or unit of government within a county.* For any change in the form of county government to occur, the change must be approved by a majority of people voting within the cities in the county taken as a unit, and in the area outside the cities taken as a unit — a double majority provision. If a change also affects a function or government structure of a village wholly within a county, the change must also be approved by a majority within the villages of the county taken as a unit — a triple majority provision (Article IX, Section 1(h)(1)). In addition, any subsequent and significant alteration in a county government is also subject to a permissive referendum (Article IX, Section 1(h)(2)).[5]

In addition to the constitutionally required referendum for certain matters concerning local government, there is no bar to the legislative authorization of the use of the permissive referendum at the local level, and the legislature has provided for it for a number of specific purposes in statute.[6]

Who Registers?; Who Votes?; Who Administers Elections?

The composition and size of New York's electorate is defined by provisions in Article II of the state Constitution. This article also specifies how the registration of voters should occur and the structure of the agencies responsible for handling the process of registration. As mentioned in the introduction, certain key provisions of Article II, dealing with suffrage and elective franchise, have been preempted or overridden by federal actions.

Currently the state Constitution provides for the right to vote for any citizen who: has reached the age of 21; is a three-month resident of the state; and is literate in English. (Article II, Section 1) But superseding federal law makes the voting age eighteen, establishes 30 days as the maximum residence requirement, and abolishes literacy tests for voting.

Most state constitutional provisions defining how the registration of the electorate is to be achieved, as well as the institutional structure for

---

5   See the discussion on "Intergovernmental Relations" in this book.

6   See, for example, *People ex rel. Unger* v. *Kennedy* 207 NY 533 (1913). Here the Court of Appeals determined that the creation of Bronx County could be conditioned on a vote of the people living in the Bronx alone. A vote of all those living in New York County, of which the Bronx was then a part, was not required.

administration of elections for local, state, and federal office, remain operative.

1. *Secret Ballot and Voter Identification.* The Constitution provides for a secret ballot. It also specifies that when personal registration is used (it is now universal) those eligible to vote will be identified upon voting by their signature except if illiterate or handicapped, and that all of those voting will be required to provide their signature (Article II, Section 7).

2. *Voter Registration.* The current Constitution provides for the creation of a system for registering eligible individuals before they may vote. The legislature is given the authority to set up such a system of registration (Article II, Section 5), which may be permanent in nature (Article II, Section 6). The adoption of statewide permanent personal registration by statute in 1965 rendered irrelevant much of the detail in Article II, Section 5, concerning different possible requirements for voter registration in localities of different sizes, and exceptions to personal registration requirements.[7]

    Election reform legislation in 1992 gave a statutory basis to agency-assisted voter registration, formerly implemented by executive order, that was designed to increase voter registration, and therefore voter participation. It anticipated portions of the federal "Motor Voter" Act. This act, passed in 1993, requires that people ". . . be offered the opportunity to register for federal elections by mail, at armed forces recruiting offices, and when applying for a driver's license, public assistance or services by mail."[8]

3. *State and Local Boards of Election.* The responsibility for registering voters and administering elections is assigned to bipartisan boards of election. The current provision states that only the two parties that received the highest vote totals in the last general election shall have representation on such boards. Exemptions to this provision are provided for towns and village elections (Article II, Section 8).

4. *Absentee Voting.* A series of amendments following the Second World War (1947, 1951, 1963) eased restrictions theretofore in

7   See Galie, at p. 73.

8   This summary is taken from the draft memorandum in support of legislation proposed by the National Voter Registration Task Force to implement the motor voter bill in New York (reproduced January 14, 1993).

place upon absentee voting. The legislature may now provide for a system of absentee voting for qualified voters absent from their county of residence on election day or "unable to appear personally at the polling place because of illness or physical disability" (Article II, Section 2).

5. *Residence.* Fearful that persons temporarily resident in a location but unfamiliar with local conditions would have undue influence on community affairs if permitted to vote locally, nineteenth-century Constitution makers added a constitutional provision that gain or loss of a residence would not occur for persons engaged in certain occupations: those in military service; civil mariners; students; prisoners; or those institutionalized in whole or in part at public expense (Article II, Section 4). Persons in these occupations must provide evidence in accord with statutory standards that allows them to overcome the presumption that they do not reside locally. Regarding college students voting in college towns, recent federal decisions have eased the evidentiary standards previously applied.[9]

6. *Loss of Franchise.* Persons buying or selling votes or betting on election outcomes are constitutionally barred from voting, but procedures set out in the Constitution to establish a violation of this provision may be contrary to U.S. constitutional provisions against self incrimination (Article II, Section 3).[10] Loss of the franchise for other reasons — imprisonment for a felony, having been judged incompetent, commitment to a mental institution — are statutory.

7. *Presidential Elections.* Special provisions are included to allow the legislature to set up special procedures for participation in presidential elections for those who have recently moved within the state, into the state, or out of the state (Article II, Section 9).

What Offices Are Elected?; How Long Are Terms of Office?; and Who Draws Districts?

The state's Constitution also denotes which offices are to be elective, when elections to fill them shall take place, and, in the case of the legislature, how the Assembly and the Senate districts are to be drawn. Regarding the

9   *Auerbach v. Rettaliata,* 765 F. 2d. 350 (1985).

10   See Galie, at p. 71.

issue of redistricting, as was the case with the age requirements and literacy tests, certain of the constitutional language contained in the legislature article (Article III) has been rendered moot due to recent court decisions and federal statutes. For example, Article III, Section 4, provides that "no county shall be divided in the formation of a senate district. . . ." The courts found, however, that this provision posed a barrier to implementing the principle of "one person, one vote," and it was ruled in violation of the United States Constitution. The provision in Article III, Section 5, providing for one assembly seat for each county was voided on the same basis.[11] Still, constitutional provisions concerning districting remain in effect, the most significant of which is the continued location of this responsibility in the legislature itself.

1. *State Elective Office(s), Terms of Office, and Election Cycles.* A governor and a lieutenant governor are to be elected (but not nominated) jointly, with each serving a four-year term (Article IV, Section 1). For both offices the individual must be at least thirty years of age and have lived in the state for five years preceding his or her election to office (Article IV, Section 2). Additionally, a comptroller and an attorney general are to be elected for the same terms as that of the governor, and must meet the same qualifications as the governor (Article V, Section 1).

2. *Election of Judges.* Most judicial positions are filled via elections within jurisdictions defined by the state Constitution. Judges are given long terms of office to assure their independence (Article 6, Section 6). Judges exempt from partisan election are those serving on the Court of Appeals, the Court of Claims, and certain judges in New York City (Article VI). Local justices are elected for four-year terms.

3. *Election of Senators and Assembly Members.* The Constitution sets an absolute limit on the number of Assembly seats (150) but allows for increases in the number of Senate seats under certain conditions (Article III, Section 2). Senators and Assembly members serve for two years (Article III, Section 2). Age and residency qualifications for legislators are also indicated (Article III, Section 7). Elections are to be held in even-numbered years (Article III, Section 2) on the Tuesday succeeding the first Monday in November. The legislature is granted the discretion to change the timing of electing state legislators (Article III, Section 8).

---

11 See Galie, at p. 83.

4. *Redistricting.* The Senate and Assembly districts are to be drawn by the legislature (Article III, Sections 4 and 5), with the federal census used to apportion districts (Article III, Section 4). The governor must approve the legislation.

5. *Local Elective Office.* Every local government (except a county wholly within a city) shall have an elected local legislature (Article IX, Section 1). City and county officers must be elected in odd-numbered years (Article XIII, Section 8), for terms ending in odd-numbered years. (This provision effectively insulates these localities from the influence of national and statewide political trends, and protects statewide elections from surges in urban turnout motivated by local concerns.) Additionally, the terms of county clerks, sheriffs, and district attorneys are constitutionally specified at three or four years, subject to legislative discretion (Article XII, Section 13). The legislature also has considerable discretion in declaring offices vacant (Article XIII, Section 6), for filling vacancies (except where, under the home rule article, there is a superseding local provision) (Article XII, Section 3), and for statutory designation of the length of term for an office when that term is not indicated in the Constitution (Article XIII, Section 2).

Statutory Regulation of the Political Process: Political Parties, Ballot Access, and Campaign Finance

Political Parties

New York is among those states in which political parties are embedded by statute in the operations of elections. Recognized parties have their own structure and procedures regulated to a significant degree by law — for example, statutes define parties' processes for creating their nominating committees and nominating candidates — but also enjoy advantages in ballot access for their candidates.

Despite their centrality to core democratic processes, the state Constitution is virtually mute on the appropriate role of the political parties in the political system. Article I, Section 1, notes that a primary election need not be held if a candidate has no opponent. A second constitutional reference to parties is the specification that the all laws regulating boards administering elections ". . . shall secure equal representation of the two political parties which, at the general election next preceding . . . cast the highest and next highest number of votes" (Article II, Section 8). Finally, the Constitution provides for an exception to the prohibition of tests in addition to the oath of office that allows parties, by rule, to provide for equal representation by the sexes at party conventions and on party committees. (Article XII, Section 1).

New York's constitutional drafters intentionally left a good deal to the legislature and governor in their outline of the electoral and political processes of the state. Dispersed throughout the Constitution is language granting the legislature discretion over the creation and enactment of the enabling legislation necessary to fulfill the state's broad constitutional provisions concerning voter registration, ballot access, procedures for election administration, and related matters. Numerous disputes over these matters have brought the judiciary into the fray; the case and statutory law surrounding New York's political process has become both extensive and infamous.[12]

Ballot Access

Statutory provisions regarding ballot access have generated the greatest controversies, and prompted the most questions about the fairness of the modern political process in New York from good government groups, third-party and independent candidates, and even some candidates of the major parties. One important study concluded that ". . . no single procedural requirement contained in New York's election law itself is so complicated that it cannot be complied with through reasonable diligence. Collectively, however, those requirements unreasonably restrict access to the ballot and thereby undermine the legitimacy of the primary process as a means of selecting nominees. . . ."[13]

In order to participate in a recognized party's primary election or run during the general election as an independent candidate, a candidate for public office is required to submit a designating petition.[14] The petition must contain a necessary number of valid signatures taken from enrolled party members, generally 5 percent of the members of the candidate's

---

12   All of New York's statutory law is contained in *McKinney's*. For a complete overview of all the court cases relevant to the state's election law provisions see Edward I. Byer, *Election Law: Decisions, Procedures and Forms*, Albany: New York Legal Publishing Corporation, 1989. In addition, New York now accounts for half of the United States' election law cases, with the litigation rate on the rise.

13   See Bruce Green, (ed.), and Introduction by John Feerick, *Government Ethics Reform for the 1990s: The Collected Reports of the NYS Commission on Government Integrity*, New York: Fordham University Press, 1991, at p. 304.

14   A candidate may also access the ballot by obtaining at least 25 percent of the votes at a meeting of a party's state organization.

party who are eligible to vote in the particular election.[15] Party members signing such a petition must reside in the jurisdiction for which the candidate is seeking office. Failure to meet the compulsory number of valid signatures, or correspond to the many other strictures posed by the law (concerning, for example, the color of a petition, or the symbol used by a party organization) may cause a Board of Elections to prevent a candidate from accessing the ballot. Even if a candidate turns in a petition containing the sufficient number of valid signatures, his or her name may still face disqualification from the ballot for other infractions of the election law, for example, faulty cover sheets.

The history of the petition process in New York is revealing. Election laws passed in 1911 and 1913 replaced nomination by convention delegates with nomination by primaries precisely to bring more public inclusion into the political process, taking away some of the control of the party machinery. The unanticipated outcome, however, was the creation of a new and more exclusionary process. Shortly after independent candidates began to avail themselves of the opportunity for designation on primary ballots by petition, the requirements and the overall petition process became more stringent. For example, the number of signatures needed was increased; open primaries disappeared; detailed signature witnessing emerged; and the "dreaded" petition cover sheet was introduced.[16]

As noted, the courts have also played a major role with regard to the petition process. Repeatedly, they have taken a ". . . judicial attitude requiring strict compliance, based on the conclusion that strict compliance reflects legislative intent because the legislature has had adequate opportunity to counter the courts' approach and has not done so. . . ."[17]

The combined effect of detailed statutory ballot access requirements and strict judicial interpretation has led numerous candidates, civic organizations, less established political parties, and even the governor to note that "the ballot access problem has — for too many years — impeded or eliminated valid candidacies, deprived voters of a choice, and damaged

---

15 See Bruce Green, (ed.), and Introduction by John Feerick, *Government Ethics Reform for the 1990s: The Collected Reports of the NYS Commission on Government Integrity*, New York: Fordham University Press, 1991, at p. 305.

16 Note, "New York State's Designating Petition Process," *Fordham Urb. L. J. 14* (1985-86): 1014. "The number of valid signatures needed for a designating petition increased markedly for some office between 1913 and 1971. For example, in 1913, a candidate for New York City Council President needed 1,500 valid signatures . . . while in 1971, a candidate for the same office needed 10,000. . . ." (quote at p. 1014 fn. 31).

17 See Memorandum by Burton Agata, "Delegate Selection and the Problem of Ballot Access," New York State Temporary Commission on Constitutional Revision (January 1994), at p. 3. Also refer to *Higby v. Mahoney,* 48 NY 2d 15 (1979).

[the political process]."[18] They advocate both more liberal construction of the ballot access requirements by the judiciary, and extensive simplification of the laws by the legislature.

The most recent attempt at correcting some of the problems facing the current system of elections in New York State was the Election Reform Act of 1992, previously noted for its provisions concerning voter registration. Additionally, this statute liberalized the requirements for witness statements on petitions for party office; reduced the number of signatures needed for designating petitions; and reduced the number of signatures needed for independent nominations. Critics continued to argue, however, that this reform package did not go far enough.

Campaign Finance

The continual concern about campaign finance is that large contributors have disproportionate influence over candidates. The state has responded to that by enacting limits on how much contributors can give. Critics have suggested that New York campaign finance limits are in reality of little consequence. The details of the law cannot all be outlined here, but a few provisions are illustrative.

The limit on the total annual political contributions, unrepaid loans, and loan guarantees by any individual for the election of others to political office is $150,000. (Contributions of family members are not included.) The limit for contributions by an individual to a party or constituted committee is $62,500 per year. Statewide candidates may receive five cents from an individual contributor per party-enrolled voter for use in a primary (but not less than $4,000 or more than $12,000, adjusted for the cost of living). The aggregate contributions from designated family members may not exceed $.025 times the number of party enrolled voters in the state. For Republicans in 1991 this total was $63,991; for Democrats it was $94,004. For the general election, contributions from any individual are limited to $25,000, and from designated family members $.025 times the number of total enrolled voters in the state, or $197,593 in 1991.

New York law does provide for periodic disclosure during the election cycle by candidates and committees of the size and source of campaign contributions. Disclosure for state elections or committees, or elections that transcend the boundaries of counties, is the responsibility of the state Board of Election. For local elections and committees within

18   Statement by Vance Benguiat, then Executive Director of the Citizen's Union of the City of New York, at a 1985 Joint Public Hearing of the Senate and Assembly Election Law Committees on Ballot Access.

counties it is up to the county boards. (For state and county parties, however, certain "housekeeping" receipts are exempt from disclosure.) Decentralized filing makes it hard to track the activity of contributors across the state. There has been criticism, too, of the relative casualness of information gathering and retention of records by state and local boards of elections in some cases, and inattention to enforcement of disclosure requirements.

Ethics

New York State's first conflict of interest laws date to the mid-1950s, and have periodically been altered in times when corruption or scandal has focused public attention on standards of behavior for persons in high public office. The most recent reforms were made in the Ethics in Government Act passed in 1987. This legislation restricts statewide elected officials, state legislators and their staff, state officers and their employees (including some in public authorities), and some political party leaders in their business relationships with the state. For example, it bars the receipt of contingency fees by these persons for representation of others before state agencies, prohibits their taking gifts or loans of more than nominal value, and prevents businesses in which they have a substantial interest from doing business with the state except by competitive bidding. The act also specifies in detail financial disclosure requirements for these officials, and sets out a two-year prohibition on their representing interests before state agencies after they leave office on matters in which they were involved while they were in government. Finally, two bodies are established to administer this law, the State Ethics Commission and the Legislative Ethics Commission.[19]

Critics have argued that this law does not go far enough. For example, the New York State Commission on Government Integrity (The Feerick Commission) has called for an absolute prohibition on state government officers and employees representing private clients before state agencies. It also proposed that executive branch employees be required to disqualify themselves from involvement in official actions likely to affect their personal financial interests in a manner different than the general public; that preemption of professional disciplinary codes by the 1987 act be repealed; and that financial disclosure be linked to policy-making responsibilities and not tied solely to levels of compensation, as currently required.[20]

---

19 Public Officers Law, Sections 73, 73a, and 74.

20 See John Feerick, "Reflections on Chairing the Commission on Government Integrity," *Fordham Urban Law Review* 18, 1 (1990-91).

Proposals for Constitutional Change

Numerous criticisms have been expressed about the Constitution and the political process in New York. In response, a great number of proposals, both constitutional and statutory, have been put forth to alter that process. The following reviews these criticisms and proposals. For each section the presumed problem is first presented. Where appropriate, the argument for not making change is also presented. The proposed change is then presented, with the focus on constitutional change.

Remove Obsolete and Superseded Provisions

As described above, a number of provisions concerning the franchise in Article II and legislative districting in Article III have been superseded by federal statute or U.S. Supreme Court decisions. In the case of permanent personal registration, the state government itself has gone beyond the minimum requirements of the state constitution, making detail in it irrelevant to the actual operation of the electoral process. Retention of superseded or superfluous language in the state constitution is positively misleading. Moreover, it has no fallback value, since federal law or state practice is most unlikely to change in these areas. Existing state constitutional language that lacks force and effect might be simply deleted. Alternatively, it could be replaced with language that is in accord with existing law and practice, giving these an additional state constitutional basis.

What Is Voted Upon?

1. *More Direct Democracy.* Many groups are advocates of citizens having the right to directly vote on some issues. Proponents suggest that a mechanism for direct democracy at the state level is a way of forcing action on issues that the legislature and governor won't consider, either because they are too difficult politically or because they are against elected officials' self-interest. Advocates often do not distinguish structural change from policy goals, and seek initiative and referendum because it has been used elsewhere for ends they favor (e.g., tax limitation). Opponents regard direct democracy as undermining representative institutions, and contributing to irresponsibility in them.[21] There are also arguments

---

21 See Gerald Benjamin, *Initiative and Referendum for New York* (unpublished essay, files of the Nelson A. Rockefeller Institute of Government) for a complete history of the debate on this issue in the state. For a more general discussion, see, Thomas Cronin, *Direct Democracy*, Cambridge: Harvard, 1989.

that poorer and less educated people vote less than others on initiatives, and thus results from this process have a class bias.[22]

Constitutional and statutory initiative and referendum have been intermittently debated in New York for a century. A number of different proposals have been made in recent years, but none has been given serious consideration, including one by Governor Cuomo for indirect initiative (the capacity of voters by petition to compel legislative consideration of a matter). The Constitution might be altered to add the right of citizens to use the initiative.

2. *Extended Use of the Referendum in Localities.* It is difficult now to change local government structures. The provisions vary, depending upon the type of local government. Critics argue that this allows entrenched interests to block serious debate on structural issues even if a significant portion of the local community seeks such a debate.[23] Those who are uneasy about rapid change find the current arrangements acceptable.

The Constitution might be altered to include a provision that would allow the use of initiative and referendum to require consideration of structural change in local government.

3. *Ease the Referendum Requirement for Local Government Consolidation.* The double and triple majority requirements make altering local governmental arrangements and structures more difficult than in many other states.[24] They are barriers for municipalities and public administrators attempting to "reinvent government" at the local level, for example to begin a process of regionalization. Some would alter them for this reason. Others argue that these provisions protect the interests of all persons and governments potentially affected by structural change, and assure that decisions on these matters will be local and consensual.[25]

A provision might be added that would allow a simple majority of those voting to consolidate local governments or specific functions across local governments.

---

22   See Diana Dwyre, Mark O'Gorman, Jeffrey M. Stonecash, and Rosalie Young, "Disorganized Politics and the Have-Nots: Politics and Taxes in New York and California," *Polity* (forthcoming).

23   See Frank Mauro, *Finance and Budget Issues (Both Good and Bad Depending on Your Perspective) that Might be Considered by a Constitutional Convention,* Albany, New York: Fiscal Policy Institute, 1993. (Copy in files of Commission.)

24   See George Carpinelli and Patricia Salkin, *Legal Processes for Facilitating Consolidation and Cooperation Among Local Governments: Models From Other States,* Albany: The Rockefeller Institute, Local Government Restructuring Project, 1990.

25   See the chapter on "Intergovernmental Relations" in this book.

Who Is Elected?; Terms of Office?; Districting?

1. *Elective Offices.* There is continual debate about whether there should be changes in who is elected and who is appointed. There are proposals that some state and local elected offices should be filled by appointment to assure competence in performance of essentially nonpolitical functions. Proposals reach such offices as attorney general, most judgeships, sheriff, highway superintendent, town clerks, assessors, and tax collectors. Proposals have been made to abolish certain offices (lieutenant governor) or add statewide elected offices (commissioner of education). Some of these changes would not now require constitutional revision, but might be taken up at a convention. Debates turn on whether the offices in question involve policy making and the sorts of functions that ought to be directly accountable to the people, or whether effective executive management and the need for special expertise requires appointment. In moving from election to appointment, the identity of the potential appointing authority is, of course, central to the discussion.[26]

2. *Term Limitation.* Critics of legislatures argue that many problems do not get addressed because incumbents avoid controversy. Generally, advocates of this change are hostile to the idea of careers in legislative office, to incumbency advantage in elections, and to what they regard as increasingly entrenched and nonresponsive state political institutions. Opponents see term limitation as antidemocratic, and as oversold in its potential for enhancing political competition. Additionally, they fear its potentially damaging impact on the legislature as an institution.[27]

A two-term limit for the governor, now present in almost half the states, has also been proposed for New York. In fact, some would welcome such a limitation for all statewide elected officials. Proponents of such a change argue that long tenure in the governorship or other statewide office, helped along by the capacity to attract campaign funds and other incumbency advantages, closes down political opportunity, preventing periodic renewal of the political system by new leadership, and is therefore not healthy for New York. Moreover, they point out that a limita-

---

26   See discussion of specific offices in the chapters "Structures of New York State Government" and "Intergovernmental Relations" in this book.

27   For an extensive discussion see Gerald Benjamin and Michael Malbin, *Limiting Legislative Terms.* Washington: CQ Press, 1992; see also Benjamin and Malbin, "Why Is There No Real Term Limits Debate in New York?" *Empire State Report* (November 1992).

tion of two four-year terms appears to have had no systemic negative effect at the national level or for states that now have it.

Proponents of the current system point out that the potential to run again is a great source of strength to the governor in relationships with legislators and others within the state political system. A term limit would create an automatic lame duck status in the governorship every eight years, and would not be good for the state. The potential to continue to serve, they continue, has also allowed New York governors to develop relationships and reputations that help them better serve the state in the national arena and, not insignificantly, make them more competitive for the presidential nomination.

As term limits for state and local legislators have become more widely adopted in the last several years, including for New York City council members, a number of proposals to limit legislative terms have been advanced in New York State. As in other states where there is no initiative and referendum process, none of these have been given serious consideration here. Given the lack of an initiative process, and the disinclination of the legislature to establish a limit, a constitutional convention would be necessary to establish limits at the state level in New York.

3. *Redistricting.* Many argue that allowing legislators to design their own legislative districts creates a conflict of interest. The record in New York State and elsewhere shows that legislatures tend to focus on the two goals of preserving partisan advantage and protecting incumbents when they redistrict themselves.[28] District plans also get caught up in complications involving the federal constitutional and statutory requirements. Almost inevitably, the record also shows, the results of such a process end up in litigation.

Advocates of redistricting commissions recognize that such quintessentially political decisions cannot entirely be removed from politics, but suggest that such an arrangement places a salutary distance between the legislature and these choices. Such a distancing, they argue, also takes a very contentious matter out

---

28   See Richard Lehne, *Legislating Reapportionment in New York*, New York: National Municipal League, 1971; David Wells, "The Reapportionment Game," *Empire State Report* (February 1979): 8; Gerald Benjamin, "The Political Relationship," in *The Two New Yorks*, New York: Russell Sage Foundation, 1988, at pp. 132-145; and Jeffrey M. Stonecash, "New York," in Leroy Hardy, Alan Heslop, and George Blair, editors, *Redistricting in the 1980's*, Claremont: Rose Institute of State and Local Government, at pp. 185-90.

of the legislature, making it more possible to bring it to timely closure.

Opponents argue that resolving the value choices about representation involved in redistricting is a core legislative function. Commissioners, they say, may often have their own political agendas. Finally, it is not clear from experience that commissions do a better, more efficient job than do legislatures in the states.[29]

Thirteen states have constitutional provisions for redistricting outside of the legislature. In ten the responsibility is given to a commission; in three others it is left to the governor and/or others appointed by him or her. (Where the governor has a principal role, a separation of powers question is present.) In almost all cases where a commission is used, careful steps are taken to provide for multiple appointing authorities and partisan diversity in the resultant group. Often, there are requirements for geographic representativeness, as well. In several cases, service on the commission precludes members from later candidacy for the legislature for a defined period of time.[30]

---

29   See Tim Storey, "Dickering Over the Districts," *State Legislatures* (February 1992): 22-23.

30   The provisions are as follows:
Alaska: reapportionment is the governor's responsibility, with an appointed advisory board;
Arkansas: the governor, the secretary of state , and the attorney general reapportion districts;
Colorado: has a commission consisting of (11) members, three selected by the governor, four by the legislature and four by the judiciary, with geographic and partisan distribution prescribed;
Hawaii: has a commission consisting of (9) members, two each selected by four legislative leaders and a ninth selected by the eight so selected;
Maryland: reapportionment is the governor's responsibility;
Massachusetts: the governor and Executive Council reapportion representative districts;
Michigan: employs a commission consisting of (8) members, four of whom are selected by each of the state organizations of the two major political parties, with a geographic distribution, a bar to service by government officials or employees, and bar from election to legislature for two years after service;
Missouri: has the two parties nominating commissioners from each of the Congressional Districts for separate districting committees for the House and Senate. The governor appoints from these lists. Committee members are barred from legislative candidacy for four years after service.
Montana: uses a commission consisting of (5) members, one picked by each leader, and a fifth by those so selected (with the Supreme Court acting if they cannot decide within twenty days), and none of whom may be public officials or run for the legislature for two years following service;
New Jersey: employs a commission consisting of ten members picked by the chairs of the two major parties, with an eleventh selected by the majority of the Supreme Court if they cannot agree in a specified time;
Ohio: the governor, comptroller, secretary of state, and two representatives from the legislature are the commission that reapportions districts;
Pennsylvania: uses a commission made up of the majority and minority leaders of each house and a fifth member chosen by them.
Washington: has selection of four of five commission members by each leader in each house, with the four selected picking the final member.

The Charter of the City of New York specifies a commission for districting its City Council. [31] In Iowa, the task is given by law initially to a nonpartisan Legislative Service Bureau. In Connecticut a nine-member bipartisan commission appointed by the governor, with two members each designated by the leaders of the legislative bodies and the chair then selected by these eight, is charged with reapportionment if the legislature fails to act by a specified date.[32] Finally, the Constitution prepared for New York State by the 1967 Convention provided for a redistricting commission. Four members of this five-person body were to be appointed one each by the speaker, the majority leader and the minority leaders of the Senate and Assembly, with the fifth member and chair selected by the Court of Appeals.[33]

Eligibility to Vote and Election Administration

1. *Continued Registration Once Registered.* Registration in the state is not continuous. If a voter moves he or she must re-register. Critics argue this suppresses political involvement and voting. They also argue that voter fraud is of less concern than in years past. Others are less troubled by this because they argue the current practice limits the possibilities of fraud and systematically cleans the registration rolls.

   A package of reforms to facilitate voter registration has been proposed by the state's National Voter Registration Task Force as a consequence of the adoption in Washington of the Motor Voter Bill. Almost all of these are statutory. However, one amendment to Article II, Section 6, has been offered by the Task Force to "bring our law into compliance with the requirements of the federal statute." It permits the continued registration of a person who changes addresses so long as he or she remains within the jurisdiction of the same local board of elections. Some will oppose this constitutional change because it will facilitate the continued registration of college students in their communities, once they are first registered. Failure to act, however, may well result in two-tiered registration system, with one set of rules for national elections and another for state and local elections.

---

31 For descriptions of the experiences of the commission see Frank J. Macchiorola and Joseph G. Diaz, "Minority Political Empowerment in New York City," *Political Science Quarterly* (Spring 1993): 37-57; "Decision Making in the Redistricting Process: Approaching Fairness," *Journal of Legislation* (1993): 199-222; "The 1990 New York City Redistricting Commission," *Cardozo Law Review* (April 1993): 1175-1235.

32 Connecticut Constitution Article XXVI, Section 26.

33 Article II, Section 2(a).

2. *Election Day Registration.* As in many other states, voter turnout has declined in recent years. There are few people who are not troubled by the trend. Considerable research indicates that the primary reason for failure to vote is failure to register.[34] Additional steps to ease registration requirements, therefore, may be desirable. Most may be taken by statute, but election day registration will require constitutional change.

Registering voters when they appear to vote on election day has been the practice in Wisconsin and some other states since the mid-1970s. Its proponents argue that even the relatively close cut-off date for registration permitted by federal law prohibits voters from becoming eligible just as they are beginning to pay attention as a result of the political campaign. Opponents say, however, that such a change would enhance opportunities for election fraud and make election administration very difficult. Such a change could be accomplished in New York only if the constitutional requirement that "registration be completed at least ten days before each election" (Article II, Section 5) were repealed.

3. *Alteration of Structure for Election Administration.* The provision that the state and local boards of elections be headed by representatives of the two major parties has been controversial. Since all action on challenges regarding violation of election procedures must be approved by commissioners of opposing parties it is often difficult for them to reach agreement to resolve disputes. Minor parties, insurgents within the major parties, and independent candidates contend that the two major parties' representatives on these boards are preoccupied with protecting their candidates. Governor Mario M. Cuomo remarked in the spring of 1993 that the current constitutional provision "locks New York's many thousands of Independent voters out of a voice on the State Board."[35] Defenders of the arrangement argue that the presence of party officials creates individuals with a strong incentive to detect improper behavior, and is a valuable mechanism for providing scrutiny of the process.

Regardless, changing the current arrangement would require altering the constitutional designation of their role on boards of elections.

---

34 See Raymond Wolfinger and Steven Rosenstone, *Who Votes?*, New Haven: Yale University Press, 1980; and Steven J. Rosenstone and John Mark Hansen, *Mobilization, Participation and Democracy in America*, New York: MacMillan, 1992, at pp. 205-209 and citations at note 85.

35 See Governor Mario M. Cuomo. *Real Reform: A Special Message to the People*, 1993.

a. *Increase the Membership of State and County Boards of Election to Five Members.* One solution would be to increase the membership of these boards to five, perhaps with a provision barring the fifth member from membership in either of the major parties. Such a change would require amending the constitutional provision (Article II, Section 8) that requires equal major party representation on these commissions. Such a change would assure a means of breaking deadlocks on the commission. Issues would surely arise, however, on how to tell the "true partisan colors" of any potential fifth commissioner.

b. *Remove the Idea of Party Representation From Election Administration.* The constitutional guarantee of equal representation on election boards for the major parties is an attempt to assure that neither suborns the process by allowing each to watch the other. But this structure forces much of election dispute resolution in New York into the courts. Moreover, both experience and theory brings into question the efficiency and effectiveness of multiheaded government departments. Finally, sensitive matters are handled in other areas of governmental concern without use of this representational model in department organization. An alternative approach would be to have a single-headed department at the state and county levels for election administration, with a quasi-judicial process to handle dispute resolution. Special professional qualifications might be established in law for the department head, with statutory prescription of strict neutrality and significant penalties for violation.

Ballot Access

As noted, there is concern that there are too many obstacles for candidates to get on the ballot. Much of the reform agenda is statutory. Some of the constitutional changes proposed include:

1. *Liberal Construction.* A constitutional "substantial compliance" provision (Article II, Section 5) could be written that would direct the courts to depart from strict compliance with regards to statutory provisions concerning candidate petitions and other highly detailed aspects of the election laws. Experience with a similar directive to the courts on home rule suggests that such an approach might not be fruitful.

2. *Constitutional Basis For Primary Elections.* Another approach is to require primaries for all offices. Arizona's Constitution directs its legislature to enact a direct primary law for nomination of candidates to all elective offices (Article VII, Section 10). Similarly, the Constitution in California provides for primary elections for all partisan offices (Article II, Section 5). The Oklahoma Constitution provides for "a mandatory primary system" for nomination to all offices, except presidential elector, and directs the state legislature to provide by law for nomination of independent candidates by petition (Article 3, Section 1). A similar provision for New York, depending upon its precise language, might provide the basis for eased ballot access requirements.

Campaign Finance

The role of money in campaigns is troubling to many. There is concern that only the well financed have a chance to be elected, and that the lack of money inhibits challengers and prevents competition. Constitutional provisions concerning campaign finance are found in some states.

1. *Public Financing.* The Constitutions of Hawaii and Rhode Island require public financing of elections. In Hawaii the legislature is constitutionally directed to ". . . establish a campaign fund to be used for partial public financing of campaigns for public offices of the State and its political subdivisions. . . ." The Rhode Island Constitution provides that the general assembly ". . . shall provide for the adoption of a plan of voluntary public financing and limitations on total campaign expenditures for campaigns for governor and such other general officers as the general assembly shall specify."[36]

2. *Contribution and Spending Limits.* Another approach is to place more stringent limits on the role of money in campaigns. In both Hawaii and Rhode Island, the requirement for public funding legislation is linked to limits on campaign spending and on

---

36   Hawaii: Article II, Section 5; Rhode Island: Article IV, Section 10.

contributions to a candidate or a candidate's authorized political campaign organization.[37]

3. *Sunshine Provisions.* New York statutory law now provides that candidates file campaign finance disclosure statements. Some states provide a constitutional basis for such requirements. For example, Arizona's Constitution directs its legislature to require public disclosure of campaign contributions and expenditures. The Rhode Island Constitution includes a provision requiring the passage of disclosure legislation covering campaign spending by or in behalf of each candidate in primary, special, and general elections, though discretion is allowed the legislature to exclude smaller contributions.[38] As noted before, the practice in New York has been to engage in only limited review of financial disclosure forms, and there is almost no effort to analyze the information or present it to the public. Provisions might be inserted to change how such information is assessed and used.

Campaign Practices

There has been considerable concern about the general deterioration of the quality of public discourse, and especially with increased mudslinging and negative campaigning in elections at every level in recent years. The California Constitution contains a provision, adopted in 1984, that removes from office a person ". . . found liable in a civil action for making libelous statements against an opposing candidate during the course of an election campaign . . . where it is established that the libel or slander was a major contributing cause in the defeat of an opposing candidate."[39] Though a number of cases have been brought, no successful candidate for public office has ever been removed under this provision.

Ethics Commissions

There has been considerable debate about whether enough is done in New York about the scrutiny of the ethics of public officials. One solution is to establish a constitutionally based independent statewide ethics commission, as has been done in other states.

---

37   Hawaii: Article II, Sections 5 & 6. (Added by the 1978 Constitutional Convention, and ratified by the public in that year.); Rhode Island: Article IV, Section 10.

38   Arizona: Article II, Section 5; Rhode Island: Article IV, Section 9.

39   Article VII, Section 10.

The Constitutions of Texas, Hawaii, and Rhode Island mandate the creation of a state ethics commission. In Texas an eight-member bipartisan commission with four members appointed by the governor, and two each by the assembly speaker and lieutenant governor (the Senate presiding officer) seems somewhat misnamed. Its duties are left entirely to legislative discretion, except that it is given broad authority to set legislative compensation, subject to public referendum.[40]

In Rhode Island the commission must be "independent and nonpartisan" and adopt a code of ethics dealing at minimum with ". . . conflicts of interest, confidential information, use of position, contracts with government agencies and financial disclosure" applicable to all elected and appointed state and local officials. The commission is given powers to investigate, to impose penalties, and to remove officials not subject to removal by impeachment.[41]

The constitutional ethics provision in Hawaii is most extensive. It directs the legislature, each political subdivision and even any constitutional convention to adopt a code of ethics applicable to all elected and appointed officials. Each code is to be administered by a commission, with members ". . . selected in a manner which assures their independence and impartiality . . ." and who are barred from an active role in any political campaign. At minimum, ethics codes must cover ". . . gifts, confidential information, use of position, contracts with government agencies, post-employment, financial disclosure and lobbyist registration and restriction." Disclosure statements of all elected officers, candidates for elective office, and others designated by law (but including all those with ". . . discretionary or fiscal powers . . .") must cover ". . . sources and amounts of income, business ownership, officer and director positions, ownership of real property, debts, creditor interests in insolvent businesses and the names of persons represented before government agencies."[42]

40   Article 3, Section 23(a).
41   Article III, Section 8.
42   Article XIV.

Reforming New York's Constitutional System of Election Administration[1]

Gerald Benjamin

New York is one of two states that provides in its Constitution for a role for political parties in state and local election administration. The exceptional nature of these provisions leads to a questioning of whether election administration is an appropriately constitutional matter. An additional concern is for whether the structures and processes entrenched in the constitution for this purpose affect the fairness of the electoral process, and its efficiency.

Constitutional Provisions for Election Administration

The New York State Constitution has required since 1894 that "All laws creating, regulating or affecting boards or officers charged with the duty of registering voters, or distributing ballots to voters, or of receiving, recording or counting votes at elections, *shall secure equal representation of the two political parties which, at the general election next preceding that for which such boards or officers are to serve, cast the highest and the next highest number of votes.*" Additionally, the Constitution directs that "All such boards and officers shall be appointed or elected in such manner, and *upon the nomination of such representatives of said parties respectively,* as the legislature may direct.[2]

The Constitution exempts town and village elections not held at the time of the general election from the constitutional requirement for bipartisan supervision of their elections. By provision of a statute passed

---

1   Michael Owens and Ben Thomases provided research assistance for the preparation of this paper.

2   Article II, Section 8. An amendment in 1938 changed the wording of one phrase from "distributing ballots at the polls" to "distributing ballots to voters" in response to a court decision permitting absentee ballots to be distributed by county clerks (*Matter of Adams* v. *Flanagan* [1922]) cited in Peter Galie, *The New York Constitution: A Reference Guide* (Westport, CT: Greenwood, 1991), p. 74.

in 1986, boards of elections may run village elections at local request and expense. School districts and other special districts conduct their own elections, using voter lists provided by boards of elections.

The Election Law and Election Administration

Detailed statutory provisions further implement the state constitutional provisions concerning election administration.

The election law creates a state Board of Elections, comprised of four commissioners, appointed by the governor for two-year terms. Two of these are recommended by the chairs of the state committees of the major parties, and two by the leaders of the major parties in each legislative house. One of the legislative leaders' designees must be named as board chairman by the governor and the other as vice chairman.[3]

County elections commissioners serve for two years, though the term may be extended to four years at local option, and is now four years in New York City and Schenectady county by state law. Local commissioners are appointed by the county legislative board outside New York City, and the City Council in that city, upon the recommendation of the major parties. There are two commissioners in each county outside New York City and ten in the City (two for each county within it); outside the City at local option the number of commissioners may be increased to four in counties with populations that exceed 120,000.[4] Currently, all counties operate with two commissioners. Additionally, 48 employ two deputies, each appointed by a commissioner and serving at his or her pleasure.

The state Board of Elections is responsible in New York for the promotion of "fair, honest and efficiently administered elections." A revision of the election law in 1974 removed the remaining powers of the secretary of state and attorney general concerning election administration, and consolidated them in the Board.[5] To accomplish its mission, the Board of Elections is given the power to adopt regulations concerning election administration, campaign practices, and campaign finance. In addition it is authorized to encourage voting, study election processes and recom-

3   Election Law 3-100.1

4   Election Law 3-200.2; 3-202; 3-204.

5   Chapter 607, Laws of 1974. See generally, New York State Assembly, Standing Committee on Election Law, *Is Anybody in Charge Here?* (March 24, 1988). Prior to the passage of Chapter 607 of the Laws of 1974, the responsibility of election matters was shared by the secretary of state, who administered the election laws, and the attorney general, who enforced them.

mend improvements, oversee local boards, investigate alleged wrongdoing, and compel the production of evidence.[6]

State election law requires that state and local boards of elections operate by majority vote.[7] Because boards are comprised of an even number of members selected equally from each of the two largest parties, this requirement effectively means that no decision is possible without the approval of appointees recommended by both major parties. By not voting, the board member or members of a party may block an official action. This may have the effect of driving increased numbers of election disputes into the courts for decision; New York is reputed to have half of the election litigation in the country. According to one inside account, ". . . each year, in the month preceding the primary election, the judicial system must prepare itself for an 'avalanche' of cases involving challenges to candidates' petitions. . . ."[8]

New York boards of elections are structured in this way, as history (detailed below) indicates, to create an internal check in the agencies and prevent dominance by either major party of the electoral process. It is now conventional in American administrative practice to avoid agencies headed by boards, except for quasi-judicial functions. Even where they are used, to prevent deadlock even-numbered member boards are rarely created. Among the minority of states that use boards to administer the electoral process, only two besides New York — Illinois and Kentucky — have agencies with an even number of members.

Moreover, when boards head agencies executive authority is almost always vested by law in the head of the board. For example, the chairman of the state Civil Service Commission, which like the Board of Elections is required to be bipartisan, is by statute "head of the department."[9] The arrangement for the Public Service Commission is similar.[10] Before the state tax department was reorganized in 1986, the functions of the tax commission and of the commissioner as department head were distinct in the law.[11]

---

6   New York State Election Law, Section 3-102.

7   Election Law 3-100.4; 3-28.23

8   Katherine E. Scheulke, "A Call for Reform of New York State's Ballot Access Laws," *New York University Law Review* Vol. 64 (April, 1989) p. 190, citing Lewis. "Election Petition Cases in New York," *New York Law Journal* August 8, 1980, p. 1. The proportion of all election litigation that occurs in New York is given in *The New York Times* May 23, 1987, p. A26.

9   Civil Service Law. Article I, Section 5.

10 Public Service Law. Article I, Section 3.

11 See Tax Law — Article 8.170.1 — Until reorganization the Commissioner of Taxation and Finance was "head" of the department and *ex officio* chairman of the Commission. Under Article 8.170.6 the law provided that he was also "the executive of the State Tax Commission, and shall have sole charge of the administration of the department. The two other members of the commission shall join with the commissioner of taxation and finance in exercising the powers and performing the duties specifically imposed by law on the commission as a body."

The state Board of Elections in New York and its local counterpart agencies are distinctive not only because of their even number of members, but because their quasi-judicial and administrative functions are not distinguished, and executive authority for the latter is not vested by law in them in a single person. Weakness in executive direction of the agency resulting from this structure was cited as a problem in a state Assembly Election Committee Study in 1988.[12]

Historic Development

Over the course of New York's history, local election administrators have been chosen by appointment, by election or by a combination of these. Whatever the method used, a principal goal was to produce an honest unbiased electoral process. When election was employed to fill these jobs, statutory directives about the number of officials elected and the voting system used sought to assure that partisans of both major parties were included in the administrative process. When appointment was employed, provisions concerning the appointing authority, the number and source of appointees, and the partisan balance among them were designed to produce the same ends.

Though they differed in detail, all methods for administering elections in New York shared two basic assumptions. The first was that New York State had and would have a two-party system. The second was that a neutral, professional nonpartisan system of election administration was not possible.

Finally, despite the best efforts of reformers, all methods resulted in the domination by political parties and their leaders of the election machinery. When election administrators were elected, the parties controlled their nomination; when they were appointed, the parties were able to gain a legal and constitutional role in the appointing process. The result, one critic contends, is a system that makes the agencies that administer elections in New York "wholly-owned subsidiaries of New York's major political parties."[13]

Early Constitutional Provisions

The first state constitution was silent on the question of election administration or procedure, except that it explicitly left to the legislature whether voting

---

12   op. cit., *Is Anybody in Charge Here?* (1988).

13   Travis Plunkett, "The Case Against the State Board of Elections," *Empire State Report* (November 1992), p. 45.

would be by voice vote or ballot. The second constitution, adopted at the 1821 Convention, provided for the first time that elections be "... by ballot, except for such town officers as may by law be directed to be otherwise chosen."[14] A provision also added in 1821 directed the state legislature to make laws "... for ascertaining, by proper proofs, the citizens who shall be entitled to the right of suffrage ..." established in the Constitution.

Constitutional provisions added in the mid-nineteenth century focused not on election procedure but voter eligibility. For example, the 1846 Convention directed that a residence for voting purposes not be gained or lost as a consequence of federal service; employment at sea or on the waters of the state or nation; student status; residence in an almshouse or asylum at public expense; or imprisonment.[15] An amendment adopted in the midst of the cIvil War added that "... in time of war, no elector in the actual military service of the United States, in the Army or Navy thereof, shall be deprived of his vote by reason of his absence from the state...." and required the legislature to provide for voting by military personnel and counting these votes.

Statutory Provision for Election Administration

In Revolutionary and post-Revolutionary New York local officials were appointed, not elected, and the conduct of elections was their responsibility, or that of their designees. For example, administration of elections under New York's first election law, passed in 1778, was the duty of the town supervisor, clerk, and assessors acting as election inspectors in rural areas and the city of Albany (where the clerk, however, could not be an inspector), and of inspectors appointed in each ward by a group that included the mayor, recorder, aldermen, common councilmen, assessors, or vestrymen in New York City. Later laws retained this early model for towns, but generalized the practice of a group of officials, most often the Common Council, acting as the appointing authority for election administrators in the state's cities.[16]

Jacksonian Democracy brought broadened participation in local elections, the transition of the position of mayor from an appointive to an elective office in cities, and the practice of filling a large number of local offices by election. An 1840 statute mandated the division of New York City wards into election districts of approximately 500 people. Initially the Common Council appointed three election inspectors in

---

14   Article II, Sections 3 and 4.
15   Article II, Section 3.
16   Charles Z. Lincoln, *Constitutional History of New York*, Vol. III, pp. 114-116.

each district. Thereafter the law required the election of three commissioners of registry in each ward and three election inspectors in each district with voters limited to two votes for three positions. In geographic areas where one party dominated, nomination to these positions was tantamount to election, giving majority party leaders effective power to name two-thirds of those running elections locally. The limited vote provision made it likely (but not certain) that the other one-third of these officials would be chosen by the minority party leadership.

A law passed a year later, in 1841, directed the division of other cities in the state into election districts, with explicit provision that one of the initial appointees to three member Boards of Election Inspectors ". . . shall belong to a different party from the other two." Following initial appointments, the limited voting system adopted for New York City was to be used to fill these posts.[17]

The post-Civil War period in New York State was one of great political competitiveness between the major parties, considerable corruption, and, concomitantly, great efforts at reform. One retrospective turn of the century account catalogued these evils: party preparation and distribution near the polls of distinctive ballots, eliminating secrecy in voting; ballots printed on tissue paper, marked, folded together and "stuffed" in the ballot box; control of the electoral process by the locally dominant party; no means of identifying voters, leading to padding of the rolls with fictitious names; purchase of votes with liquor or cash; organized gangs of "repeaters" voting at different locations under fictitious names; party adherents lining up at the polls and not moving, blocking access by opposition voters; voter intimidation, with complicity of police appointed through partisan processes; and damage or falsification of ballots during counting, and then their immediate destruction to remove any evidence of fraud.[18]

Reform achievements during the late nineteenth century included the establishment of voter registration, government responsibility for ballot preparation in a form prescribed by law, the secret ballot, and bipartisan administration of elections.

Bipartisan Administration of Elections

An 1872 law applicable to New York City provided for the first time for equal party representation in election administration. At the time, conduct-

---

17 *Ibid*, pp. 116-117.
18 Robert H. Fuller, *Government by the People* (New York: The Macmillan Company, 1908), pp. 5-6.

ing elections in the city was the responsibility of a bureau of elections within the police department headed by a four-member commission, appointed to six-year terms. Under the terms of the statute, the police commission appointed four election inspectors in each election district to one-year terms, with the minority party police commissioner or commissioners recommending the minority party inspectors. Interestingly, and despite this provision concerning appointment authority, there appeared to be no statutory requirement that the police commission itself be bipartisan.[19]

This bipartisan system for New York City was imposed by a Republican legislature on the Democratic city, creating Republican patronage at local expense. In contrast, for upstate cities and rural areas state law provided for three to five election inspectors in each election district. Posts were filled by a system of election, appointment or a combination of the two that assured majority party control (almost always Republican), not equality, in election administration outside New York City.[20]

Equal party representation in a board with overall supervisory responsibility for elections within a city, rather than at the actual voting level, first appeared in Brooklyn in 1880. Under the provisions of a statute adopted in that year, each of the two major parties had two members of a city Board of Elections. Five year terms were provided to assure them a degree of independence. The mayor appointed his party's members. The first appointment of the minority party members was by the city comptroller, with subsequent appointments by the mayor. The appointments of registers, poll clerks, and inspectors, all by the mayor, was to be similarly bipartisan.[21]

When they gained control of the state government in 1892, Democrats moved to establish their control of the electoral process in New York City. "If boards of inspectors, a majority of whom are Republicans, are safe and economical in Republican strongholds of the state," Democratic Governor Roswell P. Flower argued, "boards of inspectors, a majority of whom are Democrats, ought to be equally safe and economical in the Democratic strongholds."[22] The Consolidated Election Law of 1882

19   Chapter 675, Laws of 1872. Recodified as Chapter 410 Laws of 1882.

20   For a general review of election law development in early New York see Lincoln, *Constitutional History*, Vol. III, pp. 114-131. Ballot Reform Law Chapter 262, Laws of 1890. This statute consolidated previously adopted election law provisions. Though the statute provided for five inspectors, the secretary of state, with the support of an attorney general's Opinion, decided three were sufficient. See *Revised Record of the 1894 Constitutional Convention*, Vol. III, p. 255. Remarks of Jesse Johnson of Brooklyn.

21   Chapter 528, Laws of 1880. Troy had a similar system between 1881 and 1892. See Lincoln, Vol. III, p. 123.

22   *Messages From the Governor* (1892), p. 103.

(which recodified provisions first adopted in 1872) was amended to provide for appointment by the police commission to one-year terms of three inspectors for every election district, two from the majority and one from the minority party. Additionally, they provided that appointments be made by the commission from lists provided by chairs of the party executive committees, and even established a procedure for determining which recommendations would be used if a ". . . political party is divided in said city into two or more factions."[23] This marked the further development of a statutory basis for the involvement of political party leaders in election administration when officials were appointed rather than elected, provisions for which first appeared in state election law for New York City in 1887.[24]

On the eve of the 1894 Constitutional Convention, Republicans recaptured control of the state legislature, but Flower remained governor. A compromise was reached, which established bipartisan election administration throughout the state. In rural areas two inspectors were to be elected and then two appointed, to assure partisan balance. In New York City and all other cities an appointment process would be used that included selection from lists provided by party leaders.[25]

What began as a reform thus evolved into bipartisan agreement to create a major patronage resource at public expense. By one estimate, at the turn of the century as a result of state provisions for bipartisan election administration each of the major parties could reward 18,400 trustworthy adherents with jobs paying at least $5 each on election day.[26]

Boards of Election in the Constitution

". . . [The 1894] constitutional convention," one leading historian of the period wrote, "gave the Republicans the opportunity to embed the reforms in fundamental law."[27] The Convention Committee on Suffrage sought, in the language of its chairman Edward Lautenbach, to "secure in perpetuity" the provisions of this compromise, even before it went into effect.[28] The committee's first draft required equal representation of the two major parties on boards of elections, but with no role in their selection by party

---

23   Chapter 410 Laws of 1882.

24   Lincoln, Vol. III, p. 124.

25   Chapter 348 Laws of 1894.

26   Howard F. Gosnell, *Boss Platt and His New York Machine*, New York: Russell and Russell, 1924, reissued 1969, p. 146.

27   Richard L. McCormack, *From Realignment to Reform: Political Change in New York State, 1893-1910* (Ithaca: Cornell, 1981), p. 52.

28   *Revised Record of the 1894 Constitutional Convention*, Vol. III, p. 111.

officials. Upon submitting the question for debate on the floor of the convention (and after consultation with the Committee on Cities, which was also interested in the question) Lautenbach immediately added an amendment providing a constitutional role in nominating board members for party leaders, similar to the provisions of the 1894 statute. When an objection was raised about the substantial nature of this change by John Cochran, a Brooklyn Democrat and committee member, the matter was laid over so that the committee could meet again. It later reported the provision with the party leader role intact.[29]

During the debate on this question, Benjamin Dean, a Republican of Jamestown, observed that this approach would entrench in the Constitution the power of the state chairman of each of the major parties to ". . . decide the regularity of the election officials in every city in this State. . . ." A later effort was made by John Bowers, a Democrat of New York, to remove party leaders from the process. The idea of their inclusion was defended on the grounds that no appointing authority selected through a partisan process (for example, the governor) should be situated to choose the watchdogs of the opposing party. Bower's amendment failed in a voice vote.[30]

Charles Z. Lincoln, who served as a delegate to the 1894 Convention, points out in his *Constitutional History of New York* that it was not Lauterbach's intent to have the bipartisan requirement apply to ". . . central boards of elections or police boards or commissioners or other officers who might be charged with the duty of appointing local election officers, and that it was intended to apply only to officers in election districts."[31] This is why Lauterbach and Bowers amended the constitutional language requiring bipartisanship to apply to "officers [who] shall distribute ballots *to voters at the polls.*" (The Constitution notwithstanding, an early twentieth century account of election administration in New York notes that responsibilities for election administration were ". . . performed by a Commissioner of Elections in the city of Buffalo and the County of Westchester and by county clerks or town clerks in other parts of the state.")[32]

Additional issues arose about the application of bipartisan election administration to town meetings and village charter elections held at times different than the general elections. Rural delegates pointed out that elected justices of the peace and town clerks traditionally presided at these

---

29   *Revised Record*, Vol. III, p. 244.
30   *Revised Record*, Vol. III, pp. 248 and 270.
31   Lincoln, p. 129.
32   Fuller, 1908, p. 88.

meetings, and argued that without an exception for these, ". . . big men of their respective localities . . ." would mobilize sentiment against the entire constitution.[33] After a long debate on the appropriate language, delegates voted to exclude "town meetings and village elections" from the reach of this constitutional provision. An attempt to similarly specifically except nonpartisan school district elections failed, perhaps because it was proposed by the gadfly, Benjamin Dean.[34]

Dean was the only convention delegate to raise general objections to the bipartisan election procedure, which he described as one more reform "fetich." He pointed out the difficulty that might arise in getting a decision if the parties were divided on a matter before a board with an even number of members, and argued that an elected board accountable to the public was preferable, even if controlled by one party. Later, Nathan Woodward, a Batavia Republican, also questioned the capacity of a bipartisan board with an even number of members from each party to decide controversial matters. Defenders of the provision acknowledged that hypothetically, deadlocks on such a board were possible, but argued that experience showed that they were rare. Moreover, the annoyance of occasional deadlock between parties was a risk worth taking, Jesse Johnson of Brooklyn said, to ". . . avoid the much greater . . . danger and menace of the majority party having practically the control over the election."[35]

Though strongly influenced by reform elements in the Republican party, the 1894 state Constitutional Convention was comprised of members elected on a partisan basis from the two major parties. Perhaps this explains why, in this era of civil service reform and third party activity nationally, advocates of fairness in election administration at the 1894 Constitutional Convention gave little attention to three sets of issues: possible circumstances in which the interests of leaders of the major parties converged, undermining their incentives to check each other; the protection of the interests of minor parties in election administration; and the possibility of a nonpartisan system for running elections.

The 1915 Convention

Election administration was not a controversial matter when the 1915 Constitutional Convention met. There was public discussion prior to the convention of a procedure for selection of election officers by competitive civil service

---

33   Revised Proceedings, Vol. III, p. 246. Remarks of William Dickey of Newburgh.

34   *Revised Record*, Vol. III, p. 245.

35   *Revised Record*, Vol. III, p. 254.

examination, rather than ". . . leaving the choice of these important officers to the two great party Machines as represented in their local organizations." Opponents pointed out, however, that such a step would compromise bipartisan election administration as required by the state Constitution.[36] Four proposals for changes in provisions concerning election administration were offered at the 1915 Convention, one of which suggested a neutral, civil service approach. None reached the floor for action.

The 1938 Convention

In reaction to a court decision in 1922, which found it constitutional for a town clerk to perform the task, the 1938 Constitutional Convention amended Article II to make clear that issuance and receipt of absentee ballots was to be the responsibility of bipartisan boards.[37] The task for bipartisan boards was changed from "distributing ballots at the polls to voters" to "distributing ballots to voters." This undid the amendment added at the 1894 Convention that sought to apply the bipartisanship in election administration only to the actual site of voting but not to higher administrative levels. In a 1942 decision the Court of Appeals then determined that the bipartisan requirement "apparently applies not only to the local boards of inspectors who actually perform "the duty of registering voters, or of distributing ballots . . . at elections," but also to the members of the county and New York City boards of elections which administer the election machinery generally."[38]

The 1967 Convention

The draft 1967 Constitution, rejected at the polls, retained bipartisan boards of elections, but removed nomination of their members by party organization representatives. School board elections were specifically excluded from the jurisdiction of these boards, as were ". . . a village or special district election where candidates of neither such parties were on the ballot at the preceding election therein." The retention of the village exclusion, a goal of rural upstate Republicans in the convention minority, survived narrowly. The exclusion for towns, however, was eliminated.[39]

---

36   Fuller, 1908, p. 175.

37   *Matter of Adams* v. *Flanagan* 201 App. Div. 735 (2nd. Dept., 1922) aff'd 234 N.Y. 540 (1922).

38   Temporary State Commission on the Constitutional Convention, *The Right to Vote,* Albany: The Commission, Pamphlet #4, 1967, p. 54; *Thomas* v. *Wells* 288 N.Y. 155 (1942).

39   Article II, Section 2. *Proceeding of the 1967 New York State Constitutional Convention,* Vol. II, pp. 392-402.

Research prior to the convention questioned whether boards of elections required constitutional status, especially since their operation was subject to judicial review. The mechanism of bipartisan boards was defended as providing the necessary checks and balances to keep elections impartial, and for their capacity to mobilize large numbers of part-time workers through the parties on election day. Detractors questioned their impartiality with regard to third parties and in administering primaries in which one board member by definition had no interest. Two alternative approaches suggested were multiparty representation on election boards or replacement of the board system with a corps of professional county and city election administrators. Under the latter model, boards (though perhaps not with an even number of members) would be retained for quasi-judicial functions.[40]

The inclusion of a provision for bipartisan boards was twice challenged at the convention in ways that indicated discontent with the system among reformers and third parties. David Bromberg proposed in an amendment to delete all reference to such boards from the convention, leaving the question to the legislature. He argued that the provision cemented control by the major parties of the election machinery in a manner "neither fair nor just." ". . . [A]ll too often the major party representatives on Boards of Elections tend to combine in favor of the regular organization designees of the major parties and to exhibit . . . a bipartisan lack of sympathy with insurgents." Third-party candidacies were equally disadvantaged, Bromberg said, before such boards. Moreover, he argued, the bipartisan board structure automatically produced deadlock, protected the status quo, and was inefficient in that it resulted in "...two partisan groups [of staff], working more or less independently under different members of the board and often at cross purposes." Though taking the matter out of the Constitution would not automatically produce change, it would, he concluded, make change more likely over the long run.

Bromberg's amendment failed by a vote of 128 to 17, proving at least to his satisfaction the bipartisan interest in the constitutional status quo that he had earlier identified.[41]

In a later effort at amending this provision, Alex Rose, long-time head of the Liberal Party, suggested a nine-member Honest Ballot Association to oversee boards of elections so as to ". . . establish and guarantee the principle of observing the ethics and morality of an honest election count. . . ." No more than three of the members of such a board, Rose said, would be of a single party. He argued that such a change would facilitate representation of

---

40   Temporary State Commission on the Constitutional Convention, *The Right to Vote* (Document #4), 1966, pp. 56-57.

41   *1967 Proceedings*, Vol. II, pp. 417-419.

unenrolled voters in the process, and build confidence in what had become a poorly functioning and two-party dominated process of election administration. It would also, of course, allow third parties to gain representation in the process. The idea failed in a voice vote.[42]

Other States' Provisions

Constitutional Treatment

Thirty-six of the 50 states deal with election administration entirely by statute and regulation; they do not have constitutional provisions on the subject.[43] Distinctions among these states are few. New Hampshire's Constitution is totally silent on the question. The others direct their legislatures to provide for the basics of a democratic electoral system — pure, free, and equal elections, the use of the secret ballot and voting machines, and a defined system of voter eligibility and registration.

Alabama, Arkansas, Delaware, Louisiana, Massachusetts, Minnesota, Ohio, and Pennsylvania do maintain provisions that establish some constitutionally based organization to handle the administration of elections and the resolution of disputes. But they do not establish a partisan role of any kind on election boards nor do they mention any other form of party involvement and activity in the election process. For example, the Delaware Constitution provides only that judges are to be charged with mediating election disputes and establishing penalties for election related crimes.[44] In Minnesota a board of canvassers, comprised of the secretary of the state (whose office administers the elections), two disinterested district court judges, and one or more supreme court justices, is empowered to examine election returns and declare results. Pennsylvania's Constitution provides for district election boards, comprised of one judge and two independent inspectors elected at municipal elections.

Only six state constitutions (those of Illinois, Michigan, New Mexico, New York, Oklahoma, and Virginia) have provisions authorizing partisan membership on state entities overseeing elections. Most provide no affirmative role for parties or party officials, but seek to prohibit

---

42 *1967 Proceedings*, Vol. II, pp. 423-425.

43 The states are Alaska, Arizona, California, Colorado, Connecticut, Florida, Georgia, Hawaii, Idaho, Indiana, Iowa, Kansas, Kentucky, Maine, Maryland, Mississippi, Missouri, Montana, Nebraska, Nevada, New Hampshire, New Jersey, North Carolina, North Dakota, Oregon, Rhode Island, South Carolina, South Dakota, Tennessee, Texas, Utah, Vermont, Washington, West Virginia, Wisconsin, and Wyoming.

44 Delaware statute provides for a state election commissioner, appointed by the governor, with local county boards of elections having six nonpartisan members. Del. Code tit. 15, Secs. 301 and 105 (1975).

domination of any one party. The Illinois Constitution instructs the legislature to create a board of elections to supervise registration and elections, on which "no political party shall have a majority of the members." Michigan's Constitution mandates legislative establishment of four-member state boards of canvassers, and provides that "a majority of any board of canvassers shall not be composed of members of the same political party." New Mexico's Constitution provides that "not more than two members of the board of registration, and not more than two judges of election shall belong to the same political party at the time of their appointment." Similarly, Oklahoma's Constitution establishes a state election board empowered to supervise elections, of which "not more than a majority of said board shall be selected from the same political party."

Virginia's constitutional provision is closest to New York's in its affirmative provision for a party role. It provides for three-member county and city electoral boards, and requires that "in the appointment of the electoral boards, representation, as far as practicable, shall be given to each of the two political parties which, at the general election next preceding their appointment, cast the highest and next highest number of votes." It also stipulates the appointment of election and registration officers in accordance with the partisan representation scheme mentioned above. Though Virginia, like in New York, has a bipartisan state Election Board, this is not constitutionally required, nor are the boards in that state composed of an equal number of members from each major party. Currently, by statute, the deciding member of the three-member Virginia election boards is selected from the party that controls the General Assembly.[45]

Board for Administration

Also in 36 states, prime responsibility for administration of elections is vested in a single individual. Usually it is an elected secretary of state or his or her appointee, but in three states (Alaska, Hawaii, and Utah) it is the lieutenant governor, and in one (Delaware) it is a commissioner appointed by the governor. In these states, a board comprised of officials serving *ex officio* is often used to certify election results. Three New England States that administer elections through the secretary of state's office — Massachusetts, New Hampshire, and Connecticut — maintain a separate board to perform quasi-judicial functions. In Georgia, Iowa, Kentucky, Oklahoma, Rhode Island, South Dakota, and Wisconsin, the

---

45 Virginia Constitution, Article II, Section 8. A.E. Dick Howard, *Commentaries on the Constitution of Virginia* (Charlottesville: University Press of Virginia, 1972), pp. 424-428. The Virginia statute declares that "A majority of the board shall be of the political party having the highest number of members in the General Assembly" [VA. Code Sec. 24 1-19 (Supp. 1977)].

secretary of state acts with or under the supervision of a bipartisan board in administering elections. Finally, in the seven remaining states, including New York, boards are given full authority.[46]

The pattern at the local level is similar, with election administration most commonly made the responsibility of an elected county clerk or similar official of different title. Even within states patterns vary, with boards or other special structures commonly used, for example, in big cities or larger counties. Additionally, the use of boards, and the provision for party balance in the process, is more common at the local level, where actual voting takes place, than at the state level. Interestingly, in many local jurisdictions the voter registration function is kept distinct from election administration. This dispersal of responsibility is an additional check on corruption, and is similar to that commonly used for fiscal functions.

Reforming New York's System of Election Administration

The goal of New York's Article II, Section 8 is to foster fairness in the administration of state and local elections. However, as Governor Roswell Flower noted over a century ago, "the mere fact that election [administrators] are divided equally among the two great parties adds not an iota to the honesty of the elections."[47] What it does achieve is substantial control of the political process by the two major parties, additional costs in election administration because of duplication and overlap, and increased burdens on the courts, which must resolve candidate and party conflicts when poorly structured administrative processes become deadlocked.

The history of New York's constitutional provisions for election administration, and a review of the constitutions of other states, does not produce a convincing case for treating this subject in a state constitution. Moreover, other states' practices suggest alternative, statutory-based frameworks that might allow New York to achieve greater fairness in running its elections while both narrowing the influence that the major political parties have over the process and perhaps reducing the need for election litigation.

One reform study suggests that a "model election administration system" would "fix responsibility for general supervision of elections in a single officer of state government," and "clearly assign responsibility

46   Brian Hancock, "The Administrative Structure of State and Local Election Offices," *Technical Report 3,* Washington: Federal Election Commission, February 1992.

47   *Messages from the Governor,* Vol. IX, 1892, p. 105.

for conduct of elections to single county and city officers." It also recommends that the responsible state official should serve ". . . under the merit system of civil service for an indefinite term under the Secretary of State . . ." and should appoint single officials in counties or cities, also through the civil service, to register voters and conduct elections.[48]

The creation of such a system in New York would require constitutional amendment. Whether or not it follows these recommendations precisely, however, an alternative system in the state might seek to:

❋ establish an effective center of executive authority by law in the election administration agency;

❋ remove control of the process by regular party organization leaders in the two major political parties;

❋ provide for professional administration by persons selected on a competitive basis and accountable to an official appointed by a neutral authority (perhaps an *ex officio* board chaired by a judge of the state's high court) and serving for a relatively long term;

❋ allow for policy guidance for the administrator by that *ex officio* board; and

❋ establish a quasi-judicial forum to resolve election disputes and penalize election law offenses in a strictly neutral manner.

An alternative to the model outlined above would:

❋ give the executive director of the State Board and a single person in the counties and New York City statutory-based executive authority to manage these agencies;

❋ retain state and local election boards for policy making and quasi-judicial functions but enlarge them so that they are comprised of an odd number of members — perhaps five as is now the case in Maryland, North Carolina, and South Carolina — and prohibit any party from having more than two members on a board.

While likely to improve management, opening the process to minority party interests and guaranteeing against stalemates, this alternative would retain partisan dominance of the state's electoral process.

---

48   George Hallett, *Model Election Administration System,* New York: National Municipal League, 1961, pp. 6 and 8.

Individual Liberties and "Positive Rights"

O ne reason that the Founders did not at first include a Bill of Rights in the United States Constitution was that citizens' rights were regarded as protected in already existing state constitutions. As a result of the debates over ratification, the amendments that now comprise the U.S. Bill of Rights were proposed by the first Congress and ratified by the states. They are now regarded as an integral part of the original document. At the same time, state Bills of Rights remained. When it comes to individual rights, the U.S. Bill of Rights as interpreted by the national Supreme Court provides a floor but not a ceiling for citizens. State constitutions as interpreted by state courts may not diminish rights protected by the national Constitution, but may augment them. And often they do.

The New York Constitution puts rights first, in Article I. Burt Agata notes in his introductory essay in this section that the New York State Court of Appeals, the state's highest court, has extended the state constitutional protections for speech in New York beyond those provided under the national Constitution. Agata provides an overview of the history of the New York Bill of Rights, summarizes current interpretations, and draws upon the constitutions of other states to suggest areas in which a constitutional convention might define additional rights, for example, to privacy; against discrimination based on gender, sexual preference, or disability; and to give special protections to children.

In recent years critics have argued that state courts have gone so far in using the New York Constitution to raise protections for the accused above the federal floor that a debate on this subject is likely if a convention is held. In a second essay in this section, Burt Agata looks at the constitutional rights of criminal defendants as part of an overall examination of state constitutional provisions that shape the criminal justice system.

Bills of Rights are conventionally understood as sources of protection for citizens against abuses by government. One distinctive characteristic of state constitutions is that they also include "positive rights" of citizens to receive something from government. For example, the New York State Constitution says that "The legislature shall provide for the maintenance and support of a system of free common schools. . . ." It also says that "The aid, care and support of the needy are public concerns and shall be provided by the state. . . ." The essay in this section by Robert Stone explores the history and meaning of New York's education article. Litigation notwithstanding, and unlike the situation in many other states, this article in New York has not been the basis of major reform in educational finance or organization in recent years. Looking at the several state constitutional provisions concerning social policy, Gerald Benjamin and Melissa Cusa consider the implications of New York's unique constitutional requirement upon the state to help the poor. This provision gained considerable publicity in 1996 when Congress passed welfare legislation giving increased flexibility to the states. The obvious question raised is how New York's constitutional provision to care for the poor will affect the state's response to this new federal approach.

New York's constitutional provision to keep the Catskill and Adirondack Preserves "forever wild" was an early achievement of the conservation movement in the United States. William Ginsburg explores the history and later interpretation of this provision and others of significance to environmental policy, and outlines nascent efforts to create a positive right to a safe and clean environment.

Individual Liberties

Burton C. Agata

This chapter deals with those provisions in the New York State Constitution that are concerned with individual liberties, i.e., those matters usually included in a Bill of Rights.[1] Mention of individual liberties protected by a Bill of Rights commonly causes focus on the Bill of Rights in the United States Constitution. But as originally conceived and enforced by the courts, the federal Constitution's Bill of Rights was intended to protect against the acts of the new national government and not those of state governments.[2]

The Bill of Rights comes at the beginning of the New York Constitution, not at its end as in the national document, and that is significant. In theory, the national government is one of limited, delegated powers. The Bill of Rights in the national Constitution is an added assurance of limits on national government achieved in the Constitution by other means. In contrast, the powers of state governments are plenary, except as specifically limited. It is therefore necessary to set out individual protections in state constitutions at the outset.

From the beginning of the Republic until shortly after World War II, the state constitutions were at least as much of a focus for defining the rights of the individual as was the federal Constitution. However, it is also true that there were very few cases significantly involving individual liberties under the state constitutions (or the federal Constitution, for that matter). One view is that individual liberties issues were just not seen as litigable questions throughout most of the nineteenth century.[3] Moreover, much of the concern about individual liberties, particularly with respect to racial issues and free speech and assembly, was attributable to sometimes oppressive state actions.

---

1   The provisions concerned with criminal justice will not be covered in this chapter. They are dealt with in the chapter on Criminal Justice in this book.

2   In *Barron* v. *Baltimore*, 32 U.S. (7 Pet.) 243 (U.S. 1833), the Supreme Court held that the federal Constitution's Bill of Rights was a limitation on the national and not the state governments.

3   See, Kincaid, "The State and Federal Bills of Rights: Partners and Rivals in Liberty," *Intergovernmental Perspective* 17, 31 (1991): 32.

The idea at the founding was that the state constitutions would define the people's protection from state government, for here the people had some degree of control. Most of the language and ideas for the federal Bill of Rights, added to the Constitution after its ratification as a condition of adoption, were derived from the state constitutions.[4] Until the passage of the post-Civil War Thirteenth, Fourteenth, and Fifteenth Amendments to the federal Constitution, the United States Constitution's protection of individual liberties was against federal and not state government action.[5]

Significant federal court involvement in Bill of Rights claims against state action began in the 1920s.[6] Until shortly after World War II, the results were mixed in terms of the expansion of individual liberties under the federal Bill of Rights. Selectively applying its provisions to the states through various provisions of the post Civil War amendments, the United States Supreme Court greatly extended the protections of the national Bill of Rights during the third of a century following World War II. But with the changes in its membership during the past 15 to 20 years, there has been a slowing of the expansion of those rights achieved by the Court under Chief Justice Earl Warren.

Currently, and over the past decade or more, there has been a revived interest in state constitutions as important vehicles for defining individual liberties. This is due in part to the less sympathetic posture the current Supreme Court has taken with regard to reliance on the Bill of Rights as a limit on state government action. But it is also due to attempted expansion of constitutional protections to areas heretofore not deemed to be reached by the federal Bill of Rights. Some argue, in fact, that states were intended to ". . . remain the principal protectors of individual rights — 'the immediate and visible guardian(s) of life and property.'"[7]

Of course, the Bill of Rights in the federal Constitution remains fundamental for determining individual rights. The United States Supreme Court's determination of its scope, when applied to the states through the Fourteenth Amendment and the rights guaranteed by the

---

4   The main sources for the federal Bill of Rights were the Virginia Bill of Rights, the 1780 Massachusetts Constitution, and some of the colonial charters.

5   Prior to that time, there were some limited areas where the federal Constitution protected against state action. For example, the "privileges and immunities" clause of the original Constitution was held to guarantee freedom of movement across state borders without interference by the states. *Crandall* v. *Nevada*, 6 Wall. 35 US 1868. However, the subject matter of these areas was very limited when compared with the expansive and expanded view of individual liberties that developed later. Also consider *Dred Scott* v. *Sandford*, 19 How. 393 US 1857 and the view of federal courts as a protector of civil liberties which it fostered.

6   See *Gitlow* v. *New York*, 268 US 652 1925. (Court began to apply Bill of Rights to states on a theory of incorporation through the Fourteenth Amendment).

7   See Judith Kaye, "Dual Constitutionalism in Practice and Principle," *Record* 42 (1987): 289.

Thirteenth and Fifteenth Amendments, serves as a floor under the constitutional rights of the individual. States may build upon these, but may not diminish them. Perhaps equally important, Supreme Court Bill of Rights decisions strongly influence many state courts in the construction of their state constitutions. Moreover, there are areas, particularly matters of First Amendment concern, where the current Court can be and is viewed as expansionist or, at least, as holding the line. However, state courts may independently interpret their constitutional provisions. Further, "(h)istory tells us that the independent protection of individual rights under state constitutions is not new; nor is it an illegitimate assumption of authority by state courts."[8]

While there currently is significant support for turning to state constitutions as an important source of individual liberties protection, there are also misgivings, based upon four factors: lack of confidence in the states based on the sometimes sorry history of individual liberties under state constitutions; concern that popular control of the state courts unduly influences the actions of those courts on controversial issues; concern that too great a reliance on the state constitutions would relieve the pressure on the federal judiciary to continue its role as an active protector of individual liberties; and belief that the definition of individual liberties is more properly a national function and that those liberties should not depend on the geographic location of the person.[9]

In response, proponents suggest that, "[T]he argument that the states are incapable of protecting rights adequately seems to have little merit in the context of the 1980s. . . . [T]he states often take the lead in defining and expanding individual liberty." Moreover, they say, in determining where the major focus on protection of individual liberties should be, the question "is not always a matter of more or fewer rights." It can be a matter of balancing conflicting rights, and ". . . where state courts have recognized the legitimacy of the rights claimed on both sides of a conflict, they have struck different balances among them, seeking to accommodate both claims in keeping with its (sic) own state constitutional tradition."[10]

---

8   *Ibid.*

9   For more extended discussions, see: Hall, "The Legacy of 19th-Century State Bills of Rights," *Intergovernmental Perspective* 17, 15 (1991); Advisory Commission on Intergovernmental Relations, "The States and Civil Liberties," *State Constitutions in the Federal System, Selected Issues and Opportunities for State Initiatives*, 49 (1985).

10   See Advisory Commission on Intergovernmental Relations, "State Constitutional Law: The Ongoing Search for Unity and Diversity in the American Federal System." *State Constitutions in the Federal System, Selected Issues and Opportunities for State Initiatives*, 49 (1985): 119 and 120-21.

Finally, they argue, "[t]oday, a total dependence on the national government for a uniform definition of rights would, in all likelihood, diminish the scope of individual liberty in the United States. The development of an independent state constitutional law of civil liberties, on the other hand, would not only be likely to expand individual rights but would also encourage experimentation in developing appropriate balances when rights are in conflict."[11]

The New York State Constitution's Bill of Rights

The New York State Constitution's Bill of Rights (Article I) currently has fifteen sections (there is a separate article, Article II, which deals with suffrage).[12] The first New York State Constitution, adopted in 1777, had only four provisions in its Bill of Rights. They were: a prohibition on denying "a member of the state" the right to vote or any other right or privilege "unless by the law of the land or[13] the judgment of his peers"; a guaranty of trial by jury; and religious liberty.[14] These three provisions, as subsequently amended, are in the current state Constitution, as Article I, Sections 1, 2, and 3 and 6, respectively.

The development of the state Constitution's Bill of Rights is a product of responses to specific issues of the day and cautionary action to assure that rights recognized by some state statutes had constitutional status. The language of the amendments to the state's Bill of Rights often was the exact language of the federal Constitution or of an existing state statute. In some instances, the reason for proposing an

---

11   See Chapters 4, 6, and 10, Advisory Commission on Intergovernmental Relations, *State Constitutions in the Federal System, Selected Issues and Opportunities for State Initiatives,* (1985); Kincaid, "The State and Federal Bill of Rights: Partners and Rivals in Liberty," *Intergovernmental Perspective* 17, 31 (1991): 21.

12   The last section in Article I is 18, but there only are fifteen sections because §§10, 13, and 15 were repealed in 1962.These repealed sections dealt with real property. Section 10 dealt with escheat, allodial tenures, and the abolition of feudal tenures. In large measure, they were the result of the rent wars or revolts in New York State's Hudson Valley by tenants against such landowners as the Van Rensselaers. Sections 13 and 15 dealt with purchase of Indian lands and grants under the English charters. The provisions were largely of historic interest and their repeal as late as 1962 provides some insight into one of the basic criticisms of the New York State Constitution, i.e., it requires pruning, which rarely occurs. In all likelihood, any continuing substantive effect of the repealed provisions are now governed by the due process clause. For extended discussion, see "Problems Relating to Bill of Rights and General Welfare." *Report of the New York State Constitutional Convention Committee* VI, XIV (1938) (hereafter, *Poletti Report).*

13   The original provision said "and" instead of "or." The change was the product of the 1938 Convention.

14   Interestingly, the Declaration of Independence was set out verbatim in this first New York State Constitution, but it did not contain an extensive detailed Bill of Rights.

amendment does not appear in the records of the convention that proposed it.[15]

Trial by Jury in Civil Cases

Article 1, Section 2, provides that "[t]rial by jury in all cases in which it has heretofore been guaranteed by constitutional provision shall remain inviolate forever."[16] The constitutional provision permits waiver of a jury in civil cases[17] and authorizes the legislature to provide that, in a civil case, a jury verdict may be rendered by not less than five-sixths of the jury.[18]

A number of other constitutional provisions bear upon trial by jury in civil cases. Part of the article on the judiciary (Article VI, Section 18(a)) states: "Trial by jury is guaranteed as provided in article one of this constitution." The provision then goes on to authorize the legislature to provide for jury trials of six or twelve persons.[19] Another section of that article (18[b]) abolished a right to a jury trial in claims against the state. Additionally, the right to a jury trial in workers' compensation cases has been abolished by Article I, Section 18.[20]

Freedom of Worship and Religious Liberty[21]

Article I, Section 3, of the New York Constitution provides that:

> The free exercise and enjoyment of religious profession and worship, without discrimination or preference, shall forever be allowed in this state to all mankind;[22] and no person shall be rendered incompetent to be a witness on account of his opinions

---

15 Rights having to do with criminal justice and "affirmative rights" included in the state Constitution but not in Article I are discussed in other chapters in this book, and will not be taken up here.

16 For a discussion of the origins of its provision, and its evolution, see the chapter in this book on "Criminal Justice." It should be noted that to the extent this provision by its terms seeks to prevent future changes by constitutional amendment with respect to the right to a jury trial, it cannot be effective. Of course, any amendment would have to satisfy federal constitutional requirements as well as state constitutional amendment procedure.

17 Added by the 1846 Convention. Waiver of jury criminal trials is considered in the chapter on "Criminal Justice."

18 Added by amendment in 1935. The number of jurors required for verdict and the number required to constitute a jury in criminal cases are considered in the chapter on "Criminal Justice."

19 For discussion of criminal jury trials and Article VI, Section 18, including an unconstitutional aspect of the section, see, the chapter on "Criminal Justice" in this book

20 This is discussed in the context of Section 18, below.

21 The prohibition of state aid to religious schools (Article XI, Section 3), is discussed in the chapter on "Education" in this book.

22 In the 1777 Constitution.

on matters of religious belief;[23] but the liberty of conscience hereby secured shall not be so construed as to excuse acts of licentiousness, or justify practices inconsistent with the peace and safety of the state.[24]

In comparison the relevant parts of the first amendment to the United States Constitution read:

Congress shall make no law respecting an establishment of religion, or prohibiting the free exercise thereof;

Professor Peter Galie offers a succinct comparison between these provisions. He notes that whereas the federal Constitution addresses two matters, establishment of religion and free exercise, the state Constitution has three parts ". . . the first guarantees religious liberty, the second forbids any religious qualifications for competency as a witness, and the third, an abuse-of-liberty clause, preserves the state police power to prevent conduct inconsistent with the peace, welfare, and safety of the state." Galie observes further: "There is no reference to establishment of a religion or to government action, as in the federal provision. While the federal provision speaks in absolute terms, the state provision speaks in terms of balancing interests.[25]

Subject, of course, to the limitations on state action concerning "free exercise" and "establishment" that the Supreme Court applies to the states through the Fourteenth Amendment, the relation of the state to religion has been characterized generally as one of accommodation and the balancing of interests. Constitutional provisions require that state agencies place children in places governed by the same religious persuasion of the children where possible (Article VI, Section 32); and afford religious institutions tax exemptions for property (Article XVI, Section 1). The courts have displayed sympathy for religious organizations in decisions that permit building of places of worship in residential areas.[26]

---

23   Added by the 1846 Constitution. "Up to 1846, except in a few cases witnesses were not permitted to testify unless they professed a belief in the existence of the Supreme Being and in a future and present state of punishment and rewards. . . . In addition, ministers and priests were ineligible to hold office. (Constitution of 1777 Article XXXIX; Constitution of 1821 Article VII, Section 4). In 1846 the disability of ministers and priests was removed by eliminating Article VII, Section 4 . . ." Although the 1846 Constitution contained the clause concerning competency of witnesses, it was not until 1903 that the Court of Appeals in *Brink* v. *Stratton*, 176 N.Y. 150, held that the provision "prohibited all discrimination against witnesses because of their religious opinions. It was decided that not only was a witness entitled to testify regardless of what his religious opinions were, but his credibility could not be attacked because he did not believe in the Supreme Being or a future state of punishment and rewards." *Poletti Report*, at pp. 27-28.

24   In the 1777 Constitution.

25   See Galie, at p. 38.

26   See Galie, at p. 39.

A recurring area of concern involves the conflict between prison inmates' rights to religious freedom under the state Constitution and the interests of the correctional authorities. The verbal formula for judging these conflicts under the state Constitution differs from the one used under the federal Constitution. The federal constitutional formula would uphold a prison regulation "if it is reasonably related to legitimate penological interests."[27] The state standard "requires the balancing of the competing interests at stake: the importance of the right asserted and the extent of the infringement are weighed against the institutional needs and objectives being promoted."[28]

Potentially, the divergence of these approaches could lead to different results. One intermediate appellate court has held, however, that the difference between the two approaches is "more verbal than substantive."[29] It is likely that this area of prisoners' rights will continue to be a testing ground for Article I, Section 3.

The Due Process Clause

Article I, Section 6, *inter alia*, provides:[30]

No person shall be deprived of life, liberty, or property without due process of law.

The language is practically the same as the due process clause in the Fifth Amendment to the federal Constitution. It was added to the state Constitution by the 1821 Convention, and, as a practical matter, replaced the "law of the land" provision in Article I as an active concept in New York state constitutional law.[31]

The due process clause has a procedural scope and a substantive scope. Until the mid-1930s, the substantive scope of the state provision, like the United States Supreme Court's use of the Fifth Amendment's due process clause, was a barrier to much social welfare legislation, particularly that concerned with issues involving labor.[32] The state provision still has the substantive scope, but the basic approach of the New York state courts

---

27 *Turner* v. *Safley*, 482 US 78, 79 (1988).

28 *Matter of Lucas* v. *Scully*, 71 NY 2d 399, 406 (1988).

29 *Matter of Bunny* v. *Coughlin*, 187 AD 2d 119 (3d Dept. 1993). For a recent attempt to apply the standards, see *Jackson* v. *Coughlin*, 156 Misc. 2d 975 (Sup. Albany 1993).

30 Section 6 also contains provisions relating to the Grand Jury, self-incrimination and waiver of immunity by public officers. Each is discussed in the chapter on Criminal Justice. This paper deals only with the due process clause of Section 6.

31 See *Poletti Report*, at p. 2.

32 See *Poletti Report*, at pp. 295-97.

when a fundamental right is not involved is to determine whether there is a rational basis for legislation and a valid legislative purpose against the backdrop of a presumption of constitutionality of enactments by the state legislature. When fundamental rights are involved, the legislation is judged by the so-called strict scrutiny test.[33]

State courts have found broader rights under the state's due process clause than were required by the federal constitutional provision. Former Chief Justice of the Court of Appeals Sol Wachtler offered this summary:

> Due process is guaranteed by both state and federal constitutions and is one of the cornerstones of American jurisprudence. The concept is said to have been derived from a statute enacted in New York, and it always has had a special significance in this state. The ideal of basic fairness which is at the core of due process, applies across the spectrum of civil and criminal cases. In recent years, it has been held to entitle the citizens of this state to contact visits with family members while detained awaiting trial, to refuse unwanted medication, and to receive prior notice of a garageman's intent to sell a car to satisfy a lien for repairs. In each of these cases, the result under the Federal Constitution would either be uncertain or else certain rejection of the argument on behalf of the individual.[34]

In some states, state constitutional substantive due process doctrines have been developed by high courts so as to provide a barrier to regulation of contract and property as formidable as the so-called *Lochner* era cases posed for state and federal regulatory action under similar interpretations of the federal Constitution's due process clause.[35] This has not happened in New York.

Compensation for Taking Private Property

Article I, Section 7(a), states that "Private property shall not be taken for public use without just compensation." The language is the same as that

---

33   For a short statement of the issues, see *Galie*, at pp. 47-49.

34   Wachtler, "Constitutional Rights: Resuming the State's Role." *Intergovernmental Perspective* 15 (1989): 23-24, citing *Cooper* v. *Morin*, 49 NY 2d 69 (1979), *Rivers* v. *Katz*, 67 NY 2d 485 (1986), and *Sharrock* v. *Dell Buick-Cadillac, Inc.*, 45 NY 2d 152 (1978). Also see, *McMinn* v. *Town of Oyster Bay*, 66 NY 2d 544 (1985) and *People* v. *Lee*, 48 NY 2d 491 (1983) (striking down a zoning ordinance and a criminal statute, respectively, because they bore no rational relationship to a valid purpose).

35   See Advisory Commission on Intergovernmental Relations, "State Courts and Economic Rights." *State Constitutions in the Federal System, Selected Issues and Opportunities for State Initiatives* 7 (1989), reporting well over 100 state cases striking down economic regulation under state constitution due process and equality provisions on the same or nearly the same theories discarded by the United States Supreme Court.

in the Fifth Amendment to the federal Constitution, and it was added to the state Constitution by the 1821 Convention.

Although its language is familiar and the principle appears obvious today, one legal historian has observed that "[T]he principle that the state should compensate individuals for property taken for public use was not widely established in America at the time of the Revolution. Only colonial Massachusetts seems rigidly to have followed the principle of just compensation in road building. New York, by contrast, usually limited the right of compensation to land already improved or enclosed or else it provided that compensation should be paid by those who benefitted from land taken to build private roads."[36]

By 1800, only three states had just compensation provisions in their state constitutions. Vermont and Massachusetts in their original constitutions were joined in 1800 by Pennsylvania. However, the Pennsylvania courts still permitted some uncompensated takings on the grounds that those which they permitted were established by long practice and were not intended to be barred by the new constitutional provision. "Even by 1820 a majority of the original states had not yet enacted constitutional clauses providing for compensation," though statutory provisions for compensation were common. Only South Carolina's court "continued to uphold uncompensated takings of property."[37]

Prior to the adoption of the "just compensation" amendment, the New York courts relied on several theories to require compensation. Chancellor Kent steadfastly enjoined state officials "from undertaking any activity for which there was no advance provision for compensation."[38] In the absence of statute or constitutional provision, the basis for this position was never clearly established. A taking without provision for compensation was characterized by a New York court as "against natural right and justice" and despite the absence of a constitutional provision at the time, as violative of an "equitable and constitutional right to compensation."

Other New York decisions looked to the Magna Carta and the common law. A provision of the state Constitution continued in effect the common law as of April 19, 1775,[39] and the court concluded that compensation was part of the common law.

---

36   See Horowitz, *The Transformation of American Law, 1780-1860*, New York: Oxford University Press, 1992, at pp. 63-64, *passim*.

37   *Ibid.*, at p. 64.

38   *Ibid.*, at p. 64.

39   The provision, now Article I, Section 14, of the state Constitution, was part of the original 1777 Constitution.

Interestingly, there were some arguments and cases which held that the New York constitutional provision on just compensation was a "disabling" and not an "enabling" clause and that, consequently, while it limited takings for public purposes by requiring just compensation, the legislature could authorize private takings without just compensation. This was based on the theory, noted above, that the state legislature had plenary power, subject only to specific limitations. The ultimate conclusion was that the state could take only for a public purpose and had to provide compensation for the taking. In *Taylor* v. *Porter*, decided in 1843, "a sharply divided New York court" struck down a much-used colonial statute that had been used to build private roads through other persons' property. It held that the Court would decide "what was and was not public use"[40] and it restricted the takings to those for a public use.

Article I, Section 7(c), authorizes the taking of private property for private roads and provides that the property benefiting from the private road will pay the costs. It was adopted in 1846 as a direct response to *Taylor* v. *Porter*, which cast doubt on the state's power to authorize such a taking. Its purpose was to provide access to property that otherwise would not be accessible.[41]

Finally, Article I, Section 7(d), was a response to the economic needs of farmers. It enabled them to improve their land by drainage and permitted the owners of land requiring drainage to build dams and dikes for that purpose on the property of others. The section also provides for payment for the damage caused or the adverse effects on the use of that property. It was adopted by the 1894 Convention and in effect declares such uses of another's property to be a public purpose.[42]

Freedom of Speech and Press, Criminal Prosecution for Libel and Right of Assembly

Article I, Section 8, was added to the Constitution by the 1821 Convention, and has not been amended since its adoption. It contains two sentences:

> Every citizen may freely speak, write and publish his sentiments on all subjects, being responsible for the abuse of that right; and no law shall be passed to restrain or abridge the liberty of speech

---

40   4 Hill 140 NY (1843). Horowitz, *The Transformation of American Law, 1780-1860*, New York: Oxford University Press (1992), pp. 65-66 and 260.

41   *Poletti Report*, at pp. 138-140. Also see, Galie, at p. 50.

42   For a summary of the economic, political, and legal forces involved, see Horowitz, *op. cit.*, note 46, *supra*, at pp. 259-61. Also see *Poletti Report*, at pp. 140-45; and Galie, at pp. 50-51.

or the press. In all criminal prosecutions or indictments for libels, the truth may be given in evidence to the jury; and if it shall appear to the jury that the matter charged as libelous is true, and was published with good motives and for justifiable ends, the party shall be acquitted, and the jury shall have the right to determine the law and the fact.

The first sentence directly recognizes or confers, and prohibits legislation that interferes with, the rights to speak, write, and publish. Unlike the federal Constitution it is not explicitly directed to state action. Moreover, the state provision makes the citizen "responsible for the abuse of" these rights.

The second sentence covers criminal (not civil) libel. It states the points argued to the jury by Andrew Hamilton in his famous successful defense of Peter Zenger in the middle of the eighteenth century. The inclusion of the sentence fairly can be viewed as an effort to preserve that landmark victory. Today, there is no criminal libel statute in New York; it was repealed with the adoption of the current Penal Law in 1967 and seditious libel has not been a subject of prosecution in New York.[43]

1. *Background.* At the time of the adoption of the federal Constitution and the original state constitutions, there were some who believed that no constitutional provision concerning freedom of expression was required because no government would interfere with that right. Nevertheless, adoption of the federal Constitution's First Amendment was a condition for ratification by a number of states.

    In 1798, the attacks on freedom of speech and the press found expression in the Alien and Sedition Laws. Their constitutionality was not finally adjudicated, but in large measure, these enactments revived concern about the security of the rights of speech and the press and were an important issue in the election of Thomas Jefferson to the presidency.

    Thereafter, up until World War I, few issues arose under the First Amendment free speech provisions of the U.S. Constitution, despite vigorous criticism of the government during the Mexican and Spanish-American wars. Indeed, these freedoms were neither substantially challenged nor curtailed even during the Civil War. However substantial attacks on political expression by the federal

---

43   See: *Poletti Report*, at pp. 156-158; Galie, at pp. 51-52.

and state governments, including New York, emerged during World War I and continued into the 1950s.[44] During this period the New York legislature and courts have been described as concerned primarily with the individual's "abuse" of speech and press freedoms, and not with the protection of speech against government action.[45]

2. *New York and Federal Constitutional Limitations; New York Goes Beyond Federal Protection.* In the 1960s, the federal courts substantially changed direction, and most of the previous judicially approved legislative condemnations of "abuses" of speech did not withstand federal constitutional attacks. The New York courts adapted rather easily to the federal constitutional decisions that protected political speech of the kind previously condemned by the New York legislature and its courts and upheld by the federal courts.

It is commonplace and accurate to observe that New York, in many instances, can be expected to be more hospitable to freedom of expression than required by the federal Constitution.[46] The current attitude of the New York Court of Appeals is captured in its statement in *People ex. rel Arcara* v. *Cloud Books*:

"We, of course, are bound by Supreme Court decisions defining and limiting Federal constitutional rights but 'in determining the scope and effect of the guarantees of fundamental rights of the individual in the Constitution of the State of New York, this court is bound to exercise its independent judgment and is not bound by a decision of the Supreme Court of the United States limiting the scope of similar guarantees in the Constitution of the United States' (citations omitted). The Supreme Court's role in construing the Federal Bill of Rights is to establish minimal standards for individual rights applicable throughout the Nation. The function of the comparable provisions of the State Constitution, if they are not to be considered purely

---

44 It should be noted, however, that early on New York condemned prior restraints on speech as part of a deep concern about government censorship. See the following, which condemn injunctions as prior restraints akin to censorship: *Brandreth* v. *Lance*, 8 Paige 246 NY (1839); *Marlin Firearms* v. *Shields*, 171 NY 384 (1902). *Cf. Near* v. *Minnesota*, 283 US 697 (1931).

45 See, *Poletti Report*, at pp. 150. n.4 and 163-176; Galie, at pp. 51-52. Cases referred to in the cited volumes include *People v. Bohnke*, 287 NY 154 (1941) (ordinance prohibiting distribution of material on residential property without occupants consent upheld) and *People* v. *Feiner*, 300 NY 391, affirmed 340 US 315 (1950) (disorder conduct conviction for street speech upheld). Earlier cases include *People* v. *Most*, 171 NY 423 (1902) (advocacy of violence not protected) and *People* v. *Ruggles*, 8 Johns 211 NY (1811) and *People* v. *Muller*, 96 NY 408 (1884) (upholding prohibitions on blasphemous or obscene materials).

46 E.g., see Wachtler, "Constitutional Rights: Resuming the States' Role," *Intergovernmental Perspective* 15 (1989): 23- 24.

redundant, is to supplement those rights to meet the needs and expectations of the particular State.

Freedom of expression in books, movies and the arts, generally, is one of those areas in which there is great diversity among the States. Thus it is an area in which the Supreme Court has displayed great reluctance to expand Federal constitutional protections, holding instead that this is a matter essentially governed by community standards (citations omitted). However, New York has a long history and tradition of fostering freedom of expression, often tolerating and supporting works which in other States would be found offensive to the community (citation omitted). Thus, the minimal national standard established by the Supreme Court for First Amendment rights cannot be considered dispositive in determining the scope of this State's constitutional guarantee of freedom of expression."[47]

In *Arcara* the U.S. Supreme Court held that it was permissible for the state to close down a bookstore where the patrons are committing illegal acts not protected by the First Amendment, even if the store owner is wholly innocent.[48] The New York Court of Appeals required that before a bookstore that is entitled to First Amendment protection is closed, the state must "show that no other measures, such as prosecution of the offending patrons, will eliminate the nuisance."

A second example is the greater specificity required by the New York Court of Appeals in the application for warrants to seize allegedly pornographic films than is required by U.S. Supreme Court standards under the First Amendment.[49]

Finally, in the area of civil libel, the federal Constitution has been construed to protect false statements about public figures and about private persons by requiring that there can be no recovery in a civil action for libel unless statements about public figures are made with knowledge of their falsity or in reckless disregard of the risk they are false (i.e., malice) and unless statements about private figures are made negligently with respect to the risk of falsity. New York imposes a greater burden on the plaintiff in a civil libel suit against a private party — the false

---

47   *People ex rel. Arcara* v. *Cloud Books*, 68 NY 2d 553 (1986), pp. 557-58.

48   *Arcara* v. *Cloud Books*, 478 US 697 (1986).

49   *People* v. *P.J. Video, Inc.*, 68 NY 2d 296 (1986).

statement must be the product of "grossly irresponsible" conduct. In addition, the Court of Appeals has created a presumption that "statements included in an article or broadcast do involve [a matter of] public concern."[50]

3. *The Right to Assemble and Petition.* The right to assemble and petition the government in Article I, Section 9, was also adopted by the 1821 Convention.[51] It has not been amended since its adoption as part of the 1822 Constitution and has not developed separately from New York State Constitution Article 1, Section 8, dealing with speech, or from the First Amendment to the federal Constitution.[52]

Equal Protection of Laws and Discrimination in Civil Rights

Article I, Section 11, added to the state Constitution in 1938, provides that:

No person shall be denied equal protection of the laws of this state or any subdivision thereof. No person shall, because of race, color, creed or religion, be subjected to any discrimination in his civil rights by any other person or by any firm, corporation, or institution, or by the state or any agency or subdivision thereof.

The equal protection clause contained in this section is similar to the one in the Fourteenth Amendment to the United States Constitution, except that it does not by its terms require "state action." However, it has been construed to require state action by the state courts, defined in a manner similar to the federal court construction of the Fourteenth Amendment.

The second sentence of the section, by its terms, applies to private parties. However, it is not self-executing.[53] What constitutes a "civil right" within the meaning of the provision is determined by legislation or some source other than the constitutional provision itself.

---

50 See *Galie*, at p. 52. *New York Times* v. *Sullivan*, 376 US 254 (1964) (first amendment and public figures); *Gertz* v. *Welch*, 418 US 323 (1974) (first amendment and public figures); *Chapadeau* v. *Utica Observer-Dispatch, Inc.*, 38 NY 2d 196 (1975) ("gross irresponsibility" for private figures); *Gaeta* v. *New York News*, 62 NY 2d 340 (1984) (presumption statement is matter of public concern).

51 This section also prohibits the granting of a divorce by other than a judicial proceeding and also authorizes lotteries and other games of chance under stated restrictions.

52 See Galie, at p. 55. For earlier, but no longer accepted judicial views, see *Poletti Report*, at pp. 154-55 and 163-87.

53 For a more extensive discussion of self-execution see the chapters, "Social Policy" and "Education," in this book.

Until the adoption of this provision in 1938, "all existing [state] provisions against discrimination on the grounds of race, creed or color" were contained in the Civil Rights Law and the Education Law. (Additionally, of course, there was the equal protection clause of the Fourteenth Amendment and the Thirteenth and Fifteenth Amendments to the U.S. Constitution.) The state statutory provisions prohibited: disqualification of a person as a juror and denial of access to public accommodations, resorts, and places of amusement on account of race, creed, or color; inquiry concerning religious affiliation of a job applicant for a position with the public schools; discrimination by a public utility on account of race, color, or religion; and exclusion of a person from a public school on account of race or color.[54]

The *Poletti Report* identified a number of concerns not addressed by the existing statutes or the federal Constitution as then interpreted. In the case of public accommodations, retail and wholesale establishments apparently were not covered. Except for public utilities, there was no prohibition against discrimination in employment. With respect to education, there was a provision in the Education Law that permitted segregation on the basis of race. A final concern addressed was residential segregation and discrimination in housing. In fact, New York courts, at the time, were enforcing restrictive racial and religious covenants.[55]

The impact of the adoption of the state constitutional equal protection-antidiscrimination provision has not been dramatic. The impetus for major changes has come from the application to the states of the equal protection clause of the Fourteenth Amendment by the post-World War II federal courts.

Nevertheless, there are a number of less dramatic cases where the state court has held a statute to be violative of the equal protection clause of the state Constitution. As one author has pointed out, the state clause serves a useful purpose in this regard, because it is not certain and not even likely that these situations would ever get United States Supreme Court review.[56]

Common Law and Acts of the Colonial and State Legislatures

Article I, Section 14, is part of a more extensive provision included in the 1777 Constitution, which preserved the law in effect (common law and colonial legislative enactments) that was in force on April 19,

---

54   *Poletti Report*, at pp. 221-22.

55   *Poletti Report*, at pp. 224-227.

56   See *Galie*, at p. 58.

1775,[57] and the acts of the subsequent colonial and state legislatures in force on April 10, 1777,[58] thereby providing a legal system for the new state. It also provided that parts of the common law inconsistent with the new Constitution would not remain in effect.[59] In the absence of constitutional protections in some areas, the common law was relied on as a source of some liberties. For example, some courts found a common law right to compensation for property taken for a public purpose.[60] The adoption of this clause in 1777, it has been stated, "amply justifies the wisdom of the men who, even in the excitement and turmoil of a great political revolution, calmly determined to preserve in the Constitution the personal rights and the principles of organized society which are such distinguishing features of the common law."[61]

The Labor Provisions

1. *Wrongful Death Actions.* The constitutional protection for wrongful death actions without statutory limits on the amount recoverable in Article I, Section 16, was added to the state Constitution by the 1894 Convention after heated public debate. In common law, there was no right of recovery by the survivors of one who had suffered wrongful death. In 1846, England adopted Lord Campbell's Act, which for the first time recognized the pecuniary interests of the survivors. Many states, including New York in 1847, followed suit. Two years after the passage of the original New York statute, it was amended to limit recovery to $5,000 regardless of actual pecuniary damage as a result of pressure from employers concerned about payment for employees who were killed on the job. The preservation of the right to recover damages and the elimination of the ceiling became hotly debated questions. The 1894 Convention proposed the current article in response to the pressures and the debate. It was approved by the electorate as part of the 1894 Constitution and remains unchanged in the current state Constitution.[62]

---

57   The Battle of Concord was fought on April 19, 1775.

58   April 20, 1777, was the date of the adoption of the first New York State Constitution.

59   The original provision provided that the common law should not be construed to "establish or maintain any particular" religious denomination. This provision was repealed in 1821. *Poletti Report*, at pp. 205-210.

60   See text accompanying notes 36 and 37, *supra.*

61   *Poletti Report*, at pp. 207-28, quoting from Lincoln, *Constitutional History of New York from the Beginning of the Colonial Period to the Year 1905, IV*, Rochester, NY: Lawyers Cooperative Company, 1905, p. 176.

62   See Special Legislative Committee on the Revision and Simplification of the Constitution, *Inter-Law School Committee Report on The Problem of Simplification of the Constitution*, Staff Report No. 1, Leg. Doc. No. 57 (1958), pp. 47-51 (hereafter *Staff Report No. 1*).

Peter Galie has noted that this provision only preserves the right "now existing," construed to mean prior to January 1, 1895. In addition, the Constitution does not prevent: (1) the enactment of statutes of limitations: (2) legislative limitation of damages to pecuniary loss; and (3) judicial remedies to deal with "excessive" awards.[63]

2. *The Workers' Compensation Provision.*[64] Article I, Section 18, permits the establishment of a workers' compensation system which could include, *inter alia*: liability without fault; a limitation on the amount of a recovery; and determination of the amount by a method other than one that uses a jury. The history of this provision provides an interesting example of an unanticipated consequence of the adoption of another constitutional provision, in this case, the wrongful death provision.

    After extensive study and debate, New York enacted a workers' compensation statute which the New York Court of Appeals declared unconstitutional in 1911 on the grounds that it violated the state's due process clause.[65] It has been suggested that while a workers compensation statute probably would survive constitutional attacks based on denial of due process and denial of the right to a jury trial, the wrongful death provision (Article I, Section 16) could prove a serious barrier to a workers' compensation statute if it were not authorized by a constitutional provision such as Article I, Section 18.[66]

    This provision therefore was added to the Constitution in 1913 to remove constitutional barriers to a workers' compensation statute.

3. *The Labor Bill of Rights.* Article I, Section 17, labor's "Bill of Rights," was added as a result of the 1938 Convention. In the context of the rise of organized labor in the era of the Great Depression, it gave constitutional status to a number of principles or policies that had already found their way into federal or state

---

63 See Galie, at p. 64.

64 Generally see *Staff Report No. 1*, at p. 52, *et. seq.* and *Poletti Report*, at pp. 288-92.

65 *Ives* v. *South Railway Buffalo Co.*, 201 NY 271 (1911). The statute also had been challenged as a denial of the state constitutional right to a jury trial, but the Court could not agree on this ground of attack.

66 See *Poletti Report*, at p. 289. In 1958, repeal of Sections 16 and 18 were recommended on the grounds they were unnecessary and that Section 16 has had and could continue to have unanticipated effects. Moreover, if Article I, Section 18, is repealed, it has been noted that Section 16 also must be repealed so as to remove it as a potential barrier to a workers compensation statute. *Staff Report No. 1*, at pp. 59-60.

statutes, protecting them from future changes in the legislature or adverse court decisions. This provision has three major elements. First, a declaration that labor is not a commodity removed labor organizing from the reach of anti-trust law which had been used to restrict union activity. Second, constitutionalization of hours and wages policy — the eight-hour day and five-day week for those engaged in any "public work" and a requirement that wages of those engaged in such work not be less than that which prevails in the locality where the work is performed — gave state constitutional basis to previously enacted statutes. And finally, a guarantee of the right to organize and bargain collectively had similar effect (though it did not prohibit state laws barring strikes by public workers or require the state to allow supervisors to organize and bargain collectively.) According to one authority, federal law has preempted this section.[67]

Proposals for Constitutional Change

There is little doubt that a constitutional convention in New York would bring considerable efforts to redefine existing rights (both more broadly and more narrowly), and to add new ones. Experience demonstrates that ideas would arise out of a range of sources: dominant issues and passions in the current political environment; decisions of the courts; and the thinking of leading commentators on state law and policy, to name just a few. The constitutions of sister states will be another rich source of ideas. One recent survey offers a sampling of "distinctive state constitutional guarantees" not now paralleled by explicit provisions in New York: a right to privacy (Montana); a right to a legal remedy (Connecticut); gender equality (Hawaii); a right to bear arms (Nebraska); a right to bail (Ohio); and freedom from excessive punishments (Utah).[68] Any or all of these, and others not cited here, might be considered.[69] *The ideas below are a brief and suggestive, not definitive, list of issues that might arise. Detailed consideration of their merits is beyond the scope of this summary.*

---

67 See Galie, at pp. 64-66.

68 See G. Alan Tarr, *Judicial Process and Judicial Policy Making*, St. Paul: West Publishing, 1994, at p. 379.

69 E.g., Massachusetts provides that no provision shall be construed as permitting the death penalty, while Michigan has a provision that prohibits enactment of a law that provides for the death penalty. Glasser and Kincaid, "Selected Rights in State Constitutions," Intergovernmental Perspective 17 (1991): 35 and 42.

Article I, Section 3 (Religious Freedom)

Consideration might be given to adding a clause to the current section on freedom of religion prohibiting enactment of any law establishing religion. Litigation in New York on the establishment issue centers around the federal Constitution's provision and the United States Supreme Court's interpretation of the federal provision.[70] Arguably a more complete state constitutional provision would include a clause with respect to the establishment of religion.

Article I, Section 8 (Freedom of Speech and Press; Criminal Libel)

1. Consideration should be given to repeal of the provision concerning criminal libel in view of the federal and New York state constitutional law governing civil libel. It is practically certain that a statute expressed in the language of this sentence would not pass muster under the federal Constitution.[71]

2. Consideration could be given to defining the journalist's privilege in the Constitution.

Article I, Section 11 (Equal Protection of Laws and Discrimination in Civil Rights)

This provision could be the focus of some significant current controversial issues:

1. prohibition of discrimination based on gender;

2. prohibition of discrimination based on sexual orientation;

3. prohibition of discrimination based on disability;

4. designating some civil rights in the constitution, for example:

---

70 The most recent establishment case decided by the New York Court of Appeals, *Grumet, et al. v. Board of Education of the Kiryas Joel Village School District*, 81 NY 2d 518 (1993), was decided solely on the federal Constitution's establishment clause and the Fourteenth Amendment, which, according to the opinion, was the only basis relied on by the plaintiffs.

71 As part of the consideration to be given to the removal of state constitutional provisions currently declared to be in violation of the federal Constitution, consideration should be given to eliminating the requirement of Article II, Section 1, that as a condition of being permitted to vote, a person be literate in the English language, a provision that has been declared to be in violation of the federal Voting Rights Act and consequently is unconstitutional under the supremacy clause. *Katzenbach* v. *Morgan*, 384 US 641 (1966).

a. prohibiting discrimination in employment by public and private employers, and

b. prohibiting discrimination in housing;

5. adoption of a children's Bill of Rights or a Bill of Rights for persons under 18 years of age; and

6. establishment of equality in education funding.

Reserved Rights

1. Consideration might be given to a provision that holds rights that are not enumerated are retained by the people. The similar federal constitutional provision has been the basis for recognizing such rights as a right to privacy and is the foundation of the federal limitation on governmental power to limit abortions.

2. Consideration might be given to including a provision similar to the one in the Rhode Island Constitution, which provides that rights guaranteed by the state constitution are not dependent on those guaranteed by the United States Constitution.[72]

---

72 See May, "Amending State Bills of Rights: Do Voters Reduce Rights?" *Intergovernmental Perspective* 17, 45 (1991): 48 n. 14; and the chapter on "Criminal Justice."

Criminal Justice

Burton C. Agata

A principal objective of government in any society is to assure that citizens are safe. Toward this end, governments define crime in law and establish processes through which laws are enforced and sanctions are imposed if they are broken. These sanctions may include the taking of a person's liberty or property, or even that person's very life. But the protection of all of these — life, liberty, and property — is also a fundamental objective of government in a liberal democracy.

The objectives that democratic government must meet are thus in tension. It is balance among them that the constitution writer seeks: to provide the government sufficient power to assure the security of the citizenry, while constraining that power through specific limitations, and in the very design of the system itself, to assure the protection of life, liberty, and property.

In the American federal system the obligation to keep the citizenry safe falls primarily upon state (not national) government. This is no accident. Rather it is a first purposeful step in decentralizing government's power in relation to the individual, while safety and order are simultaneously being assured.

Within state constitutions, state bills of rights, like their national counterpart, define limits on government that protect individuals suspected or accused of crimes against arbitrary process or punishment. The development of American constitutional law has come to regard rights under the national Constitution as a floor; rights guarantees under state constitutions can build upon, but not diminish, those provided by the national document.

State constitutions also structure state governmental systems both horizontally and vertically to further fragment power in areas in which life, liberty, or property may be at stake. In New York this is evidenced by the multiplicity of institutions at the state level that deal with criminal justice matters. Several of these — elected judges and the attorney general (to the extent that this office has criminal justice responsibility) — are directly elected to further assure their autonomy. Additionally, significant responsibilities for enforcement, prosecution, defense, trial, and punish-

255

ment are further decentralized to the local level where they are performed by a range of departments responsible to elected heads of general purpose governments — cities, counties, towns, and villages — or by independently elected officials — judges, district attorneys, and sheriffs.

In recent years, the growth of crime and the fear of crime has led many citizens to believe that the balance has been lost between the capacity of government to assure safety and the constraints upon it to protect liberty. Some have come to think that the protections given those suspected or accused of crimes have become too great. Others believe that the design of governmental institutions for dealing with criminal justice matters is outmoded. A contrasting view, however, is that rights protections and structural constraints upon government are most essential during times in which the majority is most likely to sacrifice these because of concerns about personal security. This debate enters the constitutional realm because both methods for limiting government as it tries to assure public safety and security are rooted in the state constitution.

The New York State Constitution
Bill of Rights Provisions

Jury trial, a right of an accused person regarded so fundamental that it appears in practically all seventeenth-century colonial charters and grants, was one of only four rights guaranteed in the original New York State Constitution. (Unlike the constitution of most other states, New York's original document lacked a Bill of Rights.) Currently Article I, Section 2, provides that "[t]rial by jury in all cases in which it has heretofore been guaranteed by constitutional provision shall remain inviolate forever." It applies to both civil and criminal cases. Despite the language enjoining violations of its guarantees "forever," it is clear that this provision did not and cannot prevent changes by constitutional amendment concerning the right to a jury trial if both federal constitutional requirements and state constitutional amendment procedure are satisfied. Indeed, the Article was amended in 1935 and 1938, and the current language dates to 1938.

> New York's first Constitution, enacted in 1777, guaranteed trial by jury in all cases "in which it hath *heretofore been used [. . . shall remain inviolate forever]*" (N.Y. Constitution of 1777 Article XLI). The import of that provision was to include in the constitutional guarantee all cases in which a jury trial had been provided under common law. . . . Subsequent Constitutions, up to and including the Constitution of 1894, adopted the "heretofore

been used" clause without change. The effect was to include in the constitutional guarantee those cases to which the right to jury trial had been extended not only at common law before 1777 but also by statute between the 1777 and 1894 Constitutions. The Constitution of 1938, whose relevant sections remain unchanged today, abandoned the "heretofore been used" language and provided that "[t]rial by jury in all cases in which it has *heretofore been guaranteed by constitutional provision* shall remain inviolate forever" (N.Y. Constitution of 1938, Article I, Section 2).[1]

Earlier, a 1935 amendment permitted the defendant to waive a jury trial in all criminal cases, "except those in which the crime charged may be punishable by death." However, by virtue of additional changes made in 1938 the section also requires that the waiver be "[1] in writing [2] signed by the defendant [3] in person [4] in open court [5] before and with the approval of" the court.[2] The legislature is empowered to legislate concerning the form, content, manner, and time of presentation of the waiver instrument.

Article VI, Section 18, approved in a 1961 referendum as part of the adoption the Unified Court System reiterates Article I, Section 2's guarantee of jury trials, but permits the legislature to provide for trials by twelve or six-person juries and also for trials without a jury, except that criminal cases require 12-person juries for crimes prosecuted by indictment. The U.S. Supreme Court has held that a defendant has a federal constitutional right under the Sixth Amendment to a jury trial where imprisonment for six months or more is authorized. As a consequence, a New York statute requiring nonjury trial under some circumstances where the authorized punishment exceeded six months has been held unconstitutional.[3] Amendments altering the size of juries continue to be regularly proposed in the legislature.

The habeas corpus provision in Article I, Section 4, of the New York State Constitution, originally added in 1821, was made identical to that in

---

1   *Motor Vehicle Mfrs. Assn. of U.S.* v. *State of New York*, 75 NY 2d 175, 180-81 (1990) (emphasis supplied; citations omitted). Also see, In re *DES Market Share Litigation*, 171 AD 2d 352 (Dept. 1991); *John W. Cowper Co., Inc.* v. *Buffalo Hotel Development Venture*, 99 AD 2d 19 (Dept. 1984); Galie, *The New York State Constitution: A Reference Guide,* Westport, CT: Greenwood Press, 1991, at p. 36.

2   Although judicial approval of the waiver of a jury trial is required, the accused has a right to be tried without a jury and the waiver must be accepted by the Court if the accused knows and understands what he is doing. *People* v. *Davis*, 49 NY 2d 114 (1979).

3   *Baldwin* v. *New York*, 399 US 66 (1970). See *Morganthau* v. *Erlbaum*, 59 NY 2d 143 (1983), upholding criminal procedure law provision requiring nonjury trials in the City of New York where less than six months is maximum authorized imprisonment.

Article I, Section 9, of the United States Constitution in 1938. It reads: "The privilege of a writ or order of habeas corpus shall not be suspended, unless, in case of rebellion or invasion, the public safety requires it." Habeas corpus, the basic right to be free from unlawful detention, is commonly traced to the Magna Carta. It is utilized in criminal matters and in such civil matters as child custody.

Excessive bail, excessive fines, and cruel and unusual punishment are prohibited in Article I, Section 5, of the New York State Constitution with language practically identical to that in the Eighth Amendment to the United States Constitution. These parts of the state provision were the product of the 1846 Constitutional Convention, which was called as the result of strong popular pressure and resulted in substantial democratization of the Constitution.[4] The 1846 Convention also included in this section *a prohibition on unreasonably detaining witnesses,* a subject not expressly covered by the United States Constitution.

Unreasonable Searches and Seizures. The New York State Constitution's prohibition against *Unreasonable Searches and Seizures* in Article I, Section 12, Paragraph 1, is identical to the prohibition against unreasonable searches and seizures contained in the Fourth Amendment to the United States Constitution. It states: "The right of people to be secure in their persons, houses, papers, and effects against unreasonable searches and seizures, shall not be violated, and no warrants shall issue, but upon probable cause, supported by oath or affirmation, and particularly describing the place to be searched, and the persons or things to be seized."

Interestingly, New York had no state constitutional protection against unlawful searches and seizures until this language was added to the Constitution by the 1938 Convention.[5] This identical language notwithstanding, the state guarantee has been the occasion for divergent approaches to searches and seizures between the federal and New York State courts, demonstrating the importance of state rights provisions. Thus, in *People* v. *Bigelow*, 66 N.Y.2d 417 (1985), the New York Court of Appeals refused to adopt for the state Constitution the so-called "good-faith" exception for warrantless searches that the United States Supreme Court previously had adopted for the Fourth Amendment in *United States*

4   See State University of New York, "Constitutional Developments in New York 1777-1958," *Bibliography Bulletin* 82, New York State Department of Education (1958): 30-31.

5   "A proposal at the 1867 Constitutional Convention to make this section [prohibiting unreasonable searches and seizures] a part of the Constitution was rejected. There was, however, a statutory provision embodying the protection which goes back to 1928." Galie, at p. 59.

v. *Leon.*[6] On the same day in *People* v. *Johnson,* 66 NY 2d 398 (1985), the Court of Appeals rejected for Article 1, Section 12, of the state Constitution a recently announced Supreme Court interpretation of the Fourth Amendment concerning the test for establishing the reliability of informants for warrantless searches.[7] Instead, the New York State Court of Appeals adhered to the earlier stated Supreme Court test as a matter of state constitutional law.[8]

The 1938 Convention also added a provision to Article I, Section 12, which deals with the interception of telephone and telegraph communications. It contains various mandates concerning the issuance of *ex parte* orders and warrants. The United States Constitution has no equivalent provision. As a practical matter, however, wiretapping and related policies currently are governed by federal statutes and the state Constitution plays little or no role. Finally, a proposal at that Convention, supported by Governor Lehman and others, to prohibit the use of unreasonably obtained evidence was rejected by the Convention.[9] Adoption of the proposal would have anticipated the requirement of the landmark United States Supreme Court case of *Mapp* v. *Ohio.*[10]

Grand Jury Indictment, Double Jeopardy, Counsel, Information, Confrontation of Witnesses, Self-Incrimination, and Due Process. In language practically the same as that found in the Fifth and Sixth Amendments to the United States Constitution, Article 1, Section 6, of the state Constitution provides for *grand jury indictment for capital and "infamous crimes," protection against double jeopardy, right to counsel, the right of an accused to be informed of charges and confront witnesses, protection against self-incrimination and due process of law.* Most of these provisions date to the 1821 or 1846 Constitutions. The right to be informed and confront witnesses was added in 1938. The 1777 Constitution guaranteed a right to counsel, and the state Constitution later was amended to expressly provide that the accused shall be permitted "to appear and defend in person," a provision not found in the United States Constitution.

In 1973, an amendment to Article I, Section 6, was passed and approved that permits an accused to *waive grand jury indictment* and consent to be tried on a district attorney's information. The amendment

---

6   104 S. Ct. 3485.

7   *Illinois* v. *Gates,* 462 US 213 (adopting the so-called "totality of circumstances" test).

8   The three-pronged or Aguilar-Spinelli test established in *Aguilar* v. *Texas,* 378 US 108, and *Spinelli* v. *United States,* 393 US 410, and later changed by *Illinois* v. *Gates.*

9   See Robert Allan Carter, *New York State Constitution: Sources of Legislative Intent,* Littleton, CO: Fred Rothman Co., 1988, at p. 11, n. 1.

10   367 U.S. 643 (1961).

recognized that a defendant might wish to expedite the trial or that, in the case of a guilty plea, there was no need for grand jury indictments; needless costs and delay could be avoided by permitting intelligent waiver.

Public Official's Misconduct. The 1938 Convention, meeting at a time of great public concern about corruption and official misconduct, added provisions *requiring public officials and former public officials to testify before a grand jury concerning their public employment and to waive immunity against prosecution on penalty of losing or being disqualified from holding public employment.* These have been practically superseded by a series of U.S. Supreme Court cases that condemned as violating the Fifth Amendment the coercion of a person to testify by the threat of loss of public employment and then the use of the testimony in a criminal prosecution against that person. However, a public official must testify on those matters narrowly related to the office or employment and can be discharged if the testimony provides a basis for discharge. Neither the testimony nor its fruits may be used against that person in a criminal proceeding.[11]

The 1938 Convention also added a provision that explicitly provides for grand jury power to inquire into "willful misconduct" of public officials in public office.

Due Process. The provision in Article 1, Section 6, that "No person shall be deprived of life, liberty or property without *due process of law*" is identical with the due process clause in the Fifth Amendment to the United States Constitution. It was added by the 1821 Convention, before the adoption of the due process clause in the Fourteenth Amendment to the United States Constitution, the important vehicle for imposing federal constitutional limits on the states, which applies only where there is so-called "state action." The state Constitution's due process clause does not explicitly require "state action." Nevertheless, the state provision has been construed to require some state involvement, although the state involvement in private action need not be as extensive or pronounced as the requirement of state action under the Fourteenth Amendment. Obviously, "state action" easily is found when the criminal justice system is involved.

The due process clauses apply to criminal *and* civil matters, and are used both to assure that government adheres to procedural requirements and often to monitor its substantive conduct. The due process clause in

---

11   For a summary of the cases and the applicable doctrines, see *Matt v. Larocca*, 71 NY 2d 154 (1987).

the New York State Constitution has been the basis for a right to a speedy and public trial, protections not specifically provided by the state Constitution but that are specified in the Sixth Amendment to the United States Constitution.[12]

In addition, the state due process clause, like its provision concerning unlawful searches and seizures, has been construed to provide broader rights than the federal provision. For example, in *Cooper v. Morin*, 49 NY 2d 69 (1979), there was a claim that federal and state constitutional rights had been denied a pretrial jail detainee with respect to allowable visits. The New York Court of Appeals held that the complainant's federal constitutional rights had not been violated, but that there had been a violation of her state constitutional rights under the state's due process clause.

A provision taken from Article 39 of the Magna Carta and that dates to the original New York Constitution, now in Article 1, Section 1, assures that no person shall be disenfranchised or deprived of any of the rights or privileges secured to any citizen, *"unless by the law of land or the judgment of his peers."*[13] As a practical matter, the provision has been considered coterminous with the due process clause in Article 1, Section 6. In modern times the "law of the land," "judgment of his peers" formula does not appear to have had an independent life in criminal matters. There is no counterpart provision in the United States Constitution.

Other Provisions: Civil Rights, Criminal Libel. Two additional Bill of Rights provisions that could affect criminal justice include the *equal protection clause and the prohibition against discrimination based on race, color, creed, or religion in the exercise of civil rights* in Article 1, Section 11, and the provision in Article 1, Section 8, that makes *good faith truth* a defense in criminal libel cases, with the jury the judge of the law and the facts. These provisions surely affect how crimes may be defined and how the system may be operated. The equal protection clause, added in 1938, is substantially the same as the one in the Fourteenth Amendment to the United States Constitution.

---

12   Of course, there are statutory speedy trial provisions.

13   The original provision said "law of the land and judgment of his peers"; in 1821, it was amended to add "any citizen." The cases in which this provision has played a significant role concern voting and elections. A 1959 amendment to the section permits the legislature to provide for no primary election when a party nomination for public office or an election to a party office is uncontested.

Organization of the Criminal Justice Functions of State Government

The New York Constitution makes provision for the election of the attorney general at the state level and judges, district attorneys, and sheriffs at the regional and local levels. It also specifies the criminal jurisdiction of the superior state courts and the limits on the criminal jurisdiction of other courts that may be conferred by statute. Additionally, there is some constitutional provision for the delivery and oversight of correctional services. In general, however, the criminal justice functions and duties of state and local government are largely defined by statute.

The Attorney General. The state Constitution creates the elective office of attorney general, filled at the same time and for the same term as the governorship, with the legislature empowered to make provision for filling vacancies (Article V, Section 1).[14] The attorney general heads the Department of Law (Article V, Section 4). The state Constitution requires that he or she (1) provide the legislature with an opinion on the effect on other constitutional provisions of a proposed constitutional amendment under Article XIX, Section 1; (2) seek the forfeiture of the office of a public officer who fails to answer grand jury inquiries concerning his or her conduct of the office (a 1959 amendment to Article I, Section 6); and (3) be served with notice of any citizen's suit alleging a violation of the Conservation article of the state Constitution (Article XIV, Section 5).

There may be some residual common law powers remaining with the attorney general acting as "the peoples' lawyer," but these are quite vague. Absent specifics in the Constitution, therefore, the duties of this office, criminal justice or otherwise, are largely left to the legislature to define.

The attorney general originally was the state's chief prosecutor, but lost this function with the emergence of the office of elected district attorney and the decentralization of the prosecutorial function in the first half of the nineteenth century.[15] Though now New York's chief law officer, the representative of the state in all litigation, the attorney general is no longer the chief law *enforcement* officer.

---

14   The current provisions for election of the attorney general result from a 1919 *Report on Retrenchment and Reorganization of State Government*, the recommendations of which were approved by 1925 referendum on amending the Constitution, and some additional amendments stemming from the 1938 Constitutional Convention. For details about the powers and duties specified for this office in the Constitution see "Structures of New York State Government" in this book.

15   See, below the description of the district attorney.

Whether the attorney general should be elected or appointed has been an issue in New York throughout its history. During the colonial period, the attorney general was appointed by the governor. When New York became a state the first appointment was by the state Constitutional Convention; thereafter, until 1821, the power of appointment was exercised by a Council of Appointment. The 1821 Constitutional Convention provided for election of the attorney general by the two legislative houses, meeting jointly. Direct popular election emerged as a result of the 1846 Convention. The office continues to be elective, but many heavily debated proposals to change it to an office appointed by the governor have been seriously considered into this century.[16]

Judges. The New York State Constitution provides for the election of almost all *judges* to serve in the courts in which criminal matters are originally decided, and to which these decisions are first appealed. Election is highly decentralized, to towns, cities, counties, or judicial districts, and is for long terms to assure judicial independence (with the exception of the four-year term of the justice of the peace). Even where the Constitution provides for appointment — by the mayor to the Criminal Court of New York City, for example, the term of office is ten years.[17] Though there is provision made in the Constitution for central administration of the courts, and temporary assignment of the judges outside of the jurisdiction in which they were elected, their high status, local electoral base and this decentralized selection process makes them quite independent actors in both the state and local criminal justice systems.

Criminal Jurisdiction. The Constitution also specifies in some detail the original and appellate *jurisdiction of courts in New York State in criminal matters,* making alteration of these arrangements more difficult than if they were established in statute. The Supreme Court has ". . . general original jurisdiction in law and equity . . ." and "In the city of New York, . . . exclusive jurisdiction over crimes prosecuted by indictment, provided, however, that the legislature may grant to the city-wide court of criminal jurisdiction in the city of New York jurisdiction over misdemeanors prosecuted by indictment and to the family court in the city of New York jurisdiction over crimes and offenses by or against minors or between spouses or between parent and child or between members of the same family or household." The court of citywide criminal jurisdiction of New

---

16   A history of the elective-appointive debate can be found in Burden, "Problems Relating to the Office of New York State Attorney General," *Essays on the New York Constitution*, Littleton, CO: Fred Rothman Co., 1966, at pp. IV-5-7.

17   See generally, Article VI. judicial organization and selection is further detailed the chapter *Structures of New York State Government* in this book.

York City also is given jurisdiction by the Constitution over ". . . crimes and other violations of the law, other than those prosecuted by indictment. . . ."

County courts outside New York City have original jurisdiction ". . . over all crimes and other violations of law . . . ," and appellate jurisdiction over criminal matters over which the legislature has given jurisdiction to district, town, city, or village courts. Family courts outside New York City share the same constitution-based jurisdiction as such courts within the City. The criminal jurisdiction of the district courts is determined by statute, but it may not be greater that the jurisdiction of the New York City Criminal Court. The criminal jurisdiction of town, village, and city courts outside of New York City is established by the legislature and may not exceed that of the District Court. Appeals in criminal cases must be taken to the appellate division from the Supreme Court and in any case prosecuted by indictment or where indictment has been waived. In other cases where there may be a right to appeal to the Appellate Division, the appellate division can establish an appellate term. Appeals from town, village, and city courts outside of New York City are to the County Court, unless the legislature provides they are to be taken to the appellate term.

Finally, under the Constitution the Court of Appeals takes appeals "In criminal cases, directly from a court of original jurisdiction where the judgement is of death, and in other criminal cases from an appellate division or otherwise as the legislature may from time to time provide."[18]

Corrections. Insofar as the corrections system is concerned, the state Constitution authorizes the legislature to establish and maintain prisons and a system of probation and parole and requires the state Commission of Corrections to inspect adult correctional facilities (Article XVII, Section 5). These are not only the basis of activity in these areas by the state government itself, but provide the authority for oversight of and mandates upon local governments, especially counties. The state board of social welfare is required to inspect juvenile facilities (Article XVII, Section 2). As part of the Local Finance Article (Article VIII, Section 1) the Constitution permits local authorities to provide for the care, maintenance, and education of inmates of correctional facilities. There are no other provisions on this subject in the Constitution.

District Attorneys are independently elected in each county of New York State, including the five counties of New York City. According to Shapiro,

---

18   Article VI, Sections 3(a), 7(a), 8(a), 11(a) & (c), 13(b).7, 15(c), 16(d), 17(a).

the office of district attorney evolved in several stages in the state's early history. The office was not always elective, but has been so since 1846.

Prosecution of criminal offenses was originally the responsibility of the attorney-general. The first attorney-general was authorized by the constitution of 1777, and in 1796 the legislature provided that assistant attorneys-general be appointed to assist in criminal prosecutions. The state was divided into seven districts, and an assistant attorney-general was appointed for each district. In 1801 the assistant attorneys-general were renamed and became district attorneys. In 1821 the system of appointing district attorneys was modified, and district attorneys were appointed in the counties by the county courts. In the 1846 constitution a provision was adopted for the election of district attorneys, and that provision remains in Section 13 of Article XIII of the present constitution.[19]

The duties of district attorneys are almost entirely defined by statute. An exception is a responsibility to prosecute persons violating the Public Officers provisions of the state Constitution (Article XIII, Section 13(b)). As permitted by the Constitution, the legislature has made the term of this office four years. Where a county is operating under an alternative form of county government, the county charter may abolish the office of district attorney (Article XIII, Section 13).

Sheriffs, like district attorneys, are county-based elected officials, whose term may be set by the legislature at three or four years. The office of sheriff, the powerful local agent of the king, dates to the tenth century in England, but was in relative decline in powers and functions there by the time it was transferred to the British colonies in America in the sixteenth century. Early constitutional arrangements indicate a clear desire to constrain the person serving in this office. Under New York's first Constitution the sheriff was appointed to a one-year term with a four-year limit on service. The office became elective in 1821, with a three-year term and a bar on immediate reeligibility. Only in 1938 did a constitutional amendment make possible service in the office of sheriff for multiple consecutive terms.[20]

---

19   See Shapiro, "Local Law Enforcement in New York State," *Essays on the New York State Constitution*, Littleton, CO: Fred Rothman Co., 1966, at p. V-9 (footnote omitted).

20   See New York State Constitutional Convention Commission, "Problems Relating to Home Rule and Local Government," *Reports*, Albany: The Commission, 1938, at pp. 124-126.

For the sheriff, as for the district attorney, constitutional definition of powers and duties is quite limited. Sheriffs are constitutionally barred from other office and are required to regularly "renew their security." Counties are specifically removed from responsibility for sheriffs' actions (Article XIII, Section 13(a)).

Sheriffs have both criminal and civil functions under state law. In the criminal justice area, they are mandated to maintain and operate the county jail, and may at local discretion perform law enforcement functions through a "road patrol." The office of sheriff has been abolished in New York City, and like that of district attorney, may be abolished if a county adopts an alternative form of government under home rule authority provided in the state Constitution. This step has been taken in Westchester County.

Elected judges at the county, city, and town levels are critical actors in the local criminal justice systems in New York. Additionally, a number of criminal justice functions are performed at the city and county levels by general purpose governments, including incarceration, public defense, defendant-based advocacy, probation, and alternatives to incarceration programs. Mandates in state law give state agencies authority to direct the actions of local officials. In such a highly fragmented system, the presence of two constitutionally based, county-wide independently elected officials is regarded by some as an additional barrier to the coordination of criminal justice activities in New York State.

Criminal Sanctions

Criminal sanctions are only minimally addressed in the Constitution. There is, as has been discussed, a prohibition of excessive fines and cruel and unusual punishments. Additionally, the governor is given the power to grant reprieves, commutations, and pardons except in cases of treason and impeachment, which actions must be reported to the legislature annually (Article IV, Section 4). In treason cases, the governor may only suspend execution of sentence and then must report this action to the legislature, which makes the final decision.

Article III, Section 24, which restricts contracting-out prison labor, but permits prisoners to be required to work, might be viewed as a provision dealing with sanctions. However, arguably it is mostly concerned with protecting free labor from the threat of prison labor.

Finally, provisions for the removal of public officials from office under certain conditions may be regarded as sanctions for behavior that might include (but not be limited to) criminal behavior. Article XIII, Section 5, requires that the legislature make provision in law for ". . . the removal for misconduct or malaversion in office of all officers, except judicial, whose powers and duties are not local and legislative and who shall be elected at general elections. . . ." Elsewhere in this article, the governor is empowered to remove sheriffs, clerks, registers, or district attorneys for cause, after providing them an opportunity to be heard (Article XIII, Section 13(a) and (b)). The governor, lieutenant governor, and judges are subject to trial by impeachment, and additional separate provisions establish procedures for disciplining or removing judges (Article VI, Sections 22-24).

Proposals for Constitutional Change

A review of current state constitutional provisions in the area of criminal justice, their history, and recent developments suggests a number of issues that might be addressed at a constitutional convention should one be called. They include: the scope of the state Bill of Rights and its relation to the federal Bill of Rights; modifying Bill of Rights provisions dealing with the grand jury, the composition of the jury and the right to bail; coordinating or centralizing law enforcement; alleviating court logjams; adopting or altering criminal sanctions; and preserving or assuring victims rights.

The State Bill of Rights and Criminal Justice. During the last 40-45 years the federal Constitution as interpreted by the United States Supreme Court has been a significant touchstone for evaluating and understanding "Bill of Rights" provisions in state Constitutions, including those of New York. This has been and is the case regarding all Bill of Rights provisions, whether or not they address crime and the criminal justice system. The intensity of the crime problem has, with some notable exceptions (e.g., abortion, obscenity, and pornography), caused the focus to be primarily on those provisions that directly affect the criminal justice system.

In considering the state constitutional Bill of Rights provisions related to crime and the criminal justice system in the context of our federalism, therefore, several basic propositions should be borne in mind:

※ The proscriptions and commands of the federal Bill of Rights [the first ten Amendments] originally were limitations on federal action and did not apply to the states.

✳ These now are applied to the states in whole or in part by virtue of the later-adopted Fourteenth Amendment to the federal Constitution, primarily by judicial construction of the Fourteenth Amendment's due process clause.

✳ The federal constitutional limitations on state action are a floor on the rights that the states must recognize, and the states are free to recognize broader rights under their own state Constitutions. As noted above, this has been the case in New York State with regard to the "search and seizure" and "due process" provisions of its Constitution.

✳ The state court's construction of its own state Constitution will be accepted and bind the Supreme Court.

✳ The language of the various state provisions may be the same as or different than the federal constitutional provision on the same subject. Moreover, a state constitution may have additional provisions or it may have no provision at all that deals with matter explicitly addressed in the federal Constitution. The presence or absence of a state constitutional provision or how, if at all, the language of that provision differs from the relevant federal Constitution may or may not, depending on the state and the right involved, have a decisive bearing on how the federal definition of the right is used by the state court in construing the state constitution.

✳ As noted, it is not uncommon for some states, including New York, sometimes to recognize broader state constitutional rights than those accorded by the federal Constitution; by like token, it is not uncommon for a state always or often to construe its own constitution to provide no greater rights than those accorded by the United States Supreme Court's interpretation of the federal Constitution. Of course, no provision or construction of the state Constitution may stand that seeks to enforce narrower rights than those afforded by the federal Constitution.

1. With these contextual factors in mind, New York may wish to consider constitutional changes making *federal rights a ceiling as well as floor on state constitutional rights.* A variety of approaches might be used to require or encourage the state courts to recognize only those rights recognized under the federal Constitution as construed by the United States Supreme Court. In

recent years states have been moving towards constitutional Bill of Rights provisions that are textually the same as those found in the federal Constitution. If limiting the state courts is the sought end, it might be served simply by more generally adopting the language of the federal Bill of Rights for the state Constitution (with or without eliminating some state constitutional provisions covering other matters). A change in the constitutional language would not necessarily accomplish the result of limiting state courts to federal interpretations of the language; different reasonable constructions may flow from both the terminology employed and the provision's history. And there is no reason to conclude that the federal courts, including the United States Supreme Court, have a monopoly on reasonable construction. But such a move by a constitutional convention, accompanied by a developed record of the reasons for it, would surely be highly directive of interpretive behavior by state judges.

In Florida and California the referendum has been used in attempts to make rights as federally defined constraining upon state high court interpretation of rights under state constitutions. In 1982, Florida tied constitutional rights in that state with respect to searches and seizures to the United States Supreme Court's interpretation of the federal Constitution's Fourth Amendment by adding the following *italicized* language to the Florida Constitution's Declaration of Rights:

. . . *This right shall be construed in conformity with the 4th Amendment to the United States Constitution, as interpreted by the United States Supreme Court.* Articles or information obtained in violation of this right shall not be admissible in evidence *if such articles or information would be inadmissible under the decisions of the United States Supreme Court construing the 4th Amendment to the United States Constitution.*[21]

The California electorate approved an even broader provision prohibiting its courts from going beyond defendants' rights as construed by the Supreme Court in a number of areas in addition to search and seizure. In 1990, the California amendment was declared unconstitutional under the California Constitution for procedural reasons.[22]

21 Florida Constitution Article I, Section 12.

22 For more detail see the description in the chapter "Amending and Revising the New York State Constitution" in this book. *Raven* v. *Deukmejian*, 801 P2d 1077 (CA 1990).

In contrast to the initiatives in Florida and California, Rhode Island in 1986 adopted a constitutional provision which expressly states that the rights under the state Constitution are not dependent on the federal Constitution. It provides:

The enumeration of the foregoing rights shall not be construed to impair or deny others retained by the people. The rights guaranteed by this Constitution are not dependent on those guaranteed by the Constitution of the United States.[23]

The explicit purpose of this provision, according to one authority, was to ". . . add to the Constitution [of Rhode Island] a concept that the state Constitution is to be interpreted as expanding and not limiting individual rights, even though similar rights in the federal Constitution may be more narrowly defined.[24]

Persons who wish to constrain state courts in their interpretation of the rights of criminal defendants argue that these courts have been "too liberal." They disagree in substance with the distinctions these courts have made between federal and state constitutionally based rights, and the more expansive interpretation of rights under state constitutions in some states that has occurred in response to the more "conservative" trends in the Burger and Rhenquist Courts in this area of the law in recent years. Persons who favor allowing state courts greater latitude in interpreting rights under state constitutions, in contrast, are more likely to be supporters of the substantive outcomes these courts have been reaching. Thus, and perhaps counterintuitively, in this area of federal relations it is the "conservatives" who seek greater centralization or at least uniformity and the "liberals" greater decentralization.

2. *Abolition of the grand jury.* Periodically, including recent years, there have been proposals to abolish grand juries altogether or to retain them only for the purpose of investigating and reporting on government operations. The factual impetus for these movements has come largely from a view that in practice grand juries are primarily an extension of the prosecutor's will and rarely, if ever, make independent judgments that justify the cost and delay they entail. On the other hand, some deny these facts and point to instances of independence, and in any event believe the secrecy

---

23   Rhode Island Constitution Section 24.

24   Quoted in Janice May, "Amending State Bills of Rights: Do Voters Reduce Rights?" *Intergovernmental Perspective* 17, 45 (1991): 48 n. 14.

of the investigation that protects the innocent is worth the cost. Still others would not disturb what was historically viewed as a protection against arbitrary government action.

In considering whether the grand jury should be retained either as one method or a required method of initiating felony prosecutions, consideration should be given to the fact that not all states have or ever did have required grand jury proceedings. Some employ a prosecutor's information based on probable cause shown at a hearing; others give the prosecution the option of proceeding by indictment or information. The experience of those states should be examined in any consideration of the disposition of the grand jury in New York.[25]

3. *Bail.* Whether denoted "preventive detention" or otherwise, constitutional revision might consider the scope of the constitutional right to bail as involving more than a determination as to whether the accused will appear in court when required.

4. *Exemption from Jury Service.* There is current discussion concerning the multitude of exemptions from jury service. Many are thought by substantial numbers to be unjustified, but the day-to-day political pressures make it difficult to change the law and practice concerning jury exemptions by legislation. Consideration might be given to a constitutional provision that defines permitted exemptions or even bans exemptions by class.

5. *Victims' Rights.* A number of states, including Florida, California, Arizona, Michigan, Rhode Island, Texas, and Washington, have adopted so-called victims' rights provisions for their constitutions. Others have statutes dealing with the subject. The idea of a Victims' Bill of Rights is an obvious response to the existence of defendants' protections in traditional Bills of Rights. While the reasons for each set of rights rests on different goals, each does impose limitations on state government by giving individuals the right to make defined demands. Victims include surviving relatives of a deceased or incapacitated victim.

As for the kinds of provisions included in a victims' Bill of Rights, the Arizona Victims' Bill of Rights appears to be the most detailed and specific. It includes the right to be given notice

---

25   For a chart setting forth the various provisions related to initiation of criminal proceedings, see Glasser and Kincaid, "Selected Rights Enumerated in State Constitutions," *Intergovernmental Perspective* 17, 35 (1991): 42.

of all proceedings from the commencement of an action, trial, sentencing, and parole hearings; the right to be advised of and to be heard with respect to any disposition, including plea bargains; the right to be present and heard at sentencing and the right to examine pre-sentence reports; the right to a speedy trial; the right to restitution; the right to refuse to speak to defendant's attorney; and the right to be informed of the defendant's release or escape. It also contains a provision that requires that evidentiary rules and rules of procedure protect victims' rights.[26]

The Michigan[27] and Texas Constitutions also contain some detailed specific rights.[28] Texas provides that while a "victim or guardian or legal representative of a victim has standing to enforce the rights enumerated in [the Victims' Bill of Rights, they do] not have standing to participate as a party in a criminal proceeding or to contest the disposition of any charge."[29]

The California Constitution's Victims' Bill of Rights takes a different tack than the others.[30] It begins with a broad statement about the "grave statewide concern" for victims and the need to meet the expectation that people who commit crimes will be punished. The opening statement specifically refers to the need for safety in the schools and the need for broad reforms in criminal procedure and the disposition and sentencing of convicted persons.[31] It then declares a right to restitution and right to "safe schools."[32] The bail provision, described as "public safety bail," declares "public safety shall be the primary consideration" for pretrial release.[33] It does not explicitly provide for the presence of the victim at a bail hearing (or at any other aspect of a criminal proceeding, for that matter.)

The article contains what is described as a "right to truth-in-evidence," which requires the receipt of all relevant evidence unless excluded by a statute enacted by a two-thirds vote of each house of the legislature. Existing statutory privilege and hearsay

---

26 Arizona Constitution Article II, Section 2.
27 Michigan Constitution Article I, Section 24.
28 Texas Constitution Article I, Section 30.
29 Texas Constitution Article I, Section 30(d).
30 California Constitution Article I, Section 28.
31 *Ibid.*, Article I, Section 28(a).
32 *Ibid.*, Article I, Section 28 (b) and (c).
33 *Ibid.*, Article I, Section 28 (e).

rules are excluded from the operation of this mandate. So are the traditional rules that give the court discretion to exclude relevant evidence which is substantially outweighed by the danger of prejudice, and rules which prohibit the use by the prosecution of evidence of defendant's character to prove he or she acted in conformity with that character.[34] Prior convictions are admissible without limitation for impeachment and sentence enhancement purposes.[35]

There is scarcely any, if any, provision in the constitutionally established Victims' Bills of Rights that cannot and has not been the subject of legislation in other states, including New York. It is unclear, except for the opportunity to declare an important policy during tumultuous times, what function is served by the inclusion of these provisions in a state constitution that is not already served by thoughtfully drafted statutes.

Organization of the Criminal Justice System. It has been suggested at least since the 1938 Constitutional Convention that the fragmentation of the criminal justice system in New York is a barrier to effectively and efficiently protecting public safety. A number of approaches have been proposed to deal with this problem through constitutional change, some functional — focusing on such elements of the system as criminal prosecution or policing — and others more comprehensive, for example, seeking the creation of a Department of Criminal Justice.

1. *A Department of Criminal Justice reporting to the governor* for New York State was seriously debated at the 1967 Constitutional Convention. A constitutional amendment that received support from a majority of members present for the vote, but not the majority of those elected to the Convention necessary for passage, proposed that: "The governor shall be the chief law enforcement officer of the state and shall exercise his powers in relation thereto through a department of criminal justice to be established for such purpose. . . ." The amendment further provided the governor with power, through a department head he appointed with advice and consent of the Senate, to ". . . coordinate and supervise district attorneys, sheriffs, police and other law enforcement officers. . . ."[36]

---

34 *Ibid.*, Article I, Section 30(d).

35 *Ibid.*, Article I, Section 28(f).

36 See State of New York, *Proceedings New York State Constitutional Convention IX*, Proposition No. 1333 (1967).

The model for this proposal was the United States Department of Justice. Its chief advocate, Court of Appeals Judge Bernard Botein (formerly counsel to Governor Dewey and later chief judge of the Court) argued that to be effective against organized crime, which used the latest technology and did not respect local boundaries, state criminal justice activities had to be organized on a statewide basis. Botein and others who favored this proposal suggested that this department should report to the governor, and not to the attorney general, because the governor was already primarily responsible for execution of the laws and because all key operating functions of state government should be directed by the state's chief executive.

Opponents suggested that concentrating authority over prosecution, policing, and punishment in this manner was too dangerous to personal liberty. They argued that the system in place was more effective than opponents acknowledged, and had the virtue of being responsive to local leaders and local community values. District attorneys, represented at the convention by Aaron Koota from Queens County among others, were especially resistant to the criticism of their performance they saw as embedded in this proposal, and to the control over their discretion that might flow from it.[37]

2. *Centralization of the Prosecutorial Function in the Attorney General.* There are states, New Jersey for example, where centralized direction or coordination of the prosecutorial function is given to elected or appointed attorneys general. Some have the power to appoint prosecutors instead of relying on elected district attorneys. As noted above, in New York State, election of the attorney general and district attorneys as constitutionally independent officers presents issues concerning the efficiency and effectiveness of law enforcement and the establishment and coordination of statewide policy. One commentator argues that the mode of selection of the attorney general may significantly affect the organization of the criminal justice function. That is, because the attorney general has an independent electoral base, the governor and legislature are reluctant to give this office a coordinating role in the criminal justice

---

37   See the debate on Proposition 1333. "*Proceedings of the Constitutional Convention IX,*" (1967), pp. 678-725. The vote on the proposition was 85-74.

system by statute, or even to restore to it a substantial prosecutorial function.[38]

This option raises a number of constitutional issues:

a. *Appointment of the Attorney General by the Governor, With the Advice and Consent of One or Both Houses of the Legislature?*

Proponents of appointment say that this approach gives recognition to the governor's duties to execute the laws. Additionally, it paves the way for an integrated approach to criminal justice, as described above. An attorney general appointed by the governor is not likely to be a political rival; he or she would have the chief executive's confidence and would therefore more likely be delegated the range of responsibilities necessary to achieve greater efficiency and effectiveness in criminal justice administration. Such an appointed attorney general might act at first as a chief prosecutor, and then later come to have more general responsibilities for this area of policy as the office evolved. Additionally, proponents say, confusion and overlapping would be avoided; that might be the case if there was a separate criminal justice department and a department, headed by the attorney general, for other legal functions of state government.

Opponents to appointment of the attorney general by the governor say that this would make more powerful a governorship that is already too powerful in New York. They argue that having a statewide elected official in the attorney general's office, a potential political opponent of the governor either within or outside his or her party, is a salutary check upon the chief executive and therefore a benefit for the people of the state. More generally, opponents say, a certain number of state-wide elected offices are needed that provide political exposure and broad experience to potential governors. Less in New York State than nationally at the state level, the attorney general's office performs this function. But, especially if term limits are instituted in New York

---

38 See Gerald Benjamin, *The Governor and the Attorney General in New York,* Albany: The Rockefeller Institute, 1986; and "A New York State Department of Justice," *Empire State Report* (April 1985): 15-18, and 22.

for statewide office, the attorney generalship might come to be used in this way here as well.[39]

Moreover, opponents continue, concentration of the prosecutorial function in the attorney general does not require gubernatorial appointment to that office as a necessary condition. In fact, keeping the office elective is one reassurance that may be given to those who fear the threat to liberty that, they say, inheres in any concentration of power in the criminal justice area. Of course, if the prosecutorial function is centralized in an elected attorney general, attention must then be given to legal relationship between that office and the governor in order to assure greater coordination of law enforcement policies, especially with regard to specific statewide crimes or problems. For under these conditions, less is likely to be achieved informally, by coordination within the governor's administration.

b. *Appointment of County Prosecutors and Their Oversight.*

However the attorney general or head of a criminal justice department is chosen, the question remains as to whether the chief prosecutor in each county (or in groups of counties, in less populated areas) should be elected. Proponents of the current system favor its decentralized quality, and find merit in the direct accountability of the district attorney to the local majority, and therefore to majoritarian values in the locality. New York, they remind us, is a very large state. The great differences in the views and needs of New Yorkers in different parts of the state demand local flexibility and discretion in the administration of justice that the current system provides.

Opponents remind us that appointed deputy attorneys general were the local prosecutors in the early history of New York. They suggest that election does not always produce the best qualified people in the prosecutorial role. (Indeed, county-based election in very rural areas produces part-time prosecutors who may frequently find themselves in conflict-of-interest

---

39   See generally Larry Sabato, *Goodbye to Goodtime Charlie*, Washington: CQ Press, 1983.

situations because of their continued involvement in the private practice of law.) If the power to appoint and assign prosecutors for counties or other defined areas were in the hands of an elected or appointed attorney general or commissioner of criminal justice, they argue, the result would be greater coordination of law enforcement and preservation, and better allocation of resources. Additionally, a career prosecutorial service could be developed in the state, resulting in a higher and more consistent quality of work.[40]

Even if district attorneys continue to be elected, a constitutional amendment might be passed that would allow the attorney general, the governor or a commissioner appointed by the governor to coordinate their activities, in a manner similar to that proposed in 1967. Whether such an approach would be successful is an interesting question. An analogy is the creation by constitutional amendment of a central mechanism for coordinating the activities of locally and regionally elected state judges. Though a good deal of order, discipline, and coordination has been brought to this system as a result of these changes, there remain important decentralizing pressures within it.

c. *Abolition of the Office of Sheriff, or Appointment of the Sheriff by a County-Level Appointing Authority.*

Advocates of abolishing the office of sheriff regard it as an anachronism. The independence that the office derives from its elective status leads to inefficient, uncoordinated, and sometimes destructively competitive delivery of police services among local departments and between local and state police in rural areas of the state. The technical competence that is required for effective command in modern policing requires that trained, qualified leaders be selected, they say, and these are best identified by an appointive, not an elective, process. In fact, they say, in many areas of the state most police work might best

---

40 In this connection, it should be noted that the district attorney can be abolished in the case of an alternative county government; however, it has been held that it may only be abolished and not retained and be subject to changes in the constitutional election requirements.

be done by the highly trained and professional state police.

An additional consideration is that the control by the sheriff of the county jail is a barrier to effective cooperation between the corrections function and alternatives to incarceration programs at the county level. Even if the office of sheriff must be maintained, critics argue, at minimum it should be filled by appointment by the general purpose county government, for reasons parallel to those given for gubernatorial appointment at the state level.

Opponents suggest that county sheriff's departments perform very important police services that otherwise would not be provided in many areas of the state. Sheriffs have been reasonably effective and professional in performing their duties, usually under very difficult conditions dictated by state mandates. There is no convincing evidence that abolishing the office would produce the benefits claimed for such a move. Centralization of police services, a traditionally local function, is contrary to New York's dedication to home rule and could therefore present questions under Article IX. Current arrangements have widespread public support.

Sanctions

1. *Right of Prosecution to Appeal Sentences.* The prosecution and the defendant may appeal an illegal sentence. The defendant may now appeal an otherwise legal or authorized sentence on the grounds that it is harsh or excessive, but the prosecution cannot appeal a sentence on the grounds that it is too lenient. Constitutional revision could consider providing the prosecution with the right to appeal an otherwise authorized sentence that, under the circumstances, may be too lenient or which undermines an important state policy. Prosecution appeals of sentences also could support policies of uniformity in the state or region.

2. *Death Sentence.* Suggestion has been made to include in the Constitution a provision requiring that the state have an authorized death penalty. Without commenting on the difficulties of

developing an acceptable appropriate provision in this regard, inclusion of this kind of provision is a possibility when revision of the Constitution is undertaken, and its debate in a committee of a convention and/or on the floor is most likely in the current political environment.

Education

Robert D. Stone

Current provisions of the New York State Constitution concerning education date largely from 1894 and fall into five categories: recognition of education as a state obligation and function; establishment of the governance and oversight structure; relief from certain constitutional limitations concerning state finance; structuring of local finance limitations; and limiting use of public funds for the support of denominational institutions. Summaries of the current status and history of provisions in each of these categories are given below, followed by a discussion of a number of current or persistent constitutional issues concerning education in New York.

Education as a State Function

The Constitutional Convention of 1894 evidenced the broadest, and perhaps most intense, interest in education of any constitutional effort to that date. For the first time, it mandated free public education. Article XI, Section 1, is a model of brevity and conciseness. It reads:

> The legislature shall provide for the maintenance and support of a system of free common schools wherein all the children of this state may be educated.[1]

As though to emphasize the clear mandate expressed in this provision, Article IX, the local government article added in 1963, provides in Section 3(a) that:

> Except as expressly provided, nothing in this article shall restrict or impair any power of the legislature in relation to: (1) the maintenance, support or administration of the public school sys-

---

1   Constitution 1894, Article IX, Section 1; renumbered Article XI, Section 1, 1938. All 50 states have constitutional provisions requiring the maintenance of a system of public schools. In 22 of them, the word "free" expressly appears. One authority asserts that constitutional provisions of an additional eight states might be construed to require "free" public education. Only in Mississippi does the constitution expressly provide that there is no right to education at public expense. Such a provision in Alabama was overturned in *Alabama Coalition for Equity Inc.* (ACE) v. *Guy Hunt and Mary Hunter, et al.*, 624 SO 2d 107 (1993).

tem, as required or provided by article XI of this constitution, or any retirement system pertaining to such public school system. . . .

State Function. With respect to Article XI, Section 1, the *Report of the Committee on Education and the Funds Pertaining Thereto* of the 1894 Constitutional Convention said: "There seems to be no principle upon which the people of the commonwealth are so united and agreed as this, that the first great duty of the State is to protect and foster its educational interests. . . . This requires not simply schools, but a system; not merely that they shall be common, but free, and not only that they shall be numerous, but that they shall be sufficient in number, so that all the children of the State may, unless otherwise provided for, receive in them their education."[2]

Despite the fact that the New York public school system is comprised of individual school districts (currently 715), governed by locally elected (or in some cases appointed) boards of education, it has long been settled that Article XI, Section 1, makes administration of public education a state function.[3] Education was further confirmed as a state responsibility by the expressed preservation of legislative authority for this function in the home rule article. This provision "constitutionalized" a frequently expressed opinion of the Court of Appeals that education was a state concern, and that legislation dealing with matters of state concern, even though of localized application and having a direct affect on the most basic of local interests, did not violate constitutional home rule provisions.[4]

"Free" Schools. The term "free" has consistently been interpreted to mean without tuition or other charge to resident students of each school district. For example, a school district may not impose a charge for such nonrequired instruction as music or driver education.[5] The right to a free public education extends as well to delinquent, neglected, and dependent children.[6] While the right of children with handicapping conditions to appropriate education is significantly buttressed by federal law, Article XI, Section 1, is also the predicate for New York's statutory provisions for such children, set forth primarily in Article 89 of the Education Law.[7]

---

2   1894 Convention Document no. 62, at pp. 3-4.

3   *Lanza* v. *Wagner*, 11 NY2d 317 (1962), app. dism. 371 U.S.74, cert. den. 371 U.S. 901; *Board of Education* v. *New York*, 41 NY2d 535 (1977).

4   See *Lanza* v. *Wagner,* 11 NY2d 317 (1962); *Divisich* v. *Marshall*, 281 NY 170 (1939); *Board of Education* v. *New York*, 41 NY2d 535 (1977).

5   *Matter of Gordon*, 14 Ed. Dept. Rep. 358 (1975); 497 Op. St. Comptr. .(1981).

6   *Wiltwyck School* v. *Hill,* NY2d 182 (1962).

7   *In re Levy,* 38 NY2d 653 (1976), app. dism. 429 US 805, reh. den. 429 US 966.

The constitutional mandate to provide a free public education does not, however, give a student a right to monetary damages based on the alleged inadequacy of the education provided. The state courts have held, for example, that a complaint by the recipient of a high school diploma that he could not comprehend written English did not state a cause of action for damages because statutes ". . . designed (to) confer a benefit upon the general public do not give rise to a cause of action by an individual. . . ." Some advocates argue that modern minimum standards legislation confers benefits "not simply on the general public, but more specifically on '[e]very citizen in [New York] state,' therefore increasing the body of law that might be taken by the courts to create an implied right of action . . . to sue."[8]

Moreover, there is no constitutional right of a parent, the Court of Appeals has said, to dictate *where* educational services to children must be offered. Thus members of a religious sect who live within their own incorporated village were not denied any constitutional right by placement of their handicapped children in public school programs.[9]

Financing Education as a State Constitutional Issue Under the Education Clause. With respect to the state's system for financing public elementary and secondary education, the Court of Appeals held in 1982 that the then-current statutory provisions for allocation of state aid to school districts violated neither the "free common schools" provision of Article XI, Section 1, nor the equal protection clauses of either the state or federal Constitutions, even though they resulted in substantially disparate per-capita expenditures for education from one district to another.[10] This result diverges from the outcome of similar cases in five other states based upon the education provisions of their constitutions: Kentucky, Montana, New Jersey, Texas, and Washington. Equal protection arguments have been the basis for finding unconstitutional the education finance schemes of Arkansas, California, and Georgia. Decisions invalidating the education finance systems of Connecticut and West Virginia were based upon both the equal protection and education clauses in the constitutions of those states.[11] The most recent "third wave" of litigation in the states seeking equity in educational finance is largely based upon

---

8   *Donohue* v. *Copiague Union Free School District* 47 NY2d 440 (1979) at p. 880. See also James Liebman, "Implementing Brown in the Nineties: Political Reconstruction and Litigatively Enforced Legislative Reform," *Virginia Law Review* 76, 3 (April 1990): 405.

9   *Board of Education* v. *Wieder*, 72 NY2d 174 (1988).

10 *Board of Education* v. *Nyquist*, 57 NY2d 27 (1982).

11 See Edwin Margolis and Stanley Moses, *The Elusive Quest: The Struggle for Equality of Educational Opportunity*, New York: The Apex Press, 1992, at pp. 152-155.

education clauses in state constitutions.[12] Litigation seeking to reopen the question of equity in school financing in New York — based upon the education clause, the equal protection clause, and the bar against racial discrimination in the state Constitution — has been unsuccessful on Long Island, and is pending in New York City.[13]

Governance and Oversight

Two provisions dating to the 1894 Constitution establish the structure for governance and oversight of New York's educational system. Building upon these, the drafters of the extensive 1938 constitutional revisions retained the long-standing concept of The University of the State of New York as a corporate entity governed by a Board of Regents, with powers assigned by the legislature. Comparative research has found no other state in which a single education authority has been assigned, either by constitution or by statute, the breadth of responsibilities assigned to the Board of Regents/Commissioner of Education.[14]

Section 2 of Article XI provides that:

> The corporation created in the year one thousand seven hundred eighty-four, under the name of The Regents of the University of the State of New York, is hereby continued under the name of The University of the State of New York. It shall be governed and its corporate powers, which may be increased, modified or diminished by the legislature, shall be exercised by not less than nine regents.[15]

Article V, the officers and civil departments article, in Section 4, provides in part that:

> The head of the department of education shall be the Regents of the University of the State of New York, who shall appoint and at pleasure remove a commissioner of education to be the chief administrative officer of the department.

---

12 See Molly McUsic, "The Use of Education Clauses in School Finance Reform Litigation," *Harvard Journal of Legislation* 28 (1991): 307-340.

13 *Reform Educational Finance Inequities Today, et al.* v. *Mario M. Cuomo, et al.* 152 Misc. 2d. (1991); *Campaign for Fiscal Equity, Inc.* v. *the State of New York* (Supreme Court of the State of New York, County of New York, Index # 93111070).

14 See New York State Constitutional Convention Committee, *State and Local Government in New York,* IV (1938), at pp. 67 and 245-249.

15 Constitution 1894, Article IX, Section 2; renumbered Article XI, Section 2, 1938.

Constitutional Status. One researcher concludes that constitutional status was given to the Board of Regents well after its hundredth birthday "to insulate it from capricious legislative action and partisan politics."[16] The Education Committee of the 1894 Convention gave a different view, stating that "The section simply crystallizes into a constitutional mandate the settled policy of the State for over one hundred years. . . . The University of the State of New York is the oldest institution of the State and has survived unchanged the vicissitudes of more than a century. In the regard of other states and countries it is this university which has given New York her reputation and her position in the literature of education. . . . Moreover, in the history of this State, as elsewhere, the great historical truth, which is often lost sight of has been made manifest, namely, that education works downward from the higher institutions of learning, and by no means, as might be supposed on superficial thought, from the common schools up."[17]

Two significant changes to this article as reported from the Committee were debated on the floor of the 1894 Convention. The outcome of both debates gave or left considerable power with the legislature. An amendment was passed that gave the legislature express authority to increase, modify, or diminish the Regents' powers. Another failed that placed in the Constitution the Regents' power to appoint the superintendent of public instruction (now commissioner of education), thus leaving appointing authority with the legislature. It was not until 1925 that a separate amendment (Article V, Section 4) gave constitutional status to the statutory authority given the Regents in 1904 to appoint and remove the commissioner of education.[18]

Governance and Policy Consequences. The authority, roles, and functions of the Board of Regents, the commissioner of education, and the Education Department stem from a combination of the constitutional provisions discussed above and the extensive statutory scheme set forth in the Education Law.[19] One of the results of that scheme is that the Regents/Commissioner/Department have responsibility for standard-setting and oversight of very nearly all organized educational activity within the state, both public and nonpublic, from preschool through graduate and professional education, and including libraries, museums, public radio and television, and historical societies. The Board of Regents is the only state educational governing body recognized by the United States Depart-

---

16 See Peter J. Galie, *The New York State Constitution: A Reference Guide*, Westport, CT: Greenwood Press, 1991, at p. 26.

17 1894 Convention Document No. 62, at pp. 5-6.

18 See New York State Constitutional Convention, *Revised Record III*, (1915), at pp. 696-719; Chapter 40, Laws of 1904.

19 Book 16, *McKinney's Consolidated Laws of New York* (1994).

ment of Education as an accrediting agency for colleges and universities. It can fairly be assumed that such recognition and reliance stem, at least in part, from the responsibility assigned to the Regents by state law for oversight of all higher and professional education. The Court of Appeals has held that a purpose of the constitutional and legislative system for public school governance is to make all matters pertaining to the public school system within the authority and direction of the State Education Department, and to remove them so far as practicable and possible from controversies in the courts.[20]

Vacancies in New York City Community School Boards. A final provision of the New York Constitution having to do with governance in education that, though minor, should be noted here for completeness, allows vacancies in elected New York City community school boards to be filled by appointment for a period longer than otherwise permitted under Article XIII Section 3.[21] This is another area in which a constitutional change was made to overcome a decision of the Court of Appeals. In 1972 the court held that vacancies in community school boards in New York City could not be filled by appointment for periods beyond the next ensuing December 31. The sponsors of the amendment in 1977 argued that "The term 'political year' in the constitution, applied by the Court of Appeals in this case, was never meant to refer to the State school system."[22]

State Finance Provisions

The state finance provisions applicable to education create exceptions to what otherwise would be constitutional limitations or prohibitions. These exceptions involve gifts or loans of the state's money or credit; borrowing for the state university without referendum; and permitting a lottery for education despite a general prohibition on gambling.

Gifts and Loans Exceptions. Article VII, Section 8, Subsection 1, the so-called "gifts and loans" provision, prohibits the use of state funds or credit in aid of any "private" person, corporation, association, or undertaking, with exceptions that include educational purposes. Subsection 2 of this section extends the exception to education of ". . . the blind, the deaf, the dumb, the

---

20   *James* v. *Board of Education*, 42 NY2d 357 (1977).

21   Constitution 1846, Article X, Section 5; renumbered Article XIII, Section 8, 1938; renumbered Article XIII, Section 3, 1962; Amendment 1977 (added provision pertaining to boards of education).

22   *Roher* v. *Dinkins*, 40 AD2d 956, affd. 32 NY2d 180 (1972); Bill Memorandum accompanying A.1568 (1977).

physically handicapped, the mentally ill, the emotionally retarded or juvenile delinquents." These exceptions are consistent with the priority given education in Article XI, Section 1, and recognize state practices in place in 1984, when these provisions were written.

In 1938, Article VII, Section 8, Subsection 2, of the Constitution was altered to assure to the legislature authority to provide for health or welfare services to children through school districts, subject to the limitations on indebtedness and taxation, the gifts and loans prohibition notwithstanding. At least one observer believes that "There were factors that would make it difficult for delegates [to the 1938 Convention] to ignore social and economic issues . . . ," including his view that "The Great Depression had forced public officials to re-evaluate their understanding of the role of government in society."[23]

Issues occasionally arise in the courts as to the genuineness of an "educational purpose." The use of space in the student union of a campus of the State University for a non-state student activity has been held to not violate the gifts and loans provision because of the education exception. And a not-for-profit corporation formed to provide educational, health, and social services information to community residents comes within the exceptions to the gifts and loans prohibition.[24]

State University Debt. Article VII, Section 19, permitted the legislature to authorize the creation of state debt, up to $250 million, without submission to the people, for expansion and development of the State University and community colleges. (Whereas state universities in many other states have constitutional status, this provision is the only mention of the State University of New York in the New York Constitution.) The Board of Trustees of the State University, in its "Annual Reports to the Governor and the Legislature for 1955 and 1956," detailed the capital needs of the State University in a period of postwar expansion, and urged the submission of a $250 million bond issue proposal to the voters. The proposal was approved by the legislature at its 1956 and 1957 sessions, and by the voters in 1957. In its 1957 Report the Board of Trustees expressed gratitude that "In the first opportunity ever provided for the people of our State to express their attitude toward the State University, the constitutional amendment . . . was approved. . . ."[25] However, rejection of a constitutional amendment permitting an additional $500 million in borrowing for additional construction in 1961 led to the funding of the

23   See Galie, *supra*, at p. 26.

24   *Cavages, Inc.* v. *Ketter*, 86 AD2d 753 (1982); 1976 Op. Att'y. Gen. (f.9.)

25   1956 Leg. Doc. No. 89; 1957 Leg. Doc. No. 8; 1958 Leg. Doc. No. 112.

later expansion of the state university through public authorities, bypassing constitutional limits.

Lottery for Education. An amendment to Article I, Section 9, Subsection 1, adopted in 1966 permits the operation of a state lottery ". . . the net proceeds of which shall be applied exclusively to or in aid or support of education in this state as the legislature may prescribe. . . ." The principal justification for the 1966 amendment was to create a new source of revenue for the state without additional taxation. The linkage of this revenue source to education, a then-popular area of expenditure with the voters, was a means to generate support for it.[26]

The 1966 amendment, following those permitting pari-mutuel betting on horse races in 1939 and bingo in 1957 over the vociferous objection of many, suggests a change in public attitude since the adoption of the stern injunction against gambling by the 1894 Constitutional Convention. This proposition will be further tested as a result of the recent burgeoning growth of gambling on Indian reservations in New York and elsewhere as a result of federal law. In its 1972 report, the New York State Commission of Gambling recommended a constitutional amendment eliminating the lottery provision of Article I, Section 9, and giving the legislature discretion to authorize any kind of gambling.[27] Such an initiative would remove the linkage between gambling and education in the state Constitution. The root issue, of course, is the question of whether a state should not only permit gambling, but should profit from it.

Local Finance Provisions

Article VIII embodies a great range of restrictions upon the finances of counties, cities, towns, villages, and school districts, reflecting an underlying assumption ". . . that local governments cannot be trusted to act responsibly, especially in incurring debt and contingent liability that will not have to be paid until future years."[28] These restrictions are detailed elsewhere in this briefing book.[29] In general, the exceptions to these limits, like those to the limits on state debt, demonstrate the special status of education as a public policy concern of the state.

---

26   See Galie, *supra*, at p. 56.

27   *See New York State Commission on Gambling Report,* February 1972, at p. 5; *Ibid.,* (February 1973), at p. 3.

28   See Galie, *supra*, at p. 185.

29   See the chapter "Intergovernmental Relations" in this book.

Gifts and Loans Exceptions. As with the parallel provision of Article VI, the local "gifts and loans" prohibition in Article VIII, Section 1, provides an exception for county, city, or town spending to provide for the ". . . secular education of inmates or orphan asylums, homes for dependent children or correctional institutions . . . whether under public or private control. . . ."

These exceptions are consistent with the philosophy underlying other education provisions of the Constitution discussed in this section, which is that the secular education of children occupies a preeminent place in the spectrum of governmental responsibilities.[30]

Debt Limitation Exceptions. Article VIII, Section 4, dealing with limitations on local indebtedness, provides the sole exception to the five percent of average full valuation limit on debt for school districts in cities with fewer than 125,000 people (the so-called "small cities") ". . . *for specified objects or purposes with (1) the approving vote of sixty percent or more of the duly qualified voters of such school district voting on a proposition therefore . . . (2) the consent of the Regents . . . and (3) the consent of the State Comptroller.*"[31]

Prior to 1951, the debt limits of the "small city" school districts were tied to the limits for the cities in which the school districts were located. All levels of government in the post-World War II environment found themselves prevented by these constitutional debt limitations from constructing needed public improvements, such as schools. In 1947 the state comptroller appointed a Committee on Constitutional Tax and Debt Limitations and City-School Fiscal Relations. This committee reported in 1950 that the small city districts were being unduly inhibited from constructing facilities anticipated to be needed for future years, and recommended that they be able to borrow without securing the consent of the city, within a separate debt limit. They also proposed that the voters of such school districts be permitted to authorize them to exceed the initial 5 percent limit by a 60 percent vote, with the consent of the Regents and the Comptroller. Such flexibility was required, the committee said, because of prospective needs for school buildings in future years.[32] Addi-

---

30 Judicial decisions, opinions of the attorney general and the state comptroller, and judicial decisions of the commissioner of education as to what uses of school district funds are or are not permissible under the gifts and loans prohibition are voluminous. See the annotations to Article VIII, Section 1, in *McKinney's Consolidated Laws of New York Annotated* or *Consolidated Laws Service Laws of New York* (1994).

31 Constitution 1894, Article VIII, Section 10; renumbered Section 4 and Amendment 1938; Amendment 1951 (section revised generally).

32 See The Committee: New York State Comptroller, *Third Report* February 27, 1950.

tionally, according to Galie, "The separate debt limits for cities and school districts would permit school reorganization in and near cities without bringing the school debt within the city's debt limit."[33]

Article VIII, Section 4, further provides that in ascertaining the power of a small city district to contract indebtedness, debts contracted for purposes other than the financing of capital improvements and to be redeemed within two years, and debts incurred in anticipation of taxes or state aid, are excluded. It can be fairly inferred that short-term debt and debt incurred in contemplation of taxes for state aid was not seen as necessitating constitutional inhibition.

Finally, Article VIII, Section 7, pertaining to the debt-incurring power of New York City, provides in Subdivision E that certain indebtedness contracted for school purposes on which annual amortization would be paid from state aid may be excluded from the debt limit. Apparently, the exemption was meant to aid New York City in financing school construction and other capital improvements.[34]

Support of Denominational Education

A much-debated and litigated section of the state Constitution adopted in 1894, the so-called "Blaine Amendment," provides that:

> Neither the state nor any subdivision thereof, shall use its property or credit or any public money, or authorize or permit either to be used, directly or indirectly, in aid or maintenance, other than for examination or inspection, of any school or institution of learning wholly or in part under the control or direction of any religious denomination, or in which any denomination tenet or doctrine is taught. . . .

An exception to the very stringent prohibition against public support for parochial education was added in 1938 to permit

> the transportation of children to and from any school or institution of learning.

This amendment was intended to overcome the then-current decision of the Court of Appeals in *Judd* v. *Board of Education of Union Free School District No. 2 Town of Hempstead* barring such transportation to

---

33   See Galie, *supra,* at p. 197.
34   See Galie, *supra,* at p. 203.

denominational schools under Article IX, Section 4 (now Article XI, Section 3). The overturning of Judd led some wags to proclaim "Poor Judd is dead!" Proposals that the 1938 Convention act to authorize health and welfare services and textbooks, state or local support of denominational schools, and religious instruction in the public schools were defeated.[35]

The 1967 Constitutional Convention would have completely removed the Blaine Amendment ban on aid to sectarian schools, reflecting a more accommodating approach to religion, but the Constitution proposed by that body was rejected by the people by a three to one margin, with the proposed repeal of Blaine a very important factor in determining the outcome.[36]

Origins of Blaine Amendment. Professor Peter Galie attributes the inclusion of the Blaine Amendment in the 1894 Constitution to "the growth of the Catholic population" in New York State, and suggests that Blaine was precipitated by a proposal in the 1893 legislature that parochial schools should receive a pro rata share of state school aid. "Because it had been the policy of New York for all its history to combine religious and secular instruction in public schools without serious objection," Galie observes, "the proposal marked a radical change of opinion concerning the legitimate function of public education. . . . Concentrated in the cities and Democratic in political affiliation, Catholics wished to create and maintain their own schools and social institutions. This alarmed many Protestants, extremist and non-extremist alike."[37]

The education committee of the 1894 Convention, in its report to the Convention, put it differently but equally forcefully. "In the opinion of the Committee there is no demand from the people of the State upon this Convention so unmistakable, widespread and urgent; none, moreover, so well grounded in reason and right, as that the public school system of the State shall be forever protected by constitutional safeguards from all

---

35 Constitution 1894, Article IX, Section 4; Amendment and renumbered Article XI, Section 4, 1938; renumbered Article XI, Section 3, 1962. *Judd v. Board of Education of Union Free School District No. 2 Town of Hempstead*, 278 NY 200, reh. den. 278 NY 712 (1938); New York State Constitutional Convention 1938, *Revised Record*, II, at pp. 1055-56. The vote was 135-9. For further information see *Education in the Constitutional Convention 1938*, New York: The University of the State of New York Press, 1943, at pp. 12-15.

36 A discussion of the desirability of repealing the Blaine Amendment may be found in *Inter-Law School Committee Report on the Problem of Simplification of the Constitution*, 1958 Leg. Doc. No. 57, pp. 115-133; For the full text of the education article proposed by the 1967 Convention, see *Proceedings of the Constitutional Convention of the State of New York, 1967*, XII, at pp. 25-26. For an analysis of the Blaine Amendment debate at the 1967 Constitutional Convention see Henrik Dullea, *Charter Revision in the Empire State: The Politics of New York's 1967 Constitutional Convention*, Ph.D. Dissertation, Department of Political Science, Maxwell School, Syracuse University, 1982, at pp. 339-428.

37 See Galie, at p. 20.

sectarian influence or interference, and that public money shall not be used, directly or indirectly, to propagate denominational tenets or doctrine." But the Committee intended two exceptions in the language it proposed: the reading of the Bible in public schools should, it thought, continue; and the state should continue to "examine and inspect" all schools, public and parochial at state expense. Interestingly, the Committee proposed an additional sentence excepting "schools in institutions subject to the visitation and inspection of the State Board of Charities" from the effect of this amendment, but this exception was removed on the floor of the Convention.[38]

Examination and Inspection: Formula Aid. The constitutional exception allowing "examination or inspection" of denominational schools was viewed for many years as simply authorizing the expenditure of state funds to enable the Education Department to universally perform its oversight responsibilities. In 1970, however, gubernatorial and legislative interest in providing some measure of direct financial assistance to nonpublic schools resulted in the enactment of a law apportioning funds to such schools on a formula basis ostensibly to assist in meeting expenses incurred in complying with examination and inspection requirements. The appropriation for this so-called "Mandated Services Law" was $28 million.[39]

The constitutional validity of the Mandated Services Law was promptly challenged in the federal courts and its implementation enjoined. The law was invalidated by the United States Supreme Court in 1973 as an establishment of religion prohibited by the First Amendment of the national Constitution. The statute, the court said, provided no means to ensure that internally prepared tests used by denominational schools, which were an integral part of the teaching process, were free of religious

---

38   1894 Convention Document No. 62, *supra*, at pp. 15-16. The reasons for and against the adoption of Article IX, Section 4 (now Article XI, Section 3) given in Convention debate are far too extensive to examine here in detail. See, e.g. New York State Constitutional Convention, *Revised Record III*, (1915), at pp. 739-762, 766-806, 955-970, 981-986, and IV, at pp. 746-754, 761-772, and 777-797. Most of the debate revolved around the primary question whether state financial support of denominational education is desirable. A secondary question concerned state support of denominational *charitable* institutions that house and care for, as well as educate. Revisions of the amendment were defeated on the floor; the language prohibiting State support of denominational schools was approved, on a roll call, by a vote of 77-60. See New York State Constitutional Convention, *Revised Record II*, (1915), at p. 986. Following further debate on third reading, proposed Article IX (now Article XI) was approved in its entirety by a vote of 108-37. *Revised Record IV*, (1915), at pp. 857-881.

39   Chapter 138, Laws of 1970, as amended by Chapter 501, Laws of 1971. The money was to be for "services for examination and inspections in connection with administration, grading and the compiling and reporting of the results of tests and examinations, maintenance of records of pupil enrollment and reporting thereon, maintenance of pupil health records, reporting for personnel qualifications and characteristics and the preparation and submission on the state of various other reports as provided for by law or regulation."

instruction. Moreover, it provided no mechanism for assuring that these exams did not have the effect of inculcating students in the religious precepts of the sponsoring church.[40]

Examination and Inspection: Reimbursement of Costs. In response to this development the legislature took a different approach, seeking to provide reimbursement to nonpublic schools for their actual cost of complying with the requirements of the state's pupil evaluation program, the basic education data system, the statewide evaluation plan, the uniform procedure for pupil attendance reporting, similar state-prepared examinations and reporting systems, and the administration of Regents examinations. This method of aiding parochial schools while remaining in compliance with both the state and national Constitutions — reimbursement for actual costs of providing noninstructional services subject to audit by the state comptroller — was upheld in the courts.[41]

Aid to the Student. A third exception to the ban on public aid to parochial education has been carved out by the legislature and the courts in the so-called "Textbook Loan Law," which requires every school district to purchase textbooks, and to loan them upon individual request to all children enrolled in a public *or private* school in the district.[42] The reference to private schools of course includes denominational schools. Given its effect, it was inevitable that the Textbook Loan Law would be challenged under both the state and federal Constitutions. In the landmark cause of *Board of Education* v. *Allen* both the Court of Appeals and the United States Supreme Court sustained the validity of the statute under Article XI, Section 3, of the state Constitution and the Establishment Clause of the U.S. Constitution, on the ground that it did not intend to assist parochial schools as such but rather benefited their students.[43]

Despite the holding and rationale of *Allen,* the Supreme Court later decided that although the loan of textbooks to students attending denominational schools is permissible, the loan of other instructional materials and equipment, such as maps, charts, films, and projectors, and recording and laboratory equipment, constitutes an impermissible establishment of

---

40   *Levitt* v. *Committee for Public Education and Religious Liberty,* 413 US 472 (1973). In response to the injunctive relief granted in the lower federal courts with respect to Chapter 138, the Legislature in 1971 enacted Chapter 822, constituting a new Mandated Services Law designed to ensure that payments to sectarian schools would not support religious instruction. Predictably, that Chapter was also challenged.

41   Chapters 507 and 508, Laws of 1974. *Committee for Public Education and Religious Liberty* v. *Regan,* 444 US 646 (1980).

42   Education Law, Section 701.

43   20 NY2d 109 (1967), affd. 392 US 236.

religion, in violation of the Establishment Clause. The Court's primary rationale for the distinction was its view that the materials and equipment were to be loaned to the schools, rather than to the students.[44]

School Prayer, Released Time, Oath of Allegiance. On another critical issue, a practice intended to be permitted by the drafters of the Blaine Amendment, prayer in the schools, was found in violation of the national Constitution. The United States Supreme Court in the "Regents Prayer" case held that the recital in public schools of a nondenominational prayer composed by the Board of Regents violated the Establishment Clause.[45] But released time from public school for religious instruction and the inclusion of the phrase "under god" in the oath of allegiance recited in school were upheld by the state high court.[46]

Policy Consequences. The estimated total identifiable state cost for 1993-94 of programs and services for students attending nonpublic schools, both nonsectarian and denominational, is $219 million. This includes: transportation — $65.4 million; health services — $6.64 million; textbooks — $13.92 million; computer software — $1.38 million; library materials — $.92 million; mandated services — $38 million; school breakfast, lunch, and milk programs — $2.9 million; and programs for students with disabilities — $90 million. Not all these costs result from aid to children in denominational institutions, but methods developed to circumvent the strictures of the Blaine Amendment generally involve aid flowing to all nonpublic institutions or children in them.[47]

Probably reflecting the bruising nature of the 1967 attempt at repeal of the Blaine Amendment, and subsequent successes in gaining some assistance for denominational schools by the means outlined above, recent efforts to gain additional state aid for nonpublic schools have been linked to the general movement for school reform, especially in inner cities. They have focused upon evidence that the educational results gained by paro-

---

44   *Meek* v. *Pittenger*, 421 US 349 (1975), reh. den. 422 US 1049.

45   *Engel* v. *Vitale*, 370 US 421 (1962).

46   *People ex. re. Lewis* v. *Graves*, 245 NY 145, reh. den. 245 NY 620 (1967), the Court of Appeals upheld the practice of excusing public school youngsters from school for one-half hour per week for the purpose of attending religious instruction. In *Lewis* v. *Allen*, 14 NY2d 867 (1960), cert. den. 379 US 923, the Courts sustained a regulation of the commissioner of education that recommended for use in the schools a version of the Oath of Allegiance that contains the words "Under God."

47   See "General Aids and Services," New York State Education Department (August 1993); and "Handbook on Services to Pupils Attending Nonpublic Schools," New York State Education Department (1990).

chial schools with disadvantaged students has been better than those achieved by public schools with similar students.[48]

Proposals for Constitutional Change

1. Equity in School Finance. The 1967 draft Constitution sought to bring equity to school finance by a provision calling for ". . . equality of educational opportunity . . . to . . . all the people of the state . . . ," by providing that ". . . the legislature shall provide necessary programs to develop the educational potential of each person. . . ." and by specifying aspects of the educational aid formula designed to be more redistributive.[49] Since the Court of Appeals decision in the Nyquist case in 1982, a number of constitutional amendments have been proposed to alter the language of the education clause of the state Constitution, most recently one that would require a "uniform and efficient" system of free common schools, and which would ensure that all common school educational facilities and services are equal throughout the state.[50]

Comparative research suggests that ". . . the more demanding the relevant language in a state Constitution, the more likely it is that the supreme courts [sic] will find the education financing provision deficient."[51] Such research also shows that New York's constitutional language places it among those states where there is ". . . little prospect for reform . . ." of school finance based upon the education clause.[52] Proposed changes in the education clause are thus clearly attempts to bring language into the New York Constitution that, in the constitutions of other states, New Jersey for example, has resulted in a finding that equality of state spending is required across school districts. In Kentucky, the state Supreme Court invalidated not only the education financing mechanism but the entire state system of common schools on the grounds that it was not "efficient" in accord with the mandate of the state Constitution.[53]

---

48   See Blue Ribbon Panel on Catholic Schools, "Report to New York State Commissioner of Education Thomas Sobol." (June 1993); See also Paul T. Hill, Gail E. Foster, and Tamar Gendler, *High Schools With Character*, Santa Monica: The Rand Corporation, 1990.

49   Article IX, Sections 1(c) and 1(d).

50   S.3324/ A.6825 (1993) and A.1533 (1993).

51   See Bill Swinford, "A Predictive Model of Decision Making in State Supreme Courts: The School Financing Cases," *American Politics Quarterly* 19, 3 (July 1991): 347.

52   See William E. Thro, "The Third Wave: The Impact of the Montana, Kentucky and Texas Decisions on the Future of Public School Finance Reform Litigation," *Journal of Law and Education* 19 (Spring 1990): 248.

53   *Rose v. Council for Better Education*, 709 S.W. 2d. 186 (1989). For a discussion of this case by one of the principals see Kern Alexander, "The Common School Ideal and the Limits of Legislative Authority," *Harvard Journal of Education* 28 (1991): 341-378.

Critics to this approach argue that even if constitutional change can be used to achieve a court mandate requiring substantially equal educational spending throughout the state's school districts, equality of spending is not likely to result in equality in educational outcomes. Moreover, if it is equality of opportunity that is desired (which might well result in *disproportions* of spending in much different directions than is now the case) different language is required. Models are available. The education clause of the Montana Constitution, for example, directs that the state provide "a system of education which will develop the full education potential of each person. Equality of educational opportunity is guaranteed to each person of the state." The Illinois Constitution declares that ". . . the educational development of all persons to the limits of their capacities . . ." is a ". . . fundamental goal for the People of the state."[54]

Another proposal by advocates of school finance reform would amend the state Constitution to place the distribution of school aid among local jurisdictions in the hands of an independent commission. Under this plan, the legislature would be left with responsibility for determining the overall level of resources to be devoted to education.[55]

2. Constitutional Authority of the State to Assure Effective Local Delivery of School Services. New York's Constitution is among those that requires the establishment and maintenance of a system of public schools, but does not commit the state to an educational standard. In contrast, the Illinois Constitution requires the state to "provide an efficient system of *high quality* public educational institutions and services"; the Montana Constitution speaks of "a basic system of *free quality public elementary and secondary schools*"; and the Virginia Constitution requires its legislature to "ensure that *an educational program of high quality* is established and maintained."[56] This focus on outcomes might allow the state to selectively intervene based on the performance of local school districts, while at the same time being generally respectful of the long-established local role in educational service delivery in New York. Additionally, since the assurance of quality results or outcomes is the focus of the constitutional requirement, and not equality of spending or inputs, this approach is likely to be less costly to the state. A potential problem, however, is devising appropriate outcome measures that would trigger state intervention.

---

54   Mont: Article X, Section 1 (1); Ill: Article X, Section 1. Both cited in McUsic, at p. 334.

55   See Margolis and Moses, at pp. 110 and 111.

56   Ill: Article X, Section 1; Montana: Article I, Section 1 (1); Va.: Article VII Section 1. Cited in McUsic, at p. 307.

In its decision in the *Rose* case cited above, the Kentucky Supreme Court used the constitutional requirement that the state educational system be "efficient" to establish "seven basic capacities" that an adequate education system must seek to develop in each child. That is, the court began to define broad outcomes measures for the state's educational system. According to the court, the seven basic capacities were: "1) oral and written communications skills; 2) knowledge of social, economic, and political systems; 3) understanding of governmental processes; 4) knowledge of mental and physical wellness; 5) grounding in the arts; 6) training or preparation for academic [sic] or vocation sufficient to choose or pursue life work intelligently; and 7) sufficient academic and vocational skills to compete favorably with counterparts in surrounding states."[57]

The fundamental criticism of state Supreme Courts acting in such a far-reaching manner on the basis of constitutional provisions concerning education is that they are inappropriately entering the bailiwick of state legislatures. The rationale of the New York State Court of Appeals in the *Nyquist* case was built upon a philosophy of judicial restraint that had this notion at its core. "The ultimate issue before us is a disciplined perception of the proper role of the courts in the resolution of our State's educational problems, and to that end, more specifically, judicial discernment of the reach of the mandates of our State Constitution in this regard. . . . Primary responsibility for the provision of fair and equitable educational opportunity within the financial capabilities of our State's taxpayers unquestionably rests with [the legislative] branch of our government."[58]

Moreover, there is some thinking in the state that the Constitution need not be changed in order for the Court of Appeals to act more aggressively in the area of education. Measurable educational standards, it is argued, have already been enacted in statute, or adopted by the Board of Regents. Current constitutional language can be used by the courts to require the legislature, the governor, and the Regents to move more effectively towards achievement of the standards they themselves have adopted.

3. Constitutional Right to Safe Schools. An amendment proposed in 1993 would add language to Article XI providing that all students and staff of "primary, elementary, junior high and senior high schools shall have the inalienable right to attend schools which are safe, secure and peaceful."[59] This language is similar to that in the California Constitution that

---

57   *Rose* 790 S.W. 2d. at 212 (1989).

58   *Board of Education* v. *Nyquist*, 57 NY 2d. 27 (1982), at p. 49.

59   A.3088 (1993).

". . . public safety extends to public primary, elementary, junior high and senior high school campuses, where students and staff have the right to be safe and secure in their persons."[60]

The apparent motivation of this provision in New York is increased reports of violence in the schools. Its underlying assumption is that education cannot go forward effectively in an unsafe or threatening environment. Opponents would argue, however, that a constitutional amendment in this area might inappropriately redirect scarce educational resources.

4. Right to Education Not Limited to Children. The language of both the Montana and Illinois Constitutions, cited above, also suggests that educational opportunity not be limited to children, but should be made available to all people. This point becomes especially important in an era in which rapid technological change is transforming the workplace. Some New Yorkers have argued that the underlying intent of the constitutional requirement that the state provide free public education is to assure that people be prepared to be productive citizens. Therefore the right to education, they suggest, should not end with the awarding of a diploma or at a specified age, but should continue until a person has gained the capacity to serve as a productive citizen. If this capacity is seriously marred by social or economic circumstances outside the individual's control, this view continues, then the right to education should be structured so as to assure the free access to reeducation or retraining.[61]

As noted above, the courts have found that the state is not liable for the alleged shortcomings of the free education it offers. One difficulty with a generalized right to education, opponents might argue, is that it reopens the question of the liabilities to which the state might be exposed for outcomes. Additional arguments concern the massive potential expense of such a definition of a positive right to education, and the practical difficulty of determining how claims upon the state for educational support might be limited.

5. Constitutional Status for the State University. Linked to the idea of an expanded right to education is the idea that public higher education be given constitutional status. State universities in many states have a con-

---

60   Section 28 (a). See also California State Department of Education and School Climate and Student Support Services Unit and California Office of the Attorney General, Crime Prevention Center, *Safe Schools: A Planning Guide for Action*, Sacramento, CA: State Department of Education, 1989.

61   Remarks made by Dr. Laura Fleigner, BOCES Superintendent of Schools for Ulster County, at a meeting held by the Constitutional Revision Commission for community leaders in New Paltz, New York, on October 21, 1993.

stitutional base; in some — Colorado, Nevada, and Michigan, for example — their Boards of Trustees are elected by statewide ballot. In New York, the State and City Universities have seen constitutional status as a way of escaping oversight by the Board of Regents.[62] The draft Constitution of 1967 directed that the legislature ". . . establish and define a system of higher education, for all the people of the state, encompassing both public and non-public institutions." It left the Regents with authority over higher education, but provided for the first time for the "continuation" of the State University of New York and the City University of New York, leaving each of these responsible for ". . . the control and administration of the institutions and facilities therein." A major battle for a constitutional guarantee of free higher education led by Convention president Anthony Travia resulted in a provision for "programs which may include free tuition, grants, fellowships and scholarships."[63]

6. Abolition of the Board of Regents. A constitutional amendment proposed in 1993 would repeal Article XI, Section 2, and amend Article V, abolishing the Board of Regents.[64] Presumably, this would result in selection of the head of the Department of Education in a manner similar to other departments, by appointment of the governor with the advice and consent of the Senate. There have been some proposals, however, that New York's education commissioner be a statewide elected official, as in California.

Proponents argue that a very large portion of the state budget is devoted to education, and that therefore this activity should be more directly under the control of the governor and the legislature. Additionally, they say, the current system, designed to shelter educational decision making from politics, has not achieved this end. Rather, it has shifted educational politics to a different arena, less accountable to the public.[65]

Opponents argue that the Regents are sufficiently accountable through the current process of their selection, election by the legislature. Moreover, the legislature and governor retain very substantial power over education through the budgetary process, and may act by statute to shape

---

62 Henrik N. Dullea, *Charter Revision in the Empire State: The Politics of New York's 1967 Constitutional Convention*, Doctoral Dissertation, Department of Political Science, Maxwell School, Syracuse University, 1982, pp. 433-434. A revised version is being published by the Rockefeller Institute Press as a companion to this volume.

63 Draft Constitution of 1967. Article IX, Sections 1b.1, 3, and 4.

64 S.4939 (1993).

65 Memorandum accompanying S. 4939 (1993). Concurrent Resolution of the Senate and Assembly proposing an amendment to the Constitution, in relation to abolishing the Regents of the University of the State of New York and repealing certain provisions relating thereto.

and direct educational policy. The current organizational arrangement, they add, provides the commissioner of education some shelter from direct legislative and gubernatorial pressure, and thus allows for greater impact of professional training and values on policy implementation.

7. Repeal of the Blaine Amendment. Those who favor repeal suggest that this amendment is anti-Catholic in intent and effect, and has no place in the Constitution of a diverse and progressive state. The national Constitution, they assert, has a sufficiently strong general safeguard against the establishment of religion; a specific state provision focused on education is not needed. Moreover, they argue, this provision limits the state's options for the delivery of this service at a time in which conventional approaches are not working and when it should be exploring innovative alternatives. Finally, though methods have been found and will continue to be found to circumvent Blaine, these unnecessarily add to the cost and complexity of state government.

The arguments against repeal are both principled and practical. On principle, it is suggested that the strongest possible statement of separation of church and state is necessary as New York grows even more diverse, and the number of religions in the state with large numbers of adherents increases. Experience shows that federal and state constitutional provisions may be mutually reinforcing, yet have independent effects on policy. Additionally, education of children is an especially sensitive area for parents and families, one in which they demand and appreciate specific constitutional safeguards of religious neutrality.

Furthermore, as a practical matter, the 1967 experience demonstrated the power of this issue for distracting from other desirable constitutional changes. Results favorable to those who advocate additional state support for denominational education have been achieved without repeal. In light of the current demand for educational reform and the attention being directed to the success of parochial schools with inner-city children, further concrete results in this direction are possible if the energy of advocates is not dissipated on largely symbolic goals.

Social Policy

Gerald Benjamin
with
Melissa Cusa

S ocial policy in New York State is affected by every aspect of the state Constitution. This chapter will consider only those constitutional provisions that specifically address or define the state's role in the areas of social welfare, health, mental health, and housing.

Current Provisions

The Social Welfare article in the New York State Constitution (Article XVII) identifies the ". . . aid, care and support of the needy . . . " and "the protection and promotion of the health of the inhabitants of the state" as "public concerns," and mandates that the state provide these ". . . in such manner, and by such means, as the legislature may from time to time determine."[1] More permissive language is used in the areas of mental health and corrections. The article provides that "The care and treatment of persons suffering from mental disorder or defect and the protection of the mental health of the inhabitants of the state *may* be provided by state and local authorities," and that "The legislature *may* provide for the maintenance and support of institutions for the detention of persons charged with or convicted of crime and for systems of probation and parole of persons convicted of a crime."[2] Additionally, two boards — the state board of social welfare (now moribund) and the commission of correction — and the head of the department of mental hygiene are charged with oversight responsibility for public and private institutions in the areas of social welfare, mental health and corrections. Finally, the article creates an exception to the constitutional prohibition on the loan of state, municipal, or public corporation credit in the case of construction of hospitals or other health care facilities.

---

1   Article XVII, Sections 1 & 3.
2   Article XVII, Sections 4 & 5.

Under Article XVIII of the state Constitution the legislature is authorized but not mandated to provide low-rent housing and nursing home accommodations for low-income persons, and to engage in slum clearance and housing rehabilitation activities. The article specifies the state's authority to borrow money and enter into financial relationships with cities, towns, villages, and public corporations (but not counties) in pursuance of its goals. It also details the authority of these classes of municipalities to borrow (beyond constitutional limits specified elsewhere), lend money, guarantee borrowing, offer tax exemptions, and otherwise facilitate the development of housing and nursing homes for the poor by certain regulated corporations. State full faith and credit borrowing up to $300 million for low-income housing without a popular referendum was permitted. Conditions for securing and repayment of borrowing, and legislative authority to provide localities powers to condemn property needed to achieve the purpose of this article, but in excess of that required for public use after the purpose is accomplished, are also specified.

The Appropriateness of Inclusion of Social Policy Provisions in the New York State Constitution

A threshold question is whether the Constitution is an appropriate place in which to specify the state's role in welfare, health, mental health and housing policy, or indeed in any particular area of policy. Many would argue that constitutions should be used only for creating basic governing institutions, allocating powers and duties to them, specifying fundamental governance procedures, and limiting government's capacity to infringe upon individual rights and liberties. In fact, however, state constitutional provisions in the United States have been widely used to charge state governments with affirmative responsibility to act in areas of policy regarded to be of special importance, or to block state action in policy areas thought to require special protection. Constitutionalization of selected values gives them a relative priority and permanence in the state's political system. Thus, for example, New York's constitutional provisions regarding social welfare, health, mental health, and housing seek to insure that citizens' basic needs in these areas will be met, whatever the pressures upon those who have temporary control of the state's political system.[3]

---

3   For further detail on the functions of state constitutions as contrasted with the national Constitution see the chapter "State Constitutions in the Federal System" in this book.

Delegates to the 1967 Constitutional Convention debated whether much of the specific social policy language should be retained in the New York Constitution, and ultimately proposed a Constitution that eliminated the Social Welfare and Housing articles, despite the argument that their elimination could jeopardize the security of the needy, leaving services and programs for them subject to special interest influence. The Constitution proposed in 1967 had in its Bill of Rights a statement regarding the state's obligation to "foster and promote the general welfare and to establish a firm basis of economic security for the people," but in language that was careful to express "public concern" rather than spell out an "actionable right."[4] (Additionally the document did, of course, "provide for the transfer to the state of responsibility for the administration of all programs of public assistance. . . . ")[5]

Those favoring elimination of these provisions perceived their constitutional status as superfluous and limiting on legislative flexibility. This was in accord with the view expressed by a committee of law professors in 1958 that specific constitutional language concerning health and social welfare was "superfluous because the state has the (authority) to act under its inherent police powers. . . . There is no reason to believe that absent any such (specificity) the extensive . . . (legislative programs) of the state . . . would be any less constitutionally secure."[6] Moreover, a study done for the 1967 Convention a decade later concluded, "The problems which lie at the very heart of the present (social welfare) system cannot be remedied directly by constitutional enactment (i.e. spiraling costs, the growing number of dependent persons on assistance, and the complexities inherent in administration of welfare programs)."[7]

Though the debate concerning the inclusion of policy goals or mandates in a constitution is conducted in theoretical terms — What is appropriately constitutional? How much discretion should be left to the legislature? — the choices made have substantial practical consequences. The presence of such social policy provisions in a constitution may shift the forum in which policy is decided. Constitutionalization of issues not only limits or binds the legislature, but also potentially gives a greater voice to courts in policy making, for they are the final arbiters of the

4   See Proposed New York State Constitution, Article I, Section 10. See also State of New York, *Proceedings of the New York State Constitutional Convention, 1967*, XI Doc. #48, at p. 15.

5   Proposed New York State Constitution, 1967, Article 10 Section 16(a).

6   See Special Legislative Committee on Revision and Simplification of the Constitution, *Inter-Law School Committee Report on the Problem of Simplifying the Constitution* 1 (1958), at p. 188.

7   See State of New York, "Welfare, Health, and Mental Health," *Temporary State Commission on the Constitutional Convention* 11 (March 1967): 88-95.

constitution. Thus, those who favor including a value in the state Constitution are likely to be less confident that they can prevail in the legislature, or that they will continue to prevail there over time.

In an influential essay on "positive rights" published in 1989, Burt Neuborne of New York University Law School argues that "[i]f it were possible to derive a set of judicially enforceable rights in the areas of education, health, nutrition and shelter that could co-exist with democratic political theory, we might be able to use those enforceable floors to break the political log-jam threatening to saddle us with a permanently outvoted economic 'underclass.'"[8] Here the clear objective is to use a state constitutionally based argument to move the locus of decision from an unsympathetic arena, the legislature, to one that may be more sympathetic, the courts.

Of course, creating an opportunity for supportive judicial action does not assure that such action will occur. As detailed below, even when constitutional language mandates state action in a number of social policy areas, the courts in New York State have been generally respectful of the legislature's role and deferential to its decisions.

Evolution of Constitutional Provisions on Social Policy

New York's constitutional provisions concerning social policy have evolved through two distinct phases. In the 1894 Constitution, building upon earlier action (mostly statutory but in one instance constitutional), provisions were adopted to permit aid to local governments and private charitable activities and to provide oversight once aid was given. In 1938, based upon experience under the 1894 Constitution and as the demands upon government for social services grew and views of the role of state government changed as a result of the Great Depression, amendments were added to specifically mandate or permit greater direct state involvement in specified areas of social policy.

1. *State Oversight.* Historically in New York care for the needy was a local responsibility and services were delivered by local governments and by private institutions and charities. Although the state government did not directly deliver services it did provide aid to these private institutions under the "police powers" of the legislature. In addition to promoting the general welfare, it was

---

8   See Burt Neuborne, "State Constitutions and the Evolution of Positive Rights," *Rutgers Law Journal* 20 (1989): 888.

assumed that "without state aid private charities could not care adequately for those in need. . . . (T)he state would (then) be required to undertake this burden at a significantly higher cost."[9] Thus initially provisions concerning social policy were included in the state Constitution to except this aid from mid-nineteenth century constitutional prohibitions against the gift or loan of state money or credit to private entities.

Concomitantly, the Constitution was altered to create oversight institutions within the state government to assure that the money given to private institutions or local governments for social purposes was properly spent, both fiscally and programmatically. The state looked favorably on "private sector efficiency" but sought proper supervision and control. Oversight was achieved through providing a constitutional base of authority for a number of boards: the Board of Charities, the Commission of Lunacy, and the Commission of Prisons.

The legislature (upon the recommendation of the governor) created and empowered a state Board of Charities by statute in 1867. Though this board, as noted, was given constitutional status in 1894, a decision of the Court of Appeals raised questions about its authority to visit and inspect institutions that received no public funds.[10] An amendment in 1925 transferred responsibility for institutions for the blind, deaf and dumb to the Department of Education. In 1931 the agency was changed to the Department of Social Welfare, and the Board to the Board of Social Welfare, and limited power was granted to inspect private child care institutions.[11]

A Commission on Lunacy was created by statute in 1889 to oversee institutions serving the insane and "feeble minded." It too gained constitutional status in 1894. The 1915 Convention debated but did not act upon a proposal to consolidate its activities with oversight of all hospitals, under a general Commission on Hospitals. A 1925 amendment changed the name of the agency to the Department of Mental Hygiene and extended the agency's

9   See State of New York, "Revised Record." *Proceedings of the 1938 Constitutional Convention* VI, at p. 488.

10 *People ex rel State Board of Charities* v. *Society for Prevention of Cruelty to Children,* 161 NY 233 (1900).

11 See Peter J. Galie, *The New York State Constitution: A Reference Guide,* Westport, CT: Greenwood Press, 1991.

jurisdiction. A 1938 amendment authorized commission staff, not just the director, to make personal visits and inspections.[12]

State inspection of prisons dates to an 1846 constitutional provision for the statewide election of three prison inspectors. The Commission of Prisons was a reform adopted in the 1894 Constitution. Also in 1925, its name was changed to the Commission of Corrections.[13]

2. *State Responsibility.* Local governments and private agencies could no longer financially meet the social welfare needs of people during the Great Depression in the 1930s. As a consequence, the state stepped in on a temporary basis to provide financial assistance to people in need.[14] By 1938, delegates at the Constitutional Convention agreed that the need for state involvement had become permanent. The result was Section 1 of Article XVII, which establishes the affirmative duty to provide for the aid, care, and support of the needy. The chairman of the 1938 Convention described this provision as a "charter of human protection for the underprivileged, the destitute and the handicapped of our state."[15] The provision allowing the legislature to determine the "manner and means" of implementing this section was meant to provide flexibility for experimental social welfare programs.[16]

The growth of the constitutionally based responsibility of state government for social policy can also be seen in the development of the public health provision. The Constitution was silent in this area until 1938, with the state's authority assumed to be inherent in its police powers. Historically, local governments provided certain public health functions, including local health departments and local health officers.[17] One reason for the inclusion of Section 3 of Article XVII, in 1938, providing that it is the responsibility of the state to protect and promote the public health, was a fear that absent such a provision oversight of the localities and related activities by the Public

---

12 *Ibid.*

13 See the chapter "Criminal Justice" in this book.

14 See State of New York, "Revised Record," *Proceedings of the New York State Constitutional Convention 1938*, at p. 486.

15 See State of New York, "Revised Record," *Proceedings of New York State Constitutional Convention 1938*, at p. 2125.

16 See Christine Ladd, Note: "A Right to Shelter for the Homeless in New York State," *N.Y.U. L. Rev.* 61 (1986): 272.

17 See generally, N.Y. Public Health Law, Article 3, *McKinney's* 1990.

Health Department might at some point not be permitted by the courts under the police power.[18]

Additionally, the provision of health insurance by the state had been debated since at least the 1915 Constitutional Convention. During the 1938 Convention, delegates again considered this issue. As finally drafted, the public health section of Article XVII allowed but did not mandate state provision of health insurance.

Finally, Article XVIII, providing for and encouraging state and local responsibilities and roles in providing housing for the citizens of the state, was also added to the Constitution in 1938. Among other effects, it established clear authority for the state and its localities to take advantage of federal housing assistance becoming available at that time.

Court Interpretation

Because of its affirmative language, the first section of Article XVII — providing that the "aid, care, and support of the needy are public concerns and shall be provided by the state and by such of its subdivisions, and in such manner and by such means, as the legislature may from time to time determine" — has been pressed hardest by advocates for the poor in the courts. Over several decades, they have sought an expansive judicial definition of the mandate this language places upon the legislature and the executive departments so as to increase the resources available to poor people for food, clothing, shelter, health care, and housing. (In contrast, court action concerning Article XVIII, the housing article, has focused on the extent of government's power to provide low-income housing, should it choose to do so.)[19]

Two cases decided in 1977 illustrate the parameters within which the Court of Appeals has dealt with this litigation. In *Tucker* v. *Toia*, the court gave force to the constitutional right of the poor to assistance,

18   See Galie, at p. 264.

19   Research for the Commission by Patricia E. Salkin indicates that the courts have determined that "low rent" and "low-income" in Section 1 of Article XVIII do not mean lowest possible rent or lowest possible income, and "persons of low-income," "families of low-income," and "low-rent housing," are now defined in law to include persons of moderate means and middle-income to qualify for public housing programs. See *Neufeld* v. *O'Dwyer*, 192 Misc 538 (1948) and *Minkin* v. *City of New York*, 203 NYS 2d 692 (1960). See also NY Public Housing Law Article 3 Section (18) (23) (*McKinney* 1989). The Court has also held that the Urban Development Corporation may override local zoning laws to further the goals of this section. But it has also said that the article does not permit the condemnation of property for "public use" that will result not in the later operation of housing by a municipality but in its sale to low-income persons. See *Floyd* v. *New York City Urban Development Corporation*, 33 NY 2d 1 (1973).

emphasizing the obligation of the state to assist those it defined as needy under the law. The case concerned the denial of assistance to home relief applicants under the age of 21. Home relief benefits for minor children living alone was being conditioned upon the institution and completion of court proceedings against parents (wherever they may be).[20] An order of disposition of child support was required by the state to establish proof that home relief was the only available option. Relying on Article XVII, Section 1, the Court of Appeals ruled this state action unconstitutional. It wrote:

> In New York State, the provision for assistance to the needy is not a matter of legislative grace; rather, it is specifically mandated by our constitution. . . .
>
> . . . [T]he Constitution imposes upon the state an affirmative duty to aid the needy and although it provides the legislature with discretion in determining the amount of aid, and in classifying recipients and defining the term 'needy,' it unequivocally prevents the legislature from simply refusing to aid those whom it has classified as needy.[21]

But in *Bernstein* v. *Toia,* the court emphasized the broad discretion of the legislature in giving substance to the constitutional right, in the same manner that it has in interpreting the constitutional provision on education.[22] A regulation of the state Department of Social Services providing flat grants for housing, rather than grants that took into consideration the situation and need of individual clients, was challenged as an unconstitutional violation of Article XVII, Section 1. Writing for a five-judge majority of the court, Judge Hugh Jones said: "We do not read this declaration and precept as . . . commanding that, in carrying out the constitutional duty to provide aid, care and support of the needy, the State must always meet in full measure all the legitimate needs of each recipient." Judge Jones made specific reference to the *Tucker* decision in this opinion. "We explicitly recognized in *Tucker* that the legislature is vested with discretion to determine the amount of aid; what we there held prohibited was the legislature's "simply refusing to aid those whom it has classified as needy."[23]

---

20   *Tucker* v. *Toia*, 43 NY 2d 1 (1977).

21   *Tucker* v. *Toia*, 43 NY 2d 1, 400 N.Y.S. 2d 728 (1977); see also *Lee* v. *Smith*, 387 NYS 2d 952 (1976).

22   For a detailed discussion and comparisons with other states see the chapter "Education" in this book.

23   43 NY 2d 437 and 448-449.

Writing in 1986, one critic of the development of the law in New York State summarized it in this way: "Under current judicial interpretation, the only reviewable legislative decisions are those which flatly deny aid to persons the legislature has classified as needy. . . . The classification itself is not reviewable and any inquiry into the sufficiency of aid is precluded."[24]

In fact, it appears that the recent approach of the Court of Appeals has been to continue to find statutory or other means to grant relief in particular circumstances, often reversing lower courts, while at the same time maintaining a deferential posture toward the legislature.

In *McCain* v. *Koch*, decided in 1986, several poor families sought and obtained an injunction from the state Supreme Court requiring New York City agencies ". . . when they have undertaken to provide emergency housing for homeless families with children, to provide housing which satisfies minimum standards of sanitation, safety and decency."[25] Relying on the Bernstein decision, the Appellate Division "reluctantly" vacated this order. The Court of Appeals, relying on the absence of departmental regulations to distinguish the case, overturned the Appellate Division. Quoting the Supreme Court's observation that "[i]n a civilized society, a 'shelter' which does not meet minimum standards of cleanliness, warmth, space and rudimentary conveniences is no shelter at all," the Court of Appeals remarked: ". . . in providing subminimum shelter the defendants were, in effect, denying *any relief* to the homeless in contravention of their statutory and constitutional obligations."[26]

In *Jiggetts* v. *Grinker*, a 1990 case in which plaintiffs were recipients of public assistance whose shelter costs exceeded the maximum allowable, the Court of Appeals again confirmed that ". . . broad policy choices which involve the ordering of priorities and the allocation of finite resources, are matters for the executive and legislative branches of government and the place to question their wisdom lies not in the courts but elsewhere." The high court did state, however, the statute establishing shelter allowances requires that such allowances "shall be adequate to maintain a family," and that therefore the commissioner "should be compelled to implement that legislative decision."[27]

---

24 See Ladd, at p. 279.

25 *McCain* v. *Koch*, 117AD 198, 502 NYS 2d 720 (1986).

26 *McCain* v. *Koch*, 502 N.Y. 2d. 720, at pp. 119-120.

27 *Jiggetts* v. *Grinker*, 75 NY 2d 411 (1990). The case was sent back for further arguments. Closing arguments were made in January 1992, and as of the summer of 1993 no decision had yet been rendered.

A final example is provided by a case now pending before the Court of Appeals, *Hope* v. *Perales*.[28] The Appellate Division affirmed a decision of Supreme Court Judge Carmen Ciparick (who just joined the Court of Appeals) finding a violation of the state Constitution's social welfare provisions and due process clause in the legislature's failure to fund abortions in a 1989 statute that provided prenatal and postpartum care for low-income women. "Having acknowledged that pregnant women with family incomes between 100 and 185 percent of the poverty level are needy and require help in obtaining pregnancy related health services," the court said, "the legislature violated Article XVII, Section 1, as well as Article XVII Section 3, dealing with the protection and promotion of the health of the state's citizens, by conditioning aid to this needy class on a standard totally unconnected to need or health."[29] An interesting aspect of this decision is the partial reliance by the court on the constitutional provision concerning protection and promotion of public health (Article XVII, Section 3) which has rarely been the basis for litigation.

Proposals for Constitutional Change[30]

1. *Enhanced Rights to Social Welfare Benefits, Shelter, and Health Care.* The nature and tone of recent litigation indicates that there will continue to be significant efforts to strengthen positive rights to social welfare benefits, health care, and housing in New York State. Such efforts might involve the alteration of the current Article XVII and XVIII, or attempts at additions to the state Bill of Rights — the definition of new rights — in discrete areas.

   The social welfare provision of New York's Constitution is among the strongest in the nation.[31] Altering general language or specifying further positive rights would therefore primarily serve as a signal to the courts that Constitution makers expect the courts to act differently, perhaps more aggressively, in the interpretation of these rights. The experience with home rule, of course, indicates that

---

28   595 NYS 2d 948 (1993).

29   *Hope* v. *Perales*, 595 NYS 2d (1993), at pp. 948 and 953.

30   Portions of this section (numbers 2, 5, 6, and 7) are drawn from a memorandum, "Social Policy and the NYS Constitution," by Patricia E. Salkin, Esq., Director, Government Law Center, Albany, NY, October 1993.

31   See Dann Braveman, "Children, Poverty and State Constitutions," *Emory Law Journal* 38 (1989), for a categorization of state constitutional provisions concerning the poor. For other writing on legal strategies to develop positive rights protections for needy people see Neuborne, *op. cit.*; and Bert Lockwood, et al. "Litigating State Constitutional Rights to Happiness and Safety," *William and Mary Law Quarterly* 2 (1993).

such signals are not always well received by the courts.[32] Certainly, few state high courts have been willing as yet to use their state constitutions to consider the sufficiency of welfare benefits. (Montana is an exception. In one case it ruled that the state may not constitutionally limit certain recipients to only two months of benefits.)[33]

Proponents and opponents divide on ideological lines. Those in favor of an expansion of positive rights seek to make the commitment of state resources to alleviating social ills a permanent priority in New York. They suggest the right to human welfare should be viewed as analogous to the right to property, and not simply as a "gratuity." "Benefits as a right" would remove individual blame and acknowledge the conditions that cause need.[34] They envision the development of a contemporary "community-based" rather than "individual-based" concept of society and social welfare. New York State should break new ground in establishing rights in these essential areas of life, they would argue, taking fundamentally new directions in its Constitution as it did in 1938.

Arguments against an enhancement of positive rights in these areas oppose the fundamental assumption: that individuals have a claim upon society as a matter of right to meet their basic needs. Opponents reject the redefinition of social policy on communitarian rather than individualistic premises. They adhere to the notion that each person is fundamentally responsible for him- or herself, and believe that it is government's role to enter these areas when others cannot or will not, and then with the goal of restoring self-reliance. Opponents, too, fear the economic impact of broadly defined positive social rights: the effect on incentives to work; the potential cost to government of such an approach; and the consequences for the state's private economy if it assumes burdens that its sister states do not. Finally, including such rights in the state Constitution raises the concern of transferring key decisions in New York from the more democratic legislature to the less democratic courts.

---

32 See the chapter "Intergovernmental Relations" in this book.

33 *Deaconess Medical Center* v. *Department of Social and Rehabilitative Services* 700 P. 2d 1165 and 1168 (1986); *Butte Community Union* v. *Lewis,* 712 P. 2d 1309 and 1311-13 (1986).

34 See *Goldberg* v. *Kelly,* 397 US 254 1970 and Charles Reich, "The New Property," *Yale Law Review* 73, 5 (April 1964): 785.

2. *Alteration of Article XVII, Section 1, to Limit the Courts' Discretion.* Those who oppose the expansion of rights and the extension of judicial power in New York are disquieted by many of the recent decisions cited above. Their agenda for constitutional change would be to place more limiting language in Article XVII, Section 1. For example, in 1993, Senator John Marchi and Assemblymembers William Bianchi and Elizabeth Hoffman introduced a joint resolution to change the word "shall" to "may" in this section.[35]

3. *Transfer of the Health and Welfare Functions to the State.* State assumption of the costs and operation of the welfare system was proposed at the 1967 Constitutional Convention. The national health care debate currently dominates the domestic agenda, while state takeover of Medicaid is currently a key focus of reform efforts in New York. Issues at the forefront when constitutional change is considered will color and influence the agenda of those involved in the change process.[36]

4. *Extensive Modification of the Housing Article, or Replacement With a Broadly Constructed Community and Economic Development Article.* Delegates to the 1967 Constitutional Convention agreed that the existing housing article was ineffective in meeting the housing needs of the state. To remedy this, several delegates proposed (1) legislative flexibility in the "scope and nature of the state's housing program"; (2) modification of the gift and loan prohibitions "so as to encourage private sector participation"; and (3) substitution of the "present housing article with a comprehensive community and economic development article."[37]

As finally drafted, the 1967 Constitution authorized the state and local governments to acquire ". . . property necessary for any economic or community development purpose."[38] Economic and community development purposes were defined very broadly, ". . . to include the renewal and rebuilding of communities, the development of new communities, and programs and facilities to enhance the physical environment, health and social

---

35 S.3426 (1993); A.6787-A (1993); A.6709 (1989). See "Constitutional Amendment Proposed by Legislators," *N.Y.L.J.*, (March 11, 1993): 1 col. 5.

36 For further detail see the chapter "Intergovernmental Relations" in this book.

37 See State of New York, *Proceedings of the 1967 Constitutional Convention,* XI Doc.#48, at p. 58.

38 Article XV, Section 2.

well-being of, and to encourage the expansion of economic opportunity for, the people of the state."[39] Moreover, the draft
Constitution explicitly permitted the grant or loan of public
money to private persons, associations, or corporations for economic or community development, and the enactment of general
or special laws for these purposes.

Though permissive in nature, this language removed significant constitutional barriers to creative approaches to housing
policy, and indeed to a range of social policy concerns. The dual
goals of economic development and meeting the housing needs of
New York are as important, or more important, than they were a
quarter century ago. The approach captured in this draft provision,
and other ideas in this area of policy, are likely to be significantly
addressed in any serious constitutional revision effort.[40]

5. *Adding Counties to General Purpose Local Government Types
Permitted to Contract Indebtedness for Housing.* This idea has
long been debated. Article XVIII specifically authorizes cities,
towns, and villages to contract indebtedness, but does not mention
county government. Since counties have a larger tax base than
other municipalities, they could potentially contribute significant
resources to make certain types of housing projects feasible. For
example, county-owned land from tax foreclosures could be used
for siting housing. This relatively small change has received serious consideration, as noted below, and is likely to be considered
seriously if the housing article is retained.

In 1989 and 1991, Senator James Lack and Assemblyman
Richard Brodsky sponsored legislation to provide for a constitutional amendment to allow counties to participate in low-income
housing construction like other political subdivisions. The bill
passed in 1989, but not in 1991.[41]

A 1948 opinion of the state comptroller states that counties
may not provide emergency housing facilities.[42] In 1992, the
attorney general was asked to reconsider a 1978 Informal Opinion
which found that counties are not authorized by the Constitution
to contract indebtedness for housing purposes.[43] The latest Opin-

---

39 Article X, section 15.
40 See the chapter"The Private Economy" in this book for further discussion of this point.
41 S.2933-A (1989); A.9181 (1991); A.1363 (1993).
42 4 Op. St. Compt. 339 (1948).
43 1978 Op. Att'y Gen. (Inf. 162).

ion does state that although counties were intentionally omitted from the authorization contained in Article XVIII, counties do have the power under home rule, or Article IX, to engage in this activity.[44] The attorney general relied on Section 10, which provides that this Article shall not be construed as imposing additional limitations. Since the opinions of the attorney general are advisory and not mandatory on the courts, and due to the high level of county interest in providing low-income housing, this is one issue that is ripe for an amendment.

6. *Extending the Reach of the Current Housing Article.* A constitutional amendment proposed in the Senate and Assembly regarding municipal housing powers included counties as described above but also made additional changes.[45] The joint resolution extended the article to include owner-occupied as well as rental housing; included moderate-income as well as low-income persons; and also specifically incorporated elderly individuals as among those eligible for service. A final provision specifically provided that counties could not override town or village zoning to achieve their housing programs. The proposal failed to win support during two successive legislative sessions.

An alternative approach is to change the language in Article XVIII, so that it concerns "affordable housing" rather than "low-income" housing. This would confirm the direction taken in court decisions in this area, and would explicitly encompass efforts to meet the needs of citizens of moderate income. Additionally, some would argue that special-needs housing, such as housing for the elderly, be included.

7. *Removal of Little Used Provisions and Consistency in Language.* The 1967 Temporary State Commission questioned the necessity for several of the provisions of Article XVIII since they are infrequently used or are repetitive. For example, Section 5 is infrequently invoked since every state loan to a local housing authority or urban renewal agency is supported by a corresponding state contract that provides for periodic subsidies. Section 7 is also infrequently used, except for a few cases in New York City. Section 10 has been interpreted to simply repeat Section 1. Finally, Section 4 of this article bases borrowing limits on "assessed valuation," while limits in Section 4 of Article VIII, as a result of a 1951

---

44 1992 Op. Att'y Gen. (Inf. No. 92-4).
45 A.8717 (1989).

amendment, are based on full valuation. A 1966 attempt to make Article XVIII read the same as Article VIII was defeated.[46] A switch to full valuation would both provide consistency and grant local governments the authority to contract increased indebtedness to further the goals of Section 1.

---

46   See Galie, at p. 273.

The Environment

William R. Ginsberg

Introduction

Environmental issues, as they have come to the forefront of public consciousness in the past three decades, do not appear to have been on the minds of the framers or amenders of the New York State Constitution. The exception is Article XIV enacted in 1895 and amended several times since.

There are, however, other constitutional provisions that have a substantial impact on the relationship between government and the environment, even though they may not have originally been written for that purpose. These include the Local Governments Article IX, which establishes the power of local governments and their relationship to state powers as exercised by the legislature; Article XVI, Section 1, concerning exemptions from taxation; and Article XV, Section 1, prohibiting the disposition of canals and canal properties.

Finally, there are provisions of the New York State Constitution that, from a jurisprudential point of view, are central to the environmental field but are duplicative of provisions of the U.S. Constitution. In these instances the issues that arise are usually resolved in a federal context. These include subjects such as due process,[1] equal protection,[2] and regulatory takings.[3] These subjects, although certainly important, are not discussed in this paper because the federal Constitution's "Supremacy Clause"[4] renders them less relevant to the New York State constitutional framework.

---

1   See U.S. Constitution Amendment V and Amendment XIV, Section 1, and N.Y. Constitution Article I, Section 6.

2   See U.S. Constitution Amendment XIV, Section 1, and N.Y. Constitution Article I, Section II.

3   See U.S. Constitution Amendment V and Amendment XIV, Section 1, and N.Y. Constitution Article I, Section 7.

4   U.S. Constitution Article IV, Section 2.

Article XIV

Section I of Article XIV is known as the "Forever Wild" Provision. Originally in Article VII of the 1894 Constitution, it gives constitutional status to the "Forest Preserve," created by the legislature in 1885.[5] There is no similar provision in any other state constitution, and it is generally regarded as the most important and strongest state land conservation measure in the nation. It has enjoyed widespread public support since its enactment.

The critical language of the 1894 provision now appears in the first two sentences of Article XIV, Section 1:

> The lands of the state, now owned or hereafter acquired, constituting the forest preserve as now fixed by law, shall be forever kept as wild forest lands. They shall not be leased, sold or exchanged, or be taken by any corporation, public or private, nor shall the timber thereon be sold, removed or destroyed.

The lands referred to were in certain counties in the Adirondack and Catskill regions of New York.[6] However, within those counties are the so-called Adirondack and Catskill "blue-line" parks.[7] Today, state-owned lands within those counties but outside of the legislatively created "blue-line" may be used for "forest or wildlife conservation," notwithstanding the provisions of Section 1.[8]

The commitment to forest preservation and a strict interpretation of the "Forever Wild" clause was reaffirmed by delegates to the 1915 Constitutional Convention.[9]

Considering the century-long history of the Forest Preserve, amendments to Article XIV, Section 1, have been relatively few, attesting to the importance of the provision. Of nine amendments in the past half century, four provided for the exchange of parcels of Forest Preserve for other

---

5   The Forest Preserve was created by Chapter 283, Sections 7 and 8, Laws of 1885. Scandals plagued the Forest Commissions established to administer the Preserve and led to the adoption of the constitutional provision.

6   The Forest Preserve was defined by Chapter 283, Section 7, Laws of 1885, and included: ". . . the counties of Clinton, excepting the towns of Altona and Dannemora, Essex, Franklin, Fulton, Hamilton, Herkimer, Lewis, Saratoga, St. Lawrence, Warren, Washington, Greene, Ulster and Sullivan."

7   The Adirondack Park was created by Chapter 707, Laws of 1892. The Forest Preserve and Adirondack Park were re-enacted in Chapter 332 Sections 100 and 120, Laws of 1893.

8   Article XIV, Section 3 (1).

9   See New York State Constitutional Convention, *Unrevised Record*, Albany: New York State, 1915, at p. 1336.

parcels of equal or greater acreage and value.[10] Amendments in 1941, 1947, and 1987 authorized the construction of ski trails on Whiteface, Belleayre, Gore, South, and Peter Gay Mountains. Amendments in 1957 and 1959 permitted up to 400 acres of Forest Preserve to be used for eliminating dangerous curves and grades on state highways and up to 300 acres to be used in the construction of the interstate "Northway."

Section 2 of Article XIV, also originating in the 1894 Constitution, permits the legislature to provide for the use of up to three percent of Forest Preserve lands for the construction and maintenance of municipal water supply reservoirs and canals. Section 3, as already noted in the discussion of Section 1,[11] concerns the use or disposition of Forest Preserve lands lying outside of the blue lines. Separate Forest Preserve parcels not exceeding 100 contiguous acres and located outside of the blue lines may, by legislative action, be used for forest or wildlife conservation, recreation, or other state purposes or may be sold, exchanged, or disposed of provided that the proceeds are used to acquire land within the blue lines (Article XIV, Section 3(2)).

Section 4, adopted in 1969 and effective January 1, 1970, provides that:

> The policy of the state shall be to conserve and protect its natural resources and scenic beauty and encourage the development and improvement of its agricultural lands for the production of food and other agricultural products. The legislature, in implementing this policy, shall include adequate provision for the abatement of air and water pollution and of excessive and unnecessary noise, the protection of agricultural lands, wetland and shorelines, and the development and regulation of water resources.[12]

---

10 The 1963 amendment provided for the conveyance of ten acres to the village of Saranac Lake in exchange for 30 acres owned by the village. A 1965 amendment permitted the conveyance of 28 acres to the town of Arietta in exchange for 30 acres. In 1979 an amendment authorized an exchange with the International Paper Company of 8,500 acres for an equivalent number of acres, and in 1983 an amendment authorized the conveyance of ten acres, including buildings to the Sagamore Institute, Inc., in exchange for 200 acres.

11 See footnote 8 and related text.

12 Subsequent to the passage of this section, the legislature has enacted laws dealing with air and water pollution (N.Y Environmental Conservation Law Section 19-0101 *et seq.* and Section 17-0101 *et seq.*), Tidal and Freshwater wetlands (N.Y. Environmental Conservation Law Section 25-0101 *et seq.* and N.Y. Environmental Conservation Law Section 24-0101 *et seq.*) and other environmental issues. It cannot be ascertained whether these statutes were to some degree a consequence of the constitutional mandate or a reflection of nationwide federal and state legislative activity concerning the environment in the 1970s and 1980s.

The section also establishes the state nature and historic preserve consisting of certain state-acquired lands outside of the Forest Preserve counties. It has not been amended, nor has it been the subject of litigation.

This section is similar to provisions of other state constitutions that mandate state legislatures to enact environmentally protective legislation.[13] The efficacy of such provisions is limited. Courts usually refused to compel legislatures to act on the basis of constitutional mandates.[14] Since the judiciary is a coordinate branch of government, it does not have the power to compel the legislature to act in its purely legislative function.[15]

This section may, however, have a role with respect to environmental litigation. The New York Court of Appeals has mentioned the provision in a solid waste decision, although the purpose of the reference is ambiguous, since it was not the basis of the Court's holding.[16]

Section 5 of Article XIV, which dates back to Article VII of the 1894 Constitution, addresses how violations of Article XIV may be enjoined. Actions for this purpose may be brought by the state, but may also be brought by a citizen with the consent of the appellate division of the Supreme Court and on notice to the attorney general. The section is unusually restrictive in its limitation on citizens' suits. It also may prohibit other remedies such as damages.[17] Thus, if trees are wrongfully destroyed in the Forest Preserve, the wrongdoer can be enjoined from further cutting, but a court may not be able to award damages to the state for the value of the trees destroyed.

Article IX: Local Governments

The legal and historic relationship between local governments and state governments and the respective powers and responsibilities of each have

---

13   *See e.g.*: Alaska Constitution Article 8, Section 7; Hawaii Constitution Article 9, Section 8; Florida Constitution Article II, Section 7; and North Carolina Constitution Article 14, Section 5. Other states have adopted provisions that establish a constitutional right to a decent environment. *See, e.g.*: Illinois Constitution Article 11, Section 2; Massachusetts Constitution Amendment 49; Pennsylvania Constitution Article 1, Section 27; Rhode Island Constitution Article 1, Section 17; and Texas Constitution Article 16, Section 59.

14   See, e.g., *State ex rel Walker* v. *Board of Comm'rs*, 141 Neb. 172, 3 N.W.2d 196 (1942), holding that a court is powerless to enforce a state constitutional mandate since the duty exclusively belongs to the legislature, and *Southern Ry.* v. *Virginia*, 200 Va. 431, 105 S.E.2d 814 (1958), holding that a constitutional mandate to the legislature is not self-executing. For a general review of this question see Jose L. Fernandez, "State Constitutions, Environmental Rights Provisions, and the Doctrine of Self-Execution: A Political Question?" *Harvard Environmental Law Review* 17 (1993): 333-387.

15   *Brewer* v. *Gray*, 86 So. 2d 799 (Fla. 1956).

16   See Town of Islip footnote 26 *infra*, and related text discussion of Article IX, Sections 2 and 3.

17   See *Oneida County Forest Preserve Council* v. *Wehle*, 309 N.Y. 152, 128 N.E. 2d 282 (1955).

been important factors in the evolution of environmental law. New York, like most northeastern states, is regarded as a strong home rule state — that is, local governments appear to have important powers that are jealously guarded. As a practical and legal matter, however, local governments are creatures of the state, formed by the state and subject to the superior powers of the state, except to the extent that the state Constitution grants authority to sub-state jurisdictions.

Certain governmental functions such as land use and zoning, solid waste and sewage collection and disposal, water supply, and police and fire protection have historically been the responsibility of local government. Gradually, however, it has become apparent that in the environmental field, as in other areas, regional and statewide regulation, coordination, and cooperation are essential.

The problems may be most obvious in dealing with solid waste, where development and increased population density have made it impossible to find and operate adequate new disposal sites in many jurisdictions. The issue has been most difficult, however, in the land use area, particularly since the primary source of local revenue is the real property tax. Perceptions, true or false, concerning the relationship between different types of development and the tax base are often substantial influences on land use decisions. The construction of a shopping center or industrial plant in one community may raise important issues for adjacent communities with respect to traffic, residential development, retail trade, air pollution, or waste disposal, yet those adjacent communities will have no right to participate in the land use decisions of their neighbor.

In recent years the state has enacted environmentally related land use statutes to address particular issues such as fresh water wetlands,[18] tidal wetlands,[19] and mined land reclamation.[20] However, New York has developed no statewide or regional approaches to land use planning, with the exception of the Adirondack Park Agency and the Long Island Pine Barrens Act, which affects only Suffolk county.[21]

---

18   N.Y. Environmental Conservation Law Section 24-0101 *et seq.*

19   N.Y. Environmental Conservation Law Section 25-0101 *et seq.*

20   N.Y. Environmental Conservation Law Section 23-2701 through 2727.

21   N.Y. Executive Law Section 800 *et seq.*; and (Chapter 262, Laws of 1993); This latter legislative action was in response, at least in part, to a plea by the New York Court of Appeals in *Long Island Pine Barrens Society* v. *Town of Brookhaven*, 80 NY 2d 500, 606 N.E.2d 1373 (1992). A much earlier judicial appeal to the legislature to create a system of statewide or regional land use planning has gone unheeded. See *Golden* v. *Town of Ramapo*, 30 NY 2d 359 (1972), at p. 376.

Section 1 (h) of Article IX, the "Bill of Rights for Local Governments" has an impact on environmental functions. While the purpose of this section is to preserve the principle of home rule for localities in New York, its provisions are mainly structural and not exclusive; that is, it does not necessarily prevent the state, acting through the legislature, from acting in the area.[22] There is, however one provision of this section, Subparagraph (h), that does have an impact on environmental functions. It provides that a county with an alternative form of county government (including charter counties) can transfer functions of local governments in the county (including land use functions) to itself, but only by a triple referendum. That is, such a transfer must be approved by a majority of voters in the county, in the area of the county outside of cities and in the cities of the county. While the provision protects the interests of all concerned, it has been suggested that the cumbersome procedure permits a minority of voters to defeat the interests of the majority of voters in the county and severely inhibits the consolidation of functions on a county level.[23]

Section 2 of Article IX seeks to define the distribution of powers between the state and its localities. In particular, Subparagraph 2 provides that the state legislature:

Shall have the power to act in relation to the property, affairs or government of any local government only by general law, or by special law only (a) on the request of two-thirds of the total membership of its [the locality's] legislative body or on request of its chief executive officer concurred in a majority of such membership, or (b) . . . on certificate of necessity from the governor. . . .

While the section appears to limit the state's powers substantially, the restriction is more apparent than real. The state can supersede the right of local governments to home rule by enacting a valid general law.[24] In addition, and of central importance, Section 3(a) of Article IX states,

---

22 For example, the legislature could abolish a local office existing at the time the section was adopted, provided that the function of the office, if retained, could be exercised by some other officer of the jurisdiction. *Wilcox* v. *McClellan*, 185 NY 9, 77 N.E. 986 (1906). For a detailed review of this section also see the chapter "Intergovernmental Relations" in this book.

23 See Report of the Temporary State Commission on the Powers of Local Government, Part I, (1974):92-94. The Commission recommended that a charter county should be able to transfer functions from cities, towns, and villages by a referendum approved by a majority of voters in the county.

24 See *Toia* v. *Regan*, 54 A.D.2d 46, affd, 40 NY 2d 837, 356 N.E.2d 276 (1976). This raises the question of what constitutes a general law. The term (as well as "Special law") is defined in Article IX, Section 3 (d) as "A law which in terms and in effect applies alike to all counties, all counties other than those wholly included within a city, all cities, all towns or all villages."

"Except as expressly provided, nothing in this article shall restrict or impair any power of the legislature in relation to: — (3) Matters other than the property, affairs or government of a local government."

State legislation regulated the disposal of solid waste in Nassau and Suffolk counties in order to protect the drinking water of a substantial part of the state's population.[25] The Court, while noting that the law involved ". . . is in form a special law and applies only to a limited territory" held that such laws are valid if they deal with matters of state concern, citing Article IX, Section 3 (a) (3).[26] The Court also mentioned the constitutional mandate to the state legislature contained in Article XIV, Section 4, to provide for the abatement of water pollution.[27] This raises the question whether, with respect to environmental protection, Article XIV, Section 4, might influence to some extent the interpretation of the prior provisions of Article IX, Sections 2 and 3.

Article XVI, Section 1: Exemptions from Taxation

This section is an example of a constitutional provision that has substantial environmental impact, although this is not widely understood. It states, among other things, that "Exemptions may be altered or repealed except those exempting real or personal property used exclusively for religious, educational or charitable purposes as defined by law and owned by any corporation or association organized or conducted exclusively for one or more of such purposes and not operating for profit." As a result of this section, thousands of acres of land, owned by conservation organizations such as The Nature Conservancy, National Audobon Society, Trust for Public Land, Mohonk Preserve, and various local land trusts are available to the public.

The land in question is used by individuals and groups for educational and recreational purposes and serves to protect watersheds, aquifers, plants, wildlife, and scenic vistas. Such land serves public purposes and meets public needs without imposing acquisition or managerial expense on the public. It has a relatively minor adverse effect on the local real property tax base, while substantially limiting local expenditures for functions such as schools and roads. If these preserves were subject to real

---

25   *Town of Islip* v. *Cuomo*, 64 NY 2d 50, 473 N.E. 2d 756 (1984).

26   *Ibid.*, at pp. 52 and 55.

27   *Ibid.*, at p. 57. See footnotes 16 and 17 *supra* and related text for a further discussion of this issue.

property taxation, the not-for-profit organizations owning them would be unable to hold them for public use. The New York Court of Appeals has consistently found such lands to be exempt as charitable and educational.[28]

While property held as nature preserves constitutes a minuscule portion of exempt real estate, it has, over the years, been the object of legislative proposals to limit exemptions, including proposals to place acreage limitations on the size of properties that can be exempt. Such proposals might run afoul of the constitutional provision or might be permitted, on the basis that the section permits the exempt purposes to be "as defined by law." To date, however, the constitutional tax exemption protection afforded open space held by not-for-profit organizations has been a primary factor in open-space preservation, and as indicated, the courts have supported an interpretation that makes this possible.

Article XV: Canals

Stemming from the Constitution of 1846, and amended several times in the nineteenth and twentieth centuries, this provision applies to the canal system that was a major factor in the state's economic development.[29] Section 1, the heart of the article, prohibits the sale, lease, abandonment, or any other disposition of the state barge canal, including its terminals, and states that ". . . such canals and terminals shall remain the property of the state and under its management and control forever." This includes the Erie, Oswego, Champlain, Cayuga, and Seneca canals. The section was amended in 1991 to permit the legislature to grant revocable permits or releases for the occupancy or use of such lands.

Section 2 of the article provides that when canal lands or terminals are no longer "necessary or useful" for canal or terminal purposes, they may be disposed of by the legislature.

The framers' original concern was clear — to prevent the system, or parts of it, from being transferred to private ownership. Time has changed the function of many parts of the canals but not their importance. They are now an integral part of the state's water system, and the canals themselves, as well as the adjacent lands, are extensively used for recreational purposes.

28   See e.g., *Mohonk Trust* v. *Board of Assessors of Town of Gardner*, 47 NY 2d 476, 392 N.E.2d 876 (1979), In the *Matter of North Manursing Wildlife Sanctuary, Inc.*, v. *City of Rye*, 48 NY 2d 135, 397 N.E. 2d 693 (1979) and In the *Matter of New York Botanical* v. *Assessors of the Town of Washington*, 55 NY 2d 328, 434 N.E.2d 703 (1982).

29   The Article was amended in 1874, 1882, 1894, 1921, 1933, and 1991.

It is evident, however, that use of the canal system for recreational purposes is both "necessary" and "useful." It has been held that the use of canal lands for state park purposes does not alter the sovereign nature of the state's holding and that title to such lands remains constitutionally inalienable.[30] In addition, Section 3 of Article XV, which originally prohibited the imposition of tolls for the use of the canal system, was amended in 1991 to authorize leasing and fees. Revenue collected from the disposition of unnecessary canal lands or the use of the canals must be placed in a special account to be used for maintaining and improving the canals.

The legislature, in enacting the amendment, stated, ". . . it is essential that the beauty and environmental integrity [of the canal system] be preserved for future generations."[31] The legislature also described the popular support for preserving the canals,[32] created a Canal Recreationway Commission, and gave the New York State Thruway Authority managerial responsibility for the system.[33] Finally, Section 4, adopted in 1959, permits the legislature to lease or transfer the barge canal to the federal government for inclusion in the national system of inland waterways. This authorization has not been exercised.

Conclusion

The foregoing review indicates that the current environmental agenda for the New York State Constitution has four major focal points:

1. *Defending Crucial Provisions Now in the Constitution.* A number of provisions of the New York Constitution have been powerful resources for protecting and advancing environmental values. These include the "Forever Wild" Forest Preserve provision of Article XIV, provisions in Article XVI concerning the use of property tax exemption to advance environmental goals, and the provisions of Article XV with respect to state ownership of the canal system. Should a constitutional convention occur, one goal would be to assure that these provisions remain intact and retain the meaning and effect they have been given.

---

30 See *State* v. *Case*, 86 Misc. 2d 43 (1976).
31 Chapter 766, Section 1, Laws of 1992.
32 *Ibid.*
33 Chapter 766, Section 138, Laws of 1992.

2. *Moving Toward "Self-Executing" Status for the Existing Constitutional Statement of Environmental Goals.* As the foregoing review indicates, state constitutions have their limitations as tools to reach environmental objectives. They can impose specific restrictions on governmental action (as in Article XIV, Section 1, Article IX, Section 2, Article XVI, Section 1, and Article XV, Section 1) and can confer specific powers (as in Article XIV, Sections 2, 3, and 4, Article IX, Section 1, and Article XV, Sections 2, 3, and 4). They are very limited, however, in their ability to force particular legislative action (see discussion of Article XIV, Section 4). The Pennsylvania Constitution is interesting in this respect. It contains a brief but broad environmental mandate:

"The people have a right to clean air, pure water, and to the preservation of the natural, scenic, historic and esthetic values of the environment. Pennsylvania's public natural resources are the common property of all the people, including generations yet to come. As trustee of these resources, the Commonwealth shall conserve and maintain them for the benefit of all the people."[34]

The Pennsylvania lower court held that this provision is "self-executing."[35] That is, its implementation does not require any legislative action, but rather it is a directive to be followed by the courts in reaching their decisions. It is not an "absolute" but requires a judicial balancing of environmental and social concerns to determine whether the environmental harm resulting from the challenged action will clearly outweigh the benefits.[36]

As indicated, it is very uncertain whether Article XIV, Section 4, in the New York Constitution, as now written, will achieve substantive results. It has been on the books for over three decades with questionable effect. Some changes in its wording might result in an interpretation similar to that achieved in Pennsylvania and at least one other state.[37]

---

34 Pennsylvania Constitution Article I, Section 27.

35 *Commonwealth, National Gettysburg Battlefield Tower, Inc.*, 8 Pa. Cmwlth. 231, 302 a.2d 886 (1973), affirmed, 454 Pa. 193, 311 A.2d 588.

36 *Ibid.* at 895. See *Payney, Kassab,* 11 Pa Cmwlth. 14, 312 A.2d 86 (1973), which establishes ". . . a threefold standard: (1) Was there compliance with all applicable statutes and regulations . . . ? (2) Does the record demonstrate a reasonable effort to reduce the environmental incursion to a minimum? (3) Does the environmental harm . . . so clearly outweigh the benefits . . . that to proceed further would be an abuse of discretion?

37 In *Askew* v. *Game and Fresh Water Fish Comm'n*, 336 So.2d 556 (Fla. 1976), the Florida court held that legislation that might otherwise be unconstitutional was constitutional, since it furthered the policies set forth in Florida Constitution Article II, Section 7.

3. *Access to the Courts to Enforce Environmental Laws.* In the environmental area, as on many other issues, constitutional provisions provide guidance for, and define access to, the courts. With respect to access to the courts for enforcement of environmental laws, the New York Constitution is restrictive (Article XIV, Section 5). Addition of a constitutional "Citizen's Suit" provision similar to those in federal environmental legislation that guarantee access for this purpose would be a major advance.

4. *Easing Constitutional Provisions for the Transfer of Functions Among Local Governments.* Such a change might permit land use decision making to go forward in the state on a more comprehensive basis, taking into consideration regional values in the decision-making process.

Amendment and Revision Process: Experience and Issues

A s New Yorkers consider whether to call a constitutional convention, we must weigh the potential risks against the possible benefits. To do this, we must consider whether the things we would call a convention to do might be accomplished at less expense or with less risk by other means. Such an assessment requires a thorough knowledge of how legislative procedures to amend the Constitution have been used in the past and the record of past conventions. (There have been seven.) It also requires an understanding of how delegates to a convention would be selected, who they are likely to be, and how a convention is likely to be organized.

Burton Agata's essay in this section provides an overview of methods for amending and revising the New York Constitution. It introduces a number of concerns about the delegate selection process, including the questions that would surely arise if a convention is called as to whether the processes prescribed in the state Constitution in 1894 conform to the Federal Voting Rights Act of 1965. These questions are more thoroughly discussed in Section V of this volume.

Both Peter Galie and Henrik Dullea explore the historic record of conventions as a means for constitutional change. Concern has been expressed about the absence of a means in New York State to limit the agenda of a state constitutional convention should one be called. Galie, the leading contemporary student of New York constitutional history, explores this "Pandora's box" question. He finds no record of "runaway" conventions in New York history.

Henrik Dullea's essay in this section suggests that the experience of New York's most recent constitutional convention held in 1967 has been misunderstood. The Constitution produced by that convention, Dullea argues, included valuable and needed reforms of state government. According to Dullea, it was defeated at the polls because of political miscalculations by the convention's leadership on how to offer the results of their work to the public. Some argue that the 1967 experience shows that if a convention is called it will be dominated by those already in power. Michael Owens' profile of the delegates to that convention shows that sitting legislators and judges were a relatively small numerical minority. However, those with experience in the "government industry" did predominate, and importantly the legislative leadership of the time was also the convention leadership.

Finally, Gerald Benjamin and Melissa Cusa examine the point made by some that a convention is unnecessary because changes may be made by the alternative route that the state Constitution provides, passage of amendments to the state Constitution by two separate sessions of the legislature followed by ratification at the polls. The record since 1967 reveals that significant structural alterations in state government, especially changes directly addressing the institutional powers of the legislature or individual interests of its members, are rarely achieved through this route.

Amending and Revising the New York State Constitution

Burton C. Agata

Article XIX of the New York State Constitution, adopted in 1894, currently provides two methods for constitutional change:

1. amendment initiated by the legislature and followed by a referendum (Article XIX, Section 1); and

2. revision or amendment initiated by constitutional convention followed by a referendum (Article XIX, Section 2).

Commonly, change by amendment is viewed as limited in scope, while revision involves more extensive change or adoption of an entirely new document. Whether these differences have legal significance in New York has not been judicially determined.

Legislative Proposal-Referendum Method of Amendment

A legislative proposal for amendment or amendments may be introduced in either the Senate or the Assembly. After it is introduced, the Constitution requires that the proposal be referred to the attorney general for an opinion concerning its effect on existing provisions of the Constitution. The attorney general must render this opinion within 20 days. A 1941 amendment provides, however, that his or her failure to provide a timely opinion, or even to render one at all, does not affect the validity of the amendment or the legislative action on the amendment.

After a proposed amendment is introduced, a majority of each house of two successive separately elected legislatures must approve it, with the "ayes and noes" recorded. The proposal must be published for at least thirty days before the second legislature acts, and the versions approved by each legislature must be identical. An attorney general's opinion states that though initial legislative approval may occur in either the first or second session of that legislature, the second approval must come in the first session of the succeeding legislature.[1]

If approved by the second legislature, the proposal *must* be submitted to a referendum for approval (or disapproval) by the electorate. "[U]nder the Constitution it is only the succeeding Legislature . . . which had the authority and 'the duty to submit each proposed amendment or amendments to the people in such manner' as it shall prescribe (New York Constitution, Article XIX, Section 1)."[2] It is thus within the legislature's discretion to decide whether it shall be a special or regularly scheduled election and whether the amendments, if more than one, shall be submitted separately or as one proposal. If approved at the referendum, the proposal or proposals become law on January 1, following the approval.

The Constitutional Convention Method of Amendment

The constitutional convention method of amendment involves the submission to the people of proposals to amend or revise the Constitution previously approved by a popularly elected constitutional convention. Article XIX, Section 2, of the state Constitution requires that every twenty years the following question must appear on the ballot at the general election: "Shall there be a convention to revise the constitution and to amend the same?" The question was last submitted in 1977, and a majority of the voters voted "no." The next time the question *must* appear on the ballot is for the general election in 1997.

In addition to, but not in lieu of, the mandatory submission of the question every twenty years, the legislature may provide for submitting the same question to the people at such other times as it decides. The question was submitted by the legislature in 1965, the people approved and a convention was held in 1967. However, the Constitution produced by that convention was rejected by the people in a 1967 referendum.

If the people vote to hold a convention, delegates are elected at the next scheduled general election. The Constitution provides that there shall be three delegates elected from each senatorial district by the voters of the respective district and fifteen delegates-at-large elected by voters from the entire state. Thus, if the people approve the calling of a convention in 1997, election of delegates will take place during the 1998 general election.

---

1   1959 Op. Att'y Gen. (f. 36).

2   *Frank* v. *New York*, 44 NY 2d 687, 405 NYS 2d 454 (1978).

The Constitution does not presently state what procedures shall be followed in electing delegates; the legislature provides and may change the method of election by statute. The current general provisions of the election law govern the nomination, designation and election of delegates to the constitutional convention. There is only one specific reference in the election law to the delegates; it concerns the place for filing campaign finance statements.[3]

The convention must convene at the Capitol in Albany on the first Tuesday in April after the delegates are elected and continue until they decide to adjourn. Beyond establishing the first meeting date, the Constitution contains few directions on how the convention shall be run, leaving adoption of rules, election of officers, and organizational decisions to those elected to serve as delegates. It does provide that a majority of those elected constitute a quorum and that an affirmative vote of a majority of those elected is required as a condition for submitting a proposal to the people. It also provides that the "ayes and noes" on any proposal be recorded in a journal.

The convention is the "judge of the election, returns and qualifications of its members." Although the Supreme Court has jurisdiction under the election law to determine the accuracy of a tally by the Board of Elections, the convention may ignore the court's determination and seat someone other than the person the court declares to have received the most votes.[4] In 1967, an election for convention delegate was certified by the New York City Board of Elections to have ended in a tie. The Democratic majority of the Convention seated the Democrat, Alfred Santangelo. After considerable wrangling and litigation, the Convention asked Governor Rockefeller to call a special election to settle the matter. He did. The Republican, Charles Rice, prevailed and was seated in Santangelo's place.[5]

Should a vacancy arise, the Constitution prescribes how it is to be filled. A district delegate vacancy is filled by the vote of the remaining delegates from that district;[6] an at-large delegate vacancy is filled by a vote of the remaining at-large delegates.

---

3 Section 14-110 provides for filing of campaign finance statements by delegate candidates with the state Board of Elections and such other places designated by that board.

4 The convention did exercise its power in the situation involving *Rice* v. *Power*, 19 NY 2d 106, 278 NYS 2d 361 (1967); also see, *Rice* v. *State*, 55 Misc. 2d 964 (1968).

5 *New York Times*, May 17, 1967, p. 51; July 12, 1967, p. 30.

6 The Constitution is silent in the event there are no remaining delegates from the district which has the vacancy or vacancies. (Presumably, if there is only one remaining delegate from the district that delegate will choose the other two). It also is silent in the event of a tie vote with respect to either district or at-large delegates.

Finally, the Constitution provides that each delegate shall receive the annual compensation of a member of the Assembly and travel expenses received by members when the Assembly is in session. Compensation, including the certification of a payroll, is a matter for the convention and neither the court nor the comptroller will interfere unless there is a violation of the Constitution. A determination by the convention concerning pro rata payment was held to be beyond review.[7] The convention may hire employees and assistants and set their compensation and provide for printing "and other expenses of the convention."

The convention determines when to adjourn and whether proposals will be submitted to the voters in two or more parts or as one package. The convention also determines the time and manner that proposals for a constitution or a constitutional amendment will be submitted to the people, but submission cannot be sooner than six weeks after the convention adjourns. If the proposed "constitution or constitutional amendment" is approved at the referendum, it becomes law on the following January 1, as is the case with proposals approved by the "legislative-referendum" method of amendment.

When a legislative proposal and a convention proposal "relating to the same subject" are submitted at the same election, and if both are approved, the Constitution provides that the convention proposal supersedes the legislative proposal. This provision was added to the 1894 Constitution and amended by the 1938 Convention in an immaterial respect. "This choice" one authority has written "is consistent with the view that the convention as a constituent body chosen for the specific task of amending the constitution is closer to the sovereign will of the people than the legislature."[8]

History and Background of Provisions Governing Amendments to the New York State Constitution[9]

The first New York State Constitution was adopted on April 20, 1777, at Kingston, New York, by the Fourth Provincial Congress. The preceding Third Provincial Congress had ratified the Declaration of Independence and, in accordance with the urging of the Continental Congress, resolved to establish a new government. The Third Provincial Congress, anticipating a British attack on New York where it was meeting and doubting

---

7   *Rice v. State*, 55 Misc. 2d 964 (1968).

8   See Galie, *The New York State Constitution: A Reference Guide*, Westport, CT: Greenwood Press, 1991 at p. 281.

9   See various sources, but primarily Swindler, *Sources and Documents of U.S. Constitutions*, Dobbs Ferry, NY: Oceana Publications, 1982; and State University of New York and New York State Education Department, "Constitutional Developments in New York 1777-1958," *Bibliography Bulletin* 82 (1958).

whether it had the authority to adopt a new form of government, directed that a Fourth Provincial Congress be elected and meet at White Plains on July 8, 1777.

The Fourth Provincial Congress was charged with establishing a new government, as well as with other duties. It changed its name to the Convention of Representatives of the State of New York. Military duties of the members and exigencies of threatened British attacks caused it to move from place to place; it appears that a majority of the delegates never met together. Nevertheless, a committee was appointed to and did draft what became the first New York State Constitution. It was adopted on July 9, 1777, in Kingston, New York. This first Constitution was not submitted to the people for approval, and it contained no provision for its amendment or for calling future conventions.

The absence of a method for amending the 1777 Constitution presented a dilemma when questions arose concerning the number of members of the legislature, reapportionment of legislative districts, and the interpretation of the constitutional provisions concerning the locus of the powers of nomination and appointment. The legislature met the problem by enacting a statute that authorized the election of delegates to a convention and that "proposed to the citizens of this State [that they] . . . elect by ballot delegates to meet in convention, for the purpose of considering parts of the Constitution of this State respecting these matters.[10] The legislature did not submit to the people the question of whether they wanted a convention or the subject of the convention; consequently "some posited this convention may have been held against the people's will."[11]

It should be noted that the call of the convention by the legislature was a limited call. That is, the subject matter for the 1801 Convention was stated in the call; it did not confer authority by its terms for the convention to consider matters not stated in the statute which provided for the Convention, and the convention appeared to recognize that its powers were limited to the terms of the call.[12]

At the very outset, then, it was recognized that changing the state Constitution was an extraordinary process that required the participation

10 Opening paragraph of amendments to New York State Constitution adopted in 1801.

11 See Lincoln, "Constitutional History of New York from the Beginning of the Colonial Period to the Year 1905 IV," Rochester, NY: Lawyers Cooperative Company, 1905, at p. 606.

12 The preamble to the amendments adopted by the 1801 Convention states, in relevant part: "And whereas the people of this State have elected the members of this convention for the purpose above expressed; and this convention having maturely considered the subjects thus submitted to their determination, do, in the name and by the authority of the People of this State, ordain, determine and declare:"

of the people and could not be accomplished by legislative action alone. While recognizing that the legislature had called the Convention and set its agenda, the 1801 Convention declared that its action to amend the Constitution was taken "in the name and *by the authority of the people of this State*" (emphasis added).[13] Nevertheless, the Constitution itself still did not provide a method for amending the state Constitution.

The third [1821] constitutional convention came as the result of popular dissatisfaction with the existing government and growing demand for democratization. The Council of Revision and Council of Appointment were becoming unpopular and public pressure mounted still higher when the Council of Revision vetoed a bill in 1820 calling for a constitutional convention. The following year a law was passed . . . whereby the question of holding a convention was to be submitted to the people. [In 1821], [t]he people overwhelmingly voted for a convention.

The 1821 statute authorizing the convention provided broad authority for the convention and specifically called for an amendment process. It declared the purpose of the delegates to be "considering the Constitution of this State, and making such alteration in the same as they may deem proper; and to provide the manner of making future amendments thereto." The statute also provided for the election of delegates and required that any proposed amended Constitution be submitted to the people for approval.[14]

The new Constitution proposed by the 1821 Convention was adopted by the people in 1822 and became effective on December 31, 1822. It effected several democratizing reforms including provision for legislative initiative of proposals to amend the Constitution.[15]

The current Article XIX, Section 1, and Article VIII of the 1822 Constitution are practically identical. They each provide for two successive legislatures to approve a proposal and for the approved proposal to be submitted to a referendum. One difference, however, is that the 1822 provi-

---

13 Also, in addition to amending the constitutional provisions concerning the numbers and reapportionment of the legislature, the Convention performed what presently we would call a judicial act when it construed the existing Constitution in response to the legislature's call of the Convention. It stated:
"[T]he convention . . . in the name and by the authority of the people of this State, ordain, determine and declare . . . the true construction of the twenty-third article of the constitution of this State [concerning the locus of the powers of nomination and appointment]."

14 See State University of New York and New York State Education Department, "Constitutional Developments in New York 1777-1958," *Bibliography Bulletin* 82 (1958): 28; Lincoln, "The Constitutional History of New York from the Beginning of the Colonial Period to the Year 1905 IV," Rochester, NY: Lawyers Cooperative Company, 1905, at p. 629.

15 The 1822 Constitution was a more complete Constitution than the 1777 Constitution. It also effected several additional democratizing reforms by expanding suffrage and abolishing the Council of Revision and the Council of Appointment.

sion required approval of two-thirds and not simply a majority of the second legislature voting on the proposal, and the 1822 provision did not set a fixed effective date (currently, January 1) for an approved amendment. The 1822 provision simply provided that upon approval by the people the amendment become part of the Constitution. Moreover, the 1822 provision did not contain a requirement that a proposal be referred to the attorney general for an opinion.

The state's third Constitution, the 1846 Constitution, was the product of the 1845 Convention. The Convention itself was the product of intensive and long-time agitation for constitutional reform in the context of a general reform movement.[16] When 24 counties demanded that a convention be called, the legislature referred the question to the people. The response was overwhelmingly affirmative.[17]

The Constitution framed by the 1845 Convention and approved by the people in 1846 continued the process of democratization begun in 1821.[18] Reflecting this thrust, the convention method of amending the Constitution was included for the first time, while the legislative-referendum method of constitutional change was retained with two changes.[19] The first of these eliminated the requirement that two-thirds of each house of the second legislature approve the proposal in favor of requiring only a simple majority (the current requirement). The second changed the language referring a proposal to the second legislature, from "the legislature next chosen" to "the legislature to be chosen at the next general election of senators."

This language change was influenced by the simultaneous reduction in the term of Senators from four to two years. Members of the Assembly continued to be elected annually. The effect was to permit the possibility that two years would pass before the next legislature had to deal with a previously approved proposal.[20]

---

16 This general reform movement was marked by the codification of law under David Dudley Field, the formation of a labor party, an organized program for women's rights, temperance societies, and several anti-slavery organizations. Swindler, *Sources and Documents of U.S. Constitutions*, Dobbs Ferry, NY: Oceana Publications, 1982, at p. 154.

17 See State University of New York and New York State Education Department, "Constitutional Developments in New York 1777-1958," *Bibliography Bulletin* 82 (1958): 30.

18 In addition to democratization of the amending process, important democratizing constitutional changes included the election of the judiciary and many state officers and the reduction of the term of Senators from four to two years. See State University of New York and New York State Education Department, "Constitutional Developments in New York 1777-1958," *Bibliography Bulletin* 82 (1958): 30.

19 *Ibid.*

20 In 1937, the term of a member of the Assembly was increased from one to two years, and in 1938, the legislative-referendum provision was amended to read that the proposal be referred to the "next regular legislative session convening after the succeeding general election of the assembly" which is the current language of Article XIX, Section 1.

Article XIII, Section 2, of the 1846 Constitution added the convention-referendum method by directing that every twenty years beginning in 1866, and at such other times as the legislature may provide, the following question be put to the people in referendum: "Shall there be a convention to revise the constitution and amend the same?" If the vote was in the affirmative, the legislature was to provide for the election of convention delegates the following year.

Unlike the current Article XIX, Section 2, the 1846 provision contained: (a) no requirement of a referendum on the convention's proposals; (b) no provision governing when and how the convention's work would take effect; and (c) no provision concerning the makeup of the convention delegates. Also, the 1846 provision had none of the detail in the current provision concerning filling vacancies and determining disputed delegate elections and no reference as to how the convention was to be organized. All these questions were left to the legislature.

In 1866 the people approved calling a convention under the 20-year rule of the 1846 Constitution. The Convention's proposals were submitted to the people, although, as has been noted, the 1846 Constitution did not make this a specific requirement. To enhance the possibility that a key judicial reform proposal was accorded public approval, the submission to the people was in two parts — a judiciary article and all other changes. The former was approved; the latter was rejected.[21]

In the wake of this outcome and in response to the governor's continued urging of reform, the legislature created a commission of 32 members for the purpose of proposing constitutional amendments to the legislature. "The creation of the commission was an innovation in the State's constitutional history." The commission offered 11 proposals, including many rejected as a result of the 1867 constitutional referendum. These were approved by the legislature and then by the voters in 1874.[22]

Pursuant to the 20-year rule, the question of whether a convention should be called was submitted to the people in 1886. It was approved by a vote of 574,993 to 30,766. Nevertheless, there was a deadlock on calling the convention, because Democratic Governor Daniel B. Hill and the

---

21 See State University of New York and New York State Education Department, "Constitutional Developments in New York 1777-1958," *Bibliography Bulletin* 82 (1958): 33; Swindler, *Sources and Documents of U.S. Constitutions*, Dobbs Ferry, NY: Oceana Publications, 1982, at p. 154.

22 See State University of New York and New York State Education Department, "Constitutional Developments in New York 1777-1958," *Bibliography Bulletin* 82 (1958): 35; Swindler, *Sources and Documents of U.S. Constitutions*, Dobbs Ferry, NY: Oceana Publications, 1982, at p. 154. See also Robert Williams, "The Role of the Constitutional Commission in State Constitutional Change" in this book.

Republican legislature could not agree on how delegates were to be chosen. In the course of the deadlock, Governor Hill vetoed several convention bills.

With the election of a Republican governor in 1892, Roswell P. Flower, the deadlock on calling the convention approved by the people in 1886 was broken. Legislation authorizing the method of electing delegates was enacted in 1892 and delegates elected at a special election in 1893.

Section 2 of Article XIX of the 1894 Constitution retained a slightly revised version of the 1846 Convention referendum provision[23] and added detailed provisions designed to avoid repetition of the just-experienced delay encountered in holding a convention resulting from partisan differences between the legislative and executive branches. Thus, it provided "the method of selecting delegates, prescribed the date for a convention to assemble, quorum requirements . . . [,] the manner in which proposed amendments were to be submitted to the people and the effective date of approved amendments." With one exception concerning the timing of the submission of the mandatory constitutional convention question, these provisions are the same as the current Section 2 of Article XIX.

The constitutional question was submitted by the legislature in 1914 to avoid the presidential election year.[24] Following the approval at referendum of a convention, a New York Constitutional Convention Commission was created by the legislature and charged with the duty of making a comprehensive study of the form and substance of state constitutions in general with special reference to the needs of New York. The Commission was aided in its studies by many specialists in law and the social sciences, the New York Bureau of Municipal Research, the Legislative Drafting Research Fund of Columbia University, and the State Library.[25] The 1915 Convention's work, though rejected at the polls in 1916, did bear fruit over the next decade and a half, as major portions of its work were incrementally submitted to the voters and approved.[26]

The Constitutional Convention of 1938 resulted from an affirmative vote upon automatic submission of the question in 1936. Governor Lehman's suggestion of a bipartisan commission to help prepare

---

23   The amendment made clear that approval of the call of the convention required only a majority of those voting on the question and not a majority of those voting at the election. There had been some debate on this point at the 1867 Convention. It was resolved in the 1894 Constitution.

24   The constitutionally required submission of the question in 1916 resulted in rejection.

25   See State University of New York and New York State Education Department, "Constitutional Developments in New York 1777-1958," *Bibliography Bulletin* 82 (1958): 43.

26   See Robert A. Caro, *The Power Broker: Robert Moses and the Fall of New York*, NY: Knopf, 1974, ch.6.

for the convention was rejected by the legislature. Consequently, the governor appointed Justice Charles Poletti to chair a committee for that purpose. The result was the now famous and then invaluable 12-volume "Poletti Report."

The 1938 Convention passed 58 proposals, submitted to the people in nine parts.[27] Six of the nine submitted proposals were adopted. The division of the Convention's proposals into several parts undoubtedly was critical in the approval of so many of them. Those that were rejected were recognized at the time as the most partisan. They dealt with expansion of the courts, reapportionment, and a prohibition of proportional representation. Among the changes passed was an amendment to Article XIX, Section 2. It made 1957, not 1956, and every 20 years thereafter the years for the regular 20-year submission to the people of the mandatory convention question. The apparent object was to separate this question from statewide general elections in presidential years.

In contemplation of aiding a convention if one was held, following the mandatory referendum on the convention question in 1957, the legislature established the Temporary Commission on the Constitutional Convention, headed by Nelson Rockefeller. The people responded in the negative to the 1957 question. Nevertheless, after Rockefeller's election to the governorship, he and the legislature continued the commission's work in a Special Committee on Revision and Simplification of the Constitution and then the Temporary Commission on Revision and Simplification of the Constitution. Each produced several reports on a variety of subjects. The last named was the source of the home-rule amendment adopted in 1963. One authority suggests that the Commission was permitted to expire in 1961, "because it took up the [controversial] question of reapportionment."[28]

In 1965 the legislature, as earlier noted, placed a convention question on the ballot and the people approved the calling of a convention. In 1967 this Convention produced a new Constitution, but the people rejected it by a vote of almost three to one. The Convention decided to submit the proposal as a whole to referendum and to provide no opportunity to vote for one or more changes individually. It is widely believed that this tactic resulted in a devastating combination, not necessarily an alliance, of each

---

27 The Convention entertained 694 proposals. 76 were reported out of committee, and 58 were adopted by the Convention. See State University of New York and New York State Education Department, "Constitutional Developments in New York 1777-1958," *Bibliography Bulletin* 82 (1958): 52.

28 See Galie, *The New York State Constitution: A Reference Guide*, Westport, CT: Greenwood Press, 1991, at p. 28.

group or interest that strongly opposed even one part of the proposal.[29] The 1967 strategy provides a striking contrast with the deliberately different strategy and substantially successful outcome of the 1938 Convention.

The draft Constitution of 1967 significantly revamped the provisions for amendment and revision of the state Constitution in Article XIX. Among its provisions was a prohibition of convention service by the governor, the lieutenant governor, the attorney general, the comptroller, the chief judge, and the associate judges of the Court of Appeals, but not by members of the legislature. An amendment passed by the legislature in 1970 and 1971 was substantially similar to the 1967 proposal. In addition to the prohibitions on service listed above, it included a slight alteration of the text of the referendum question; age and residency requirements for delegates; a specification of procedures for recording votes to submit amendments; a provision for the presiding officer to resolve tie votes for delegates; and a provision allowing the proration of salary for convention service beyond a year. The change that attracted the most attention, however, was one that postponed the automatic referendum question from 1977 to 1985. ". . . [s]uch postponement," the *New York Times* remarked, "would have the effect of leaving the state's basic law generally intact for half a century, which is much too long in this era of rapid change."[30] The amendment was defeated by a significant margin.

Issues Presented by the Amending Process

The Federal Voting Rights Act. Election of three delegates from each senatorial district and 15 at-large from the entire state could present two problems under the Federal Voting Rights Act. One of these (arising under 42 United States Code Section 1973(b)) involves a potential violation of the provision prohibiting denial of the vote to a person on account of race or color (the "protected class"). Discrimination is established if "under the totality of circumstances" it is determined that the "political processes leading to nomination or election in the state or political subdivision are not open to members of the protected class . . . in that its members have less opportunity than other members of the electorate to participate in the political process and to elect representatives of their choice."[31] In general,

---

29 See Swindler, *Sources and Documents of U.S. Constitutions*, Dobbs Ferry, NY: Oceana Publications, 1982, at p. 155; Galie, at p. 29.

30 *The New York Times*, November 3, 1972, p. 38.

31 The provision also states that it does not establish a right to have members of the protected class elected in numbers equal to their proportion of the population. However, it also provides that the extent to which members of the protected class have been elected can be considered as part of the totality of circumstances.

federal courts have been very questioning of the use of at-large elections in multimember districts when Voting Rights Act criteria are applied. Though current New York State Senate districts have survived Justice Department review under the Voting Rights Act, they have not been reviewed as multimember districts. Nor has statewide at-large election of delegates to a collective decision-making body been considered by the courts.

While no voting rights case has been found that deals with delegates to a state constitutional convention, there appears to be no reason that the language should not be held applicable to the election of delegates.[32] However, even if applicable, whether the state Constitution's delegate election provisions do or do not violate the provision is a question of fact based, as the statute says, on the "totality of circumstances."

An additional facet to this delegate election issue under the Voting Rights Act is the question of the timing of potential court action to resolve the question. Consider that the constitutionally required referendum will be held in November 1997, and the election of delegates would be in November 1998. The "totality of circumstances" now or in the immediate future may be quite different than those extant on or after November 1997 or 1998. A court may well be reluctant to rule on the question so far in advance of a possible election, one which may never take place.

However, should the legislature seek to avoid the problem in advance by proposing a constitutional amendment to Article XIX, Section 2, changing the manner of electing convention delegates, there may be an additional problem. This second question could arise under the provisions of 42 United States Codes Section 1973c, that requires pre-clearance for any changes with respect to districts that previously have been found to be subject to Voting Rights Act. Senate districts in three counties in New York City are subject to this provision.[33] Thus, if changes are made in the delegate election provisions, 1973c could come into play.

Limiting the Call. One of the concerns expressed with respect to calling a constitutional convention is that the convention would control its own agenda. Some would favor a convention if it could be limited to specified subject matter. The wisdom of restricting the call of the convention is debatable, and the language of Section 2 would seem to preclude that possibility at present. The provision contains the precise language of the

---

32 Cf., *MacGuire* v. *Amos*, 343 F. Supp. 119 (Ala. 1972) (delegate to Democratic National convention).

33 Pre-clearance of the Justice Department was sought in connection with the recently adopted New York City Charter.

question to be posed whether it is posed at the required 20-year referendum or by the legislature acting at other times. The very first convention called by the legislature in 1801 did contain restrictions on the call, but this was prior to the inclusion of any amending clause in the Constitution.

Should There Be Special Statutory Provisions for Election of Delegates? Subject to certain exceptions contained in Article XIX of the New York State Constitution noted above, the regular election law provisions are applicable to the election of delegates to a constitutional convention. Thus, the at-large delegates would be subject to those provisions of Article 6 of the election law which concern designation and nomination of candidates elected by the entire state (e.g., 6-104[1]; 6-136[1]; 6-142[1]) and those delegates elected from Senatorial districts would be subject to the counterpart provisions that cover elections from Senatorial districts (e.g., 6-142[2](f) and its counterparts). These provisions address such questions as the number of signatures required on petitions, the form and contents of petitions, and the like. Moreover, as noted above, delegates are subject to campaign finance laws.

There can be little dispute that the complex and sometimes technical construction and application of the election law favors those most familiar with it. This includes political party leaders, office holders, and other professional politicians who have the resources and experience to plumb the complexities of the election law. Some have expressed concern that it would be relatively more difficult for those who are not a part of an existing political party or organization to become candidates for convention delegates. This is not only a criticism of the election law but also an expression of the view that, regardless of the rules applicable to everyday political elections, there should be afforded to persons not normally involved in partisan politics a greater and more open opportunity to become involved in the special process of constitutional revision.

In a draft Constitution prepared in anticipation of the 1966 convention, Judge Jack Weinstein made two proposals to address this concern. The first provided that convention delegates be elected by a nonpartisan process. The second required that delegates be chosen at a special election, and not the general election. Also before the 1967 Convention, Senator Robert Kennedy unsuccessfully sought Republican and Democratic party cooperation in assembling a nonpartisan slate for statewide convention delegates.[34]

---

34 See Lewis B. Kaden, "The People 'No:' Some Observations on the 1967 New York Constitutional Convention," *Harvard Journal of Legislation* 5 (1968): 343-371.

Comparative research in the 1960s did show that nonpartisan selection of convention delegates significantly affected the work of constitutional conventions. Nevertheless, critics have resisted the use of nonpartisan election in New York, arguing that they advantage the richest and most organized elements of society. The political parties, they say, are most likely to mobilize the poor and less educated and therefore to protect their interests. They also reject nonpartisan politics as not in accord with the state's political culture.

With regard to special elections to choose delegates to a constitutional convention, it is arguable whether these would be a greater disincentive to the domination of a convention by established political leaders and forces than their selection at a general election. If the general election were used, state legislators would have to run simultaneously for legislative office and a seat at the convention. Under some circumstances, this might provide a considerable disincentive.

Should There Be Changes In Who May Be a Delegate and In the Compensation of Delegates?

1. As noted, serious proposals have been offered in the past making several elected state officers and officials ineligible to serve as constitutional convention delegates. Supportive sentiment for this idea, extended to include barring legislators from service at a convention, persists in the state.

   Those who favor excluding state elected officials and judges from service at a convention argue that they are likely to be resistant to considering serious structural change in a system they have mastered and that benefits them. It is suggested, further, that past experience with conventions demonstrates this point to be true. Those who oppose excluding those officials argue that such a provision constitutes discrimination and would keep knowledgeable and experienced New Yorkers from service at a convention. This would both diminish the quality of the convention's work, and open greater possibilities for its domination by single issue groups and advocates.

2. A question also arises as to whether those who are already being paid by the state (e.g., legislators, judges, and others) should be permitted to receive both their regular salaries for state office and the compensation for delegates provided for in the Constitution, i.e., an amount equivalent to the annual salary of a member of the Assembly and travel reimbursement a member would receive

when the legislature is in session. An important ancillary issue is the affect of the receipt of two salaries in one year on the calculation of an official's pension benefits. It is possible, without constitutional change, that the impact of a second salary on pension benefits might be mitigated by statute.

3. There are questions of whether the legislature may provide for delegate qualifications and whether there are any limitations on the power of the convention to judge the qualifications of its members. A constitutional provision clarifying the legislature's power to establish delegate qualifications or providing for quali- fications in the Constitution would be desirable.

    Current Section 2 of Article XIX does not contain qualifi- cations of delegates to a constitutional convention. The only reference to delegate qualifications is in the provisions that make the convention the judge of the qualifications of its members.[35] In *Powell* v. *McCormack*, 395 US 486 (1969), the Court held that Congress could not modify the qualifications for members of Congress stated in the United States Constitution; however, its power to expel a member was not limited by the qualifications provisions in the Constitution.[36]

    Although this case is not binding on the state with respect to the power of the New York State Legislature to legislate qualifications for convention delegates, its reasoning could sup- port a similar limitation on the state legislature's power with respect to delegate qualifications. However, there are significant factual differences, both historical and textual, which could lead to a different conclusion. First, the historical background of the federal Constitution's text lends clear support to the Court's conclusion. The historical background of Article XIX, Section 2, provides no such support, clear or otherwise. Second, the federal constitutional provision contains qualifications for a member of Congress. The state provision in question contains no statement of qualifications at all. Moreover, the consequence of a total limitation on legislative power could mean that infants and non- residents and noncitizens of the state would be eligible for elec-

---

35   In *Powell* v. *McCormack*, 395 US 486 (1969), the Court stated that this provision in the federal Constitution contemplated that qualifications would be established elsewhere to provide a standard for judging qualifications of members.

36   See *Alamo* v. *Strohm*, 74 NY 2d 801, for a similar view of the power to expel a member. Also see Public Officers Law Section 30.

tion and to serve as delegates without the power of the legislature to provide the contrary.[37]

Amendment and Revision — Do They Differ for Purposes of Article XIX?

A question that could arise in New York, but apparently has not yet been presented to the courts, is whether there is any difference between the scope or subject matter of constitutional alteration under Article XIX, Section 1 (legislative referendum method) and Section 2 (convention referendum method). The language of the two provisions presents the question.

Section 1 speaks of "amendment or amendments" to the Constitution proposed by the legislature and submitted to the people. Section 2 states the question of holding the convention in terms of "a convention to revise the constitution and amend the same." It also provides for the submission to the people and their approval of any "proposed constitution or constitutional amendment."

There is no question that a constitutional convention can propose a new Constitution and extensive or very limited revisions and amendments. Thus for the constitutional convention we need not distinguish between revisions and amendments.

On the other hand, Section 1 speaks only of an "amendment or amendments." Clearly, the legislature has the power to submit for approval as many amendments as it wishes, i.e., the number of amendments alone should not be viewed as a limit on the legislature. But are there other limits? Can an "amendment" embody a new or revised Constitution? Can several amendments submitted at the same time be considered a "new" or "revised" Constitution? If the answer to either or both of these questions is in the affirmative, has the power of the legislature been exceeded?

---

37 The 1894 Constitution first referred specifically to delegates; it was clear that prior to its adoption the legislature had the power to prescribe delegate qualifications. Interestingly, the legislation that provided for the 1894 Convention appears to have been the only one that specifically provided qualifications for delegates. It provided that any male or female citizen of the state over the age of 21 may be a delegate. Chapter 8, Section 7, Laws of 1893. Arguably, it is not likely that simply by providing for delegates, it was intended that even minimal qualifications could not continue to be established by the legislature.
Also see 1937 Op. Att'y Gen. (f. 136), in which the attorney general concluded that all judicial officers and public officials, except sheriffs, are eligible to serve as delegates because nothing in the Constitution disqualifies them. The attorney general also relied on a provision of the statute establishing the 1938 Convention that provided:
A disqualification imposed by general or local law upon any person by reason of his holding another office is hereby removed so far as concerns his rights to be a delegate to such convention. The attorney general's opinion did not discuss the constitutional power of the legislature to establish delegate qualifications.

These can be important questions. Some are pessimistic about the prospects of a future convention proposing a new or acceptable Constitution.[38] Moreover, since 1938, New York has relied on legislative proposals to amend the Constitution, sometimes extensively. If it is desired that there be no limit on what the legislature can propose, perhaps Section 1 should be altered to include an explicit reference to the power to recommend revisions of the Constitution.

This is not an uncommon provision.[39] Several state courts have attempted to distinguish the terms "amendment," "revision," and "new constitution." The dispute appears to revolve around whether a court concludes that the fact that the people must approve the proposed amendment or new constitution should override what may be limitations on methods of amendment found in the state Constitution. Relying on the former factor, some state courts have held that although the only constitutional provision for a new or revised constitution described the method for the legislature to call a convention, this did not preclude the legislature from submitting a new or revised constitution to the people, because, in any event, the people are sovereign and would have the final say on whether to approve a new Constitution.[40]

Other state courts, in the context of the use of initiative to amend the constitution have sharply distinguished between amendment, on the one hand, and revision of a constitution or adoption of a new constitution, on the other. The distinction requires the court to examine the quantity and quality of the changes. Even a short simple provision may have so great an effect on the structure of government or existing constitutional provisions as to constitute a revision. Where initiatives are limited to "amendment," the initiatives construed to have been revisions have been held invalid.[41]

Should the Appointment of a Commission to Study and Recommend Changes in the Constitution Be Regularized? As noted, a number of commissions have been established over history to provide recommendations to the legislature and to aid conventions in advance of their convening. The Florida Constitution calls for the periodic creation of a

---

38 See Galie, *at pp. 29-30.*

39 See California Constitution Article XVIII, Section 1.

40 *Gatewood* v. *Mathews,* 403 S.W. 2nd 716 (Ky.1966); *Wheeler* v. *Board of Trustees,* 200 Ga. 323, 37 S.E.2d, 322 (1946) (concluding that constitutional provision for calling a convention for a new constitution was not the exclusive method for adopting a new constitution); also see dissents in *Adams* v. *Gunter,* 238 So.2d 824 (Fla. 1970).

41 See *Amador Valley School District* v. *State Board of Equalization,* 22 California 3d 208, 593 P.2d 1282 (1978); *Raven* v. *Deukmejian,* 52 California 3d 336, 801 P.2d 1077 (1990); *Adams* v. *Gunter,* 238 So.2d 824 (Florida 1970).

constitutional revision commission to propose constitutional changes to the people. Utah has a statutory bond commission.[42] It would be worth considering whether a commission of a more permanent character might be useful in New York to monitor constitutional developments and develop proposals for the legislature and for conventions. While recognizing that the subject matter often is infinitely more controversial than most of the matters considered by the Law Revision Commission, a similar body dedicated to the study of the New York State Constitution could be as useful as the Law Revision Commission is in its usual sphere.[43]

Leadership, Organization, Procedures, and Presentation of Results: Decisions for the Convention. Some aspects of the constitutional convention process may not be addressed in statute or by constitutional amendment; they may only be settled by the convention itself. These include such matters as selection of leaders; organization of the convention, including committee structures and work flow; adoption of rules; and the presentation of the results to the public for action. Structural arrangements that might affect the delegate selection process if known in advance can therefore not be specified before a convention's first meeting.

Consider, for example, a concern, based upon the professional and demographic characteristics of the delegates at 1967 Convention, that a future constitutional convention might attract insufficient representation by New Yorkers from a range of professions and walks of life.[44] There has been a suggestion that a more diverse group of candidates for delegate might be attracted if the body met over a longer period of months, but only in two or three day stretches of time at a single sitting. (Such a schedule, of course, would not preclude staff work on a more conventional schedule. Indeed it is the pattern during the regular sessions of the state legislature.) People with less flexible employment schedules might be able to serve under such a scenario. A decision to organize a convention in this way, however, would have to be made by the delegates in organizational sessions after they were elected.

With regard to the presentation of a potential convention's work to the public, it has been widely noted that the 1967 Convention's decision to offer a single package at referendum for an up or down vote resulted in

---

42   See the chapter "The Role of the Constitutional Commission in State Constitutional Change," in this book.

43   See, Advisory Commission on Intergovernmental Relations (ACIR), "The Question of State Government Capability," Washington DC: ACIR, 1985, pp. 58-59 and Chapter 3, *passim.*

44   See the paper prepared for the Temporary Commission on Constitutional Revision by Michael Owens on "The 1967 Constitutional Convention Delegates" (1993), included as an appendix to the commission's first interim report (1994).

failure, while that of the 1938 Convention to offer nine questions, with some of the most controversial matters offered to the voters for separate action, resulted in the adoption of six. The apparent lesson is that presentation of a number of questions by a convention is a better strategy. Some might argue, however, that the results of any serious convention will be a bundle of intricately negotiated compromises not easily amenable to disassembly. If a constitution has an organic quality as it should, they would say, it is best considered as a whole. Moreover, the use of separate questions does not guarantee positive action. The results of the 1915 Convention were offered to the voters in five separate questions; none were adopted.

A Pandora's Box?
Holding a Constitutional
Convention in New York

Peter J. Galie

If each generation were allowed and expected to build its own houses, that single change, comparatively unimportant in itself, would imply almost every reform which society is now suffering for. I doubt whether even our public edifices . . . ought to be built of such permanent materials as stone or brick. It were better that they should crumble to ruin, once in twenty years, or thereabouts, as a hint to the people to examine into and reform the institutions which they symbolize.

> Nathaniel Hawthorne
> *The House of the Seven Gables*

Each generation . . . has . . . a right to choose for itself the form of government it believes most promotive of its own happiness, and it is for the peace and good of mankind that a solemn opportunity of doing this every nineteen or twenty years should be provided by the constitution, so that it may be handed on, with periodical repairs from generation to generation. . . .

> To Samuel Kercheval, July 16, 1816,
> *Thomas Jefferson Writings,* Ed., Merrill D. Peterson,
> NY: Library of America, 1984, p. 1402

. . . Every twentieth year thereafter, and also at such time as the legislature may by law provide, the question "Shall there be a convention to revise the constitution and amend same?" shall be submitted to and decided by the electors of the state. . . .

> New York Constitution, Article XIX

"People elected to conventions are strikingly similar to people elected to state legislature." One legislator interrupted to say

"That may be of great comfort to you professor, but it scares the hell out of me."

Perry & Weber, *Unfounded Fears, Myths and Realities of a Constitutional Convention*, (Westport, CT: Greenwood Press, 1989, p. 103, n. 44

The prospect of opening a "Pandora's Box" has been a principal argument against calling a state constitutional convention. Democratic theory tells us that such a convention is called by the people to reconsider first principles in governance; its agenda is therefore unlimited. Consequently, the possibility exists that the delegates, elected in the historic moment and responsive to its passions, might propose changes to the state's Constitution that compromise fundamental rights, undo hard won achievements of the past or entrench ill-considered changes for decades into the future.

These reservations about a state constitutional convention echo fears about what might flow from a national convention called in the present political environment. Some regard such an event as a prospective forum for "reactionary populism," an opportunity for delegates chosen by an electorate in an angry and resentful mood to write into the U.S. Constitution provisions requiring a balanced budget, authorizing the death penalty, limiting abortion, prohibiting flag burning, and the like. About a decade ago, when such a convention seemed possible, respected constitutional scholar, Gerald Gunther worried in print about "Constitutional Roulette" and "Constitutional Brinksmanship."[1] Former Associate Justice William Brennan declared the prospect of a national constitutional convention "The most awful thing in the world."[2] Expressing a similar apprehension, Professor Walter Murphy has argued that certain provisions of the Constitution are so fundamental that they should not be subject to amendment.[3]

Each of these proposals, whatever their intellectual merits, reflect a distrust of the people's judgment in the context of contemporary movements to amend and revise our constitutions. On the question of calling a

1   "Constitutional Brinksmanship: Stumbling Towards a Convention," 65 *American Bar Association Journal* (1979), p. 1046.

2   As quoted in Russell L. Caplan, *Constitutional Brinksmanship*, NY: Oxford University Press, 1982, p. VIII.

3   Walter Murphy, "An Ordering of Constitutional Values," 53 *Southern California Law Review* (1980), p. 755.

national constitutional convention we have moved from "Gay Abandon" to "Cautious Resistance."[4]

Unlike the national government, states have had more experience with conventions, having held over two hundred in the last two centuries. The governmental functions of state constitutions, and their symbolic import in the polity, differ substantially from that of the national document, and therefore not all the arguments raised by opponents of a national convention are apposite at the state level.[5] Nevertheless there has been a reluctance in states to call constitutional conventions in recent years. And, as New York approaches its mandatory consideration of the question of whether to call a convention in 1997, there is a concern that delegates might address issues not related to those which provided the basis for its existence; adopt extreme measures on the issues they were called to address; or perhaps the ultimate fear, address issues unconnected with those prompting its calling and propose extreme and "divisive" amendments on those issues.

What constitutes a radical or extreme action is a contextual matter, to be determined from the range and distribution of public sentiment or belief at any given historical period. For this analysis the conventions of 1801, 1821, 1846, 1867, 1894, 1915, 1938, and 1967 will be examined to identify the issues debated in the press, the legislature, and elsewhere before and during the delegate selection process. These issues will be compared with the recommendations produced by the conventions. Three core questions will provide focus for this examination of delegate behavior at these nine constitutional conventions: "What has been the relationship between issues which precipitated the conventions and the recommendations they produced?"; "Have conventions produced measures which could fairly be called radical or extreme in that historical context?"; and, "If so, have those recommendations been approved by the voters?" Finally, an assessment of the "extremeness" of the proposals will be made, using the judgments of those involved in the ratification debates and scholarly assessments of the conventions.

---

4   Linda Healy, "Past and Present Convention Calls: From Gay Abandon to Cautious Resistance," paper presented at Southern Political Association, Savannah, GA, November 1, 1984.

5   This point is detailed in Richard Briffault. "State Constitutions in the Federal System," in this book.

1777 Constitution

The 1777 Constitution was adopted by the Fourth Provincial Congress without ratification by the public, and contained no method for amendment. Even the first Constitution did not create *ex nihilo*. The structure established was remarkably similar to the institutions and practices in place in colonial New York, beginning a constitutional tradition that has emphasized continuity and gradualism.

1801 Constitution

The 1801 Convention was called by the legislature to consider only two matters: the number of senators and assemblymen, and the correct interpretation of the governor's power as a member of the Council of Appointment.[6] This convention, the only one in New York's history called for limited purposes, confined itself to those two matters. The amendments were not submitted to the voters for their approval.

1821 Convention

The 1821 Convention was called as much from a desire of Tammanies and other anti-Clintonians to destroy the power of Governor De Witt Clinton as it was in response to demands for reform on the part of the electorate. The major issues debated in the legislature and in the press concerned the Council of Appointment, the Council of Revision, suffrage, reorganization of the judiciary, and changes in the document imitating provisions admired in the U.S. Constitution such as the Bill of Rights and a veto power for the chief executive.[7]

Members of both parties wished for a limited convention "with no other power or authority whatsoever."[8] However, voters in the newer sections of the states, in need of an expanded judiciary and wishing to reduce their dependence on the more settled regions, supported an unlimited one.[9]

The Democratic-Republicans, led by Martin Van Buren, controlled the convention. Their agenda was set forth in the recommendations of an Assembly Committee advocating a convention to reform the appointive

---

6 *Laws of New York V*, 24th Session, Chpt. 159.

7 John Casais, "The New York Constitutional Convention of 1821 and Its Aftermath" (unpublished Ph.D. thesis, Columbia University, 1967), p. 9-17.

8 *Assembly Journal*, 41st Session (1818), p. 345.

9 Casais, *op. cit.*, p. 14.

power, replace the Council of Revision with an executive veto, expand suffrage, and reorganize the judiciary.[10]

The convention abolished the Council of Appointment, dividing the appointment power between state and local governments and eliminated the Council of Revision, replacing it with a governor's veto modeled after that in the national Constitution. Delegates expanded the suffrage just short of universal manhood suffrage, but added a property qualification of $250 for African-Americans. These measures passed by overwhelming margins.

The one measure that could be considered "extreme" was an attempt by some "Radical Republicans" to abolish the Chancery Court and create a new common law court system. There was strong support for judicial reorganization. The judiciary as constituted wasn't able to dispose of judicial business. This support was undergirded by a hostility to the judiciary that was pervasive in early nineteenth century America.[11] Additionally, judges in New York made themselves personally unpopular by engaging in partisan electioneering.[12] The Court of Chancery, unlike common law courts, functioned without a jury and became a lightning rod for Republican ire.

The proposal to abolish the judiciary was defeated by the moderate Republicans. Chancery Court was preserved, though it would now share jurisdiction with common law courts. "Radical Republicans" did succeed in restructuring the Supreme Court in such a way as to eliminate the sitting Federalist judges. The Court of Errors and Impeachment continued but without the participation of Supreme Court judges. The moderates had rescued the judiciary from "a too great dependence on the will of the legislature."[13]

The convention added a Bill of Rights imitating the form of the national model, though the substantive provisions were drawn from a variety of sources.

Opposition during the ratification debates consisted of Federalists from older counties displeased with the extension of suffrage and with the reorganization of the judiciary; a minority of Western Republicans dissat-

10   *Assembly Journal*, 43rd Session (1820), pp. 110f.

11   James Willard Hurst, *The Growth of American Law: The Law Breakers,* Boston, 1950, p. 155. Dixon Ryan Fox, *The Decline of Aristocracy in the Politics of New York,* NY, 1919, p. 97.

12   Helen Young, "A Study of the Constitutional Convention of New York State in 1821," unpublished Ph.D. thesis, Yale University, 1910, p. 84.

13   Casais, *op. cit.,* p. 266.

isfied with the duty on salt; and a faction of the Tammanies. The final vote tallied 75,000 for and 45,000 against.

The judgment of students of the convention has been uniform: Dixon Ryan Fox called it a victory for "prudent democracy";[14] Helen Young, a victory for "moderate Republicans";[15] and John Casais called its reforms "mild."[16]

1846 Convention

The issues that generated support for a convention in 1846 were, by and large, the same issues addressed by delegates when it met. These were demands for greater use of elections to fill key posts, reform of the judiciary, control over legislative power to incur debt, modernization of the law on ownership and tenure of land, and alterations in how corporations were formed and their powers. This convention resulted in widespread changes in the way New York was governed. It may be regarded as the state's most "radical" convention, yet the choices it made for the Constitution were not the most extreme it considered.

The decisions of the 1846 Convention reflected the democratization movement that had been sweeping the country between 1820 and 1850. More statewide offices in the executive branch and local posts were made elective. Senate terms were reduced from four to two years. The judiciary was also subject to the Convention's exercise in participatory democracy; it was made elective and, in theory, open to service as judges by lay persons.

This democratic impulse notwithstanding, the Convention's decision to divest the senate of its power, as part of the Court for the Corrections of Errors, to pass on the constitutionality of legislation, gave the newly created Court of Appeals the position of the highest court in the state. This placed judicial review exclusively in the hands of the judicial department.

Another major reason for the calling of the Convention was the financial morass created by the state's funding of canals. The Convention adopted a series of limits on the use of the state's credit by private individuals or associations, and placed a one million dollar limit on the aggregate debt the state could accumulate. Additional long-term debt had to be approved by the people in a referendum. Restrictions placed on legislative power to pass special or local legislation included a provision

---

14   Fox, *op. cit.*, p. viii.

15   Young, *op. cit.*, p. 136.

16   Casais, *op. cit.*, p. 266.

that prohibited creation of corporations by special law, a practice used to advantage some and exclude others. Even here exceptions were permitted. More radical attempts to cripple corporations, for example by eliminating their limited liability, were rejected in spite of great public resentment of them. Delegates both recognized that more extreme measures might cripple corporations entirely and found it difficult to draft constitutional language that would address abuses without creating unwanted consequences. Finally, they left the matter to the legislature under a broadly worded provision meant to provide no more than general direction.

A third problem that prompted the 1846 Convention was the system of land tenure, especially in the communities along the Hudson and in much of the southeastern third of the state. An anti-rent movement had grown out of discontent with the limitations on ownership connected with manorial leases. Farmers rioted in the 1840s in protest. The Convention ratified already existing legislation, removing the last vestiges of the feudal system in New York. But it refused to make these provisions retroactive, doing little for those remaining tenants currently bound to the land.

Concerning rights, the Convention added to the Constitution protections against excessive bail and cruel and unusual punishment and eliminated the prohibition against clergy serving in office. Divided on the issue of African-American suffrage, they left the matter to the voters to resolve in a separate amendment on property qualification. It was soundly defeated.

As mentioned above, the 1846 convention reorganized the judiciary, laying the basis for New York's modern court system. It established the Court of Appeals (replacing the old Court for the Correction of Errors and Impeachment), abolished the chancery, and established a new Supreme Court with jurisdiction at law and equity. Finally, delegates added the provision which required that the question of whether to hold a constitutional convention be submitted to the voters every twenty years.

No doubt there were constitutional provisions adopted in 1846 that did not have their intended effect. Some created new problems, as was the case with the decentralization and diffusion of power in the executive branch. Others even compounded the problems they were meant to solve, e.g., the provisions limiting the legislature's ability to accumulate debt or lend its credit. However, one would be hard pressed to point to any major or controversial issues taken up by the convention that were not part of the pre-convention debates and for which it provided an extreme or divisive solution.

1867 Convention

The 1867 Constitutional Convention was the first to meet as a result of the every twenty year requirement. It was supported by the "Radical Republicans" who had gained control of New York in the 1860s under the leadership of Governor Reuben Fenton and saw it as the capstone to their postwar reconstruction program. Their major goals were elimination of the property qualification for African-Americans, canal reform, reform of the judiciary, and elimination of corruption. A committee on legislative reorganization also recommended major restructuring of the legislature.

The Convention rejected most of these recommendations regarding legislative restructuring. It did, however, place additional restrictions on the power of the legislature. Many of these were prompted by the belief that the legislature was abusing its power by favoring special interests, particularly the railroads.

Confusion regarding the governor's veto power was eliminated and that power was strengthened by the requirement that two-thirds of all members *elected* rather than two-thirds of those *present* was required to override a veto. Some executive consolidation was undertaken.

The judiciary was subject to major overhaul, with the objective of depoliticizing the courts. A Court of Appeals was created, with six associates and one chief justice, as were eight intermediate appellate districts. Supreme Court judges would no longer sit on the Court of Appeals. Terms of the Supreme Court were extended from eight to fourteen years. With the exception of the Court of Claims, these reforms were submitted as separate amendments and approved by the electorate. An amendment to be submitted in 1873 on whether to make the judiciary appointive was, however, voted down.

The convention was the first to address the status of cities; it had as one of its major goals the granting of a degree of relief for them from the "intermeddling of the legislature."[17] Some modest home rule powers were granted to cities, and their mayors given more responsibility and leadership in city government.

The convention added a new article dealing exclusively with corruption, and attacked it too in provisions concerning canal administration. Additionally, it provided in the Constitution for free common schools. Alterations in the state Bill of Rights included a prohibition against

---

17 *Proceedings and Debates of the Constitutional Convention of the State of New York, 1867-1868*, 5 vols., Albany, NY: 1868, IV, p. 2927.

unreasonable searches and seizures, addition of a right to confront witnesses, and allowance for fewer than twelve jurors for trials in justice courts.

The omnipresent African-American suffrage question was caught up in the rapidly changing politics of race in New York and the Northeast. Again it was submitted as a separate amendment. Along with the Constitution itself, it was again defeated.

The initial judgment of the proposed Constitution was negative. The major newspapers in New York City and the *Nation* magazine, for example, judged its accomplishments unworthy. Whatever the immediate reaction, the accomplishments of the convention could in no sense be termed radical or extreme. Indeed, the subsequent judgment of the state's citizens was positive, as most of its major recommendations, in one form or another, have been incorporated into the constitutional law of the state.

1894 Convention

In the 1890s in New York, concerns about party machines, bosses, and political corruption exercised the minds of reformers organized in burgeoning nonpartisan municipal reform organizations.[18] When Republicans finally gained control of the 1894 Constitutional Convention they formed a loose alliance with these independent activists, assuring that their concerns and approach received a sympathetic hearing.

The 1894 Convention sought through electoral reform to "purify" the electoral process, that is, to reduce the control of the party machinery in the cities, particularly New York City and Buffalo. In this they were partly successful. Closely related, and deeply affected by the issue of corruption, was the question of home rule for the cities. The measures taken to achieve home rule were, however, far less substantial than reformers desired for two reasons. First, big cities were Democratic bastions (and home rule might therefore mean Tammany rule). Second they continued to be regarded as centers of corruption and incompetence, not worthy of self governance.

The most partisan results of the 1894 Convention were constitutional provisions for reapportionment that subordinated New York City in

---

18   The following passages on the 1894 Convention draw on the research of Samuel T. McSeveney, *The Politics of Depression Political Behavior in the Northeast 1893-1896,* NY: Oxford University Press, 1972; Richard L. McCormick, *From Realignment to Reform: Political Change in New York, 1893-1910,* Ithaca, NY: Cornell University Press, 1981; Robert Crosby Eager, "Governing New York: Republicans and Reform 1894-1900," unpublished Ph.D. thesis, Stanford University, 1977.

state politics and assured Republican legislative dominance far into the future under almost all foreseeable electoral circumstances. A measure to prohibit all sectarian aid to education, the anti-Catholic "Blaine Amendment," was the most controversial measure approved by the convention. But an even more "radical" proposal was defeated; it would have prevented aid to the many charitable institutions run by the various religions.

The reorganization of the courts was the major nonpartisan and noncontroversial measure adopted by the convention. Additionally it dealt with canal policy, revised the militia article, established the first statewide system of education in the country, and adopted a conservation article that included the famous "Forever Wild" provision protecting the major forests of the state. Progressive in their day, accepted in ours, none of these can be characterized as extreme.

In light of Republican dominance of the convention and that party's apprehension concerning immigration, the growth of the cities, and all the changes associated with these developments, it is remarkable that more radical changes were not adopted in 1894. The delegates rejected a proposal recommending to the Congress of the United States an amendment that would prohibit the state from granting citizenship to aliens. No votes were even taken on proposals to require English for voting or a requirement for literacy. And the convention rejected an attempt to mandate naturalization six months before exercise of the right to vote, settling instead on ninety days.

If the 1894 Convention can be faulted, it would not be for proposing radical and dangerous constitutional provisions, but for failure to take bolder measures to confront industrial and urban problems.[19] Restoration of decent municipal government seemed far simpler than the profound and complicated questions raised by the Depression of 1893, the rise of organized labor, and increased monopolization in the corporate world. Avoidance and caution would be descriptors most appropriate to the work of the 1894 Convention. Buried in committee were proposals that: protected labor unions from anti-conspiracy laws; broadened employers' liability for accidents; created a court of labor management; limited workings hours in nonagricultural jobs; barred women and children from working in "exhaustive occupations"; granted municipal home rule; provided for the initiative and referendum; and mandated public ownership of transportation facilities and utilities.[20]

---

19   Crosby, *op. cit.,* p. 52; McCormick, *op. cit.*, p. 53.

20   McSeveney, *op. cit.*, p. 81.

1915 Convention

The 1915 Convention was held without the benefit of any significant popular agitation or support, and in contrast with that of 1894, reflected a convergence between Democratic party and reform interests. The convention was called by Democrats in 1914, two years before the date specified in the 1894 Constitution for the consideration of the mandatory question. Confident of their political strength and buoyed by recent political success in capturing all branches of the government, Democrats were anxious to undo the reapportionment provisions of the 1894 Constitution.

Simultaneously, a collection of reform groups, loosely aligned under the label "Progressives," had been advocating reorganization of the government, especially the executive branch. This goal had numerous supporters in academia, government, and among business executives. Its elements included consolidation of administrative activities in fewer single-headed departments; focus of executive authority and responsibility in the governor's office; adoption of an executive budget system for the state; and reduction in the number of statewide and local elected officials, "the short ballot."

A third constitutional issue likely to be addressed again at the 1915 Convention was home rule. As noted, the 1894 Convention made only token efforts to provide autonomy for cities; two decades later, most observers agreed that these steps were inadequate.

The lack of excitement concerning a convention was manifest in the fact that, despite growth in the electorate, the total vote on whether to call it was less than half that on the question in both 1866 and 1886. Holding a convention was approved by the slim margin of 153,322 to 151,969. When, to the consternation of the Democrats, the Republicans won a majority of delegate seats, the question of a change in the reapportionment provisions became moot. That left executive authority, departmental reorganization, efficiency in government, and nonpartisanship as the central issues.

The Constitution adopted by the Convention provided for an executive budget, consolidated and streamlined executive offices and departments, and a shortened list of elective state offices. In addition it addressed problems plaguing the judiciary, authorizing the legislature for the first time to establish juvenile courts. The Convention also granted more meaningful home rule powers for the cities, proposed women suffrage, provided for absentee registration, and added an equal protection clause to the New York Constitution. It overhauled the canal policy of the state, for the first time comprehensively defining the canal system. Though not particularly sympathetic to the demands of labor, delegates did extend the section dealing with workers' compensation to injuries and deaths, and prohibited manufacturing tenements known as "sweatshops."

The proposed Constitution was defeated overwhelmingly, two to one against approval. There was a lack of interest by the public (foreshadowed by the meager turnout for the convention call). Opponents, strange bedfellows, were numerous: organized labor, the Progressive Party, regular Tammany Democrats in New York City, and upstate Republicans. The reasons were varied: some voted against the Constitution because they thought it too radical (upstate Republicans) and some because it was too conservative (labor). Tammany Democrats disliked the status quo on apportionment and the "weak" home rule provisions. Progressives felt the Constitution to be a threat to their party's status in the state.

Undoubtedly the Constitution contained bold initiatives, but were they radical or dangerous? The verdict of history is "No." In the following twenty years most of the major recommendations of the convention became the constitutional law or public policy of the state.

1938 Convention

Proponents of the 1938 Constitutional Convention had a variety of goals. The Citizen's Union argued for greater home rule for cities, and suggested that the piecemeal amendments adopted between 1894 and 1938 had created much obsolete or partially inapplicable matter in the state Constitution, which needed to be excised. Democrats who supported the convention still had reapportionment on their minds. The American Labor Party desired measures that would deal with social and economic problems, advance civil liberties, and ban discrimination based on race, nationality, or religion. Other civic groups urged an appointed judiciary, appointment rather than election for the comptroller and attorney general, permanent voter registration, and reform of the tax and debt provisions concerning local finance.

A major reason for the lack of a concerted statewide effort for constitutional reform was the fact that between 1915 and 1937 reformers had achieved a number of their major goals: executive organization, an executive budget, and a degree of home rule for the cities. The convention question passed, though it was opposed by most of the state's major dailies.

When convened, convention delegates were not inclined toward bold innovations. This moderation was rooted in its lack of a popular mandate for significant constitutional change, Republican control of the proceedings and the constitutional traditions of the state. The advanced social welfare policies added to the constitution — concerning welfare, housing, and a labor bill of rights — entrenched policies previously enacted by the legislature.

The convention did create a single comprehensive article on local finance, but rejected proposals for: public takeover and development of the power resources of the state; compulsory automobile insurance; and banning all billboard advertisements on scenic highways and parkways. An attempt to provide state finance to denominational schools died in committee. A proposal to allow religious instruction in public schools in the faith of pupils with parental consent was also rejected, but aid in the form of transportation costs was approved.

In summing up, the leading students of the 1938 Convention called its work "middle of the road conservatism."[21]

1967 Convention

Between the public's rejection of the mandatory constitutional convention question in 1957 and 1967, when the legislature in New York put the question to a vote, organized pressure from a variety of sources was brought to bear on behalf of constitutional reform. The focus of these efforts was upon general simplification and modernization of the document. Additionally, despite the passage in 1961 of an amendment revising and expanding local government powers, the fiscal problems of municipalities operating under tax and debt limits continued in the state. Other groups called for amendments to achieve court reform. The problems plaguing the courts had been the subject of a number of reports by temporary commissions and Bar Associations. But U.S. Supreme Court reapportionment decisions in 1964, declaring parts of the state Constitution's provisions on reapportionment void, were the decisive factor in the decision of the legislature to call for a convention.[22]

Democrats, benefiting from the Lyndon Johnson landslide, captured both the Senate and the Assembly in 1964. Interested in continuing themselves in power, they sought and gained voter approval of a convention, which

21 Vernon A. O'Rourke and Douglass W. Campbell, *Constitutional Making in a Democracy: Theory and Practice in New York State,* Baltimore: John Hopkins Press, 1943, p. 211.

22 *WMCA* v. *Lomenzo*, 322 U.S. 633 (1964).

they believed, accurately as it turned out, they would control. In the election for delegates, "repeal of the Blaine Amendment was by far the most significant popular issue."[23] Not surprisingly, other issues that surfaced included judicial reform and legislative reapportionment.

The convention's main work concentrated on state and local finance, home rule, judicial reorganization, the Blaine Amendment, the voting age, reapportionment, and welfare reform. Court merger proposals floundered on the political arguments for separate courts, especially surrogate courts. On suffrage the convention did not muster sufficient votes to reduce the voting age to 18, but did authorize the legislature to choose an age between 18 and 21.

One of the most radical proposals submitted at the convention was for a 150-person unicameral legislature; it did not make it out of committee, though it generated banner headlines. A bipartisan redistricting commission was approved to decide future reapportionment decisions. Referendum and legislation by petition proposals were defeated as they had been by every convention since 1894. The Blaine Amendment was repealed. With the Democratic and Republican leaders of the convention, most of the political leadership throughout the state and most delegates committed to its repeal, the result was not surprising.[24]

In the face of Republican skepticism, the Democratic convention majority gave state and local governments greater power and flexibility to cooperate with each other to meet the challenges facing the state.[25] One example is a finance proposal that would have freed the state from the referendum provision requiring approval for long-term debt. The new proposal allowed the state to accumulate debt for capital expenditures without referendum approval when the debt service amounted to less than 12 percent of the state's average revenue in the prior two years.

The convention also added a new community development article that authorized a comprehensive array of programs to achieve community development, job training, creation of jobs, and housing. A new conservation bill of rights sought to significantly broaden the role of the state in protecting and fostering scenic beauty, as well as conserving and protecting natural resources.

---

23 Henrik Normann Dullea, *Charter Revision in the Empire State: The Politics of New York's 1967 Constitutional Convention* (unpublished Ph.D. thesis, Syracuse University, 1982), p. 145. A revised version of this thesis is being published under the same title by the Rockefeller Institute Press as a companion to this volume.

24 *Ibid.*, p. 344.

25 *Ibid.*, pp. 209-213.

Regarding rights, an attempt to place a right to bear arms in the state constitution failed. Instead the convention called for further restrictions on the sale of firearms. A proposal to ban busing used for integration purposes was also defeated. In fact, the convention strengthened the anti-discrimination clause of the constitution — including sex, age, and physical handicaps — thus adding for the first time a "little" equal rights amendment to the New York Constitution. An amendment banning abortion went down by voice vote, as did one barring from public employment those who advocated overthrow of the government. A move to allow for preventive detention was also rejected.

In contrast, a requirement that state and local agencies open their records to the public was adopted. Delegates also adopted bold measures that transferred the cost of the welfare system to state government and committed the state to the goal of providing free higher education to all who qualified.

After the new Constitution was placed before the public, opposition came from most major newspapers, civic groups such as the League of Women Voters, the New York Civil Liberties Union, the NAACP, and Protestant organizations. Governor Rockefeller remained noncommittal, but his budget director warned of an 80 percent rise in state taxes to pay for some of the provisions.[26] Republicans opposed the document, while Democrats conducted what has been described as a "non-campaign."[27]

The convention's bold initiatives proved too much for the state's voters to swallow all at once, but they could not be said to be particularly dangerous or extreme. The politics of rejection centered ultimately on the repeal of the Blaine Amendment. Even here, opponents agreed that the amendment had become largely symbolic and would not alter in any significant way the state's relationship to sectarian educational institutions. State and national legislation and court decisions had moved government to a more accommodationist position with regard to public aid to religious schools.

As in previous years, although the voters rejected the Constitution, many of its recommendations have subsequently been approved by constitutional amendment or legislation.[28]

---

26   *Ibid.*, p. 499.

27   *Ibid.*, p. 500.

28   Henrick Normann Dullea, *The 1967 Constitutional Convention: Outcome and Impact* (Albany, NY: Rockefeller Institute Special Report, Series No. 3, SUNY, 1984), p. 14.

Conclusion

New York's nine constitutional conventions have remained near the center of the political spectrum, sometimes moving in the direction of a pragmatic liberalism, other times toward a moderate conservatism. Though theoretically unlimited, conventions have in fact been limited by the constitutional tradition they inherit, the resistance of major parties to further political experimentation in the forms and techniques of government, and the particular configuration of interest groups of the time pursuing their various objectives.

As the most careful scholarly review of the 1938 Convention concludes, although conventions may be legally unrestrained as to the scope and character of their actions "the empirical evidence . . . makes it clear than any convention functions within very effective practical limitations."[29] The notion that a politically organized and well established community is a *tabula rasa* upon which a constitutional convention may inscribe whatever is agitating the minds of delegates is "scarcely a credible one."[30]

In New York, constitutional change has taken place incrementally, creating a tradition of continuity, and resulting in a heavily detailed, policy oriented document. Legal guarantees that a convention will not adopt extreme and divisive measures are not possible, but the state's constitutional tradition, the inevitable need for compromise in a state characterized from its beginnings by religious, ethnic, and social pluralism, and the fact that the state's voters must approve all the proposals of the convention, make the specter of "Pandora's Box" a theoretical possibility rather than a real probability.

---

29   O'Rourke and Campbell, *op. cit.*, p. 26.
30   *Ibid.*

Constitutional Revision in 1967: Learning the Right Lessons From the Magnificent Failure[1]

Henrik N. Dullea

The notion of a periodic constitutional convention to reshape the structure and policies of government has been with us in New York for a century and a half. Since 1846 the state Constitution has required that New Yorkers have presented to them every 20 years the question of whether a constitutional convention should be convened to amend and revise the state's basic charter. Sometimes the answer has been in the affirmative; sometimes not. Sometimes the end products of a convention have been ratified and put into place immediately; other times they have been rejected.

In almost every instance, however, the occasion for a convention has generated intense debate about fundamental public policies as well as about the structure of state and local government.

Why People Fear Constitutional Change

For many people, the very notion of such a fundamental debate is frightening. Whatever their ideological approach to everyday politics, New Yorkers, like most American voters, are increasingly conservative when it comes to their institutions of government. We are less and less inclined to tinker with our structures. In large measure, that is because our society has been relatively free from widespread social turmoil. But it is also because more and more people (judges, legislators, governmental officials, special interest group representatives, and so-called public interest

---

1   The material contained in this paper is drawn substantially from Henrik Normann Dullea, *Charter Revision in the Empire State: The Politics of New York's 1967 Constitutional Convention,* unpublished Ph.D. dissertation, Syracuse University, 1982. A revised version of this work is being published by the Rockefeller Institute Press as the companion to this volume.

group lobbyists alike) have such an enormous stake in the accumulation of policies, benefits, and perquisites reflected in our constitutions as currently crafted.

In fact, most residents of the state are unaware that New York has a *state* Constitution. Those who do know the document exists guess that the state Constitution is something like the one that governs the federal government — a brief document that protects individual rights and liberties and defines the responsibilities and structure of the major branches of government. They therefore come to its consideration with a view inculcated by generations of elementary and secondary school civics teachers, emphasizing respect for the Constitution as one of the fundamental sources of stability in our society. These citizens would never imagine that the state Constitution contains, sometimes in excruciating detail, everything from the width of ski trails in the Adirondacks to procedures for the issuance of local debt for water and sewer systems.

New York's Constitution, like those in other states, contains the accumulated results of literally thousands of political debates. From the rights of persons accused of crimes, to the exemption from real property taxation afforded to charitable organizations, the Constitution is a living political document that reflects the balance of political forces at many different points in history.

Constitutional conventions are a threat to that balance. They essentially provide the opportunity to reassess the sum product of all those ad hoc decisions. If we were to use a fiscal analogy, they take a giant step toward zero-based budgeting as opposed to incrementalism. They afford the opportunity to question whether those collective decisions of the past can deal *effectively* with the challenges of today, let alone those of tomorrow.

Changing a constitution thus creates uncertainty and risk. For many, even people who acknowledge the need for change, when their specific interests are engaged the devil they know is preferable to the devil they don't. From this derives *Dullea's First Law of Constitutional Revision Dynamics*: For every group passionately committed to the reform of a particular constitutional provision, there is an equal and opposite group fiercely determined to preserve that same provision, which has provided it with either an important benefit or protection over the years.

With the next constitutionally mandated referendum on whether or not to hold a constitutional convention scheduled for November 1997, the debate has begun on the desirability of such an event. Former Governor

Cuomo has spoken out frequently and strongly in favor of such a gathering. When not antagonistic, the general response has been cautious. For many observers, the proof of the pudding was the history of the 1967 Constitutional Convention. It produced a dramatically shortened document that would have totally replaced the 1894 Constitution that remains in force today. But it was rejected by the voters by a three-to-one margin at the polls.

If the voters defeated that Constitution by such an overwhelming margin, skeptics ask, how could anyone seriously suggest that we now march down that particular path of constitutional revision once again?

The 1967 Experience

What did happen in 1967?

If you listen to many of the skeptics today, you'd hear these descriptions: "The legislators ran the entire show and nothing got done." "They gave away the store to New York City." "The policies they adopted would have bankrupted the state." "The only thing they were interested in was fattening their own pensions." "The interests of the people were never represented."

Are these descriptions accurate?

Taking our cue from former Governor Al Smith, that great genius of New York State's political history, "Let's look at the record."

Why Was the Convention Called?

Who was responsible for New York State's last constitutional convention in 1967? When you think about it carefully, one possible answer is Lee Harvey Oswald.

Without the assassination of John F. Kennedy, we would not have had the Johnson landslide; nor would we have had the initiation of the Great Society, the election of Robert F. Kennedy as New York's junior senator, and the first transfer of political power in the New York State Legislature since the Great Depression. Each of these events played a major role in the decision of the electorate in November 1965 to set the wheels in motion for the 1967 Convention.

It has been said repeatedly by casual commentators on this last encounter with comprehensive constitutional revision that "We should learn the lessons of history." Well, history may in some ways be instructive, but the specific forces that led to the creation of our last constitutional convention are certainly unlikely to repeat themselves.

Pressure for a convention had been building up for some time. It was an article of faith in Democratic party platforms during much of the century that a constitutional convention would be necessary to end the pattern of political discrimination against New York City.

Governor Averill Harriman's first Annual Message to the Legislature, in 1955, called for a constitutional convention to reapportion both houses of the Legislature on the basis of population, and it repeated Governor Herbert Lehman's request for the popular initiation of constitutional amendments.

Nelson Rockefeller's first New York State job was service as chair of the Temporary State Commission appointed by Harriman and the legislative leaders to review the issues to be considered by the voters in 1957. That referendum narrowly failed to secure approval. Although 61 percent of the New York City voters who cast a ballot on the referendum supported the call for a convention, that margin was insufficient to overcome the 38 percent vote against throughout the rest of the state.

A second major factor contributing to the public's desire to hold a convention was the structural chaos in the Legislature arising from "one man, one vote."

The three famous cases to remember are: *Baker* v. *Carr, Reynolds* v. *Sims,* and *WMCA* v. *Lomenzo.*

In December 1964, the lame-duck Republican majorities in the Senate and Assembly passed the infamous redistricting Plans A, B, C, and D (the Reapportionment Compliance Act) in the wake of the Johnson landslide. All but Plan A were found by the federal courts to be unconstitutional, and the State Court of Appeals invalidated that plan as well, as violative of the state Constitution. The Court of Appeals directed the legislature to adopt a new apportionment plan and recommended that a constitutional convention be convened as soon as possible. The state's highest court's order was subsequently set aside by the federal courts. Chaos reigned.

A third, driving force behind the call for a convention was Howard J. Samuels of Monroe County. Long before he was appointed president of the New York City Off Track Betting Corporation and became popularly known as "Howie the Horse," the "upstate Canandaigua industrialist" was pushing his message of structural reform. As a prelude to seeking the 1966 gubernatorial nomination, Samuels formed his Citizens Committee for a

Constitutional Convention to promote the view that a new, modern Constitution would allow state government to be run in a businesslike fashion. He favored dropping arcane provisions, strengthening the executive's ability to manage, and switching to a unicameral legislature.

The popular mood in the mid-1960s was also affected by the startup of Lyndon Johnson's Great Society. Responding to urban unrest and a new presidential determination to alleviate the incidence of poverty in America, Great Society programs raised fundamental questions about the ability of existing governmental structures — including those relationships that exist between and among the federal, state, and local agencies — to meet the complex demands for the generation and implementation of social policy.

In its faith in the ability of government to meet social needs, this era was far different from the Clinton-Gore "reinventing government" activities of today. Basic to the time was an assumption that government *could* solve the nation's problems; it simply had to be given the wherewithal to do so.

The 1965 Referendum

The 1965 referendum was approved by a comfortable margin of 233,000. In view of the almost total lack of organized opposition, however, the victory was surprisingly narrow. As in 1957, New York City was overwhelmingly in favor. The difference was that the remainder of the state voted only narrowly in opposition. Upstate editorial support for reapportionment combined with general demands for constitutional simplification, legislative reform, court consolidation, and local government home rule to provide the enthusiasm required to overcome the latent negativism present in all New York State referenda.

Generally less than half of the voters who go to the polls in a general election choose to cast their ballots for or against the myriad propositions, questions, and constitutional amendments presented for their judgment, informed or otherwise. In 1965, 52 percent of those who went to the polls cast a ballot on the Convention referendum, 48 percent in New York City and 55 percent in the rest of the state.

How Were the Delegates Selected?

Many of the delegates ultimately elected to serve in the 1967 Convention had no knowledge of constitutional conventions until *after* the 1965 referendum campaign. More of the district delegates had evidenced an early interest than those who served at-large. Many nonlegislators had little sense of the issues that would be likely to be voted upon at such a convention, but simply wanted to be where the action was.

Often aspiring delegates were political leaders in their own right and therefore did not have to go to anyone else to secure their nomination. On the Democratic side, there were former New York City Mayor Robert F. Wagner, Assembly Speaker Anthony Travia, Assembly Majority Leader and Queens Democratic Chairman Moses Weinstein, long-time Albany Mayor Erastus Corning, Erie County Chair Peter Crotty, Liberal Party Statewide Chair Donald Harrington, and the Liberal party's labor leaders, Alex Rose and David Dubinsky. On the Republican side, Senate Majority Leader Brydges, Assembly Minority Leader Perry Duryea, and Monroe County Executive Gordon Howe called the shots on their own nominations. (New York's senior United States Senator, Jacob Javits, ran but was defeated on the Republican at-large slate.)

Geographic balance was important upstate in multicounty senatorial districts, as were ethnic and racial considerations in the New York City metropolitan area.

The at-large slates were named by each party's state convention. The Democrats, led by Robert Kennedy, had tried to get a bipartisan slate with the Republicans, but the latter were not interested. The Democratic slate was put together by Robert Kennedy, Frank O'Connor, the 1966 gubernatorial candidate and Queens county district attorney, and Binghamton's John Burns, the state chairman.

Many of the Democrats thought the Republican at-large slate was unbeatable. It included Javits, former U.S. senator and then Court of Appeals Judge Kenneth Keating, former Comptroller and Lieutenant Governor Frank Moore, Syracuse Mayor Bill Walsh, J. Lee Rankin (John Lindsay's corporation counsel), Fordham Law Dean William Hughes Mulligan, and Bill Benseley, the head of the New York State Farm Bureau. The GOP even nominated two enrolled Democrats — Mrs. Ruth Gross of Great Neck, past president of the New York State Association for the Help of Retarded Children, and Santiago Grevi, a member of the State Narcotics Control Commission. Both Gross and Grevi said they were "Rockefeller Democrats."

The Democrats had primary contests in 17 of 57 districts; Republicans in 7 of 57; and the Conservatives had two. Not surprisingly, there were no primaries for the Liberals. Republican primaries were most likely in competitive districts; they were rare in rural and strong Republican suburban areas. Despite all the time, effort, and money expended in the 27 primaries occurring in 24 districts, only two insurgents were able to defeat the regularly designated candidates of either major party. The designating process alone constituted election in the 19 safe districts (ten Democrats, nine GOP) that had no primary contests.

The 1966 General Election Campaign

In the general election, convention candidates were often lost in the shuffle of other campaigns, either intentionally or unintentionally. Many delegate hopefuls never campaigned at all. There was a low rate of voter interest in the campaign, abetted by the effort of many delegates to avoid being forced to take public positions on issues.

The overwhelming impact of the Blaine Amendment debate, concerning constitutional restrictions on aid to parochial education, was readily apparent in the general election: 90 percent of the delegates I surveyed for my study of the convention mentioned this issue as a subject of concern throughout the campaign, while no more than one-third referred to any other subject.

Reapportionment and judicial reform were subjects mentioned overwhelmingly by Democrats, not Republicans. By contrast, local government and matters related to the forest preserve were mentioned as popular subjects much more frequently by Republicans than by Democrats. The "frequency of amendment, cumbersome document" issue was mentioned by only one delegate in my interview cohort, hardly indicative of a broad-based mandate for fundamental constitutional reform.

The general election produced a Democratic/Liberal convention majority, with the former holding 102 seats and the GOP/Conservatives had 84. As Donna Shalala noted in her study of the convention, the key to the Democratic victory at the district level was their ability to pick up 13 seats in nine districts that were simultaneously sending a Republican to the Senate. By contrast, the Republicans were able to gain only one seat in each of two districts electing a Democratic Senator. The Democratic strategy of selecting well-known public officials as candidates was a big factor, as was the issue of third-party endorsements.

The 13-member Democratic/Liberal at-large slate was elected, while the two Democrats who had not received Liberal endorsements (due to the Liberals' desire to endorse Javits and Rankin) were defeated by the GOP/Conservative endorsements for Moore and Benseley.

Who Were the Delegates?

Lawyers comprised 66.7 percent of the convention delegates. The at-large slates had fewer lawyers, 40 percent versus 69 percent for the district delegates. There were more "other professionals" (academics and social workers) elected on the at-large slate than in the district delegate slots. The only farmer among the delegates was the GOP's at-large delegate, Bill Benseley.

Religious representation among the delegates generally reflected the estimated population of the state at the time.

Only 17 percent of the delegates had no prior governmental service, whether appointed or elected. Thirteen delegates, six Democrats and seven Republicans, or 7 percent of the total, were presently serving as state legislators, joined by one Democratic member of Congress. No incumbent legislator seeking election at the district level was defeated, although Nassau GOP chairman Senator Edward Speno lost as a member of the Republican at-large slate. If you add former legislators to the mix, 19 of the 101 (18%) Democrats had served in the Senate or Assembly; for the Republicans, the ratio was 26 of 85 (31%). Of the total convention membership, 45 of 186 or 24 percent had state legislative experience.

As striking were the 28 delegates who had served in one or more capacities in the state's judicial system: 15 percent of the total. Fourteen Democrats and five Republicans were sitting judges.

In total, 50 percent of the Democrats and 48 percent of the Republicans had held some form of political party office in their careers.

What does all this show? As I have written previously, "The political process employed in the nomination and election of delegates produced a Convention membership strikingly similar in personal characteristics to that found in the State Legislature. The absence of significant interest in constitutional issues at the time of their selection was likely to produce a Convention geared to political pragmatism rather than to structural reform."[2]

If There Were Only 13 State Legislators Among the 186 Delegates, Why Does Everyone Say That It Was Dominated By Legislators?

The image of legislative control of the Convention stemmed from Assembly Speaker Anthony Travia's rapid and successful drive to lock up the

---

2   Ibid. at 175.

convention presidency immediately after the election. None of the other potential candidates (for example, former chief judge of the Court of Appeals Charles J. Desmond, Mayor Wagner, or Bernard Botein, presiding judge of the Appellate Division's First Department covering Manhattan and the Bronx) made the required effort.

With the defeat of Frank O'Connor in the gubernatorial election, Travia was the dominant Democratic leader in the state. Once Travia's leadership of the convention was clear, the Republicans saw no alternative but to select Senate Majority Leader Earl Brydges of Niagara County as their leader. The subsequent appointment of Assembly Majority Leader Moses Weinstein and Assembly Minority Leader Perry Duryea to comparable positions only solidified the image.

The Rules of Procedure for the Convention were based on the Rules of the Assembly, giving to the president of the convention an enormous power to appoint all committee chairs and members and to control the flow of debate. All committee power for the last three months of the convention shifted to the Rules Committee, which the President both chaired and controlled.

The replication of the legislature's leadership structure in the convention strongly affected the public's perception of the convention as a truly separate body with the potential to adopt significant reforms, particularly reform of the legislature itself. I conclude elsewhere, however, that ". . . the actual demise of the prospects for structural reform was far less the product of the elevation of the legislative leaders to positions of power than to the predisposition of the rank and file delegates elected by the people."[3]

Were The Convention's Leaders United In Their Goals?

Convention President Travia announced his goal on opening day: "a new and simple Constitution that will permit our State and localities to solve their problems in a working partnership with the federal government." The Constitution should be amended, Travia thought, to let governments — or at least the state government — govern.

Alone among the opening speakers, Senator Jacob Javits referenced the politically volatile specific subjects of replacing the Blaine Amendment with the First Amendment to the Federal Constitution, reducing the

---

3   Ibid. at 207.

voting age from 21 to 18, encouraging intergovernmental compacts, and broadening the taxing and borrowing powers of the state and local governments. His Republican colleagues were much more cautious, proclaiming their willingness to amend the document but not to sacrifice its many protections against governmental activism.

Was There Nothing But Partisan Fighting in the Convention?

While there was substantial partisan conflict within the convention, unanimous and near-unanimous votes did occur on many articles, especially those incorporating verbatim the text of the existing Constitution. Especially regarding the tax and finance article, arguments for simplification and consolidation gave way before considerations of stability and familiarity.

In the convention, 1,405 propositions were introduced, 1,322 by individual delegates and the rest by committees. By contrast, that year 6,091 bills were introduced in the Assembly, 4,545 were put forward in the Senate, and 1,129 were ultimately sent to the governor. Individual propositions did influence the outcome of committee deliberations and contributed to the drafting of committee-offered propositions — a practice in sharp contrast with the legislature's up or down verdict on individual legislator's bills.

Of 198 total roll calls at the convention, 29 were completely unanimous and 43 others had less than 15 percent in opposition, for a total of 36 percent. There was a fairly high degree of conflict involved in the debates over the Bill of Rights, the proposed repeal of the Blaine Amendment, and the Education, Judiciary, and Suffrage articles, as well as over the format for presentation of the Constitution to the people.

Ninety of the 198 votes, and 71 percent of the controversial votes, were party opposition votes — that is, roll calls with a majority of each party's delegates in opposition to each other. The level is significantly higher than that found in the Assembly in this same period.

Twenty-six (30 percent) of the 88 party opposition votes — involving the Bill of Rights, Executive, Judiciary, and Suffrage articles — saw the convention minority Republicans on the prevailing side. Even on party votes — that is, those with more than 90 percent of each party's votes against each other — the Republicans twice prevailed, once on an Education article dealing with school district aid from the state, and again on the effort to reconcile two sections of the proposed local government article. In both instances, the hour was late and Democratic absences from the chamber allowed the Republicans to deny them the absolute majority vote required to adopt the provision.

There were several additional issues that generated very intense party conflict. No Republican votes were given in support of constitutional provisions reducing the governor's appointment power over the Public Service Commission by sharing it with the two houses of the legislature meeting in joint session, eliminating his power to appoint a comptroller and an attorney general when the legislature was not in session.

Other significant, controversial, party-opposed issues included: dropping the voting age to 18; creating a system of "free higher education"; state assumption over a ten-year period of the local costs of welfare; increasing the ability of the state to insure debt without recourse to public referendum; and applying the "one man, one vote" principle to units of local government.

Fourteen significant and controversial measures were placed in the Constitution with the majority support of both parties. These included the repeal of Blaine and the final passage of the Suffrage and Judiciary articles.

Two proposals were adopted by a majority of Republicans and a minority of Democrats — the attempt by a conservative Democratic delegate from Queens to block the reduction of the voting age to 18; and a Nassau Republican's amendment to insure that the proposed state funding of the courts would include the district courts in the New York City metropolitan area.

Both parties were united in support of the Labor article. Public employees had just received the Taylor Law in 1966, and state leaders wanted to avoid further conflict. Additionally, judicial determinations on reapportionment brought the same reaction from delegates on both sides of the aisle.

Democrats were split on the proposed creation of a state Department of Criminal Justice and on the Judiciary article. The Republicans, on the other hand, had more difficulty uniting on votes involving the legislature, future constitutional conventions, and local government.

There was no significant difference in the average party support score for delegates from the two parties. The average Democrat was with his or her party 87.25 percent of the time, and the average Republican 86.08 percent of the time with his or hers.

Legislators as a group in both parties had average party support scores lower than those of their parties as a whole. This was the case for the sitting judges as well, although it was not as pronounced for the Republican judges. It may well be that the greater political experience of legislators and judges gave them slightly greater confidence in staking out independent positions than was the case for those who were relative newcomers to a legislative-style political environment.

Interestingly, the upstate/downstate dichotomy evident in the vote on whether to call a convention remained a better predictor of voting behavior than party affiliation.

The highest average index of cohesion was attained by the Democratic at-large delegates. This reflects their role as the Convention's leadership team and their greater-than-average commitment to many of the reform measures that divided their party colleagues. The least cohesive Democratic delegation was its largest — the senatorial district delegates elected from Kings County.

The Result and Its Presentation

When the Democratic majority made the determination to present the revised Constitution to the voters in a take-it-or-leave-it single package, the fate of the proposal was probably sealed.

Anthony Travia was true to the goal he had established on opening day. He and his colleagues, from their perspective, had indeed crafted "a new and simple Constitution that will permit our State and localities to solve their problems in a working partnership with the federal government." They had cut in half the size of the existing cumbersome document. They had prohibited discrimination based on sex. They had empowered the state and its localities to grapple with emerging problems such as community development, urban education, and social services, setting forth a new vision of social policy that they believed would maintain the state as a major partner with the federal government in the domestic agenda. The state assumption of the costs of welfare, provided for over ten years in their draft Constitution, is a transfer of responsibility still called for today, 27 years later, by local officials in every region of the state. Though less than radical in structural reform, they had prohibited "gerrymandering" of any kind and had established a legislative redistricting commission.

While the voters and the editorial writers may have had some level of enthusiasm for structural reform in the legislature and the judiciary at the time of the referendum on whether to hold the convention, the overwhelming majority of delegates actually elected to serve in the convention had given precious little attention to these issues. Once they had succeeded in substituting the Federal Constitution's First Amendment for the text of the Blaine Amendment, many of the delegates felt that they had fulfilled whatever campaign promises they had made.

These social policy innovations in the state Constitution had come at a price. Not only did they suggest the possibility of future massive state tax increases, but they were to be accomplished in part by removing the requirement for voter approval of all general obligation state debt. Along with the popular antagonism to the convention generated by its style of legislative leadership and the intensity of its religious controversy, the removal of the referendum requirement for the creation of new state debt gave the opponents of the draft charter a phenomenally appealing rallying cry.

Why were not such issues as Blaine and the debt referendum stripped out of the basic document and submitted directly to the people for determination? Some have argued that the reason was Travia's commitment to the Catholic hierarchy that he would give them the best hope of the repeal of Blaine by burying it in the entire document. I would disagree. He and other members of the convention's leadership recognized the political difficulties associated with their determination, and even the Church's leadership ultimately took pains not to be associated with the all-or-nothing approach.

Rather, those in command of the convention concluded that they had done what they sought out to do. They had come together for six months and debated an extraordinary litany of issues, from wiretaps and eaves-dropping devices to relations between church and state, many of which would have received only fleeting consideration in the day-to-day operations of the state legislature. Their product was not a consensus document, but it was one that had been forged in the crucible of sharply divided partisan debate. It was a new document, not a series of piecemeal amendments to the charter of 1894. Its articles were woven together into a coherent whole. While its provisions might not appeal to one and all, it deserved to be judged, they thought, as a whole on its merits.

Rejection at the Polls

And judged it was.

The voters in every county of the state rejected the proposed Constitution. The relatively narrow statewide approval of the referendum calling for the convention was based on a solid foundation of Democratic support, no organized or visible Republican opposition, consistent media endorsements, and the enthusiasm of reform-oriented groups. The ratification vote, by contrast, retained a hard core of Democratic support, but it generated near-universal opposition from the Republican leaders, the media, and good government organizations. The final vote was 3,487,513 against; 1,327,999 in favor.

Many of the proposals included in the 1967 Constitution were adopted through the legislative amendment route. Others remain under debate decades later.

"Was the process worth it?," you ask.

I can only reply, "You should have been there!"

1967 Constitutional Convention Delegates

Prepared by Michael Leo Owens

Table 1
Occupation at the Time of
the Constitutional Convention

Occupation	District	At-Large	Total
Attorney*	85 (49.5%)	3 (20%)	88 (47%)
Business	35 (20%)	1 (7%)	36 (19%)
Judge	22 (13%)	2 (13%)	24 (13%)
State Legislator**	13 (7.5%)	0 (0%)	13 (7%)
Union Official	4 (2.5%)	2 (13%)	6 (3%)
Professor	3 (2%)	2 (13%)	5 (3%)
Media Professional	3 (2%)	1 (7%)	4 (2.5%)
Mayor	3 (2%)	0 (0%)	3 (2%)
Congressman	2 (1%)	0 (0%)	2 (1%)
UN Official	0 (0%)	1 (7%)	1 (.5%)
Clergy	0 (0%)	1 (7%)	1 (.5%)
Farmer	0 (0%)	1 (7%)	1 (.5%)
Other	1 (.5%)	1 (7%)	2 (1%)
Total	171 (100%)	15 (100%)	186 (100%)

Sources: the 1967 Convention Directory of Delegates and Henrik Dullea's *Revision in the Empire State* (Ph.D. Dissertation, Syracuse University, 1982).

*   Those that categorized themselves as full-time practicing attorneys.
**   19 state legislators (12 Assembly and 7 Senate) were elected as delegates to the convention during the 1966 election cycle. However, 10 did not seek or gain reelection to the legislature during that same election.

Table 2
Government Professional Experience*
(Not limited to time of Constitutional Convention)

Level (total #)	District	At-Large	Total
Elected (87)			
Executive	0 (0%)	1 (6.7%)	1 (.5%)
Judiciary	20 (12%)	2 (13.3%)	22 (12%)
Assembly	25 (14.5%)	0 (0%)	25 (13.4%)
State Senate	7 (4%)	0 (0%)	7 (3.7%)
Assembly and Senate Combined	8 (4.5%)	0 (0%)	8 (4.3%)
Congress	3 (1.7%)	0 (0%)	3 (1.6%)
Mayor	4 (2.3%)	1 (6.7%)**	5 (2.6%)
Other Local***	15 (9%)	0 (0%)	15 (8%)
Appointed (66)			
Executive or Agency Dept.	21 (12%)	0 (0%)	21 (11%)
Legislative Staff	8 (4.5%)	1 (6.7%)	9 (5%)
Judicial Staff	6 (3%)	0 (0%)	6 (3.3%)
Federal	1 (1%)	2 (13.3%)	3 (1.6%)
Local****	28 (16%)	0 (0%)	28 (15%)
None (33)			
No Experience	25 (14.5%)	8 (53.3%)	33 (18%)
Total *****	171 (100%)	15 (100%)	186 (100%)

*	Elective experience (47%); appointive experience (35%); none (18%).
**	This person also had state legislative experience bringing the total of delegates with legislative experience to 41.
***	Includes district attorneys, town supervisors, city council members, etc.
****	Includes assistant district attorneys, commissioners, career civil servants, etc.
*****	15 (8%) of the delegates had at one time or another served on a NYS Constitutional Revision Commission.

Table 3
Political Party Affiliation

Party	District	At-Large	Total
Democrat	89 (52%)	10 (67%)	99 (53%)
Republican	82 (48%)	2 (13%)	84 (45%)
Liberal	0 (0%)	3 (20%)	3 (2%)
Total	171 (100%)	15 (100%)	186 (100%)

Table 4
Gender

Gender	District	At-Large	Total	1967 State Percentage
Men*	163 (95%)	13 (86%)	176 (95%)	48%
Women**	8 (5%)	2 (14%)	10 (5%)	52%
Total	171 (100%)	15 (100%)	186 (100%)	100%

* Includes 9 Blacks and 5 Hispanics
** 8 Whites, 1 Black, and 1 Hispanic

Table 5
Racial Background

Race	District	At-Large	Total	1967 State Percentage
European-American	158 (93%)	12 (86%)	170 (91%)	80%
African-American	8 (5%)	2 (13%)	10 (6%)	11%
Hispanic-American	5 (2%)*	1 (7%)	6 (3%)	7.5%
Other	0 (0%)	0 (0%)	0 (0%)	1.5%
Total	171 (100%)	15 (100%)	186 (100%)	100%

* One of the delegates was a Republican.

Table 6
Religious Background

Religion	Delegation Total*	State Percentage
Catholic	76 (41%)	40%
Protestant	68 (36%)	40%
Jewish	37 (20%)	15%
Other	5 (3%)	5%
Total	186 (100%)	100%

Source: Henrik Dullea's *Charter Revision in the Empire State* (Ph.D. Dissertation, Syracuse University, 1982).

*   Estimations

Amending the New York State Constitution Through the Legislature

Gerald Benjamin

and

Melissa Cusa

One of the two means for obtaining constitutional change in New York State is the passage by the legislature of an *amendment* at two sessions separated by an intervening general election. That amendment becomes a part of the Constitution if it is then ratified by the people at referendum (Article XIX, Section 1). The second method of change is *revision* through a constitutional convention. Again if ratified by the people, revisions proposed by a convention become part of the Constitution. In the extreme case, revision may encompass the complete replacement of one constitution by another.[1]

The distinction between amendment and revision is significant. Though amendments may be quite extensive in scope and effect, amendment through the legislature is generally used for more limited changes. Revision, through the convention, is almost always more widespread, encompassing the entire document. It thus becomes evident that choice of a method of constitutional change has implicit within it a second choice, about the desired scope of change.

Those who oppose a constitutional convention for New York argue that necessary changes may be obtained through the legislative route. They assert that this more focused method is both less costly and less politically

---

1   As argued in the chapter "Amending and Revising the New York State Constitution" in this book, the distinction between revision and amendment is more clearly established in other states than it is in New York. In states with a constitutional initiative process, courts have used this distinction to determine whether a change through initiative is an amendment, and therefore permissible, or a revision, and therefore impermissible. The distinction is made in this chapter for New York based on conventional understanding and clarity of analysis, not definitive determinations by the New York courts.

risky than a convention. Those who favor a constitutional convention say, in contrast, that the legislative route has not produced necessary changes in recent years. This is especially a problem, they suggest, when possible amendments are seen by legislators to be contrary to their own political interests, or the institutional interests of the legislature as a whole.

In order to inform this debate, this chapter seeks to examine systematically what constitutional changes have been proposed in the legislature in recent years, and what action has been taken upon them. In addition to exploring the workings of the process of constitutional change through the legislature, such an analysis is useful for establishing the range of matters that have been placed by at least one legislator on the state's agenda for constitutional change in the recent past, and that therefore might find their way onto that agenda again should a convention be held.

Even if efforts at constitutional change through the legislature are found to have produced limited results in recent years, easing this process may provide an alternative to holding a constitutional convention. In addition to examining the New York experience, this chapter therefore explores the methods of change through the legislature employed in other states. The object here is to determine whether alternative approaches make this avenue easier than the approach employed in New York, with an eye again toward the implications for New York.

Amendments Introduced

Legislators may introduce constitutional amendments for any number of reasons. Consider the following possibilities:

* to act on *personal conviction* or ideological commitment — conservative members seek to insert a definition of "family" that excludes homosexual partner relationships, or liberal members seek an affirmative "right" to shelter;

* to please a *constituency* group — members from the Hudson Valley introduce a provision allowing casino gambling in reaction to requests from the hotel industry;

* to make a *partisan* statement — minority party members introduce proposals in each legislative house that would weaken majority control;

* to align themselves with good government or "reform" movements within or outside the state — this category includes

proposals for a unified judiciary, "merit" judicial selection, term limitation, initiative, and referendum;

※ to further *empower their house or branch* of government, or weaken another branch — for example, the proposal adopted allowing the legislature to call itself into special session;

※ *to react to a court decision* by the Court of Appeals, interpreting the state Constitution, or the U.S. Supreme Court, interpreting the national Constitution — for example, amendments that would permit the distribution of political leaflets in shopping malls, or extend the rights of criminal defendants;

※ to change a provision regarded negatively after it has gained visibility *as a result of political events* — proposals altering the budgetary process, or the method of filling vacancies in statewide elective office;

※ to remove detail, largely technical, that prevents the government from *taking advantage of more efficient ways of doing business* — for example, debt reform provisions adopted in 1993; or

※ to *allow some government action that can only be taken by amendment,* because of the nature of restrictions or constraints put into the Constitution in the past — proposals adopted in recent years, permitting certain construction in the Catskill and Adirondack preserves.

This wide range of potential motivations encourages the introduction of constitutional amendments by legislators. Moreover, there is no limitation in New York, as in some other states, on the number of bills or resolutions a member may introduce, and considerable staff assistance is provided for drafting and other technical work. There is thus little disincentive and are few barriers to the introduction by members of constitutional amendments.

A Senator or Assembly member may have a serious commitment to a constitutional amendment he or she proposes. But often amendments are advanced without such a commitment. A proposal may be put in the legislative hopper with little expectation that it will pass, or even receive serious consideration. Members who have no intention of pushing a matter may introduce it to take political pressure off themselves, or to take credit for its introduction while campaigning. Or they may simply be seeking to start a debate, with an understanding that their proposal may come to be taken seriously years later, after it gains visibility, or when the political environment changes. Staking out political and policy turf is also involved. By putting an amendment in early, a legislator effectively "claims" it as his or her issue for the future.

Under these circumstances, it is likely that numerous constitutional amendments will be offered in the New York State legislature. In fact there have been 4,437 proposed in the state during the 26 years between 1967 and 1993, or an average of 171 a year (Table 1). Legislators were most active in proposing amendments in the period immediately following the 1967 Constitutional Convention. A peak was reached in 1969, when 417 ideas for constitutional change were filed in the legislature. Average levels of activity have been much lower in recent years. In 1988, only eighty amendments were proposed. In general, too, there has been more activity in odd than in even-numbered years, reflecting the need to reintroduce measures after the election of a new legislature to keep them alive.

Table 1 also looks at how frequently amendments to the New York State Constitution have been proposed, by article. Such an analysis cannot separate the more serious proposals from the less serious, nor can it distinguish wide-reaching ideas from those that are more narrowly focused. It is useful, however, for understanding those areas in which legislators felt some impulse, however small, to put a matter on the legislature's agenda, and to take the responsibility for sponsorship in doing so.

The table reveals that patterns of amendment introduction in New York have varied substantially since 1967, when the last state constitutional convention was held. Based upon average numbers of amendments proposed, and the persistence of proposals over time, five categories emerge.

Some articles have been the focal points for frequent amendment efforts for most years over the entire quarter of century. These include the state Bill of Rights (Article I), the judicial article (Article VI), state finance provisions, including the budgetary process (Article VII), the provision concerning officers and civil departments (Article V), the legislative article (Article III), and the local finance article (Article VIII).

A second group is made up of articles that, on average, attracted moderate levels of amendment activity, largely but not entirely in the decade or so immediately following the last constitutional convention. These include the provisions on suffrage (Article II), the executive (Article

Table 1 — Number of Bills To Amend the Constitution From 1967-1993

	Article																				
	1	2	3	4	5	6	7	8	9	10	11	12	13	14	15	16	17	18	19	20	Total
1967	11	19	5	5	4	3	8	10	5	1	1	0	11	6	1	3	1	1	9	0	104
1968	30	24	1	7	14	10	29	2	1	5	13	1	0	13	5	8	4	8	11	1	187
1969	36	28	32	10	34	61	40	59	19	6	22	0	10	6	2	15	13	16	8	0	417
1970	37	50	25	9	20	37	29	27	5	1	12	0	9	6	1	7	5	14	4	0	294
1971	34	17	42	11	24	37	29	35	3	0	8	0	6	6	3	14	8	13	6	0	296
1972	18	12	32	12	17	29	16	17	6	1	3	0	3	3	3	8	4	8	4	1	197
1973	24	11	28	13	12	47	34	17	7	0	1	0	9	5	7	8	5	9	5	2	244
1974	18	4	24	9	9	33	26	19	2	0	0	0	8	6	2	4	0	1	7	5	177
1975	22	3	37	9	20	50	35	18	5	0	0	0	12	3	1	5	2	2	6	9	240
1976	10	3	25	10	16	34	33	5	1	3	2	0	11	5	0	5	2	1	8	7	181
1977	6	10	22	12	11	60	25	13	5	7	3	0	7	3	1	9	0	1	3	11	209
1978	20	5	9	3	11	13	9	3	3	3	0	0	7	2	2	7	3	1	5	12	118
1979	11	9	14	1	13	17	11	13	2	2	1	0	4	4	3	14	1	0	3	15	136
1980	27	1	5	0	9	20	6	3	2	1	0	0	1	2	2	2	1	0	3	13	96
1981	15	5	7	3	20	31	14	9	2	4	1	0	2	5	2	10	0	0	2	11	142
1982	19	3	12	1	12	21	8	5	4	5	1	0	2	4	2	8	0	0	1	6	114
1983	17	5	6	2	16	38	12	8	3	4	1	0	3	6	1	8	1	0	2	6	139
1984	20	4	6	4	15	6	15	6	1	2	2	0	1	3	0	7	0	1	1	5	99
1985	15	4	6	13	15	28	16	8	2	4	1	0	1	6	0	7	3	1	2	5	137
1986	14	2	7	4	11	23	6	3	1	1	1	0	2	7	0	4	0	2	1	3	92
1987	13	4	12	12	12	26	11	3	1	1	3	0	3	6	0	3	0	4	0	5	119
1988	11	2	8	6	7	19	7	0	0	0	1	0	3	6	0	3	0	2	0	5	80
1989	12	5	4	11	6	21	28	2	1	2	2	0	2	4	7	0	0	5	0	6	118
1990	11	3	5	6	9	22	11	6	2	5	2	0	2	4	3	2	0	1	0	6	97
1991	12	5	7	8	8	37	27	3	2	2	5	0	2	4	5	1	0	2	0	10	140
1992	11	3	16	7	9	14	29	6	2	2	5	0	3	5	0	1	0	1	2	9	123
1993	11	2	17	11	14	24	20	6	5	1	4	0	2	4	0	1	1	1	5	8	137
Average	18.0	9.0	15.3	7.4	13.6	28.2	19.8	11.3	3.4	2.3	3.6	0.0	4.7	4.7	1.9	6.1	2.0	3.5	3.6	6.0	
Sum	485	243	414	199	368	761	534	306	92	61	96	1	126	127	52	164	54	95	96	161	
Grand Total	4,437																				

IV), public officers (Article XIII), conservation (Article XIV), and taxation (Article XVI). (Article XX is included in this category because various entirely new provisions have been proposed by legislators with this number.)

A third category includes articles that show low levels but relatively persistent change effort: These are the articles on home rule (Article IX), education (Article XI), and housing (Article XVIII). The final group of constitutional articles appear to be relatively settled. Some have attracted virtually no interest at all. For others, attempts to amend them have been infrequent in recent years, though a few have experienced brief bursts of activity. These are the articles on corporations (Article X), defense (Article XII), canals (Article XV), social welfare (Article XVII), and amendment of the Constitution itself (Article XIX).

Substance of Proposed Changes

A substantive review of proposals to amend the New York State Constitution from 1967-1993 is indicative of the agenda for constitutional change that has emerged from the legislative process during the period. It is through this first step that certain matters enter the political environment. The themes and tendencies that may be elicited from these proposals is thus revealing of what has been on New York State's "mind" concerning constitutional change in recent years. These tendencies can be categorized as focusing on: (1) state and local relations; (2) distribution of power between the executive and legislative branches; (3) rights; (4) structure and scope of government; and (5) judicial reform.

State and Local Relations. Proposed constitutional amendments in this category are largely concerned with state and local spending and local authority in decision making. Combining both themes, many ideas introduced either directly or indirectly affected fiscal discretion. In the 1967-77 period, suggested amendments to articles on State Finance, Local Finance, Public Corporations, and Taxation (Articles VII, VIII, X, and XVI) and the amendatory process itself (XIX) addressed increased local control of total spending, the incurrance of debt, and allowable tax exemptions. Proponents sought increases in state liability for financing local improvements and public corporations; expansion of projects for which bonds might be issued; greater flexibility in bond type and repayment schedules; increases in both exclusions to debt and tax limits; and greater allowable percentages of revenue that might be raised by taxes. These reflect an interest in expanding New York State's ability to work for economic development and an interest in allowing a greater flexibility to localities, especially the largest ones, in financing their own operations.

During the late 1970s and early 1980s, the legislative agenda for constitutional change continued to suggest an interest in greater fiscal discretion for local governments and a desire for redistribution of power from the state to localities. Typical proposed amendments sought to require the printing of local fiscal impact on bills; increase local control over land uses; increase local options in debt and tax management; restrict legislative authority to create or dissolve counties; and enhance local authority to create laws and perform duties not directly prohibited by the Constitution. Matters specific to social welfare (Article XVII) also describe the home rule constitutional agenda. The consistent concern is state takeover of public assistance and medicaid programs.

Distribution of Power Between Branches. The last several decades are commonly regarded as ones of legislative resurgence in New York. It is thus not surprising that struggles to strengthen legislative authority, vis-à-vis the executive, have been part of the legislature's agenda for constitutional change. For all years studied, proposed changes to the Executive (Article IV) have been restrictive of the executive while expansive of the legislative branch, or have linked changes desired by the executive to proposals strengthening the legislature. (Exceptions were a few efforts in the early 1970s to increase the governor's authority to reorganize the executive branch.) For example, proposed increases in the time allowed to the governor to act on legislation, offered in the early 1970s, were tied with concomitant proposals submitted to increase legislative power to convene itself, act on its own agenda, and override the executive veto. Other constitutional changes proposed by the legislature have sought to limit the number of the executive's terms in office while increasing the length of legislative terms; grant the legislature appointment power for the office of lieutenant governor; allow legislative discretion in determining succession to executive offices; and create limitations on executive authority to grant reprieves, commutation, and pardons. Additionally, attempts to remove the need for a message of necessity from the governor to overcome the three-day constitutional waiting period for legislation, would enhance legislative and restrict executive power.

Another avenue for increasing legislative authority or restricting the executive is altering of the constitutional provisions relating to Officers and Civil Departments and Public Officers (Articles V and XIII). Some amendments offered sought legislative control over appointment and removal of the heads of state departments, for example, the Education

Department and the Public Service Commission. Alternatively, other proposals called for the election of the heads of these departments. Attempts to allow the legislature to bypass the twenty-department limit now in the Constitution were also advanced to permit the creation of specific departments, for example, a department of criminal justice.

In the last decade studied (1983-1993), efforts to restrict legislative authority have become more common, reflecting the antigovernmental environment of the era. Some proposals sought to limit the length of legislative sessions. The prime examples, however, are efforts to institute term limitations for legislators and authorize initiative and referendum (Articles XIX and XX).

Rights. Amendments concerning the Bill of Rights (Article I) are introduced into the New York State Legislature with relatively high frequency. However, examination reveals that almost half of all the ideas for changes to Article I were to authorize gambling throughout the state or in specific locations within the state. Gambling restrictions and attempts to change them in New York State happen to be in the section of the Constitution concerning rights, but they are not typically regarded as "rights " in a constitutional sense. These proposals are better classified as examples of desires to generate revenue and increase control of the fiscal environment.

Amendments concerning rights have involved both rights enhancing and rights constraining proposals. Within the traditional notion of constitutionally defined rights — limits on government's capacity to regulate the behavior of individuals — rights enhancing proposals included expansion of the freedom of speech and extension of rights to privacy, private property, abortion choice, and gender equality. These were most prevalent during the first part of the period of study. In contrast, rights constraining proposals, more evident during the latter portion of the period, included defining "family" to exclude homosexuals and alternative family structures, eliminating the right to abortion, and establishing English as the "official" language of the state.

Due process proposals are somewhat harder to classify. Waiving the right to a grand jury trial in criminal proceedings and protecting witnesses from intimidation appear to be restrictive of the rights of the accused. However, some believe grand jury trials in practice have little effect on verdicts, and that removing them from the Constitution may be an attempt to facilitate court proceedings.

Amendments concerning rights were also advanced in other parts of the Constitution. For example, proposed changes to the Suffrage article

(Article II) would facilitate voting, by establishing less restrictive registration procedures. Attempts to increase enfranchisement to diverse populations through the repeal of certain discriminatory age and literacy requirements were also introduced by members.

Scholars have noted the special place of positive rights in state constitutions. These are obligations placed upon the state to meet the social or human needs of its residents. Amendments to the New York State Constitution have been offered during the last quarter century that would advance "positive rights" to a quality and equal education, a healthful environment, and a decent place to live.

Structure and Scope of Government. As frustration with governmental gridlock has grown over the past decade, and as governments at all levels increasingly have been regarded as part of the problem rather than part of the solution, ideas for altering the structure of government and limiting its scope have gained. Term limitation and initiative and referendum have already been mentioned. Additional ideas have included a proposal for a unicameral legislature and a range of suggestions for the reform of the budget process to force timely action. Proposals to limit government also have included caps or restrictions on spending, taxing, and borrowing.

Judicial Reform. The Judicial article (Article VI) comprises about a quarter of the New York State Constitution. It therefore may be expected that it would be the focus of a large portion of the proposals addressing constitutional amendment. Topics of interest to some legislators concerning the judiciary article include: manner of nomination, selection, and determination of qualifications; the supervision of individual judges (conduct) and the system; the scope of duties and jurisdiction of courts; the structure of the system; and financial administration and responsibility. It has been argued that the detail in the Constitution regarding the third branch is attributable to the judiciary's interest in establishing its independent authority over itself. The courts are, after all, the final arbiters of the Constitution. The irony is, however, that to have this final say the leaders of the judiciary trade ease of change, even when they come to regard change in their institutional interest. The difficulty of achieving judicial reform has led recently to calls by leaders of the judiciary for a constitutional convention.

The number of amendments proposed to Article VI is also particularly interesting because this is the only article that maintains the same rank in Tables 1 and 2. That is, a proportionately large number of changes regarding the judiciary are both proposed in the legislature and offered to the voters for action. Proposals that involved major structural changes concerning the judiciary were voted on and passed at referendum during the period of this study. However, questions of unification and district representation in election processes and the selection of judges still remain unaddressed and on the agenda.

Changes That Have Passed the Legislature

During the period under study 61 constitutional amendments were passed by the legislature, or 1.4 percent of the number proposed (Table 2). This rate of "success" for amendments offered is substantially lower than for ordinary legislation either passed or adopted in New York, notwithstanding the fact that there is no gubernatorial veto possible for amendments.

Of amendments passed by the legislature, 41 (or 67.2%) were adopted by the voters at referendum. These constitute .9 percent of all amendments proposed during this period. This record is roughly comparable to rates of public acceptance in other states of constitutional amendments offered by state legislatures. It does appear, as intended by those who designed the amending process, that it is more difficult to amend the New York Constitution than to enact a statute in the state.

The legislature was most inclined to pass amendments to articles on the Judiciary (VI), Conservation (XIV), Local Finances (VIII), State Finances (VII), Corporations (VI), The Legislature (III), and Public Officers (XIII). As noted above, four of these areas were among those for which amending proposals were most frequent. The exceptions were the articles on Public Officers and Conservation, for which there were moderate and persistent levels of proposed amendment activity.

For each of five other articles, one amendment was passed over the quarter of a century period under study. These were Officers and Civil Departments (V), Canals (XV), Social Welfare (XVII), Housing (XVIII), and the Amending Clause (XIX). No amendments were proposed to the voters regarding the constitutional provisions concerning Suffrage (II), Home Rule (IX), Education (XI), or Defense (XII). The rank order correlation of constitutional articles for which amendments were proposed and articles actually amended by the legislature is statistically significant (Spearman's Rho = .48, significant at .05).

No more than a quarter of the constitutional amendments passed by the legislature in the twenty-six years under study involved fundamental changes in the structure of state government. The three amendments concerning the state judiciary passed in 1977 and approved by the voters

	(1) Introduced by Legislature (mean)	(2) Passed by Legislature	(3) Passed by Voters (#)	(4) Passed by Voters (%)
ARTICLE				
I	18.0	2	2	100%
II	9.0	0	0	—
III	15.3	5	2	40%
IV	7.4	0	0	—
V	13.6	1	1	100%
VI	28.2	16	9	56.25%
VII	19.8	6	5	83.33%
VIII	11.3	7	4	57.14%
IX	3.4	0	0	—
X	2.3	6	4	66.67%
XI	3.6	0	0	—
XII	0.0	0	0	—
XIII	4.7	4	4	100%
XIV	4.7	8	6	75%
XV	1.9	1	1	100%
XVI	6.1	1	1	100%
XVII	2.0	2	2	100%
XVIII	3.5	1	0	0%
XIX	3.6	1	0	0%
XX	6.0	0	0	—
TOTAL	164.40	61	41	67.21%

**Table 2
Constitutional Amendments Acted Upon
1967-1993**

NOTE: For an explanation of the data contained in column 1 (Amendments Introduced by Legislature) refer to Table 1.

were most important. They altered the selection processes for judges of the Court of Appeals, moved the state toward a unified system of court administration, and established a commission on judicial conduct. (There was a failed attempt to accomplish some of these goals through two amendments offered in 1975.) Five other amendments adopted during the period, several based on ideas developed at the 1967 Constitutional Convention, were of some structural significance. These provided the legislature the power to call itself into special session, removed the head of the state department of corrections from the chairmanship of the commission on corrections, permitted the waiver of grand jury indictment in certain cases, and permitted legislative extension of the terms of district attorneys, sheriffs, and county clerks from three to four years by ordinary legislation. If they had passed at the polls, the proposals extending local powers in community development, establishing a fifth judicial department, altering the amending process, altering the rules for erecting new counties and incorporating an equal rights amendment in the state Bill of Rights would have also provided for changes of some significance in the governmental system.

Though many of the remaining amendments that reached the voters during this period were of *policy* significance, they were not of structural significance. Exceptions to constitutional debt limitations for certain kinds of local borrowing and the extension of the borrowing limit for state guaranteed authority bonds for economic development are two examples of amendments that fall into this category. (Many other amendments were required for marginal change of detailed constraints upon the legislature.) Because of the "forever wild" provision in Article XIV, for example, eight constitutional amendments were needed to allow construction within the Catskill or Adirondack preserves or to permit the disposal or exchange of preserve land. Similarly, the detailed nature of the Judicial Article required constitutional amendment to alter the jurisdiction of certain state and local courts, provide flexibility in the assignment of judges, and allow their service beyond retirement.

Areas in which the public was most skeptical of legislative proposals for constitutional change were those that appeared to allow more spending, borrowing, or taxation. In seeking greater resources for economic development the legislature proved most persistent. For example, voters were asked six times to extend the limit on state guaranteed public authority borrowing for this purpose. The answer?: three times "Yes," three times "No."

One widely cited example of the voters reluctance to agree if the word "taxes" appears in a referendum question concerning constitutional change involves the attempt to allow incorporating federal tax provisions in state law by reference. Seeking to block the use of this technique to sneak matters past legislators unnoticed, the state Constitution forbids this practice. An exception was sought in this instance in order to simplify the process of achieving intergovernmental tax compatibility, and ultimately the process of filing tax reports by taxpayers. No new tax was involved. But the voters saw the word tax on the ballot, and twice voted this proposal down.

Summary: Change Through the Legislature in New York

Large numbers of constitutional amendments have been filed by legislators in New York State over the past quarter century. Key focal points have been judicial reform, state/local relations, the financing of government, governmental restructuring, individual rights, and the size and scope of government. In contrast, some areas of the Constitution — for example, the articles concerning corporations, defense, canals, and social welfare — have attracted very few change proposals.

Ideas for amendment often reflect or are reactions to developments in the larger political environment, both in New York State and elsewhere. Members' reasons for the introduction of constitutional amendments vary, with the actual hope of constitutional change only one of many possible motivations.

The passage of amendments does indeed appear more difficult to achieve than the passage of statutes. Few amendments seeking to restructure government or reorder the powers of the major branches actually emerge from the legislative amending process. This process is likely to bring to popular referendum ideas that enhance the power and discretion of elected decision makers, and relatively noncontroversial technical changes. The detail already in the Constitution concerning some policy matters produces the need for amendments to implement changes that might otherwise be handled by statute. The public is most skeptical of changes that appear to involve money, whatever their actual purpose or impact.

Comparisons With Other States

"A good amending process should guard against the extreme facility which would render the Constitution too mutable," James Madison wrote in the *Federalist Papers,* "and on the other hand it should guard against the extreme difficulty which might perpetuate its discovered faults."[2] Following this prescription, the initiation of constitutional amendments through the legislature in most states is purposely made more difficult than is the passage of ordinary legislation. Generally, this greater difficulty is achieved by one or more of three means:

1. requiring the maximum denominator for the recording of a majority (all members elected to the body, rather than those present or those voting);

2. requiring extraordinary majorities (three-fifths, two-thirds, or three-quarters); and/or

3. requiring passage more than once, often by separately elected majorities.

Additionally, constitutional amendment is made more difficult in some states by limiting the number of proposals that may be offered in any one year; by limiting the number of articles of the Constitution that may be changed in any year; and by limiting the substance of an amendment to a single purpose (though more than one article may be affected).

As noted above, the New York Constitution currently requires a majority vote of those elected in each house of two separately elected legislatures in order to offer a constitutional amendment to the public at referendum. It includes no limit on the number of amendments that may be made in a year, the number of articles that may be affected, or the content of amendments.

The Majority Required

Thirty-six states including New York require in their constitutions that a majority of members *elected* to each house vote affirmatively to pass ordinary legislation, making a majority more difficult to obtain than if the majority need only be of those voting. Twelve of the remaining states constitutions specify that ordinary legislative action be by a majority; a majority of those present; a majority of those present and voting; or a majority of those voting. In Massachusetts, New Hampshire, South Carolina, and Texas, the state constitution is silent on this matter.

---

2   See Quote by Wesley L. Lance in *Proceedings of the New Jersey Constitutional Convention,* August 21, 1947, at p. 695.

For constitutional change forty-five states require that legislative majorities in each house be of all those elected. Only Hawaii, Maine, Montana, Vermont, and Mississippi are exceptions. But all of these states require either dual passage or extraordinary majorities to amend their constitutions, adding extra hurdles to the process. In Massachusetts the majority must be of all members of both houses *sitting in joint session.* In Mississippi a two-thirds majority of those voting in each house must include a simple majority of those elected.

Extraordinary Majority as an Alternative to Dual Passage Requirements Like New York's

As illustrated in Table 3, there is a clear and strong relationship between the legislative majority required in each house for passage of a constitutional amendment and the number of times passage is required. The two passage requirement is negatively related to the extraordinary majority requirement. Most jurisdictions require either an extraordinary majority or passage at two sessions, but not both.

Half the state constitutions provide that an extraordinary majority of those elected to each state legislative house may act at a single session to offer a constitutional amendment for popular ratification. (Pennsylvania also provides this option for emergencies.) Four additional states require extraordinary majority action at some stage, with passage required at two sessions. Of these, Delaware requires two-thirds of each house to vote twice, but has no popular referendum requirement for amendment approval. South Carolina requires two-thirds of each house at first passage, and a majority at second passage *following* referendum approval. In Tennessee a simple majority of each house must be obtained for first passage, followed by a two-thirds majority at second passage. In Vermont two-thirds of the Senate must approve on first passage, along with a majority of the house; a majority of both houses then must be obtained on second passage. In Oregon a constitutional distinction is made between amendment and revision. Amendment may be by simple majority and single passage, but more extensive change through revision requires two-thirds in each house.

In eight states (including Massachusetts, where the joint session is used, as noted), a simple majority in each house with passage twice is required. Nine states require a simple majority at a single session to initiate amendment.

Finally, three states — Hawaii, New Jersey, and Connecticut — all with relatively recently adopted constitutions, offer two alternatives: passage at two sessions with simple majorities or single passage with

Table 3
State Constitutional Amendment
Through the Legislature
(Number of States and Percentage)

		Frequency of Passage Required	
		Once	Twice
	Ordinary	9	11
		17.0%	20.8%
Majority Required			
	Extraordinary	29	4
		54.7%	8.5%
			N = 53
			Tau b = -.4615

Note: Connecticut, Hawaii and New Jersey are included twice. They each have two different methods of constitutional amendment. Pennsylvania's ordinary, nonemergency method was used in preparing this table.
Source: Derived by the author from *Book of the States 1992-93* (Lexington, Ky.: Council of State Governments, 1992) pp. 22 - 23.

extraordinary majorities: three-fourths in Connecticut, two-thirds in Hawaii, and three-fifths in New Jersey.

New Jersey was the first state to allow the legislature to propose constitutional amendments by two different means. Between 1844 and 1947 amending the New Jersey Constitution required passage by two legislatures and then ratification by the voters at a special election. In an address to the 1947 New Jersey Constitutional Convention, Governor Driscoll described this process as "time consuming," "costly," and "substantially unworkable." In fact, the highly visible cost of holding a special election, $750,000 in 1947, was a major disincentive to constitutional amendment through the legislature. As summarized by one delegate, adopting these alternative methods "gives speed where it is necessary . . . and deliberation where it is proper."[3]

The Connecticut provision was adopted at its 1965 Constitutional Convention. Before the change, constitutional amendments in that state

---

3   See *New Jersey Proceedings*, August 21, 1947, at p. 606.

could be initiated in one house only and had to be passed by two-thirds majorities in two successive sessions before they could be submitted to the people. Many leaders regarded this process as too slow and too difficult. The possibility of acting in a single session with majorities of three-quarters in both houses allowed for swift action when there was a "an obvious emergency or an obvious correction to be made and where [there is] general approval."[4] The majority requirement was lowered when dual passage was used, allowing for careful consideration over time but making action somewhat easier.

It is unclear on its face whether the requirement of an extraordinary majority is a greater or lesser barrier to legislative proposal of constitutional amendments than a requirement for dual passage. But an analysis of state experience with amendments proposed in this manner during the period 1986-1991 indicates that a dual passage requirement for constitutional amendment is the greater barrier (Table 4). States that employed single passage and required a simple majority proposed 2.3 amendments a year during this period, about the same number of constitutional amendments proposed annually through the legislative process as in states that employed single passage and required an extraordinary majority. In contrast, states like New York that employed simple majorities and required passage at two sessions offered slightly less than one amendment a year on average (.9/year), while states that employed extraordinary majorities and dual passage offered an amendment about every two years (.6/year). Dual passage requirements, including New York's, resulted in strikingly fewer amendments offered through the legislature whether a simple or extraordinary majority was required.

Evidence from an earlier half-decade, 1966-1970, confirms this finding (Table 5). In those years, states that required single passage and extraordinary majorities for amendments proposed through the legislature actually offered more amendments on average annually (4.1/year) than states that used single passage and simple majorities (2.9/year). But as in the more recent period, these averages were higher than in states that employed dual passage, whether simple (2.2/year) or extraordinary (1.3/year) majorities were required.

These findings are reinforced by evidence from states that offer alternative means for constitutional change through the legislature. Presumably, with both alternatives available, the one most used will be

---

4   See Remark of Delegate Bernstein. *Proceedings of the Connecticut Constitutional Convention*, III, (October, 15, 1965) at p. 821. See generally at pp. 814-826.

Table 4
Average Number of Constitutional Changes Offered
Through the Legislature, 1986-1991

		States With	
		Single	*Dual Passage*
	Ordinary Majority	2.3	.9
States With:			
	Extraordinary Majority	2.3	.6

Note: 1. Amendments with local effects only not included.
2. Table is based upon data from 47 states. New Jersey, Hawaii, and Connecticut are excluded because they allow two methods of constitutional change.
Source: Calculated by the author from data supplied by Professor Janice May, University of Texas.

that which is easiest. According to the Deputy Counsel in the Office of Legislative Services in New Jersey, since 1981 dual passage with simple majorities has been used there three times, while single passage with extraordinary majorities has been employed about three times as frequently.[5] Contrary to the expectation when the alternative methods were adopted in Connecticut, single passage with three-quarter majorities in each house has become the norm there, as well. In the era in which options were available, dual passage was used only once, in a failed attempt in 1974 and 1975 to amend the Constitution to remove the straight party ticket lever from the voting machines there. This measure finally passed in 1985.[6]

Popular Ratification

The sovereign people, as the original source of their constitutions in democratic theory, must agree to changes in these basic documents. This is why all constitutional change processes in the American states (except that of Delaware) require popular ratification of constitutional amendments, however they are initiated. In most states ratification of legisla-

---

5   Telephone interview with Mr. Leonard Lawson, Office of Legislative Services, State of New Jersey, December 22, 1993.

6   Data on Connecticut was provided by the state library and is in the files of the commission in Albany.

		States With	
		Single	*Dual Passage*
	Ordinary Majority	2.9	2.2
States With:			
	Extraordinary Majority	4.1	1.3

Table 5
Average Number of Constitutional Changes Offered
Through the Legislature, 1966-1970

Note: 1. Amendments with local effects only not included.
2. Table is based upon data from 47 states. New Jersey, Hawaii, and Connecticut are excluded because they allow two methods of constitutional change.
Source: Calculated by the author from data supplied by Professor Janice May, University of Texas.

tively initiated constitutional changes is by simple majority vote on the amendment question. In a small number of states, minimum majorities or dual majorities are specified. There appear to be three reasons for this: experience with "voter fall-off" on constitutional amendments and other referendum questions; the particular geographic impact of some state constitutional provisions; and a perceived special need to protect particular constitutional arrangements from change.

Hawaii and Nebraska require a majority of at least 50 percent of the votes cast in a regular election to pass a constitutional amendment. At a special election, the minimum vote for passage is 30 percent of the registered voters. In Louisiana, if fewer than five civil subdivisions of the state are affected by an amendment, a majority must be achieved in them as well as within the state at large for passage. In Illinois the minimum majority is half of those voting in the election, and 60 percent of those voting on the question. In New Mexico, amendments on certain elective franchise and education matters must receive support from three-fourths of those voting in the state and two-thirds in each county. In Tennessee passage of amendments requires a majority of the number of citizens voting for governor.

New York's standard for passage of a constitutional amendment proposed through the legislature is the one most commonly used, and offers the lowest threshold for a positive outcome.

Annual Limits on the Number of Amendments Offered

An additional barrier to constitutional amendment in the states is a restriction on the number of amendments that may be offered in any one year, or on the number of articles that may be amended annually. Three states limit the number of amendments: Arkansas (to 3), Kansas (to 5), and Kentucky (to 4). Illinois limits the number of articles that may be changed in one year to three, and Colorado to six. In New Jersey, an amendment that fails at the polls may not be reoffered until three general elections have passed.

Adding requirements similar to these in New York would make constitutional change through the legislature more difficult.

Options for New York

If New York wishes to ease its method for proposing constitutional change through the legislature by adopting one or more practices currently used in other states, this review suggests three alternatives that are relatively widely employed:[7]

1. Replace the current requirement of dual passage by simple majorities in both houses of those elected with single passage by extraordinary majorities in both houses;

2. Change the base of the majority from those elected to those voting, while either retaining the current dual majority system or altering it as described in 1 above; and/or

3. Add a procedure for adopting an amendment through single passage of both houses by extraordinary majorities to the current provision, emulating the current practice in Connecticut, Hawaii, and New Jersey.

---

7   The *Model State Constitution* provides for constitutional amendments to be proposed by simple majorities of all members in both houses in a single session (New York: National Municipal League, 1963) Section 12.01 (b). The method used by Oregon for proposing constitutional amendment through the legislature (as distinct from revision) — single passage by a simple majority of those present — offers the lowest barrier to action of any method currently used. The first is not used in any state. The second is unique. Neither makes a distinction between the standard for proposing an amendment and that for passing ordinary legislation.

The Delegate Selection Process

A several year delay in calling a constitutional convention in the late nineteenth century because of a dispute over the method of delegate selection resulted in the 1894 provision detailing the delegate selection process in the Constitution itself. The Interim Report of the Temporary Commission on Constitutional Revision, issued in 1994, addressed concerns about whether this hundred-year-old process conforms to current federal constitutional requirements for the fair representation of minorities. It also considered criticisms about how the delegate selection process operated in the past, and offered proposals about how it might be improved. In this report, reproduced as the introductory essay to this section, the Commission recommended eased ballot-access rules and public financing for convention delegate campaigns, single-candidate voting for delegate elections, and prohibitions against "double-dipping" (for salary) by those elected to serve as delegates. The commission majority rejected, however, an idea widely under discussion that sitting legislators and judges be barred from service at a constitutional convention.

In the second essay in this section, Burton Agata explores the effects of applying the procedures generally applicable to elections in New York — partisan election with relatively restricted ballot access — to constitutional delegate selection. In the third, Richard Briffault demonstrates why one element of the delegate selection method prescribed in the Constitution — the use of State Senate districts for the election of three delegates, with each vote casting three votes — would make litigation under the federal Voting Rights Act almost certain.

Both Agata and Briffault suggest reforms that could be achieved by statute before the vote on whether to hold a convention to make delegate elections more competitive and avoid or mitigate the effects of potential federal constitutional litigation concerning the process. In his essay, Agata also outlines alternative approaches that would ease ballot access for convention delegate candidates. The second Briffault essay in this section explores alternative voting systems that would conform to both the requirements of the state Constitution and the federal Voting Rights Act. Also in this section, Michael Malbin looks at ideas suggested by some to make delegate selection more competitive, public campaign finance for delegate elections.

The Delegate
Selection Process

Temporary State Commission
on Constitutional Revision

The Opportunity for Constitutional Choice

Once every 20 years our state Constitution requires that New Yorkers vote on whether we wish to hold a constitutional convention. The next such required vote will be held on November 4, 1997, when a referendum will pose the question: "Shall there be a convention to amend the constitution and revise the same?" Whatever its outcome, this vote will provide a rare opportunity for New Yorkers to grapple with basic issues of governance as we enter the twenty-first century.

For any number of reasons, we may decline to call a convention. Or we may opt for a convention and thus begin a deliberative process that could result in our later being offered either an entirely new Constitution or a series of amendments to the existing Constitution.

Whatever our eventual decision, we will be participating in a constitutional choice of great importance to New York and its people that, absent a legislative initiative, will not arise again for another 20 years. It is therefore of fundamental importance that this opportunity be used wisely.

Political choices are rarely clearly defined. Moreover, they are rarely made with sufficient time to fully understand their implications. The time we have between now and November 4, 1997, thus makes our opportunity for constitutional choice even more exceptional. We know today the question we must answer. We know today when it will be asked. And we have more than three years to weigh the merits and consequences of alternative answers.

To use the time we have well, this Commission intends to foster a statewide discussion of the opportunity and risks presented by the mandatory constitutional convention question. We seek in this initial report, therefore, to begin a process of deliberation and debate — an open, robust, and informed airing of views on constitutional change in New York. Such a process will allow us to arrive at November 4, 1997, more knowledgeable about the state Constitution, more aware of ideas for changing it, more familiar with the change process itself, and clearer in our sense of priorities for state government in the twenty-first century.

If the people of New York decide to call a constitutional convention, the Commission believes that this convention should be as open, as fair, and as representative of the state as practically possible. With this objective in mind, the Commission chose early in its deliberations to explore how these goals might best be achieved. The result was an initial focus upon the delegate selection process for a possible convention.

Delegate Selection As a Priority Concern

Assigning priority to consideration of the delegate selection process for a possible constitutional convention is the consequence of four interrelated factors:

* First, if the voters vote "yes" on the referendum question, the selection of delegates is the initial step in achieving constitutional amendment or revision by the convention method.

* Second, any change in the delegate selection process for a convention that might arise from the 1997 referendum will require sufficient time to effect, whether by statute or constitutional amendment.

* Third, because of the fundamental importance of constitutional change, the Commission believes that obstacles to running for delegate should be removed and that the state's minority groups should have a fair opportunity to select delegates of their own choice. Reducing barriers to participation in the delegate selection process will aid in assuring that the broadest array of interests is heard at any constitutional convention.

* Fourth and finally, at the time of the Commission's establishment, public debate on delegate selection had already commenced, with several state interest groups expressing concern that the present system was too narrow and too difficult. Some interest groups pointed to the 1967 Constitutional Convention as an exercise in "closed politics." (Although this last convention did much good work, and some

of the fruits of its efforts were later adopted as amendments to the state Constitution, its overall product was rejected at the polls and its process left a bad aftertaste for many observers.) Other interest groups appear prepared to condition their judgment on whether to support or oppose a future constitutional convention on how participatory the delegate selection process for it proves to be. Consequently, the Commission thought it essential to examine, early on, the criticisms of the process that produced the 1967 convention and, where these seemed substantial, to explore alternative potential remedies.

The Existing Process

The selection of delegates to a constitutional convention is regulated by both Constitution and statute. According to the New York State Constitution (Article XIX), for each Senate district (presently 61 under a formula established in Article III, Section 4) there are to be three convention delegates, for a total of 183. Article XIX also provides for 15 delegates to be selected on a statewide (at-large) basis. Delegates must be elected at the general election next ensuing after the voters authorize a constitutional convention at referendum.

Subject to certain exceptions contained in Article XIX of the New York State Constitution, the regular election law provisions are applicable to the election of delegates to a constitutional convention. Thus, the at-large delegates would be subject to those provisions of Article 6 of the election law that concern designation and nomination of candidates elected by the entire state (e.g., 6-104[1]; 6-136[1]; 6-142[1]) and those delegates elected from senatorial districts would be subject to the counterpart provisions which cover elections from senatorial districts (e.g., 6-142[2](f) and its counterparts). These provisions address such questions as the number of signatures required on petitions, the form and content of petitions, and the like. Candidates for delegate would also be subject to the campaign finance laws.

Issues that arise as a consequence of the application of the election law to delegate selection are taken up in Section IV, below. The details of the existing process and its history are discussed in the paper by Professor Burton C. Agata of the Hofstra University School of Law (see page 435), and the chapter titled "Amending and Revising the New York State Constitution" on page 331.

Five Areas for Consideration

The Commission has divided its consideration of the existing process into five discrete areas: (I) *equity in representation*; (II) *ballot access*; (III) *financing delegate campaigns*; (IV) *incentives for service*; and (V) *qualifications for service*.

Equity in Representation

The Voting Rights Issue

Based on the analyses presented by its consultant, Professor Richard Briffault of the Columbia University Law School, and its counsel, Professor Eric Lane of the Hofstra University School of Law, the Commission concludes that the federal Voting Rights Act of 1965 (as amended) almost certainly covers the election of delegates to a state constitutional convention. The Commission has substantial concern that the use of existing Senate districts as multimember districts combined with at-large elections, as prescribed in the state Constitution for choosing delegates to such a convention, may violate the requirements of Section 2 of that act.

Multimember districts are red flags in the voting rights environment and they have been successfully challenged in a large number of voting rights cases. The reason for this is that multimember districts with at-large electoral mechanisms allow "a block-voting racial majority to control all the elected positions. Fifty-one percent of the population consistently decides 100 percent of the elections. In addition, although everyone had one vote, some voters were qualitatively less important than others because of the voter's or the candidate's race or both. As a result, the black minority was permanently excluded from meaningful participation."[1] It is more than reasonable to suggest that, based on New York's political demography and voting rights experience, the multimember delegate districts engender considerable potential for denying protected classes an equal opportunity to elect candidates of their choice.

While the Commission has not undertaken an exhaustive or dispositive analysis of the evidentiary information (see *Thornberg* v. *Gingles*, 478 U.S. 30, 1986), a preliminary review of relevant data suggests that a challenge under the Voting Rights Act might be sustained. For example,

---

1   Lani Guinier, "The Triumph of Tokenism,"*Mich. Law Rev.* 89, 1077, 1094; reprinted in Guinier, *The Tyranny of the Majority,* Free Press, 1994.

as Professor Briffault has written with respect to African-Americans and the multimember districts:

> Currently, African-Americans hold 5 of the 61 Senate seats, or 8.2 percent of the total, but African-Americans account for 21 of the 150 Assembly seats, or 14 percent of the total. Since New York's population is 16 percent African-American it appears that African-Americans are currently receiving nearly proportional representation in the Assembly, but much less representation in the Senate. Moreover, all the African-American senators are from New York City, whereas four of the African-Americans in the Assembly are from outside the City, suggesting that African-Americans outside New York City would be far more able to elect representatives of their choosing in smaller districts.

The historical lack of statewide minority electoral success would suggest that the provision for 15 at-large seats may minimize minority representation among their number. It is worth noting, however, the fact that two minority delegates were elected as delegates-at-large to the 1967 Constitutional Convention as a result of slating efforts of the Democratic party. While such minimization may be sustainable on the basis of the smaller number and proportion of at-large seats, and a need for a statewide perspective, their use remains somewhat in question, particularly in a context where the multimember districts themselves are open to attack. A Voting Rights Act analysis of the present electoral mechanisms, prepared by Professor Briffault, appears on page 445.

Voting Rights Remedies

Based on its conclusion that there is a reasonable possibility that the electoral mechanisms for delegate selection would, in whole or in part, be found in violation of the Voting Rights Act, the Commission has considered two broad categories of alternatives to counter the majority-enhancing effects of the constitutionally mandated electoral system: (1) those that retain the at-large and multimember districts, but moderate majority dominance of those districts by altering the electoral system; (2) those that replace the multimember districts with single-member districts.

In the first category we considered proportional representation briefly, and explored single- and double-candidate voting and cumulative voting. In the second category we explored creating 15 districts to replace the at-large seats, subdistricting present Senate districts, and utilizing

Assembly districts to replace the multimember districts. For a number of reasons discussed below, including especially the difficulty of effecting change through constitutional amendment, the Commission favors the retention of statewide at-large and Senate district based multimember districts for any convention that might result from the 1997 referendum. For the multimember districts the Commission proposes that the delegates be selected by a single-candidate[2] voting mechanism with each voter allowed one vote, rather than the present three votes.

The rationale for these recommendations is summarized below. For a detailed discussion of the various alternatives addressed by the Commission see the article by Professor Briffault on page 473.

1. Timing

The Commission is of the view that any revision to the delegate selection process should be accomplished prior to the constitutionally mandated 1997 referendum on whether there should be a constitutional convention. This view is based on two judgments by the Commission. First, the representativeness issue is an important factor in the debate over whether or not to hold a convention. Second, if a constitutional convention is mandated by the voters, waiting until after the 1997 referendum to address the Voting Rights Act issues may throw the convention process into chaos.

2. Statewide At-Large Delegates

The Commission believes that there is a compelling rationale for the preservation of at-large representation at a constitutional convention — the presentation of a statewide perspective by persons of statewide stature and reputation. Moreover, the opportunity to vote for a statewide at-large slate provides a real opportunity for supporters of historically weaker political parties in specific Senate districts to have a practical effect on the selection of the partisan majority at the convention. There are no sensible alternatives to statewide at-large seats for assuring the achievement of these ends. Either the abandonment of the at-large seats or the creation of fifteen single-member districts would sacrifice the statewide perspective.

The Commission has therefore concluded that the presence of statewide delegates in such a small number and proportion (7.6 percent of the total delegates) adds an appropriate perspective to constitutional

---

2   In voting rights law, this system is called "limited voting" as a term of art.

deliberation and, *in conjunction* with changing the electoral system for the selection of convention delegates in (multimember) Senate districts, will not adversely affect the opportunity of protected minorities to participate in the political process. Although it is possible that these statewide at-large seats may be found in violation of the Voting Rights Act (which can be judged entirely separately from the question of the validity of the use of an alternative electoral system within multimember districts), the Commission believes the relatively small risk is worth taking in light of the substantial potential they offer for enriching the deliberations of a constitutional convention, should one be called.

3. Alternative Voting Systems for Senate District Delegate Selection

a. The present multimember districts with single-candidate or double-candidate voting. Single- or double-candidate voting is a system under which a voter casts fewer votes than the total number of seats to be filled in a three-member district. Where there are three seats to be filled, each voter would be permitted to vote for one or two candidates, but not three. One effect of this voting system is to assure that a large enough and cohesive enough minority within a multimember district has a fair chance to win a seat.

The "threshold of representation" in a multimember district with single-candidate voting may be calculated using the formula $R = V/(V+N) + 1$, where R is the percentage of the vote that assures election, V is the number of votes a voter may cast and N is the number of seats to be filled. Thus with the use of state Senate districts to select three constitutional convention delegates as required by the state constitution, and with each voter casting one vote, a minority of 25 percent plus 1 is guaranteed to elect a delegate. And with each voter casting two votes, a minority of 40 percent plus 1 is guaranteed to elect a delegate.

A simple example further clarifies this point. Assume that a district is comprised of 100 voters who are to elect three delegates with each voter casting one vote. If an organized group within the district can deliver 26 votes to a single candidate, it would be guaranteed one of the three seats. This is because no distribution of the remaining 74 votes could result in three candidates each with 26 or more votes.

The Commission favors retaining multimember districts with each voter given one vote as a remedy to voting rights problems raised by the current state constitutional requirements for electing delegates to a constitutional convention for five reasons:

1. It is likely to provide protected minorities a fairer opportunity to select convention delegates of their choice;

2. It can, in all probability, be effected by statute (as opposed to requiring constitutional amendment);

3. It maintains the traditional Senate district base with all voters in the district facing the same choices;

4. It is the easiest of the multimember district mechanisms for the voter to understand and the government to implement. The voter will only be asked to vote for one candidate. Current voting machines can be employed with this system.

5. It has been accepted by federal courts as a remedy to voting rights problems in jurisdictions with multimember districts — Alabama, North Carolina, and Georgia in recent years. In this connection Professor Briffault notes in his memorandum:

> Limited voting systems have been adopted as part of settlement agreements in Voting Rights Act cases in twenty-one municipalities in Alabama. One study of 14 of those municipalities found that the number of seats in the local legislature was either 5 or 7, and the number of votes a voter could cast was either 1 or 2. Due to limited voting, African-Americans were elected to local legislatures in communities where they constituted 10.2, 14.6, 23.5, 26.3, 32.2, and 38.5 percent, respectively, of the population. African-Americans have been elected to county commissions and school boards in North Carolina under limited voting arrangements that provided for one vote per person in elections to three-member at-large boards in jurisdictions in which blacks accounted for 31 to 36 percent of the voting age population. Limited voting arrangements have also been adopted as a result of settlements of vote dilution lawsuits in Augusta, Georgia, and the Phoenix Union High School District School Board. (For footnotes, see page 473.)

The Commission's recommendation of one vote per person reflects its desire to optimize the possibility that federal voting rights requirements will be met within the confines of the use of Senate districts as multimember districts for the selection of convention delegates. Adherence to these requirements will maximize the likelihood that each voter will have some impact on delegate selection. This recommendation is made with the understanding that such an approach may reduce the number of delegate choices that each voter can affect. As noted above, however, under the Commission's recommendations each voter does retain a role in selecting statewide delegates and therefore in influencing the overall distribution of power at a potential constitutional convention.

The Commission also considered a system that would retain the current multimember districts with each voter given two votes. This would increase the number of convention delegates each voter might help to elect, but might make it more difficult for voters, including protected minorities under the Voting Rights Act, to select a representative of their choice, as mathematically demonstrated above.

b. The present multimember districts with cumulative voting. Under a cumulative voting system, each voter may cast as many votes as there are positions to be filled, and voters may allocate these votes in whatever way they deem fit. For example, in a three-member district each voter would have three votes that he or she could cast for a single candidate; or allocate among two candidates on a two-for-one-candidate, one-for-another basis; or cast on a one-for-each-candidate basis. Here the "threshold of representation" is calculated on the basis of the formula $R = 1/(1+N)+1$ where R again represents the percentage of votes required to assure victory, and N is the number of seats to be filled. As can be seen, in three-member districts like those required under the New York Constitution, a vote of 25 percent plus one under a cumulative voting system guarantees a candidate victory, just as it does under single candidate voting with each voter casting one vote.

The advantages of cumulative voting are that, of all the available electoral systems, it is least likely to require constitutional amendment. Voters retain the same number of votes and the range of candidate choice that they have had under the system traditionally used for the selection of constitutional convention delegates, yet minority groups gain a fairer opportunity to elect candidates of their choice.

The disadvantages of this mechanism that caused the Commission to favor single candidate voting are its unfamiliarity, its complexity, and the possibility that its implementation would overly tax the capacity of the state's voting machines. Additionally, in the American political culture, voters may feel uncomfortable with the idea that any one person could vote two or three times for one candidate in one election.

c. The present multimember districts with proportional representation. The Commission recognizes that a variety of proportional representation electoral systems offer technical solutions to the voting rights problems raised by multimember districts with candidates running at-large. The relative unfamiliarity of such systems and their comparative complexity for both voters and election administrators has caused the Commission to forego these options.

d. Dividing each of the present multimember districts into three subdistricts. The Commission considered a proposal to subdistrict Senate districts. While the Commission recognizes that such a choice might, in theory, best maximize the opportunity of geographically concentrated minorities to participate in the political process, it does not favor this alternative. Such change would require constitutional amendment and therefore be far harder to accomplish than statutory changes to adjust the electoral system for convention delegate selection. Also, the Commission is of the view that the political process of drawing lines prior to the 1997 referendum or after could be extremely contentious and therefore work to undermine attempts to create a rich and informed public debate on the procedural and substantive issues involved in state constitutional change.

e. Employing Assembly districts. The Commission also considered using the existing Assembly districts as single member districts for delegates. This position was not favored because it, also, would require constitutional amendment.

Ballot Access

Historically, the election of delegates to New York State constitutional conventions has largely been governed by the generally applicable election law. This is still the case today. The provisions of this law, and their strict interpretation by the courts, have been criticized repeatedly as raising substantial barriers to ballot access. The Commission believes that the special and fundamental nature of a constitutional convention requires that the opportunity to serve be open to as many interested New Yorkers as possible. Moreover, it regards the prospect of election of constitutional convention delegates as an opportunity to test ideas for reform of the election law in a practical manner that will be minimally threatening to and disruptive of current institutional and political arrangements in the state.

The Problem

1. Delegates From Senate Districts:
The Petition Process

Under New York law, a valid petition is the basic method for appearing on the primary ballot as the candidate of an established party. Candidates for convention delegates from Senate districts must collect either 1,000 signatures, or signatures of 5 percent of the enrolled party voters residing in the district, whichever is less. [3]

An independent candidacy for delegate is difficult, but possible. A person may appear on the general election ballot as an independent candidate if he or she obtains the signatures of 3,000 voters in the senate district, or a number of signatures equal to 5 percent of the votes cast in the district in the last gubernatorial election, whichever is less.[4] Petition signers, however, may not include persons who voted in a primary election for delegate, or who earlier signed another valid nominating petition.[5] A write-in candidacy is also possible.

Experienced candidates for public office in New York generally seek two to three times the number of signatures legally required so that they are assured of weathering any challenge and gaining a place on the ballot. This is because the election law contains minutely detailed requirements for a valid petition. For example, state law reproduces the actual required form of petition pages and a cover sheet; specifies who may sign and who may witness signatures and each element of information required of a signatory and witness; and even details page numbering and binding rules.[6] For independent petitions the color of paper is specified (it is white); within New York City the Board of Elections is given statutory permission to make paper color requirements for those seeking party designation.[7]

Reacting to pressures for reform and the massive amount of election law litigation that this level of detail has generated, the state legislature made some changes in petition requirements in 1992. Customary abbreviations of names and addresses are now permitted, and failure to complete some detail no longer necessarily invalidates specific signatures or petition pages. Most interestingly, the legislature provided that two sub-

---

3   Election Law, Section 6-136 [2] (h).
4   Election Law, Section 6-142 [2] (f).
5   Election Law, Section 6-138
6   Election Law, Section 6-132.
7   Election Law, Sections 6 - 132 [4] and Section 138.

divisions of the election law having to do with petition and cover sheet preparation "... should be liberally construed, not inconsistent with substantial compliance thereto and the prevention of fraud." It also mandated in the same section, however, that "The provisions of this subdivision shall in no way be construed to restrict or expand the construction of any other provisions of this chapter or any other requirements applicable to the petition process."[8] Thus, with some significant exceptions, the courts continue to be encouraged to enforce the detailed requirements of the election law in a strict and uncompromising manner, as they have in the past.

The combination of the nature of the law and the posture of the courts places a premium on the electoral, legal, and political expertise of the party organization and political professionals, and has operated in the past to deny ballot access to persons with clear popular support but technically defective petitions. The Commission believes that these barriers are unfairly high for service at a constitutional convention, and must be reduced to make the delegate selection process for such a convention open, fair, responsive, and credible.

2. State Committee Designation of Delegates-At-Large

The general authority of state party committees to designate statewide candidates includes the power to designate constitutional convention delegates-at-large. By design, the election law thus empowers the state's political party leadership. Under these provisions, the person receiving the majority of a state party committee's votes is that party's designee for nomination, and if unopposed, the candidate for election. Although the designee may face opposition in the primary, he or she will appear on the primary ballot. Opposition on the primary ballot may be by a person who has received at least 25 percent of the vote of the state committee; or has obtained sufficient valid signatures on a petition in accord with the election law; or has successfully petitioned to be a write-in candidate. Independent candidacies by the write-in route are possible as well.

Remedies

Apart from a general overhaul of the election law, easing ballot access for potential convention delegate candidates may be achieved by either continuing the application of the election law and creating an exception for convention delegates, or by enacting an entirely separate approach to the election of convention delegates.

---

8   Election Law, Section 6-132 [15].

1. A Grace Period

The Commission favors a grace period as an alternative to easing the existing technical restrictions on ballot access. During the grace period delegates would have time to bring technically defective petitions into compliance. If corrections could be made during the designated period so that the corrected petition would satisfy the strict compliance standard, litigation would be reduced and deserving candidacies could be preserved.

2. Reducing the Number of Signatures Required

Even if a potential candidate for convention delegate negotiates the technicalities of the petition process, the number of signatures required alone may be a significant barrier to ballot access.

The New York State Commission on Government Integrity recommended in 1990 that the required number of signatures for a valid petition be reduced as a means of increasing ballot access. Such a step is consistent with the original purpose of adopting the petition method for nomination of candidates early in this century, weakening the parties' control of the process. This Commission endorses the enactment of a separate statute governing convention delegate selection that reduces the minimum number of signatures required both for party nomination and for independent candidacies for convention delegate by half, to 500 and 1,500, respectively. When combined with the adoption of a grace period, such a step could significantly open the process to less politically experienced candidates.

3. Substantial Compliance

In addition to these steps, the legislature may wish to extend the "substantial compliance" it has already enacted into law to cover a greater range of provisions used to determine whether a petition is sufficiently valid to permit a candidate for constitutional convention delegate to appear on the ballot. Under this approach, either the appropriate boards of elections or the courts would have the authority to determine whether a particular petition had substantially complied with election law.

4. Nonpartisan Election of District Delegates

Nonpartisan elections are used in a number of states for elections to constitutional conventions. Election without party designation on the ballot is generally employed in New York State for village and school board elections, and has been recently adopted for elections to fill city council vacancies in New York City.

Proponents argue that the use of nonpartisan elections, combined with easier petition requirements for ballot access, will weaken the grip of political parties on the convention delegate selection process, opening it up to persons with a greater diversity of experience and alternative bases of support. Additionally, they point to comparative research that indicates that nonpartisan election of delegates has substantially altered the tone, process, and focus of constitutional conventions in the states in which it has been recently used.

Opponents say that parties, in general, perform valuable functions in recruiting political leadership and mobilizing voters in the political process. They also reduce the likelihood that well-financed special interests will dominate an election. They should not be barred from doing this, they argue, for this very fundamentally important election. Moreover, they say, New York is a strong party state. The effect of adopting a nonpartisan process for delegate selection will not be to exclude parties from the process, but to drive their involvement behind the scenes where it is less visible and accountable.

Although the Commission reached no consensus regarding partisan versus nonpartisan elections for convention delegates, at least one commissioner (Commissioner Eberly) strongly favors nonpartisan elections.

5. Elimination or Provision of Alternatives to State Committee Designation of Candidacies for Delegates-At-Large

The current practice for nominating delegates at-large is even less accessible to those outside the major parties than nominations for delegates selected within state senate districts. The difficulty is in envisioning a statewide process that is both orderly and broadly accessible. The Commission urges consideration of alternatives for statewide delegate nominations — for example, a petition process or nonpartisan election of statewide delegates.

Financing Delegate Campaigns

Because of inequalities in access to campaign funds and the advantages current and former elected officials and other well-known persons are likely to have in races for delegate to a state constitutional convention, the

Commission favors the adoption of a public financing scheme for these campaigns. Public financing might also encourage persons to run for convention delegate who otherwise might not consider running, increasing the prospect of diversity in the composition of the convention. Such an initiative also promises to decrease the need for candidates to rely on special interest funds and therefore to reduce the influence of special interests in the delegate races.

A particular problem in designing a public finance scheme for delegate selection is the advantage present or former elected officials would have in such races. They include: the visibility generally gained from public service, constituency service, and repeated campaigning; access to the use of government resources to remain in regular touch with constituents; and a disproportionate ability to attract campaign contributions. The result of the cumulative effect of these advantages upon even the best situated potential opponents is also critical. Seeing the deck stacked against them from the outset, they often choose simply not to run, making the incumbent's position even stronger.

Moreover, if a constitutional convention is called, the election for delegates will be held in 1998, an election year for the state legislature and all statewide elected officials. Senators and Assembly members who seek to continue in those offices while also becoming delegates will be required to run simultaneously for two posts. The need to do this may discourage some candidacies. But for those who do choose this option, the synergistic effect of their campaigns may overwhelm the campaigns of their opponents for delegate.

The current system for campaign finance regulation is summarized in a memo prepared for the Commission by Professor Michael Malbin of the Rockefeller Institute (see page 491). New York has recently been subjected to close scrutiny by the State Commission on Government Integrity (The Feerick Commission). It identified a reform agenda that includes: the creation of an independent campaign finance enforcement agency; detailed and timely disclosure of contributions; "drastically" reduced contribution limits and bans on direct contributions from unions, corporations, and those doing business with the government; public funding of elections for statewide office and removal of barriers to public funding of local elections; and (conditioned on public funding) carefully prescribed expenditure limits.

This Commission believes that the election for constitutional convention delegate may offer an opportunity to test elements of these proposals without challenging all those with a stake in the current system.

Public Campaign Financing

The Commission recommends that an appropriate public financing system for the election of constitutional convention delegates be adopted. An example of such a system might be the following:

1. *Expenditure limitation:* $50,000 for each election (the Primary and the General Election). This contemplates a campaign using mailings and phones, with some paid staff support.

2. *Matchable contribution:* a contribution of not more than $250 from a natural person who is a resident of the state of New York.

3. *Threshold:* a total of $2,500 from at least 50 natural persons, at least 30 of whom reside in the district from which the candidate wishes to run. After the threshold is reached, it will be matched on a two-for-one basis.

4. *Matchable contribution after threshold is reached:* up to $250 on a two-for-one basis.

5. *Contribution limitation:* no more than $2,000 from any contributor, per election cycle.

   The Commission believes that any campaign finance system should include the following components:

6. *Incentives for participation:* A candidate who is opposed by a "serious" candidate, who does not opt into the public financing system, will be entitled to spend twice the expenditure limit and will receive a three-to-one match for all the matchable contributions, including the threshold amount. A serious candidate will be defined as a candidate who has raised and/or spent a substantial amount of money.

7. *Non-participants:* Candidates running for any other elective office at the same time they are running for delegate would be ineligible to participate in the campaign finance program and would be deemed as opting out of the program, thus triggering the provisions of paragraph six, above.

8. *Source of funds:* Experience elsewhere suggests that to assure the availability of sufficient resources, a public financing plan for convention delegate candidacies should be financed from the general fund. The Commission staff, based on the experience of

New York City Council races, estimates roughly that the total cost to the state for a public financing system covering senate district candidates would be between $7,000,000 and $9,000,000.

9. *Disclosure requirements:* Candidates opting into the public campaign finance system would comply with greater disclosure requirements than currently required under state law by listing the occupation of contributors, the name of all contributors' employers and by listing intermediaries (bundlers) who deliver contributions to the candidate.

10. *Administration:* The Commission believes that the legislature should consider delegating the administration of a public financing system for convention delegates to the New York City Campaign Finance Board. While this may cause some political difficulties, the Board is the only entity in the state that has had any experience with public financing programs and it would be wasteful to establish a new bureaucracy for the purpose of a single election.

Voter Pamphlets

The Commission believes that publicly financed voter pamphlets should be provided to publicize convention delegate candidacies. The messages in these pamphlets should be prepared by candidates in their own words, within reasonable space limitations. Such pamphlets are one relatively inexpensive way to treat better-known and less well-known candidates for delegate equally and to distinguish the race for delegate from the numerous other elections that will be taking place in 1998. An approximate cost estimate for voter pamphlets produced and mailed for both the primary and general election is $5 million to $6 million. This does not include the estimate for a campaign finance program.

Incentives For Service — Delegate Compensation

One of the concerns raised in public discussions about a potential constitutional convention, based upon the 1967 experience, is that legislators and judges who might be elected delegates will receive two full public salaries and concomitant pension benefits. In response to this concern the Commission considered both this specific issue and the more general question of double compensation for all public officials who might be elected to serve at a convention.

State Legislators and Judges: Combined Effect of Current Constitutional Provisions

If a constitutional convention is called, Article 19, Section 2, of the state Constitution provides that delegates be paid " . . . the same compensation as shall be annually payable to the members of the Assembly, and be reimbursed for actual traveling expenses, while the convention is in session, to the extent that a member of the Assembly would be entitled thereto in the case of a session of the legislature."

Elsewhere, the state Constitution also prevents the reduction of legislative or judicial salaries by statute during the term of service.[9]

The provision making convention delegates' annual salaries equivalent to those of Assembly members was included in the state Constitution in 1894. At that time, Assembly service was considered part-time, an Assembly salary level reflecting this understanding was specified in the state Constitution, and legislative sessions were unlikely to be longer in duration than a constitutional convention. In contrast, today many Assembly members regard elective office as their principal employment, regular legislative sessions may extend for half a year or more, and additional special sessions are common. Compensation levels are in accord with these realities; moreover, they have not been fixed in the Constitution since 1947.

The combined effect of the three constitutional provisions concerning legislative, judicial, and convention delegate salaries is to permit state legislators and judges who are elected as delegates to a constitutional convention to receive two full annual salaries during the year of the convention. From the historical record it is reasonable to conclude that this effect was unintended. But because of its constitutional basis, the clearest, simplest way to address this situation is by constitutional amendment.

Statutes passed in anticipation of the last two state constitutional conventions further assured that legislators and judges who were elected as delegates would receive significant pension benefits as a consequence of service at a convention. Specific provision for inclusion of service at

---

9   Article 3, Section 6; Article 6, Section 25.

the 1938 and 1967 constitutional conventions as "government service" for pension purposes may be found in the pension law in several places.[10]

Other Public Officials as Delegates

Local elected or appointed officials, state employees or officials, employees of public authorities, or federal elected officials or employees may, of course, run for the position of convention delegate. In advance of the 1967 Constitutional Convention, a state law was passed that permitted local elected officials to include the salary received for convention service in their compensation for the year for pension purposes.[11]

Apart from state legislators and judges, full double compensation of delegates in state and local public service does not arise as a result of constitutional provisions, and has not yet been identified as a problem in contemporary assessments of the record of past conventions. Any restrictions on double compensation of individuals in these categories could constitutionally be achieved by state statute, or through policy decisions of the employing government or entity regarding acceptance of ordinary salary while absent for service as a convention delegate, but not by restricting receipt of delegate compensation.

Double Compensation of Staff at the Convention

A significant portion of the staff of a constitutional convention may be drawn from legislative staff or from other people in full-time public service. Extra work should be fairly compensated, and there are well-established policies for the compensation of state workers for extra service. However, concerns about avoiding the receipt of two full-time public salaries and concomitant pension benefits by delegates may extend as well to professional staff. These may also be addressed by state statute.

The Criticism of Dual Compensation

Critics of dual compensation have two fundamental arguments:

The first is the straightforward idea that it is wrong for an elected official or any person to be paid two annual salaries for public service in the same year. Outside of the major metropolitan areas of the state, it is the public perception that the $57,500 annual base salary currently paid

---

10   Article 2.11a; Article 8.302.12.a.1.
11   Article 2.44(a).

Assembly members and Senators (frequently augmented by additional pay for added duties) is very generous, especially in the absence of a statutory or constitutional requirement for full-time legislative service and in light of the fact that convention service is likely to be for six months or less. The regular base pay of judges is generally higher than for legislators.

In the case of simultaneous service in the state legislature or on the bench and at a convention, the issue is not only the fact of dual compensation but the level of that compensation. For example, at current pay levels a legislator who was also a delegate would receive at least $115,000 in salary for the year of the convention, plus expenses. Again, the figure for judges might be even higher. And a significant lifetime pension benefit would flow from the boost in the three consecutive highest paid years' average compensation for these officials that would result from this dual compensation.

The second argument of critics is that the salary and pension benefits that flow from convention service summarized above give sitting elected officials a special incentive to serve at a convention. But, it is argued, these officials are precisely the ones who should not be encouraged to seek convention service because they are already in power and therefore likely to be self-interested and predisposed to protecting the status quo.

Value of the Current Provision
Concerning Delegate Compensation

The primary virtue of the current New York state constitutional provision on delegate compensation is that it removes this potentially contentious question as an issue that would require settlement in the legislature prior to the convening of a convention. If the question were left open, failure to settle it might actually block a convention after it was authorized by the voters.

A rationale for the salary level fixed in the Constitution is that a convention is a deliberative assembly somewhat similar to the legislative session; the salary of an Assembly member is a convenient benchmark for compensation for this kind of statewide service. Moreover, the work of the convention delegate — the careful consideration of the design of the state's entire governmental and political system, and its redesign if needed — is at least as important as that of the legislator, and should be compensated accordingly.

Convention service is by its very nature temporary and additional to a person's regular work. This is true for legislators or judges, as it is for others. Like others who choose to do this additional work, it is argued, legislators or judges who are elected as delegates should be additionally compensated without discrimination.

Alternative Analogies

There are a number of examples in New York of public officials paid two salaries for the simultaneous performance of two jobs. Town supervisors in some counties who serve both as members of the town board and the county board, for example, are paid by both governments. But in this and other similar cases the salary for each post is relatively small and each salary is established in contemplation of the other.

More generally, however, state law and practice regarding state employees seeks to preclude payment twice for work done on the same day and at the same time. The approach taken by the state when its employees face an obligation that arises only periodically, e.g., when they are intermittently called away from their ordinary work for jury duty, offers an alternative approach. Jurors are currently compensated $15 per day and mileage for service. Since 1991 state employees called to jury duty continue to receive their regular pay, and may accept mileage, but may not accept the juror's stipend.

By analogy service as a convention delegate is periodic and reflects assumption of the highest level of service and obligation. In accord with its general practice, the state may therefore reasonably provide that a convention delegate who is also on a state or local payroll may either receive his or her regular salary and any additional expenses that accrue as a result of convention service, but not additional pay for this service, or alternatively the salary and expenses of a delegate but not his or her ordinary compensation.

Prohibitions Against Dual Compensation

The Commission recommends that steps be taken to bar dual compensation for government employees who serve as delegates or staff at a constitutional convention. For officials whose salary is protected by the Constitution, this must be achieved by constitutional amendment. For others, it may be achieved by statute.

1. A constitutional amendment to limit double compensation to legislators or judges who serve as delegates might be written as an exception to the compensation provision in Article XIX, Section 2. It might read (new matter in bold):

> Every delegate shall receive for his **or her** services the same compensation as shall then be annually payable to the members of the Assembly and be reimbursed for actual traveling expenses, while the convention is in session, to the extent that a member of the Assembly would then be entitled thereto in the case of a session of the legislature, **except that for an official whose compensation is protected against diminution during a term of office or service by provision of this constitution, the combined compensation for service in his or her principal position and for service as convention delegate may not exceed the level of his or her annual salary for the principal position.**

Such an amendment would remove special financial incentives for legislators and judges to serve as convention delegates, without barring their service absolutely. This general approach would also limit added compensation for service as a convention delegate by the governor and lieutenant governor. And by restricting these officials to one salary, such an amendment would also eliminate the added pension benefits that might otherwise result for these officials from convention service.

To have an effect before an election for delegates to a convention called in 1997, first passage of such an amendment would be most timely if it were achieved in 1994. This would allow second passage by a separately elected legislature in 1995 and submission to the voters in that year. First passage in 1995 or 1996 would still allow second passage in 1997 and adoption at referendum in that year.

2. The Commission recommends that a statute be passed in advance of the 1997 convention referendum that would limit other delegates at a constitutional convention who are compensated full time from a governmental or public authority payroll to a single salary. Since delegate compensation is constitutionally protected, this end could be achieved by adjustments to the elected delegate's regular annual salary. This statute should also assure that persons in public service who are elected delegates have the opportunity

to serve without risk of loss of their regular governmental position.

The view of the Commission is that once double compensation is ended, pension benefits for public employees who serve as convention delegates be linked to the salary they receive. That is, if their salary as delegate is higher than their regular salary, and this becomes their annual salary, they then should receive the pension benefit that flows from this level of compensation. Such an arrangement might provide an additional incentive for lower paid state and local workers to run for delegate, which also might increase diversity at a convention.

3. The Commission further recommends that practices regarding compensation and pension benefits for staff at a constitutional convention who are regularly employed by the legislature, the executive, or the departments and agencies of state government adhere to the principle that dual compensation be avoided.

Statutory Limitation on Pension Benefits for Service as a Convention Delegate by Legislators and Judges

Even if a constitutional amendment is not passed, the Commission believes that it is both possible and desirable to limit the enhancement of pension benefits for legislators or judges as a result of convention service.

By statute in New York State, membership in state and local pension systems is made mandatory for all persons in "government service." Moreover, Article V, Section 7, of the state Constitution provides that ". . . membership in any pension or retirement system of the state or of a civil division thereof shall be a contractual relationship, the benefits of which shall not be diminished or impaired."

But since a constitutional convention has not yet been called, delegates to it have not yet been selected, and even if their service is defined as "governmental" for pension purposes no contractual obligation has yet been incurred. Moreover, as noted above, special legislation was passed in anticipation of both the 1938 and 1967 conventions to specifically include service as a convention delegate within the definition of "government service" under the pension law. The implication is that these actions had to be specifically taken by the legislature to assure that pension benefits would accrue for convention service, and that absent such action, or if contrary action is taken, pension benefits for convention service would not accrue.

The Commission recommends that if the prohibitions against dual compensation (see page 427) are not adopted, that for government employees who would receive more than one annual salary by virtue of being delegates or staff to a future constitutional convention, or one called as a result of the 1997 referendum only, the state legislature act to preclude service at the convention from inclusion in the definition of "government service" in the pension law. The Commission is aware that, if passed, such statute might be challenged by disadvantaged convention delegates as contrary to long practice and in conflict with the intent of Article V, Section 7. But should it survive a challenge, such a statute would remove this incentive to run for delegate from those who might receive a special pension benefit for doing so.

Qualifications for Service

After serious consideration and several extended discussions, the Commission recommends against barring state legislators and/or sitting judges from service as delegates at a constitutional convention. The Commission also recommends against barring those who serve as convention delegates from later service in state elective office, including judicial office, for a period of years, which might not only exclude sitting members of the legislature and judges from a convention but also those who hope or expect to serve in those capacities in the future.

Legislative Dominance?

One argument made against holding a constitutional convention is that the people most likely to be elected as delegates to a convention are also those least likely to be sympathetic to the goals of reform for which the convention was called. More specifically, critics suggest that a convention is likely to be dominated by state legislators, who will use their powers as delegates to protect their own interests and those of their institutions, thus thwarting reform.

Those who expect legislative dominance at a convention point to the constitutional provision that most delegates be elected from state Senate districts, and suggest that legislators already well known in their home districts have a significant advantage in this sort of low visibility election. They also point to the 1967 experience, in which: the convention leadership was the legislative leadership; much of the convention's staff was recruited from those on legislative staff; the rules of the convention were adapted from the legislature's rules; and the convention met in the Assembly chamber, taking on the coloring of the legislature from the physical setting itself.

In response, other observers point out that unlike the convention that might be called as a result of the 1997 question, the 1967 Convention was the direct result of legislative initiative. Under such circumstances, active legislative involvement was more likely. In fact, they point out, sitting legislators actually comprised a relatively small portion of the 1967 convention delegates. Only 13 of the 186 people elected (7%) were Senators and Assembly members. Twenty-eight others (15%) had previously served, and nine (5%) held legislative staff positions. (An analysis of the occupations and demographics of delegates to the 1967 convention is set forth on page 381.) And, they argue, the 1967 convention proposed some significant "anti-insider" structural changes, including the creation of a reapportionment commission for future legislative districting.

Dominance by the "Government Industry"?

A reformulation of this argument suggests that a constitutional convention is likely to be dominated by people in the "government industry" in New York. These are not just state legislators, but judges, local officials, and others with a substantial stake in the current system. Evidence for this is that fewer than one in five delegates to the 1967 Convention came from entirely outside government. Even if they have their internal disagreements, it is argued, people in the "government industry" will be inclined, at best, to incremental change, not the fundamental government reform desired by many convention advocates.

The response to this point of view questions whether the perception that there is a monolithic "government industry" with a single interest is accurate. It is natural that the prospect of a constitutional convention will attract the attention and involvement of persons already involved or interested in government. The public positions of elected officials in New York reflect a great range of views on questions of policy and government structure. The legislative minorities in both houses, for example, have been a consistent source of serious proposals for system change. Moreover, sitting officials have led the state through great periods of constitutional change in the past; there is no reason to think that this group would not produce leaders who would do so again.

The Commission's Position

Over the course of their deliberations, most members of this Commission came to the view that to ban from service at a constitutional convention any group — legislators, judges, or others — defined solely by their occupation was not desirable.

It is the general view on the Commission that democratic governmental processes should be inclusive, not exclusive. Entire groups should not be barred from participation in a defining event for the state political system, especially when these groups are constituted on the basis of the capacity of their members to win popular nomination and election. Moreover, most commissioners think such a prohibition would deny the convention the experience of some people deeply knowledgeable about state government and experienced in balancing the various pressures that are placed upon elected representatives. It might also turn influential state leaders against the idea of a constitutional convention, not on the basis of the merits but rather on the basis of the act of exclusion itself.

The Commission does believe that if a constitutional convention is held, its membership should represent the great diversity of New York as we enter the twenty-first century. This includes not only our racial and ethnic diversity, but the broad spectrum of education and experience and the range of professional and vocational backgrounds present in New York. But the way to achieve such a convention, most commissioners concluded, is not by banning legislators or others, but by altering the process of delegate selection to make it more likely that less politically experienced candidates can successfully compete in that process, and by removing special incentives that may attract legislators and judges to convention service.

All other recommendations in this report are designed to encourage diversity at future constitutional conventions and openness and fairness in the process that selects delegates to attend it. The recommendations seek also to remove special incentives for legislators and judges to run for positions as delegates. These recommendations are supported unanimously by all members of the Commission. It is in the framework of the overall thrust of this report that the Commission's recommendation against barring legislators and judges from service as convention delegates should be read.

An Alternative View

While all commissioners support these recommendations, which seek to provide an open, fair, responsive, and credible process, two commissioners would go further. It is their view that a ban to service at a constitutional convention is an essential precondition to the calling of a convention, and to its success if called.

Recent history demonstrates, these commissioners believe, that state constitutional conventions tend to be dominated by entrenched political interests. Reducing financial incentives or raising political barriers to service will be insufficient to diminish the likelihood that this will occur again, they think, because the core issue remains the threat a convention poses to control by those in power over levers of power.

It is their view that legislators seek to serve at a convention to protect their fundamental positions and interests, and that, similarly, judges seek convention service to control the definition of the role, jurisdiction, structure, and function of the judiciary, set out in so much detail in the Constitution precisely to restrain the legislature's discretion regarding these questions. Therefore, they say, only an absolute ban will deny these officeholders the capacity to define any convention's agenda and undermine the purpose of those who might vote to call it.

Moreover, they point out, even if the disincentives to service by judges or legislators will work, we cannot know this until after the vote on whether to call the convention. But to support a convention voters must be convinced that it will not be dominated by legislators and judges before they vote on the convention question in 1997. Only an absolute ban, they conclude, will provide voters with certainty on this issue.[12] The views of Commissioner Malcolm Wilson are set forth in a concurring statement to be found on page 434.

---

12   This view is subscribed to by Commissioners Eberly and Wilson.

Concurring Statement Of
Commission Member Malcolm Wilson

With three exceptions, I concur wholeheartedly with the report of the Commission in the form dated March 1994.

One exception is my belief that there is no logical basis for permitting judges to serve as convention delegates and the second is that I discern no logical basis for permitting members of the legislature to serve as delegates.

Men and women are elected to judicial office solely to discharge the responsibilities of dispute resolution through the judicial process. Period.

Men and women are elected to the state legislature for the purpose of participating with the governor in the lawmaking process. There is no logical basis for them to serve as delegates to a constitutional convention. They are empowered to participate in the process of amending the Constitution by passing a proposed amendment in two separate sessions of the legislature with an election intervening.

The third exception is the failure of the report to provide that no delegate to a constitutional convention shall be eligible by election or appointment to any public office in New York State or local government for a minimum period of at least three years (preferably five years), after the adjournment *sine die* of the Convention. The obvious purpose of this proposal is to help assure complete objectivity and minimize the possibility of a delegate's vote for what might be considered a nonmonetary bribe.

Delegate Selection and the Problem of Ballot Access

Burton C. Agata

The Problem of Ballot Access Under The Election Law

Background

In the event a constitutional convention is called, the New York State Constitution provides that there shall be three delegates from each senatorial district and fifteen elected at-large statewide.[1] In view of the state Constitution's silence on the procedure for the election of constitutional convention delegates, the legislature has made the election law applicable to convention delegate nominations and elections.[2] Access to the ballot by potential candidates under the New York election law has been long recognized as a serious problem and was addressed in detail in a 1988 study, which called for fundamental reform.[3] Consequently, there are access problems with respect to the election of convention delegates.

Historically, election of delegates to all New York State constitutional conventions has been governed by the generally applicable election law, plus some additional specific provisions in the enabling legislation for the earlier conventions. Until the adoption of the 1894 Constitution, the state Constitution either contained no provision for a convention or after adoption of the 1846 Constitution, it included a provision for a convention but contained nothing about delegates or

---

1   NY Constitution, Article XIX, Section 2.

2   The Temporary State Commission on the Constitutional Convention, *First Interim Report, February 19, 1957*, p. 13. Article 6 of the election law governs the election to public office and party position (Section 6-100, Election Law).

3   *Government Ethics Reform for the 1990s: The Collected Reports of the NYS Commission on Government Integrity*, Bruce A. Green, Ed. (New York: Fordham University Press, 1991), pp. 302-313, chapter 9, "Access to the Ballot in Primary Elections: The Need For Fundamental Reform."

aboutconvention procedure.[4] During that period convention enabling acts included provisions concerning the election of delegates and often contained details concerning the method of conducting the convention. However, all of the enabling acts also explicitly provided that the general act regulating elections then in force also should be applicable to the election of delegates.[5] After the adoption of the 1894 Constitution, which contained substantially the same convention provisions in the current state Constitution, the content of the enabling legislation changed. The enabling legislation in contemplation of the 1915 Convention practically relied entirely on the election law then in force.[6] Legislation in contemplation of the 1938 Convention assumed that the election law applied to the election of delegates and made no reference to it other than a departure with respect to publication requirements.[7]

One of the issues presented during public hearings held by the Temporary Commission on the Constitutional Convention was "Should the Constitution specify the manner of electing delegates-at-large?"[8] Although the proponents of the 1967 Constitution addressed many reform issues, the question of ballot access for delegate candidates does not appear to have attracted attention, and the proposed 1967 Constitution did not deal with the ballot access issues presented by the election law.[9]

Access to the Ballot Under Current Election Law: By Petition and By State Committee Designation

1. **Petition.** Much of the problem of ballot access revolves around the petition process. Four main factors are involved:

   a. Under New York's election law, a valid petition is the basic method for appearing on the primary ballot in

---

4   See "History and background of provisions governing amendments to the New York State constitution," of Agata memorandum to Commission, pages 160-167, and the chapter "Amending and Revising the New York State Constitution" in this book.

5   For the 1801 Convention, Laws of 1801, c. 69; for the 1821 Convention, Laws of 1821, c. 90, s. III; for the 1846 Convention, Laws of 1845, c. 252, s. 2; for the 1867-68 Convention, Laws of 1867, c. 194, s. 2; for the 1894 convention, Laws of 1893, c. 8, s. 6.

6   Laws of 1913, c. 819, s. 4.

7   Laws of 1938, c. 376, s. 6.

8   Temporary State Commission on the Constitutional Convention, *1967 Convention Issues; Introductory Report,* p. 71.

9   Article XIV, Section 2, of the proposed 1967 Constitution did specify qualifications for delegates.

order to become the candidate of a party or on the ballot on election day as an independent candidate; [10]

b. A second factor is that the election law contains detailed — sometimes minutely detailed — requirements for a valid petition.

c. Third, the courts enforce those detailed requirements in a strict and uncompromising manner and "substantial compliance" has been rejected as a sufficient standard to satisfy compliance with the detailed statutory requirements.

d. Even if a potential candidate would comply with all of the technical requirements for a valid petition, the number of signatures required may be a significant barrier.

The petition method for ballot access was introduced in 1911 as a reform measure designed to open the process to voters generally and to take it out of the control of the party machinery.[11] However, the result has been to place a premium on the electoral, legal, and political expertise of the party organization and the political professional, on the one hand, and, on the other, often has served to deny a place on the ballot to individuals with obvious popular support but with technically defective petitions. Moreover, the costs and potential hassle that individual candidates are likely to face discourage many without party support from seeking office at all. In addition, the cost to the system in terms of judicial resources can be astounding.[12] Nevertheless, the judicial attitude requiring strict compliance, based on the conclusion that "strict compliance" reflects legislative intent because the legislature has had adequate opportunity to counter the courts' approach and has not done so, remains unrelentingly strong.[13]

---

10   For an outline of the election law requirements concerning petitions, see Memorandum, "Law governing election of delegates to a New York State constitutional convention," from Lane and Agata, dated November 1, 1993.

11   *Government Ethics Reform*, p. 312, chapter 9, "Access to the Ballot in Primary Elections: The Need For Fundamental Reform."

12   See *Government Ethics Reform*, pp. 302-309, chapter 9, "Access to the Ballot in Primary Elections: The Need For Fundamental Reform," for a detailed survey of the problems summarized in this paragraph.

13   *Higby* v. *Mahoney*, 48 N.Y.2d 15 (1979).

2. **State committee designation of delegates at-large.** The general authority of party state committees to designate statewide candidates includes the power to designate convention delegates at large. This presents another problem of ballot access. Under this method, the person receiving the majority of the state committee votes is the party designee for nomination, and if unopposed, its candidate for election. Although the designee may face opposition in the primary, he or she will appear on the primary ballot.[14] This method, by design, places power in the hands of party leadership.

Remedies for Consideration

Of course, the problem of ballot access is not unique to those who would become delegates or candidates for delegate to a constitutional convention. Nevertheless, if convention delegates can be distinguished validly from other elective positions, it might be possible to mitigate the ballot access problem for convention delegates without, at this time, undertaking the complex and daunting task of attempting a complete overhaul of the state election law.

Other than a general overhaul of the election law, consideration should be given to two main categories of remedies: (1) those that continue the application of the election law but invoke some exception for convention delegates; and (2) a basically separate approach to the election of convention delegates.

Legislatively Enacted "Substantial Compliance"
Rule for the Election Law and Other Changes in
Election Law

A "substantial compliance" standard. The kinds of details with which filers of petitions must be concerned include, for example, such requirements as: (1) a signature on a petition must include the date of signing and the address, Assembly district, and election district of the signatory; (2) that the petitions for candidates for local office be filed between 9:00 A.M. and 5:00 P.M.; and (3) various requirements concerning numbering

---

14 Opposition on the primary ballot may be by a person who has received at least 25% of the vote of the state committee, by a person who successfully obtains valid signatures on a viable designating petition (Election Law, Section 6-104), or from a write-in candidate as a result of a valid petition to permit write-in candidates (Election Law, Section 6-164, 6-166). An independent candidate may appear on the election ballot as a result of petition, as well (Election Law, Section 6-142[1]).

of pages, binding of volumes of petitions, and information on cover sheets.[15]

But even one of the severest critics of the way in which the petition process has been treated by the courts has conceded that the requirements have a basically legitimate purpose — to prevent fraud and to facilitate counting signatures — and has concluded that "[n]o single procedural requirement contained in New York's election law is itself so complicated that it cannot be complied with through reasonable diligence. Collectively, however, [it also was concluded] those requirements unreasonably restrict access to the ballot and thereby undermine the legitimacy of the primary process as a means of selecting nominees who command the support of a party's members, not just the party's leaders."[16]

The New York State Commission on Government Integrity (The Feerick Commission), concerned with all aspects of the election law, recommended that a study be made with a view to a complete overhaul of the election law and, in the interim, that the legislature enact a "substantial compliance" rule for determining whether a petition is sufficiently valid to permit a candidate to appear on the ballot. Legislative adoption of a "substantial compliance" standard would be a useful step in improving the election law generally and would benefit candidate ballot access for all potential candidates, including convention delegate candidates. However, the difficulty of enacting any generally applicable mitigation of the "strict compliance" approach could be as great as achieving a complete overhaul of the election law.

"Substantial compliance" rule limited to election of convention delegates. As an alternative, consideration could be given to adoption of a "substantial compliance" standard limited to candidates for convention delegate. However, it is submitted that broader considerations counsel that a "substantial compliance" rule should not be adopted that only applies to the election of constitutional convention delegates. Its adoption, by implication, needlessly would reinforce the position that by failure to mitigate the "strict compliance" rule generally, the legislature thereby had approved the courts' current strict compliance approach to elections for positions other than convention delegates.

---

15 For form and contents of designating petitions, Election Law, Sections 6-130, 6-132, and 6-134 (primary election), 6-138, 6-140, and 6-142 (for independent nominations) and Section 6-166 (to permit write-in candidates).

16 *Government Ethics Reform*, p. 310, chapter 9, "Access to the Ballot in Primary Elections: The Need For Fundamental Reform."

Convention as judge of elections. Despite the appropriate concern about the judicial application of substantial versus strict compliance standards in adjudicating disputes about petitions under the election law, in the case of the election of convention delegates the courts are only one level of adjudication and not the final level at that. It should be borne in mind that ultimately the convention is the judge of the election (and qualifications) of delegates, and presumably even a judicial application of the strict compliance rule could be overcome by the convention applying a substantial compliance rule and seating (or not seating) a delegate.[17]

Simplifying petition requirements. In the absence of substantial compliance rule, enactment of legislation that reduces the pitfalls for convention delegate petitions should be considered. For example, simpler provisions concerning what must accompany the signature of a petition signatory and a witness and less stringent requirements concerning the binding and numbering of petitions could be adopted. Clearly New York has the most complex requirements, which have fostered more than one-half of the election litigation in the United States; reduction of the complexities (even if due care would result in compliance) should not increase fraud and would reduce the costs of the election process.[18]

A Grace Period to Bring Defective Petitions Into Line With the Election Law

Another method of dealing with the strict compliance standard would be to permit a candidate to bring defective petitions into compliance during some designated grace period. For example, a candidate could be afforded the opportunity to correct technical errors in filed petitions within a defined period after filing the petition or, when the petition is a subject of judicial challenge, within a defined period after the commencement of the lawsuit. If corrections could be made during the designated period so that the corrected petition would satisfy even the strict compliance standard, valuable judicial resources could be saved and deserving petitions given effect. Moreover, petitions that could be brought into strict compliance by this method would, in all likelihood, have been in substantial compliance

---

17　The convention is the "judge of the election, returns and qualifications of its members." Although the Supreme Court has jurisdiction under the election law to determine the accuracy of a tally by the Board of Elections, the Convention may ignore the court's determination and, as judge of the elections and returns under Article XIX, Section 2, of the Constitution, may seat someone other than the person the court declares to have received the most votes. The Convention did exercise its power in the situation involving *Rice* v. *Power,* 19 N.Y.2d 106, 278 N.Y.S.2d 361 (1967). Also see, *Rice* v. *State,* 55 Misc.2d 964 (1968).

18　*Government Ethics Reform,* pp. 302-304 and n. 43, at 310, chapter 9, "Access to the Ballot in Primary Elections: The Need For Fundamental Reform."

with the statute in the first place. This remedy could be limited to delegates to constitutional conventions in order to avoid the difficulties of enacting a generally applicable ameliorative.

Any concern about the possibly unusual procedure of involving the courts directly in a corrective process could be met by requiring a lawsuit to be preceded by a notice of alleged defects served directly on the candidate by the challenger or through the Board of Elections. Within a specified time of receiving the notice, the defender of the petition would have the opportunity to make corrections. In the event he or she refuses to do so, the judicial proceeding could be instituted.

Reducing the Number of Signatures Required for Petition; Combining It With a Grace Period

The Feerick Commission recommended that the required number of signatures for a valid petition be reduced as a means of increasing ballot access. Reducing the number of required petition signatures would be consistent with the original purpose of the petition method of placing candidates on the ballot, which was intended to ameliorate the access problems caused by relying solely on party caucuses for candidates.[19] While alone this would not significantly, if at all, affect the strict compliance requirement, it would make it easier for candidates with lesser resources to satisfy the number of signature requirements. Moreover, if the required number of signatures is reduced in conjunction with adoption of the grace period proposal discussed in the previous paragraph, it could significantly open the process to so-called outsiders or independent candidates.[20]

Registration Fee

Another method would be to permit persons to appear on the ballot by filing a declaration of candidacy and paying a registration fee or, in the

---

19 Some states require that delegates to a constitutional convention *must* be nominated by petition apparently as a means of opening the nominating process to the voters at large. See, e.g.: Ark. St. s. 7-9-304; Neb. Rev. St. s. 49-214; Ohio Const. Art. XVI, s. 2. In Missouri, party candidates from senatorial districts may be designated according to party rules, but candidates for delegate from the state at-large must be nominated by petition. Missouri Const. Art. XII, s. 3(a).

20 The current signature requirement for the primary is 15,000 signatures or 5% of the enrolled party voters in the state, whichever is less, with at least 100 or 5%, whichever is less, from 1/2 the congressional districts for at-large delegate and 1000 signatures or 5% of the enrolled voters in the senatorial district, whichever is less, for senatorial district delegates may create difficulties for a person without an experienced organization. Election Law ss. 6-104[5], 6-136[2](h). To appear on the ballot from a senatorial district as an independent candidate, a petition containing the signatures of 3000 registered voters or 5% of those who voted in the previous election for governor, whichever is less, is required.

alternative, by filing a petition.[21] The amount of the fee could be nominal or could be determined on the basis of striking a balance between opening the process and clogging it with so-called frivolous candidates. Payment of fees as a means of appearing on the ballot has been employed in other states for all kinds of elections.[22] While it is true that in some instances the field becomes very crowded and voter confusion results, it may be an acceptable risk in exchange for opening the process. The declaration of candidacy and registration fee method should be considered in contrast with its polar opposite in the search for increasing open access to the ballot — permitting a person to have an absolute right to appear on the ballot as a candidate for delegate-at-large solely because he or she is the state committee's designee.

Elimination of State Committee Designation of Candidates for Delegate At-large

Consideration should be given to eliminating the designating power of the party state committee with respect to convention delegates at-large. This is the most direct contradiction to popular control over candidate selection and while perhaps the most difficult to change politically, mechanically it could be relatively easy. The question of what would replace the designation process remains an issue, but whether it is petition, declaration, and

---

21   See, e.g., Louisiana: ". . . Each person desiring to be become a candidate for election as a delegate from a representative district shall qualify as a candidate from the particular representative district he seeks to represent by filing a statement of candidacy with the secretary of state not later than. . . ." LSA Constitution 1972 Conv. s. 1;
New Hampshire:
Any person who by the laws of this state is a qualified voter in the town, ward, or unincorporated place from which he may be elected is eligible to be a delegate to the constitutional convention. NH R.S.A. 667:7
A declaration of candidacy shall be filed with the town or city clerk on or before a date 36 days before the date of the election. All declarations shall be forwarded by the town or city clerk to the secretary of state for preparation of the ballots at least 35 days before the date of the election. NH R.S.A. 667:8
At the time of filing a declaration of candidacy, each candidate shall pay to the town or city clerk a filing fee of $2 for the use of the town or city.   NH R.S.A. 667:9
On or before the closing date for filing declarations of candidacy with the town or city clerk as provided by RSA 667:8, any candidate for delegate shall file with the town or city clerk a declaration of candidacy in substantially the following form, which shall be prepared and furnished by the secretary of state:
I, _____ , candidate for office of delegate to the constitutional convention from District No. ___ of _____ county hereby certify that I am at least 18 years of age; that I am domiciled in ward _____ of the city of _____ (or town or unincorporated place of _____) county of _____ state of New Hampshire; that I am a qualified voter therein and at the present time am an inhabitant of District No. _____ of _____ county.   NH R.S.A. 667:10

22   See, e.g., Texas Election Code Ann, Section 172.021 which for most offices requires a candidate only to pay a fee and as an alternative permits using the petition method in order to avoid unconstitutionally excluding persons who cannot pay the fee. For other statutes, see, Note, *New York's Designating Petition,* 14 Fordham Urb. L. J. 1011, 1024, n.94 (1985-86), discussed in *Government Ethics Reform,* chapter 9, "Access to the Ballot in Primary Elections: The Need For Fundamental Reform," at 304.

payment of a fee or a nonpartisan election of at-large delegates it would be an improvement over the current method from the point of view of improving ballot access. There may be a cost to eliminating the state committee's power to designate candidates to the extent this method could assure that some of the most experienced of our citizens will become convention delegates. If this is considered a significant factor, it might be useful to determine who have been past designees of state committees.

Variations on Nonpartisan Elections for Convention Delegates

New York's delegate elections, as with other New York elections, as a practical matter, are largely dependent on political party organization, and markedly so with respect to the state committee designation of candidates for delegates at large. Some states require that convention delegate elections be nonpartisan.[23] Missouri seeks to assure that more than one political party will be represented in the convention from the senatorial districts and also provides that election for at-large delegates will be nonpartisan.[24]

The New York experience with so-called nonpartisan elections often has been that the candidates are known surrogates for established political parties. This also may be the case in other states that purport to conduct nonpartisan elections. However, nonpartisan delegate elections nevertheless could increase ballot access by the elimination of the power of state committees to designate candidates. In addition, primary elections also would be unnecessary.

---

23 E.g., Arkansas:
(c) The election of delegates to the convention shall be on a nonpartisan basis, and no candidate shall designate political party affiliation at the time he files for election. Ark. C. A. s. 7-9-302. Also Ohio Const. Art. XVI, s. 2; South Dakota Const. Art. 23, s.2. *Cf.* Mont. Const. Art XIV, s. 4 (". . . The legislature shall determine whether the delegates may be nominated on a partisan or a nonpartisan basis.").

24 Missouri Constitution Art. 12, s. 3(a):
To secure representation from different political parties in each senatorial district, in the manner prescribed by its senatorial district committee each political party shall nominate but one candidate for delegate from each senatorial district, the certificate of nomination shall be filed in the office of the secretary of state at least thirty days before the election, each candidate shall be voted for on a separate ballot bearing the party designation, each elector shall vote for but one of the candidates, and the two candidates receiving the highest number of votes in each senatorial district shall be elected. **Candidates for delegates-at-large shall be nominated by nominating petitions only,** which shall be signed by electors of the state equal to five percent of the legal voters in the senatorial district in which the candidate resides until otherwise provided by law, and shall be verified as provided by law for initiative petitions, and filed in the office of the secretary of state at least thirty days before the election. All such candidates shall be voted for on a separate ballot without party designation, and the fifteen receiving the highest number of votes shall be elected. (emphasis supplied)

In any event, introducing nonpartisan elections would require a new election law scheme for delegate election. It could be characterized by one or more of the following:

1. by requiring persons who wish to be candidates to employ a petition method simpler than the one currently in place;

2. by permitting qualification as a candidate to rest on a declaration of candidacy and the payment of a registration fee;

3. by distinguishing between at-large and senatorial district candidates and requiring only the at-large delegates to be nonpartisan and requiring qualification by a simplified petition process or registration fee alone for the at-large delegates.

The Voting Rights Act and the Election of Delegates to a Constitutional Convention

Richard Briffault

This paper considers the application of the federal Voting Rights Act to the New York State constitutional provision for the election of delegates to a constitutional convention. It finds that the election of delegates to a constitutional convention probably falls within the scope of the Voting Rights Act and that the central features of the convention delegate selection process are similar to electoral mechanisms which, in other settings, have been found to infringe upon minority voting rights. These mechanisms, however, are not per se unlawful. The highly fact-specific nature of Voting Rights Act jurisprudence, the need for more precise demographic and statistical data, and the lack of any directly applicable precedents make it impossible to venture a prediction as to how a Voting Rights Act challenge to the New York delegate selection process would turn out.

The paper proceeds as follows: The first section, "The Voting Rights Act," provides a description of the Voting Rights Act, with particular attention to its implications for electoral structures that dilute minority representation. Section two, "The Procedure for Electing Convention Delegates," presents the state constitutional provision for the election of constitutional convention delegates. The following section, "Does the Voting Rights Act Apply to the Election of Constitutional Convention Delegates?," considers whether the election of delegates falls within the Voting Rights Act. "The Application of Section 2 of the Voting Rights Act to New York's Constitutional Convention Delegate Election Process" analyzes the delegate election rules in light of the governing principles and case law of the Act. Finally, "Alternative Strategies for Addressing the Voting Rights Act Questions" considers some strategies for obtaining further resolution of the Voting Rights Act questions.

445

The Voting Rights Act

The Concept of Vote Dilution

First enacted in 1965, and subsequently amended and extended in 1970, 1975, and 1982, the Voting Rights Act protects members of racial and language minorities from interference with the right to vote. For present purposes, the crucial provision of the Act is Section 2 (42 U.S.C. 1973), which prohibits any "voting qualification or prerequisite to voting or standard, practice, or procedure . . . which results in a denial or abridgement of the right of any citizen of the United States to vote on account of race or color" or membership in a language minority.

Initially, both government enforcement actions and private litigation under the Act focused on the elimination of formal barriers to participation, such as literacy tests and discriminatory registration practices. Soon, however, attention shifted to "vote dilution," that is, the use of electoral mechanisms that permit minority voters to register and cast ballots but that "operate to minimize or cancel out [minority] voting strength."[1]

Vote dilution is frequently an issue in reapportionment. Racial gerrymandering in which minority populations are fragmented into a number of different districts so that the minority is unable to elect the candidate of its choice in any one district is a form of vote dilution, as is gerrymandering that "packs" the minority into one district, thereby minimizing the number of districts in which minority voters can determine the outcome.[2]

Vote dilution is often alleged when candidates are elected at-large or from multimember districts rather than from single-member districts. As the Supreme Court has observed, "[t]he theoretical basis for this impairment is that where minority and majority voters consistently prefer different candidates, the majority, by virtue of its numerical superiority, will regularly defeat the choices of minority voters."[3] In 1993 the Court noted that "multi-member district plans, as well as at-large plans, generally pose greater threats to minority voter participation in the political process than do single-member districts."[4] The central problem with at-large or multimember systems is that they extend the range of the majority's domination, thereby making it more difficult for minorities than for whites to elect representatives of their own choosing.

---

1   *Burns v. Richardson*, 384 U.S. 73, 88 (1966).

2   See, e.g., *Thornburg v. Gingles*, 478 U.S. 30, 46 n.11 (1986).

3   *Ibid.* at 48 (1986).

4   *Growe v. Emison*, 113 S.Ct. 1075, 1084 (1993).

Assuming that a jurisdiction is to elect ten representatives, that the electorate is 60 percent majority and 40 percent minority, and that the minority is territorially concentrated in certain areas within the jurisdiction, then, if the jurisdiction is divided into ten single-member electoral districts, the minority has a fair chance of electing its candidates in four of the ten districts. But if the jurisdiction serves as a multimember district, with all ten representatives elected from the jurisdiction at-large, and if there is voting along racial lines, then it is quite possible that the majority will elect all ten representatives, "leaving the minority effectively unrepresented."[5]

Very early on, the Supreme Court determined electoral structures that dilute the voting strength of minority groups could violate the constitutional and statutory bans on racial discrimination in voting. In *Whitcomb* v. *Chavis*,[6] and *White* v. *Regester*[7], the Court held that at-large elections and multimember districts are not *per se* violative of minority voters' rights but that they can be unlawful where, under the totality of the circumstances, they operate to minimize or cancel out the ability of minority voters to elect their preferred candidates.

In *City of Mobile* v. *Bolden*,[8] decided in 1980, the Supreme Court made it significantly more difficult to bring a vote dilution case. Although *Bolden* confirmed that vote dilution could be a form of racial voting discrimination, a plurality of the Court determined that it would no longer use an "effects" analysis in determining whether an electoral mechanism constituted vote dilution. Instead, *Bolden* held that to establish vote dilution a plaintiff must prove that the electoral mechanism was adopted or maintained intentionally for the invidious purpose of excluding minorities.

The 1982 Amendment

In 1982, Congress amended Section 2 to reject the *Bolden* "intent" test and reinstate the prior "effects" analysis. Specifically, Congress rewrote Section 2 to make it clear that the Act applies to any standard, practice, or procedure "which results in a denial or abridgement" of the right to vote,[9] and Congress added a new subsection (b) which provides that a violation of Section 2 is established

---

5   478 U.S. at 48, n. 14.

6   403 U.S. 124 (1971).

7   412 U.S. 755 (1973).

8   446 U.S. 55 (1980).

9   The pre-1982 version of Section 2 had simply applied to standards, practices or procedures that "deny or abridge" the right to vote, permitting the interpretation adopted in *Bolden* that the denial or abridgement of minority voting rights must have been intended by those who imposed or applied the electoral mechanism.

if, based on the totality of the circumstances, it is shown that the political processes leading to nomination or election in the State or political subdivision are not equally open to participation by members of a class of citizens protected by subsection (a) of this section in that its members have less opportunity than other members of the electorate to participate in the political process and elect representatives of their choice. The extent to which members of a protected class have been elected to office in the State or political subdivision is one circumstance which may be considered: *Provided,* That nothing in this section establishes a right to have members of a protected class elected in numbers equal to their proportion in the population.

Amended Section 2, thus, makes it unlawful to use any electoral mechanism that, under the totality of the circumstances, results in the denial or abridgment of the right to vote of any citizen who is a member of a protected class of racial or language minorities. As the Supreme Court has explained, the "essence of a §2 claim is that a certain electoral law, practice, or structure interacts with social and historical conditions to cause an inequality in the opportunities enjoyed by black and white voters to elect their preferred representatives."[10] Section 2 rejects *Bolden*'s "intent" test, singles out as one key factor the extent to which minorities have been elected to office in the jurisdiction, and also rejects the idea that the Act establishes a right to proportional representation, but it provides no clear standard for determining when an electoral mechanism will be found to constitute unlawful vote dilution. Relying on the vote dilution jurisprudence that had developed in the decade before *Bolden,* the Senate Judiciary Committee Report that accompanied the bill that amended Section 2 elaborated on some of the circumstances that might be probative of a Section 2 violation. The Supreme Court has indicated that these factors are to be given great weight in any Section 2 analysis. These factors are:

1. the history of voting-related discrimination in the jurisdiction;

2. the extent to which voting in the elections of the jurisdiction is racially polarized;

3. the extent to which the jurisdiction has used voting practices or procedures that tend to enhance the opportunity for discrimination against the minority group, such as unusually large election

---

10   478 U.S. at 47.

districts, majority vote requirements,[11] and prohibitions against bullet voting;[12]

4. the exclusion of members of the minority group from candidate slating processes;

5. the extent to which minority group members bear the effects of past discrimination in areas such as education, employment, and health, which hinder their ability to participate effectively in the political process;

6. the use of overt or subtle racial appeals in political campaigns; and

7. the extent to which members of the minority group have been elected to public office in the jurisdiction.

The Senate Judiciary Report also noted that evidence demonstrating that elected officials are unresponsive to the particularized needs of the members of the minority group and that the policy underlying the state's or the political subdivision's use of the contested practice or structure is tenuous may also have probative value.

The Report, however, stressed that this list of typical factors is neither comprehensive nor exclusive, and that there is no requirement that any particular number of factors be proved, or that a majority of them point one way or the other. Rather, the resolution of a vote dilution claim "depends upon a searching practical evaluation of the 'past and present reality'" and "on a 'functional' view of the political process."[13]

Thornburg v. Gingles

The leading Supreme Court case construing amended Section 2 and considering its application to at-large and multimember districts is *Thornburg* v. *Gingles*,[14] decided in 1986, which involved a challenge by black voters to five multimember legislative districts in the redistricting plan of the North Carolina General Assembly. *Gingles* confirmed that under

---

11 That is, requirements that the winning candidate receive an absolute majority of all votes cast, rather than a simple plurality.

12 That is, requirements that a voter must cast votes equivalent to the total number of legislative seats that are to be filled. Bullet voting enables a minority group to win some at-large seats if it concentrates its vote behind a limited number of candidates and if the vote of the majority is divided among a number of candidates. Anti-bullet voting rules would preclude such a strategy.

13 478 U.S. at 45.

14 478 U.S. 30 (1986).

amended Section 2 vote dilution could be proven by an "effects" test without regard to intent. The Court held that to establish a vote dilution claim with respect to a multimember districting plan, a plaintiff must be able to meet three conditions.

First, the minority must be "sufficiently large and geographically compact to constitute a majority in a single-member district. If it is not, as would be the case in a substantially integrated district, the *multimember form* of the district cannot be responsible for minority voters' inability to elect its candidates."[15] As the Court explained, "unless minority voters possess the *potential* to elect representatives in the absence of the challenged structure or practice, they cannot claim to have been injured by the structure or practice."[16]

Second, "the minority group must be able to show that it is politically cohesive. If the minority group is not politically cohesive, it cannot be said that the selection of a multimember electoral structure thwarts distinctive minority group interests."

Third, the minority plaintiffs must be able to demonstrate that "the white majority votes sufficiently as a bloc to enable it . . . usually to defeat the minority's preferred candidate."[17]

Gingles gave extensive consideration to the issue of racially polarized voting. Polarized voting is central to the proof of the second and third *Gingles* factors. One way of proving minority political cohesiveness necessary is to show that minority voters tend to vote for the same candidates. Moreover, it is white bloc voting that results in the white majority "defeat[ing] the combined strength of minority support plus white 'crossover' votes."[18] Indeed, racially polarized voting is central to a vote dilution claim: it is the negative synergy of racially polarized voting with majority-enhancing devices like multimember districts and at-large elections that give those electoral systems their vote dilutive effects.

Gingles, however, provided "no simple doctrinal test for the existence of legally significant racially polarized voting."[19] The amount of white bloc voting that will "minimize or cancel" black voters' ability to elect representatives of their choice "will vary from district to district according to a number of factors," including the nature of the allegedly

---

15   *Ibid.* at 50. (emphasis in original).
16   *Ibid.* at n. 17. (emphasis in original)
17   *Ibid.* at 51.
18   *Ibid.* at 56.
19   *Ibid.* at 58.

dilutive electoral mechanism; the presence or absence of other potentially dilutive electoral devices; the percentage of voters who are minority; the size of the district; and the number of seats to be filled. In short, "the degree of racial bloc voting that is cognizable as an element of a §2 vote dilution claim will vary according to a variety of factual circumstances."

Gingles, however, did reject arguments made by the state of North Carolina that plaintiffs must prove that race (as opposed to other factors such as socioeconomic status or party affiliation) is the principal reason for voters' decisions. According to the plurality opinion, the proper inquiry under Section 2 is *whether* voters of different races favor different candidates, not *why* they do so. As Justice Brennan explained, "it is the *difference* between the choices made by blacks and whites — not the reason for the difference — that results in blacks having less opportunity than whites to elect their preferred representatives."[20] Plaintiffs could prove the voting was racially polarized by demonstrating a substantial statistical correlation between the race of voters and the candidates for whom they voted. There was no need to show that race "caused" voters to vote the way they did, that race was the primary determinant in voters' choices, or that voters were motivated by racial hostility. Substantial statistical differences in the voting patterns of black and white voters, resulting in the usual defeat of candidates supported by black voters, would suffice.

Ultimately, the Supreme Court sustained the lower court's findings of a Section 2 violation with respect to four of the five districts at issue, but reversed with respect to the fifth district because sustained black electoral success in that district had resulted in proportional representation for black residents, and, thus, the multimember election structure did not dilute black political strength.[21]

Vote Dilution Issues Since Gingles

By confirming that amended Section 2 imposed a "results" test, treating racially polarized voting as the central "circumstance" in the "totality of the circumstances" analysis, and holding that racially polarized voting could be proven by the statistical correlation of voting patterns without showing that race caused those voting patterns, *Gingles* facilitated minority challenges to a host of at-large systems for electing city and county legislators, and to multimember districts for the election of state legisla-

---

20   *Ibid.* at 63. (emphasis in original)
21   *Ibid.* at 77.

tors and state judges. These challenges have frequently been successful, although courts have repeatedly advised that "Section 2 contains no per se prohibitions against particular types of districts" and that the burden is on plaintiffs to prove that the apportionment scheme has the effect of denying a protected class the equal opportunity to elect its candidate of choice.[22]

Even after *Gingles* a number of vexing voting rights questions remain. One issue is the interplay of the "totality of the circumstances" test in the statute and the factors laid out in the Senate Judiciary Report with *Gingles'* three-factor test. A number of courts have treated *Gingles'* three factors as necessary preconditions to be met before ever getting to the totality of the circumstances. If one factor is missing — typically, if the minority is too small to constitute a majority in a single-member district — the court will not proceed to the "totality of the circum-stances."[23] Other courts have treated the *Gingles* test as if it were the sole standard to be met in a vote dilution challenge.[24] Some judges have sought proof of both the *Gingles* factors and at least some of the factors identified in the Senate Judiciary Report.[25]

In general, when plaintiffs have challenged at-large or multimember election systems and have requested single-member districts as a remedy, courts have required plaintiffs to prove all three *Gingles* factors. But the meaning of three factors is not always self-evident. With respect to the first factor, courts and litigants have divided over what constitutes a "sufficiently large and geographically compact" minority group. *Gingles* required plaintiffs to prove that they were large enough to constitute a "majority" in a single-member district. But the Court did not specify what was meant by the term *majority* — population majority, voting age population majority, or citizen voting age majority. Most courts have embraced the voting age majority position, but there are precedents in support of each definition of majority.[26] The "compactness" of the pre-dominantly minority district that could be carved out of the at-large or multimember district may also emerge as a significant issue in the after-math of the Supreme Court's recent invalidation of a "dramatically irregu-

---

22 *Voinovich* v. *Quilter*, 113 S.Ct. 1149 (1993).

23 See, e.g., *McNeil* v. *Springfield Park Dist.*, 851 F.2d 937 (7th Cir. 1988); *Sanchez* v. *Bond*, 875 F.2d 1488 (10th Cir. 1989).

24 *Gomez* v. *City of Watsonville*, 863 F.2d 1407 (9th Cir. 1988).

25 See, e.g., *Monroe* v. *City of Woodville*, 881 F.2d 1327 (5th Cir. 1989).

26 See also *Growe* v. *Emison*, 113 S.Ct. 1075, 1083 n.4 (1993) (noting but not resolving dispute over whether "majority" refers to total population or voting age population).

lar" North Carolina congressional district drawn to create a black voting majority.[27]

The meaning of "politically cohesive" minority — *Gingles'* second prong — has been contested in cases in which plaintiffs have sought to combine different racial and ethnic groups, e.g., African-Americans, Latinos, and/or Asian-Americans in a single plaintiff class. This might occur when no one minority group is large enough to constitute a majority in any single-member district. In a challenge to a three-seat multimember district where three single-member districts are sought as the remedy, a minority would have to constitute a majority in at least one possible single-member district in order to pass the first *Gingles* factor. If the minority constitutes less than one-sixth of the voting age population in the district, it probably would not pass that test. But, if two minorities, each having 10-12 percent of the district's population, are taken together then the first hurdle might be overcome. In several cases, plaintiffs have urged that different minority groups can be combined into a politically cohesive aggregation in order to cross the *Gingles* threshold. "The courts have not often allowed minority groups to be combined," although cases go both ways and "what is relevant is an empirical demonstration of whether blacks and Hispanics consistently vote together in elections in which minority and white candidates compete for office."[28] In a case decided earlier this year, the Supreme Court emphasized the special need for a showing of minority political cohesion where the minority in question is an "agglomerated political bloc" of distinct ethnic and language minority groups.[29]

The third *Gingles* factor is the existence of "legally significant" white bloc voting. As with all the *Gingles* factors, the plaintiff bears the burden of proving racially polarized voting.[30] The examination of racial polarization has two parts. The first is determining whether minority and majority voters cast their ballots differently. This has become the realm of statistical proof and clashes between conflicting expert witnesses over the proper method of determining the voting behavior of different racial groups.

The second step is deciding whether polarization is legally significant. This requires determining who the minority-preferred candidates are and how often these candidates are successful in their bids for office.

---

27 *Shaw* v. *Reno*, 61 U.S.L.W. 4819 (1993).

28 Grofman, Handley & Niemi, *Minority Representation and the Quest for Voting Equality* 72 (1992).

29 *Growe* v. *Emison*, 113 S.Ct. at 1085.

30 *Voinovich* v. *Quilter*, 113 S.Ct. 1149, 1156-57 (1993).

Courts have divided over whether the analysis should be limited to elections that include minority candidates or whether so-called white-versus-white elections, in which white candidates enjoying the support of the preponderance of minority voters are elected over other white candidates, can also be considered. In a portion of *Gingles* joined by only a plurality of the Supreme Court, Justice Brennan advocated a race-neutral approach to determining the minority-preferred candidate, but Justice White, in a separate concurring opinion, and Justice O'Connor, writing on behalf of three of the other justices, rejected Justice Brennan's approach and took the position that the race of the candidate could be considered relevant. Most courts have rejected Justice Brennan's position and have either limited their consideration to elections in which there were minority candidates or have indicated that elections involving minority candidates will be given greater weight — although at least one circuit court has opted for a race-neutral approach. It should also be noted that the Supreme Court, including Justice Brennan's plurality, upheld a district court's finding of legally significant racial bloc voting based on an analysis of only those elections in which there were black candidates.[31]

If a court chooses to focus on only those elections in which there are minority candidates, there may be only a limited number of such minority-contested elections for the office whose electoral mechanism is subject to attack. Can the court consider election contests other than those for the office under challenge? The handful of courts that have considered whether the results of so-called "exogenous elections" may be admitted into the analysis have divided over the question, with most finding that exogenous elections may be relevant, but at least one circuit court opinion held that only elections for the office in question may be considered.[32]

A fundamental uncertainty in the proof of legally significant racially polarized voting is the significance of some black electoral success. The only "circumstance" specifically mentioned in the Act itself in determining whether the local political process is equally open to participation by minority voters is "the extent to which members of a protected class have been elected to office," and the Senate Report also gives as a factor "the extent to which members of the minority group have been elected to public office in the jurisdiction." By the same token, the Act rejects any right to proportional representation. Have minority votes been unlawfully diluted where minority candidates have enjoyed some electoral success?

---

31   See generally Grofman et al., *supra,* at 75-79.

32   *Ibid.* at 79-80.

In *Gingles,* the Supreme Court held that "where multimember districting generally works to dilute the minority vote, it cannot be defended on the ground that it sporadically and serendipitously benefits minority voters."[33] Some minority electoral success, even nearly proportional representation in one recent election, does not compel a trial court to dismiss a vote dilution claim, but sustained minority success is inconsistent with the proof of vote dilution.[34]

Finally, some lower courts have considered the question of so-called "influence districts." Where the minority is too small or insufficiently geographically compact to be a majority in a single-member district that might be carved out of a multimember district, some plaintiffs have still sought the creation of single-member districts on the theory that the multimember system impairs the minority's ability to *influence* electoral outcomes even though it cannot elect its own candidates. *Gingles* considered only the claim that multimember systems impair the ability of minorities to *elect* representatives of their choice and expressly declined to consider whether multimember districts can be attacked on an "influence" theory.[35] In two decisions this year the Court again declined to pass on the viability of an "influence" critique of districting systems.[36] The lower courts have divided over whether an influence district theory may be used to attack a multimember districting scheme, although only a handful of courts have considered the issue.[37]

The Procedure for Electing Convention Delegates

The procedure for the election of delegates to a New York constitutional convention is set forth in Article XIX, Section 2, of the state Constitution. Article XIX, §2, provides that if the voters approve the call for a constitutional convention, then "the electors of every senate district of the state,

---

33   478 U.S. at 76.

34   Cf. *Nash* v. *Blunt,* 797 F. Supp. 1488, 1503-04 (W.D. Mo. 1992) (finding sufficient minority electoral success to rebut vote dilution claim where twice in a decade minority candidates won Democratic primaries with small pluralities over fragmented white opposition and then went on to win the general election).

35   478 U.S. at 46-47 n. 12.

36   See *Growe* v. *Emison,* 113 S.Ct. 1075, 1084 n.5 (1993) (multimember district plan; case remanded for deference to pending state judicial proceeding; moreover, no showing of a politically cohesive minority); *Voinovich* v. *Quilter,* 113 S.Ct. 1149, 1157 (1993) ("influence" theory used to challenge single-member districting plan that allegedly "packed" black voters into districts where they had large majorities, thereby reducing their ability to influence outcomes in other districts; but no showing of racially polarized voting).

37   See, e.g., *West* v. *Clinton,* 786 F.Supp. 803 (W.D. Ark. 1992) (assuming the argument that influence theory is legally viable, but rejecting its application to particular multimember plan, and citing other cases).

as then organized, shall elect three delegates at the next ensuing general election, and the electors of the state voting at the same election shall elect fifteen delegates-at-large."

This provision is the successor to a provision of the Constitution of 1894; the present language and number of this Section derives from an amendment submitted by the constitutional convention of 1938. This provision governed the election of delegates to the 1967 Convention. At that time, the Senate consisted of 57 districts, so that 171 delegates were elected from districts. In addition, 15 delegates were elected at large, for a total convention of 186.

Currently, the Senate consists of 61 districts, so that 183 delegates would be elected from Senate districts. With the additional 15 statewide delegates-at-large, the total convention would consist of 198 delegates.

Does the Voting Rights Act Apply to the Election of Constitutional Convention Delegates?

The Voting Rights Act almost certainly applies to the election of constitutional convention delegates. Section 2 broadly proscribes denial or abridgments of the right to vote. Another provision defines the terms "vote" and "voting" to "include all action necessary to make a vote effective in any primary, special, or general election . . . for public or party office and propositions for which votes are received in an election."[38] Although nothing in the Act refers specifically to the election of convention delegates, the Act also makes no specific reference to any other elective office. The Act has traditionally received an expansive construction, and it ought to apply to any office filled by popular election, including convention delegates.

The only basis for an argument for the exclusion of convention delegates from the ambit of the Act would be that under current case law the "one person, one vote" doctrine does not apply to the election of constitutional convention delegates. The "one person, one vote" doctrine is an application of the Equal Protection Clause of the Fourteenth Amendment to the right to vote. Under "one person, one vote," the right to vote includes the right to an equally weighted vote, so that a state or local government cannot create an electoral system in which the votes of some residents of a jurisdiction are given a greater weight than the votes of other residents of the same jurisdiction. "One person, one vote" requires that legislative districts

---

38   42 U.S.C. 1973l(c)(1) (Section 14 of the Act).

be of substantially equal population. But at least two state supreme courts and one federal district court have held that "one person, one vote" does not apply to the election of convention delegates, on the theory that a constitutional convention is not a governing body but simply a recommendatory body whose "only authority . . . is to propose amendments to be submitted to a vote of the people of the State at large."[39]

The precedential effect of the exclusion of constitutional convention delegations from the "one person, one vote" doctrine for the resolution of the Voting Rights Act coverage question was substantially eroded, if not entirely eliminated, by the decision of the Supreme Court in *Chisom* v. *Roemer,* in 1991, to apply Section 2 of the Voting Rights Act to judicial elections.[40] In *Chisom,* the defendants argued, *inter alia,* that judges are not "representatives" within the meaning of Section 2(b) of the Act, and that an earlier Supreme Court decision that had affirmed a lower court's finding that the "one person, one vote" doctrine did not apply to judicial elections[41] supported the claim that when Congress used the term "representatives" in the 1982 amendment it did not mean to include judges. *Chisom* determined that "the word 'representatives' described the winners of representative, popular elections" and did not eliminate any category of elected officials. The earlier decision that "one person, one vote" does not apply to judicial elections did not affect the scope of Section 2 since "the statute was enacted to protect voting rights that are not adequately protected by the constitution itself."[42]

In the aftermath of *Chisom,* it has to be assumed that Section 2 of the Voting Rights Act applies to the election of constitutional convention delegates.

The Application of Section 2 of the Voting Rights Act to New York's Constitutional Convention Delegate Election Process

Article XIX, §2 of the state Constitution relies on two electoral mechanisms that have repeatedly been the targets of successful Voting Rights Act challenges in other settings: at-large elections, and multimember

---

39   *Livingston* v. *Ogilvie,* 250 N.E.2d 138, 145-46 (Ill. 1969); *Stander* v. *Kelley,* 250 A.2d 474 (Pa. 1969), cert. denied sub nom, *Lindsay* v. *Kelley,* 395 U.S. 827; *Driskell* v. *Edwards,* 413 F. Supp. 974 (W.D. La. 1976).

40   *Chisom* v. *Roemer,* 111 S.Ct. 2354 (1991). See also *Houston Lawyers Ass'n* v. *Attorney General of Texas,* 111 S.Ct. 2376 (1991).

41   *Wells* v. *Edwards,* 347 F.Supp. 453 (M.D. La. 1972), aff'd mem. 409 U.S. 1095 (1973).

42   111 S.Ct.

districts. This part of the memorandum sketches some of the arguments that would be raised in a possible Section 2 attack on each on Article XIX's electoral mechanisms; some possible defenses; and some of the uncertainties in resolving these questions.

The At-Large Delegates

The state Constitution provides that 15 delegates are to be delegates-at-large, elected on a statewide basis. At-large electoral mechanisms have frequently been challenged as dilutive of minority voting power. In general, the larger the jurisdiction, the more difficult it is for candidates backed by minority groups to obtain electoral success. Greater resources are necessary to mount successful campaigns in large districts, and large districts are more likely to be dominated politically by members of the white majority. Historically, in most jurisdictions, minorities have tended to be more successful politically in smaller electoral units. A statewide district is, of course, the largest district there can be.

Applying the three *Gingles* factors, one would find, first, that both African-Americans and Hispanics are probably "sufficiently large and geographically compact to constitute a majority in a single-member district." If the 15 at-large delegates were replaced by 15 single-member districts, a minority group could elect its own representative if it constituted a majority in one-fifteenth of the state. In other words, a group that constituted around one-thirtieth of the state, or a little more than 3 percent of the state, if it were geographically concentrated, could elect a representative in one district. According to recent census figures, New York's population is 16 percent African-American and 12.3 percent Hispanic. Even if a court were to use voting age population or adult citizen population figures, which might reduce the African-American and Hispanic proportions of the relevant populations, it is still likely that each group would be large enough to constitute a majority in one out of 15 single-member districts.

This first *Gingles* factor also requires that the plaintiff minority be "geographically compact." Since African-American and Hispanic residents are, to a considerable degree, concentrated in and around New York City, it is likely that each group could dominate at least one geographically compact district in that part of the state — although any final determination would have to await more thorough and precise demographic analysis.

As for the second factor, many cases have found that African-American and Hispanic voters constitute distinct, politically cohesive units. Heeding the Supreme Court's recent warning that the political cohesiveness of minorities may not be presumed and must be proven with appropriate statistical analysis of voting records, it is still unlikely that the second *Gingles* factor would be a major impediment to a Section 2 attack on the election of delegates-at-large.

The third factor involves consideration of whether in New York State whites and minorities have different voting patterns and whether, due to any such differences, minorities are unable to elect candidates of their choice to statewide office. The first aspect of this factor — whether voting patterns are racially polarized — requires statistical proof. The second aspect — whether minorities are able to elect candidates of their choice to statewide office — is less difficult if attention is limited to statewide elections in which there have been minority candidates. As far as I can tell, no minority candidate has ever won election to any of the four statewide state offices (governor, lieutenant governor, attorney general, comptroller) or to the United States Senate, and at least four minority candidates have been defeated — Basil Paterson (running for lieutenant governor on a ticket with Arthur Goldberg); Carl McCall (defeated in 1982 Democratic Primary for lieutenant governor); Herman Badillo (defeated for state comptroller); Al Sharpton (defeated in 1992 Democratic primary for United States senator).[43] An African-American currently holds the office of comptroller but he was elected to that post by the state legislature.

On the other hand, two minority candidates were elected as delegates-at-large to the 1967 Constitutional Convention: Andrew Tyler and Antonia Pantoja.

That would mean that 1/15th, or 6.7 percent, of the at-large delegates were African-American at a time when African-Americans were 11 percent of the state's population, and 1/15th, or 6.7 percent, of the at-large delegates were Hispanic at a time when Hispanics constituted 7.5 percent of the state's population.[44]

The relative success of these minority candidates — relative, that is, to the lack of minority success in other statewide elections — appears to be a product of the party-line voting that characterized the 1966 delegate-at-large elections. Overall, Democrat-Liberals won 13 of the 15 seats. The entire Democratic slate ran ahead of the entire Republican slate by about 100,000 votes. There was surprisingly little variance within the party slates.

---

43 This is based on a cursory review of recent elections. It is quite possible that a closer examination might disclose other races in which minority candidates ran for statewide office. A court might also consider how Jesse Jackson fared in the 1984 and 1988 Democratic presidential primaries.

44 African-American and Hispanic percentages of New York's 1967 population were obtained from data supplied by the Temporary Commission on Constitutional Revision.

The most popular of 15 Democratic nominees won 2,327,300 Democratic votes; the least popular won 2,318,386 Democratic votes, or within 10,000 of the leader of the slate. On the Republican side, the most popular candidate won 2,229,316 Republican votes, and the least popular 2,217,261. The two winning Republicans won because they also had Conservative Party backing.[45] In other words, race appears not to have been a factor with the voters in the 1966 general election; the Democratic-Liberal slating had the major role in determining the ability of minorities to elect their own representatives.

Two issues, then, in any Voting Rights Act challenge to the delegates-at-large would be whether, and how much, party-line voting has declined over the last three decades, and what procedure will determine how convention delegates are nominated. On the second point, in the absence of any specific provision for delegates-at-large, I assume that the general provisions for nomination "for any office to be filled by the voters of the entire state" would govern.[46]

In short, a challenge to the delegates-at-large would probably satisfy the first two *Gingles* factors. The third *Gingles* factor creates greater indeterminacy. There is a need for adequate statistical proof of voting patterns in statewide elections. Moreover, the qualitative judgment of whether the record in the election of delegates-at-large in 1966, in light of the lack of statewide minority electoral success in the intervening three decades, indicates that minority political power is likely to be minimized or canceled out through statewide election of convention delegates is inevitably uncertain.

If a court were to find that plaintiffs can prevail on all three *Gingles* factors that might be the end of the dispute, and the at-large elections could be invalidated. It is also possible that a court might, as part of a "totality of the circumstances" review go on to other issues. In defense of the delegates-at-large electoral structure, the state might make two arguments. First, there is a public policy value in having delegates with a statewide perspective participate in the convention's deliberations. Their broad, statewide outlook can be seen as a desirable balance to those elected from the Senate districts, who are likely to take a more localist approach to the state's problems. In other words, the statewide delegates may play a role

---

45   The Conservatives provided a little over 348,000 to each of the three Republicans they endorsed. These two then defeated the two Democrats who had not received the Liberal Party's endorsement, and the two Republicans who had been endorsed by the Liberals. The Conservative-endorsed Republicans received about 23,000 votes more on the Conservative line than the Liberal-endorsed Republicans received on the Liberal line. Shalala, *The City and the Constitution: The 1967 New York Convention's Response to the Urban Crisis* 26 (table 4) (1972).

46   Election L. 6-104.

akin to that of the president in the federal government, the governor and other statewide officials in the state government, and the mayor and the two other citywide officials in New York City's government in offsetting the narrower viewpoints of those elected from smaller legislative districts. For purposes of a Section 2 "totality of the circumstances" test, the delegates-at-large can be justified as the product of a legitimate and not a "tenuous" policy.

Second, and intertwined with the first, the delegates at-large are only a small portion of the total convention membership. There would be 183 Senate district delegates and 15 delegates-at-large, for a total of 198. The delegates-at-large would amount to approximately 7.6 percent of the total convention membership. It could be argued that even if an at-large election mechanism dilutes minority representation, the dilutive effect is relatively modest and justified by the benefit in terms of statewide perspective that the delegates-at-large provide. There is some precedent for this approach. In a handful of cases, courts and the Department of Justice have approved electoral systems for local governments that combined a large number of representatives elected from single-member districts with one or a small number of representatives elected from the jurisdiction at large — although such mixed systems have also been invalidated, too.[47]

The possibility that the at-large election could survive a Section 2 challenge, even if the *Gingles* factors are met, if the court believed that the at-large mechanism assured the election of a relatively small number of delegates with a valuable statewide perspective assumes that the other delegate election mechanism — which governs the election of more than 92 percent of the convention delegates — provides minority voters fair and effective representation in the convention's deliberations. But the other delegate election procedure is itself subject to Voting Rights Act attack.

The Delegates Elected from Senate Districts

The state Constitution provides that each Senate district "shall elect three delegates" to the convention. Each Senate district thus serves as a multimember district. As previously noted, multimember districts are a frequent target of Voting Rights Act litigation, with plaintiffs contending that

---

47 See, e.g., Days, "Section 5 Enforcement and the Department of Justice," in B. Grofman & C. Davidson, eds., *Controversies in Minority Voting* 61-63 (1992) (discussing Justice Department role in development of city government for Houston that combined districts and at-large elections); *East Jefferson Coalition* v. *Parish of Jefferson,* 703 F. Supp. 28 (E.D. La. 1989) (approval of 6-1 plan instead of all single-member district system); *Williams* v. *City of Dallas,* 734 F. Supp. 1317 (N.D. Texas 1990) (invalidating Dallas' 8-3 system).

if the multimember districts are broken up into smaller single-member districts minorities will be more likely to elect representatives of their own choosing. The assumption is that in a multimember district a solid majority of racially polarized white voters will control the election for all the seats to be filled in the district but if the district is divided into smaller single-member districts a minority would be able to win some of those seats. As with at-large elections, multimember districts are not per se unlawful. Plaintiffs would have to prove that the multimember election mechanism is likely to abridge minority representation "under the totality of circumstances" in the jurisdiction.

A brief look at the degree of success in electing minority candidates to the Senate, compared with the rate of election of minorities to the Assembly, suggests that at least African-Americans might be able to argue that they would be disadvantaged by multimember elections from Senate districts and would receive more effective representation if the three delegates from each Senate district were elected from single-member districts. There are 61 Senate districts and 150 Assembly districts, so that the Assembly districts can be treated as something of a proxy for 183 single-member convention delegate districts. If anything, since single-member convention delegate districts would be smaller than the Assembly districts, the use of Assembly districts in this comparison may actually understate the dilutive effect of multimember Senate districts. Currently, African-Americans hold 5 of the 61 Senate seats, or 8.2 percent of the total, but African-Americans account for 21 of the 150 Assembly seats, or 14 percent of the total. Since New York's population is 16 percent African-American it appears that African-Americans are currently receiving nearly proportional representation in the Assembly, but much less representation in the Senate. Moreover, all the African-American Senators are from New York City, whereas four of the African-Americans in the Assembly are from outside the City, suggesting that African-Americans outside New York City would be far more able to elect representatives of their choosing in smaller districts.

It is less clear that the use of the multimember Senate districts would interfere with the representation of Hispanic New Yorkers. Currently, Hispanics hold 6.5 percent (4 of 61) of seats in the Senate but only 4.7 percent (7 of 150) seats in the Assembly. According to the 1990 census, Hispanics account for 12.3 percent of New York's population.

Both African-Americans and Hispanics won relatively few elections from the multimember Senate districts in 1966. There were 10 African-American delegates elected from Senate districts, or 5.8 percent of the total of 171 Senate district delegates to the 1967 Convention. At that time African-Americans made up 11 percent of the state's population. In 1967, there were 5 Hispanic delegates elected from Senate districts, or 2.9 percent of the total, at a time when Hispanics accounted for 7.5 percent of the state's population. On the other hand, it is not clear how much of this was due to racial bloc voting in either the nomination or the election process. Of the 15 minority delegates, ten were elected from four districts which elected either two or three minority delegates, but five were elected from districts in which only one minority delegate was elected.[48]

The Voting Rights Act analysis of multimember Senate districts is far more complicated than this brief discussion of 1993 minority membership in the Senate and the Assembly and use of 1967 delegate totals would suggest. For one thing, no one election can be dispositive; rather, a court would need to consider several elections' worth of results. In particular, this brief survey has focused on the ethnic identities of the candidates elected. Litigants and a court determining a Section 2 challenge would be at least as interested in the ethnicities of those candidates defeated.

More importantly, it is quite possible that a court would not approach the question of whether the use of multimember Senate districts abridge minority voting rights on a statewide basis, but might instead consider the use for each district separately, and evaluate the *Gingles* factors differently in each district. In the typical Section 2 lawsuit involving multimember districts, a state legislature has provided that some legislators will be elected from multimember districts and some from single-member districts, and minority plaintiffs have challenged multimember schemes in particular districts. The courts have then considered such issues as the size of the minority population, the existence of racially polarized voting, and minority electoral success in *each district* in which a multimember scheme was challenged. Although courts might consider some statewide circumstances — such as past *de jure* discrimination, or racist election appeals — the critical issues concerned whether multimember elections are dilutive in a particular district. Thus, in *Gingles,* the trial court and the Supreme Court proceeded on a district-by-district basis in considering the existence, and the significance, of racially polarized voting, and ultimately the Supreme Court upheld the invalidation of multimember elections in four districts but reversed the trial court and permitted multimember elections in the fifth district.

---

48 Again, party seemed to play the dominant role in the general election, with all the 14 minority Democrats elected from districts in which only Democrats were elected, and the one minority Republican elected from a district that elected only Republicans.

The use of multimember Senate districts for the election of convention delegates is different from other recent Voting Rights Act cases in that the state Constitution treats every Senate district as a multimember district. Because the state Constitution imposes multimember elections in all districts, it is possible that a court might treat the state as a whole as the relevant jurisdiction for consideration of the vote dilution question, but a plausible reading of *Gingles* is that any lawsuit might have to be adjudicated on a district-by-district basis since these are district elections, not statewide elections. That is, plaintiffs would have to prove for individual Senate districts that there is a minority group large and compact enough to win in a single-member district that could be carved out of the multimember Senate district; that the minority is politically cohesive in that district; and that, as a result of racially polarized voting, multimember elections would deny minorities an equal opportunity to elect candidates of their choice in a particular district.

On a district-by-district basis several outcomes are plausible. First, for those districts that are predominantly minority in population and have regularly elected minority Senators, there would probably not be a finding of vote dilution. In some of these districts it is likely that all three delegates will be minority.[49] Second, in some districts the minority population will be too small or dispersed to constitute a majority in any single-member district that might be carved out of the multimember Senate districts. In these districts, too, the vote dilution claim is likely to fail. Finally, there will be some number of districts where the minority population is large enough to pass the first *Gingles* factor, but not large enough to dominate the district politically. In each of these districts, a court (or courts) will have to consider whether the minority is politically cohesive, whether there is racially polarized voting, and whether due to such racial voting minorities have been unable to elect candidates of their choice. Without the necessary demographic data and statistical analyses of election results and voting patterns, it is impossible to know how these issues will be resolved in any district, but it is certainly possible that multimember Senate district elections will, after the application of the *Gingles* factors, be *prima facie* valid in some districts and *prima facie* invalid in others.

Are there arguments that the state could rely on to defend multimember elections in those districts where the state has found that they are *prima facie* dilutive of minority voting power? To be sure, some of the aggravating circumstances noted in the Senate Judiciary Committee Report, such

---

49 In the 1966 convention delegate elections, two Senate districts, the then-18th district (Kings) and the then-27th district (New York), elected three minority delegates apiece, and two districts, the then-29th (Bronx) and the then-31st (Bronx) elected two minority delegates apiece.

as majority vote requirements (that is, requirements of a runoff if no candidate gets more than a plurality) and prohibitions of bullet voting are absent. The presence of the other factors identified in the Report is no doubt subject to great debate. However, unlike the statewide at-large elections, it is unclear what arguments the state could present to defend multimember elections.

The fact that the multimember election system goes back decades and was adopted without racially invidious intent is, under Section 2, irrelevant. It is not clear what policy the multimember Senate district elections serve today. At one time, most Senate districts were coterminous with counties. A residue of this past practice may still be found in Article III, §4, of the state Constitution, which provides that "no county shall be divided in the formation of a senate district except to make two or more senate districts wholly in such county." The use of Senate districts as units of election may have been a means of assuring representation of county governments and discrete county interests in the convention revision process. Today, however, county lines and other political subdivision lines play little role in the districting of the legislature. In an unsuccessful challenge to the 1992 Senate reapportionment, plaintiffs pointed out that under the current districting scheme 28 out of the total 61 Senate districts cross county lines, with 11 counties having populations smaller than one Senate district and 12 counties having populations larger than one Senate district so divided. The current Senate consists of four bicounty districts, and the Bronx, which has sufficient population for four whole districts, is given only two wholly intracounty districts and is then divided by four additional cross-county districts.[50] As Judge Titone observed, the Senate apportionment "all but disregards the integrity of county borders."[51]

Nor could the state rely on the fact that the Department of Justice "precleared" the Senate district lines under Section 5 of the Voting Rights Act in 1992. Section 5 provides that certain states and political subdivisions — the so-called "covered jurisdictions"[52] — can enforce changes on their voting practices and procedures only after obtaining federal

---

50   *Wolpoff* v. *Cuomo*, 587 N.Y.S.2d 560, 565 (1992).

51   Ibid. at 567.

52   A political subdivision becomes a "covered jurisdiction" under Section 5 through a two-fold test: (1) did fewer than 50 percent of the voting age residents vote in the presidential elections of 1964, 1968, or 1972? (2) Did the jurisdiction utilize a forbidden "test or device" as a prerequisite for voting? Bronx, Kings, and New York counties "passed" this test in 1973, after a federal district court found that New York's failure to provide a Spanish-language ballot violated the Voting Rights Act, and the turnout in the three covered counties had fallen below the 50 percent threshold in the 1968 presidential election. See *New York* v. *United States* 419 U.S. 888 (1974). Since that time, any change in voting rules, including legislative districting, affecting the three covered counties has been subject to preclearance.

"preclearance."[53] Bronx, Kings, and New York counties are "covered jurisdictions" and since the early 1970s all reapportionments affecting those counties have had to obtain Justice Department approval before they can go into effect. The 1992 Senate redistricting did obtain the necessary approval. But preclearance of the current Senate district lines under Section 5 does not resolve the issues likely to arise in a Section 2 suit against the use of multimember elections from the Senate districts for the election of convention delegates.

First, as a matter of law, Section 5 preclearance is not a barrier to a subsequent Section 2 suit since the issues will be different, although admittedly the fact of preclearance might make it more difficult for plaintiffs to prevail. Second, the preclearance process focuses primarily on the effect of the redistricting on the covered jurisdictions, whereas a Section 2 suit would require a court to consider the rest of the state. Third, and most importantly, the issue in the Section 5 case was the fairness of the Senate district lines in creating single-member districts for the election of 61 senators. The Department of Justice precleared those lines, but it gave no attention whatsoever to their use as lines for *multimember* elections or for their use in the election of convention delegates.

The Senate district lines may provide fair representation in the 61-member Senate, at least for the minorities in the covered jurisdictions, but the Constitution provides for a convention that is more than three times the size of the Senate. Such a larger body would permit smaller districts. Electing convention delegates from large Senate districts in multimember elections could dilute the ability of minority voters to elect candidates of their choice to the convention, at least when compared to the smaller single-member district alternative.

In short, the outcome of any Section 2 challenge to the provision for the election of convention delegates from Senate districts in multimember elections is at least as uncertain as the outcome of a challenge to the statewide at-large elections. Indeed, it is far more uncertain since there could be 61 different outcomes. It is quite possible that in a significant number of districts — those that are either predominantly minority or that

---

53 Under Section 5, covered jurisdictions may obtain the necessary preclearance in either of two ways: (1) they may obtain a declaratory judgment in the United States District Court for the District of Columbia that the changes "do not have the purpose and will not have the effect of denying or abridging the right to vote on account" of race or membership in a language minority; or (2) they may submit the changes to the Attorney General, who, utilizing the same criteria as those given for the federal district court, has 60 days to object, and thereby block the effectuation of the proposed electoral change. In such a case, the burden of proof is on the jurisdiction seeking to change its laws that the proposed change does not have any discriminatory impact on minorities. In practice, the vast majority of preclearances go through the Attorney General process.

lack significant minority populations — the Constitution's system will not be a problem. But there may be many districts in which, once the demographic and elections data are developed, the Constitution's provisions will be seen as diluting minority participation when, as is ordinarily the case in a Section 2 lawsuit, the multimember district is compared to the single-member district alternative.

Alternative Strategies for Addressing the Voting Rights Act Questions

There are two approaches to resolving the Voting Rights Act questions. One would focus on reducing or eliminating the features of the current law that create voting rights questions. The other would be to obtain an authoritative determination of these issues before the call for a constitutional convention is submitted to the voters. The prospects may be better for the former strategy than the latter.

Limited or Cumulative Voting

Article XIX, §2, provides that "the electors of each Senate district in the state, as then organized, shall elect three delegates." This provision treats the Senate district as the unit of election. It is not clear whether this would permit subdistricting, which would be the easiest way to avoid the Voting Rights Act challenge. The Constitution, however, does seem to provide a way to use the Senate districts as units of election while ameliorating the features of multimember elections that tend to submerge minority votes. There are electoral mechanisms that limit the power of the majority or enhance the power of the minority within the context of multimember elections which could be deployed consistent with this provision of the Constitution,

One such mechanism is *limited voting*. In limited voting, the voter has a limited number of votes — fewer votes than there are seats at stake in the district. This prevents the same majority from dominating every seat. A minority group will be able to elect its preferred candidate to a seat so long as its share of the vote is V/(V+N) +1, where N is the number of seats to be filled and V is the number of votes a voter can cast. In a three-member district with voters limited to one vote apiece, an organized minority group is guaranteed a seat so long as it casts 1/(1+3) +1, or one vote more than 25 percent, of the vote. That is, even if the majority has 74 percent of the vote, and is perfectly organized so that all majority voters vote for majority candidates and the majority's vote is evenly spread among its three candidates so that there is no weak majority candidate,[54] the minority will win 1 of the 3 seats so long as it is just as organized.

An alternative mechanism is *cumulative* voting. In cumulative voting, each voter is allowed to cast as many votes as there are positions to be filled, but voters may cumulate their votes behind just one or two candidates, so that minority voters can cast three votes apiece for one preferred candidate. Under cumulative voting, a minority group is guaranteed a seat so long as its share of the vote is $1/(1+N) + 1$, where N is the number of seats to be elected. Thus, where three seats are to be elected, a minority can elect a candidate, even if no member of the majority group votes for that candidate, so long as the minority accounts for 25 percent of the vote.

Both limited voted and cumulative voting have had modest use in this country as methods of enhancing minority *party* representation. Between 1870 and 1980 members of the lower house of the Illinois legislature were elected from three-member districts through the use of cumulative voting. This tended to result in the election of more Republicans from Chicago and more Democrats from downstate than would have been the case otherwise. Similarly, between 1963 and 1982, ten seats on the New York City Council were elected on a two-per-borough basis through borough-wide limited voting. The New York system limited both the number of votes a voter could cast and the number of candidates a party could nominate to one in each borough. This limited voting system guaranteed the election of at least five non-Democrats at a time when nearly all the council members elected from districts were Democrats. The New York State Court of Appeals sustained this limited voting procedure against the claim that it violated the provision of the state Constitution guaranteeing to each qualified voter the right to vote for "all officers" elected from a jurisdiction.[55]

Cumulative voting and limited voting have become increasingly important as remedies in Voting Rights Act cases either after a court has found a voting rights violation or as part of the settlement of a voting rights dispute. In 1991, a federal appeals court found that four jurisdictions in North Carolina had agreed to limited voting in consent decrees.[56] At least a dozen Alabama communities have adopted limited voting or cumulative

---

54 That is, each candidate gets 24 and 2/3 percent of the vote. If the majority is less well-organized, so that some majority candidates get more votes than others or there are more majority candidates than there are seats, it will be even easier for a 25 percent minority to win a seat.

55 *Blaikie* v. *Power,* 13 N.Y.2d 134 (1963).

56 *Moore* v. *Beaufort County,* 936 F.2d 159 (4th Cir. 1991).

voting,[57] and the city of Alamogordo, New Mexico adopted cumulative voting as part of a settlement to a voting rights challenge to the election of its city council.[58] Some voting rights advocates have found limited voting or cumulative voting within large multimember districts to be superior to the traditional single-member district remedy in those jurisdictions where there are substantial minority populations but the minority is geographically dispersed so that is difficult to create compact predominantly minority districts.

Nothing in Article XIX, §2, bars cumulative voting, since cumulative voting entails a choice by the voter to vote for fewer candidates in order for the voter to register the intensity of her preference for one candidate. Nor does the Constitution actually mandate that each voter be able to cast three votes. All it provides is that the "electors of every Senate district" elect three delegates. That would still occur with limited voting. Given the minority-enhancing or majority-restricting features of limited voting and cumulative voting, the use of either mechanism within the multimember Senate districts might be sufficient to blunt any Voting Rights Act attack. Cumulative voting or limited voting could be adopted by statute and would not require constitutional amendment.

I am less certain that the at-large delegates could be elected by limited or cumulative voting since those devices might reduce the statewide perspective of those delegates, although it could be argued that all the term "at-large" does is preclude the use of any districting system for the election of the 15 statewide delegates — the preclusion of subdistricting is clearer here than for the Senate district delegates. Cumulative voting would enhance the ability of a minority with 1/16th of the vote to elect a delegate. The effect of limited voting would turn on the limit on the number of votes each voter could cast.

Cumulative voting or limited voting, of course, are not strategies for determining how the traditional system would fare in challenges under the Voting Rights Act; they are strategies for avoiding the challenge.

*Obtaining Advance Resolution
of the Voting Rights Act Issues*

I am not sure if any advance resolution of these issues can be obtained. One channel — the Department of Justice — is surely not open. Unlike

---

57   See *Dillard* v. *Chilton Co. Board of Educ.,* 699 F.Supp, 870 (M.D. Ala. 1988); *Dillard* v. *Town of Cuba,* 708 F. Supp. 1244 (M.D. Ala. 1988).

58   Engstrom, Taebel & Cole, "Cumulative Voting as a Remedy for Minority Vote Dilution: The Case of Alamogordo, New Mexico," 5 *J. L. & Pol.* 469 (1989).

Section 5 of the Act, the Department has no special role in interpreting Section 2. Indeed, even under Section 5 the Department is generally quite reluctant to provide informal advice before a districting plan is formally submitted for its official consideration under Section 5.

Alternatively, one could seek a judicial determination of whether the constitutional delegate selection provision violates the Voting Rights Act. Advance judicial resolution of these issues entails several procedural questions. First, who has standing to bring such an action? The Voting Rights Act cases I have seen have all been brought on behalf of minority voters. It is not clear whether this Commission or the state is a "person aggrieved" by the constitutional provision or the state or the Commission have interests that fall within the zone of interests protected by the Act. Second, if suit can only be brought by minority voters, can one suit resolve the issue of vote dilution for all the Senate districts? One lawsuit could address itself to the statewide at-large delegates and to the question of whether the Senate districts are to be resolved on a statewide basis or on a district-by-district basis, but if this is determined to be a district-by-district matter there will be a need for plaintiffs from each district, and, possibly, multiple suits.

Third, when will such a dispute be ripe for adjudication? Although declaratory judgments may be brought for the declaration of rights without seeking a final judgment, the federal statute requires that there be an "actual controversy." It is not clear whether there is an "actual controversy" before the submission of the call for a constitutional convention to the voters, let alone the voters' approval of the call. It could be argued that there will be insufficient time to resolve the Voting Rights Act questions in the brief period between the approval of the call and the start of the election cycle for the nomination and election of delegates, and, therefore, that these issues must be determined in advance. Moreover, it could be argued that for some voters the decision whether or not to vote for a convention would turn on how convention delegates are to be elected so that the issue is ripe for adjudication in advance of the placement of the call on the ballot. Even so, it is now several years before the question is, under the Constitution, scheduled to be presented to the voters, so a court might still deem the question not ripe — although it is unlikely that anything will occur between now and the year of the ballot question.

Procedural specialists and voting rights litigators might have useful insights concerning the resolution of these procedural questions. But even if the standing and ripeness issues are eliminated, the merits of the case could still take years to determine. As indicated, Section 2 cases require a close analysis of a large number of very fact-specific circumstances. The relevant facts — the existence of racially polarized voting, its affect on the ability of minorities to elect their preferred candidates, even whether the minority constitutes a sufficiently large, compact and cohesive group — are difficult to determine or assess. The judicial examination of the Senate Judiciary Report factors can entail a thorough description and evaluation of the role of race in state and local politics, as well as a consideration of the value of the policies underlying the electoral mechanism.

The difficulties would go beyond simply studying voting patterns and campaign practices — although determining these could be quite difficult — but would also involve questions of interpretation. This was illustrated by the opinions in *Butts* v. *City of New York*,[59] the lawsuit that alleged that the runoff requirement for primaries for citywide offices in New York City was racially discriminatory, in which the four federal judges (one trial judge and three appellate judges) disagreed sharply in reading the same data in their judgments as to just how much success minorities had in the local political process.

In short, I am not sure that there can be any definitive resolution of the questions considered in this memorandum any time soon, although Voting Rights Act specialists and litigators are likely to have additional insights as to both the substance of these questions and the procedures for getting them resolved.

---

59   614 F. Supp. 1527 (S.D.N.Y. 1985), *rev'd* 779 F.2d 121 (2d Cir. 1985).

The Election of Delegates to the Constitutional Convention: Some Alternatives

Richard Briffault

This paper considers alternative methods for the election of convention delegates. The Constitution provides for the election of constitutional convention delegates from multimember districts: fifteen delegates are elected on a statewide basis and the remaining delegates are elected from Senate districts, on a three delegates per district basis. Such multimember districts can pose problems for the representation of minorities. If there is a sharp political polarization between a majority and minorities in a jurisdiction, multimember election districts can extend the range of the majority's domination by enabling the same majority to determine the outcome of each election contest in the multimember district.

This paper presents two types of alternatives for addressing the majority-enhancing effects of multimember districts. One set of options would retain multimember districts but limit the ability of the majority to dominate elections within the district. Electoral mechanisms that enhance minority representation in multimember districts include limited voting, cumulative voting, and single transferable voting. Because these mechanisms are relatively uncommon in the United States they will be described in considerable detail. The other set of options would replace the multimember districts with single-member districts. For the Senate district delegates, this could be accomplished by subdistricting or by utilizing Assembly districts. For the at-large delegates, this would require the creation of new election districts.

Limited Voting

Description

Limited voting is a strategy for improving the ability of minorities to elect representatives of their choice in multimember election districts. Put simply, limited voting limits the number of votes a voter can cast to fewer than the number of seats to be filled at the election. In an election in which there are three seats to be filled, limited voting would limit each voter to voting for just one or two — but not three — candidates. This can prevent the same majority from dominating every seat and, thus, will enable a large enough and sufficiently cohesive minority to win a seat.

Under limited voting, a well-organized minority can win a seat even in the face of well-organized majority opposition. The size necessary for the minority to win a seat is determined by something known as the *threshold of exclusion*, which, in turn, is determined by the number of seats to be filled and the number of votes a voter may cast. In a three-member district, with each voter limited to casting just one vote, a well-organized minority can win a seat if the minority-preferred candidate receives one vote more than 25 percent of the vote. This can be seen by considering a district with 1,000 voters; one minority candidate; and three majority candidates. The worst situation for the minority is to be faced with a well-organized majority that spreads its strength equally across its three candidates. Even in this situation, if the minority's candidate can garner just 251 votes, then, due to limited voting, that candidate will win. If 251 votes go to the minority's candidate, that leaves 749 for the majority. If each majority voter is limited to one vote, and if the 749-vote majority divides its strength exactly evenly among three candidates, then two of the majority's candidates will get 250 votes apiece and the third will get 249. Thus, the minority candidate will squeak by. If the majority does not divide its vote evenly and, instead, gives one of its candidates more than 250 votes, then one of the majority's candidates will receive even less than 249 votes and will clearly come in after the minority-preferred candidate.

The threshold of exclusion in a three-member district with each voter limited to one vote is, thus, 25 percent + 1 — a minority-preferred candidate who receives one vote more than 25 percent of the total vote can be elected even in the face of total majority opposition (provided the candidate receives comparably unified minority support).

There is a formula for threshold of exclusion: $V/(V+N) + 1$, where V is the number of votes a voter may cast and N is the number of seats to be filled. Where there are three seats to be filled and each voter is limited to one vote, then $N = 3$ and $V = 1$, the threshold of exclusion is $1/(1+3)$ — a minority can win a seat if it receives one vote more than 25 percent. Similarly, in a three-seat district with voters limited to two votes, a well-organized minority will win a seat if it receives $2/(2+3)$ — or one more than 40 percent of the total vote. In a 15-seat district, with voters limited to five votes, the threshold of exclusion is $5/(5+15)$ or 25 percent

— so that the minority would win a seat if it received one more than 25 percent of the total vote. In a 15-seat district, with voters limited to one vote, the minority would win a seat with a little over 1/16th of the district-wide vote, or 7 percent.

History and Current Use

Limited voting has had some history in the United States. Between 1963 and 1982, ten seats on the City Council of the City of New York were elected on a two-per-borough basis through borough-wide limited voting. This system limited both the number of votes a voter could cast and the number of candidates a party could nominate to one in each borough. This guaranteed the election of at least five non-Democrats at a time when nearly all the Council members elected from districts were Democrats. The New York State Court of Appeals sustained this limited voting procedure against the claim that it violated the provision of the state Constitution guaranteeing to each qualified voter the right to vote for "all officers" elected from a jurisdiction. In so doing, the Court noted that "limited voting systems almost identical in substance with the system now under review were in effect in New York City for many years during the 19th century in connection with the election of supervisors and aldermen, the predecessors of councilmen."[1] The City Council limited voting system was discontinued because of the constitutional problem posed by giving each borough an equal number of borough-wide representatives despite the sharp differences in borough populations, and not because of any legal problems with limited voting.

Limited voting has been used elsewhere in the United States, particularly in Pennsylvania, Connecticut, and New York. According to one study, Philadelphia has used this method since 1951 for its at-large council seats, and most Pennsylvania counties, except those under home rule charters, elect county commissioners under a limited voting system in which a voter can vote for only two candidates for the three seats to be filled.[2] Limited voting has also been used in city council elections in several Connecticut cities, in local school board elections in that state, and in local elections in Rome, New York.[3] Limited voting has been used for elections to the national legislatures in Japan and in Spain. In the Japanese

---

1 *Blaikie v. Power*, 243 N.Y.S.2d 185, 190, 13 N.Y.2d 134, 142-43 (1963).

2 B. Grofman, L. Handley & R. Niemi, *Minority Representation and the Quest for Equality* 125 (1992).

3 See Leon Weaver, "Semi-Proportional and Proportional Representation Systems in the United States," in A. Lijphart & B. Grofman, *Choosing an Electoral System: Issues and Alternatives* 197-97 (1984); B. Grofman, L. Handley & R. Niemi, *supra*, at 125.

House of Representatives, most districts are three-, four-, or five-member districts, with each voter casting one vote. In Spain, the basic rule is that each province is a four-member district for the election of the Senate, with each voter casting three votes.[4]

There has been a recent upsurge of interest in limited voting in Voting Rights Act litigation. Some voting rights advocates have found limited voting within large multimember districts to be superior to the traditional single-member district remedy in those jurisdictions where there are substantial minority populations but the minority is geographically dispersed so that it is difficult to create compact, predominantly minority districts. Limited voting systems have been adopted as part of settlement agreements in Voting Rights Act cases in 21 municipalities in Alabama. One study of 14 of those municipalities found that the number of seats in the local legislature was either five or seven, and the number of votes a voter could cast was either one or two. Due to limited voting, African-Americans were elected to local legislatures in communities where they constituted 10.2, 14.6, 23.5, 26.3, 32.2, and 38.5 percent, respectively, of the population.[5] African-Americans have been elected to county commissions and school boards in North Carolina under limited voting arrangements that provided for one vote per person in elections to three-member at-large boards in jurisdictions in which blacks accounted for 31 percent to 36 percent of the voting age population.[6] Limited voting arrangements have also been adopted as a result of settlements of vote dilution lawsuits in Augusta, Georgia, and the Phoenix Union High School District School Board.[7]

Limited Voting and the Election of Constitutional Convention Delegates

1. Limited voting is relatively easy for voters to understand: all the voter has to know is that he or she can cast a certain number of votes.

2. Limited voting could be applied by statute to the election of Senate district delegates. The Constitution provides that the "elec-

---

4   See generally A. Lijphart, R. Lopez Pintor, and Y. Stone, "The Limited Vote and the Single Nontransferable Vote: Lessons from the Japanese and Spanish Examples," in B. Grofman and A. Lijphart, *Electoral Laws and Their Political Consequences* (1986).

5   Engstrom, "Modified Multi-Seat Election Systems as Remedies for Minority Vote Dilution," *Stetson L. Rev.* 21 (1992), pp. 743, 758-59.

6   *Ibid.* at 759-60.

7   *Ibid.*

tors of every senate district" elect three delegates. This would still occur under limited voting, so a constitutional amendment would not be necessary. By contrast, the creation of single-member districts for the election of convention delegates would probably require a constitutional amendment.

3. Since it would use current Senate district lines, limited voting avoids the highly charged, and often litigated, issue of how to draw new district lines. By contrast, subdistricting Senate districts would require the drawing of subdistrict lines.

4. One issue in the adoption of limited voting for the Senate district delegates is whether to limit voters to one vote or two. With one vote per voter the threshold of exclusion is 25 percent; with two votes per voter, the threshold of exclusion is 40 percent. Thus, the determination of the number of votes per voter would determine how large a minority would have to be in order to be able to win the election of a delegate. This has implications for the representation of political parties as well as racial and ethnic minorities, since limited voting would make it easier for Democrats to win in Republican districts and Republicans to win in Democratic districts, and the lower the threshold of exclusion the more likely that the smaller party in the district would win a seat.

5. Limited voting could also be used in the election of the statewide delegates. The Constitution provides that "the electors of the state . . . shall elect fifteen delegates-at-large." Even under limited voting, the 15 delegates would still be running statewide, and voters from all over the state could vote for the same candidates. So, limited voting could probably be adopted by statute. There is, however, considerably more discretion with respect to the number of votes a voter could be permitted to cast when there are 15 seats to be filled (compared to three at the Senate district level).

6. Limiting the voters to a single vote would lower the threshold of exclusion to 1/16, or under seven percent of the vote. That might be considered too low if the purpose of the statewide elections is to assure the election of some delegates who have a statewide perspective and a statewide base of support. It might also reduce the incentive to the development of balanced slates, since each voter would be voting for just one candidate. Giving voters three or five votes — that is, creating a threshold of exclusion of 16

percent or 25 percent — might be an appropriate balance of statewide perspectives and minority representation.

Cumulative Voting

Description

Like limited voting, cumulative voting is a device for enhancing minority representation within the context of multimember districts. In cumulative voting, each voter may cast as many votes as there are positions to be filled, but voters may choose to vote for candidates for all the positions to be filled or may instead *cumulate* their votes behind those candidates they prefer most intensely. Typically, the only restriction on the distribution of votes among the candidates is that the votes be cast in whole units. In a district in which three seats are to be filled, a voter could cast three votes for one candidate; two votes for one candidate, and one vote for a second candidate; or one vote for each of three candidates.

Cumulative voting can provide a minority group with an opportunity to elect a candidate or candidates of their choice without limiting the voting strength of the majority. By lifting the constraint of one vote for any particular candidate, cumulative voting permits minority voters to cast a more effective form of "single-shot" voting than is possible in a regular multimember district election. Under the usual single-shot strategy, a group's voters cast a vote for a candidate they wish to elect, but then withhold the rest of their votes from all the other candidates so as not to add to the vote totals of those candidates. With cumulative voting, the minority group members need not withhold their remaining votes, but can cast them for the candidates they prefer most intensely without contributing to the vote totals of those candidates they prefer only weakly. Cumulative voting, thus, allows minority voters to concentrate their votes to increase their opportunity to elect candidates of their choice.

Like limited voting, cumulative voting relies on the threshold of exclusion concept. The threshold of exclusion for cumulative voting is $1/(1+N) + 1$, where N = the number of seats to be filled. The formula is the same as that used for limited voting where voters are limited to just one vote. In a three-seat district with cumulative voting, a minority's candidate can win a seat if the minority casts one vote more than $1/(1+3)$ or 25 percent of the total vote. In a district with 1,000 votes, a minority with 251 votes can win a seat even if none of the other 749 voters casts a single vote for the minority's candidate, provided that all 251 minority voters cast all of their votes for the minority's candidate. That candidate would receive 753 votes. The 749 majority voters would cast 2,247 votes (749 x 3). If those votes were spread evenly over just three candidates, no one candidate backed by the majority would receive more than 749 votes, and the minority-preferred candidate would squeeze by. If the majority's vote were spread over more candidates, or if the majority gave a disproportionate share of votes to one candidate, then it would be even easier for the minority-preferred candidate to get by the third majority-preferred candidate and win a seat.

History and Current Use

Cumulative voting has also had some history of use in the United States. From 1870 to 1980, the members of the lower house of the Illinois legislature were elected from three-member districts through the use of cumulative voting. It was "based on a bargain between the major parties" that enabled Republicans to be elected from Democratic areas and vice versa. Although Illinois voters voted to keep cumulative voting in 1970 in a separate ballot question presented as part of a referendum on a new state constitution, they voted to abolish the cumulative voting system in 1980 as part of a ballot measure to shrink the size of the legislature.[8]

As with limited voting, there has been a resurgence of interest in cumulative voting because of the Voting Rights Act. Probably the most important instance of the modern use of cumulative voting was its adoption in municipal elections in Alamogordo, New Mexico, in 1987. Alamogordo replaced a seven-member at-large council with four single-member districts, and three at-large seats to be elected under cumulative voting. One of the four single-member district was majority-minority, but due to the dispersion of Hispanics — who accounted for 21 percent of the voting age population — around the city plaintiffs did not feel that a seven single-member district arrangement would provide two secure minority seats. In the initial election for the three at-large seats, there were eight candidates — seven Anglos and one Hispanic. The Hispanic candidate placed third in the total vote, and clearly benefited from cumulative voting: 50 percent of Hispanic voters reported casting all three of their votes for her, and another 23 percent reported casting either one or two votes for her.[9]

The adoption of cumulative voting also led to the election of a Native American to the Sisseton Independent School District board in South

---

8   See Weaver, *supra,* at 198-99.

9   Engstrom, supra, *Stetson L. Rev.* at 752-54.

Dakota. About 34 percent of the population in the district was Native American but Native Americans had only rarely won elections to the at-large board. Following a lawsuit, the board agreed to adopt cumulative voting, and a Native American finished first among seven candidates contesting three seats. According to an exit poll, 93 percent of the Native Americans who voted cast all three votes for the Native American candidate, who won despite receiving only 14 percent of votes cast by whites.[10]

Cumulative voting was also adopted, again as part of a settlement to a vote dilution lawsuit, by five local governments in Alabama. "Despite having African American populations that ranged from only 10.3 percent to 11.9 percent, an African American was elected for the first time to the governing board of each of these jurisdictions under cumulative voting rules."[11] Cumulative voting also enabled African-Americans to win one of five at-large seats city council in Peoria, Illinois, where they constituted 20.9 percent of the population.[12]

Cumulative Voting and the Election of Constitutional Convention Delegates

1. Like limited voting, cumulative voting could be adopted by statute and would not require a constitutional amendment. Indeed, this question is even clearer for cumulative voting than for limited voting since under cumulative voting a voter could still choose to cast votes for as many candidates as there are seats to be filled. In this respect, then, cumulative voting like limited voting would be easier to adopt than single-member districts, which require amendments to the state Constitution.

2. Cumulative voting is also like limited voting — and differs from some of the single-member district options — in that it can utilize the existing state Senate districts and the statewide jurisdiction for the election of the at-large delegates, so that no new district lines would have to be drawn.

3. Cumulative voting differs from limited voting in two ways. On the one hand, it may be slightly superior to limited voting in the sense that no voter is deprived of the opportunity to vote for a separate candidate for each seat to be filled; rather, cumulative

---

10   *Ibid.* at 754.

11   *Ibid.* at 756-57.

12   *Ibid.*

voting gives voters an additional opportunity of voting for each seat or voting strategically to maximize the chances of success of the most intensely preferred candidate. On the other hand, cumulative voting is slightly more complex than limited voting. Voters would have to be instructed that they may cast multiple votes for the same candidate, and voting machines would have to be modified accordingly. The evidence from the jurisdictions using cumulative voting is that this can be done. Nevertheless, this complexity from the voter's perspective may be a disadvantage relative to limited voting and to the single-member district options.

4. As with limited voting, the application of cumulative voting to the statewide delegates raises an additional question. Most jurisdictions that use cumulative voting do so in the context of the election of three or five officials. The effect of cumulative voting in those situations is to permit 25 percent or 16 percent minorities to win elections. Cumulative voting in a 15-member election would allow a minority with under seven percent of the vote to win a seat. This may be seen as too low a threshold and too likely to permit representatives of small political groups to win seats. It might discourage a candidate from seeking broad support when he or she can win a seat with a narrow but intense base. It may be in tension with the apparent purpose of having statewide delegates, which is to secure the participation at the convention of delegates having a broad perspective. If cumulative voting were adopted, some thought might be given to limiting the number of votes a voter can give to one candidate to, say, three or five, thus raising the threshold of exclusion to 25 percent or 16 percent.

Single Transferable Voting[13]

Description

Single Transferable Voting (STV) is a preference voting system. Each voter is provided with a single vote, but is allowed to rank in order candidates to reflect his or her relative preferences among them. Ranking candidates in order of preference enables votes that would be "wasted" on one candidate to be transferred to another candidate. Votes can be "wasted" if they are "surplus" votes for a candidate who would win without that

---

13 See, generally, Engstrom, "The Single Transferable Vote: An Alternative Remedy for Minority Vote Dilution," *U.S.F. L. Rev.* 27 (1993), p. 781.

vote, or if they are cast in support of a losing candidate. STV saves wasted votes by providing for the transfer of the vote to the next ranked candidate on a voter's ballot. STV, thus, increases the proportion of voters in an election whose vote will ultimately contribute to the election of a candidate. This benefits electoral minorities whose votes would otherwise be "wasted" on losing candidates.

The winning candidates in an STV election are those whose votes equal or exceed a specified number. This number is based on the "Droop quota," which is the quotient obtained when the total number of ballots cast is divided by the number of seats to be filled, plus one. The formula is: $V/(N+1) + 1$, where V is the total number of votes cast and N is the number of seats to be filled. This is the lowest possible number of votes that can be required for election and yet limit the number of individuals elected to the number of seats to be filled.

If there are three seats to be filled, and 1,000 votes have been cast, the Droop quotient is $1,000/(3+1) + 1$, or 251. In an STV election, a candidate who gets 251 first-place votes is automatically elected. If a candidate meets the quota on the first ballot, then the candidate's "surplus" votes are redistributed to the second choices named by those voters, and a new set of vote totals is determined. If no candidate receives the quota on the first count, the last place candidate is eliminated, and his or her votes are transferred to the next ranked candidates on these ballots, and a new set of vote totals is determined.

Transferring the votes of losing candidates is straightforward. All of the ballots of an eliminated candidate are simply transferred to the voters' next choices. The transfer of the surplus votes of winning candidates is more complicated, and several methods are used. One is simply to declare a candidate elected once his or her vote matches the quota, and treat all remaining ballots as surplus. A second, used in Ireland where STV is the basic election system, is to select randomly among the winning candidate's ballots. A third method, "probably the preferable one now that computers can be used to count votes,"[14] is to redistribute a winning candidate's votes according to the proportion of the total ballots allocated to the winning candidate on which each respective other candidate has been identified as the next choice.

STV offers a group united behind a candidate the same opportunity to elect that candidate as does a one-vote limited voting system or cumulative voting. The Droop quota functions as a threshold of exclusion

---

14   Ibid. at 790.

for STV and it generates the same threshold as a cumulative voting or one-vote limited voting system. An organized 25 percent + 1 minority can win one seat in a three-seat jurisdiction under all three systems.

STV, however, "has a distinct advantage over these other systems in that it can better accommodate intra-group competition."[15] In a limited voting or cumulative voting election (as well as in a majority-minority single-member district), a dispersion of the minority vote across two or more minority-preferred candidates could be fatal to the election of any minority-preferred candidate. Under STV, however, there can be both intra-group competition without canceling out the group's opportunity to elect a candidate of its choice.

For example, assume an election with 1,000 voters, 300 minority voters and 700 majority voters; three seats to be filled; two minority-preferred candidates and three majority-preferred candidates. Assume also that the majority votes only for majority-preferred candidates; that it spreads its first place votes evenly (233 or 234 per candidate) and that majority voters subsequent preferences are only for majority candidates. Assume the minority voters split, 170 first-place votes for candidate A and 130 first-place votes for candidate B, and that voters for B list A as their second choice.

In order to win, a candidate needs a Droop quota, that is,

$$1000 \text{ (total votes)}/[3 \text{ (total seats)} + 1] + 1,$$

or 251 votes. On the first count, Candidate B would be eliminated. But B's voters would have listed A as their second choice, and on the second round B's votes go to A, giving him 300 and a seat. Subsequently, the weakest majority candidate would be eliminated and the other two majority representatives elected.

In effect, STV can function as both a primary election and a general election simultaneously, with voters registering both their most intense preference, and their second (and more) choices who may have a better chance of election. Under STV voters can also cross group lines, perhaps naming as their first choice a member of their own racial or ethnic group but also listing members of other groups as lower-ranked choices, thus giving them an opportunity to support their own group's candidate and also — once their candidate has either clearly won or clearly lost — giving support to the most attractive candidates of other groups. This may also encourage candidates to appeal across group lines for the second- or

---

15   Ibid. at 791.

third-place votes of members of another group since those votes might enable such candidates to win seats without undercutting the principal choices of the other group.

History and Current Use

Approximately two dozen cities adopted STV for elections to city councils in the period between 1917 and 1950, although only Cambridge, Massachusetts, uses the system today. STV was used for the election of the nine-member city council in Cincinnati, Ohio, from 1924 to 1957 and there is currently a major initiative led by the local Rainbow Coalition to restore STV in Cincinnati.[16] STV is also used in the election of the New York City community school boards. STV is used for all public elections in the Republic of Ireland and for the election of the upper house of Parliament, and some provincial elections, in Australia.

STV and the Election of Constitutional Convention Delegates

1. Like limited voting and cumulative voting, STV could be adopted without constitutional amendment since delegates would still be elected from Senate districts or from a statewide election district.

2. Again, like limited voting and cumulative voting, STV would use existing election district lines and avoid the political and litigation issues implicated by district line-drawing.

3. As noted, STV has one advantage over cumulative voting and limited voting in that it permits intra-group disagreement without forfeiting group strength. STV gives voters more choices than does limited voting: An STV voter has just one first-place choice but can rank order as many second-, third-, fourth-place, etc. candidates as there are seats to be filled. And unlike cumulative voting, there is no risk of "wasting" votes, that is, of voters unnecessarily giving a candidate "surplus" votes, since those votes can be counted towards a voter's second-choice candidate once the first-choice candidate is elected.

4. STV also has one major drawback: it is a relatively complicated system. Voters have to be instructed concerning the opportunity

---

16   Ibid. at 792-806.

to cast rank-order preference votes; the voting technology has to be modified accordingly; and the process of reallocating votes can be time-consuming. STV is also a relatively uncommon system. The experience with STV in the New York City community school board elections has not exactly been an advertisement for the merits of STV, although it is far from clear that the problems with the school board elections are attributable to the use of STV.

5. Like cumulative voting and limited voting, STV may also lead to too great a representation of small minorities in the statewide delegate elections. The Droop quota for the election of statewide delegates is 1/16th of the total vote — although this is attributable to the limitation of voters to just one first-place vote (as in limited voting with a limit of one) and not to the ability to transfer that vote to second- or other lower-ranked choices. It might be possible to raise the threshold of exclusion by allowing voters to cast, say, three ballots, and rank up to five choices; or five ballots, with three choices. Needless to say, this would make the system even more complicated.

Subdistricting Within Senate Districts

The most common response to the claim of minority vote dilution in multimember districts is to create single-member districts out of those multimember districts. With respect to the delegates elected from state Senate districts this could be accomplished by maintaining the Senate districts but then dividing the districts into equally populous thirds and electing one delegate from each subdistrict.

A. *The advantage* of subdistricting is that it is quite straightforward, and the resulting elections will be easy for voters, parties, and candidates to deal with. In a Senate district with significant geographically concentrated minorities, subdistricting ought to result in the creation of a majority-minority subdistrict.

B. *The disadvantages* of subdistricting, compared to cumulative voting, limited voting, and STV are: (1) it may require a constitutional amendment; (2) it may not increase minority representation in districts where the minorities are geographically diffuse; and (3) it will entail drawing new subdistrict lines within each affected Senate district.

1. The Constitution provides: "the electors of every senate district of the state, as then organized, shall elect three delegates at the next ensuing general election." (Art. XIX, §2). It is an open question as to whether this permits subdistricting. It could be argued that Senate district lines are still being used, and that the purpose of using Senate districts — of obtaining local, as opposed to statewide representation — is still being served. On the other hand, the operative lines in a subdistrict-based election would be the subdistrict lines and not the Senate district lines. Moreover, it could be argued that when it comes to provisions like that in Article XIX, §2, what counts is the letter of the law and not the spirit, and the letter of the law is violated when the Senate districts are not being used as the unit of election. I do not know if this issue can be definitively resolved in advance of the election of constitutional convention delegates. As a result, it may be necessary to amend the Constitution to authorize the use of subdistricts.

2. The creation of single-member districts enhances minority representation only when the minority population is sufficiently large and geographically concentrated to be dominant in one of the resulting single-member districts. It is possible that in some Senate districts subdistricting will be less effective in enhancing minority representation than limited voting, cumulative voting, or STV would be if the minority is territorially scattered and subdistrict lines cannot be drawn that would place most of the minority in one subdistrict.

3. By definition, subdistricting requires the drawing of new lines — two new lines within each affected Senate district. This line-drawing will, of course, be the focus of considerable political activity, and would be subject to various legal requirements, including the "one person, one vote" doctrine, other constitutional requirements, and the Voting Rights Act. The resulting lines could be the target of legal challenges.

Using Assembly Districts
Instead of Senate Districts

The Constitution provides for the election of three delegates from each Senate district. With 61 Senate districts, that would result in the election of 183 delegates. The Assembly currently consists of 150 single-member districts. If the multimember Senate districts were replaced by the single-member Assembly districts, the size of the district-based convention delegation would be only modestly affected and the voting rights issue posed by the use of multimember districts would be eliminated.

A. The use of Assembly districts has one advantage over the subdistricting within Senate districts: the Assembly district lines already exist, so that the political conflicts and the potential legal challenges to new lines could be avoided.

B. The use of Assembly districts shares one of the problems posed by subdistricting the Senate districts: it will certainly require a constitutional amendment. There is no argument that the existing constitutional language can be construed to include the Assembly district option.

C. In addition, the use of Assembly district lines may not benefit all minority groups. African-Americans plainly do better with Assembly districts than Senate districts. Currently, African-Americans hold five of the 61 Senate seats (8.2%), but 21 of 150 Assembly seats (14%). But Hispanics actually do better with Senate districts than with Assembly districts. Currently, Hispanics hold four of the 61 Senate seats (6.5%), but only seven of the 150 Assembly seats (4.7%).[17]

D. Moreover, although use of Assembly districts would avoid the highly politicized process of drawing new Senate subdistricts, the switch from Senate to Assembly districts would be fraught with political significance. Currently, Republicans dominate the Senate by a nearly three-to-two margin, while Democrats control the Assembly by approximately two to one. The legislative district lines clearly play a role in the sharply different partisan composition of the two houses. The use of Assembly district lines instead of Senate district lines could have obvious implications for the partisan composition of the convention.

---

17 Under the 1990 Census, African-Americans constituted 16 percent, and Hispanics 12.3 percent, of New York's population.

Single-Member Districts and the
Statewide Delegates-at-Large

There is no Assembly district-type alternative for the creation of single-member districts for the election of the 15 delegates-at-large. The only single-member district option would be the creation of 15 new convention delegate districts. These would be roughly the size of two congressional districts.

A. The creation of single-member districts to replace the at-large election of these delegates would surely require a constitutional amendment. The Constitution plainly calls for the election of "delegates-at-large." Whereas a statewide election using limited voting, cumulative voting, or STV could probably fit within the constitutional language, single-member districts surely would not.

B. The creation of single-member districts would require the drawing of new lines, with all the attendant political and legal conflicts. These districts could not be constructed out of congressional districts — by adding two congressional districts together — since there are 31 congressional districts and these could not be mechanically turned into 15 convention delegate districts. If congressional district lines were adopted directly, that would significantly increase the number of "large district" delegates (from 15 to 31) while simultaneously shrinking the size of these districts. By contrast, electing these 15 delegates statewide on a cumulative voting, limited voting, or STV basis would avoid the need to draw lines.

C. As with all districting alternatives, creating 15 single-member districts will enhance minority representation only when the minority population is sufficiently large and geographically concentrated to be dominant in one or more of the resulting single-member districts. It is possible that districting will be less effective in enhancing minority representation than limited voting, cumulative voting, or STV for minorities that are territorially scattered, for whom lines cannot be drawn that would make the minority dominant in a district.

D. Replacing the 15 delegates-at-large with delegates elected from 15 single-member districts is in sharp tension with the whole purpose of having the delegates-at-large, that is, that there is a public policy value in having delegates with a statewide perspective participate in the convention's deliberations. Their broad, statewide outlook can be seen as a desirable balance to those elected from the Senate (or Assembly) districts, who are likely to take a more localist approach to the state's problems. In other words, the statewide delegates may play a role akin to that of the president in the federal government, the governor and other statewide officials in the state government, and the mayor and the two other citywide officials in New York City's government in offsetting the narrower viewpoints of those elected from smaller legislative districts. It is hard to see what purpose there would be in having 15 delegates elected from districts that are too large to be local but too small to represent the interests of the state as a whole or even necessarily of distinctive regions.

With respect to the 15 delegates-at-large, then, the principal alternatives would appear to be:

1. Defending this electoral mechanism in the face of a Voting Rights Act attack on the theory that the delegates-at-large have a public policy value and that since they account for only 15 of the 198 convention delegates (7.6%) their vote-dilutive effect is quite modest.[18]

2. Retaining the statewide unit of election but using limited voting, cumulative voting, or STV to limit the majority's dominance and enhance minority opportunities to elect minority-preferred candidates.

3. Eliminating the delegates-at-large altogether.

The fourth option — creating 15 large single-member districts — would require a constitutional amendment, would require extensive line-drawing, and would not seem to have much purpose.

---

18   There is some precedent for this approach. In a handful of cases, courts and the Department of Justice have approved electoral systems for local governments that combined a large number of representatives elected from single-member districts with one or a small number of representatives elected at-large — although such mixed systems have at times been invalidated.

Public Campaign Financing

Michael J. Malbin

At the last meeting of this commission, the members discussed whether to recommend a system of partial public financing for the election of delegates to a constitutional convention. My understanding is that the commission is interested in this both for its potential direct affects on convention delegate elections and as a possible model for elections to other offices (governor, lieutenant governor, attorney general, comptroller, Senate, and Assembly). This paper will address both of these issues, but will place them in a more general framework.

The outline of the chapter will be as follows:

❋ First will come a factual description of the programs that now exist in the 50 states.

❋ Next will come a brief delineation of two different kinds of purposes campaign finance reform is typically meant to achieve: reducing the undue influence of special interest groups and promoting electoral competition.

❋ Third is an examination of the positive effects that disclosure, contribution limits, and supplementary regulations can have on the role of interested money. This section will end, however, by urging a broader look at questions of governmental ethics and not letting this discussion rest solely, or even primarily, on the role of campaign contributions.

❋ Finally will come an extended look at the problem of electoral competition. This section will argue that public funds can make a difference under some conditions, but it will also be laced with some cautionary words and a healthy dose of skepticism. Specifically, the commission needs to be aware of the magnitude of the problem it is thinking of taking on. For reasons I shall explain later, I believe that the presence of officeholders in the election, the size of the district, and the likely low visibility of the elections will combine to make the competitiveness problem more difficult — and its solution potentially far more expensive — than any problem any jurisdiction so far has addressed successfully through public financing. Therefore, after I finish discussing campaign finance options, the final section of this paper will conclude with an alternative suggestion for improving competition in races for convention delegate that will focus on what I think is a new way to look at multimember districts.

The Range of Programs and Purposes

Only 20 years ago, most election campaigns in this country were financed in what was virtually a laissez-faire market place. There were rules on some statute books, but the loopholes were large enough to make the rules all but useless. Since 1973, the states (and the federal government since 1971) have adopted what might seem like an almost limitless array of proposals. These combinations, however, have been built out of four basic building blocks: public disclosure, limits on the maximum size of contributions, public financing for candidates and/or political parties, and spending limits for candidates.

Disclosure: At this time, almost every state has some form of a public disclosure law, and 45 states require pre-election as well as post-election disclosure for candidates. (Two states require post-election disclosure only and the remaining three require disclosure by political committees but not by candidates.) Thirty of these 45 states require documents to be filed with an independent commission, although the effectiveness and budgets of these commissions vary a great deal.

Contribution Limits: Contribution limits exist in 29 of the 50 states. On the low end, Florida limits contributions to all covered offices to a $500 maximum per person; Arizona allows $550 contributions to gubernatorial candidates and $220 for other offices. Wisconsin's allows contributions of up to $10,000, and 21 states have no limits.

Public Financing: Public financing and spending limits are much less common than disclosure or contribution limits. Depending on what you want to count, about 20 states have some form of public financing provision on the books. Twelve of these programs are funded by income tax check-off provisions that, like the federal government's, does not add to the taxpayer's liability. Seven other states use "add-ons" — voluntary contributions collected through check-offs on the tax form that are in addition to (instead of substituting for) a portion of one's tax liability. Finally, Florida, which has no income tax, abandoned using general appropriations in 1990 to pay for the program with vanity license plate income.

The public participation rate, not surprisingly, depends on the kind of program. Add-on programs tend to have very low rates of participation — typically well below one percent. Standard check-offs do better, but everyone has experienced significantly declining rates over the past decade. According to the most complete recent study, the rate dropped from an average of 21 percent in 1984 to 14.5 percent in 1990.[1] (Federal participation went down from 29 percent in 1980 to 18 percent in 1991.) With the decline in revenues has come a decline in outlays and a corresponding decline in the incentive for candidates to participate.

The most common uses for public funds are for grants to political parties and to statewide candidates. Fourteen states give money directly to political parties, eleven give flat or matching grants to gubernatorial candidates, and three have programs for legislative candidates. Many of the gubernatorial programs are significant, but all three of the legislative programs are small. Hawaii gives flat grants of only $50 each to legislative candidates. Wisconsin and Minnesota are more generous, but the maximum amount in both states is less than $10,000 per lower house candidate and the spending limits only about twice that amount — or less than about 15 percent of what a competitive Assembly race often costs in this state.

Spending Limits: Spending limits, as you know, cannot constitutionally be forced upon candidates. As a result, the eleven states with spending limits include one purely voluntary program (Vermont), one in which spending limits are accepted in return for a waiver of filing fees and petition requirements (New Hampshire), and nine in which accepting a spending limit is a condition for receiving public funds. This latter group includes all eight states in which a check-off funds candidates, plus Florida. In contrast, the two states that give very small grants to candidates from voluntary add-on money (Massachusetts and Montana) do not impose spending limits as a condition for getting the money.

Purposes: These four kinds of provisions — disclosure, contribution limits, public financing, and spending limits — are generally put forward as serving two quite different purposes: (1) to promote electoral competition and (2) to reduce the fact or appearance of public corruption or excessive interest group influence on government. However, I believe —

---

1   Herbert E. Alexander, Eugene R. Goss and Jeffrey A. Schwartz, *Public Financing of State Elections,* Los Angeles, CA: Citizens' Research Foundation, 1992.

and will argue in this paper — that it is confusing to treat all four methods as if they equally serve both of these ends. As a result, the remainder of this paper will be organized around the ends to be achieved.

Reducing Corruption and the Power of Special Interests

Effective pre-election disclosure, and limits on the maximum size of a contribution, are both well tested and potentially quite effective tools for reducing the appearance of corruption or undue influence stemming from campaign contributions. On the federal level, contribution limits significantly decreased the importance of $100,000+ gifts to presidential campaigns for at least a cycle or two after Watergate. Unfortunately, we also know from the federal experience that candidates and contributors can be very resourceful if they want to make or receive large gifts. As a result, we can now feel confident in saying that if a jurisdiction wishes to achieve the purposes contribution limits were meant to achieve, it also has to be prepared to regulate:

* ※ contributions to political party organizations that are permitted to engage in activities directly or indirectly in support of an identified candidate;

* ※ the practice known as "bundling," in which one person or organization collects many legal individual contributions and then passes them on in an identifiable form to the candidate, even though the amount exceeds what the organization legally may contribute on its own;

* ※ unlimited and often undisclosed expenditures by labor unions and other interest groups;

* ※ ostensibly nonpartisan, but politically well coordinated and targeted registration and get-out-the-vote drives.

Some of these activities probably should be made subject to contribution limits. For example, all contributions *to* a political party could be limited (although the limits should be higher than the ones on candidate contributions). At the same time, the organization-building activities *of* a political party should not be limited in the same way as activities in support of an identified candidate — although even these organization-building activities should be fully disclosed. (Federal law exempts contributions *to* organization-building activities from contribution limits, thus creating a huge "soft-money" loophole.) Others activities on the above list, such as the voter-mobilization activities of labor unions and not-for-profit organizations, probably should be treated like organization building by the political parties: not limited, but subject to pre-election disclosure.

Even the most complete set of regulations, however, cannot prevent people or organizations from spending unlimited amounts on constitutionally protected activities. Most discussions on this subject focus on independent expenditures that explicitly advocate a particular candidate's election or defeat. Among other things, it would surely be wise for most jurisdictions to draft regulations to define what kinds of activities are truly "independent." But there are other activities beyond independent spending that would be even harder to reach. For example, almost any political consultant could draw up a constitutionally protected issue advertising campaign for an interest group that would merely comment on an officeholder's official performance, without directly advocating defeat or re-election. ("Incumbent X Coddles Cop Killers," etc.) This level of interest group influence would almost surely fall outside the scope of constitutionally permissible campaign regulation.

The impossibility (whether desirable or not) of putting an airtight lid on interest groups' campaign activities should lead to a broader question: Are campaign contributions the only, or even the most important, activity to be regulated in the relationship between interest groups and government officials? No state expects its legislators to work at that job full time, all year. All of them — unlike the U.S. Congress — expect members to earn outside income. As a result, the potential for conflicts of interest are boundless. Therefore, I would argue that it is at least as important for a state to look directly at ethics and conflict-of-interest regulation as to look at campaign finance. Specifically, most states could do with strengthened disclosure requirements, stronger independent monitoring agencies, and an expectation (if not a rule) that members will recuse themselves from voting on any issue that affects their own, their families', their clients', or their other regular business relationships' financial well-being.

Electoral Competition

The second major purpose most supporters of campaign finance reform say they are trying to achieve is to foster electoral competition by equalizing the candidates' campaign resources. In fact, my understanding is that some members of this commission are looking at public campaign financing precisely because they would like to promote competition in races for convention delegate. In addition, it has been suggested to me that at least some not only want to foster competition, but would also like serious nonpoliticians to have a reasonable chance to win a seat at the convention, even in a contest in which he or she has to run against an incumbent state legislator.

I personally believe that public financing can help stimulate challengers and open-seat candidates, but that the problem of enhancing electoral competition (and therefore the solution) is NOT the same for all offices. That is because the character or content of "incumbency advantage" varies with an office's public visibility and its responsibilities. The advantage is probably at its peak under the following set of conditions:

* The district is too large for most voters to know most of the credible officeholders and potential candidates personally;

* Officeholders, through effective use of their offices and good press coverage, have almost universal name recognition;

* The voters' knowledge of the officeholder is based almost entirely on locally noncontroversial issues; and

* The voters know very little about the challenger at the start of the campaign and the local press gives the campaign less prominent coverage than it gives others.

This situation almost perfectly describes the situation of most members of the U.S. House of Representatives or the New York Assembly.

By contrast, chief executive officers (the President, governors, big-city mayors) face a sharply different kind of politics. They are much more likely than legislators to be forced into unpopular or highly controversial decisions. *If* some of these decisions, or other circumstances, attracted good quality challengers into the field, the challengers almost surely will be able to raise significant amounts of money, and will become almost as well known as the incumbents — with both campaigns attracting almost daily, and free, press coverage. Thus, two of the main advantages of incumbency for low-visibility legislators (favorable images based on consensus issues and low-visibility challengers) simply do not apply to most chief executives.[2] The executives' one compensating advantage —

---

2   U.S. Senators fall somewhere between lower-level legislators and chief executives along these dimensions. Senators, like all legislators, can try to emphasize the consensus issues on their agendas. But most Senators represent more diverse constituencies than most representatives, and therefore have a harder time finding issues that are purely consensual statewide. In addition, Senate races frequently attract experienced opponents with good name recognition of their own.

and this is one Governor Cuomo often mentions — is that incumbents can use the power of their offices to raise a great deal of money easily.

As a result, it is fairly easy to use campaign finance laws in chief executives' elections to give a slight boost to competition in what is already a fairly competitive situation. If you put a lid on campaign spending, you theoretically can take away the incumbents' ability to out-raise the challenger. I say "theoretically" because most laws in fact permit incumbents to raise unlimited funds for their political parties.

The picture looks different for legislative races and other low-visibility races. As I argued in the *Bulletin,* most U.S. House challengers are starved for funds. The same is true for both chambers of the New York State Legislature as well as the 51-seat New York City Council. Getting *significant* amounts of money to these challengers would make a real difference to the level of competition. Nothing else in the typical legislative arsenal, including spending limits, would do much to help challengers. Low spending limits would hurt challengers. High spending limits would not hurt challengers, but neither would it do much to help them. About the only legislative remedy that would clearly improve competition would be to give money (or free postage, etc.) to all qualified candidates who pass a reasonable threshold.

If you do want to consider this option, you should do so with a full awareness that this is NOT cheap. The figure most people who seriously want to help challengers have mentioned for the U.S. House is about $200,000, and both the House and Senate balked at providing anything like this in the bills the two chambers sent to conference in 1993. Note that in a situation where this $200,000 will make a real difference, it will be understood as seed money by experienced politicians who will be able to raise another $300,000 or so on their own.

Candidates for state legislature and city council — not to mention convention delegate — are even less visible than congressional challengers. But the races can still be quite expensive. In recent election cycles, competitive races for the Assembly often hit $150,000, state Senate races about $250,000, and the city council at least $100,000. Providing matching funds, or modest-sized grants, probably would help an experienced politician who has already decided to take on an incumbent. It may even help that politician make the decision to run. But modest levels of partial funding are not likely by themselves to attract a new style of politician into the fray. After all, the challenger would still have to raise a significant amount of money on his or her own.

As evidence for this assertion, I urge the commission to look at the election results for the last two elections to the New York City Council. The city makes up to $40,000 in public funds available to qualified council candidates. In 1991, 32 incumbents ran for reelection for 51 seats to the newly expanded council. Of these 32, one lost in the primary, one lost in the general election, and eight others faced close races (60 percent or less of the top-two-candidate vote) in either the primary or general election. The two winning challengers spent well over $100,000 each. In the eight close primaries, spending in the $75,000 range for the primary seemed common. I have not looked at comparable spending figures yet for 1993, but there were fewer competitive races this time. Forty-nine incumbents ran for reelection and 47 won both the primary and general election.

These numbers should be sobering if you hope to use public funds to make a big difference in the level of competition and in the occupations of candidates for delegate elections. If officeholders are permitted to serve in a convention, they would have many of the advantages of incumbents in a district that has about twice the population of a city council seat. I would suspect that it would take a minimum of $100,000 in public funds (or about twice the level the New York City Campaign Finance Board has recommended for city council) to make much of a difference in a contest to defeat a sitting state legislator, and even that would assume a candidate who could raise significant money on his/her own. But if you work that out — assuming only *one* candidate per convention seat took the money, this would cost $15,000,000 — or about the same amount that New Jersey appropriated for its gubernatorial election in 1993. And if you want to give a nonpolitican with valuable experience a serious chance to *defeat* a sitting incumbent, or even defeat a well-known, recently retired officeholder, you may have to think about doubling that figure per candidate. (That, of course, would also induce more candidates to make the race, thus raising the total some more — to $45 million if there are 1.5 publicly funded candidates per seat, $60 million with 2 candidates per seat.)

At this point you have to face a tough question. Do you really believe the people are prepared to pay $15 million (let alone $45-$60 million) to elect delegates? (Not to mention: do you think legislators will fund free opposition to themselves, if they are allowed to be delegates?) As I said earlier, the evidence of declining support in *every* jurisdiction with a check-off is not favorable. Of course, you could always recommend a token amount of public money. But my opinion is that if a jurisdiction is not prepared to give challengers real money — lots of it — then the funds are not likely to have a major effect on the occupation pool of the candidates who run, or on the overall level of competition. Maybe there would be another reason to consider the idea even without adequate challenger funds, but competition would not be it.

One important caveat: the specific numbers above (all of them, from $15 to $60 million) were based on two key assumptions: (1) that political amateurs would be running against incumbent officeholders, and (2) that three delegates would be elected at large from multimember Senate districts. Changing either assumption could have a major impact on the bottom-line cost. For example, single-member districts with 85,000 populations could be reached with only 1/3 the mailing costs of a three-person, 250,000-person district. If you used nonpartisan districting commissions that were instructed to draw compact and contiguous districts (consistent with the Voting Rights Act), you would also make it easier for nonprofessional politicians to build upon existing nonpolitical networks and community organizations.

On the other hand, nonprofessional challengers would still be unlikely to defeat sitting officeholders in single-member districts, no matter how small the district. You might even be able to make a case for saying that nonofficials would have a better chance in a multimember district. But once you decide to let public officials run for delegate, the only real way to *insure* that others come to the convention is to make sure that nonpoliticians do not have to beat politicians to come.

One way to do this could be to "earmark" your three seats. For example, you might say that current elected officials (specific offices to be defined) could hold no more than one seat per district and that current and former elected officials (or current + former + current public employees) could hold no more than two seats combined. That would, in effect, create an "open seat" race among nonofficials for the third seat. In an open seat contest, less money would go a long way toward making a difference. In fact, if you create such a stratified election, you might even consider a rule that would limit public financing to candidates who are eligible to run for the nonofficials' seat. If you did that, you presumably would still want a threshold test of some kind — either signatures, money, or a combination — to limit the potential liability, but the spending total would be significantly less than any of the ones I suggested earlier.

Of course, if you do create a nonofficials' seat, the next question you would have to face would be how to handle interest group employees who — like delegates to the major party national political conventions — are really there to represent their interest groups. Having raised the issue, I will not try to answer it. It takes us too far afield from campaign finance.

Finally, you should not forget that voter pamphlets are an extremely valuable, low-budget form of public finance that can and should be adopted, no matter what you decide about cash subsidies. The importance of these pamphlets as a source of voter information increases in low-visibility races that are held congruently with other elections on the same ballot — and this election is sure to fit that description. It is awfully hard for a candidate in a low-visibility race to get a message through all of the "noise" created at the top of the ticket. Voter pamphlets are probably the single most cost-effective way to cut through this problem.

Appendices

The Temporary State Commission on Constitutional Revision

Commission Members   503

Commission Biographies   505

Commission Staff   511

Author Biographies   513

COMMISSION MEMBERS

Commission Biographies

Peter C. Goldmark, Jr.

Peter C. Goldmark, Jr. has been the president of the Rockefeller Foundation since 1988. He has been senior vice president of the Times Mirror Company; executive director for the Port Authority of New York and New Jersey; director of the New York State Division of the Budget; and secretary for human services for the Commonwealth of Massachusetts. Mr. Goldmark has also held various positions with the city of New York and the Federal Office of Economic Opportunity. Mr. Goldmark is a member of the board of directors of Knight-Ridder, Inc., a director of the Dreyfus Third Century Fund, and a member of the Council on Foreign Relations.

Terry Anderson

Terry Anderson is a writer and former foreign correspondent for The Associated Press. Other than the Commission, his activities include The Committee to Protect Journalists, of which he is a director, and the Vietnamese Memorial Association, a nonprofit group building elementary schools in Vietnam, of which he is co-chairman. He was the longest-held American hostage in Lebanon, from 1985 to 1991, and the book he and his wife wrote about that experience, *Den of Lions,* became a national best-seller. He is a strong proponent of political reform in New York, and a frequent speaker on this and other topics around the nation.

Amalia Victoria Betanzos

Amalia Betanzos is president of Wildcat Service Corporation, a nonprofit multimillion dollar employment program to bring the chronically unemployed into the regular labor force. Ms. Betanzos has served as a member of the Citizens Commission on AIDS; commissioner of the New York City Youth Services Agency; a member of the "Sovern Commission" on Integrity in Government; a member of the New York City Board of Education; and in various other capacities for the city of New York during the Lindsay, Beame, Koch and Giuliani administrations. Ms. Betanzos is currently a member of the New York City Private Industry Council; the New York City Citizens Union; and the National Puerto Rican Coalition. She serves as a trustee of Catholic Charities and Chair of the Commission on the Status of Women.

Jill M. Considine

Jill Considine is president of the New York Clearing House Association. She has been managing director and chief administrative officer of American Express Bank Ltd. and served as the New York State Superintendent of Banks and as a director on various New York State Economic Development Boards.

Ms. Considine was also president and chief executive officer of the First Women's Bank of New York and held various positions with Bankers Trust Company and The Chase Manhattan Bank. She is a member of the board of directors of Atlantic Mutual Insurance Company, a U.S.-Japan Leadership Fellow, and a member of the Council on Foreign Relations.

Peggy Cooper Davis

Peggy Cooper Davis is the Shad professor of law at New York University, where she has taught since 1982. Her publications have been influential in the fields of family law, legal process, and critical race theory. Before joining the N.Y.U. faculty, Professor Davis practiced law in both the private and public interest sectors and served as a judge of the Family Court of the state of New York.

Dr. Henrik N. Dullea

Henrik N. Dullea is Vice President for University Relations at Cornell University. From 1983 to 1991 he was director of state operations and policy management for Mario M. Cuomo. Among his previous positions were those of acting president of the State University of New York College at Purchase, assistant secretary for education and the arts for Governor Hugh L. Carey, associate vice chancellor for employee relations personnel and deputy to the chancellor for governmental relations in the State University system, and a legislative budget analyst for the New York State Assembly Ways and Means Committee. He is a recipient of the Nelson A. Rockefeller Award of the New York State Academy for Public Administration and the Distinguished Service Medal of the State University at Albany. He received his B.A. degree in government from Cornell University and his Ph.D. in political science from the Maxwell Graduate School of Citizenship and Public Affairs, Syracuse University.

Shirley W. Eberly

Shirley W. Eberly is a biostatistician with the University of Rochester School of Medicine and Dentistry. She is a past president of the League of Women Voters of New York State. She is a member of the Budget

Committee of the League of Women Voters of the U.S. and serves on the Advisory Board of the National Women's Hall of Fame.

Margaret Fung

Margaret Fung is currently the executive director of the Asian American Legal Defense and Education Fund. Ms. Fung was a law clerk for the United States Court of Appeals for the Second Circuit in New York City. She is a member of the board of directors for the National Asian Pacific American Legal Consortium; the New York Civil Liberties Union; the New York Foundation; and Japanese American Social Services, Inc. She serves on New York City Community Board #1.

Stanley Hill

Stanley Hill has served since 1987 as the executive director of District Council 37 AFSCME, the largest public employees union in New York City. He also chairs the Municipal Labor Committee and serves as an International Vice President of AFSCME. Mr. Hill is a member of the National Democratic Committee. He also serves on the New York City Central Labor Council Board and as a vice president of the New York State AFL-CIO. Additionally, he is a member of the Black Leadership Commission on AIDS, Catholic Interracial Council Board, Histadrut Afro-Asian Institute Board, and 100 Black Men Board.

James L. Larocca

James L. Larocca is a lawyer and consultant. From 1985 to 1993 he was president of the Long Island Association, the region's largest business and civic organization. Mr. Larocca has served as commissioner of the New York State Department of Transportation; commissioner of the State Energy Office; was the governor's counsel in Washington under Governor Hugh Carey; and has served as trustee of the New York Power Authority. He is active in a wide range of community and civic organizations and serves on the advisory boards of Hofstra and Polytechnic Universities. Mr Larocca is a member of the Stony Brook Council, the Marine Sciences Research Center, the Human Rights Advisory Council, and the Regional Economic Development Council. He is Chairman of the Board of Touro Law School, a director of the Brooklyn Union Gas Company, and sits on the European American Bank Board.

Nathan Leventhal

Nathan Leventhal has served as president of Lincoln Center for the Performing Arts since 1984. In 1994 he was elected chairman of Citizens Union. Mr. Leventhal has also served as deputy mayor for operations of New York City; commissioner of the Department of Housing Preservation and Development of New York City; commissioner of rent and housing maintenance for New York City; chief counsel to the Senate Subcommittee on Administrative Practice and Procedure, chaired by Senator Edward Kennedy; fiscal director of the New York City Human Resources Administration; assistant and special assistant to Mayor John Lindsay; special assistant to the executive director of the U.S. Equal Employment Opportunity Commission; and secretary of the New York City Charter Revision Commission. He was an associate and a partner in the law firm of Poletti, Freiden, Prashker, Feldman & Gartner from 1974 to 1978.

Murray Light

Murray Light was appointed managing editor of *The Buffalo News* in 1969, editor and vice president in 1979, and senior vice president in 1983. He began employment at *The Buffalo News* as a reporter in 1949. Mr. Light was formerly employed by the *New World Telegram* and served in the United States Army during World War II. He has been a member of the Pulitzer Prize Nominating Jury in Journalism; the New York State Citizen's Bee Steering Committee; the Judicial Screening Committee for the Fourth Judicial Department; and various committees related to universities in the Western New York Area.

Richard P. Nathan

Richard Nathan is a professor of political science and public policy at the State University of New York at Albany; the director of the Nelson A. Rockefeller Institute of Government; and provost of the Rockefeller College of Public Affairs and Policy. He was formerly professor of public and international affairs at Princeton University; senior fellow at the Brookings Institution; associate director for the National Commission on Civil Disorders, also known as the "Kerner Commission"; assistant director for the United States Office of Management and Budget; and deputy undersecretary for the United States Department of Health, Education, and Welfare.

Keith C. St. John

Keith St. John, a graduate of Vassar College and the Cornell Law School, is a clinical instructor/staff attorney at the Albany Law School of Union University. Prior to joining the law school faculty, Mr. St. John was a legal services attorney with the Legal Aid Society of Northeastern New York, Inc. and engaged in the private practice of law in Albany. Mr. St. John, a former fellow at the Kennedy School of Government at Harvard University, is also an Alderman on the City of Albany Common Council.

David Sive

David Sive is senior partner at Sive, Paget & Riesel, P.C., and a Professor of Law at Pace University Law School; has been a member of the New York State Energy Research and Development Authority; a lecturer at Columbia Law School; and a visiting professor at other law schools. He has been a founder and trustee of the Natural Resources Defense Council, the Environmental Law Institute, and the Environmental Planning Lobby. Mr. Sive served as the director of staff of the Committee on Natural Resources and Agriculture at the 1967 constitutional convention; counsel to the Rockland County Charter Commission; and a member of the Court of Appeals Committee on Women and the Courts. He has authored numerous law review and other articles and is the co-author of *Rowley on Partnership Planning*.

Peter G. Ten Eyck, II

Mr. Ten Eyck is president of Indian Ladder Farms Inc., an apple orchard, cold storage, cider mill, and retail farm market located two miles west of Voorheesville, New York. He is a graduate of Cornell University and lives on the farm with his wife Rose-Marie, a professor at the University at Albany. He is in business with his daughter, Laura, who is the 11th generation of the family in Albany.

Besides his farming duties, Mr. Ten Eyck is a director of the New York State Agricultural Society, chairman of the Advisory Council of the New York State College of Agriculture and Life Science at Cornell, and is a member of the Agricultural Advisory Council of the New York State Department of Environmental Conservation. He serves as a delegate to the Council of Agriculture Organizations and in recent years has been the President of the New York State Horticultural Society as well as a member of the New York State Commission on Constitutional Revision.

Malcolm Wilson

Malcolm Wilson is former governor of the state of New York. He was first elected to public office in 1938 and held elective state office for 36 consecutive years — 20 years as an assemblyman and 15 years as a lieutenant governor, until he became the 50th governor of New York in 1973. Governor Wilson has served as chairman of the board and chief executive officer of the Manhattan Savings Bank. He has been associated with his law firm in White Plains since 1936.

COMMISSION STAFF

Gerald Benjamin
Director of Research
Temporary State Commission on
Constitutional Revision
Rockefeller Institute of Government

Melissa Cusa
Assistant to the Director
Center for New York State and Local
Government Studies
Rockefeller Institute of Government

Sheila Davidson
Keyboard Specialist
Secretary to the Director of
Communications
Temporary State Commission on
Constitutional Revision

Irene Pavone
Keyboard Specialist
Center for New York State and Local
Government Studies
Rockefeller Institute of Government

Eric Lane
Counsel and Staff Director
Temporary State Commission on
Constitutional Revision
Hofstra University

Pauline Toole
Director of Communications
Temporary State Commission on
Constitutional Revision

Michael Owens
Researcher
Temporary State Commission on
Constitutional Revision
Rockefeller Institute of Government

Author Biographies

Burton C. Agata

Burton C. Agata is the Max Schmertz Distinguished Professor of Law at the Hofstra University School of Law where he was a member of its founding faculty in 1970. He has been on the law faculties of Houston, Montana, and New Mexico and has visited at Wisconsin and New York University. Professor Agata received his A.B. in 1950 and his J.D. (with distinction) in 1951 from the University of Michigan where he was a member of the *Michigan Law Review*. In 1951, he received an LL.M. (in trade regulation) from New York University where he held a fellowship. After service in the United States Army, he practiced law and served in several positions in New York State government where he was intimately involved in the legislative process as counsel to a division of the New York State Banking Department and as special counsel with the office of the Counsel to the Governor. He also has served as special counsel to the New York State Senate Minority, as consultant to the New York State Temporary Commission on Constitutional Revision, as senior counsel and consultant to the National Commission on Reform of Federal Criminal Laws, as consultant to the New York City Charter Revision Commission, and as reporter and consultant to several other state and federal agencies and judicial and bar associations. He is an elected member of the American Law Institute and a Life Fellow of the American Bar Foundation. Professor Agata currently serves on several New York State and American Bar Association committees and has published on constitutional law and the other subjects that he has been teaching since 1961.

Gerald Benjamin

Gerald Benjamin is interim dean of the College of Arts and Sciences and professor of political science at the State University College at New Paltz. Formerly director of the Center for the New York State and Local Government Studies at SUNY's Rockefeller Institute of Government in Albany, between May of 1993 and March of 1995 Professor Benjamin served as research director of New York's Temporary State Commission on Constitutional Revision. He holds a doctorate in political science from Columbia University and, alone or with others, has written or edited thirteen books and numerous government reports and articles, most of them on state and local government in New York.

513

Richard Briffault

Richard Briffault is professor of law and director of the Legislative Drafting Research Fund at Columbia Law School. He received a B.A. from Columbia College and a J.D. from Harvard Law School. He was assistant counsel to Governor Hugh Carey of New York in 1980-82 before joining the Columbia faculty in 1983. He is the author of *Balancing Acts: The Reality Behind State Balanced Budget Requirements* (Twentieth Century Fund Press, 1996) and of articles in the Columbia, Stanford, University of Chicago, and other law reviews on various topics in state and local government law. He was a consultant to the New York City Charter Revision Commission, the New York City Council Districting Commission, and the Temporary New York State Commission on Constitutional Revision, and was a member of the New York City Real Property Tax Reform Commission.

Melissa Cusa

Melissa Cusa is currently employed as budget analyst for Albany County Human Services. Formerly, she was assistant to director of the Center for New York State and Local Government Studies at the Nelson A. Rockefeller Institute of Government in Albany. She helped author several chapters of *The New York State Constitution: A Briefing Book* for the New York's Temporary Commission on Constitutional Revision and was involved in every stage of the editing and production of that document. Ms. Cusa holds a Master of Social Work from the Nelson A. Rockefeller Graduate School of Public Affairs and Policy and a Master of Arts in Sociology from the State University of New York at New Paltz.

Henrik N. Dullea

Henrik Dullea is vice president for university relations at Cornell University. From 1983 to 1991 he was director of state operations and policy management for New York Governor Mario M. Cuomo. Among his previous positions were those of acting president of the State University of New York College at Purchase, assistant secretary for education and the arts for Governor Hugh L. Carey, associate vice chancellor for employee relations personnel and deputy to the chancellor for governmental relations in the State University system, and legislative budget analyst for the New York State Assembly Ways and Means Committee. He is a recipient of the Nelson A. Rockefeller Award of the New York State Academy for Public Administration and the Distinguished Service Medal of the State University at Albany. He received his B.A. degree in government from Cornell University and his Ph.D. in political science from the Maxwell Graduate School of Citizenship and Public Affairs, Syracuse University.

Peter J. Galie

Peter J. Galie, Ph.D., University of Pittsburgh, is professor of political science at Canisius College in Buffalo, New York. He is the author of numerous articles on aspects of state constitutional law and two books: *The New York State Constitution: A Reference Guide* (1991) and *Ordered Liberty: A Constitutional History of New York* (1996).

William R. Ginsberg

William R. Ginsberg is distinguished professor of environmental law at Hofstra University School of Law, and holds the Rivkin, Radler, Dunne & Bayh Chair. He is of counsel to the firm Sive, Paget & Riesel, P.C., in New York City. A graduate of Antioch College and Yale Law School, he was a partner in the firm of Ginsberg, Schwab & Goldberg, served as deputy and acting executive assistant to the president of the New York City Council and commissioner and first deputy administrator of the New York City Parks, Recreation and Cultural Affairs Administration. He was counsel and director of research of the New York State Temporary Commission on the Powers of Local Government.

Robert P. Kerker

Robert P. Kerker was the principal author of *The Executive Budget In New York State: A Half-Century Perspective* (Albany: New York State Division of the Budget, 1981), a study of the origins and development of the state's budget system. He has also contributed essays on state budgeting history to *Governing New York State*, edited by Jeffrey M. Stonecash (3rd edition; Albany: State University of New York Press, 1994), the *Yearbook* of the Council of State Governments, and the *Empire State Report*. A graduate of Columbia University (B.A., M.A. in Public Law and Government), Mr. Kerker served in the New York State Budget Division in a variety of capacities until his retirement as deputy chief budget examiner in 1992.

Michael Malbin

Michael J. Malbin is professor of political science at the State University of New York, Albany, and director of Legislative and Political Studies at SUNY's Nelson A. Rockefeller Institute of Government. His most recent books are *Limiting Legislative Terms* (Gerald Benjamin, co-author and co-editor) and *Vital Statistics on Congress, 1997-98* (Norman J. Ornstein and Thomas E. Mann, co-authors). Appearing in 1997 will be a book co-authored with Thomas L. Gais entitled *The Day After Reform: Sobering Campaign Finance Lessons from the American States*.

515

Frederick Miller

Frederick Miller of Albany is an attorney, and graduate of Siena College and the Albany Law School. He is executive director and counsel of the New York Lawyers' Fund for Client Protection, and an adjunct professor of legislative law at the Albany Law School. Between 1974 and 1983, Miller held the post of legislative counsel for the state's Unified Court System, and was the principal draftsman of statutes implementing the 1978 constitutional reorganization of judicial administration in New York State, judicial discipline and a merit selection process for judges of the Court of Appeals.

Michael Leo Owens

Michael Leo Owens is a senior research aide at the Nelson A. Rockefeller Institute of Government's Urban Studies Group. In addition, he is a Ph.D. candidate in political science at the Rockefeller College of Public Affairs and Policy, the University at Albany. Prior to his current position at the Rockefeller Institute, Mr. Owens served on the staffs of the New York State Temporary Commission on Constitutional Revision and the New York State Senate Majority Program Office.

Robert D. Stone

Robert D. Stone, of Delmar, New York, has been engaged in the private practice of law since 1987. Following ten years of private practice in Binghamton, New York, from 1959 to 1986, he served in various capacities in New York State government, including executive deputy secretary of state, deputy commissioner of General Services, appointments officer to Governor Rockefeller, and general counsel to the Board of Regents and the State Education Department. He attended Hamilton College and Columbia Law School, and is admitted to practice in all state and federal courts in New York, and in the United States Supreme Court.

Jeffrey M. Stonecash

Jeffrey M. Stonecash is professor of political science at the Maxwell School, Syracuse University. His research focuses on state political parties, their electoral bases, and their roles in shaping state policy debates about state-local relations, state assumption of fiscal responsibilities, and intergovernmental aid. He also does work on campaign finance. He has published in *American Political Science Review, American Politics Quarterly, Legislative Studies Quarterly, Polity, Public Budgeting and Finance, Publius, Social Science History, Western Political Quarterly, Political Parties*, and other journals. He is the editor of *Governing New York State*, published in 1994, and is now preparing a fourth edition, to be published in 1998. His textbook, *American State and Local Politics*, was published by Harcourt and Brace in 1995. He is now completing a study of changes in the role of the state in New Jersey from 1950 to 1995.

Stonecash does polling and consulting for political candidates in New York, covering races from Congress to county legislatures. He is also professor-in-residence for the New York State Assembly Intern Committee. In that position he teaches a course on New York politics and conducts seminars with legislators, lobbyists, legislative staff, and journalists.

David I. Wells

David I. Wells was associate director of the Political Department of the International Ladies' Garment Workers' Union, AFL-CIO, from which he retired in 1995. In 1990, he was appointed by Mayor David Dinkins as a member of the New York City Districting Commission, to draw new City Council district boundaries. Wells also served as redistricting advisor to national COPE, AFL-CIO, following the 1970, 1980, and 1990 censuses and was a consultant to political, labor, and reform groups in many states on problems relating to Congressional and state legislative redistricting. Wells received an M.A. in American history from Columbia University.

Robert F. Williams

Robert F. Williams is distinguished professor of law at Rutgers University School of Law in Camden, New Jersey. He received his B.A. from Florida State University in 1967 and his J.D. from the University of Florida College of Law in 1969. Prior to attending law school, he served as legislative assistant in the Florida Legislature during the 1967 Constitutional Revision Session. He practiced law with Legal Services in Florida and represented clients before the 1978 Florida Constitution Revision Commission. Professor Williams received an LL.M. from New York University School of Law in 1971, and an LL.M. from Columbia Law School in 1980. He teaches civil procedure, state constitutional law, and legislation at Rutgers Law School in Camden, New Jersey, in addition to writing and practicing in that area. He is the author of *State Constitutional Law: Cases and Materials* (2d Ed., Michie Co., 1993), and *The New Jersey Constitution: A Reference Guide* (Westport, CT: Greenwood Press, 1990) and numerous journal articles about state constitutional law and legislation. He is also coauthor (with Hetzel and Libonati) of *Legislative Law and Process* (2d Ed., Michie Co., 1993).

Joseph F. Zimmerman

Joseph P. Zimmerman is the author of many books, including *The Government and Politics of New York State*, and a professor of political science in the Graduate School of Public Affairs of the State University of New York at Albany. He has been a consultant to several United States government agencies, including the Advisory Commission on Intergovernmental Relations, state governments, and local governments.

Index

A

Abrams, Robert, 83
absentee voting, 197-198
Adirondack "blue-line" parks, 318
Adler v. *Deegan*, 170
advance resolution, of Voting Rights Act
   issues, 469-471
African-Americans, *See also* minority
   groups
   at-large delegates, 459
   delegate selection issues, 410-411
   senators, 462-463
   suffrage, 357, 358
Agata, Burton C., 409
agencies, structure of, 65-66
Alien and Sedition Laws, 245
amendments, 331-349, *See also* legislative amendments
   constitutional convention method of,
      332-334
   constitutional provisions, 42-43, 59
   debt reform, 102-103
   defined, 331
   initiation of, 14-15
   issues involved in process, 341-344
   legislative method, 331-334, 385-404
      introduction of, 386-390
      judicial reform, 393-394
      passage of, 394-397
      power distribution between branches,
         391-392
      rights, 392-393
      state comparisons, 397-404
      state and local relations, 390-391
      structure and scope of government,
         393
   limits on number offered, 404
   number of, 14
   provisions governing, 334-341
   ratification of, 15-16
   relative ease of, 15
   revision vs., 346-349, 385
   of state constitutions, 28
Anderson v. *Reagan*, 84
Appellate Divisions, 65, 128

establishment of, 131
jurisdiction, 264
reforms, 138, 141-145
apportionment
   constitutional provisions, 34-35
   Equal Protection Clause and, 8
   federal regulation of, 25
   pre-1964 process, 106-107
   vote dilution and, 446
appropriations
   current provisions, 82, 83
   federal funds, 84
assembly, freedom of, 248
Assembly
   election of members, 199-200
   role of, 61
   sharing of powers, 58
   size of, 119-120
   term length, 73
Assembly districts
   coterminality, 120-121
   for delegate selection, 416, 487
   pre-1964 districting process, 106-107
at-large delegate selection, 409, *See also*
   delegate selection
   alternatives to state committee designa-
      tion, 420
   applicability of Section 2 of Voting
      Rights Act to, 458-461
   ballot access and, 435
   creating single-member districts for,
      488-489
   cumulative voting and, 481
   limited voting and, 476-477
   petition process, 417
   single transferable voting and, 485
   state committee designation, 442
   vote dilution and, 446
   voting rights and, 412-413
at-large districts, U.S. Supreme Court
   interpretation, 449, 452
Attorney General, 61
   appointment of, 275-276
   constitutional provisions, 37
   election/appointment of, 263

proposed centralization of prosecutorial
function in, 274-278
role of, 65, 262
sharing of powers, 59
autonomy of local governments, 184-191
components of, 184-185
constitutional ban on special acts,
186-187
fiscal, 187-188
immunity against state interference,
185-186
lack of, 175-176
presumption in favor of local authorities
to act, 185
true local control of local governments,
187
autonomy of the states, 6, 8-9
Axelrod, Donald, 87

B

backdoor financing, 102, 104
bail, 271
excessive, 257
balanced budget, 84-85
certification, 99
legislative requirements, 100
proposed changes, 97-98
balance of powers, 57
ballot access, 201-203, 435-444
delegate petition process, 416-420
proposals for constitutional change,
212-213
banks, chartering of, 149, 152
Bartlett, Richard J., 137-138, 139
Bellacosa, Joseph W., 92, 140
Benjamin, Gerald, xix
Bernstein v. *Toia*, 308
Bianchi, William, 312
biannual budgeting, 97
bicameralism, 68-69
Bill of Rights (New York State), 32-34,
233-234, 235-254
civil rights, 248-249, 261
colonial laws and legislatures, 249-250
common law, 249-250
compensation for taking private
property, 242-244
corruption and official misconduct, 260
counsel, 259
criminal justice and, 267-273
criminal libel, 261

development of, 238-239
due process clause, 241-242, 260-261
equal protection of laws, 248-249
excessive bail, excessive fines, and
unusual punishment, 258
freedom of speech and press, 244-248
grand jury indictment, 259-260
habeas corpus, 257-258
labor provisions, 250-252
legislative amendments, 392-393
proposals for constitutional change,
252-254, 267-273
provisions, 238-252, 256-261
religious freedom, 239-241
trial by jury, 239, 256-257
unreasonable search and seizures,
258-259
U.S. Bill of Rights and, 268-269
Bill of Rights (United States), 7, 233,
235, 241
civil rights, 249
freedom of speech and press, 246-247
significance of, 235-238
Bill of Rights for Local Governments,
39, 155, 322
bills, legislative process, 61, 62
bills of rights, criminal justice and, 255
bipartisan gerrymandering, 110-111, 125
Blaine Amendment, 290-292, 294, 360,
364, 365
1966 debate, 373, 379
proposed repeal of, 300
"blue-line" parks, 318
Board of Charities, 305
Board of Education v. *Allen,* 293
Board of Elections, 197
composition of, 218-220
constitutional provisions, 224-226
proposals for constitutional change, 212
responsibilities of, 218-219
structure of, 218-220
Board of Regents, 284-286
proposed abolition of, 299-300
bond anticipation notes (BANs), 87-88
borrowing, constitutional provisions,
25-26
Botein, Bernard, 134, 274
boundaries, local governments, 190-191
Boundary and Powers Review
Commission, 190-191

Breitel, Charles D., 83, 89, 95-96, 136-137, 138
Brennan, William, 352, 451, 454
Briffault, Richard, 1, 410, 414
Brodsky, Richard, 313
Bromberg, David, 228
Bryce, Lord James, 16
budgeting and finance, 81-85
  appropriation of federal funds, 84
  balanced budget, 84-85, 97-98, 99, 100
  executive, 63, 81-84
  impoundment, 84
  item veto, 83-84
  proposals for constitutional change, 96-104
  public authority proposals, 103-104
  reform, 53, 82
budget process
  biannual budgeting, 97
  debt proposals, 101-103
  disincentives to lateness, 98
  executive and legislative roles, 100
  fiscal year, 97
  global budgeting, 99-100
  openness in, 96-97
  proposals, 96-100
  proposals for constitutional change, 96-100
  revenue estimation, 98-99
  spending caps, 100
  taxation proposals, 100-101
business activities, restrictions on public grants and loans and, 151-153
Butts v. City of New York, 471

C

California, 269, 272
  Proposition 13, 25
campaign financing, 203-204, See also public campaign financing
campaign practices, proposals for constitutional change, 214
canals, 41, 324-325
Cardozo, Benjamin, 170
Carey, Hugh L., 78, 83, 138, 139
Carey v. Oswego County Legislature, 175
Catskill "blue-line" parks, 318
Chancery Court, 355
Charter Revision in the Empire State: The Politics of New York's 1967

Constitutional Convention (Dullea), xxii
chief administrator of the courts, 130
chief judge, 130
Chisom v. Roemer, 457
Ciparick, Carmen, 310
cities, See also local governments
  integrity of, 115-116
  status of, 358
citizenship, 55
"citizen taxpayer" challenges, 92
City of Mobile v. Bolden, 447, 448
Civil Court (NYC), 129
civil departments, constitutional provisions, 36-37
civil rights
  Bill of Rights, 248-249, 261
  proposals for constitutional change, 253-254
Civil Rights Law, 249
Clinton, De Witt, 354
Cochran, John, 225
colonial legislative enactments, Bill of Rights and, 249-250
Comereski v. City of Elmira, 177
Commission on Constitutional Revision, xxii
Commission of Corrections, 306
Commission on Government Integrity (Feerick Commission), 419, 421, 439, 441
Commission on Judicial Conduct, 38, 65
Commission on Judicial Nomination for the Court of Appeals, 37-38
Commission on Lunacy, 305
common law, Bill of Rights and, 249-250
compactness, of legislative districts, 114, 124-125, 450, 458
compensation, See also delegate compensation
  of legislators, 70
  for taking private property, 242-244
comptroller, 61, 67
  balanced budget certification, 99
  constitutional provisions, 37
  proposals for constitutional change, 75-76
  role of, 64-65
  sharing of powers, 59
conflicts of interest, state legislatures, 72-73

Congressional districting, 124
Connecticut, 400-401
conservation, constitutional provisions,
41
Consolidated Edison v. *Town of Red
Hook*, 173
Consolidated Election Law of 1882,
223-224
Constitution
1777 Constitution, 334-335
1846 Constitution, 94, 337
1867 Constitution, 94
1894 Constitution, 290, 291, 304, 305
1934 Constitution, 304-305
amendment provisions, 42-43, 59,
334-341
Article I: Bill of Rights, 32-34, 233,
256, 288
Article II: Suffrage, 34, 196-198, 205,
231
Article III: Legislature, 34-36, 88, 147,
151, 153, 205
Article IV: Executive, 36
Article IX: Local Governments, 39, 155,
156-161, 167-168, 171, 174, 175,
178, 180, 185, 189, 317, 320-323
Article V: Officers and Civil
Departments, 36-37, 262, 284
Article VI: Judiciary, 37-38, 127-146,
256, 393-394
Article VII: State Finance, 38-39, 81-82,
87, 88, 94, 147, 148, 150, 151,
286-287
Article VIII: Local Finance, 38-39, 147,
148, 151, 155, 161-165, 288-290,
336-337
Article X: Corporations, 39, 88, 93, 147,
148, 149, 152, 153
Article XI: Education, 39-40, 281-284,
287
Article XII: Defense, 40
Article XIII: Public Officers, 40-41, 156,
338
Article XIV: Conservation, 41, 318-320,
325, 326, 327
Article XIX: Amending the Constitution,
42-43, 332, 336-337, 338, 340, 341,
342, 345, 346-349, 409
Article XV: Canals, 41, 324-325
Article XVI: Taxation, 41-42, 85-86,
147, 149, 317, 323-324

Article XVII: Social Welfare, 27, **42**, **88**,
90, 301-302, 306-310, 312, 314
Article XVIII: Housing, 42, 89, 302,
307, 313-315
historical adoption of, xvi
major revisions, xvi
as model for other states, 30
number of amendments to, 14
as a social compact, xvii
Constitutional Commissions
1872 Commission, 45-46
1890 Commission, 49
1912 Commission, 50
1915 Commission, 49
1938 Commission, 49
origination of, 45-46
permanent, 348
role of, 45-52
as study commissions, 48-49
Constitutional Convention Committee
(1938), 93
Constitutional Conventions
1777 Convention, 354
1801 Convention, 354
1821 Convention, 221, 263, 336, **354-356**
1846 Convention, 258, 337
election administration, 221
issues, 356-357
judicial reforms, 131
1867 Convention, 134-135, 358-359
1872 Convention, 94
1894 Convention, 250, 281, 285
election administration, 226
issues, 359-360
1915 Convention, 339, 349
election administration, 226-227
issues, 361-362
1938 Convention, 251, 260, 339-340,
341, 349
election administration, 227
issues, 362-363, 366
social policy, 306
1967 Convention, 54, 93, 273, 291,
340-341, 343-344, 349, 367-384
delegates, 374-375, 381-384
delegate selection, 371-373, 408-409
election administration, 227-229
1966 general election campaign,
373-378
issues, 363-366
legislative control of, 374-375

legislative districting, 108-110
partisan fighting, 376-378
purpose of, 369-371
1965 referendum, 371-373
results, 378-380
social policy language, 303
amendment method, 332-334
authorization of, 28
average number of, 13-14
fear of change, 367-369
fear of radical or extreme actions, 353, 366
limited call, 335, 343
mandatory 20-year consideration of, xiii, 59, 332, 338-339, 407
number of, 13-14
potential problems associated with, 352-353, 366
public opposition to, xv
Constitutional History of New York (Lincoln), 225
constitutionalism, commitment to, xvi-xvii
contiguity, of legislative districts, 113-114, 124-125
contribution limits, 492
Cooke, Lawrence, 140
Cooper v. Morin, 261
corporations, 39, 148-149, 152
public, 95
corrections system, 264-265
corruption, 259, 358
public campaign financing and, 494-495
coterminality, of legislative districts, 120-121, 124
Council for Owner Occupied Housing, Inc. v. Koch, 172
counties, integrity of, 115
county charters, 174-175
County Courts, 129, 131, 264
county prosecutors, 276-277
Court of Appeals, 58, 59, 65, 128
"citizen taxpayer" challenges to state bond issues, 92
establishment of, 131, 357, 358
freedom of speech and press and, 247, 248
jurisdiction, 264
selection of judges for, 136-137
short-term borrowing and, 89

"covered jurisdictions," 465-466
Criminal Court (NYC), 129
criminal justice system, 255-279
attorney general, 262-263
as balance between security and liberty, 255-256
"conservative," 270
corrections, 264
court structure, 65-66
criminal jurisdiction, 263-264
criminal sanctions, 266-267
district attorneys, 265
judges, 263
"liberal," 270
proposals for constitutional change, 76-80, 267-278
proposals for organization of, 273-278
sheriffs, 265-266
state government functions, 262-266
criminal libel, 261
cumulative voting, 467-469, 478-481
delegate selection and, 480-481
history and current use, 479-480
threshold of exclusion and, 478-479
Cuomo, Mario M., 52, 141-145, 211, 369

D

D'Alemberte, Sandy, 51
Dean, Benjamin, 225, 226
death sentence, 278-279
debt, 86-93, *See also* loans
constitutional challenges to borrowing practices, 91-92
legislative power to incur, 356-357
long-term, 87-88, 90-91, 364
moral obligation, 93
proposals for constitutional change, 101-103
referendum requirements, 103
reform amendment, 102-103
short-term, 87, 89-90
State University, 287-288
debt limits
constitutional provisions, 26
education exceptions, 289-290
local governments, 162-164, 176-177
proposals for constitutional change, 103
defense, constitutional provisions, 40
Delaware, 399
delegate compensation, 333-334, 345, 423-430

dual, 424-429
pension benefit limitations, 429-430
for public officials, 425
for state legislators and judges, 424
delegates
for 1967 Constitutional Convention,
371-373
eligibility, 244-246
"government industry" dominance, 431
judges as, 431-434
legislators as, 430-434
qualifications for service, 430-431
race of, 454
statutory provisions for election of,
343-344
delegate selection, 407-434, *See also*
at-large delegate selection; Senate
district delegate selection
applicability of Section 2 of Voting
Rights Act to, 457-467
applicability of Voting Rights Act to,
456-457
ballot access, 416-420, 435-444
equity issues, 410-416
existing process, 409
importance of, 408-409
nonpartisan, 443
per senate district, 409
petition process, 416-420, 436-437
procedure, 455-456
public financing, 420-423
state committee designation, 437-438,
442
"threshold of representativeness," 413
Voting Rights Act and, 410-416, 445-471
denominational education, 290-295
aid to students, 293-294
"examination and inspection," 292-293
transportation, 290-291
Department of Criminal Justice,
proposed, 273-274
Department of Law, 262
departments
limitations on, 65
proposals for constitutional change, 80
structure of, 65-66
Desmond, Charles, 134
development, environment and, 321
Dewey, Thomas, 83, 97, 132
direct democracy, 23-24, 205-206
district attorneys, 265

district courts, 65, 128
districting agencies, 121-124
Dominick, D. Clinton, 135
Dominick Commission, 135-136
double-candidate voting, 413
double partisan gerrymandering,
111-112
dual compensation
criticism of, 425-426
prohibitions against, 427-429
of public officials, 425
of staff, 425
of state legislators and judges, 424
value of, 426
due process clause, 7, 241-242, 260-261
legislative amendments, 392
workers compensation provision and,
251
Dullea, Henrik N., xiv, xxii

E

economic development, public funds for,
147-154
education, 281-300
for adults, 298
Blaine Amendment, 290-292
Board of Regents, 299-300
constitutional provisions, 27, 39-40
debt limitation exceptions, 289-290
denominational, 290-295
equity issues, 295-296
financing, 283-284, 295-296
"free" schools, 282-283
gifts and loans exceptions, 286-287, 289
governance and oversight, 284-286
local finance provisions, 288-290
lottery for, 288
proposals for constitutional change,
295-300
safe schools, 297-298
standards, 296-297
state finance provisions, 286-288
as a state function, 281-284
State University, 287-288, 298-299
transportation, 290-291
Education Law, 249
elected officials, *See also* judges;
legislators; public officials
as delegates, 344-346
election administration
bipartisan, 222-226

Board of Elections, 218-220
by commissioner, 230-231
constitutional provisions, 217-218
early constitutional provisions, 220-221
election law and, 218-220
election litigation and, 219
historical development, 220-229
political parties and, 218-220
proposals for constitutional change, 210-212
reform of, 231-232
state comparisons, 229-231
statutory provisions, 221-222
election campaigns
cost of, 497-498
public financing, 491-500
Election Reform Act of 1992, 203
elections, 193-215, *See also* delegate selection; political process; voting
elective offices, 198-200, 207
electorate, 196-198
for key posts, 356
matters voted on, 194-196, 205-206
public campaign financing and, 495-500
referendums, 195-196, 206-207
reform of, 359
electorate, 196-198
environment, 317-330
"Forever Wild" provision, 318-320, 325, 360
local government provisions, 317, 320-323
proposals, 325-327
equal protection
Bill of Rights, 7, 8, 248-249
criminal, 261
delegate selection and, 456-457
proposals for constitutional change, 253-254
ethics
in political process, 204
proposals for constitutional change, 214-215
Ethics in Government Act of 1987, 204
ethnicity, *See also* minority groups
legislative districting and, 116-118
"examination and inspection," denominational schools, 292-293

executive budget system, 63, 81, *See also* budgeting and finance; budget process
current provisions, 81-82
impoundment, 84
item veto, 83-84
reform, 82
executive powers, *See also* item veto; veto power
constitutional provisions, 36
separation of, 57-58
sharing of, 58-59
extraordinary majority
legislative amendments, 399-402
legislative districting, 123

F

Family Courts, 129, 264
federal constitution
constraints on state constitutions, 6-9
development of, state constitutions and, 5-6
grants vs. limitations, 9-11
as model for state constitutional reform, 18-20
state constitutions compared to, 9-18
federal funds, appropriation of, 84
federal law, supremacy of, 6-8
Fenton, Reuben, 358
Fifth Judicial Department, 65
financing, *See also* budgeting; budgeting and finance; debt; local finances; state finances; taxation
campaign, 203-204, 213-214
education, 286-290
local governments, 161-165, 168-170, 175-180, 187-188
fines, excessive, 257
firearms, 365
fiscal practices, 53-54
fiscal year, proposed changes, 97
Florida, 50-52, 269
Flower, Roswell P., 223, 224, 231, 339
Forest Preserve, 318-320, 323-324, 325
"Forever Wild" provision, 318-320, 325, 360
Fourth Provincial Congress, 334-335
freedom of assembly, 248
freedom of press, 244-248, 253
freedom of religion, 239-241, 253
freedom of speech, 244-248, 253

"free" schools, 282-283
Fuchsberg, Jacob D., 137
Fuld, Stanley H., 136
full-time service, state legislators, 72-73
fundamental law, state constitutions expressing, 18-19, 20
fundamental rights, xxi
  federal supremacy and, 7-8
  state constitutional provisions, 4, 24

G

Galie, Peter, xxii, 46, 88, 93, 240, 251, 291
generally accepted accounting principles (GAAP), 97
gerrymandering, 110-112, 118, 122, 125, 446
gifts, 94-96
  for education, 286-287, 289
  by localities, restrictions on, 148
  by state, restrictions on, 148
Gingles. See Thornburg v. Gingles
global budgeting, 99-100
goals, established by state constitutions, 4-5
Goldmark, Peter, 94
Gordon, Bernard G., 137
governmental structure. *See* structure
governor
  constitutional provisions, 36
  legislative districting and, 122-123
  proposals for constitutional change, 74-75
  qualifications and election of, 59-60
  role of, 63-64
Governor's Task Force on Judicial Diversity, 78
Grad, Frank P., 10-11, 31
grand jury, 270-271
grants, vs. limitations, 9-11
Graves, W. Brooke, 48, 49
Gribetz, Judah, 138
Gunther, Gerald, 352

H

habeas corpus provision, Bill of Rights, 256-257
Hamilton, Andrew, 245
handicapping conditions, children with, 282, 283
Harriman, Averill, 370

Hawaii, 72, 215, 403
health insurance, 307
Henretta, James, 47
Hill, Daniel B., 338-339
Hispanics, *See also* minority groups
  at-large delegates, 459
  senators, 462-463
Hoffman, Elizabeth, 312
Hoffman, John T., 150
home rule, 62, 184
  constitutional provisions, 27, 39, 156-159
  Court of Appeals decisions, 170-175
  environment and, 321
  history, 166-170
  proposals for constitutional change, 178
  taxation, 188
Honest Ballot Association, 228-229
Hope v. Perales, 310
housing
  authorizing counties to contract indebtedness for, 313
  constitutional provisions, 42, 89, 307-310
  enhanced rights to, 310-311
  proposals for constitutional change, 312-315
  provisions, 302
housing court, 80
Housing Finance Agency (HFA), 90
Hughes, Charles Evans, 81

I

Idaho, 71-72
Illinois, 230
impeachment, 38, 267
impoundment, 84
incumbent gerrymandering. *See* bipartisan gerrymandering
individual liberties. *See* Bill of Rights (New York State)
"influence districts," 455
interest groups, public campaign financing and, 494-495
intergovernmental relations, *See also* home rule; local finances; local governments
  local government cooperation, 160-161
item veto, 83-84, *See also* veto power

constitutional provisions, 22
proposals for constitutional change,
74-75

J

Jameson, John Alexander, 45
Javits, Jacob, 375
Jiggetts v. Grinker, 309
Johnson, Jesse, 226
joint elections, governor and lieutenant
governor, 75
Joint Legislative Committee on Court
Reorganization, 137-138
*Judd v. Board of Education of Union
Free School District No. 2 Town of
Hempstead*, 290-291
judges
chief administrator of the courts, 130
chief judge, 130
as convention delegates, 431-434
election/appointment of, 59, 64, 76-78,
128-130, 136-137, 199, 263, 265
merit selection of, 142-143
judicial departments, 79-80, 128
judicial districts, 77-78, 128
judicial system
constitutional provisions, 21, 37-38,
127-128
existing court system, 128-131
historical development, 131-137
legislative amendments, 393-394
reform, 54, 393-394
separation of power and, 57-58
unified court system, 78-79, 127-128
jury service exemption, 271
jury trial, Bill of Rights, 239, 256-257
just compensation, for taking private
property, 242-244
justice courts, 80

K

Kaye, Judith S., 30, 141-143
Kennedy, Robert, 344
Kentucky, education standards, 297
Koota, Aaron, 274

L

labor, Bill of Rights provisions, 250-252
labor issues, 360
Lack, James J., 142, 145, 313
land tenure, 357

land use, 321
Lautenbach, Edward, 224-225
Law Revision Commission, 348
legislation
constraints on, 62
passage of, 61, 62
legislative amendments, *See also*
amendments
amendments introduced, 386-390
dual passage majority requirements,
398-399, 401
extraordinary majority, 399-402
judicial reform, 393-394
limits on number offered, 404
popular ratification, 402-403
power distribution between branches,
391-392
rights, 392-393
state comparisons, 397-404
state and local relations, 390-391
structure and scope of government,
393
legislative districting
compactness, 60, 114, 124-125, 450,
458
1967 Constitutional Convention,
108-110
contiguity, 113-114
coterminality, 120-121
districting agency, 121-122
district lines, 106
elections and, 200
extraordinary majority requirement, 123
gerrymandering, 110-112, 118
governor's role in, 122-123
integrity of cities and villages, 115-116
integrity of counties and towns, 115
issues, 112-123
Orans and, 107-108, 110-112
order of priority among criteria, 118-119
political process and, 105-125, 208-210
population equality and, 112-113
pre-1964 process, 106-107
proposals for constitutional change,
208-210
race and ethnicity, 116-117
special criteria, 116
state comparisons, 123-125
legislators
compensation of, 70-72
as convention delegates, 430-434

full-time service, 72-73
qualifications and election of, 59-60
self-interest of, 70
term length, 73-74
legislature, *See also* Assembly;
  legislative districting; Senate
amending constitution through,
  331-334, 385-404
constitutional policy directives, 62-63
constitutional provisions, 34-36
districting, 105-125
as districting agency, 121-122
impeachment power, 38
openness and power sharing, 69-70
proposals for constitutional change,
  68-74
  full-time service, 72-73
  legislative compensation, 70-72
  openness and power sharing, 69-70
  term length, 73-74
  unicameralism, 68-69
public reaction to salary increases, 71
restrictions on providing special
  privileges, 147-154
separation of power and, 57-58
size of, 105, 119-120
structure and powers, 60-63
unicameralism vs. bicameralism of,
  68-69
Lehman, Herbert H., 50, 83, 339
Levitt, Arthur, 90
libel, 247-248, 253, 261
lieutenant governor
constitutional provisions, 36
proposals for constitutional change, 75
qualifications and election of, 59-60
role of, 64
sharing of powers, 58
limitations, vs. grants, 9-11
limited voting, 412*n*, 467-469, 473-478
  delegate selection and, 476-478
  history and current use, 473-476
  threshold of exclusion and, 474-475
Lincoln, Charles Z., 225
loans, 94-96, *See also* debt
  for education, 286-287, 289
  by localities, restrictions on, 148
  by state, restrictions on, 148
local courts, 65
local finances, 175-180, 187-188
  constitutional provisions, 38-39

education, 288-290
restrictions, 161-165, 168-170
Local Government Assistance Corporation (LGAC), 89
local governments, xv, 54-55, *See also*
  autonomy of local governments;
  home rule
autonomy issues, 184-191
bottom-up perspective, 181-182
boundaries, 190-191
conflict and pre-emption, 171-174
constitutional provisions, 26-27, 39,
  183-184, 186-187
debt limits, 176-177
defined, 155
elections, 200
environmental provisions, 317,
  320-323
fiscal autonomy, 187-188
formation of, 159-160
home rule, 156-159, 166-175, 321
impediments to local control, 187
intergovernmental cooperation, 160-161
legislative amendments, 390-391
local control of, 156, 166, 187
local public purpose restrictions,
  177-178
presumption to act, 185
proposals for constitutional change,
  178-180
restructuring, 160, 175, 178, 189-190
special acts, 186-187
state aid, 189
tax limitations, 176
top-down perspective, 182-183
transfer of functions to state, 179
unfunded mandates, 189
local officers, local control of, 156, 166,
  174-175
long-term debt, 87-88, 364
  bypassing limits on, 90-91
lottery, for education, 288
Louisiana, popular ratification, 403
low-income families, *See also* social
  policy; social welfare
constitutional right to assistance,
  307-310
Lutz, Donald, 4

M

McCain v. *Koch*, 309

Madison, James, 397-398
Malbin, Michael, 421
"Mandated Services Law," 292
Marchi, John, 312
Maryland, compensation commission, 72
Matter of Kelly v. McGee, 174-175
May, Janice, 17
merit selection, of judges, 77, 128,
    142-143
Michigan, 10, 230, 272
minority groups, See also
    African-Americans; Hispanics
candidate race and, 454
compactness of legislative districts, 114,
    124-125, 450, 458
cumulative voting and, 467-469,
    478-481
delegate selection issues, 410-411, 413
legislative districting and, 116-118
limited voting and, 467-469, 473-478
polarized voting, 450-451, 454, 459
political cohesiveness, 450, 453,
    458-459
senators, 462-463
single transferable voting and, 481-485
vote dilution and, 446-455
Missouri, 443
"Missouri Plan," 143
Model State Constitution (National
    Municipal League), 153-154
moral obligation debt, 93
multimember districts, See also Senate
    district delegate selection
application of Section 2 of Voting
    Rights Act to, 461-467
with cumulative voting, 415
dividing into subdistricts, 416
with proportional representation,
    415-416
U.S. Supreme Court interpretation,
    449-455
vote dilution and, 446
voting rights and, 410-416
Murphy, Walter, 352

N

National Municipal League, 18
nature preserves, 323-324
Nebraska, 403
Neuborne, Burt, 304
New Jersey, 46-47, 400

New Mexico, 230, 403
New York City
    community schools boards, 286
    court system, 65, 129
New York Constitution: A Reference
    Guide (Galie), xxii
New York State Clubs Association v. City
    of New York, 172
New York State Constitution. See
    Constitution
nonpartisan elections, delegate selection,
    419-420, 443-444

O

Oath of Allegiance, 294
"occupation of the field," 173
O'Connor, Justice, 454
Office of Court Administration (OCA),
    130
officers. See public officials
official misconduct, 260
Oklahoma, 11, 71, 230
Oneida v. Berle, 84, 85
one-person, one-vote doctrine, 456-457
open government, 69-70, 96-97
Orans ruling, legislative districting and,
    107, 110, 115
Ordered Liberty: A Constitutional
    History of New York (Galie), xxii
Oregon, extraordinary majority, 399

P

parliamentary system, 57
partisan gerrymandering, 110-112, 122,
    125
partisan selection, of judges, 77-78
Pennsylvania, 326
pension benefits, statutory limitations on,
    for delegates, 429-430
People ex. rel Arcara v. Cloud Books,
    246-247
People v. Bigelow, 258
People v. Johnson, 259
petition process (delegate selection),
    416-420
    at-large delegates, 418
    ballot access issues, 436-437
    grace period, 418-419, 440-441
    independent candidates, 417
    registration fee, 441-442
    Senate district delegates, 416-418

signatures required, 417, 419, 441
simplifying requirements, 440
strict compliance, 439, 440
substantial compliance, 419, 438-440
plural executive, 22-23
Poletti, Charles, 340
Poletti Report, 249, 340
Police Commission, 223-224
political cohesiveness, of minority
groups, 450, 453, 458-459
political parties, 200-201
delegate selection and, 420
election administration and, 212,
218-220
post-Civil War, 222
political process, 193-215, *See also*
elections; voting
ballot access, 201-203
campaign financing, 203-204, 213-214
campaign practices, 214
constitutional provisions, 193-194
ethics, 204, 214-215
proposals for constitutional change,
205-215
statutory regulation of, 200-204
popular ratification, 402-403
population equality, in legislative
districting, 112-113
positive rights, xxi-xxii, 234, 304, 311
Powell v. McCormack, 345
power sharing, 69-70
prayer in schools, 294
preclearance, 465-466
pre-emption, 171-174
press, freedom of, 244-248, 253
"prevailing wage," for legislature, 41
prison inmates
labor, 266
religious freedom of, 241
private property, compensation for
taking, 242-244
property taxes, local government
restrictions, 164-165, 169-170
prosecution
proposed centralization of function,
274-278
right to appeal sentences, 278
prosecutors, appointment of, 276-277
public authorities, 92-93
constitutional provisions, 26

proposals for constitutional change,
103-104
structure of, 67-68
public campaign financing, 491-500
corruption and, 494-495
delegates, 420-423
electoral competition and, 495-500
program types, 492-494
proposals for constitutional change,
213-214
special interest and, 494-495
voter pamphlets, 423
public corporations, loans to, 95
public disclosure laws, 203, 492
public health, 306-307
public lands, tax exemptions, 323-324
public officials
constitutional provisions, 36-37, 40-41
misconduct, 260
removal from office, 267
Public Policy Institute, 98

R

race. *See* African-Americans; Hispanics;
minority groups
racial gerrymandering, 111, 125
as vote dilution, 446
racially polarized voting, 450-451, 454,
459
racial voting discrimination, vote dilution
as, 447
ratification, 15-16, 28
reapportionment. *See* apportionment
redistricting. *See* legislative districting
referendums
borrowing, 103
proposals for constitutional change, 206
taxation, 101
topics of, 195-196
voter-initiated, 23-24
registration fee, for petition process,
441-442
religious freedom, 239-241, 253
republican form of government, 7
reserved rights, proposals for
constitutional change, 254
Resnick v. County of Ulster, 174
restructuring, local governments, 175
revenue estimation, 98-99
reverse pre-emption, 174

revision
amendments vs., 331, 346-349
political context of, 30-31
Rhode Island, 215, 270
Rich, Bennett M., 52
rights, *See also* Bill of Rights (New York
State); civil rights
fundamental, xxi, 4, 7-8, 24
individual liberties, 235-254
legislative amendments, 392-393
positive, xxi-xxii, 234, 304, 311
social welfare as, 311
U.S. Supreme Court interpretation, 8-9
Rockefeller, Nelson A., 50, 90, 134, 135,
136, 340, 370
Roosevelt, Franklin D., 83
Rose, Alex, 228-229

S

Samuels, Howard J., 370-371
Schulz, Robert, 91-92, 102, 103
Schulz et al. v. *The State of New York*, 92
secret ballot, 197
security, safe schools, 297-298
self-executing directives, 326
self-interest, of legislators, 70
Senate
coterminality, 120-121
election of members, 199
pre-1964 districting process, 106-107
role of, 61
sharing of powers, 58
size of, 119-120
term length, 73
Senate district delegate selection, 409,
See also delegate selection;
multimember districts; single-
member districts
alternatives to state committee
designation, 461-467
Assembly districts as alternative to, 416,
487-488
ballot access and, 435
cumulative voting and, 480-481
limited voting and, 476-477
nonpartisan elections, 419-420, 443-444
petition process, 416-417
single transferable voting and, 484-485
subdistricting and, 485-486
voting rights and, 410-416

sentences, right of prosecution to appeal,
278
separation of powers, 21, 57-58
sheriff, 264-265, 277-278
short-term debt, 87, 89-90
single-candidate voting, 413
single-member districts
assembly districts as, 487
for at-large delegates, 488-489
creating through subdistricting Senate
districts, 485-486
U.S. Supreme Court interpretation, 450
vote dilution and, 446, 452, 455
voting rights and, 411-412
single transferable voting (STV),
481-485
delegate selection and, 484-485
history and current use, 484
threshold of exclusion and, 482-483
Smith, Alfred E., 81, 82, 90, 93
social policy, 301-315
appropriateness of including in
constitution, 302-304
court interpretation, 307-310
evolution of provisions, 306-307
proposals for constitutional change,
310-315
provisions, 310-312
social welfare
constitutional provisions, 27-28, 42
constitutional rights to, 307-310
enhanced rights to, 310-311
transfer of functions to the state, 312
solid waste, 321
South Carolina, 399
Special Committee on the Revision and
Simplification of the Constitution, 50
special interests, public campaign
financing and, 494-495
special privileges, restrictions on,
147-154
speech, freedom of, 244-248, 253
spending limits
campaigns, 493
governments, 100, 161-162
state concern doctrine, 170-171, 173
state constitutions, *See also* amendments
average age of, 13
average number of conventions, 13
compared to federal constitution, 9-18
court interpretations of, 10-11

as documents of limitation, 9-11
federal constitution as model for
reforms, 18-20
federal limits on, 6-9
frequency of amendments to, 11, 12-16
fundamental rights established by, 4
goals established by, 4-5
grants vs. limitations, 9-11
importance of, 1-2
individual liberties defined by, 235-238
item veto provisions, 22
length, 11-12
limitations on state legislatures, 22
local government, 26-27
plural executive provisions, 22-23
principal provisions, 21-28
revision procedures, 28
roles of, 3-6
separation of powers, 21
state and local taxation and finance,
25-26
statutory provisions in, 11, 16-18,
19-20
structure established by, 3-4
substantive policies, 27-28
state finances, 81-104
budgeting, 81-85
constitutional provisions, 38-39
education, 286-288
state legislatures
constitutional amendments proposed
by, 14-15
constitutional provisions, 22, 34-36
control of constitutional commissions
by, 47-48
popular distrust of, 18, 19
states
aid to local governments, 189
autonomy of, 6, 8-9
government structures, 57-80
spending, constitutional provisions,
25-26
State University, 287-288, 298-299
statutory provisions, in state
constitutions, 11, 16-18, 19-20
Stevens, Harold A., 137
Stimson, Henry L., 81
strict compliance approach, petition
process, 440
strict scrutiny test, 242
structure, xv, 53-57

established by state constitutions, 3-4
federal supremacy and, 7
legislative amendments, 393
New York state government, 57-80
student aid, for denominational schools,
293-294
Sturm, Albert, 47, 51
subdistricting, of Senate district, 485-486
substantial compliance, petition process
(delegate selection), 419, 438-440
substantive limits, on legislative power,
62
substantive policies, constitutional
provisions, 27-28
suffrage
African-Americans, 357, 358
constitutional provisions, 34, 196-198,
205, 231
supremacy of federal law, 6-8
Supreme Court (New York), 128-129
establishment of, 131, 357, 358
jurisdiction, 263-264

T

tax-and-revenue anticipation notes
(TRANs), 89
taxation, 85-86
constitutional provisions, 25-26, 41-42,
101
of corporations, 149
local fiscal autonomy, 188
local government restrictions, 164-165,
176
passage of amendments concerning,
397
proposals for constitutional change,
100-101
public land exemptions, 323-324
referendum requirements, 101
Taylor v. Porter, 244
Temporary Commission on the
Constitutional Convention (1956),
50, 340
Temporary Commission on the
Constitutional Convention (1967),
50, 91, 436
Temporary Commission on
Constitutional Revision (1993),
xviii-xix, 52, 405
Tennessee, 399
term of office, 199

limits, 36, 60, 207-208
state legislators, 73-74
Texas, 72, 215, 272
"Textbook Loan Law," 293
Third Provincial Congress, 334
Thornburg v. *Gingles*, 449-455
  at-large districts and, 458-461
  multimember Senate districts and,
    463-464
  threshold of exclusion
    cumulative voting and, 478-479
    limited voting and, 474-475
    single transferable voting and, 482-483
Tilden, Samuel J., 49
Titone, Judge, 465
"totality of the circumstances" test, 452,
  460, 461, 462
"town and block rules," 107
towns, integrity of, 115
transportation, school, 290-291
Travia, Anthony J., 134, 299, 374-375,
  378
trial courts, structure, 128-129
trial by jury, 239, 256-257
Tucker v. *Toia*, 307-308
Tweed, Harrison, 132
Tweed Commission, 132-134

U

Ughetta, Henry L., 134
Uhlfelder, Steve, 51
unfunded mandates, 189
unicameralism, 68-69
Unified Court Budget Act, 130
unified court system, 78-79, 127-128,
  129
United States Constitution. *See* federal
  constitution
United States Supreme Court
  interpretation of federal constitution by,
    10
  multimember and at-large districts,
    449-455
  state constitutional rights and, 8-9
  unreasonable searches and seizures,
    259-260
  Voting Rights Act coverage, 457
unreasonable searches and seizures,
  258-259
unusual punishment, 257

Urban Development Corporation (UDC),
  91, 94
urban issues, 360, 362
Utah, 72

V

Van Buren, Martin, 354
Vance, Cyrus, 138
Vanderbilt, Arthur, 78, 146
Vermont, extraordinary majority, 399
veto power, 58, 61, *See also* item veto
  constitutional provisions, 36
  legislative districting and, 122, 124
  procedures, 63
  proposals for constitutional change,
    74-75
victims' rights, 271-272
villages, integrity of, 115-116
Virginia, 230
vote dilution, 446-455
  at-large districts and, 458-461
  U.S. Supreme Court-defined conditions
    for, 450
voter identification, 197
voter-initiation, 23-24
voter pamphlets, 423, 500
voter registration, 197, 210, 211
voting, *See also* elections; political
    process
  absentee, 197-198
  electorate, 196-198
  eligibility, 210
  substantive issues, 195
voting rights, federal regulation of,
  24-25
Voting Rights Act, 117, 445-471
  advance resolution of issues, 469-471
  amending process and, 341-342
  applicability of Section 2 to delegate
    selection, 457-467
  applicability to delegate selection,
    456-457
  cumulative voting and, 467-469
  delegate selection and, 410-416
  limited voting and, 467-469, 476
  Section 2, 447-449, 457-467
  "totality of the circumstances" test,
    452, 460, 461, 462
  vote dilution and, 446-455

W

Wachtler, Sol, 140, 242
Wein, Leon, 92, 95
Weinstein, Helene E., 143, 144
Weinstein, Jack, 343
Wein v. *Carey*, 83, 85
Wein v. *City of New York*, 177-178
Wein v. *State,* 85, 89
Whitcomb v. *Chavis*, 447
White v. *Regester*, 447

Wholesale Laundry Board of Trade, Inc.
    v. *City of New York*, 171-172
Williams, Robert, 10, 18
Wilson, Malcolm, 433
Wilson, Woodrow, 37
WMCA v. *Lomenzo,* 105, 107
Woodward, Nathan, 226
workers compensation, 251
wrongful death actions, 250-251

Z

Zenger, Peter, 245